The Big Book of Home Learning

Volume 1: Getting Started

Also by Mary Pride

The Way Home
All the Way Home
Schoolproof

With Bill Pride

Prides' Guide to Educational Software

The
Big Book
of Home
Learning

FOURTH EDITION
Volume 1: Getting Started

Edited by Mary Pride

A PRACTICAL HOMESCHOOLING® BOOK

Vol. 1

Learning Fourth Edition
Started
Home Life, Inc.   2000

Clip art images on pages 1, 3, 7, 9, 43, 513, and 514 provided by ©1990 Dynamic Graphics, Inc. Stock photo images on cover provided by ©1998 Corbus Corp Digital Stock, ©1999 Eyewire, and ©1997–1998 PhotoDisc.

Quotes from *Phyllis Schlafly Report* are reprinted by permission from the Phyllis Schlafly Report, PO Box 618, Alton, IL 62002. This is an indispensable source of cut-to-the-chase, thoroughly documented information on the major threats arising to our freedoms of education, family life, and citizenship. Well worth the $20 annual subscription fee.

Library of Congress Cataloging-in-Publication Data:
Pride, Mary
    The big book of home learning / Mary Pride—4th ed.
       p. cm.
    Include bibliographical references and index
    Contents: v. 1. Getting Started — v. 2. Preschool & Elementary — v. 3. Teen & adult.
      1. Home schooling—United States. 2. Home schooling—United States—Curricula. 3. Education—Parent participation—United States. 4. Child rearing—United States. I. Title.
LC40.P75 1999
ISBN 0-7403-0006-7

Liability Disclaimer

We trust our readers to be intelligent human beings who can benefit from our information in the spirit in which it is offered—as a help to making your own decisions, not as a replacement for them. We have made every effort to ensure that the information contained in this book is reliable. However, since we are only human and since products change and companies come and go, neither the editor, the reviewers, nor the publisher can warrant or guarantee this information.

It is the reader's responsibility to check out current prices, product availability, and so forth before making a final purchasing decision regarding any product or company mentioned in this book. You are also responsible to check out the company from which you intend to purchase the product, to make sure it is capable of delivering the product and offering the kind of customer service and support you expect. Although we have done what we can to check out the bona fides of companies mentioned in this book, we cannot be responsible for any problems customers may encounter with them in the future. We shall not assume any liability for any loss or damage caused or alleged to be caused directly or indirectly by suggestions found in this book or by products reviewed in it.

Trademarks

In this book we review or mention hundreds of trademarked products and company names. Rather than clutter up the book with trademark symbols, we state we are using each trademarked name only for editorial purposes and to the benefit of the trademark owner with no intent to infringe any trademark.

This edition of The Big Book of Home Learning is dedicated to my parents, Dr. Stuart B. Martin and Magda Levatich Martin. Without their support this project would not have been possible. Thank you for teaching me to believe that, with God's help, we can make the world a better place.

Table of Contents

Acknowledgments

Typically, producing a resource book this size takes an army of people. In this case, a handful of people did all the behind-the-scenes work that made this book possible—which says something about the quality and dedication of those people.

I would like to thank my son Joseph Pride (age 18) and my daughter Sarah Pride (age 16), who spent hours on the painstaking job of organizing the reviews in the proper electronic format. They also did the lion's share of the phone calling for fact checking.

My son Theodore Pride (age 20), our webmaster, updated all the home-school organization information and contacted all the organizations found in this book.

My husband Bill Pride did all the technical work, converting files from one format to another, installing new programs, and making sure the network stayed up—often in the middle of the night. He also helped look over the more challenging products (as in, "Bill, what on earth can I possibly say about *this?*") and listened to the many drafts of all the chapter introductions, giving his invaluable and sometimes hilarious advice. (Picture "Dave Barry Reviews Educational Products" and you'll have a faint idea of some of Bill's suggestions!)

All our reviewers deserve a round of thanks, with a special valentine to the three who wrote up a boatload of "very last minute" reviews in response to my panicky begging: Renee Mathis, Maryann Turner, and Michelle van Loon.

Bob Hickel did a superb job of handling the negotiations that led to this *Big Book* edition finally becoming a reality. We appreciate you, Bob!

I would also like to thank the folks at Alpha Omega Publications, with special thanks to Beth Te Grotenhuis and Christi Patterson, for stepping up to publish this book and enabling us to finish this impossible project.

Finally, I would like to thank you, the readers. Some of you were praying for us all along, and you deserve special thanks. Others helped ease the pressure by being willing to wait patiently for these volumes to be completed. Still others are brand-new to *The Big Book*—we did it for you, too! May these volumes open your eyes to a whole new world of educational freedom and delight.

It took a series of miracles to get these books finished. We humbly give thanks to the God of miracles.

Foreword

Hi! I'm Mary Pride. A lot has changed since I edited the last edition of this series:

- The homeschooling movement has quadrupled in size.
- Homeschool curriculum has become much more slick and plentiful.
- Homeschool support groups have proliferated like hamsters. If there isn't one near you, you must live in a cave in Death Valley!
- Political candidates of all stripes have endorsed homeschooling, and several state governors have declared a Homeschool Day.

On a personal level:

- I've had two more children, bringing the total to nine (so far!), ages 7 to 20. The oldest has started his own home business, and the next two are simultaneously in the process of applying to college, so our family has personally experienced the entire gamut of preschool-to-college-and-business homeschool life.
- Seven years ago, we started a magazine, *Practical Homeschooling*, to keep *Big Book* readers (and others) up-to-date on the latest homeschool products, methods, and ideas.
- Five years ago we started the "Homeschool World" website (*www.home-school.com*). Currently this site has about 350,000 visitors a year; we're glad people are finding it helpful.

The Homeschool Way

If it seems strange to you that I'm mixing news about my family with news about my company, that's only because you have not yet experienced the Homeschool Way.

Homeschooling, by its nature, is extremely personal. We are doing this out of love for our families, and that carries over into interest about other people's families.

In fact, the homeschooling movement itself resembles an enormous family! I have seen numerous instances where homeschoolers who only

Mary Pride, publisher of Practical Homeschooling and editor of The Big Book of Home Learning

What's New in This Edition

- Hundreds of all-new reviews. These are marked with the notation "NEW!" next to the review in the margin.
- Complete updates of all reviews from previous editions. In almost every case, the price and ordering information has had to be updated. Only those products that have significantly changed since the last edition have the notation "UPDATED!" in the margin.
- Supplier addresses, phone numbers, and fax numbers are right alongside each review now, instead of in a separate index. (You asked for it, you got it!)
- Plus most reviews include email addresses and World Wide Web addresses for the supplier. Technology marches on!
- We have photos of most of the products reviewed. See them for yourself!
- Brand-new chapters bring you up-to-date on the latest home-schooling methods for each subject.
- More brand-new chapters provide help for special needs and gifted education, including the thorny question of if and when to accelerate your child.
- Sidebars and other highlights provide commentary and additional points of view on chapter subjects.
- Finally, we felt it would be appropriate to celebrate the achievements of our wonderful home-schooled children by featuring some of the children themselves! So every section begins with a picture and brief description of a homeschooled student and his or her special achievement. These students were all originally featured in the "Show & Tell" section in *Practical Homeschooling,* and we are very proud of them!

knew each other through an online message board have prayed for each other's needs and sent gifts of various sorts to help when times were tough. My own family experienced this when our oldest son, Ted, had double pneumonia and had to be placed on a respirator. Dozens of people sent us gifts to make up for the loss of income while we had to suspend our normal business activities to care for Ted's urgent needs.

So it is only appropriate that this edition of *The Big Book of Home Learning* should include, for the first time, reviews from over two dozen other experienced homeschool parents. While in the past I wrote every review myself, the movement is getting too big for this. At the same time more parents have had the necessary experience to be able to evaluate curriculum. I'm glad it worked out this way, as facing the huge piles of curriculum samples all by myself was becoming rather daunting!

Genuine Reviews

Part of what makes *The Big Book of Home Learning* special is that our reviews *are* reviews. We don't rewrite catalog descriptions and call them "reviews." We don't provide laundry lists of library books, either. Our reviews are first-hand, based on years of actually receiving and testing products, not second-hand "recommendations" based on other people's writings or on an afternoon spent browsing library stacks.

The number of man-hours (actually, mostly *woman*-hours!) spent on giving you genuine reviews runs by now into many thousands. That's a lot more work than it takes to chunk out a "resource list" glued together from personal experience and public sources, but we think you'll find the difference is worth the hours we've spent laboring to give you information you can really *use*.

Ever since I decided to write the original *Homeschool Curriculum Buyer's Guide* back in 1985, hundreds of companies have graciously sent me samples of their products. This has given me the unique opportunity not only to review the entire gamut of homeschool products—not just the relatively small sample that one family can reasonably use—but to compare them.

Even though *Practical Homeschooling* magazine now has many reviewers, we have continued this method of comparing products. Typically a reviewer will be assigned many similar products, enabling him or her to see what's the same and what's different about each one. This means we are able to not only describe a product, but tell you its strengths and weaknesses. We also try to determine which type of homeschooler will benefit most from each product—or if it's one we all should skip!

One thing that has not changed is that the information in *The Big Book of Home Learning* is as current and up-to-date as we could possibly make it. After the reviews were written, we did our best to contact every supplier for verification of prices, addresses, and other such information. Even so, *it is always wise to write or call the supplier to check on prices before ordering.* The prices in this book are included only to help you compare different products for value. Prices go up and down. Too, you will sometimes have to add state tax (depending on whether you and the supplier are in the same state or not, or whether the supplier has additional offices in your state). Both you and the supplier will feel better if the supplier does not have to return your order because the check you enclosed was not for the right amount.

What's Not in This Edition

You won't find many educational software reviews in this edition. That subject requires a book of its own.

For the most part, we have also left out children's fiction. Most children's fiction isn't educational except in the broadest sense; the field changes rapidly; and you can locate and purchase an excellent selection from thousands of carefully-chosen titles arranged by historical time periods and reading levels, and described in detail, by simply sending for the excellent free catalogs from Sonlight Curriculum (1-303-730-6292) and Greenleaf Press (1-800-311-1508).

We also deliberately left out lengthy lists of educational web sites. Although we do provide the web addresses of the products reviewed, the truth is that anyone who knows how to use a search engine can assemble a list of hundreds or even thousands of educational web sites in an afternoon. Our feeling is that unless a writer takes the time to check out and write up a site's content in detail, "laundry lists" of topical web sites are a waste of the reader's time and the writer's space. Happily, several good books of web site reviews do exist; you can find them in your local bookstore.

The Big Book on CD-ROM

Very few people have the means to try thirty different phonics programs or twenty different Spanish courses. And very few books can hold the thousands of resulting reviews. This one is no exception! We had a choice between increasing the number of Big Book volumes from four (believe it or not, the last edition was four books this size!) to even more (the *Big Book Galactic Encyclopedia,* maybe?).

Rather than fill up your entire bookshelf, with this edition we have chosen to be as exhaustive as possible when covering the essentials—curriculum packages and phonics, for example—and to settle for the "best of" in other areas. This means we had to leave out hundreds of deserving and specialty products. But modern technology has the answer! If you need to get your hands on all our reviews, you can get the CD-ROM edition of this book, due out in winter 2000. If all goes as planned, it will include full-color graphics, sound clips, and video clips of many of the products. (A postcard enabling you to purchase it at a discount is bound into this book.)

How to Talk to Us

We have done our best to make this the most comprehensive, easy-to-use, up-to-date homeschool book around. But we are always willing to make it even better! So if you have any suggestions for how we can improve the next edition (assuming I can survive the almost-endless process of putting together *The Big Book* one more time), please send those cards and letters in! You can write to us at Home Life, Inc., P.O. Box 1190, Fenton, MO 63026.

Of course, you can also keep in touch by subscribing to *Practical Homeschooling.* Information on how to do so is bound into this book.

One last note: This book would not have been possible without the active cooperation of many of the companies listed. Those who supplied me with samples and free catalogs bravely ran the risks of review, and I and the other reviewers have not hesitated to point out their products' shortcomings. I would like them to feel they gained more than a critical going-over by their generosity. Both the publisher and I would be grateful if you would mention *The Big Book of Home Learning* when you contact a supplier whose product is mentioned here.

It's a Real Resource List If . . .

- You write in-depth reviews of the products with which you are personally familiar, making it clear at the same time that there are many more products out there.
- You share your tips and ideas for using those products. This is especially appropriate if you are writing a book about how to implement a particular homeschool method, since you can be highly knowledgeable about the smaller group of products—e.g., Latin curriculum—that fit your method—e.g., classical studies.
- You don't waste your precious book pages on long lists of addresses, library books, or web sites. EXCEPTION: if you have taken the time to read the books and work through the sites (and decide which is great and which is not), and if what you found is significantly more than the reader could find out in a couple hours online or by browsing the Greenleaf Press and Sonlight catalogs, please do share the fruits of your research.
- If you don't really have the time or experience to write pages and pages of reviews, just tell your publisher you'd rather use the extra pages for your own original ideas, or that you'd rather save your readers some money by making the book smaller. Then take just one page to tell your readers where they can find all the reviews and recommendations they need—in the few genuine homeschool resource books, including this one.

A Note to The Writers and Publishers of Homeschool Books, and Those Who Read and Review Them

Years ago, homeschool books did not include extensive resource lists. That is because there were no resource books.

Back then, homeschool authors used the pages of their books to present their original ideas, or to explain a particular homeschool method, or to analyze public education v. homeschooling, or to share their unique experiences.

This happy situation persisted for more than a decade after the first edition of *The Big Book of Home Learning* came out. Homeschooling was a small market, and the only people writing for this market were, like myself, those who felt a real mission to share what they'd learned.

But times have changed.

Nowadays publishers who a few years ago didn't even know homeschooling existed are saying, "We need to do a homeschool book." These publishers are demanding that their new homeschool books include dozens or hundreds of pages of resource recommendations and listings.

Since the authors they are signing up quite understandably have not had tens of thousands of hours to review a wide range of products, how can these authors provide the lists the publishers demand?

The easy way is to copy large chunks of contact information from this book and the few other genuine resource books, just adding a few extra resources so the "borrowing" won't be embarrassingly obvious.

When authors fail to fact-check their information, regardless of where they got it from, sometimes the results can be comical. One "resource list" I spied in a brand-new homeschool book had our PO box wrong, our *state* wrong (it's news to me we are situated in Montana!), our area code wrong, and the phone number in any case was our *fax* number. Yet I can imagine the reviews right now, praising that author's "extensive resource list."

A few hours in the library can also yield a huge list of "recommendations." Usually these "resource lists" are just lists of titles and authors, since it takes extra time to actually read the books and determine which are useful, let alone to find out if they are still in print, how much they cost, and where they may be purchased. Novices and uninformed reviewers are easily impressed by such lists, but they are practically useless for the reader.

A few hours on the Internet can produce a laundry list of web sites, which again will impress book buyers and reviewers who don't take the time to actually follow up on these "recommendations."

It is even possible to collect resource books (such as this one) and back issues of *Practical Homeschooling* and write "recommendations" or "reviews" based on what the real reviewers said, without ever having owned, used, or handled the curriculum. In a writer's mind this may be justified as "distilling down the best of what other have said" and thus "saving the readers money" (since now these readers presumably will feel little need to buy a genuine resource book).

Do you find these approaches disturbing and unethical? I do. But the only way publishers will stop putting out homeschool books that are padded with hundreds of pages of "borrowed" or worthless information is if you, the readers and book reviewers, demand it. You deserve better than this. That's why we worked for years to bring you this new edition of *The Big Book of Home Learning*, and spent thousands of dollars double-checking every bit of information in it that we could. It is our hope that you will find it informative, inspiring, indispensable . . . and inimitable.

Introduction

Welcome to the fourth edition of *The Big Book of Home Learning!* We're really happy to see you.

We are the homeschool community, and whether you're

- determined to teach your children at home
- thinking about possibly teaching your children at home
- interested in helping your children with their education after school

you've come to the right place!

What's In This Book?

First, let's talk for a minute about what you'll find in each book of this three-volume series.

Volume 1, the book you are now reading, is about "getting started" in homeschooling. This is the place to have your basic questions about homeschooling answered . . . to find out what homeschooling is *really* like . . . to discover the steps to homeschooling success . . . and to find out what homeschooling methods and styles best fit your family. Volume 1 is also where you'll find detailed reviews of packaged curriculum, online academies, planners for your homeschool records, and information on study skills and standardized testing. Helps for special homeschooling situations—such as educating children with special needs, including the gifted—are also included, as is a whole new chapter on contests your homeschooled children can enter.

The first step to educational success is discovering which teaching and learning methods work and which don't. That's why I devoted several chapters in this book to explaining how people really learn. It's also why you will find so many resources in this book to help you learn how to learn and teach.

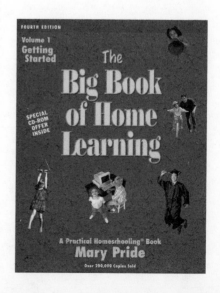

What's in the Other Big Books?

Volume 2 covers preschool and elementary education in more depth, with reviews of products that teach all academic subjects for these age groups, plus teaching tips, subject by subject. While Volume 1 includes reviews of packaged curriculum—which enables you to purchase an entire grade level of curriculum from one source—Volume 2 gives you the information you need to create your own curriculum, or supplement an existing packaged curriculum or school situation.

Volume 3 takes homeschooling from junior high through college. Again, we provide detailed reviews of hundreds of courses and educational products for these age groups, plus detailed information on preparing for college admissions tests, choosing a college, and alternatives to college.

We have designed this edition of the *Big Book* so there is very little overlap between volumes. There was no realistic way to duplicate all the reviews in Volume 1 in the the other volumes, and we didn't think you'd want to pay for a lot of repetitious material! This means **you need at least two of the volumes for a complete homeschool picture**. If you have a preschool or elementary-aged child, you need volumes 1 and 2. If your child is junior-high age or above, you need volumes 1 and 3. In this way, you will have full information about both packaged curriculum and all the many attractive options for teaching individual subjects, including courses such as art and music which often aren't included in pre-packaged material.

If you have children in both age groups, or simply want to be prepared for your young child's future options, you should get all three volumes. It's a big help to know what lies ahead; the elementary years are not too soon to start thinking about your child's ultimate academic destination, whether it will be college, a business of his own, a home of her own, or vocational training.

We'll Help You Become a Homeschool Expert

It isn't hard to provide your child with a home education that's far superior to what most kids today are getting in school. But it does take some research and study. Decisions need to be made. Goals have to be determined. Teaching methods have to be learned. You have to pick the curriculum you'll be using, and have the confidence to either stick with it, or know when it's time to move on to a customized curriculum of your own.

Thanks to the growth of the homeschool movement, you have a bewildering array of teaching methods and philosophies to choose from, and an even more bewildering array of homeschool products. (If you have trouble making up your mind at a smorgasbord restaurant, don't even *think* about attending a modern homeschool curriculum fair without some preparation!)

That's where we come in.

Everyone who contributed to this book has years—sometimes decades—of homeschooling experience. We have all spent money on products that turned out to be lemons, and wasted weeks on highly-hyped material that did not perform as advertised. We've seen our little angels sneaking off when we told them to do their schoolwork . . . and we've seen them eagerly digging into curriculum that sparked their interest. Our children have all sorts of learning styles; some would have been labeled "learning disabled" had they gone to school. We've taught our children one-on-one and in groups. We've sat down on the couch and heard three pencils snap underneath the cushions. In short, we've been in the trenches. We know what works and what doesn't.

In that sense, we are experts—the only kind of experts that count. Not degreed and credentialed experts (although most of us do have degrees and credentials), but hands-on experts who have really succeeded at what we write about.

We wrote this book to share what we have learned with you.

Now, you can become an expert too!

PART 1

Getting Started

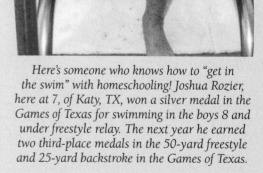

Here's someone who knows how to "get in the swim" with homeschooling! Joshua Rozier, here at 7, of Katy, TX, won a silver medal in the Games of Texas for swimming in the boys 8 and under freestyle relay. The next year he earned two third-place medals in the 50-yard freestyle and 25-yard backstroke in the Games of Texas.

Joel Dobney, a homeschooled student from Evanston, IL, recently participated in the Midwest Talent Search Scholarship Awards Ceremony at Northwestern University. He took the second-place medal for the reading section of the ACT.

In order to qualify for the awards ceremony, entrants needed to place in the 99th percentile in selected categories of the SAT, ACT, or Iowa Test of Basic Skills, in the seventh or eighth grade, instead of eleventh or twelfth grade, the usual age to take these tests.

Joel, 14, has participated in the Midwest Talent Search for two years and in the Midwest Talent Search for Young Students in fifth and sixth grades. He and his brothers, Brad (16), Bryan (12), and Jared (10), have been home educated for their entire academic careers.

CHAPTER 1

What's So Great About Homeschooling?

Are you one of those people who was not in the 99th percentile on every test? Have you learned to think of yourself as an "average" person, or perhaps even "slow"? Are you one of the millions who entered kindergarten with bright-eyed enthusiasm but who lost their love of learning along the way? If you are, then this book is for you.

Or perhaps you *were* in the 99th percentile. You soared gracefully through school while others waddled. This book is for you too.

Has your child been labeled "learning disabled" or "dyslexic" or "retarded" (or even "gifted")? Have you have gone around and around with the school trying to find out what the label means and what the school plans to do about it? Are you looking for a sensible way to help your child, one that doesn't depend on federal funding or special programs? Would you like to see *dramatic* improvement in your child's academic progress? The sources that can help you are right here.

Maybe you have already decided to teach your children at home. You look at the schools near you and are not thrilled at the prospect of incarcerating your children in them for thirteen years. You have precious values that you want to pass on, and you are determined to fight for your children's souls and minds. This book is *especially* for you!

Learning at home is the magic key that millions of people have used to unlock the educational treasure-chest. No longer must you or your children climb the academic beanstalk in competition with a hundred other Jacks, each of whom can only succeed by knocking his fellows off into the depths. No longer must you spend a fortune on college credits for knowledge offered elsewhere for a pittance. No longer must you watch your child shrivel up under the burden of a "label" that some trendy educrat has stuck on him or her. In the comfort and privacy of your own home you can learn whatever you want to, whenever you want to—and so can your children.

> The massive National Adult Literacy Survey made by the U.S. government in 1993 concluded that 40 to 44 million adults are functionally illiterate and that another 50 million are only marginally literate.
> —*The Phyllis Schlafly Report*

> "When 40 percent of our eight-year-olds cannot read as well as they should, we have to do something."
> —*President Bill Clinton*

DRUG USE IN THE PUBLIC SCHOOLS

In 1994, 33 percent of tenth graders reported using an illicit drug during the previous year. The percentage that reported using alcohol during the previous year was 64 percent. Almost half of all high-school seniors (48.4 percent) reported using drugs.

Though drug use has declined slightly since then, in and around school is still where most children are pressured to try drugs.

Current estimates now place the number of homeschooled children at about 1.5 million. That's a lot of practical, one-on-one teaching experience homeschoolers have gained over the past decade, since the movement changed from a tiny trickle into a full-grown flood.

While homeschoolers cover the entire political and lifestyle spectrum, we do have one thing in common:

We believe that parents can do a great job of teaching their children at home.

No, let me put that more strongly:

We know from experience that you can do a great job of teaching your children at home!

Homeschooled children consistently test academically ahead of public-schooled children. (See detailed research summary in Appendix 1.) In most categories, they even surpass the test scores of children from the finest private schools. The one exception? Math computation speed. Moral: homeschool moms don't like math drills!

Generally, homeschooled children are at least one year ahead academically. When it comes to reasoning skills, homeschooled children test an unbelievable *seven years* ahead of public-school children!

The academic rocket boost homeschooling provides often translates into homeschooled children winning competitions. Although homeschooled kids are just a fraction of the schooled population, and most homeschoolers don't enter competitions (a situation I expect to change as information about contests become more accessible—see the chapter and appendix devoted to contests in this book), it's becoming more and more common for homeschoolers to win, place, or show in academic competitions of all kind. Just recently here in St. Louis, for example, a homeschool high-school math team consisting of the available high schoolers padded out with the second-string junior-high students (the first-stringers were *on* the junior-high team!), trounced the teams from local Christian schools, scoring 1200 points to the next team's 800 points. Homeschoolers took every first place in individual scoring, and many of the second and third places as well. This is just one example out of thousands: homeschooled kids have performed brilliantly in everything from music competitions, to science fairs, to writing competitions, to Latin and mythology competitions, to sports and martial arts.

Homeschool graduates have been accepted into Ivy League universities such as Harvard and Yale. They have served with distinction in the military. They have joined apprenticeship programs, served as missionaries, and started their own businesses.

Often, they have done this at younger ages than their schooled counterparts. While nobody in the homeschool movement advocates whizzing through school for its own sake, thousands of homeschoolers have been mature enough and well enough prepared academically to start taking community-college or Advanced Placement courses at age 16 or earlier. Both are favored options for these younger children, because it saves money, allows students of high-school age to accumulate credits toward a college degree in a more prominent institution, and allows kids to live at home when they might be too young to go away to college.

GUNS OUT OF CONTROL

In 1994, 10 percent of tenth graders reported carrying a weapon to school "at least once," and 4 percent reported that they had brought a weapon to school for 10 or more days.

In 1999, students in a Columbine, Colorado, high school were mowed down by gun-toting peers. Columbine High, not coincidentally, was one of the pioneers in "death education" courses.

Freed by homeschooling from the necessity of following rigorous school schedules or attending class in one physical location, some families have shared adventures that range from sailing trips around the world to professional and semi-professional careers in theatre, dance, circus, and other performing arts. Still others have become expert cyberspace "netizens," creating their own World Wide Web sites, writing their own programs, publishing their own electronic newsletters, or attending online academies.

Take a look at the homeschooled kids featured on the section pages throughout these three volumes, for just a small taste of the success homeschoolers are enjoying. Truly, homeschooling has more than proved itself as a road to success in education . . . and in life.

But man does not live by test scores alone; most parents choose homeschooling for reasons beyond academics. The list of public school deficiencies is familiar and depressing:

The 15 Habits of Highly Defective Schooling

- drugs
- violence
- gangs
- morally and theologically questionable curriculum
- peer pressure
- an alarming number of teachers who can't pass basic competency tests
- censorship of religion
- plummeting test scores
- dumbed-down curriculum
- age segregation (the notion that people learn best in the company of dozens of people exactly their own age)
- isolation from community life
- busywork
- little to no one-to-one interaction with the teacher
- lockstep learning (your child has to learn at the same speed as everyone else)
- lack of opportunities to pursue special projects and interests

In all these areas where public schools fall short, homeschools excel.

Ten Ways Homeschool Beats "Regular" School

1. **"Isolation from community life?"** Not a chance! For most homeschool families, Friday is Field Trip Day. Everyone piles in the car to visit local businesses and educational attractions. Many homeschool children volunteer or work in the community on a regular basis. And *all* of us hang out at the library!

Unusual Homeschool Fact: According to *Library Journal*, homeschoolers now account for a staggering 20 percent of all library checkouts!

2. **"Drugs, violence, and gangs."** Not in my backyard! It's extremely rare for a homeschooled child to be charged with any crime. In the few instances we're aware of, the child had until recently been educated in a school situation. Jails are not packed with homeschooled kids; they are packed with people who have had the benefit of 10 or more years of being "socialized" in public schools. Added benefit: homeschooled children don't have to cope with increasingly unsafe school environments.

3. **"Little to no interaction with teacher."** You wish! As opposed to regular school classes, where the teacher asks all the questions, homeschool provides children with the chance to ask *their* questions, with-

out fear of other children calling them names for doing so. This means you answer a *lot* of questions!

4. **"Lockstep learning."** Not a problem at home. If your child doesn't "get it," you can always come back to that lesson in a day, a week, a month, or even a year. If, on the other hand, he wants to zoom ahead, you can feed him the advanced courses he craves without the social problems he would face in public school.

5. **"Censorship of religion."** At home we are free to move beyond the Easter bunny and Santa Claus.

6. **"Peer pressure."** Did you know that the number one predictor of whether your child will be a genius or not is how much time he spends with adults? It's true! As the Bible says, "He who walks with the wise becomes wise, but a companion of fools suffers harm."

7. **"Lack of opportunities to pursue special projects and interests."** We have a section in our magazine, *Practical Homeschooling,* where we print photos of homeschooled kids who have won various contests or done special projects. Over the years these have ranged from model rocketry to designing stamps for the Post Office. It's a lot easier to talk Mom and Dad into letting you do these things than to get a classroom teacher to redesign the year's curriculum to accommodate your child's special interest!

8, 9, and 10. **"Dumbed-down curriculum . . . busywork . . . morally questionable curriculum."** Not a problem if you own this book!

Three Big Advantages of Homeschooling

Three advantages of learning at home that you'll notice right away are *price, freedom,* and *options.* Home educational products come wrapped in Kraft paper and delivered by the mailman. Classroom products come wrapped in classrooms (very expensive) and delivered by the school administration (likewise, very expensive). Home learning can be done at your convenience, and in most cases there are no deadlines at all.

At home, you have thousands of choices at your fingertips through the *Big Book of Home Learning* series alone. Away from home, you either are limited to whatever options are offered in your geographical area—or forced to pay exorbitant sums for transportation in order to get to that great seminar in San Diego or that workshop in Bangor, Maine. At home nobody nags you or grades you unless you want them to. Schools, however, *run* on grades and you must do the work *they* require when *they* want you to do it and in the way *they* want you to do it, or you come away empty-handed.

Let's look at how you can reap the advantages of price, freedom, and options by learning at home.

PRICE

What do you think you'd pay for private guitar lessons from blues/jazz legend Clarence Gatemouth Brown? $100 per hour? $200? More? Homespun Tapes will sell you three solid hours of this Grammy Award winner on cassette, teaching you all his tricks for just $37.50. This amounts to actually ten or more hours' worth of lesson, as in person you would be taking a considerable amount of lesson time practicing the techniques. Further, you can rewind the tapes and hear Mr. Brown over and over again. No real-life teacher is *that* patient! When you count these latter factors in, the price of a lesson from a musical master comes to less than the price your next-door neighbor would charge.

WITHOUT A CLUE
The schools have reduced the time spent on academic subjects to about one-fourth of the school day. The majority of the day is spent on psychological courses, counseling, social services, and other non-academic activities. Even worse, these non-academic courses use a methodology that used to be called values clarification and is now known by its generic name of non-directive. That means that schoolchildren are presented with dilemmas, situations, and various problems of modern living, but given no direction as to the correct or expected behavior.
—*The Phyllis Schlafly Report*

What would it cost for you to send your child to one of the top private schools in the country? The going rate is now over $7,000 per year for these elite schools, and even those who have money are often turned away because there are fewer places than would-be students. You can, however, get the entire Calvert School program, including teacher grading and counseling, for just a tad over $500. Calvert's home-taught graduates consistently demonstrate the same achievement as its classroom students. You have thus purchased virtually all the benefits of one of the nation's most exclusive schools at a fraction of the in-person price.

Every volume of this series is loaded with bargains like these. What are you looking for? Personal online tutoring for your daughter? (Right here in Volume One.) The same kind of phonics instruction given at the most exclusive private schools? (Volume Two.) Video lessons in geometry for your high schooler? (Volume Three.) Thanks to audio, video, computers, and the written word, you can have private lessons from the best teachers in the world—at home, and at prices that won't make your checkbook scream.

FREEDOM

School, like time and Amtrak, waits for no man. The oldest grandfather in graduate school has no more freedom than the youngest preschooler when it comes to deciding *when* he wants to learn. The whole class must lurch forward at once, and laggards are left holding a lonely "F."

Under our present inefficient "credentialing" system, which focuses more on classroom attendance than actual knowledge and experience, education becomes a form of involuntary servitude. You give up control of your own life in order to (you hope) gain that coveted credential. You are not allowed to proceed at your own pace, or select the educational content or method you prefer. This applies equally to children and adults, with the major difference being that adults can switch from one institution to another or walk away from the whole thing if they are totally disgusted, whereas children usually have no choices at all.

At home, you are in control. You can pick and choose from a variety of sources instead of being tied down to whatever is physically available in your area. You can do the work when it is convenient for you. If you are looking for knowledge, not credentials, you can skip the whole stupefying mass of busywork and tests, and concentrate only on what interests you. Learning becomes a pleasant adventure rather than a burden.

OPTIONS

Lovers of the offbeat and unusual are sure to be delighted with the educational offerings available at home. From talking globes to authentic pioneer stories to science riddles, the homeschool market is popping with surprises! Buy a bridge-building construction kit for your granddaughter! Find out how to teach decimals with colorful "french fries"! Dance about the room to grammar songs! Cut out and assemble a Viking village! Play a grammar card game!

Some items you need are available *only* at home. You can't just bop down to the local Wal-Mart and pick up the organizers reviewed in this volume, for example. And I am seeing an increasing number of products specifically designed for families learning at home, from the National Writing Institute creative-writing program (Volume Two) to do-it-yourself calligraphy courses (Volume Three).

On reading instruction, are you stuck with whatever method the local school uses, no matter how poorly your children respond? Not at all! There

THE ROLE OF PARENTS IN EDUCATION

My son, hear the instruction of thy father, and forsake not the law of thy mother;

For they shall be an ornament of grace unto thy head, and chains about thy neck.

—*King Solomon (Proverbs 1:8,9)*

are dozens of excellent programs, and although most public schools and even a goodly number of private schools pass them by (witness our national illiteracy), that doesn't mean *you* can't rescue *your* children by reaching for *Play 'n Talk* or *Sing, Spell, Read and Write*.

Change Your Child, Change the World

In the long run, any positive transformation of our culture has to begin at home. If everyone lived the way most homeschool families live, there wouldn't be any crime, broken families, or wars.

You're in the right place to make a real difference in the lives of your children and everyone whose lives they touch. At home you can give your children a safe, happy childhood . . . a superior, caring education . . . and help them grow into people who will care for their own children, and reach out to make a difference in the lives of others.

There is no more important task.

CHAPTER 2

Twenty Questions

If you're considering homeschooling, you have lots of questions. If you've been homeschooling for any length of time, you've been *asked* lots of questions.

Here are some of the biggies:

- "What about socialization?"

- "Can homeschooled children get into college?"

- "Is it true that all homeschoolers have to bake their own bread and raise goats?"

"FAQ" stands for Frequently Asked Questions. On the Internet, an FAQ list is where "newbies" (new users) find the answers to their questions, so veteran users don't have to answer them again and again.

Homeschoolers definitely need an FAQ list.

And here it is!

"What does the research show about homeschooling?"

Who better to answer that question than the National Homeschool Research Institute (NHERI)? Turn to Appendix 1 for an easy-to-follow illustrated overview of research about homeschooling.

The answers in this chapter are adapted from the *Practical Homeschooling* FAQ list. This regularly updated list of questions and answers is available through the Homeschool World web site (found at *www.home-school.com*). Contributors to the original list include PHS reviewers, support group leaders, homeschooling parents, and yours truly. This group of people has heard *all* the questions—hundreds of times each. And they are *still* homeschooling, so you can be confident that they have good answers!

See Appendix 3...
...for an overview of the homeschool laws for every U.S. state and territory.

Homeschool Laws Online
For the text of the homeschool law in your state, and your state homeschool group(s)' interpretation of how best to comply with that law, visit the Homeschool World web site at www.home-school.com and select the button "Legal Requirements by State."

"Is it legal?"

Homeschooling is legal, under varying conditions, in every state. Some states (mercifully, the number is few) require you to register with the authorities. This is the most restrictive situation. Most allow you a range of options by which to show you are making a good faith effort to homeschool. Standardized testing, keeping a portfolio of the children's work, using a recognized curriculum, and/or keeping a log of the hours each child spends on school subjects are some common options. Some states also require certain subjects to be taught. For example, Missouri requires high school graduates to have a unit of Missouri history, and lists some broad subjects (e.g., language arts) that must be taught. But Missouri law also specifically forbids the state to require any specific *content* in that subject area. So the authorities in Missouri can't require your child to read any specific book or engage in any specific activity that homeschool parents might find offensive.

One important apiece of advice you *must* follow:

Very Important: Check with your state homeschool group for their recommendations on compliance.

For example, if a state law *allows* you to register your homeschool, but does not *require* it, the state group will probably recommend you *not* register, so as to discourage any attempts to build up a state database of all known homeschoolers.

The state leaders know the ins and outs of the law—after all, they probably helped draft parts of it!—and they are well aware of the battles that have been fought over how the law is to be interpreted, so my advice is to follow *their* advice.

"What about socialization?"

SERIOUS ANSWER #1. A person who is well socialized is able to relate to people from a wide variety of age groups and lifestyles. Homeschooling is the ideal option for this type of training, as it affords the opportunity to relate to people in the real world rather than a fabricated world which is limited in scope to those who are within one or two years of being the same age of the student. Study after study has shown that homeschooled children excel in every area of "socialization."

NOT-QUITE-SERIOUS ANSWER #2. The jails are full of the products of public school socialization. Are homeschoolers likely to do worse?

SERIOUS ANSWER #3. There are two types of socialization: peer-group socialization ("babies teaching babies") and adult-child socialization (otherwise known as "mentoring," "walking with the wise," or "training"). In public schools, the adults are outnumbered as much as 30 to 1, so the main form of socialization is peer-group socialization. If the peers are paragons of virtue and fountains of wisdom, this is not a problem. Unfortunately, in real life peer groups tend to fall to the level of the worst influences among them. Which is why you hear so much about "peer pressure" today and why public school children even have to worry about just saying no.

THOUGHT FOR THE DAY. Did you know that the greatest predictor of genius is the amount of time a child spends with adults? In other words, the more time your child spends with you and other adults, the more likely he or she is to exhibit advanced intellectual abilities.

SERIOUS ANSWER #4. I thought children went to school to *learn!*

"How do I find out what materials are available?"

You have this book.
Now, get the CD-ROM!

"What about college?"

THOUGHTFUL ANSWER #1. Many, many colleges currently accept homeschoolers (some even court them, giving preference to homeschoolers!) and those who haven't yet, just haven't realized what a goldmine we are!

As your student gets closer to college age (say, ninth grade), start looking at colleges that he or she would like to attend. Then write the colleges, tell them you're interested, and ask what kind of records, tests, and so forth they like to see from homeschoolers.

If your *student* writes the initial letter to the college (and it sounds good), and continues a correspondence up through the time he actually applies, he will have a valuable contact there.

Some colleges only require a standardized test, like the SAT or the ACT. Most like to see a sample of the student's writing. They look very closely at this to see how well the prospective student expresses himself. Sometimes they want a reading list (all the impressive books read during the high school years). Occasionally, they want a real transcript. Usually, you can do these yourself—but you have to have some kind of justification for why you gave which grade, and how you decided when a credit was earned.

THOUGHTFUL ANSWER #2. Going to college *at home*—in other words, homeschooling right up to the (hopefully not bitter) end—is becoming more of a real option these days. Just about every state college offers some correspondence courses, and a growing number of colleges have full degree programs. Also available are several legitimate programs that allow you to cobble a potpourri of distance education courses, plus credit for "passing" courses via tests, plus credit for life experience, into genuine degrees. For more details, see Volume 3.

THOUGHTFUL ANSWER #3. Don't neglect to investigate other options for post-high school education: video courses, tutorial software, library books, magazines, TV and satellite courses, seminars, apprenticeships, and starting your own business!

"What do I tell my in-laws?"

FOOLISH ANSWER #1. "Hi! We've gone insane and decided to ruin our children's future by homeschooling them!"

FOOLISH ANSWER #2. (to your parents). "I am so upset at the job you did raising me, Mom and Dad, that I refuse to follow in your footsteps by sending *my* kids to the public school!"

BETTER ANSWER #1. It's common for in-laws, especially parents, to "read" your choice of homeschooling as a rejection of them and the way they were raised or the way they raised you. Also, in spite of all the bad publicity public schools have garnered over the past few decades, many older people still have sentimental memories of public school days, and fear you will be depriving your children if they can't be on the football team or go to the prom. (NOTE: By the time you read this, homeschooled children in your town *may* be able to play public school sports and join after-school clubs such as the theater club or chess club. But your parents don't know this!) So don't panic if their first reaction is negative. What counts is the long run!

To find out more about how homeschoolers can prepare for college, including taking the major tests, picking and applying to college, and applying for financial aid, see Volume 3 of *The Big Book of Home Learning*.

We've found that the best approach, if at all possible, is a gradual approach devoid of any defensiveness on your part. Find common ground from which you can build. Are your in-laws concerned or alarmed about the state of the public schools? Have your in-laws ever mentioned the negative effects of peer pressure? Do they want your children to be taught a Biblical worldview? Do they in any way share some of your vision for your family? If so, you can discuss these areas of common ground and share how you believe homeschooling is the best solution for your family.

Most in-laws will probably be initially skeptical and will have a lot of questions. Some will accept your answers; others will need "hard facts" from "experts." The hard facts, including numerous studies showing that homeschooling really works, are readily available from sources such as your state homeschool group, Homeschool Legal Defense Association (HSLDA), homeschool books found in your public library, and this very book you now hold in your hands!

When your in-laws respond to this onslaught of well-researched information with pursed lips and dire pronouncements of doom, calmly reply, "We are sorry if you don't agree with our decision to homeschool, but we are convinced this is what we should be doing. We really don't want to argue about it." Families we know, who have faced strong opposition from relatives, have found that a calm, no-nonsense statement of this sort will prevent many disagreements and nasty scenes.

BETTER ANSWER #2. After you have been homeschooling a while, invite your in-laws to a "Show and Tell" day. Let the children give oral presentations of their work, complete with visual aids (flip charts, projects they have made, etc.). Make this a formal occasion, with the guests seated nicely and served refreshments. Some really anti-home-school relatives have been won over when they saw how well-behaved and informed the children were. (Of course, it helps if you have been training your children to be well-behaved and informed!)

BETTER ANSWER #3. Head off trouble at the pass, podner, by inviting your in-laws to help you teach! The same Grandma and Grandpa, or Aunt Joan and Uncle Fred, who have been disparaging your homeschool will often become its biggest boosters once they have a part in it. Grandparents are great at teaching hands-on skills such as cooking and woodworking. Or if your skeptical family members have any special skills, such as piano proficiency or math, ask them to come over a few times and help teach in these areas.

These "in-law classes" don't have to be daily, or even weekly, to be effective at the socialization that really counts—socializing your in-laws to the benefits of homeschooling!

BETTER ANSWER #4. Frequently in-laws are *thrilled* to find out you'll be homeschooling!

"How can I meet other homeschoolers?"

THE TRADITIONAL ANSWER. The best way to meet other home schoolers is through your local support group. Many states have a statewide group that will give the phone numbers of groups in your area. If you hear of a church that has lots of homeschoolers, contact them. Homeschoolers are generally very helpful to new families. Most support groups have experienced leaders who can steer you in the right direction to find information, encouragement, and support. Get involved in your local homeschool group by volunteering to help in even a little job and you will be amazed at the friends you make. Just as a Christian needs fellow Christians, so homeschoolers need others for fellowship and support.

Your local library often has information about local homeschool groups and events. So may your local "teacher's supply" store. In fact, the library and the teacher's supply store may be sponsoring some of those events. It doesn't hurt to ask!

THE WIRED ANSWER. Join an online service. America Online (AOL), Prodigy, and CompuServe (CIS) all have vigorous homeschool forums. To find them:

On AOL: go to keyword PIN. (It stands for Parent Information Network.) There's also a Christian Homeschoolers forum in the Religion-Christian area.

On Prodigy: you're on your own here, as none of the contributors to this book are Prodigy members! We know there's a homeschooling forum there, though, because every now and then someone emails us some gossip from it. Presumably searching around in the Educational area will unearth it.

On CompuServe: go to the Education forum. The Homeschool forum is a part of this area.

Also on CompuServe: the private Christian Interactive Network area (go CIN to join) has a very active homeschool forum. It actually gets more posts than the "regular" CIS homeschool forum! (NOTE: Christian Interactive Network is an additional charge on your CIS bill, and you have to agree to a very basic statement of faith to join.)

THE OVERWHELMING ANSWER. Attend your state homeschool convention. There you'll have a chance to meet between 200 and 10,000 homeschool families—all at once!

"How do I know we're covering everything we need to?"

Public schools use a tool called a "scope and sequence." This chart or list tells you, for each subject in each grade level, what skills are supposed to be covered.

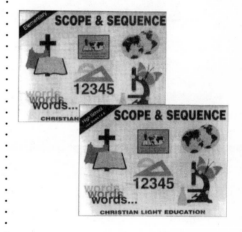

Big-time homeschool curriculum publishers such as A Beka Book and Bob Jones University Press also have scope and sequences. You can request them to send you one, usually for a very small sum or even free.

Smaller curriculum publishers sometimes include a scope and sequence in their catalogs.

A publisher's scope and sequences, of course, just tells you what the publisher's materials cover, not necessarily what they *should* cover.

So here's an important fact to remember:

There is nothing sacred about the particular subjects taught in school, or the order in which they are taught!

With the exception of math, phonics, and some math-based science topics, which really do need to be taught in a step-by-step sequence, almost everything taught in school can be taught in just about any order. Someone somewhere just sat down and *decreed* "this shall be taught in second grade." But they could just as easily have decreed it should be taught in fourth grade, or eighth grade, or not at all!

Who says Earth Science should be taught before Chemistry, anyway? And why? Why do college-bound high school graduates have to spend three years (at least) in science class, but not one single term learning CPR and basic nursing care?

Why should American History be taught before European History? Or vice versa? And what American History do we study—the newly fashionable "multicultural" kind which ignores George Washington, or the old-fashioned kind where you had to memorize "The Midnight Ride of Paul Revere"?

Is there any good reason for teaching nouns before verbs? (The most popular homeschool grammar program teaches *prepositions* first!)

In public school, a subject is educational because the teacher (or more likely, some Curriculum Facilitator somewhere) says it is. This means public schools waste lots of time doing things they *don't* need to—such as spending a week building Valentine's Day villages out of shoeboxes. (I am not making this up. *Instructor* magazine actually ran a how-to article suggesting that elementary schoolteachers do this project.)

At home, *you* are the teacher. You can decide *which* subjects to cover and *when* to cover them. This book you are now reading tells you which subjects other homeschoolers are teaching, and where to find resources to teach them. You will be covering "everything we need to" when:

- Your children have learned to read
- Your children have learned to write and type
- Your children have adequate grammar and spelling
- Your children have learned to cipher (do basic math)
- Your children have read a lot of books (both fiction and non-fiction)
- You have determined what your goals are for your children, and what their goals are for themselves, and picked out the materials that will help them meet those goals.

"What age should I begin homeschooling?"

THE LONG ANSWER. You already have! If your child has learned to speak, or play "Peek A Boo," or is toilet trained, you are a home educator!

What you mean is, "What age should I begin *formal academic* homeschooling?" The obvious answer is, "When your child is ready for it."

Boys tend to be about a year behind girls in seatwork and reading skills, for example. In public school, the boys are pushed before they are ready and then many of them are labeled "hyperactive" or "ADD" (Attention Deficit Disorder). At home, you can afford to offer a subject every so often until the child appears able to handle it.

Famous people throughout history have learned to read any time between age 2 and age 10. Sir Isaac Newton, the great scientist and mathematician, was slow in math until he became motivated to outshine a fellow student. While we would not use these examples to encourage homeschool "slacking"—letting kids goof off—we encourage you to observe your student's progress and be flexible enough to accommodate his maturity and skill level.

While public schools are set up for steady progress and everyone working at the same rate, in real life children grow in spurts. The same child who just doesn't "get" his phonics flashcards will suddenly surprise you by knowing them all perfectly! And his little brother or sister may be ready for the same lessons a year sooner than he was—or a year later.

Remember also that you don't have to do the same grade level of every subject. Quite often a child will be ready for fourth-grade work in math but only second-grade in language arts, or vice versa. A customized education is just one of the benefits of homeschooling!

"What kind of schedule should I follow?"

THE FBI-WARNING ANSWER. Figure it out fast, because the federal agencies are hanging around outside your house ready to nail you if you pick the wrong scheduling option. (We're just kidding. Actually, they're sitting in your bushes trying to catch you copying a videotape.)

THE AVERAGE ANSWER. Devotions and breakfast first, chores second, then school lessons. Most families wrap this up by early afternoon, and spend the afternoons on outside activities, fun projects, recreational reading, community service, or whatever. And don't forget Friday is for field trips!

THE DAD WORKS NIGHT SHIFT ANSWER. Switch morning and afternoons, and you can spend mornings with Dad!

THE WE-LIVE-ON-A-BOAT ANSWER. Do whatever you want. Everything you do on a boat counts for something educational, and can lead to a valuable future career, assuming you're silly enough to ever leave home and get a job. Even so, you probably use the Calvert curriculum, judging by the number of you who write in to their newsletter. Just don't forget the sunblock.

THE YEAR-ROUND ANSWER. Why stop homeschooling in the summer? The kids will just forget a lot of what they've learned. (Mary's advice: take it a little easy on this philosophy if it's really beautiful outside. Unless you live on a boat, in which case the rest of us will feel better if we know you're inside slaving over work pages.)

THE SIX-ON, TWO-OFF ANSWER. Six weeks of homeschool followed by two weeks of vacation. Lather, then repeat.

THE REGULAR SCHOOL YEAR ANSWER. You have less to explain to the neighbors when your children are on vacation during regular vacation time. This also helps if your curriculum publisher still has lesson plans that assume Christmas seasonal activities should happen in Month 4. But it really tweaks the curriculum companies when everyone tries to order at once . . . in the third week in August. So if you follow the regular school year, order early, and maybe you'll even get a special discount!

THE SPONTANEOUS ANSWER. You provide lots of great resources, make yourself available to answer questions, and never "schedule homeschool" as such. This works best if your children learn to read *early*, or if your lifestyle involves lots of hands-on, real-world activities, or both. Prepare to take a deep breath and get more organized when high school rolls around.

"How much does it cost?"

TAMMY'S ANSWER. The best analogy we have seen in reference to the cost of homeschooling is the "birthday cake" analogy (thank you, Robin Scarlata). The mom who spends time to make her child's birthday cake from scratch will spend almost no money. The mom who spends less time and uses packaged mixes and purchased decorations will spend a little more money on the cake. The mom who spends no more time than what it takes to run to the bakery to pick up a purchased cake will spend a much larger amount of money.

The same holds true in your child's education. If you choose to pursue the unit study approach and use the public library as your primary source, you can spend an absolute minimum amount of money. Between unit studies and (relatively expensive) prepackaged curricula there are many options. Your cost will be determined by which option you choose.

PEGGY'S ANSWER. In a survey I did, I found that some people spent under $100 per year, and there were others who spent well over $750 per year. The cost often depends upon the approach. If you use a textbook, you may have some higher initial costs, but you may also be able to find the book used. There is a Textbook Exchange company here in Oklahoma which offers used textbooks (Christian ones also) for $7.50 per inch. They pile up your textbooks and measure the stack. I bought five levels of Saxon math for about $40! Of course, I don't have the teacher's manuals; they were out of them at the time. But since my husband has gone through calculus and loves math, that should not be a problem.

I guess that the cost will depend upon what you feel is necessary, and what you feel would be "nice." We spend a *lot* of money on homeschooling, but we feel that we are building a library and our approach requires lots of books. Others that I know spend money for math and English, then use the library for the rest.

I wouldn't look at cost till I knew how I wanted to homeschool—whether I wanted to use textbooks, workbooks, unit studies, or other materials. Then I would look to buy as many of them as was possible from another homeschooler.

JOHN'S ANSWER. It depends on materials. We spend from $100 to $700 per year per child. It sure beats private school tuition, though. One family I know who budgeted to send their kids to a private Christian school ($3,000–$5,000/year tuition per kid) kept the same budget when they started homeschooling. Imagine all the materials you could get!

MARY'S ANSWER. The "average" homeschool family (if there is such a thing!) now spends $500–$600 per child per year.

I would encourage you not to take a bargain-basement approach to your child's education, if you can possibly help it. Dads particularly get into this mode of thought: "Here's $20 to buy all the kids' school materials, dear. Don't spend it all in one place!" This is a mistake. Homeschooling is not "cheap private school." It is an investment in your child's future and his immortal soul.

"What do I need to buy?"

What you *don't* need: School desks. Pull-down maps. Slide projectors. Filmstrips. A bell for ringing to indicate the end of class periods. School uniforms. Television. Workbooks full of "busywork."

What is *nice* to have, but not *necessary:* Whiteboard or chalkboard (also available in student sizes). Bulletin board. Maps. Videocamera. Vdeocassette player. Puzzles. Home computer with modem, online service membership, and adult-quality word processing software. Educational software.

What is *essential:* Curriculum. Pencils with good erasers. Pens (and a bottle of Liquid Paper). Paper (including different kinds of art paper). Envelopes (for writing to relatives and pen pals). Homeschool books and magazines. Camera. Cassette player. Good encyclopedia. Globe. Atlas. Dictionary. Library card. Art supplies. Some method of record-keeping.

RENEE'S ADVICE. Don't buy a formal science or history textbook for second grade or less. In fact, don't buy one at all, unless it's for reference. Use real books instead.

"Will my children respect me as their teacher?"

RESPECTFUL ANSWER #1. Do they respect you as their parent? If they don't, you need to earn their respect anyway.

RESPECTFUL ANSWER #2. Respect them as a student, and teach them to respect you. They will see more of you, more of your mistakes, but also more of your good points, more of your love and learn to like you and the rest of their family even more.

RESPECTFUL ANSWER #3. If your children have been in school, they may seriously doubt that you, a lowly Mom, could possibly know as much as a Real Teacher. However, don't let that deter you. The wonderful thing about homeschooling is that it will foster respect. Initially, there might be a bit of a struggle, some testing of the boundaries, some poor attitudes. This is not so much a homeschooling problem as it is a child-rearing problem.

Many parents have found it best not to make a formal distinction between their mothering and teaching roles. Thus, instead of saying things like "Would you talk to a teacher at school this way?" or "Pay attention to me; I am your teacher, after all!" it is best to appeal to your God-given authoritative role as their mother: "I can't allow you to talk to me this way." "When your mother is talking, you need to listen." Don't allow any sort of poor behavior during school time that you wouldn't allow the rest of the day, and vice versa. Be natural, be yourself, and give everybody room to make the adjustment to having school at home. Most important, express your love and affection for your children during school times; don't get too serious! Eventually, you will probably be surprised to discover how homeschooling has melted away all sorts of bad attitudes and replaced them with a loving respect for one another.

"How can I teach many children at once?"

DANA'S ANSWER. It seems funny that we can expect a teacher to teach 30 kids she hardly knows at the same time, but a parent can't teach when they have a large family. I'm sure that Mary has more experience with this, but I will tell you how we handle it. First, as much as possible I teach science and history to everyone together. We do a lot of reading together and then I am able to give individual assignments according to ability. As our children have gotten older they are able to do quite a bit of their work on their own . Each day I spend a set amount of time working with each child. The amount of time depends on how much attention that child needs at that time. During the rest of the school day they work on their assignments on their own. I make myself available for any questions and help they may need while they are working on their own. If they need help while I am helping someone else, they lightly tap me on the arm and wait until I can stop to answer their questions. This year a few times I have had my oldest child teach a lesson to the other children. It worked well and I plan to continue doing it.

"Help! I have a preschooler! How can I teach the older children with him around?"

CONNIE'S ANSWER. I have a four-year-old, plus children aged 11,10, and 9. My four-year-old isn't really ready for formal schooling. He likes to color, so I just picked up some beginning shape and color workbooks and we informally do things while the other kids are working. Remember that their attention span isn't very long at this age. Right now, it might be best to just lay the foundation for later, reading lots of books to him, coloring, letting her help in the kitchen etc. There are lots of good suggestions on all the homeschooling boards for curriculums for later use. It's not as hard as you might fear.

LYNDA'S ANSWER. Let him/her play, play, play. Provide new play materials . . . not necessarily toys. For example scraps of fabric, or shells or twigs. or milk jug tops and a big bottle of glue for sculpture. Go bowling with an orange and toilet paper tubes. . . . And most of all, *relax!* Have fun.

MARY'S ANSWER. Crowd control is important. I like to have the little one in the middle of the room, with the older ones on couches and chairs around the edges. I know some of you are adamantly anti-playpen, but when they are at the age of no common sense and great speed, I find it saves me lots of grey hairs if the crawler is trained to be good in the playpen. Of course, if a preschooler wants to scrunch up next to the others with a book, that's great! He doesn't have to be able to read, either. For all of our nine children, books were their favorite toys . . . probably because they saw all of us spending so much time with them. Have a variety of toys handy, and keep switching the toys week by week. Take some away and put others out. Let a preschooler "do school" with simple activities, five minutes here and there with flashcards, simple crafts, etc. Important rule: spend time with the little one *first*. This fills up his "love bucket," and keeps him from being restless and overly demanding when you have to spend time with the older children. Speaking of the older children, they can also help by taking turns spending time with the baby or toddler. Another rule: take him with you when you do chores. Then you know where he is, plus if he is old enough he can learn to "help"!

"Do I have to do ALL the teaching?"

Here's a little secret: we *call* it "homeschooling," but it's really "real-world schooling." For once, the whole village actually gets to teach the child—*if*, and this is a big "if," you, the parents, feel any particular village member is trustworthy and a good mentor for your child.

So, where do you find these mentors? Here are some answers.

- **First, the homegrown mentors.** Older children can help a lot with the younger ones. Reading books aloud to the little kids is a favorite activity. So is playing educational games with them. Do you have an older relative living with you? A family member living nearby? Does this person have any valuable knowledge and enjoy your children's company? Well, then!
- **Kids can drill kids.** Even better, educational software can do the drilling. Lots more fun than flashcards!
- **Charles Dickens** makes a great history and literature tutor. For writing style, you can't beat C. S. Lewis. David Macaulay knows a thing or two about science and engineering, too. Do you see where I'm going with this? Yup, right to the bookstore and library!
- **Volunteering** is a great way for teens to gain all sorts of useful skills. Every community has dozens, if not hundreds, of organizations that can use a helping hand. See the chapter on Volunteering in Volume 3.
- **Your church or house of worship** likely offers classes in a variety of topics—at times that don't conflict with your regular school hours, too!
- **Seminars and camps** are available year-round for all ages. Some popular options: short-term missions assignments, space camp, computer camp, leadership conferences for youth, and worldview training institutes. You will want to make sure the staff is trustworthy and supports your spiritual and moral outlook.
- **Homeschool co-ops** are increasingly popular, especially for those using unit-study curricula. In this scenario, several families get together and share the major teaching chores. One mom might teach piano, while another does math and science. Or one might arrange to purchase all the supplies (with costs shared evenly), while another supervises the creative activities. The options are endless!
- **Your local homeschool support group** likely offers social events, and some of its members teach classes. Art, music, and creative-writing classes seem especially popular.
- **Online academies** provide trained teachers, usually for the upper grades. See that chapter in this volume!
- **Local private schools** might offer classes just for homeschoolers, or welcome homeschool enrollment in just a class or two, such as lab science.
- **To be used with caution:** In some locations, the public schools allow homeschoolers to enroll in extracurricular activities. Be sure they re-

spect your right to control the rest of your curriculum if you select this option.

- **Can you spell Y-M-C-A, A-W-A-N-A, and 4-H?** Local children's clubs of all sorts offer educational opportunities and welcome homeschoolers. Our local Y even has special classes during school hours just for homeschoolers!
- **If a student has a job**, often the company will teach a motivated teen as many skills as the teen is willing to learn.
- **Don't forget videos, software, and the World Wide Web!**

One cautionary note: There should still be *some* "home" in "homeschooling." It's possible to get so excited about all the great educational opportunities out in the big beautiful world that you miss out on one of the greatest beauties of homeschooling: family togetherness. When in doubt, go for more time to think and to be together.

"What if my child REALLY wants to go to school?"

THE INSIGHTFUL ANSWER. Before you even think about this question, you need to find out *why* your child is so anxious to attend school. Usually the reason is "friends." Less often, it's some special activity, such as cheerleading or sports. I have yet to encounter a child who wants to attend school because he or she believes the school will provide a better education.

If you are firmly convinced that homeschooling is best for your child, but you are meeting resistance over the "friends" issue, you can handle this two ways. First, you can arrange for your child to get together with his existing friends outside school hours. Invite them over. Take them to the mall. Arrange skating parties. Whatever works. Second, you can help your child make some new homeschooled friends. If the group offers "Homeschool Skating Hour" at the local rink, be there. Sign up for the art fair. Enroll in the YMCA classes scheduled during school hours just for homeschoolers (they do this in our area!). Invite the new friends over. Maybe even start a co-op class.

If your child craves involvement in some special activity, perhaps he can still be involved as a homeschooler. Or maybe the homeschoolers in your area have their own marching band, or basketball team. Ask! But the bottom line has to be that your child's spiritual development, character, and academics come before social activities.

THE WORLDVIEW ANSWER. The more your child knows about what education *should* be like, and what's wrong with the schools, the more likely he is to support the homeschooling solution. So share your reading with him.

THE LITTLE KID ANSWER. If your child has never been to school, but is sure he wants to, a few facts of life regarding time on the bus, hours in the classroom, needing to ask permission to go to the bathroom, school bullies, and homework should quell any romantic fantasies. As an alternative, let him read "Calvin and Hobbes."

THE HOLLYWOOD ANSWER. If you're willing to break your family rule against letting the preteens and teens watch "R"-rated movies, then a viewing of *187, The Substitute, Stand and Deliver,* or *Lean on Me* will reveal that all is not roses in big city high schools. Even the TV show *Buffy the Vampire Slayer* shows the general meanness and put-downs of the less-than-perfectly-fashionable-and-beautiful that are daily fare in the best-groomed suburban middle and high schools. Who knows? Your child may decide to homeschool *and* choose teaching as a career (because those schooled kids really need help) all in one night!

"What if my child has ADD or needs special help?"

THE ACRONYM ANSWER. What you really mean is, "What if my child has been *labeled* as having ADD, ADHD, or one of those other vague-yet-scary acronyms?" See the chapter on How Real Are Learning Disabilities.

THE PROFESSIONAL ANSWER. First, breathe a sigh of relief. There is no law saying you have to be the expert in every area just because you are taking on the responsibility of your child's education. Instead, think of yourself as choosing from a vast array of other professionals and their expertise when necessary. Speech therapy? Vision problems? Auditory difficulties? All these are areas that you may need to seek outside assistance with if needed. The good news is that you as a loving, concerned parent are in the best place to make those decisions on behalf of your child.

THE NEIGHBORLY ANSWER. Check with state and local support groups for more info, or post your questions online. You'll probably find someone who has been there, or been in a worse situation. Homeschoolers really do like to help each other!

THE AUTHOR'S ANSWER. Check out the chapters on Help for Distractible Learners and Help for the Challenged. Relax—thousands of other families have successfully traveled this road before you!

"What if my child is gifted?"

Amazingly, we have a chapter on this topic, too!

"Where can I find more information about homeschooling?"

MARY'S ANSWER. With this huge book in your hand, you need *more* information? But seriously . . .

Don't forget Volumes 2 and 3 of *The Big Book of Home Learning.* They provide detailed subject-by-subject reviews and information for preschool through elementary, and junior high through college, respectively.

Also, there are state support groups, local support groups, conventions and seminars, online services, homeschool web sites, homeschool magazines, homeschool books, and your friends that homeschool. To name a few sources!

Where *not* to start: your local school or state Board of Education. Although homeschooling is legal everywhere, sometimes local and state officials are not aware of this. Although many school and state officials are wonderful, friendly people, those who are less enlightened may try to bully you out of exercising your rights or act unpleasantly towards you in other ways.

If you have a computer with a World Wide Web browser, the quickest way to pick up information is by surfing over to Homeschool World (*www.home-school.com*). This site, sponsored by *Practical Homeschooling* magazine, will put you in touch with more information about homeschooling than you know what to do with!

If you're not sure where to start, check your library. They most likely have a good selection of homeschool books, and may know about or sponsor events for homeschoolers. See also chapter 6, "What to Read," and the chapters on homeschool methods for leads to books in your particular subjects of interest.

All set? Great! Now on to the next chapter, where we'll answer the questions you *didn't* think to ask!

CHAPTER 3

Seven Things I Wish Someone Had Told Me Before I Started Homeschooling

In the last chapter we looked at the Frequently Asked Questions that friends, relatives, and total strangers throw at new homeschoolers—and that new homeschoolers ask themselves.

In *this* chapter, we're looking at the Frequently *Un*-Asked Questions.

These are all the questions you don't know enough to ask, but that will save your life when you find the answers! We asked veteran homeschoolers to share their most valuable piece of advice—in a nutshell. And here's what we got.

Protect Your Time

YOUR UNASKED QUESTION: "How do I say, 'No,' when well-meaning people ask me to take the time I should be spending on homeschooling and put it into various other worthy projects instead?"

TAMMY SAYS: If the word "No" is not in your vocabulary, add it now. Friends, your church, your son's scout troop . . . These people and more will see you as a stay-at-home parent with time on your hands. You're not.

So practice saying, "I'm sorry, Sue, but, NO, I can't talk right now. We're in the middle of school." "I would love to help with the church social but, NO, I really won't have enough free time." "I know you're in a bind, Bill, but, NO, I don't believe I could take over the scout troop right now."

Dear Friends,

You ask whether this is anything we wish we had known before we started homeschooling. First, we expected we could make school completely fun for our child...

Second ... we expected our child to naturally love learning. The advertisements for curriculum materials all show happy and motivated students, don't they?

Third, we got the idea that if our child was having difficulties, it must be the curriculum's fault.

A fourth part of faulty thinking on our part was that it wouldn't take that much of our time to homeschool. Even with an "independent study" type of curriculum like Christian Light Education, some time must still be taken for preparation.

Then, we somehow got the notion that it would not take our child long to do his work. This did not prove to be true either.

Also, we expected our little pupil to be able to work quite independently without a lot of supervision. While this picture may have some validity in the upper grades, plan on spending several hours each day working with very young children, especially those who are just learning to read.

Finally, we expected things to go smoothly.

When we actually began homeschooling, however, we were in for a bit of a shock.

We spent much time and effort trying to make up games and exciting ways of presenting the material, but our little pupil was not nearly as enthralled ... as we thought he would be. We finally realized that no matter how well the material is presented, it still takes a certain amount of effort to learn it. Our little pupil simply did not want to work. When we finally realized this, we stopped expending so much effort on making things fun and concentrated on the discipline of learning. Now when we

Now, obviously, you won't be telling *everyone,* "No." There are many enriching things you can do and will make time for if necessary. I can almost guarantee, however, that you will have many opportunities to use this new addition to your vocabulary.

ANOTHER MOM SAYS: I never could say, "No," easily. So I would say, "Let me check my schedule and get back to you." This made it easier to determine if I really wanted to do something extra and allowed me to consult with spouse and others involved.

_____ Check calendar

_____ Check money

_____ Check baby sitter

_____ Check feelings

If these feel uncomfortable in any way, the answer is always NO!

RICK SAYS: My/our bit of advice is this: when homeschooling, make sure *that* time is only for homeschooling. Put the phone on auto-answer, make no appointments during that time because it is "convenient," and dedicate your attention to your children and their learning. This teaches prioritization, gives structure, and lets the kids know that their learning is very important to you. They will respond with a much more serious attitude about their own learning, knowing that both parents are also committed to it (and that you walk the talk).

PAM SAYS: You are pouring your life into the next generation of leaders. That is a very time-consuming and worthwhile investment. Give it your all, not your leftovers. God bless you as you persist. May you not take any comments or reactions from others personally, but may you bless them. Our esteem comes from the Lord— being true to His Word, not our peers. Isn't that what we are teaching our young ones?

Don't Expect Amazing Results Overnight (It Takes a Few Years)

YOUR UNASKED QUESTION: "How do I know when I'm doing enough? Shouldn't my child be discovering nuclear fusion or at least building perfect scale models of the Eiffel Tower by our second week of homeschooling?"

REBECCA SAYS: Often, even as a veteran homeschooler, I wonder if I'm doing O.K. by my child. Remember, the only frame of reference we have is the institutional setting—it's what we grew up with. Don't judge what you are doing by what the schools are doing. Relax, they are learning more than you may realize.

MARY SAYS: I used to wonder the same thing. Then, as my children got older, they began doing the exciting things that they were too young to attempt for the first years we homeschooled. What made the biggest difference to this overanxious momma was when they started entering contests. Even when they didn't win, their skills improved measurably and they made some great-looking projects. So I'd say, "Give time a chance, and try a few contests." The Spelling Bee, local homeschool science fair, and local homeschool art competition are great places to start.

Build Lots of Bookshelves

YOUR UNASKED QUESTION: "Where am I going to put all of the books I will eventually end up buying?

KEN SAYS: We started in one room we naturally call the library, then added two walls in our daughter's room. Now we are in the process of putting two walls of shelves in the older boys' bedroom. After that we will go over the doorways in the library and possible into the living room, but just up high. It seems like all the children have the same habit of collecting good books, so their rooms seem like the appropriate place. I just keep wondering who in the world would buy this house if we decided to move!

ANOTHER PARENT SAYS: We built bookshelves down our long narrow hallway using cinder blocks and eight-foot boards. Now all our encyclopedias and etc. are available to us. There are no nail holes in the wall. And it keeps the hallway from being wasted space.

MARY SAYS: If I had it all to do over again, when we bought our house I'd have lobbied for a relatively inexpensive wall of bookshelves in our living room instead of the expensive fireplace which actually makes our house *colder* on the few occasions we've used it. We've lined half the walls in our basement with bookshelves, plus most of our bedrooms, and *still* it's not enough shelf space!

Update Your Insurance

YOUR UNASKED QUESTION: "What disaster am I forgetting to prevent?"

"D LADY BUG" SAYS: Go get your home owner's or renter's insurance updated. We had a fire that wiped out everything from the stairs up. Sit and think about the replacement cost of all those books you buy, and shudder. Don't think it can't happen; you just never know. Educational materials are very expensive. Update the insurance value frequently, especially after a large purchase.

MARY SAYS: When you hear on the news that an entire community is devastated by floods, or a hurricane, or an earthquake, this means that the homeschooling families in that community suffer the loss of their curriculum. We've seen the homeschool community pull together to help such families, but prevention is better than cure! If your home and possessions aren't insured, or aren't insured sufficiently, now is the time to get up to date. And that goes double for life insurance. Sufficient life insurance means you will be able to continue homeschooling—and providing that continuity in your children's lives—when they need it most.

Say Thank You

YOUR UNASKED QUESTION: "How can I be a blessing to other homeschoolers right from the start?"

REBECCA SAYS: I hesitate to put this in, lest someone think I'm asking for a pat on the back . . . but here goes. Say, "THANK YOU!" to your support group leaders! One simple card can go a *long* way to encouraging him or her. And a card or note is better than a phone call—they can pull it out and refresh themselves when the going is bumpy. Believe me, I know, and the times I have gotten one are the best!

TAMMY SAYS: You've actually gotten a thank you? Golly. . . . All kidding aside, folks. I wouldn't have thought to say it myself, but I've been a leader since before we started homeschooling our sons five years ago (the word "drafted" comes to mind). I did consider giving it up last year and a large part of it was that I didn't feel like I was getting anywhere. Ah . . . I won't go into it. . . . but, yeah, a "thank you" is a wonderful idea.

RENEE SAYS: Me too! And I read those notes over and over! Actually, let's get real here: what we'd really like is an offer to baby-sit our kids and a

do have games, they are more appreciated!

We tried several highly touted (and rather expensive!) reading and math packages with indifferent results. After these experiments, we finally came to the conclusion that there is no "perfect" curriculum. . . . In the end we decided to pick a curriculum that lines up with our Christian convictions as closely as possible and just stick with it. . . . Now, we may add or subtract a few things, but we are not constantly looking for something bigger and better.

What we discovered is that homeschooling tends to show up our own character flaws. It can be hard to admit our own weaknesses, but as we do so we have a chance both to grow ourselves and to teach our children. It's been encouraging to discover that one does not have to be perfect to get the job done. Remember, we trust in our wise heavenly Father for grace to persevere and for wisdom to learn the lessons He has for us. We have found that He is indeed faithful!

Letter from "a Virginia homeschool family," Christian Light Education LightLines, Homeschool Edition

gift certificate to an adult restaurant (one where they don't give you crayons when you are seated). Did you ever wonder why leaders always get nice gifts upon quitting? Seems like we should give them gifts to encourage them to stay on.

MARY SAYS: Believe it or not, even curriculum publishers and book writers appreciate a bit of encouragement now and then. If a writer, speaker, webmaster, tutor, neighbor, or relative has helped you be a better homeschooler, spread the sunshine around a little. After all, someday *you'll* be the one helping others!

Don't Buy It Until You Need It

YOUR UNASKED QUESTION: "Should I stock up on curriculum for future years?"

TAMMY SAYS: I was given this advice in my first year of homeschooling (ignored it, of course) and ended up with a houseful of junk which I later had to get rid of because it took up more space than it was worth, tied up more money than it was worth, etc. I've found that, no matter how much I think I might need something in the future, when the future gets here I generally have plenty of time to go out and buy it. I suppose the only exception to this would be if a generous set of grandparents were to say, "Buy whatever you need to get started and I'll foot the bill." I'd still try to be realistic, though, because you later find yourself feeling guilty about the things you're not using.

Don't Be Scared To Buy It If You Think You Need It

YOUR UNASKED QUESTION: "Do I dare to buy *anything?* I'm panicked thinking I might end up with a product I don't like or can't use."

MARY SAYS: You are going to spend money on products you will never use. This happens to all of us (see Tammy's advice above!). Even if you're careful to wait until you need it *right now,* you may find you don't enjoy it, it doesn't work, you find something better, and so on. Don't let this worry you. First, you usually can find another homeschooler who'll buy it from you at a discount. Second, every time you buy a homeschool product, you're not just buying "stuff for the kids," you're buying an education for *yourself.* When you start saying, "I could do better than that packaged curriculum," or "I disagree with the way this grammar course works," you're *really* saying, "This product has taught me something important about what works and what does not work." Think of it this way: it would cost you tens of thousands of dollars, and years of time, to get an education degree. If you end up spending even hundreds of "wasted" dollars to become an expert homeschooler, that's a tremendous savings in comparison!

CHAPTER 4

You Can Do It!

L ife is what happens while you're making other plans. Homeschool is what happens while you're living your life.

You don't need a special, ideal set of circumstances in order to successfully homeschool. You just have to start. Read this chapter and you'll see that, if there's a will, there's always a way to homeschool!

You Don't Have to be Home All Day Doing Nothing but Homeschooling

The ideal homeschool situation is for Mom and Dad to be home all day, and relatively free to supervise and instruct the children. That's why many homeschool families start home businesses.

Many of you reading this are not blessed with this ideal situation. You might be the primary homeschool parent and be

- raising your children alone, due to death, divorce, or desertion of a spouse
- working outside the home part-time
- working outside the home full-time
- working at home part- or full-time
- working odd shifts

Families can and do homeschool in all these situations. It just takes more creativity—and a curriculum that doesn't exhaust you, preferably one where the children can do most of the work on their own. A lot depends on how reliable the children are, so character training *must* come first. In practical terms, this is best accomplished by teaching your children to do the household chores. This will uncover any areas that need character education quicker than you could imagine! It also accomplishes another essential goal—freeing up enough of your time to actually teach them.

If a child is highly motivated, you can use any method compatible with his and your goals. If a child is less motivated, you'd be wise to consider "back to basics" textbooks (assign X pages a day and you can immediately see if the work for each day is done), educational software (in this case, your child needs noneducational computer games to be *in*accessible during homeschool hours), Robinson Method, and online academies. Contests can be highly motivating, but success often requires extra help from parents (e.g., drilling spelling words), so use sparingly.

You Don't Have to Have a Small Family

A large family is a blessing, and homeschoolers tend to have families larger than the national average. With more kids, it works well to "cluster" them in groups of two or even three, doing the same projects and contests and studying the same books. Older students can amplify their studies with additional reading.

Money is a factor in two ways: you probably have less of it per kid, but on the other hand a reusable resource also costs less per kid. So a $299 Odyssey Atlasphere costs $299 per child in a family with one child, but only around $33 per child for my nine kids!

As a mother of nine, I would definitely urge other large families to go for reusable quality. Hardbound textbooks. Laminated wipe-off maps. Sturdy construction kits with storage cases (so the parts don't get lost and you end up having to rebuy the kit for another child). I can't think of a single time I've been sorry that I paid more for quality. But if you fall in love with a workbook series (such as Key Curriculum Press's wonderful Key to Geometry series), don't beat yourself up over having to buy it again and again for each child. Kids like to have *something* that wasn't passed down from an older sibling!

Use any homeschool method that fits your available time and goals. As you teach the same curriculum year after year, you'll just get better and better!

You Don't Have to be Rich

In spite of the fact that one in twenty Americans is a millionaire (true fact: I did *not* make that up), in 44 years I have yet to meet anyone who describes himself or herself as "rich." Let me help you figure out where you stand as a homeschool shopper—and show you that *anyone* can homeschool, no matter how much or little they have to spend.

- **If you want something and are able to buy it immediately**, you are rich. But you don't have to admit it. Such families typically spend $900 and up per child per year for homeschool curriculum and supplies. This is great for the high-school years especially, when online academies can make advanced studies so much easier.
- **If you can buy *most* things you want right away** and only have to budget and save for *some* things, you are well off. This type of family typically spends $600–$900 per child per year for homeschool curriculum and supplies. This puts you in the market for an online course or two per child, plus more ordinary curriculum for other subjects.
- **If you have to budget and save for *most* things**, you are average. Expect to spend $300–$600 per child per year. This will get you a full year of most packaged curriculum, plus some extras.

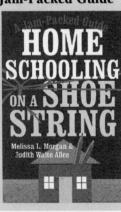

- **If you are losing ground each month and don't know why**, you probably don't *have* a budget and need to contact Christian Financial Concepts immediately (800-722-1976, *www.cfministry.org*). Founded by noted Christian financial author and speaker Larry Burkett, their books, tapes, and free phone advice have helped tens of thousands of families get out of the debt trap. Trust me. Call them. And plan your curriculum around a lot of trips to the free public library.
- **If you are out of work, on welfare, or some combination of the above**, this would qualify as "poor" in America—which still is "rich" compared to three-fourths of the present world and 99 percent of those who lived in the past. I say this as someone who lived for many years on *less* than people on welfare were getting, so I'm not unsympathetic to your plight. Here are some things you can do: (1) Get together with others in the same situation to pool your resources. (2) Buy used curriculum. You can find advertisements for companies that sell used curriculum in the *Practical Homeschooling* classifieds. (3) And here's a special tip. **Libraries often buy materials recommended by their patrons.** If you'd like to see homeschooling books, magazines, videos, and reference materials in your library, *just ask for them*. It doesn't cost a dime to ask!

You Can Learn Along with Your Kids

Rule of thumb:

The better the parent's education, the less the child's curriculum has to cost.

I don't mean just *school* education, mind you. If you are a voracious reader, you probably know a *lot* more than you did when you completed your school education. Your life experiences have also taught you a lot, which you can and should share with your children for valuable character education.

A highly educated person *who has learned how to teach* can take a student up to college level in all subjects using only library books, pencils, and paper. A less highly educated person, or one who has not yet learned how to teach will need some help. That where all the thousands of curriculum products reviewed in this and the other volumes of *The Big Book of Home Learning* come in.

The most cost-effective education is the one you give yourself. But if you lack the energy, time, or motivation to stay a year or two ahead of your student, then learning along with him or her works just fine. Most homeschool curriculum is designed to be used this way. High-school curriculum may not even require you to know *or* learn the subject, just grade the homework with the grading key. Online academies provide teachers, too!

A good homeschool curriculum will teach you how to teach. As you follow the lesson plans and teaching instructions, you'll automatically pick up teaching techniques and learn how teaching works. That's why I recommend new homeschoolers *use a packaged curriculum* from among those found in the Curriculum Buyer's Guide *for at least one full school year.* The day-after-day practice of doing it "their way" will eventually lead you either to decide you *love* "their way" . . . or to rebel and start getting your own ideas. Either response is great. If you have found the perfect curriculum for

tions that show your family may actually not be much worse off without that second income, to money-saving and budgeting tips, to home business suggestions, to ways to save on your curriculum purchases. But it goes way beyond the crop of "tightwad" tomes in its 250 oversized pages, not only in what it covers—curriculum from low-tech to high-tech, homeschooling in the teen years, art, physical education, and more—but in the depth and practicality of its advice and resources. Authors Melissa Morgan (who runs a mini-farm and two home businesses as well as homeschooling her two children and writing this book!) and Judith Waite Allen (who began homeschooling to help a foster child) have obviously done their own research and tried out their own ideas—all of which make sense!

Veteran homeschoolers will smile in recognition at many of their stories and suggestions, while pulling out a pad to take notes on the many fresh new hints. Novice homeschoolers will avoid many pitfalls and grab many opportunities by studying these pages. In fact, I feel like a more accurate title would have been *Practical Homeschooling* (but sorry, that's taken! <grin>) Even those with *huge* budgets will get a lot out of this book! *Mary Pride*

your family, why change? You'll just get better each year you teach it. If, on the other hand, this curriculum has taught you what you do and don't want to do, it has made you independent. You can't help but win!

Of course, I do not recommend picking a curriculum you are bound to eventually hate. About half of this book was written to help you avoid this ugly fate!

You Can Homeschool Anywhere

The country is definitely the place for unit studies and projects of all kinds. You have the room, the land, and the animals. You can roam around outdoors without worrying unduly about muggers or "bad air days."

The city is the place for field trips. Museum. Orchestra. Planetarium. Botanical garden. Stage shows. You name it, a large city will have it, as well as chess clubs, amateur dramatic societies, martial arts academies, and on and on.

Suburbs are usually close enough to a city for *some* field trips. They also tend to have good libraries with no spooky characters hanging around in them. Sadly, suburbs universally forbid you to own useful animals (goats, sheep, chickens) while allowing all those who are so inclined to own loud, menacing dogs. I have never been able to grasp the logic behind this, except that if you had some useful animals it might seem you *needed* them to help make ends meet and thus were *poor* (how awful!). In my suburban neighborhood, you can't put up so much as a tiny shed in your backyard with special permission (which will likely not be forthcoming). This can severely crimp the style of a would-be 4-H'er or State Fair competitor.

You can use any curriculum in any of these environments; but if you live in the city or the country, you might want to give some thought to taking advantage of the unique opportunities in your present area.

You Can Manage Three Minutes a Day

One area you won't have to worry about beating the schools in: personal time spent with the student.

Robert Doman, head of the National Academy of Child Development, has said that the average child gets only *three minutes* of individualized instruction daily in school. Three minutes!

I don't know where Mr. Doman gets his figures, but my own school experience sure validates them.

Do you think you can beat this at home? Even fifteen minutes a day is five times more personal instruction than your children get in school!

You Can Answer Questions or Look Up the Answers

Most of the time teachers spend in class is *not* spent answering questions. In fact, a survey in *Instructor* magazine several years ago showed that in the average class the teacher answered between 0 and 1 questions per hour *from the entire class*. In most cases, the teacher didn't answer *any* questions. In fact, teachers are reduced to begging the class to even answer *their* questions ("Can anyone tell us when the Declaration of Independence was signed? Anyone? Anyone?")

Since children learn best when *they* are asking the questions, right here is one of the reasons American education isn't working. For whatever reason, kids in school learn it isn't "cool" to show any enthusiasm in class. Any child who willingly answers a teacher's question without having to be drafted is labeled a "teacher's pet," "brown-noser," or "nerd." (And those are

Every issue of *Practical Homeschooling* features "Day At Our House" diaries from two to four homeschool families. So far, we've had diaries from city families, missionary families, and travelling families from across the USA and Canada and around the world!

-A DAY AT OUR HOUSE-

Hello! We're the Mosley family. We are blessed to live where we work, in Mountain Rest, SC, at our summer camp for kids and year-round group retreat center. During the summer, Rick and I work full-time as site director and personnel director. During the rest of the year, Rick runs retreats and does site maintenance. He also has charge of our four kids two days a week, while I work in the camp office where I create all our marketing materials, recruit summer staff, correspond with families, maintain our website, etc. I also use "Daddy-days" for personal errand running. It's wonderful! Pictured are Kevin (8, he likes to help Rick in the camp kitchen for retreats), Leanna (12, bookworm extraordinaire), Tessa (6, loves all of God's creatures, including Charlie), and Eric (9, loves sports). They have always been homeschooled.

The following is true. It happened Friday, November 5, 1999. No names have been changed to protect the innocent (or guilty).

Rick and Kelly Mosley were sitting near the wood stove on a comfortable (but stained and ugly) sofa in their continuous-ly-being-remodeled home at Camp Chatuga discussing all that son Eric had done that day. Said son walked through the room at that moment and mom said, "Eric, your dad and I were just talking about what a good, active boy you are."

"Yeah," Dad said. "We could write a story. We could call it Camp Boy!" (Think Farmer Boy from the Little House on the Prairie series.) And then Dad sold of Camp Boy's adventures that day:

"Camp Boy woke at the break of day (7:00), read some of his current novel, then dressed warmly, went outside, and began chopping wood. No one had asked him to do this. When he had a nice pile, he brought some in and started a roaring fire in the wood stove. Camp Boy then proceeded to the kitchen, where he cooked a delectable over-easy egg for his mother and a sunny-side-up for himself. (And he left the dirty Continued on page 59

PRACTICAL HOMESCHOOLING MARCH/APRIL 2000

We are the Newmans from Duluth, MN. This is our second year of homeschooling using the Sonlight Curriculum. We are a family of voracious readers, so Sonlight works well for us. Lots of books to read, and we love it! This is a somewhat typical day in the Newman household—Ed and Susie, Micah (11), and Christina (11).

The winter's daylight hours are still short here in the North Country. In the next couple months, when the sun begins rising earlier, I think it will be easier to get up earlier, too.

7:50 as I slowly drag myself out of bed. I had a stomach bug last night and I'm not sure how the day will go. I make my coffee, feed the dogs and let them out, empty the dishwasher, clean up the pans from last night, and start some rice cooking for the dogs' home-made dog food. (id, whose morning routine begins at six, has left for work a while ago.

8:10 Wake up the kids. They begin their breakfast while I take my shower. Micah takes his shower. Christina practices piano for ten minutes. I eat, then help Christina brush and braid her hair while Micah reads an American Heritage magazine.

9:20 The kids read their Bibles for ten minutes. We're twenty minutes behind schedule. Usually we begin by 9 am.

9:30–10:15 We sit on the couch and read together. We are using the Sonlight 6th Year Curriculum for both kids, who are 6th and 7th grade. We read from a book on the Middle Ages, followed by a few pages from Favorite Poems, Old and New, and a couple pages from the Usborne Book of Science.

10:20 The kids go out to do their morning chores. They bring water out for the goats and geese as they let them out of the barn and give them their morning feed and hay. They also feed the three rabbits.

10:35 We begin the creative writing exercise from Ed. Ed is a writer by profession and enjoys coming up with these exercises. We use them for teaching grammar as well as creative Continued on page 59

the *nice* names!) To actually *ask a question* in class is like putting on a flashing sign that says, "I am a dork. Kick me."

At home, it's just the opposite. Homeschooled kids never learn it's uncool to ask questions, so they do what comes naturally and ask you questions all day! The beauty of this is that you don't even have to know the answers. Showing kids that adults find answers by looking them up—and teaching the kids to look up answers by themselves—is an important part of a quality education.

You Can Teach Skills More Quickly Than You Expected

Here is one simple thought that can greatly reduce stress in learning. *You can master any new skill in a reasonable amount of time.*

This idea does not sound earthshaking. But when you compare it to the way schools usually teach, you'll see how revolutionary it is.

Say Johnny wants to learn to read. Does his teacher say, "O.K., Johnny, I'll teach you to read. It should take about twenty hours total, and then with practice you will be able to read anything you want"? No way! Johnny is facing up to *eight years* of reading instruction. No matter how well he can read, every year he will be reviewing his sight words, writing out spelling lists, filling out endless "reading comprehension" tests, and on and on and on. Would this discourage *you?* Of course it would! And it discourages Johnny too. The task seems endless. Nothing he does will make it shorter.

> **For dramatic results in your home program, just make it clear to the student that this task will *not* go on forever.**

If he applies himself, he *can* finish it more quickly. Promise *not* to review him constantly on his skills. Instead, immediately put those skills to work.

How do you do this? Well, let's say you are teaching your daughter arithmetic. Once she has learned addition, throw a party. Buy her a present. Treat her to a yogurt popsicle. Do *something* to celebrate. Any ceremony you come up with will help cement the fact that an era is over. Addition study is over. (Celebrating will also make her more anxious to finish the *next* step!) Now you are not going to study addition any more. Rather, you are going to *use* addition. Let her help you tally up the checks when you balance your checkbook. Have her keep running tabs on the cost of your shopping trip. Addition is used in multiplication and division, which she will be studying next, so if you don't do anything special at all she will still be using it.

If you are trying to teach your child something that he never gets any practice using in daily life, you probably didn't need to teach it in the first place.

You Can Teach the Basics Very Quickly

Another reason school seems like such a hopeless burden to many children is that it goes on so long. Thirteen years is a longer sentence than most murderers get nowadays. Yet we toss kids into school and lock the door on them for thirteen years and expect them to be enthusiastic about it!

> **Nobody needs thirteen years to learn what most schools have to teach. At the most, you need three or four.**

50 Weeks to Educate a Legend

"An American," Francis Grund remarked in 1837, "is almost from his cradle brought up to reflect on his condition and from the time he is able to act, employed with the means of improving it."

Lincoln, hardly a slouch as writer, speaker, or thinker, packed 50 weeks of formal schooling into his entire life over the twelve-year period 1814 to 1826. Even that little seemed a waste to his relatives. Unless you want to argue that those few weeks made a decisive difference to Abe, we need to look elsewhere for his education. Clifton Johnson thinks it happened this way:

He acquired much of his early education at home. In the evening he would pile sticks of dry wood into the brick fireplace. These would blaze up brightly and shed a strong light over the room, and the boy would lie down flat on the floor before the hearth with his book in front of him. He used to write his arithmetic sums on a large wooden shovel with a piece of charcoal. After covering it all over with examples, he would take his jack-knife and whittle and scrape the surface clean, ready for more ciphering. Paper was expensive and he could not afford a slate. Sometimes when the shovel was not at hand he did his figuring on the logs of the house walls and on the doorposts, and other woodwork that afforded a surface he could mark on with his charcoal.

—John Taylor Gatto, The Underground History of American Education

Let me explain why I said that. It's really pretty obvious when you see how our forebears handled education. In those olden golden days, kids didn't start school until age eight or nine. They attended classes for, at the most, three six-week sessions a year, six hours a day, and by the time they were sixteen they could read, write, and cipher rings around modern children. Nor was their instruction confined to the Three R's. American children of the 1700s through the early 1900s learned history, theology, geography, practical science, and hundreds of practical skills that are now only tackled in college, if at all.

When you add up the total time in school, it comes out to eight years of eighteen weeks each. Modern children go to school thirty-six weeks a year; so by simple arithmetic four years of old-time instruction should be all it takes for similar results.

In actual fact, it has been shown again and again that twenty hours of phonics instruction is all that children need in order to read.

As for math, I had a personal experience that might shed some light on how long it should take to learn basic math up through algebra. My father, a college professor, taught me eight years of math in the summer I turned seven. For three months, he made me do nothing but math for two hours per weekday. That amounted to 120 hours for *all* basic math, as opposed to the 1,440 hours the schools now spend. Surely I am not 12 times smarter than everyone else!

Similar reasoning applies to the other subjects: history, geography, handwriting, composition, and so forth.

WHAT THIS MEANS: *Every* child who attends school, public or private, is retarded. "Retarded" means "held back." Schools are in the business of keeping children off the street and out of the job market for twelve years. So they drag out learning needlessly for years, and fill up the time with mindless, boring exercises.

You may wonder what to do with a child who flashes through the standard school subjects. Don't worry. *He'll* know what to do! The whole point of learning the basics is to get to the good stuff—other languages, literature, serious writing, theological studies, designing and inventing, art, music, and on and on. By the time your children finish their basic education, it should be clear what subjects interest them enough to qualify for further study. Let Junior start a business. Send his articles to magazines. Patent his amazing arcade game. Give him a one-man show and invite the artistic community in to admire his work and suggest improvements. With the whole wide world out there, who wants to spend eight years with reading comprehension worksheets!

Everyone is Welcome!

The "Show & Tell" feature in *Practical Homeschooling* is where we spotlight the special achievements of homeschooled students. The section pages of this book are adorned with some of these kids and their successes.

When I first started the magazine, most of the kids whose photos I printed were white Anglos, because most homeschoolers were white Anglos. Lately I've been seeing more photos of kids from other groups, which is a good thing!

Should your race or ethnicity affect your choice of homeschooling curriculum? Probably not. You don't have to be Greek or Italian to get a classical education, as famed teacher Marva Collins' black inner-city students can attest! Your ancestors didn't need to come over on the Mayflower for you to choose the Principle Approach (mine sure didn't!). These are the only two methods that *necessarily* concentrate mostly on the works of Dead

White Males (since they concentrate most on early European and American civilization). Unit studies, Charlotte Mason Method, unschooling, etc. are all racially, sexually, and ethnically neutral.

Be aware that any homeschool curriculum that includes large amounts of readings from works published before 1960 will include some material written from an unselfconsciously racist perspective. The Robinson Curriculum, which contains many 18th-century and 17th-century works, has been particularly criticized for this (as, for that matter, has Mark Twain's classic *Huckleberry Finn,* which was written to *combat* racism!). I feel that, from a historical point of view, it is important to know what people of the past really said and thought, not what we wish they had said and thought. On the other hand, you might well feel you'd like to protect your younger children from unfairly disrespectful attitudes towards your ethnicity or race. This is a legitimate concern. Children can be strongly affected by what they read. I remember the surge of anger I had at how unfairly the fictional character Jane Eyre was treated when I first read the book by that name. Starting off a young child's study of history with a lot of anger at how his or her ancestors were treated may indeed not be the wisest course.

The only other ways your race or ethnicity will affect your homeschooling are that:

- You will stand out at the typical midwestern homeschool convention if you are not a native-born white Anglo American. (This is not as much the case in southwestern states or Pacific seaboard states.) Taking the positive outlook, at least people will remember you!
- Members of your ethnic or racial group may be less than supportive or understanding about your homeschooling, if your group is underrepresented in the current homeschool community. Look at it this way: ten years ago *everyone* had the same problem of unsupportive friends. The cure is to talk your friends into homeschooling too!

Heightened parental involvement is the greatest indicator of future educational success. By homeschooling, you are automatically entering the upper zone of parental involvement, and can expect success *whatever* curriculum and method you choose. Don't let anyone scare you off because "homeschooling isn't a thing people in our group do." You just take the lead and sooner or later your skeptical friends will be asking you how *they* can homeschool!

Independence Day

John Holt became famous for suggesting that kids can teach themselves *without* adult interference. Although this idea can be carried to extremes, it is undoubtedly easier to learn without someone hovering over you and babbling in your ear while you are trying to work.

Anyone who has a fine crop of youngsters to teach at home quickly discovers the importance of letting students do as much as they possibly can by themselves. One of my favorite lines is, "Try it. If you have trouble, come and ask for help."

Sooner or later, your child will have an Independence Day. He will discover that it's actually *more* fun to tackle a tough problem and figure out the answer on his own. At this point, he may head into areas of study that *you* never learned (e.g., website design).

When that day comes, your job as a home teacher is basically over. All you'll have to do from that point on is act as a sounding board, help him

Independence Motivates

Young people in America were expected to make something of themselves, not to prepare themselves to fit into a pre-established hierarchy. Every foreign commentator notes the early training in independence, the remarkable precocity of American young, their assumption of adult responsibility. Tom Nichols, a New Hampshire schoolboy in the 1820s, recalls in his memoir how electrifying the air of expectation was in early American schools.

Our teachers constantly stimulated us by the glittering prizes of wealth, honors, offices, which were certainly within our reach—there were a hundred avenues to wealth and fame opening fair before us if we only chose to learn our lessons.

—*John Taylor Gatto,* The Underground History of American Education

find the resources he needs, and revel in your new role as the voice of experience and wisdom. You'll be amazed that it all went so fast.

You see, it's a small job after all.

PART 2

12 Steps to a Successful Homeschool

Monique Harris, a 17-year-old homeschooler from Vilonia, TX, received a perfect 1600 on the SAT, and 34 out of 36 on the ACT. She's a national merit finalist, with a scholarship of $9,000 per year for four years. She also received the Governor's Distinguished Scholarship, which pays for complete tuition, room and board, and all mandatory expenses for four years of college. While still deciding, Monique is considering medical college.

Monique has homeschooled for her entire life, except for two years of high school. She found that "regular" school didn't offer any additional academic challenges, so she homeschooled this last year again, getting her lessons over quickly and saving time for other worthwhile activities. Monique has volunteered with Family Council, filing papers, taking notes, and performing legal research. She has been playing piano for years, and has attended the Pensacola Music Academy camp for the last three summers. Monique now gives piano lessons. It's no wonder the world's beating a path to her door!

Homeschooling can yield financial dividends! Daniel Story earned more than $9,700 in scholarship money as a National Merit Finalist. He decided to attend Christian-based Taylor University for its computer department, even through he was offered a $34,000 scholarship to Calvin College as a merit finalist. Daniel is pictured here with his family.

CHAPTER 5

What to Join

You know that homeschooling works. Your questions have been answered.

Now . . . where to start? Where to start?

In these next four chapters, you'll find twelve steps that will start you on the road to a successful homeschool.

Step One: Join HSLDA

Joining the **Home School Legal Defense Association**, otherwise known as **HSLDA** (PO Box 3000, Purcellville, VA 20134, (540) 338-5600, www.hslda.org), is a two-step process. First you send away for an application form. Upon receipt, you fill out the form, including information on what curriculum you plan to use for each child, and send it in along with a $100 check. If you are accepted (which you most likely will be), you will receive one year's worth of protection for covered legal expenses. In most cases, HSLDA can stop overbearing social workers and uninformed truant officers right at the door. In those few other cases, won't you be glad you have protection?

In addition to legal protection, benefits offered to HSLDA members include the following:

- The ability to call and speak with a legal assistant or attorney for your state about homeschooling matters or other issues ranging from social service contacts to promoting family-friendly legislation.
- A year's subscription to *The Home School Court Report*, HSLDA's newsletter
- Eligibility to subscribe to "Fax Alert" ($10 per year) or "E-Mail Alert" services that provide timely information on federal legislation that might affect homeschoolers.
- Counselling and helpful materials from the Special Needs Coordinator for those whose children face special challenges.
- A whole range of services to military homeschoolers worldwide

The purpose of the Home School Legal Defense Association is to establish the fact that responsible home schooling is legally permissible in every

The Truth About HSLDA

Some homeschoolers have made a crusade out of dissing HSLDA, claiming that it's a waste of money now that state laws are so lenient, that you can always do the legal research yourself, and that HSLDA leadership is promoting its political ambitions and agenda at the movement's expense. The truth is:

(1) It's only a waste of money if you object to defending other's rights as long as you yourself are not personally threatened.

(2) If you ever are personally threatened it's a terrific deal, especially considering that HSLDA usually manages to resolve the situation before it ever ends up in a courtroom.

(3) Yes, you can do the legal research yourself, just like you can do your own plumbing, make your own clothes, and cut your own hair. But do you really feel unempowered unless you're spending weeks in a law library?

(4) HSLDA's political agenda is consistent with its claimed mission of more rights for responsible

parents and children. To protect home educators, they have been forced to take up "side issues." But these often turn out not to be such side issues after all. HSLDA has fought for the right of homeschooled kids to have driver's licenses, for example. When a state, trying to combat the phenomenon of public-school dropouts, passes a law forbidding anyone under the age of 18 who is not enrolled in a school to drive, HSLDA is there to remind them that home-schoolers are not dropouts and the law should accommodate them. Similarly, HSLDA's response to issues ranging from the U.N. Convention on the Rights of the Child (which all but requires governments to control all aspects of a child's education and makes all children essentially wards of the state), to the free practice of religion, to how military recruits are classified, all turn out to be pertinent to homeschoolers.

(5) Mike Farris, founder and president of HSLDA, once ran for political office—vice governor of Virginia, to be exact—and made a creditable showing. That was years ago, and he has not sought political office since. HSLDA funds were not used to support his candidacy, and I am aware of no law yet making it a political crime for homeschoolers, even homeschool leaders, to run for office. In fact, one of our best friends is a homeschool dad who is a Missouri state representative, and I personally wish more homeschoolers were in political offices! So I'm not sure exactly what the issue is supposed to be here, but I present the facts for your consideration all the same.

state. They will provide experienced legal counsel and representation by qualified attorneys to every member family who is challenged in the area of home schooling. The attorney's fees will be paid in full by the Association.

Run by Concerned Women for America's former legal counsel, Michael Farris, this is a reputable organization with over 65,000 member families. Knowing you can obtain quality legal counsel is enough to dissuade potential persecutors in some cases. So is knowing what the law says, if your state law is favorable to home schooling. Ask your local homeschool group for a copy of the law (someone should have it on file). Then, if you feel you need more protection, or if you just want to contribute to the defense of those families that are on the hot seat, join the Association.

HSLDA also provides a slew of valuable services to the homeschooling community, such as their monthly packets for state leaders with summaries of bills submitted to state and federal legislatures. They personally contact government officials when some new policy impinges on our freedoms. Example: HSLDA recently persuaded the military to upgrade homeschoolers who wish to enlist from "correspondence school graduate" rank (the lowest possible) to a higher rank, over a test period of five years. If the enlisted homeschoolers perform well, the change will be made permanent.

Most people never need HSLDA's services, but the dues from those of us who never get hassled support the legal firepower to keep the whole movement strong. Think of it as a charitable contribution or think of it as insurance: either way it's a great investment. Total cost: $100 per family per year.

For those whose children have grown up and graduated, or those who have no children, or whose children haven't yet reached school age, HSLDA has launched their "Friends and Alumni Program." For $85 per year, "Friends and Alumni" members can receive the same benefits offered to homeschooling families.

WHY YOU NEED THIS STEP Because living in fear of the social worker, your nosy neighbor, and your irate in-laws is no fun. Because even if *you* have great neighbors, a friendly school district, supportive in-laws, and enlightened social workers, that doesn't mean everyone else does. Because $100 a year just isn't that much for peace of mind.

Step Two: Join Your State Homeschool Group

You can get your state group's name, address, and phone number from the appendix in the back of this book, or from the listings on our website, Homeschool World, at *www.home-school.com. And pay the dues!* These pay the overhead for the sacrificial folks who have spent years struggling to make homeschooling safe and legal. They also usually entitle you to the state newsletter, which includes info on the local support groups and their activities, and may garner you other goodies as well, such as a discount on the cost of attending the state convention or an invitation to attend your local Six Flags Homeschool Day. If you have a state group membership card, you also can request the "educator's discount" at teacher's stores and bookstores. Tell them you're a home educator, show them your membership card, and most establishments that offer educator's discounts will grant you one. This discount is usually worth somewhere between 5 percent and 20 percent off the goods you purchase in that store. Total cost of state group dues: around $20 or so.

WHY YOU NEED THIS STEP Because without state homeschool groups, there would *be* no homeschool movement. Because homeschooling operates under state laws, and your state group has spent years working with the legislators on your behalf. Because the annual state convention is really great. Because you might be able to get an educator's discount at the bookstore. Because it's the right thing to do.

Step Three: Join Your Local Support Group

While your state group provides major events, such as annual conferences and "Days at the Capitol" for meeting with legislators, your *local* group is a place to make friends, ask your questions, and be a part of ongoing activities with likeminded people.

Here is a partial list of opportunities available through support groups in my area. Please note that this is *not* an especially amazing list of opportunities. I get dozens of homeschool newsletters from different states, and can honestly say that the following list is pretty typical of the kinds of social and academic opportunities creative homeschool parents everywhere are making available to their groups:

- Bible Quiz teams
- Graduation ceremony for homeschooled high-school and 8th-grade graduates
- Speech and Theatre Club
- Marching band
- Fine Art competition
- Tutoring in forensics, public speaking, creative dramatics, create writing, beginning Latin, literature, speech, drama, English, reading, math, and physics
- Standardized testing
- Art classes
- Roller skating
- Bowling
- Swimming
- Special classes at the YMCA for homeschooled kids, during regular school hours
- Choir
- Scouts
- Math Olympics
- Field trips (I still remember our group's field trip to an Amish farm! We had to ride a rented school bus two hours each way. Bounce, bounce, bounce. Talk about spinal pain! I wonder how kids can stand to ride a bus like that every day.)
- Spelling Bee
- Lending Library and Resource Center

Let's take another look at that last option. Many support groups now have lending libraries of popular homeschool resources and of other items that are hard for individual families to afford. A set of travel videos or college counseling books might be too expensive for an individual family, but very affordable when a group clubs together to buy them.

But most of all, a support group makes it possible for new homeschoolers to find friends and mentors who have "been there" and can help you put your fears—and overoptimistic hopes—both in perspective. You can find out how others who have tried a new resource *really* liked it, or get answers on how to deal with learning obstacles from experienced homeschoolers.

The best groups are those where everyone helps. Even if you're a neophyte homeschooler, you may be a math whiz or a terrific organizer. Try to find some way to be useful, and show your appreciation a *lot*. It's the best

---

No Local Support Group? (It's Unlikely, But Anyway Here's How to Start Your Own)

NEW!
The Leader's Manual
$15 plus $4 shipping.
Christian Home Educators of Cincinnati, 4320 Tower Ave., Cincinnati, OH 45217.
(513) 398-5795.
Email: Blue.Herron@goodnews.net.
Web: w3.goodnews.net/~herronrj/

If the thought of starting your own support group fills you with fear and trembling, take heart. **The Leader's Manual: A Guide for Christian Home School Support Groups** will take you by the hand and walk you step by step through the entire process. Even if you are involved in an established group, you'll find ideas here for events and activities guaranteed to please your members. (Hint: if you want to please your support group leaders, why not buy this book and offer to coordinate one of the activities yourself?)

Meeting ideas, leadership helps, burnout prevention, basic group structure, and more are all included. Most helpful are the 25 reproducible forms: field trip planners, new member forms, schedules for planning special events, detailed instructions for science fairs, certificates, and more.

Most of these ideas can be implemented by any size group, but be prepared! Using this book will probably make your group so successful that you will experience some rapid growth. On this point I share a philosophical difference with the authors. While they include a chapter on how to split your group when it gets too large, I would prefer to see some discussion on how a larger group can operate effectively in its own right. All support groups don't have to be small, there are valid reasons for embracing growth and learning to take advantages of the resources offered by a larger group.

Regardless of the age or stage of

your particular group, you'll find *The Leader's Manual* a valuable help. *Renee Mathis*

NEW!
Help! I've Gotta Organize This Group!

Parents. $14.95.
Valerie Royce Coughlin, 13428 Cedar St., Hesperia, CA 92345.
(760) 947-3982.
Email: famfare@gte.net.

Help! I've Gotta Organize This Group is (no surprise) for use by homeschool support groups. It's smaller (80 pages) than Valerie Royce Coughlin's other book, *Help! I've Gotta Organize This Stuff* (reviewed in the chapter on organizing), and contains a few of the forms in the first book: calendars, group activities, awards, certificates, posters, even greeting cards. *Renee Mathis*

way to make sure those incredible people who plan all those fun activities keep energized and happy to do more for you!

WHY YOU NEED THIS STEP Because you're a brand-new homeschooler. Because you have no idea what you'll be missing if you *don't* join. Because you bake great cookies. Because your kids need friends. Because *you* need friends who understand what your life is really like now that you're homeschooling.

Step Four: Join Other Homeschoolers Online

Join your friendly international online support group. For no more than the cost of monthly online service—currently as little as $9.95—you can be part of a support group that is open 24 hours a day, every day of the week, and that numbers thousands of members from every state and province in America, Canada, and every English-speaking country in the world.

Online, you can:

- **Ask questions anonymously** that would embarrass you to blurt out in front of your neighbors. If your older child still wets his bed, or is having real problems with reading; if a non-custodial spouse is trying to make trouble for your homeschool; if your in-laws are being less than supportive of your decision to homeschool; you can ask for help and suggestions online without violating any of your near-and-dear's privacy or getting yourself in trouble. Just pick a "screen name" that's not identical to your real name, and ask away!
- **Find advice** for all kinds of homeschooling situations, from the rare to the common. "My child has been diagnosed with ADD. What do I do?" "I am blind and homeschooling a sighted child. Suggestions appreciated." "We are moving next week to Okinawa—can anyone tell me about the homeschooling situation there? Is there a group we can join?" If you can ask it, someone out there can and will answer it.
- **Locate and ask advice about resources** of all kinds, from the unusual to the popular. Whatever you want to know about, *someone* out there has already tried.
- **Share your opinions and concerns** (politely), tell jokes (clean ones), make friends (almost guaranteed)! Online is great!

WHY YOU NEED THIS STEP Because it's one of the few great reasons for having bought a computer in the first place. So you can "let it all hang out" when things *aren't* going great. So you can tell the world when things *are* going great. So you can have people around the country praying for you. So you can find answers to difficult questions. So your kids can make online pen pals, thus vastly improving their typing, spelling, and vocabulary. So you can really *feel* part of a million-person movement. As the first confidence-building step to maybe someday signing the kids up for an online course.

Even if you are a family of hermits living in the wilds on an island off the coast of Alaska, you can still join HSLDA and your state homeschool group. Most everyone else is within shouting distance of a hungry Internet Service Provider and a local homeschool support group. We're all anxious to meet you and get to know you. So don't be a stranger; drop in now, you hear?

CHAPTER 6

What to Read

O K. So you're a joiner, and you've rushed out to sign up with your state and local homeschool groups. Or so you're *not* a joiner, and you're ignoring all the wonderful advice in the last chapter. Either way, here are two more steps to homeschool success—both your success as a teacher, and your children's success as learners.

INSIDER NOTE: The man and girl on the cover of the middle issue are my husband Bill and daughter Lillian. Bill lost 50 pounds and gained bunches of muscle using the fitness program we described in that issue.

Step Five: Magazines

Subscribe to my magazine, **Practical Homeschooling**, also known as **PHS**. If you're a "newbie," you'd be smart to also snap up any back issue sets that are still available. Just call 1-800-346-6322 with your credit card handy. For the price of a couple of pizzas, PHS will bring you up-to-date on all the latest educational trends and resources. Regular PHS features include columns by some of the best-known names in homeschooling, oodles

of reviews of the latest new curriculum products and educational software (many from the people who brought you this book!), special research articles that take a complex topic such as special education and "open it up" to make it understandable, "Day at Our House" diaries from homeschool families around the world, story contests for the kids (with prizes!), a gallery of envelope art from our kid readers, "Show and Tell" highlights about homeschooled kids who do something special, cartoons and jokes, a lengthy letters section, and lots more. The magazine's tone is friendly; we don't care if you have a messy house, and we don't expect your kids to be perfect. PHS's viewpoint is Christian, but meekly so—this is a practical "how to" magazine, not an evangelistic treatise.

Other homeschool magazines are, of course, available. The bimonthly **The Teaching Home** carries political news, inspirational stories, a collection of the best tips from state newsletters, and "themed" how-to articles, all from a pointedly Christian viewpoint. This is the granddaddy of Christian homeschool magazines, founded in 1986. At least one song has been written about TTH's practice of featuring a perfectly posed, prettily dressed family on every cover. This is a magazine that strongly believes in presenting a "good testimony," meaning a serene home with obedient kids and the parents firmly, but lovingly, in control.

The bimonthly **Homeschooling Today**, also Christian, is best known as "more than a magazine—it's a curriculum!" In practical terms, this means you'll find discussion questions, exercises, unit studies, pull-out art units, and so on, along with a mix of Christian parenting advice from a psychologist, an occasional feature, and a review or two.

Growing Without Schooling, or GWS, has also been around a long time. Founded many years ago by John Holt, this is the most philosophical of the major homeschool magazines, and the least fancy graphically. It resembles a thoughtful discourse about home education and how children learn, with lots of readers writing in and sharing detailed observations of their children's learning experiences. The main perspective favored is often called "unschooling." (For more about unschooling, see Chapter 22.)

Other homeschool magazines exist. You'll likely be presented with a chance to subscribe when you visit your local curriculum fair or read your state newsletter.

So why do you need a homeschool magazine? Here are some possible reasons:

- To stimulate your thinking, or . . .
- To confirm your already-set opinions, or . . .
- To tell you what the publishers consider the "one best way" to homeschool. (You *won't* find the last two in PHS!)
- To increase your confidence and give you a "lift."
- To keep you up with the latest resources—including those nobody in your support group has heard of, or been brave enough to buy.
- To provide answers to questions that involve a lot of research, such as how to get your homeschooled child into college and which colleges to consider.
- To keep you up with current political news that affects homeschooling.
- To keep you up with current educational news that affects homeschooling.
- To find out what major homeschool thinkers think about an issue or subject.
- To give you a number of ways to teach a subject, so you can pick the one that fits best.

I'm sure you can think of other reasons, but these will do for now. As you can see, reasons *for* reading one magazine might be reasons *against* reading another! It depends what you're looking for. However, no matter which magazine(s) you choose, a magazine has an "immediacy," a feeling of belonging to an ongoing dialog, that a book lacks. A magazine also has a sense of permanence that a support group or online discussion lacks. Finally, a magazine can tackle issues and questions that are too short for an entire book but require too much research for you to spend the time yourself.

As a magazine publisher myself, I'm acutely aware of what a bargain a good magazine can be. We publish around 450 pages of *Practical Homeschooling* in a year, most in color and adorned with fancy graphics. A book with this much color and detail would run you at least $49, and more likely closer to $99. But a year's subscription will get you the finest minds in home education, the latest educational news, and reviews of the hottest new products, all for $19.95. Plus it comes in handy doses, is delivered directly to your mailbox, and you can enter one of our contests and win a prize worth more than the entire cost of your subscription. Even if you don't win a prize, it's a good—and inexpensive—way to quickly catch up on what homeschooling is all about.

WHY YOU NEED THIS STEP To get "connected" to what's going on right *now*. So you won't feel left out or like you're missing something. Because it's fun. Because there's a lot to learn, and magazine articles are more approachable than entire books. Because you like the cover. Because you're curious.

Step Six: Books!

Read a bunch of books about education, about public school, and about homeschooling. If you do this right, you'll end up knowing everything worth knowing about education that an education student pays tens of thousands of dollars to learn. Plus you'll know what the hopeful future teacher *doesn't* learn—what went wrong with public education and how to do a better job.

Your first step, of course, is reading *this* book. You paid for it, or at least borrowed it from the library or a friend, so why not go for the gusto and get your money's worth? We've tried to do a good job of distilling down for you what it would take thousands of hours to learn on your own. If we've succeeded, we hope to get the kinds of letters we received from readers of the previous editions. Typical example: "I used to be so confused about homeschooling, but after reading your book I feel like an expert!"

One book can't do it all, though. Even all three volumes of *The Big Book of Home Learning* can't tell you everything there is to know about home education. Luckily for us, hundreds of books are now in print explaining the fine points of everything from how to write your own unit study to the real history of how public education got a foothold in the Land of the Free and the Home of the Brave. The books reviewed in this chapter are a good place to start.

WHY YOU NEED THIS STEP To be smart. To increase your confidence. Because learning all this stuff that you never knew before is fun. Because you love your kids and want to do a great job.

Top Ten Books Every New Homeschooler Should Read

Half of you just read that subtitle and can't wait to get your hand on all these books. The other half are screaming, "Help! I don't have time to read *ten books* on homeschooling!"

Relax. You don't have to read all ten, or all at once. Some may not even apply to your particular situation. For example, Christians will be more interested in *The Christian Home School* than non-Christians, and home-schoolers of color will likely find *The Freedom Challenge* more essential reading than those of strictly European background.

This list is not an assignment: it is my personal attempt to narrow down the dozens of homeschooling books into a handy number you can start with.

The chapters on individual homeschool styles also include reviews of books explaining each method in more detail. For the truly ambitious, the CD-ROM edition of this book contains reviews of over 60 additional ti-tles—and more are coming out every day. That's why I thought you'd like a little help sorting through it all!

The Christian Home School

Parents. $14.95 plus $2 shipping.
Noble Publishing Associates, PO Box 2250, Gresham, OR 97080. Orders: (800) 225-5259. Inquiries: (503) 667-3942. Fax: (503) 618-8866. Email: Noblebooks@aol.com.

Gregg Harris's **The Christian Home School** is a delightfully refreshing, easy to follow, basic book on home schooling. The Christian Home School does simplify while it explains, and that perhaps is why it was Number Six on the Spring Arbor Distributors hotlist of Christian books when it first came out.

This is the best first how-to book for Christian homeschoolers, although veterans can learn from it, too. Gregg Harris, who has spent years presenting his justly renowned Home Schooling Workshop, leads you from the reasons for home schooling through how to answer arguments against it. He tells you how to get started, pitfalls to avoid, and why and how to link up with support groups. Even veteran home schoolers will enjoy the confident feeling you get from reading this book! *Mary Pride*

NEW!
Dumbing Us Down

Parents. $9.95.
New Society Publishers, PO Box 189, Gabriola Is., BC V0R 1X0, CANADA.

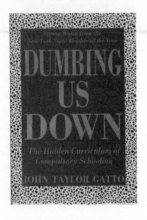

The author of **Dumbing Us Down**, New York State Teacher of the Year John Taylor Gatto, has become a legend in homeschool circles, invited to speak at dozens of homeschool conferences. His undeniable accomplishments as a "guerrilla" teacher in the public school system—smuggling *real* educational experiences into his classroom and smuggling his students *out* of the classroom to try their wings in the real world—are an inspiration to every homeschooler to break away from the mindset of imitating the public schools. But much more than this, his critique of *why* the public schools "fail" is essential reading for everyone the slightest bit interested in education.

Gatto's basic premise is that schools don't fail. They do exactly what they were designed to do, which is to dumb kids down. The "hidden curriculum of compulsory schooling," as the book's subtitle reads, is to produce a not-to-well-educated, compliant force of workers, consumers, and voters who will continue to support the mass society. How and why this plan was set into motion can be found another of his books, *The Underground History of American Education,* which is also reviewed in this chapter. How it works in schoolkids' daily lives is the burden of *Dumbing Us Down.*

The heart of the book is a speech Mr. Gatto made in 1991, on the occasion of accepting the title of "New York State Teacher of the Year." I am informed that the Regents granting the award sat there with looks of blank astonishment as Gatto informed them about the seven lessons school *really* teaches: confusion, class position, indifference, emotional dependency, intellectual dependency, provisional self-esteem, and your inability to hide from government surveillance. Other essays included in this mind-blowing book are "The Psychopathic School," "The Green Monongahela" (experiences that shaped Gatto's views on education and life), "We Need Less School, Not More," and "The Congregational Principle" (in which using historical examples Gatto shows how local control beats federal social engineering). You'll have a whole new batch of reasons for homeschooling after reading this book! *Mary Pride*

Freedom Challenge: African American Homeschoolers is unique in the annals of homeschool literature. A collection of 15 essays by homeschooling children, teens, and parents, it is simultaneously

- a "how we do it" book packed with homeschooling details and success stories
- an introduction to the "unschooling" philosophy (although some of the contributors have used traditional materials)
- an investigation into the questions and concerns that motivate biracial and African-American homeschooling families

The transcript of a "Forum for Homeschoolers of Color" held at a homeschool conference, an annotated resource list, and an index round out the book.

After reading *Freedom Challenge,* I felt that *white* homeschoolers (who comprise the vast majority at this time) should also read this book. Not only is the book an eye-opener as far as racial issues are concerned, but it's a great homeschool read. The contributors are all thoughtful and articulate, and their stories are both familiar (who among us hasn't had to deal with the dreaded "socialization" question, or with worries about educational adequacy?) and fascinating (most of us *don't* live on a boat with biracial parents or live in Japan with our military spouse).

As a first step to encouraging more non-white families to homeschool, *Freedom Challenge* is not only valuable but unique. The widely-remarked-on difference in academic achievement between racial groups in public schools has been shown by research to be eliminated by homeschooling. In other words, homeschooled black kids do as well as homeschooled white kids who do as well as homeschooled Asians, etc.

This bears out my private theory that any perceived differences in achievements between groups is simply a reflection of how much each group trusts and relies on the public education system for its children's education. While Asians (who have the highest test scores) are famous for prodding their children to go beyond school requirements, whites (in the middle) tend to take it easier, and blacks (at the bottom) tend to have a wholly misfounded trust that the "experts" in the schools will provide everything their children need. This trust is doubly betrayed as not only do black children, as a group, get inferior schooling but a vastly disproportionate number of black children are labeled "slow" or "learning disabled," thus justifying school failure in their cases. These institutional biases have led to a situation where nearly 30 percent of black student drop out before completing high school, and 25 percent of black *graduates* are nearly illiterate. As *Freedom Challenge* eloquently points out, homeschooling is an instant solution to these problems. It is also a way to emphasize one's cultural heritage, if desired, which appears to be a felt need of many black homeschoolers.

From the single mom on welfare who used homeschooling to rescue her son from a gang, to (my favorite entry) the somewhat sarcastic wit of a 14-

NEW!
Freedom Challenge
Parents. $16.95 plus $3 shipping. *Lowry House Publishers, PO Box 1014, Eugene, OR 97440-1014. (541) 686-2315. Fax: (541) 343-3158.*

FREEDOM CHALLENGE

African American homeschoolers

edited by Grace Llewellyn

Is Public Education Necessary?
The NEA: Trojan Horse in American Education

$19.95 each plus $3 shipping. *The Paradigm Company, PO Box 45161, Boise, ID 83711. (208) 322-4440. FAX: (208) 322-7781. Web: www.howtotutor.com.*

NEW!
Out of Control

Parents and mature teens. Paperback, $10.99. Hardcover, $19.99. *Huntington House Publishers, PO Box 53788, Lafayette, LA 70505. Orders: (800) 749-4009. Inquiries: (318) 237-7049. Fax: (318) 237-7060.*

year-old boy who writes just like my son Ted . . . from the "fruitarian" family who celebrate Kwanzaa, to Jamal the "bright toddler" who could read the newspaper by age three, *Freedom Challenge* is an inspiration to everyone to try the freedom of homeschooling. *Mary Pride*

Sam Blumenfeld strikes twice!

Is Public Education Necessary? is a homeschool classic. This is the first book to thoroughly document why we even have public education and who put it there. Did you know America survived just fine for over 200 years, from colonial times into the 1800s, without compulsory attendance laws, and that we had *greater* literacy *before* public education? Or that undercover socialists and Unitarians were the main forces pushing public education on us in the first place? (Hint: both the socialists and the Unitarians wanted to get children away from their parents' influence to mold them into the ideal citizen and the ideal human being, respectively.) Or that Protestant pastors went along, believing compulsory government schools could be used to transform the waves of Catholic immigrants into good mainstream Protestants? (It didn't work: the Catholics started their own schools.) Or that every single prediction the public-school promoters made, to persuade the public to accept government control of education, failed to come true? (I especially like their promise that government schooling would put an end to crime.) This, and much more that you never knew or suspected, is laid out for you, all amply documented.

The NEA: Trojan Horse in American Education shows how the schools have been turned into a political football and why our declining national intellectualism is no accident. Written in a lively, intelligent style, this is undoubtedly Blumenfeld's most important book, and essential reading for anyone concerned about curing America's educational inferiority. (The solutions are surprisingly simple.) *Mary Pride*

As could be expected from the subject matter at hand, **Out of Control: Who's Watching Our Child Protection Agencies?** is not enjoyable to read. No one at all is watching, according to this thoroughly researched and well-documented book by Brenda Scott. What with questionable statistics, denial of due process, under-educated social workers, sociological theories that scapegoat intact families as hotbeds of abuse (when research actually shows the vast majority of abuse occurs in non-biologically-related "families"—can you spell " live-in boyfriend?"—and where drugs and alcohol are involved),and medical abuse perpetrated in the name

of "therapy," it all adds up to a social nightmare of enormous proportions. Sensitive readers beware: when the back cover proclaims, "This book of horror stories is true," it isn't exaggerating!

While we don't all have a calling to fight this particular set of injustices, we should be informed of what changes are necessary and what actions we can take on behalf of our families to maintain our safety and security. These topics are covered in the last 2 chapters of the book. For coverage of this subject as it specifically relates to homeschoolers, who social workers have been known to label "educational truants" and who sometimes fall afoul of anonymous calls from neighbors who disapprove of their educational choices, I'd recommend HSLDA attorney Chris Klicka's *The Right Choice. Renee Mathis*

The Right Choice: The Incredible Failure of Public Education and the Rising Hope of Home Schooling. Is that title long enough yet? Just add "An Academic, Historical, Practical, and Legal Perspective" and you have what sounds like a college paper. To put it another way, I don't think too many folks will rush out to buy this book just because of its title. So I'd better explain what we've really got here in these 410 pages written by Home School Legal Defense Association attorney Chris Klicka and Christian Life Workshops president Gregg Harris.

First, what you *don't* have here—the one and only book a new home-schooler needs to read. Sorry, folks! That book hasn't been written yet, and probably never will be. Instead, what you have is a strong argument, backed up with much research, for the superiority of home education over public schooling, and tons of information on how the right to homeschool has been threatened in the past and is being successfully defended in the present.

The first three chapters, "The Incredible Failure of Public Education," go beyond documenting how bad the schools are. Chris Klicka tells you why they have changed so much in the past few years, and why this means we can't expect meaningful school reform any time soon. The second section, "The Rising Hope of Home Education," covers basic homeschooling history and principles. An entire chapter here is devoted to homeschooled notables, including ten presidents of the United States. The third section gives practical advice, mostly from Gregg Harris, on how to get started homeschooling.

The remainder of *The Right Choice*—almost 200 pages' worth—is devoted to legal issues. This includes what I consider the book's most valuable contribution—its detailed information on what to do when or if a government agent threatens your personal homeschool. That information, based on HSLDA's years of experience in defending homeschooling families from truant officers and social workers, is alone worth far more than the price of the book. *Mary Pride*

From the introduction of **Schoolproof**: "Schoolproofing means making sure your children get a great education, no matter what political or educational theory happens to be in vogue. It means having children who learn to read in an age of illiteracy; who learn to obey legitimate authority in an age of sullen rebellion; who learn to stand against injustice in an age of craven conformity. . . . Schoolproofing means learning how to educate, so you can recognize good and bad education. It means learning your options: different ways of presenting a lesson, different educational philosophies, different types of teaching setups."

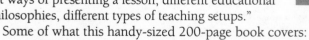

Some of what this handy-sized 200-page book covers:

- How today's popular educational philosophies treat children (as cogs, dogs, snobs, or gods) and how children *should* be treated (as unique, imperfect individuals who even so are made in the image of God)
- Organizing your learning area
- Twenty ways to present a lesson
- Twenty ways children can show you what they know (expand your horizons beyond "testing"!)
- Simple ways to multiply your teaching efforts
- How to recognize and ditch twaddle
- Learning styles and why even the same child learns at different rates at different times

NEW!
The Right Choice
Parents. $14.95 plus shipping. *Noble Publishing Associates, PO Box 2250, Gresham, OR 97080. Orders: (800) 225-5259. Inquiries: (503) 667-3942. Fax: (503) 618-8866. Email: Noblebooks@aol.com.*

Schoolproof
Parents. $12.99 plus $3 shipping. *Home Life, Inc., PO Box 1190, Fenton, MO 63026. Orders: (800) 346-6322. Inquiries: (636) 343-7750. Fax: (636) 343-7203. Email: orders@home-school.com. Web: www.home-school.com.*

An audiotape edition of *Schoolproof* is available for purchase ($17.96) or 30-day rental ($6.26) from Blackstone Audiobooks, Box 969, Ashland, OR 97520. Orders: (800) 729-2665. Inquiries: (541) 482-3239. Fax: (541) 482-9294. Web: www.blackstoneaudio.com.

> • A vision of what education could look like *with* free enterprise and *without* government coercion

Schoolproof is probably the easiest to follow book on educational philosophies and methods you can find. I wrote it for exactly that purpose—to introduce parents in general, and homeschoolers in particular, to the *whys* and *hows* that books written for teachers shroud in impenetrable prose. As such, it's a good "first" book on these topics that also goes farther and deeper than I could in *The Big Book of Home Learning. Mary Pride*

A Survivor's Guide to Home Schooling is an absolutely delightful book. Written by two experienced home-school moms who have also run a *very* large extension program/support group, it answers the nitty-gritty questions other books ignore like, "How am I ever going to get my laundry done?" The book has great stuff on subjects like Making Them Do It, reasons why *not* to hastily volunteer to teach other people's kids, ways to *realistically* schedule your days, and bushels more!

As the name implies, *A Survivor's Guide to Home Schooling* is not so much designed to enchant people with the idea of homeschooling as to help them make it work. The authors deal with questions like

> • What about the father who works outside the home and is unavailable for extended help in homeschooling?
> • What if your child is a slow learner or has difficulties?
> • How to avoid being suckered into loading up on expensive curriculum we will never, ever use
> • What experienced homeschoolers' schedules *really* look like
> • How to realistically cope with teaching many children of different ages at once.

On top of this are valuable sections with information you won't find elsewhere:

> • Plain Talk About Teaching Other People's Kids (the authors' advice is, "Don't, except in very unusual, limited circumstances")
> • Serving Other Home Schoolers (how to start a support group and make it run)
> • Mom, Will You Read Us a Story? (some fantastic insights into why and how reading aloud to your children is *the* essential preparation for their successful reading)
> • Making Them Do It (in Luanne's immortal words, "School doesn't have to be fun, it just has to be done!")

Luanne Shackelford has been called the Erma Bombeck of homeschooling, giving you an idea of the book's sense of humor. She and Susan White have lots of experience and lots of children. A very warm book, salted with humor and peppered with vivid real-life examples. When you see the cover, you'll want to buy it! *Mary Pride*

The second book you should read from the author of *Dumbing Us Down*, New York State Teacher of the Year John Taylor Gatto, is his brand-new **The Underground History of American Education**.

An oversized 412 pages, this is nonetheless a hard book to put down. *Underground History* combines the thrill of a detective story—how did traditional excellent American education turn into the morass of modern schooling, and who is responsible?—with numerous memorable stories

A Survivor's Guide to Home Schooling

Parents. $12.99 plus $3 shipping.
Home Life, Inc., PO Box 1190, Fenton, MO 63026-1190. Orders: (800) 346-6322. Inquiries: (636) 343-7750. Fax: (636) 343-7203. Email: orders@home-school.com. Web: www.home-school.com.

NEW!
The Underground History of American Education

High school and up. $30 plus $3 shipping.
Home Life, Inc., PO Box 1190, Fenton, MO 63026-1190. (800) 346-6322. Fax: (636) 343-7203. Web: www.home-school.com.

from Gatto's life. From his youth running free along the banks of the Monongahela River, to his miserable (but intellectually valuable) year in a Catholic boarding school, to his 26 years as a greatly beloved "guerrilla" classroom teacher, Gatto was always one of those special people who not only live life, or even observe life, but squeeze the juice out of life into a container they can pass on to others.

Underground History is not just a book you should read because it is informative, fun, dramatic, or even challenging, though it is all the above. This is a book you *must* read because Gatto has done what nobody else ever did—track down the roots of the centrally controlled mass society as it has taken shape in the USA, through the means of public schooling. This book names names. It explains how the great inventions based on coal and oil led to an elite group of empire-builders who feared that readily available energy would lead to an overproductive society, and took steps to stop the American Experiment of genuine political and educational freedom in its tracks. We're not talking conspiracy theories here, but well-documented historical facts that nobody ever put together in this way before. I guarantee you'll never look at prep schools, the bell curve, and the Daughters of the American Revolution the same way again!

Among Gatto's many eye-opening assertions:

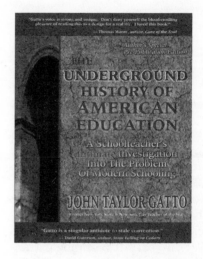

- Kids can do a lot more at a younger age than we have been trained to expect.
- People will go to outrageous lengths for the privilege of working; how to nurture rather than kill this inbuilt motivation in your students.
- Everyday people can be trusted to live their own lives well, absent compelling government intervention and mass society manipulations.
- In Gatto's own words: "Spare yourself the anxiety of thinking of this school thing as s a conspiracy, even though the project is indeed riddled with petty conspirators. It was and is a fully rational transaction in which all of us play a part. We trade the liberty of our kids and our free will for a secure social order and a very prosperous economy. It's a bargain in which most of us agree to become as children ourselves, under the same tutelage which holds the young, in exchange for food, entertainment, and safety. The difficulty is that the contract fixes the goal of human life so low that students go mad trying to escape it."

For the best results, I recommend you read Sam Blumenfeld's *Is Public Education Necessary?* before tackling *Underground History*. Blumenfeld has put together a good bit of the puzzle, and with his book under your belt, Gatto will fill in the whole picture. And, as a bonus, you will find out how the educational world really *ought* to work—a good thing to know before setting up your own little educational world! *Mary Pride*

Step 7: Attend a Homeschool Seminar

I will tell you what to expect at your first homeschool conference or curriculum fair in Chapter 8. Right now we are talking about a homeschool *seminar*: an event designed for no other purpose than to teach you how to homeschool and inspire you to tackle homeschooling with gusto.

Every new homeschooler ought to attend a homeschool seminar if at all possible. Here's why:

Any reader of *Underground History* will get an amazing education in how the world really works, and who the famous people are who made it this way. That's why I'm giving a copy to each of my teen children, with instructions to read a biography, or at least an encyclopedia entry, about each of the historical figures it names. Studying the book this way will make them better educated people than most college graduates.

NOTE: The edition I reviewed is the "Author's Edition." This is a limited-edition private printing by Gatto. He eventually plans to have the book published by a major publisher (many of them want it), and realizing that a mass publisher will most likely *not* want the book to name names, he wanted to make sure the full story was available for people such as you and me. I bought a good supply of the Author's Edition, so if you want to be sure this edition is the one you're getting, order from my company, Home Life, Inc.

- Get your specific questions answered in person
- Meet other new homeschoolers
- Get all charged up!

Now here's the seminar I've been recommending for years.

The Top Seminar for New Homeschoolers

The Home Schooling Workshop

The Basic Home Schooling Workshop: 8-tape set, $39.95; notes, $10. The Advanced Home Schooling Workshop: 8-tape set, 39.95; notes, $10. Shipping extra. *Noble Publishing Associates, PO Box 2250, Gresham, OR 97030. Orders: (800) 225-5259. Inquiries: (503) 667-3942. Fax: (503) 618-8866. Email: Noblebooks@aol.com.*

The Home Schooling Workshop by Gregg Harris is great on tape, even better in person. This is probably the best-attended homeschool workshop of all time, with hundreds of thousands of alumni.

Attending Gregg Harris's workshop in St. Louis was the high point of that year for us. Gregg Harris tells how to help our children develop an enduring taste for righteousness by giving them a taste of it, "touching their young palates" with the best of our own experience and study. He shares practical principles of child discipline and instruction that help our children in the long run rather than just providing temporary relief. He explains how to use casual family storytelling to pass on our values and national heritage to our children without even having to take time out from our household work. Find out how to achieve financial independence and give children needed work experience through a home business and how to develop a ministry of hospitality (Gregg calls this "the original Bed and Breakfast plan"!). An extra: the tapes include insights on home evangelism, one of the modern church's most neglected areas.

The Home Schooling Workshop tape sets include all this, plus the info you'd expect on the advantages of home schooling, the dangers of age-segregated peer dependency, how to begin a home-study program, how to choose a curriculum, legal considerations, and instructional methods.

Gregg is cutting down on his live workshop schedule in order to concentrate more on his writing. He has now produced a video version of his Friday evening introductory sessions, which presents strong arguments for keeping children out of conventional schools and teaching them at home. Also covered in this video is the educational strategy of secular humanism, clinic research in schooling readiness, and the Biblical answer to "What about socialization?" Gregg is not given to cliches; I promise you will get some startling new insights from this presentation!

The sets each include eight cassettes. **The Basic Home Schooling Workshop** includes Why Home School, The Battle for Your Child, Child Training God's Way, How to Do a Great Job Home Schooling, Delight-Directed Studies, The Battle for Your Legal Rights, Teaching History in the Home, and Home Schooling Hazards (passive dads, active toddlers, and teacher burnout). **The Advanced Home Schooling Workshop** covers Home School & "The New World Order," The Seasons of Life for Your Family, How to Establish an Orderly Home, How to Keep Doing a Great Job, Leading the Lost to Christ, Sunday Schools & Youth Groups, Stewardship & Family Business, Courtship for Lasting Marriages.

You also have a choice of some fascinating (and inexpensive) special-purpose workshops, thanks to Gregg's habit of leaving a session in each live workshop open to address a special topic of current interest to home schoolers. The series now includes Age-Integrated Sunday Schools & Bible Studies, Learning Disabilities or Learning Differences?, Christian Home School Support Groups, Home Schooling Teenagers, and Learning Styles.

These are *the* home-schooling tapes to buy. And if your Christian home-school support group or co-op is considering hosting a homeschooling seminar, and by some amazing miracle hasn't already hosted Gregg's basic seminar, this is the one. *Mary Pride*

CHAPTER 7

Where To Shop

For homeschoolers, shopping doesn't mean just dropping in at the mall. So far, there are no national chains of homeschool shops. This means you have to be more resourceful when hunting down homeschool goodies.

Step 8: Get These Catalogs

For your shopping pleasure, below are descriptions for a baker's dozen of what I consider the most essential homeschool catalogs. Send away for them!

WHY YOU NEED THIS STEP Because bookstores and teacher's stores don't carry everything (or even close to everything) that homeschoolers need. And one-stop-shopping beats buying products one at a time from individual vendors.

The full color **Christian Book Distributors** catalog is 64 pages of popular homeschool items, many discounted. Relatively few full curriculum items: most are fact books, fiction and fiction series, games, music, videos, and stand-alone items designed to teach a single subject. I don't have space here to list the dozens of entries in this catalog's table of contents, but I can tell you that "Harris Family," "VeggieTales," and "What Would Jesus Do?" each have a page of their own. Over 2,000 items in all. *Mary Pride*

This is a big one! **The Elijah Company Catalog** is almost 200 oversized black-and-white pages. Started about 10 years ago, this is a "native" homeschool company run by a family that has always homeschooled their children. Their motto: "More Than a Catalog! Teaching Tips, Helpful Hints, The Best Books & Teaching Materials." The catalog includes cover photos of many items, detailed descriptions, and page after page of homeschooling advice from owners Chris and Ellyn Davis. The materials they cover have all been test-

NEW!
Christian Book Distributors Homeschool Resources Catalog
Parents. Free catalog.
Christian Book Distributors (CBS), PO Box 7000, Peabody, MA 01961. (978)977-4500. Fax: (978)531-8146. Web: www.christianbooks.com.

UPDATED!
The Elijah Company Catalog
Parents. Free catalog.
Elijah Company, 1053 Eldridge Loop, Crossville, TN 38555. Orders: (888) 2ELIJAH. Inquiries: (931) 456-6284. Fax: (931) 456-6384. Web: www.elijahco.com.

ed in homeschool use, and include most popular items. Items are not discounted, and the reason for this is spelled out in detail in the back. According to *The Authentic Jane Williams Home School Market Guide*, about 175,000 copies of this catalog are distributed annually. *Mary Pride*

NEW!
Farm Country General Store Catalog

Parents. Free catalog.
Farm Country General Store, 412 North Fork Rd., Metamora, IL 61548. Orders: (800) 551-FARM. Inquiries: (309) 367-2844. Fax: (309) 367-2844. Web: www.homeschoolfcgs.com.

Farm Country General Store is hard to categorize. Established in 1991 by a homeschooling family, the current edition is 96 black-and-white pages with a two-color cover. It includes over 1,000 entries, about half with small accompanying photos. The entries are mostly not reviews, such as you'd find in the Elijah Company catalog, but sales copy that sometimes includes a decent amount of product description. Products are partly divided by publisher and partly by topic, making you really wish they had included an index. Most items are discounted. According to *The Authentic Jane Williams Home School Market Guide*, about 50,000 copies of this catalog are distributed annually. *Mary Pride*

UPDATED!
God's World Book Club Educational Catalog

Parents. Free catalog.
God' World Book Club, PO Box 2330, Asheville, NC 28802. (800) 951-2665. Fax: (800) 537-0447. Email: service@gwbc.com. Web: www.gwbc.com.

God's World Book Club was established in 1943, and has been putting out an educational catalog directed to homeschooled students and their parents for the last few years. This very attractive 64-page catalog is full color and includes both product photos and medium-size product descriptions written by over a dozen homeschool parents. As befits their "book club" roots, this catalog includes more fiction series and activity books than most. Some popular curriculum items are also included. The catalog is divided by academic areas, but does not have an index. Some "Buying Power" specials are avail-

able, and first-time buyers are offered a 10 percent discount and free shipping on their first order (Spring 1999 catalog offer). You can call their customer service number to ask curriculum questions, and they offer a free "Getting Started in Home Schooling" pamphlet. According to *The Authentic Jane Williams Home School Market Guide*, about 100,000 copies of this catalog are distributed annually. *Mary Pride*

NEW!
Greenleaf Press Catalog

Parents. Free.
Greenleaf Press, 3761 Hwy 109 N., Unit D, Lebanon, TN 37087. Inquiries: (615) 449-1617. Orders: (800) 311-1508. Fax: (615) 449-4018. E-mail: Greenleafp@aol.com. Web: www.greenleafpress.com

The 96-page, full-color, oversized **Greenleaf Press** catalog is the only one "guaranteed 100% Twaddle-Free." This must-have catalog is loaded with carefully-picked, gorgeous, fun, and useful products to enhance your homeschooling, especially in the areas of history and science. Catalog cofounders Rob and Cyndy Shearer are also authors of the immensely popular "Greenleaf Guides" to various historical periods, and their research into the best "real" books and fact books to accompany their history studies has led to a really great (and well-organized) group of products. I know the products are great because I spent my entire speaking fee, plus some, on the items at Rob and Cyndy's table when we first met them at a conference in Tennessee. (Luckily, they threw in a couple of boxes for us to carry it all in!) I know they are well-organized because I am looking at their color-coded, topic-arranged catalog as I write this.

Greenleaf is about more than history and science, of course. Other catalog topics include art, Bible, phonics and reading, language arts, math, and music.

Unique feature: their "Yuppie Specials" let you buy huge amounts of products (everything on one or more pages) all at once at discount. These collections include these history specials: Egyptian, Greek, Roman, Medieval, Renaissance/ Reformation, Explorer, Colonial America, Modern America, Art History, and Music History; a Nature Study special; a Creation Science special; a "Nutshell" special (two whole pages of science kits!), a Klutz special (goodies from the famous kit publisher), and The Grand Poo Bah Yuppie Special (which includes everything in two-thirds of the catalog, for a "mere" $8,252). Other specials range from $201 (Explorer) to $877 (Bible).

Most people don't order specials, of course; individual catalog items, of which there are thousands, range from a few dollars (for a book or workbook) to over a hundred dollars (for a complete phonics curriculum). Catalog descriptions are detailed and accompanied with color photos, and the catalog also includes pages of advice and insight from the Shearers.

Over a quarter million Greenleaf catalogs are distributed each year, according to *The Authentic Jane Williams Home School Market Guide,* so you can see I'm not the only one who goes ga-ga over Greenleaf. *Mary Pride*

The Home Computer Market, founded in 1993 by homeschooling parents Dan and Tammy Kihlstadius and now run by the homeschooling O'Sullivan family, is the only company I know of that publishes a mini software planner and product catalog just for homeschoolers. They offer over 100 software titles, all prescreened and chosen to meet the needs of Christian homeschooling families or not, and all described in length from an "I used this!" perspective. Their web site includes more product listings than fit in their 16-page catalog, as well as a list of software they recommend you *avoid* because of its lack of educational value or unwholesome content (violence, ghosts and demons, etc.). Prices are discounted. About 50,000 catalogs are distributed at a time. *Mary Pride*

Originally published as far back as 1977 as a part of *Growing Without Schooling* magazine, the **John Holt's Bookstore Catalog** was named to honor the late great unschooling advocate. Its 16 black-and-white pages contain a carefully-chosen selection, mostly books, that present and expand on this homeschooling style. There is little to no "curriculum" as such; rather, you'll find what this catalog dubs "innovative learning materials" for math, science, social studies, writing, and music, along with fiction that celebrates children adventuring on their own and many books on educational philosophy. Most books are pictured, with descriptions ranging from medium to lengthy. Some "homeschooling question and answers" sidebars, too. You won't find most of these resources in other catalogs. According to *The Authentic Jane Williams Home School Market Guide,* about 40,000 copies of this catalog are distributed annually. *Mary Pride*

NEW!
The Home Computer Market Catalog
Parents. Free catalog.
The Home Computer Market, PO Box 385377, Bloomington, MN 55438. (612) 844-0462.
Email: TheMarket@aol.com.
Web: www.homecomputermarket.com.

NEW!
John Holt's Bookstore Catalog
Parents. Free.
Holt Associates, PO Box 8006, Walled Lake, MI 48391-8006. (617) 864-3100.
Fax: (617) 864-9235.
Email: orders@holtgws.com.
Web: www.holtgws.com.

NEW!
Lifetime Books & Gifts' "The Always Incomplete Resource Guide & Catalog"

Parents. Catalog, $5.
Lifetime Books & Gifts, 3900 Chalet Suzanne Dr., Lake Wales, FL 33853-7763. Orders only: (800) 377-0390. Inquiries: (863) 676-6311. Fax: (863) 676-2732. Email: lifetime@gate.net. Web: www.lifetimebooksandgifts.com.

The Godzilla of "review" style catalogs is the **Lifetime Books & Gifts' Always Incomplete Resource Guide & Catalog**. This perfect-bound tome is as much of a book as a catalog, and its $5 cover price is certainly fair. The "Always Incomplete" part comes from the fact that it's hard to keep something this size current. As of February 2000, the latest edition was the 1997 catalog, with a 1999 supplement. A completely updated 400-plus-page catalog is due out (finally!) in October 2000.

A "native" homeschool business, established in 1987 by a Christian family, this catalog includes a hefty 3,000-plus items—all locatable through the handy index in the back. You won't find photos, but that just leaves room for longer product descriptions and chatty articles. Items are divided by subject areas, including an interesting arrangement of Science and Nature items by the seven days of Creation, and sold at retail price. According to *The Authentic Jane Williams Home School Market Guide*, about 100,000 copies of this catalog are distributed annually. *Mary Pride*

UPDATED!
Shekinah Curriculum Cellar

Parents. Free catalog.
Shekinah Curriculum Cellar, 101 Meadow Rd., Tilgore, TX 75662. (903) 643-2760. Fax: (903) 643-2796. Email: customerservice@shekinahcc.com. Web: www.shekinahcc.com.

"Shekinah" is an Old Testament Hebrew word referring to the glory of the Lord. Established in 1983, this is a "native" homeschooling business, run by homeschool moms.

Shekinah Curriculum Cellar claims, like Elijah Company, to be "More Than a Catalog!" In their case, they promise you "A Commentary on Quality Books and Teaching Aids for Home Educators." However, what you get is 36 pulp pages with no photos and short product descriptions. A little picture of a cross also appears next to items from Christian publishers.

The first hook here is discounting, accomplished mostly through taking up to 15 percent off your order (available only at certain times of year). Some individual products—not many—are also discounted. Shekinah will match any low price from another catalog.

The second hook: same-day shipping. If your order is received by 2 P.M. Central Standard Time, it will be shipped that day.

Most orders are now generated by Shekinah's complete online catalog, which features detailed descriptions and parents' reviews of many products. Contribute your own product review and get an automatic five percent off your order!

Over 1,000 products were included in the Spring 1999 edition. According to *The Authentic Jane Williams Home School Market Guide*, about 120,000 copies of this catalog are distributed annually. This catalog works best if you already know exactly what you want. *Mary Pride*

NEW!
Sonlight Curriculum Catalog

Parents. Free, one per family.
Sonlight Curriculum, Ltd., 8042 South Grant Way, Littleton, CO 80122-2705. Inquiries only, no orders: (303) 730-6292. Fax: (303) 795-8668. Email: main@sonlight.com. Web: www.sonlight.com.

You need the **Sonlight Curriculum Catalog**. The vast majority of this catalog is a treasury of children's fiction and nonfiction, divided by grade level and topic, with many titles not available elsewhere. Many of the most popular homeschool curriculum products are here, too, as well as Sonlight's own unique curriculum guides (reviewed separately in the Curriculum Buyers Guide section). Since very few items in the catalog overall are published by Sonlight, it qualifies as a general-purpose catalog, not just a "Sonlight Curriculum" catalog.

Established in 1990 by two missionary homeschooling families, this catalog's specialty is international history and Christian worldview. By far the most multicultural catalog among those listed here, it includes award-winning books about all other historical periods and cultures around the world, some of which are officially out of print and available only in these Sonlight editions. The index (hooray!) lists over 700 titles. Within each grade level, these are divided into Bible, History, Read-Alouds (in younger grades), and Readers (books children can read on their own). Within these sub-topics the books are *not* listed alphabetically (boo!), making it tough for someone like me to keep track of which kid is using which book for what subject. Of course, if you are just buying the books for your home library, this is not a problem.

The Sonlight catalog is a terrific resource for finding uplifting, thoughtful, and amusing books to enrich your homeschool program. You can also use it as a guide when you go to the library, but be prepared to discover that a large number of the books you're looking for are already checked out by other Sonlight users!

According to *The Authentic Jane Williams Home School Market Guide,* about 35,000 copies of the Sonlight catalog are distributed annually. *Mary Pride*

Established in 1982 by Seventh-Day Adventists Bill and Sandy Gogel, **The Sycamore Tree** is one of the older homeschool catalog companies. They also offer curriculum services: see description in the Curriculum Buyers Guide section of this book.

The Sycamore Tree catalog is 120 pages listing over 3,000 items. Item descriptions are short sales copy; a few photos are included. Products are divided by subject and also by type of product—e.g., games or school supplies. SDA influence is minor; most products listed are broadly popular among Christian and secular homeschoolers. According to *The Authentic Jane Williams Home School Market Guide,* about 40,000 copies of this catalog are distributed annually. A good one-stop shopping source if you already know what you're looking for. *Mary Pride*

Timberdoodle does not take credit cards or school purchase orders. I mention that right at the start, so those of you who like to call and order will be mentally prepared to give out *check* information by phone or fax. This is because of owners Dan and Deb Deffinbaugh's conviction that Christians should not go into debt, and that credit-card use can tempt the unwary into burdens they are unable to bear.

As you might expect, the Timberdoodle catalog exudes wholesome family values. This 80-page handy-sized catalog is printed on paper one step up from newsprint and decorated with black-and-white photos and line art. Catalog descriptions are lengthy, folksy, and personal; catalog selection reflects the Deffinbaugh family's own tastes and interests. These are particularly strong in the areas of math, hands-on learning, and engineering, but many other topics are covered, too: Bible tools, courtship, CPR, creationism, foreign languages, geography, handwriting, history, Keepers of the Faith, language arts, math, music, parent helps, phys ed, phonics, piano, preschool, readers/reading, science, sewing, sign language, stickers, testing, thinking skills, and typing. The engineering emphasis shows in in topics such as drafting skills, electronics/soldering, Erector sets, Fishertechnik (Timberdoodle is one of the few U.S. importers of this German construction kit system), and Rokenbok (another remote-controlled, motorized

UPDATED!
The Sycamore Tree Educational Services Catalog

Parents. Free.
Sycamore Tree, 2179 Meyer Place, Costa Mesa, CA 92627. Orders: (800) 779-6750. Inquiries: (949) 650-4466. Fax: (800) 779-6750. Email: 75767.1417@compuserve.com. Web: www.sycamoretree.com.

UPDATED!
Timberdoodle

Parents. Free catalog.
Timberdoodle Company, 1510 E. Spencer Lake Rd., Shelton, WA 98584. (360) 426-0672. Fax: (800)478-0672. Email: mailbag@timberdoodle.com. Web: www.timberdoodle.com.

construction system). I didn't have time to count them, but I estimate the catalog offers between 500 and 1,000 items. According to *The Authentic Jane Williams Home School Market Guide,* they distribute over 200,000 catalogs per year, making the unpretentious Timberdoodle Company one of the largest homeschool catalog companies. *Mary Pride*

NEW!
Whole Heart Catalogue

Parents. Free.
Whole Heart Ministries, PO Box 67,
Walnut Springs, TX 76690.
Orders: (800) 311-2146.
Inquiries: (254) 797-2142.
Fax: (254) 797-2148.
Email: whm@wholeheart.org.
Web: www.wholeheart.org.

The **Whole Heart Catalogue,** established in 1994, is very different from the others reviewed here. Over half of the elegantly designed catalog's 20 two-color pages are devoted to resources for Christian discipleship, including homeschooling methods and philosophy. The remainder consists of the topics Reading & Writing (11 entries), Favorite Read Aloud Books (11 entries), Favorite Read About Book (3 entries), and Fine Arts (12 entries). Each entry includes a photo and description of either a product or series. Descriptions are written in a highly personal "review" style.

In all, over 100 products are included.

Best known for their book *Educating the WholeHearted Child* (reviewed in the Methods or Madness chapter), catalog founders Clay and Sally Clarkson wrote or contributed to many of the discipleship and homeschool how-to resources in this catalog. The catalog includes sidebars throughout that feature the Clarksons' educational philosophy.

This is not a discount catalog, but you will find "reduced pricing on some items that tend to be universally discounted."

According to *The Authentic Jane Williams Home School Market Guide,* about 40,000 copies of this catalog are distributed annually. *Mary Pride*

Step 9: Go to the Teacher's Store

Did you know there are entire stores devoted just to educational goodies? It's true! Formerly called "teacher's stores" or "school supplies stores," many of these shops are now renaming themselves "parent and teacher stores." You can find them in the Yellow Pages under "School Supplies."

What you need to know about these stores:

- Nobody will ask you if you are a classroom teacher or demand to see your union card. These are not "teachers only" stores!
- Expect to see a terrific assortment of arts and crafts materials, writing implements, pencil toppers, posters, and bulletin-board materials. (That's why they're listed under "School Supplies.")
- You'll also find lots of fun workbooks, especially for younger grades. (If you don't think workbooks can be fun, you've never seen Frank Schaeffer workbooks!)
- Plus educational games, kits, and hands-on material of all kinds.
- Homeschoolers are welcome! In fact, many of these stores are putting in special sections just for homeschoolers.

For several years, my company has belonged to the National School Supply and Equipment Association. Their conferences are a great way for me to preview the neatest new educational products—and these are exactly the products your local teacher's store will be carrying. You will not be able to find all these goodies at Wal-Mart or Sears, or in homeschool catalogs either, for that matter. So head on down to your local teacher's store and tell them *The Big Book of Home Learning* sent you!

WHY YOU NEED THIS STEP Because it's fun. Because your kids will love the store. Because you may never need to shop anywhere else for birthday presents again.

Step 10: Attend Your First Curriculum Fair

A curriculum fair is like a homeschooling bazaar. It doesn't have the speakers and workshops you will find at a seminar or convention. What it does have: tons of STUFF!

The typical curriculum fair will have some tables manned by exhibitors who paid to be there. These are usually gracious people who are willing to explain and demonstrate their products. In return, they hope you will at least seriously consider buying something from them. You may also find tables with used curriculum, which you can purchase for considerably less than a comparable new product. To make the most of used-curriculum shopping, it would help to have read all three *Big Book* volumes before attending the fair. This will give you an idea of the products you know you want to look out for.

WHY YOU NEED THIS STEP Because otherwise you'll hate yourself when your friends tell you about the great bargains and incredible products they found at the curriculum fair.

Step 11: Bookmark This Site!

Prefer to do your shopping online? No problem. Just bookmark this site: *www.home-school.com*. This is my web site, Homeschool World. Click the "Homeschool Mall" button on the main page. This will take you to a page where links to providers of homeschool products are listed by categories (e.g., "Art," "Math," etc.). Many of these linked sites have online shopping available. And don't forget to visit our Home Life Catalog while you're at it! We offer many educational books, kits, and games not available on other sites. (Again, just click the link to our catalog on the main page of Homeschool World.) When you've done your shopping, you can relax with the huge number of helpful articles of homeschooling and family life and other fun features found only on our site.

WHY YOU NEED THIS STEP Because there's a reason Homeschool World is the most-visited homeschool web site in the world!

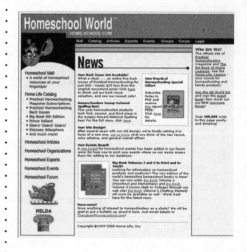

Step 12: Relax!

Take a breath. Put up your feet. Have a cup of tea or some other beverage you find relaxing. Think about how much you love your children and what a blessing it is to have them. Ask God to help you with any areas that worry you and thank Him for everything that's gone right so far.

If you're even thinking about tackling the eleven steps I outlined so far, your mind has been very active. Now it's time to realize:

It does not all depend on you and your efforts.

God wants you to succeed, and is very willing to help if you ask!

When one of my small children can't lift something and starts complaining about it, my husband Bill asks, "Why aren't you using all the strength available to you?" His point is that, if the child only asks, Bill will gladly lift the burden that's too heavy for them.

In the same way, God will lift your burdens if you will trust Him enough to ask Him for help and to do what He says. In the final analysis, this may be the most important homeschool lesson of all.

Bonus Step: Where to Find Free Stuff

NEW!
Educator's Guides to Free Materials

Parents. Complete series, $325.80, includes four free videos. Elementary Value Pack, $129.85. Secondary Value Pack, $139.50. Curriculum Value Pack, $160.56. Three free videos with any value pack. Elementary Teachers Guide, $36.95. Middle School Teachers Guide, $39.95. Secondary Teachers Guide, $47.95. Guide to FREE Computer Materials, $38.95. Guides to FREE Videotapes, Multicultural Materials, Health/Phys Ed/Recreation Materials, Science Materials, and Home Ec/Consumer Ed Materials, $32.95 each. Guide to FREE Guidance Materials, $34.95. Guide to FREE Social Studies Materials, $33.95. Guide to FREE Films, Filmstrips & Slides, $36.95. Homeschooler's Guide to FREE Teaching Aids, $34.95. Homeschooler's Guide to FREE Videotapes, $34.95. Two free videos with orders up to $95; one free video with orders up to $50. Add $3.95 shipping per guide. 15-day free trial period.
Educators Progress Service, Inc., 214 Center St., Randolph, WI 53956. (888) 951-4469. Fax: (920) 326-3127.

For over 65 years, Educators Progress Service has been producing their **Educators Guides to FREE Materials series**. That's about five times as long as I've spent on the various editions of *The Big Book of Home Learning*! You have to admire the amount of work that went into these 12 *big* books. The smallest—

Educators Guide to FREE Home Economics & Consumer Education Materials—is just over 200 oversized pages; the largest—*Secondary Teachers Guide to FREE Curriculum Materials*—is 403 oversized pages.

All materials listed in each guide are really and truly free. No "low-cost" materials are included, as in other "freebie" guides. However, many—though not all—of the videos listed do have to be send back to the sponsor at your expense. Listings are updated every year, and are double-checked with the sponsors to make sure the materials are and will be available throughout the entire school year. An effort is made to find free materials that represent a range of viewpoints. The pro-life and pro-family viewpoint is usually well represented in any given category—although Christian groups often only make their more pricey freebies available to schools, probably in an attempt to bring their messages to an often-closed-off venue. (Example: Dr. Francis Schaeffer's most excellent *Whatever Happened to*

the Human Race? video series is available for free showing to junior and senior high schools in the U.S. and Canada.) Many materials included are only available free to subscribers of this series.

Each Guide is divided into colored sections. The green pages introduce the etiquette of requesting free materials and explain the book's features. The white pages are the actual listings—over 1,000 per book—of free materials. New listings are identified with a little banner. Each listing includes a short description of the free item, its availability, suggested grade levels for use, order number if any, its format (brochure, video, booklet, or whatever), any special notes, and contact info (address alone or with phone, fax, and/or website). The availability specifically mentions homeschoolers, if we are allowed to request the product. The majority of listings are available for homeschoolers. Blue pages are the title index; yellow pages are the subject index; orange pages are the source index (with new sources for this edition in boldface); green pages are the "What's New in This Edition" index.

Some items are free because someone wants to persuade us or something or sell us something—for example, the three pro-homosexuality videos available through the *Health* volume. But quite a few include valuable information produced as a community service—for example, the Eddie Eagle Gun Safety Program (available for homeschoolers!) found in the same volume. Using the *Health* volume again as the example, the first subject listings include Abortion (four pro-life resources), Abuse (three listings of abuse recovery videos from Gospel Films), Accident Prevention (dozens of listings for different types of safety training), Acid Rain (one environmentalist listing), Acne (two listings), Activity Books (tons), Administration (a few), Adolescence (tons), Aerobics (one), Aerospace Education (one), Africa (two), Aging (twelve), Agriculture (six), and AIDS (some factual listings about blood supply etc., some "what it's like to live with this" listings, some pro-family AIDS prevention listings, some listings about AIDS therapies). Skipping through the rest of the subject index, here are some of the more interesting subjects among the hundreds more: Allergies, Beekeeping, Boats & Boating, Diseases (tons of listings on a wide variety of diseases), Driver's Ed, Ethnic Cooking, Fencing, Hurricanes, Japan (cool stuff from Japanese gardens to origami), Motion Sickness, Nuclear Power, Pregnancy (tons of listings), and an article I'm definitely going to send away for irresistibly entitled *You Mean I'm Radioactive?*

New as of the 1999-2000 school year, with fresh editions coming out annually: *The Homeschoolers Guide to FREE Teaching Aids.* This volume is in the same format as the *Elementary Teachers* Guide described below, but the over 1,200 titles listed cover *all* ages, not just elementary school and include only the titles available to homeschoolers. Also available: *The Homeschoolers Guide to FREE Videotapes.* This volume lists over 1,000 videotapes available free to homeschoolers, indexed by title, subject, and source.

The "homeschool" volumes are the ones you most likely need. But, for the benefit of the many school personnel reading this book, and since I already went to the trouble of reviewing each of the guides intended for

schools, here is what's available. Here's what each volume covers:

- *Elementary Teachers Guide to FREE Curriculum Materials, Middle School Teachers Guide, Secondary Teachers Guide*—each has resources on a wide variety of subject areas for this age group. For schools, probably your best single purchase is one or more of these volumes.
- *Guide to FREE Computer Materials*—includes many materials free through the Internet. This differs from other print and electronic lists in that, as in all the other Guides to FREE

Materials, all the items listed are guaranteed to be available through this school year. Plus listings of many brochures, catalogs, full programs, and demo disks available only through the mail. Divided into the categories of Business, Education, Graphics, and Software.
- *Educators Guide to FREE Videotapes, Educators Guide to FREE Films, Filmstrips & Slides*—the title says it all.
- *Educators Guide to FREE Multicultural Materials*—not just about diversity (although there are hundreds of listings for religious, gender, and disability diversity), but tons of resources for studying different countries, cultures, and regions.
- *Educators Guide to FREE Guidance Materials*—includes sections on career education (only 18 pages, not very com-

prehensive—includes listings such as *I Want to be a Paleontologist!*), personal health and safety (from how to brush and floss to nutrition, drug awareness and prevention, sexually transmitted diseases, fitness, dealing with chronic diseases, puberty, self-esteem, and mental illness—37 pages), conservation of our resources (from disposing of excess household chemicals to saving the rainforest—seems to exclusively represent the eco-agenda, but you do have the thrill of meeting Environmental Dog and Camouflage Kid—19 pages), social and personal materials (listings relating to psychology and belief systems, including many Christian resources—40 pages), and teacher reference materials (topics such as risk management, classroom management, violence prevention programs, Internet job searching, and tons more—25 pages)
- Subject guides: *Social Studies, Science, Home Economics & Consumer Education,* and *Health/Physical Education/Recreation*—these each include lots of fascinating listings useful in the homeschool and available to homeschoolers.

Discount collections are also available:
- The Elementary Value Pack includes the *Elementary Teachers Guide, Guide to FREE Computer Materials,* plus the Educators Guides to *FREE Films, Filmstrips & Slides* and *FREE Videotapes.*
- The Secondary Value Pack includes the *Secondary Teachers Guide, Guide to FREE Computer Materials,* plus the Educators Guides to *FREE Films, Filmstrips & Slides* and *FREE Videotapes.*
- The Curriculum Value Pack includes everything not included in the other Value Packs: the Educators Guides to *FREE*

Science Materials, FREE Social Studies Materials, FREE Guidance Materials, FREE Health/Phys Ed/Recreation Materials, FREE Home Ec/Consumer Ed Materials, and the brand-new *FREE Multicultural Materials.* New editions of each Guide start coming out in April of each year, with the last title usually available in August.   —Mary Pride

CHAPTER 8

What to Expect

Congratulations! You have now completed all 12 steps to homeschool success, or at least *thought* about completing them. You now know that, for less than the cost of one college course, you can come up to speed with what's happening in the homeschool movement. If you complete the steps outlined in the previous three chapters, you will have the connections you need to feel safe and successful. Someone will be sure to hand you a list of answers to homeschool FAQ's (Frequently Asked Questions); someone else will answer your specific questions that books and magazines can't answer. In turn, you will have less of those questions, since you have been reading the books and magazines. In less time than you think, you'll feel like an old pro, and people will be asking *you* questions!

But before you can taste the heady elixir of becoming a homeschool expert, you have to face your first homeschool month. You might also have the chance to attend:

- Your first homeschool seminar
- Your first homeschool convention

These will all go a lot better if you know what to expect. So, away we go!

Your First Homeschool Seminar

A homeschool *seminar* differs from a homeschool *convention* in these important ways:

- **A seminar usually features only one speaker.** A major seminar presenter, such as Gregg Harris, may have a guest speaker or two, but this is the exception. A convention may have only one *keynote* speaker, but you can usually count on dozens of workshops presented by dozens of people.
- **A seminar will have a single theme,** such as "How to Get Started in Homeschooling" or "Why Unit Studies are My Favorite Method, Why I Think They Should Be Yours, and How to Do Them." The seminar title typically reflects the theme. A convention's theme, if there is one, is usually something like "Homeschooling Is Great!" This provides ample room to cover whatever the workshop leaders and keynote speakers might wish to talk about.

The Future of Homeschooling

With Michael Farris

As a founder of both Home School Legal Defense Association and the National Center for Home Education, and the homeschooling dad of a *large* family, Michael Farris is one of the most influential—and knowledgeable—leaders in the homeschool movement today. He is also the author of a book entitled *The Future of Home Schooling* (reviewed in the sidebar), making him the ideal person to ask about what likely lies ahead for the homeschool movement. Christopher Thorne, then the editor of *Practical Homeschooling,* interviewed Mr. Farris:

Practical Homeschooling: We're going to take a look at where homeschooling is and the future of homeschooling. Since you literally wrote the book on the subject, we'd love to talk with you and have you share your insights.

To go ahead and get started, I was wondering what you see as the major trends in homeschooling right now.

Michael Farris: Well, on the academic side, I see a trend in Classical Curriculum as being very hot. And also high-tech educational delivery systems are starting to reach some of their potential, although there's a long way to go yet. There's still much more potential ahead. So there's two almost contrary trends, one of them going back to the past substance but the methodology of delivery of some of the extra help is very cutting edge.

PHS: So you see the trend toward Classical Education and Internet- or computer-assisted education as being complementary?

MF: Yeah. For example Fritz Hinrichs, who is the one who introduced me to the capability of high-tech delivery systems —and I would include in that DBS satellite and other broadcast forms of delivery, not just computers—he teaches classical education, world literature and history and Euclidean Geometry and so on, over the Internet. He's the one who introduced me to both. So it can be combined; one is all about content and the other's all about how you get content into the home. So they're not at all incompatible in reality, though there's a surface incongruence.

PHS: It certainly seems that many homeschooling families are going that way. Can you explain a little bit more as to why you think Classical Education has caught on and is catching on? Why more people are moving toward that methodology?

MF: Well, I think that the reason they're moving there is that . . . if I can back up just a little . . . I think that basically in the first 15 years of the modern homeschool movement, it was a big enough thing to simply break away from the methodology and to make sure we had a better version of similar content. Those are the two things that the first 15 years accomplished. And what's happening now is an examination of whether we should have different content— not just better, but different. And so I see a desire to not only emulate the methodologies of the founding fathers but a lot of their substance as well, and recognizing that if we're going to be the leaders of Western Civilization, we'd better understand the roots of Western Civilization. The way you get that is through Classical Education.

PHS: As a sidenote, you mentioned the modern homeschool movement. When would you say that the modern homeschool movement began?

MF: I would pick a particular date. Though I don't know the day, I know the event. It was April of 1982. That's when Focus on the Family and Dr. Dobson broadcast an interview with Raymond Moore. I view that as the date that really launched the modern homeschooling movement.

PHS: I know in your book you chronicle the history of homeschooling over the last decade or two. Do you think homeschooling will continue to grow, and along with that, how do you see the legal climate and attitude toward homeschooling changing and developing?

MF: The movement is continuing to grow. I'll break it into two components: the academic, or just the numerical growth, and then the legal growth. On the legal side of things, we have almost, but not completely, eradicated the idea that homeschooling is illegal. And so other than a handful of school districts out of 16,000 school districts in the country, everybody pretty well has conceded the fact that it's legal. There are some significant exceptions; for example, the chief attorney for the department of education in California thinks homeschooling is illegal. And that's not an insignificant exception. She's a politically weighty person.

But the biggest trend legally has been the harassment of homeschoolers through social workers, where they don't need to come after us with objective issues about education, but can come after us with subjective "concerns" about our family styles. All it takes is an anonymous hotline tip and you're in a bunch of trouble. So we spend more of our time dealing with social workers these days than with truant officers. Far more of our time.

PHS: Do you see that getting any better in the near future?

MF: No, I don't see any immediate change there. Fifteen years from now, I expect to sit here and tell you we've made real progress. But, if you look at the basic legal development of homeschooling, we're at the equivalent period of about 1984 for the development of the social services law in the right direction. It's going the right direction, but we're a year, year-and-a-half into it. I think it'll take about the same amount of time, about 15 years, before we see significant improvement.

PHS: Recent research has shown that homeschooling is growing at about 10–15 percent in the United States each year . . .

MF: Yeah, I think that's probably a good conservative number.

PHS: What is your impression of the growth of homeschooling in other countries?

MF: One of the trends that I see happening is that there's a real opportunity for ministry to people in other countries. Last week I visited with the ambassador to Switzerland about the homeschooling problems in his country. I went to the Czech republic earlier this year to speak to the first meeting of the brand new homeschool association, and it was really interesting, kind of a flashback for me. Being there felt just like 1982 in the United States. There were literally two homeschool families in the Czech republic, and now there are about 30. We helped them to open the law for a five-year experiment, and HSLDA gave them a small grant to get their organization going. So we had the ability to give them a hand and to observe closely what's going on there.

Chris Klicka made a similar trip to South Africa last summer, and we continue to get many requests. It's going to catch on worldwide.

PHS: That's exciting.

MF: One of the things HSLDA is doing is sponsoring a conference with American missions organizations in January, with the goal of hopefully opening the eyes of these missions groups. If they sent people to other nations where their job assignment was to help homeschoolers in that nation, they'd have a tremendous tent-making missions approach. That's one of the things I see coming.

PHS: With the growth and overall positive outlook for homeschooling, do you think there's anything that could potentially hinder the growth of homeschooling, or anything that homeschoolers should watch for or be on guard for?

MF: I think that our movement will continue to grow both in numbers and in political freedom, until and unless there are significant numbers of irresponsible homeschoolers.

PHS: Ah. That's certainly a call to parents as well to continue the high standards.

MF: One thing that bothers me, that we see happening here, is superintendents don't like to have dropouts from their schools. So if they know a student is about to drop out, they say, "No, no, you're not a dropout; you're going to be a homeschooler." So they're not listing them as dropouts, but as homeschoolers. So we're kind of getting the dregs of society thrown into our camp, even though they're not actually homeschooling. If that ruse catches hold, and we get blamed for that kind of nonsense, then our freedoms could be put in jeopardy. It's really an unscrupulous act by a superintendent. That has been rare so far and hopefully won't be repeated too much. But it's a dangerous development.

The other thing I think that could significantly hurt the homeschooling movement would be to buy us off with public funds. A lot of school districts could realize, "These kids are worth about $5,000 a head to us; if we can get them enrolled in our homeschool program and we give them $500–$1,000 worth of money, books, and services, we make about a $4,000 a year profit." And the homeschoolers will be thinking,

"There's $500–$1,000 I don't have now." I think that arrangement is a recipe for losing our freedom, losing our spark, losing all the things that have made homeschooling a success. I hope we avoid the subsidization trap.

PHS: Doesn't New Zealand have an arrangement like that now?

MF: Could be. And frankly, in the Czech republic's experiment, there's going to be a little bit of subsidization in there. Certainly HSLDA didn't ask for it, and I don't think the homeschoolers even asked for it, but it's happening. But it's a different culture. And between what goes on in a former Communist country and what goes on in America, there are different cultural expectations and I think there are different consequences. In our culture and in our legal system, I think the consequences of subsidization would be pretty bad.

PHS: Especially because it would open the door to more government control.

MF: Exactly.

PHS: To make it personal, what kind of differences has homeschooling made to your family? How are the lives of your children and grandchildren different because of it?

MF: I'm about a year away from the grandchildren business, but getting close. We have two children getting married this summer and fall. One in August and one in October. And given our philosophy about childbearing and our kids agreeing with it, about a year later we can expect to have grandkids!

The best way to answer the question is to compare my kids to myself at their age. My kids have been homeschooled for 16 years, and there's not any significant comparison. Christy was in a Christian school for kindergarten and first grade, and that's that. Nobody else has ever been in an institutional school. She's the oldest, she just graduated from college, and she's 23. I was raised in a Christian home, went to a good Bible-teaching church, was a good student, and by the world's standards I was always a good kid. By godly standards I didn't live up to everything I knew I should do, but judging by the world, I would have been one of the kids they would point to from the school and say, "Now here's an example of the way public schools work well." And I can just tell you that my kids are far more mature than I was, both in human terms and more importantly in spiritual terms.

They are at least as well-prepared academically and in some areas better. In their writing abilities, especially, they're much better prepared than I was. I graduated magna cum laude from college and was in the National Honor Society, and was in a school where two of my classmates got double-800 on the SATs, so I was in a very high-end academic program. Those of us who were in the honors program for six years— meaning 60 kids out of 600—we got great stuff. So I believe that a fair comparison is that my kids, and homeschool kids in general, get the same kind of education that those 60 of us did in this high-end program of academic excellence. But their moral life . . . the biggest thing is, they don't date, I did. And that change is a huge factor in things being better.

It's a night and day difference between where I was at their age and where they are, and I wouldn't trade it for anything in the world.

PHS: That's looking back a little bit. Now looking forward, what is the main difference that you see that the homeschooling movement will have made when history looks back from, say, 50 or even 100 years in the future? What impact will homeschoolers have had?

MF: We have been raising and will continue to raise a disproportionate number of the leaders in most of the fields of endeavor in our country. I don't think we're going to be all the leaders, but I think you'll see 15 to 20 percent of the political leaders, the business leaders, the church leaders, will have been homeschooled kids. And that's five to six times our numbers in society.

PHS: That's a significant impact.

MF: Right. We're seeing it already

in the national spelling bee, geography bees, and so on. When 20 percent of the people in Congress have been homeschooled, Congress is going to be a different place.

PHS: That's for sure.

MF: But I think we're probably 15 years from there.

PHS: In the present, how would you describe the effect that homeschooling is having on business, on the church, and on higher education here in America?

MF: I think it's had the most impact so far on the church. That churches have had to rethink their family policies and their youth group policies as a result of the dissatisfaction of homeschooling with the status quo as it was practiced for the last 15–20 years. So churches are starting to change and become more family-friendly. They used to be family-friendly in the sense that they had a room to stick every kid in when you went to church. Now they're actually becoming concerned about how the family operates as a family. There's a whole wide variety of approaches to that, and there's a lot of variance of desires among homeschoolers how they want it to be approached. Some want their kids with them at all times, others don't, but the common thread is that they want the family unit honored and supported and not ripped apart. I see churches changing that way. And I believe that 15 percent of the evangelical fundamental church in this country will homeschool their kids for at least a couple years in the very near future.

PHS: I know in my church it's certainly a growing phenomenon, with more and more families homeschooling.

MF: Turning back to my own family for a second, we've completed our 16th year of homeschooling, and we will have at least 17 more years of homeschooling by the time our youngest finishes. So I'll get to see at least the first 30 years of the modern homeschooling movement. My wife will really deserve the gold watch at the end of that time!

PHS: Are there any future plans for HSLDA?

MF: We're starting an apprenticeship-based college in September of 2000, called Patrick Henry College (*www.phc.edu*), where students would spend half the time in the classroom and half the time in an on-the-job kind of situation. The first degree will be in government. We hope to offer degrees in journalism and computer science, and eventually an accredited law school.

In the college, I think that homeschoolers will do for college education what they're done for K–12 education; and that is we're going to figure out an interesting and successful alternative to the status quo. I don't know exactly what that's going to be. What we've done is succeed remarkably at the status quo. But I think that people are looking for a change there as well.

One of the things we could do and be very successful is offer an education that's consistent with what was given in this country in the 50s and 60s in colleges, when it wasn't a crime to study the literature of dead white males. If we just did that, it would be significant. But I think it's going to be bigger and better than that. HSLDA wants to play a role as a spark—we don't want to fulfill it, but we would like to be a spark for some changes.

PHS: That is exciting. You mentioned classrooms. Will there be any way for students who can't move to its location to be enrolled perhaps through some distance learning program?

MF: Once we get the campus up and going, we are going to be looking into distance learning as well.

PHS: Do you have any personal plans for the future you would like to share with our readers, any special projects you're working on?

MF: Getting the college going, that's kind of my new project for the next few years. I'm not running for anything, and as Ollie North said, I'm not running from anything.

PHS: That's great. I want to thank you so much for your time, and for sharing your vision about the future of homeschooling with our readers.

MF: Thanks so much, and tell all your readers hello for me.

- **Conventions typically host curriculum vendors.** Lots of them. Seminars typically have a few tables where you can buy the speaker's books. (Exception: the Gregg Harris seminar, which has a *lot* of tables featuring books and resources carried in his Christian Life Workshops catalog.)

So here is what you can expect at a homeschool seminar:

> - A number of sit-down sessions, where you listen to the speaker talk about his or her area of expertise. Expect an affable presentation laced with humor, "show 'n' tell" examples, personal anecdotes, and backed up with quotes and statistics. The whole deal might last one evening, or part of a Saturday.
> - Time to browse the speaker's table and talk to him or her personally.
> - I've never heard of a homeschool speaker who charges for his or her autograph, so if you're buying a book at the speaker's table, go for it!

You might also want to keep in mind that each speaker has a favorite homeschool method, so if the speaker tells you with great authority that theirs is the One Best Way to homeschool, take notes but reserve judgment. Homeschooling is a movement based on common sense; if anything you're hearing sounds implausible, use your common sense and check it out with your fellow homeschoolers before inflicting it on your family. I know one gal, for example, who used to rave about how all homeschool moms should set up "learning centers" in their homes. A "learning center" is a table with books and materials for studying a particular topic, such as birds. Schools and museums set them up for the convenience of the large crowds of kids who use these institutions. The speaker, an ex-schoolteacher, had spent years building creative learning centers in her classrooms, and didn't have a clue that turning your home into a mini museum is educational overkill.

Which brings me to my last point about homeschool seminars—these are supposed to be *home*school seminars. Beware of seminar speakers whose main claim to fame is the years they spent teaching special ed in the schools, or math, or whatever. With rare exceptions, what's going on in today's classrooms *isn't working,* which is why we're homeschooling in the first place. Demand to see *results.* If Ms. So-and-So was such a great special ed teacher, what percent of her students did so well under her tutelage that they were ever graduated out of the special ed program? If Mr. So-and-So is such a great math teacher, how many of his students passed the AP Calculus exam, or got 800s on the math portion of the SAT I? Did he coach a math team that year after year won the Math Olympics? Did this art teacher's students become Disney animators? Teachers like this do exist, and sometimes "cross over" into the homeschool movement, but there are also opportunists out there trying to hawk their education degrees whose "years of experience" are really years of failure. That's why most homeschool seminar speakers turn out to be homeschool moms and dads, with years of *homeschool* experience.

Your First Homeschool Convention

A homeschool convention is a horse of a different color. We're talking *big.* Lots of speakers. Lots of workshops. A huge curriculum fair. Between 500 (North Dakota) and 20,000 (California) people milling around. Whole

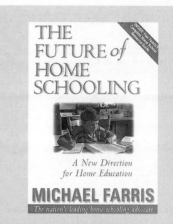

hotels reserved for homeschool guests. The biggest convention center in town rented for the show.

Your best bet is to preregister, thereby saving about $10. You and your spouse, and possibly a few of your older children, can also register at the door. Little kids are, oddly enough, not allowed at many homeschool conventions, with the exception of nursing babies. The ostensible reason is the lack of available seating. The other reason is that the convention organizers fear many new or wannabe homeschoolers have not yet trained their little darlings to behave, and the organizers don't want to spend all day chasing after misbehaving kids.

The way I've gotten around the "no little kids" rule is to be the conference speaker. Vendors also often bring their kids of all ages, for the simple reason that they can't leave them all day in the hotel room. If you're not a speaker or a vendor, make *sure* young children are allowed before you show up at the convention in your minibus with seven children of all ages.

Now it is true that little kids would be bored at most homeschool conventions. The program usually runs on Friday night and all day Saturday. Friday night, which is often open to the public, starts off with announcements, sometimes music, and a keynote address by the big-name speaker. Saturday there are workshops, and maybe some more keynote addresses or workshops by the big-name speaker. Speeches and workshops run from 45 minutes to 75 minutes long. The curriculum hall is sometimes open all the time, and sometimes closed during keynote speeches. It depends on the convention.

Your experience will go like this:

- **Show up at the door.** Either pay for or pick up your prepaid ID badge. This will have your name, so you can fraternize with other attendees. So don't take it personally when you find other people staring at your chest, or collarbone, or whatever body part you pinned your badge over.
- **You likely will also be given a "goodie bag"** of homeschool catalogs, brochures, special offers, and the like. Your best move is to immediately march out to the car and unload all the heavy material in your bag that is not directly related to the convention. If you're really smart, you will have brought along a tote, bag, or box of your own for these goodies, and others you will pick up at the curriculum tables. The key to preventing aching feet is to periodically empty the heavy purchases and goodies out into your car, instead of lugging them around all weekend. Keep the workshop schedule and floor map in your goodie bag, add a pencil and a few sheets of blank paper if you like to take notes, and return to the convention.
- **If you're timid**, sit several rows back. Some speakers have been known to select "volunteers" from the first rows for various on-stage antics.
- **If you're nursing**, sit way in the back and pick an aisle seat. I warned you about how jumpy some people (not me) get about crying babies.
- **Sit** through the announcements, music, and first speech. Then **wander outside** on the break and chat with everyone else about how good or bad the speaker is. Or sit in your seat and circle the workshops you want to attend and the booths you want to visit. Or take the kiddies to the rest room—an even more private place to chat with the other ladies about how the convention is going so far. (I know for a fact the women all chat in the bathroom in front of the mirrors; according to Dilbert's laws of male behavior, presumably the men don't do this.)
- **Pride's Law of Workshop Scheduling:** You discover all the workshops you most want to attend are scheduled at the same time. Being

clever, you and your spouse split up to cover at least two of them, or you decide to order tapes of the workshops you missed (if available).

- **If you're smart, you'll budget twice as much time** as you think you need to visit the curriculum hall. There's always at least one booth with products so fascinating you end up spending half your time there.

- **Unless you're especially fashion-conscious**, sneakers or sandals are the way to go. If you decide to cover every table in the curriculum hall, you'll be doing a *lot* of walking.

- **Lunch is usually available on-site.** If it is, pay the extra few bucks and eat right there. It's a great way to meet a few people, and the food is usually pretty good, too. (That's because the homeschooled teens made most of it!)

- **Bring lots of cash**, although credit cards and checks are accepted by most vendors. The kids will all want homeschool T-shirts and caps, and you will find some unusual curriculum and bargain opportunities as well.

- **It is not considered good manners** to roam the curriculum hall with a bargain catalog in your back pocket. It is considered even worse manners to blatantly compare prices on the table with prices in the bargain catalog. The worst of all is to make the poor curriculum vendor explain his product, demonstrate it, practically wrap it up for you, and *then* drag out the bargain catalog and tell him you're going to buy it mail-order instead. If the vendor spent a lot of time with you, consider his time as worth the few bucks extra it may cost to pick up the product right there as opposed to ordering it from a discount catalog.

- **If you want to make a lot of good friends** among the local homeschool leadership, plan to stay late and volunteer to help clean up. Older kids are also very good at this, and it's a way for them to make friends with the other responsible kids who are cleaning up, too.

Other Major Homeschool Events

I've had the pleasure of speaking at a couple of Six Flags Homeschool Days. Park attendance for homeschool days, and other special events, is lower than the 40,000 or so that can and often do jam in at other times—a mere 7,500 to 15,000. This means you don't have to stand in line for most rides, everyone in the park is a potential friend, and the tickets cost less. You can even go listen to the homeschool speaker and check out the curriculum tables if you want to.

Six Flags theme parks also host "educational" days that until now have been only marketed to school groups. In St. Louis, for example, there is Physics Day (with handouts about the physics involved in doing loop-the-loops on the roller coaster!), Science Day (with special exhibits), and St. Louis History Day (with reenactments of important historical events that occurred in St. Louis). Other Six Flags parks have similar educational days. You might want to check them out.

Also, the "homeschool vacation" is coming into its own. The idea of such events is that you can bring the whole family (including the little kids this time) and for a single package price get room, board, homeschool speakers, a curriculum fair, and lot of fun outdoors and indoors activities. I spoke at one of the first of these vacation events, at Glorieta Conference Center in New Mexico. They received twice as many registrations as they expected, leading to talk of setting up other state-by-state homeschool vacations. My hope is that such events will be coordinated with the state groups. If there is enough demand, who knows? Homeschool educational cruises, anyone? ◀ -

BELIEVE IT OR NOT
After I wrote this, I got a call from a lady who is putting together a homeschool cruise!

Your First Homeschool Month

You've read the books (or at least this one), subscribed to a magazine, attended a seminar, pre-registered for the state convention. So far so good, but now it's showtime—your first day of homeschool.

You are very excited. Either that, or you are feeling desperate. Your child, or children, are also feeling excited. Or not. We can list these alternatives thusly:

- **The Excited Homeschool Parent** Your child is about to be homeschooled for the first time, friends have homeschooled successfully, and you can't wait to start
- **The Desperate Homeschool Parent** Your child used to be in school, but for a variety of excellent reasons this turned out to be a bad idea, so now you feel you *have* to homeschool him or her, but you're not feeling very confident
- **The Excited Homeschool Child** Your child is about to start homeschool for the first time, or has been begging you to let him or her be homeschooled
- **The Unexcited Homeschool Child** Mom and/or Dad has developed convictions about homeschooling, but this previously schooled child really would rather be in school with friends

If you're excited, and your children are excited, your first month will probably go great. You have clever and creative activities planned, and they will love them.

If you're excited, and they're unexcited, you'd better resolve from the first not to take a lot of guff. Whining, moaning, and complaining can take the edge off the most prepared parent. Your best tactic is probably to demand that they "give it a chance." This is obviously reasonable. If the problem is perceived lack of friends, invite their friends over after school and on weekends, and take part in support group activities designed for kids of their age. If the problem is that they simply hate schoolwork, be patient. Hatred of learning is not natural; it was acquired in school and will take some time to evaporate.

If you're desperate, but they're excited, not to worry. Just provide library books, math workbooks, and some fun hands-on materials to start with. This will build up your confidence and keep their excitement high. In the meantime, add to your confidence by repeating Steps 1 through 12. Later on you can add more "serious" resources, once you're hitting your homeschooling stride.

If you're desperate, and they're unexcited, *rush* to the nearest support group meeting. Join an online homeschooling forum. Buy homeschooling books and magazines galore. Visit the library, the zoo, the museum, the seashore, the mountains . . . whatever new environments you can find. Your job is to jolt this child out of an acquired hatred of learning, as well as remove him from the previously corrupting or intimidating influences which caused him to withdraw emotionally in the first place. Once he gets "hooked" on *any* positive interest, you're on your way . . . because one thing homeschoolers have discovered is that *any* interest, if pursued far enough, will lead to a need to learn the academic basics.

No matter how prepared you think you are, you will encounter surprises during your first month of homeschool. The project you thought they'd love the most will turn out to be a tedious waste of time. On the other hand, simply reading aloud may be a big hit. You'll discover more about your child in this month than you did in years before. You'll also discover your personality flaws mirrored in your child. The house will not stay spotlessly clean. Nor will it clean itself. The phone will ring just when you finally got all the materials together, and when you get off it, the children will have wandered away. You will spend half a hour searching for a pencil, only to sit down on the couch and hear it go "Crack!" under the cushion. A formerly distant child will start to become affectionate. A child who has been convinced he is "dumb" will spend hours building elaborate creations with his Lego bricks. Someone will call and ask you to volunteer for a church or community function "because you don't work and have the time for it.". The UPS man will start to consider your house a regular stop. The librarian will call you by name. Some art supplies will get spilled and make a mess. You will start wondering which walls of your house are big enough to tack up a timeline on. You will sleep late by accident, and realize it doesn't matter—there's no schoolbus to catch!

Surprises aside, here are the four main things to remember if you want your first homeschool month to be a success:

(1) **No TV.** Oh, the agony! Try renting videos instead, to be played only after the school day is over. It's only for a month. See what happens.

(2) **Do the chores first.** This is the Iron Law of Homeschooling. Even if doing the chores takes all day, and *no* academic work gets done, your children must do their chores first. Trust me. This habit will do more for your homeschool success than any other. The habit of being responsible, doing a job well, and doing it completely is best learned hands-on, with chores. Without these habits, your children will become the dreaded Homeschool Slackers.

(3) **It's only the first month.** Really, it's OK if your child doesn't make it through the entire Suzuki violin book series, doesn't win a blue ribbon at the state fair for his home-bred gerbils, and doesn't invent nuclear fusion. Never mind what the kids in the homeschool magazines are doing. He has *years* to do all this. Relax.

(4) **Keep your accomplishments**, or what you may be thinking of as your *lack* of accomplishment, **in perspective.** If your child didn't do drugs, didn't get drunk, didn't stab or shoot anyone or get stabbed or shot by anyone, didn't become an unwed father or mother, didn't form a clique to reject the less-attractive kids, didn't get rejected by a clique of "in" kids, didn't swear or get sworn at, didn't engage in occult religious rituals, and didn't abandon the faith, your homeschool month was lots better than the months lots of kids were having in school. You say they learned something, as well as avoiding all that bad stuff? Then congratulate yourself—you're off to a great start!

TV Guardian

Principle Solutions, PO Box 670, Rogers, AR 72756. (501) 986-0033. Fax: (501) 986-0033. Web: www.tv-guardian.com.

Clean up any movie!

You've probably seen ads for ten or twenty programs to block out filth on the Internet, each claiming it's the best. Have you ever seen the same for TV or movies? Why not? You may have heard of the "V-Chip," which will block out entire programs with offensive material. But you've probably seen movies which had a great story, a compelling plot, lovable characters . . . and language too filthy to ever let you show them to the kids. Rather than reject the entire program, the **TV Guardian** uses the closed-captioning to block out lines with "colorful" language. We've used it and it cuts the sound for a line with any recognizable swear word, and can be set to display a cleaned-up version of the text. It can display entire cleaned-up dialogue, for the benefit of the hearing-impaired. On top of all that, you can lock the cables and the setting switches inside, so curious kids can't turn it off even if they want to!

The TV Guardian isn't perfect. If the screenwriters are inventive with their sexual allusions, some may slip by around the edges. Also, in cases where the captioning isn't timed quite right, or where there is no captioning at all, a rented video may still surprise you with some unwanted vocabulary. Nevertheless, the TV Guardian does a good job. It doesn't leave a single bad word in *Men In Black,* for example—quite an accomplishment. *Joseph Pride*

PART 3

How Kids Really Learn

Some kids learn best while moving. Others use movement to learn new skills. Katie Wise and Daniel Long, both of whom have been in Karate for 5½ years, recently received their black belts. Katie and Daniel, cousins, are both home-schooled and both study the Shito Rhu style of Karate. Katie, and another ten-year-old who got promoted at the same time, are the youngest students in the 26-year history of her Karate school to reach their black belt.

Both Katie and Daniel also took first prizes in 4-H Presentations at the district level, and went on to compete in the state competition. Katie's presentation was about Karate, and Daniel's was about Paso Fino horses. The same day, they both received gold medals for 4-H Project Records that won at the district competition. Katie won two gold awards and $100 for her Project Records. Daniel won a gold award and $50 for his Project Record.

Melissa Anne Murata, a 12-year-old homeschooler
from San Antonio, TX, won the M.S. Poster Contest for
San Antonio—A Great Place to Visit. This contest was
sponsored by the Tourism Council and Fiesta Magazine
to promote National Tourism Week and the Alamo City.
Melissa is pictured here with San Antonio Mayor
Howard Peak, who was on hand for the awards presentation at the Tower of Americas. In addition to the
recognition, Melissa received $100. Her poster was
auctioned off at the Annual Tourism Banquet and now
hangs in the River City Mall at the Imax Theater.

CHAPTER 9

The Five Steps of Learning

In this section, you will learn how children *really* learn. First, we will look at the five steps of learning—not *what* children need to know, but *how* they learn it. Next, you will discover your child's preferred discovery channel—what used to be called "learning styles." Finally, you will learn what type of thinking style your child has. Even the class clown and the daydreamer can learn rapidly and well once their individual learning needs are met.

As a no-extra-cost bonus, you can also use this section to discover *your* discovery channel and thinking style. Be careful: this could change your life!

Along the way, you'll discover why the schools, as presently conceived, cannot possibly meet the learning needs of the majority of children; why the kids the schools have the most trouble with may in fact have the gifts our society needs the most; and how you, at home, can give your children exactly the kind of education that each of them really needs.

How You Use Your Brain

Take a look at the brain. It's that roundish mass inside your skull that looks like the Green Giant's left-over chewing gum. Understand how the brain operates and you will know why some educational methods work and others don't.

Oversimplifying grossly, we see that thinking involves two main operations: storage and retrieval. You store everything that comes in through your senses in infinitesimal brain cells. If you could remember all of this, you'd probably go crazy; but you can't remember it, since you lose track of what is stored there quite easily.

> **Learning is the art of connecting your memories in a way that makes enough sense for you to be able to retrieve them rapidly.**

> **Thinking is the act of making new connections between your memories.**

> A journey of a thousand miles must begin with a single step.
> —*Lao-tsu, an ancient Chinese philosopher*

> All men by nature desire knowledge.
> —*Aristotle*

In the brain, thinking causes physical connections to grow between the brain cells. The more connections you have, the better your thinking powers. The brains of geniuses are convoluted and heavy with all the connections they have made. Newborn babies, on the other hand, have smooth brains with almost no connections.

Let us, then, develop a very simple theory of education based on these two observable truths:

(1) You can't connect what isn't there.
(2) You can't find what is there without a logical connection.

> **Thus, it is vital to expose the student, whatever his age, to a lot of raw data *before* trying to "teach" him anything concerning that data. After he has soaked up hundreds of facts and experiences, then it is equally vital to supply him with a means of connecting them all.**

You could call this the "Data-Connection Theory," but since there is actually nothing original about it, call it anything you like. It works like this:

Say you want to teach a child to read. You do not shove a book in front of his face and start teaching. First, you expose him to a lot of print. Big print, little print. Newsprint. Books. Cereal boxes. Meanwhile, you read to him. Snuggled in your lap, he is both cozy and unafraid—ideal conditions for learning. Slowly he will get the idea: those black marks are letters, letters make words, and words are what Mommy is reading to me. Once he understands what reading is all about, he will probably ask you to teach him to read. Your task, then, is to provide the logical patterns (phonics) which translate all those letters into sounds.

True, reading is a complex subject, and we haven't discussed the idea of physical readiness (i.e., brain maturation) or methods of teaching yet. But I want you to understand that there are really only four basic approaches to teaching, three of which are wrong.

✗ **Wrong: Framework Without Data** Number One is to begin laying a logical framework *without* first supplying any individual data. You can actually feel the strain on your brain of trying to learn this way. You see, you are not only trying to connect your brain cells, but to fill them at the same time! It's easy to see that a lot gets lost in the shuffle this way. Much of higher math, from algebra on up, is commonly taught this way. Which is why most kids avoid it like the plague.

✗ **Wrong: Data Without Framework** Number Two is to supply the original data, but fail to show how the individual facts hang together. This is what the schools do when they load a kid up with "Readiness" activities and then spring sight-word reading on him. He is stuck trying to memorize zillions of seemingly unconnected facts. Some kids do manage to invent their own phonics patterns and survive, but it's in spite of, not because of, the way they are taught. This rote memorization approach is used all over: in history, in math, in spelling, in my college engineering courses. Learners are handed hundreds of little "rules" or "facts" without any reasonable way of hanging them all in order. The brain does not want to work this way, and so although individual students can stuff the facts down for a test, they promptly forget it all in a week. This is not real learning.

✘ **Wrong: Erratic Data and Incomprehensible Framework** Number Three is to provide *neither* initial experiences *nor* a framework. Fluffhead professors with no communication abilities are the chief perpetrators of this style of "teaching." Others are deluded into thinking the profs are brilliant because nobody understands them. But flunking all your students is *not* a sign of genius. If a teacher gets garbage out, it's probably because he put garbage in.

✔ **Right: Data First, Framework Second** The only way that works consistently, because it is based on the way the brain operates, is Number Four: providing the learner with raw data and after he's had time to digest it, with a permanent framework for storing the data. New data can then be connected to the old with minimal effort.

In history, the framework would be a time line. In geography, the framework is a globe. The learner must have some way of getting a panoramic view of the field he is studying or he will be, as he puts it, "lost." Once he has that panoramic view, he can fill in the details as long as he lives.

Some educational products provide data (which, as you remember, includes experiences). Others provide a learning framework, such as a good phonics program. Some provide both. As we learn to discern which product does what, we can educate ourselves and our children much more efficiently.

What I am going to say now is even less original. Since the beginning of time, mothers and fathers have mastered these five simple steps of learning. Only in our science-worshiping age have we tried to bypass the wisdom of our grandparents—with the dismal results you now see. *Their generation was 99% literate, remember?*

Step 1: Playing

Let kids be kids. That's step one. *Play* is the first step of learning. Earthshaking, isn't it? Any kindergarten teacher could tell you that!

Ah, but do we *act* on this knowledge? How many times do we or Johnny's teachers try to rush him into "mastering" some new skill without giving him any chance to play around with it first?

Everyone gets ready to learn by playing.

Play is the stage where you fool around with something before settling down to get serious about it. When your husband picks up his hammer and hefts it experimentally, he is playing. When your wife tries on a new dress that she doesn't intend to actually wear anywhere today, she is playing.

Play turns the strange into the comfortable, the unknown into the familiar. Dad hefts his new hammer because he wants to know how heavy it feels before he risks his fingers using it on a piece of wood. Mom tries on her dress because she needs to feel comfortable about how she looks in it before appearing in public.

In the very same way, children need to get comfortable with new words, new objects, and new ideas before they can be reasonably expected to do anything serious with them.

Who is a Genius?

Some people have taken me to task for a what they consider a too-egalitarian view of human ability. They, quite rightly, point out that a genius, by definition, is different from other people. According to them, most children can't possibly be geniuses.

I do recognize that we are all born with a different amount of native quickness. But genius is not only, or primarily, quickness. Ask Thomas Edison. He said that genius was one percent inspiration and ninety-nine percent perspiration. And Thomas Edison should know. He invented the electric light and the phonograph, to name just a few of his contributions. Nobody has ever questioned whether Edison was a genius!

The real question, then, is why do some people perspire and sweat after knowledge, while others don't? The answer is simple—and explains why our present school system produces such an amazing shortfall of genius.

A genius is a person to whom learning is a game.

And we can help our children and students discover the game of learning.

—*Schoolproof*

Hold Me, Touch Me

Several writers on education have noticed that children who are allowed to play with learning equipment before being put through any exercises with the equipment do much better than those who are immediately forced to use the equipment for its "proper" use.

In his book *How Children Learn* (Dell Publishing Company, 1983, revised edition) John Holt tells about his friend Bill Hull's experience with the attribute blocks he invented:

"They found a very interesting thing about the way children reacted to these materials. If, when a child came in for the first time, they tried to get him 'to work' right away, to play some of their games and solve some of their puzzles, they got nowhere. . . . But if at first they let the child alone for a while, let him play with the materials in his own way, they got very different results. . . . When, through such play and fantasy, the children had taken those materials into their minds, mentally swallowed and digested them, so to speak, they were then ready and willing to play very complicated games, that in the more organized and businesslike situation had left other children completely baffled. This proved to be so consistently true that the experimenters made it a rule always to let children have a period of completely free play with the materials before asking them to do directed work with them."

If you're going to open up unfamiliar new territory in your brain, your best move is to send out some scouts. Survey the terrain. Get to know what it looks like. Then you'll feel confident about building a town out there. Play is the brain's scouting expedition.

How does this apply in real life? Here are some examples:

- **Children should *see* print and *hear* it read before trying to learn to read.** If possible, they should also *manipulate* letters (like alphabet puzzle pieces) and *write* letters before beginning their reading lessons.
- **Children should be allowed to scribble freely** before you try to help them make specific marks on the paper. Allow them to use any color they want, and to color outside the lines in the coloring book. So far, all nine of my children have gone through the scribble stage and the color-it-any-color-but-the-right-one stage, and *without any help from me* all nine have gone on to neat, accurate coloring.
- **Words like *noun* and *verb* should be used well in advance of any grammar lessons.** Ditto for all terminology and every subject. Making a student of any age learn both unfamiliar words *and* unfamiliar concepts at the same time is cruel and unusual punishment.
- **Grabbiness is part of learning.** See how quickly a baby explores the box his Christmas present came in! He is not satisfied until he has gone thoroughly over it with eyes, ears, nose, fingers, and mouth. Babies, more than the rest of us, are determined to make the unfamiliar familiar. They know they don't know, and are trying to catch up. (Incidentally, knowing we don't know and unself-consciously humbling ourselves to learn may be part of what Jesus had in mind when He said we must become like little children.)

Step 2: Setting Up Your Framework

A child learning to read and an adult studying aeronautical engineering both need the same thing: a framework to help them organize their data. This framework is like a filing cabinet loaded with files. It provides slots in which to fit the ever-accumulating new data. In history, the time line; in geography, the globe; in reading, the alphabet; in language, the web of grammar; these are frameworks under which myriads of new facts can be filed.

A good framework answers the question, "What in all tarnation is *this?*"

History is about people and movements and dates; hence the time line. Geography is about where things are; hence the globe. Engineering is about putting little pieces together to make a building (or airplane, or circuit board). Grammar is about putting words together to make a sentence. Handwriting is about making marks on paper that people can read.

A framework is the big picture, the panoramic view of your subject.

Your framework is what's going to glue together all the thousands of facts and ideas you are going to learn.

One big reason kids flounder in school is because the teachers are so wrapped up in skills and subskills and testing and grades that their students forget what they are trying to accomplish. If a student can't see the relationship between filling out fourteen workbook pages on beginning consonants and beginning to read (and believe me, the connection is pretty tenuous), his mind will not be storing the new information under the right headings. Reading will seem a succession of unrelated hoops the teacher is trying to make him jump through, and it won't "come together" for him. This is also why students shy away from those fuzzy graduate courses where the teacher wanders all over the landscape without ever making it clear what the course is *about*.

It's not hard to set up a learning framework. All classical instruction included frameworks. Just giving a subject a *name*, like Oceanography or Weaving or Renaissance Art, is the beginning of a framework. If you know what you're trying to learn—whether TV repairing or gourmet cookery or the story of Ethelred the Unready—you're on your way!

Step 3: Categories

Think of your filing cabinet, if you have one. Can you easily find papers you have filed away, or do you have to grumble your way through umpteen folders every time you need a paper?

Those of us who have expanded into several filing cabinets quickly find that we need a system to keep it all straight. Some use colored folders, some use colored dots, some use each drawer for a special purpose—it doesn't matter. The main thing is that without organization our bulging files are as useless as if they were in Timbuktu.

You see, a framework is only half the story. You can have a filing cabinet (framework) without an organized arrangement of files. Without organization, though you can happily file new facts by the ton, you can't find them except by accident.

Efficient learners make it their practice to break every new subject down into manageable categories.

They don't study the American Revolution all at once, for instance. They study Famous Loyalists, Famous Generals, Spies and Traitors, Naval Battles, the Continental Congress, or whatever categories give them most insight into what they are trying to learn.

It invariably happens that, as you go deeper into a subject, your original categories become too broad and you have to make sub-categories. In our example above, the Continental Congress quickly becomes too wide a field for the serious student. So he might break it down further into Congressional Leaders, Congressional Committees, Southern Congressmen, or other sub-categories, each of which in turn can be further divided.

Let's take another example: reading. Why do phonics courses always spend so much time talking about Vowels and Consonants and Short Vowels and Long Vowels and Blends and Digraphs and Diphthongs? Those are *categories*, that's why! Anyone can remember five Short Vowels and twenty-one Consonants. These little boxes make the data much more find-

The Learning Game

The game of learning is not adding on silly activities to serious subjects (like dishwashing and aeronautical engineering). It is making learning itself a game— getting absorbed in the problem, the answers, the process of learning. Concretely: it is a child gazing at the pattern of the tiles on her bathroom floor and devising mathematical equations to explain the regularities. It is Galileo watching the pendulum swing back and forth and timing it by his pulse to see if the swings really take the same amount of time no matter how wide they are. It is a boy making "the greatest paper airplane ever," and his younger brother secretly vowing to make a greater one. It is Grandma daringly substituting chicken for hamburger in a favorite recipe to see what will happen. It is the computer hacker hanging around the mainframe in the wee hours for "just one more run" to see if his program will compile and work this time. It is all things become new, because they are loved and admired and watched with wonder and a sense of sudden surprise.

—*Schoolproof*

able. Contrast this with the sight-word method used in 85 percent of public schools, where Junior is trying to memorize the individual shapes of all the words in the English language, and you'll have a clue as to why we have a national reading problem.

The difference in learning efficiency between a product or course that organizes the data for you into categories, and one that doesn't, is immense. Although the latter may contain gobs of useful knowledge, you'll have a real struggle walking away with any of it. Keep this in mind as you shop.

Step 4: Putting Your Data in Order

Once you've become comfortable with your object of study, the next step is to pick up more information about it. You can do this by memorizing categories of facts, but your task will be much easier if you can sort the information into patterns.

> **Patterns are your method for filing new facts into a category.**

Going back to our example of the file cabinet, let's say you have organized your file cabinet by categories. The top drawer is for family records and the bottom one is for your home business. Within each drawer you have file folders (sub-categories), also organized by topic. You have, for example, one file folder exclusively for Personal Correspondence. All is well and good so far. But if you want to quickly find the letter your Aunt Theresa wrote you six months ago, you'd better have a method for filing letters inside that folder.

You could have filed your letters with the most recent to the front of the folder and the oldest correspondence to the back. You could have filed letters by the names of the people writing to you, or by the topics on which they wrote. Although some of these schemes would be more efficient than others, *any* of them would be more efficient than simply shoving each letter helter-skelter into the folder.

In the same way, you will hold onto new facts much better if you can arrange them in order using a systematic pattern.

What do I mean by a "pattern"? As I said, *patterns are your organizing method.*

> **When you have a category of related facts (such as, in phonics, words ending with "at"), the systematic way you file them (in this case, alphabetic order) is your pattern.**

Let's look at the pattern for our example of "at" words (alphabetically, by digraphs, by diphthongs):

at	pat	plat
bat	rat	slat
cat	sat	spat
fat	vat	sprat
hat	brat	splat
mat	flat	that

Once a child gets used to writing out families of words in alphabetic order, he has a tool for generating dozens of new words from *every* word ending or category he learns.

Some facts need to be sorted alphabetically, as in our example above. Others have a natural chronological pattern (as when studying the battles in a war). Still others sort out numerically, starting with the smallest and ascending to the largest. Arithmetic is full of these kinds of patterns, e.g.:

$$1 + 1 = 2$$
$$2 + 1 = 3$$
$$3 + 1 = 4$$
$$\cdots\cdots\cdots$$
$$10 + 1 = 11$$

Learning the "one-pluses" by this pattern is much easier than trying to memorize individual "math facts" out of order.

Matter can be organized by its physical layout. You will notice that this series you are now reading follows a definite pattern. Each chapter begins with text that discusses the issues in an educational field. The text is followed by reviews, sorted in alphabetical order. Each review has contact information next to it in the margin. This makes the book easier to use than if all the information were jumbled together.

Why are we spending so much time talking about patterns? Because patterns are what make or break many educational products. If data is not patterned, or is ordered according to the wrong pattern, it becomes much harder to use. Try this simple example. Which of the following foreign language programs would be easier to use? The first categorizes phrases together that deal with, say, table manners, and leaves it at that (this one has categories, but no patterns). The second categorizes the phrases and lists them in alphabetical order (category plus pattern). The third categorizes phrases, and lists them in *grammatical* order (e.g., "I like the meal. You like the meal. He likes the meal. She likes the meal . . ."). The third program sorts the data into *the form in which you need it*, since you talk in terms of I or he or she, not in alphabet lists.

Similarly, it is easy to learn the days of the week in chronological order, which is the way we use them, whereas if you memorized them in random order, or alphabetical order, it would be extremely difficult to use them quickly.

Not every individual fact can be sorted into a pattern. You've just got to memorize the value of pi, for instance. But the vast majority of useful data does follow systematic patterns. It's the scientist's job to find these patterns, and the teacher's job to use them.

If you want to learn effortlessly, and remember what you learn, insist on products that provide both categories and patterns.

Step 5: Fusion

Have you ever had a brainstorm? Suddenly you could almost hear the clicking as light turned on inside your head. Misty ideas suddenly coalesced. Hundreds of previously unrelated facts joined arms and marched along singing.

That marvelous experience is what some writers call "synthesis," "flow," or "the genius state," and I prefer to call "fusion." Fusion is when frameworks link. All at once electrical impulses can take the express from Point A to Point B, when they used to have to make detours and swim muddy streams of consciousness to make the trip.

Go With the Flow

Flow states are critical to the development of talent. When in a flow state, one is mastering challenges that are neither too easy nor too difficult. Mastery of each challenge leads to mastery of a higher level of challenge. According to Csikszentmihalyi, the kind of person who is able to achieve flow is characterized by high curiosity, achievement and endurance, openness to experience, and strong attunement to sensory information.

—*Ellen Winner,*
Gifted Children: Myths & Realities
(1996, Basic Books)

When you're experiencing fusion, you're concentrating intensely, enjoying it, and losing track of your own physical state and the outside world. Inventors, composers, and other gifted people may experience fusion states that last for hours or days at a time. But even the rest of us have all had times when we were so immersed in a creative activity we lost all track of time. The "pieces came together" of whatever we were trying to do, and our brains made sense of it all.

Fusion *feels* good. It lets you spend the energy that used to be wasted hacking through jungles of confusion on more edifying pursuits.

Fusion is the opposite of *confusion*, which is what happens when our carefully-built frameworks turn out to be all wrong and we have to start rebuilding them from scratch. This confusion is the eternal lot of those who are heedless about looking for answers to the deep questions of life.

We live in an age when people are being taught that there *are* no answers, so one might as well not bother asking the questions. The only consistent responses if this is true are despair or ruthless hedonism. And these are the lifestyles we are seeing today.

Although the antiphilosophy of relativism—that there is no right and wrong—has had great success, it is not correct. The human brain was not constructed to be open to *everything*. People have a built-in need for right and wrong, for security, for an integrating philosophy of life. Perhaps the best books ever written on this subject, that describe our present confusion and the timeless solution, are *Escape from Reason* by Dr. Francis Schaeffer (published by InterVarsity Press) and *L'Abri* by Edith Schaeffer (published by Tyndale House). Look for them at your favorite bookstore or library.

We don't need to understand the meaning of our lives in order to eat, sleep, and park the car. But human beings are not worms in the mud; the more we learn about the world and the joys and injustices of life, the more every thinking person asks, "What is this all for?" How tragic if we, and our children, have been taught to strangle these questions before they can even be spoken. Tragic because there *is* Someone home in the universe; God is not dead; and everyone who seeks, shall find.

CHAPTER **10**

Your Child's Discovery Channels

Every trade has its tricks. A blacksmith knows how to make a horse stand still while he hammers on a new horseshoe. Fly fishermen know how to snap the rod and make the line float out over the water. Knowing these tricks makes work a sport, and sport more enjoyable.

Learning can also be a sport. The difference between the duffers and the champions is that the champions know the tricks of the sport, and care enough to put them into practice.

I would now like to share with you some very simple tricks and resources that can make a huge difference in how much you and your children enjoy learning.

Your Special Discovery Channels

Jack Sprat could learn by chat
His wife could learn by sight
Their son, named Neil, could learn by feel
They were a funny sight!

Everyone is born with a special discovery channel—not a cable network, but a favorite way to discover new facts about the world. Some, like Jack Sprat in the ditty above, learn best by listening. Others, like his wife, learn best by seeing. Still others are sensuous types who need to have real objects to handle. If you are taught through the channel that suits you, fantastic! If you're not, it's frustration time.

Educrats, in their slow grappling with reality, have recently rediscovered discovery channels and christened them "modalities." Don't expect any sudden changes in the schools from this discovery, though. The best you can hope for is that *after* your child has been labeled "dyslexic" or "hyperactive" or "learning disabled" some up-to-date remedial teacher will discover that Johnny really just has a learning channel that his classroom did not accommodate.

Now let's discover *your* best discovery channel.

Why Not "Learning Styles?"

Your overall learning style includes both

* the channel through which you learn best (eye, ear, hand)
* the ways you are most motivated to learn (your "thinking style")

We will be finding out how both of these work in this chapter and the chapter following.

The traditional classroom, which is set up to teach mostly to the auditory mode, is serving only about 34% of its students!
—*Mariaemma Willis & Victoria Hodson,* Discover Your Child's Learning Style *(Rocklin, CA: Prima Publishing, 1999)*

NEW!
The Way They Learn

Parents. Suggested donation, $11.
Focus on the Family Publishing, Colorado Springs, CO 80995. (719) 531-3400. Fax: (719) 531-3424. E-mail: mail@fotf.org. Web: www.family.org.

Of all the learning styles books I've read, **The Way They Learn** is by far my (Renee's) favorite. If you're at loggerheads with a child you just can't seem to teach, *The Way They Learn* may be just the help you need. Credit goes to author Cynthia Ulrich Tobias for making the subject matter interesting, easily understood, and applicable to all individuals—no matter where the learning takes place.

Her book is based on five sets of independent research on the way people learn. Here are the five models:

1. Four ways people perceive and order information: Abstract-Random, Abstract-Sequential, Concrete-Random, and Concrete-Sequential. Abstract versus concrete refers to the way we take in information, while sequential-random describes the way we organize it. Questions and illustrations are provided to help you get a feel for your style. Detailed chapters illustrate how what each style "looks like" in an adult or a child.
2. Ideal study environments
3. Modes of remembering (auditory, visual, and kinesthetic)

4. Analytic *v.* global approach to new information
5. Seven types of intelligence (spatial, musical, etc.)

She condenses it all in this very readable, parent-friendly 168-page hardback.

The overarching theme is that people's thinking/learning styles are distinct and follow specific patterns.

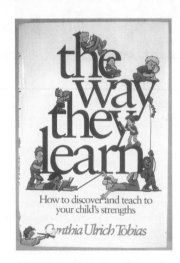

By recognizing these patterns in ourselves and our children, we can reduce needless arguments over how they should approach learning a subject and instead help them use their strengths to learn what they need to know.

Ferreting out a child's strengths using any of these models will undoubtedly give him more knowledge of himself and enable him to tackle the learning process from a perspective that suits his style. In that sense the book is both useful and correct. But we note two cautions, one of which Mrs. Tobias rightly raises herself. Don't pigeonhole someone into a particular learning style; we usually have some of the characteristics of several. We would also add: Don't rely on these secular theories as the end-all in learning styles—use them only as general guides.

This book is most useful as an easygoing introduction to the idea that we all do things differently. A good reminder for us that some conflicts and difficulties are simply a matter of not knowing how to accommodate those differences. As educators, that's something we should all be aware of. But as a Christian educator, I have to ask how Scripture comes to bear on these very issues? While there is nothing in the Bible about four personality types, there is plenty written on learning and teaching. How come a book from a Christian publisher has nothing to say to this question? Are we going to be content to let someone sift through the findings of the secular psychologists for us? Or will someone be brave enough to tackle the subject with concordance in hand? Any volunteers? *Renee Mathis and Charles and Betty Burger*

Seeing Is Believing—The Visual Learner

Are you easily distracted by new sights? Do you remember where you put things? Are you good at catching typos and doing puzzles? Are you very aware of visual details in drawings? Do you remember names better when you see them on a name tag? If you answered "yes" to these questions, you are a *visual* learner.

Visual learners need to *see* what they are supposed to do. You should write out a model, or demonstrate visually the skill to be learned. Some materials that are good for visual learners are:

- flash cards
- matching games
- puzzles
- instruction books

- charts
- pictures, posters, wall strips, desk tapes
- videos
- simulation software

The visual sense is, if anything, *over*developed in many children of the TV generation. That is why it's so easy to find instruction geared to the visual learner. The visual learner often gets an artificial "head start" in academic success, thanks to the match between his favorite learning style and the school's favored teaching style. Later on, though, visual learners can get into trouble. Being able to follow printed directions is not the same as being able to follow oral directions, for example—and neither necessarily translates into knowing how to assemble the bikes you bought the kids for Christmas!

Even though such great stress is put on visual learning in our culture, visual learners should be encouraged to develop their auditory and hands-on abilities.

Learning By Hearing or Talking: The Auditory Learner

Do you like to talk a lot? Do you talk to yourself? As a child, were you a "babbler?" Do you remember names easily? Can you carry a tune? Do you like to "keep the beat" along with the music? Do you read out loud or subvocalize during reading? Can you follow oral directions more easily than written directions? When taking tests, do you frequently know the answer, but have trouble expressing it on paper? Then you are an *auditory* learner.

Some auditory learners learn best by hearing. They need to be *told* what to do. These auditory learners will listen to you reading for hours, but you may not think they are paying attention because they don't look at you. They like to memorize by ear and can easily develop a good sense of rhythm. Naturally, auditory learners have a head start when it comes to learning music. Good materials for this type of auditory learners are:

- cassette tapes or CDs
- educational songs and rhymes (like the ABC song)
- rhythm instruments

Let's talk for a second about how musically-minded instruction can help the "I gotta hear it to understand it" kind of auditory learners. Before the movie character Mary Poppins informed her rapt young charges, "A Song Will Help the Job Along," parents and teachers were using music to teach

- the alphabet
- phonics rules
- arithmetic facts
- character lessons ("Dare to Be a Daniel!")
- Bible verses
- manners
- handwriting ("Down and Over/Down some more/That's the way we make a Four!")
- cultural history (Mother Goose)
- general history ("We fired our guns and the British kept a-coming . . .")
- science ("The hipbone's connected to the . . . Legbone")
- oh, yes, music itself
- and a few thousand other things!

Print & Picture Learners

Willis and Hodson, in their book *Discover Your Child's Learning Style,* reviewed in the next chapter, divide visual learners into "print learners" and "picture learners." According to their book, "While Picture Learners are busy trying to convert language into pictures, Print Learners are converting pictures into words."

As a Print Learner myself, I find relatively few times I need to convert pictures into words, while Picture Learners have to constantly translate the other way. *Discover Your Child's Learning style* contains many useful hints for this type of learner.

You will find musical resources sprinkled throughout the volumes of this *Big Book* series. Some of the best are in the Phonics, Geography, Bible, Foreign Languages, and of course, Music chapters. Try balancing these with a variety of interesting visual and hands-on resources to both encourage your auditory learner's natural talents and help him develop more visual and tactile learning strengths.

Finally, some auditory learners need to hear *themselves* repeat the instructions or information before they really grasp it. The Charlotte Mason method, which emphasizes students narrating what they have learned, is tailor made for this type of learner. If your child can't seem to follow written instructions, have him try reading them aloud to himself. If that makes a big difference, he's the "talking" type of auditory learner.

NEW!
Fine Tuning: An Auditory-Visual Training Program

Book 1: Primary/Intermediate, $15. Book II: Intermediate/ Advanced, $15 plus $3 shipping. *Academic Therapy Publications, 20 Commercial Blvd., Novato, CA 94949-6191. Orders: (800) 422-7249. Inquiries: (418) 883-3314. Fax: (415) 883-3720. Email: atpub@aol.com. Web: www.atp.com.*

"Ok, now listen up!"

"Did you hear me?"

Can listening be taught, exercised, and practiced? If material isn't making it from the child's ears to the child's brain, perhaps some simple drills to improve auditory skills might help.

The concept behind **Fine Tuning: An Auditory-Visual Training Program** by Ray Barsch is very simple: The child is given a grid, listens to instructions, enters the necessary information on the grid, and is rewarded with a completed picture or saying.

Two types of grids are given in this book. A Progression Grid consists of evenly spaced rows of numbers. Instructions are "Draw a line from 7 to 32." and so on, resulting in a simple line drawing. A Signs and Sayings Grid is composed of blank squares, with letters labeling horizontal rows and numbers labeling vertical ones. "Place an H in square D-5. . .place a T in square R-11" etc. etc. until you've completed a well-known saying.

The primary level grids, 40 in all, are simpler and contain fewer numbers and easier sayings. (Keep off the grass. Apartment for rent.) The 45 intermediate grids feature more numbers/letters and sayings along the lines of "To know how to wait is the secret of success."

You get masters of all grids for you to copy and re-use as needed. For those who'd like the extra drill and practice, this book might be the answer you're looking, er. . .make that listening, for! *Renee Mathis*

Learning By Moving and Grabbing: The Kinesthetic/Tactile Learner

Now for the physical types! Here are your so-called "hyperactives." As a child, did you have difficulty sitting still? Were you always grabbing for things? Did you always run your finger across the boards when walking past a fence? Do you move around a lot, and use animated gestures and facial expressions when talking? Can you walk along the curb without losing your balance? Do you prefer hugs from your spouse rather than verbal praise? Do you like to take things apart? Are you always fooling with paper or something on your desk when you're on the phone? If so, then you're a *kinesthetic* learner.

Hands-on learning is a must for kinesthetic learners. They need to mold or sculpt or whittle or bend, fold, and mutilate in order to express themselves. Kinesthetic learners learn to read best by learning to write. They like math manipulatives and sandpaper letters. Kinesthetic learners do *not* like sitting at a desk for hours staring at the blackboard—it's like blindfolding a visual learner to do this to a kinesthetic learner.

For kinesthetic learners, try:

- long nature walks
- model kits
- yard work and gardening
- textured puzzles
- typing instead of writing (it's faster and less frustrating)

Be sure to have kinesthetic learners write BIG when they are first learning. Large muscle action zips through to the brain more easily than small, fine movements. Manipulative materials and a good phonics program cure reversals in kinesthetic learners, who are the group most frequently labeled "dyslexic." Couple this with small doses of rich visual and auditory materials to increase your kinesthetic learner's attention span for these different types of learning.

You *can* be all three: visual, auditory, and kinesthetic. God designed people to learn through *all* their senses. But since most of us lean more to one learning style, you can increase your learning abilities by deliberately practicing with your weakest learning channels . . . and increase your learning enjoyment by adapting more input to fit your dominant discovery channel.

Varieties of K/T Learners

Discover Your Child's Learning Style breaks kinesthetic/tactile learners into:

- Hands-On Learners
- Whole-Body Learners
- Sketching Learners
- Writing Learners

If your child fits the k/t profile, I suggest that you try teaching using all of the above. Your k/t child may learn well through her hands, through whole-body motions (e.g., drawing letters in the air with whole-art movements), *and* through sketching, for example! This is just one more reason why all children should be taught how to draw well at a young age. See reviews of "how to draw" curricula in Volumes 2 and 3.

CHAPTER 11

Your Child's Thinking Style

Learning Style theory can be taken to extremes. The first mistake is to narrow yourself down to fit into a single discovery channel. Few people only learn visually, or auditorally, or kinesthetically.

The second mistake is to think each person falls into a single category. Categories are useful for defining major areas of interest, strength, and weakness, but they are not good for defining your total personality. Most of us fit into many categories at the same time. Take, for example, People Who like Ice Cream for Dessert and People Who Like Chocolate Candy. Or Sports Fans and Philosophers (there's more crossover between these than you think!). Or Energetic, Outgoing types and Sympathetic, Listening types (you can be each of these at different times).

There is also a danger of accepting everything about a person as that person's "style." Taken to extremes, immature or bad behavior could become enshrined as a valid temperament difference. Was it just Hitler's perfectly valid "style" to be fanatical and Himmler's "style" to be cruel? Some people are fanatical *and* cruel. Shall we call this the "National Socialist Temperament Style"? I don't think so!

Yet another problem is the introduction of occult Eastern religious techniques under the umbrella of "helping children with their learning styles." One book, for example, under the heading "Visualizing Success in Learning," says the following:

Picture a teacher that knows everything. This is your very own "inner teacher." Anytime you have a question about something, you can ask this teacher and get the answer. If you're taking a test and the answer doesn't come to you, ask your inner teacher for the right answer. If you're reading a book and see an unfamiliar word, ask your inner teacher to help you with it. If you're having a hard time understanding a new idea in school, have a conversation with your inner teacher about what is unclear, and your inner teacher will help you understand the idea.

Most Pegs Don't Fit the Holes

Classrooms, for the most part, are arranged for children who are well-practiced or naturally gifted in the Producing Skills. . . .

I have found that children with the Producing Disposition comprise between 8% and 16% of a regular classroom—or roughly, three to six students out of thirty-five.
—*Discover Your Child's Learning Style*

The Middle Ages & Temperament Voodoo

Middle Age folks were the first to invent "temperaments." They thought people were either melancholy, sanguine, choleric, or phlegmatic, depending on which bodily "humor" controlled them. Bodily fluids were thought to consist of four "humors." The one that predominated determined your personality.

Sanguine people were supposed to be cheerful because they were what we'd call "red-blooded" types. "Sang" comes from the Latin for "blood." Choleric people were easy to anger because they were bilious—full of choler. Melancholic people were sullen because they were full of black bile. 'What, me worry?" phlegmatic types were full of—you guessed it—phlegm.

Unlike more modern temperament theories, this actually had some small basis in fact. Obviously if you're healthy, you'll tend to be happier than if your liver, gall bladder, or spleen are irritating you. However, these "temperaments" are based on outdated anatomical thought. They totally ignore the spiritual aspect of our emotions, and the effect that life experience can have on people. Many a Happy Harry has turned sour under life's blows, while many a Miserable Marvin has found joy and peace through a new relationship with God.

Finally, medieval temperament classifications are useless for our study of how children learn best, since there is no way to design a method specifically for Gloomy Gus or Angry Angela—as if you'd want to! We don't want our children to settle for being chronically gloomy, angry, or apathetic. We want them to know how to *overcome* feelings of despair, anger, and unconcern.

If the author of that book really believes this "inner teacher" is just the child talking to himself, he is making unrealistic promises. If the child doesn't know a word, he doesn't know it, and no amount of chatting inside his head will substitute for looking the word up in the dictionary. However, if the author actually expects the "inner teacher" to provide information the child does not know, what we're looking at is boys and girls being encouraged to call upon supernatural beings other than God (our forebears called these "demons") and to submit to them as infallible guides.

Long-dead psychologist Carl Jung, a favorite of many involved in learning type theory nowadays, actually had frequent experiences of this nature, although he never recognized that the "beings" he was chatting with could have been more than simple projections of his subconscious mind.

I find it ominous that Jungian theory is being repackaged for Christians nowadays, via the Jung-derived Myers-Briggs Type Inventory. The bottom line of all these Jungian "discover your temperament" books and packages is their insistence that character flaws like self-centeredness and the refusal to bow to any absolutes are perfectly valid temperament styles. Some of these books go even further and insist that even our basic beliefs are simply reflections of our temperaments. This amounts to saying, in an exceedingly doctrinaire fashion cleverly disguised by the rhetoric of tolerance, that Jung was right and Jesus Christ was wrong.

The buyer, in other words, must learn to beware. Just because a theory claims to be cutting-edge doesn't mean it is scientifically valid or religiously neutral.

Temperament, in any case, is not an inflexible king to whom we are doomed to submit. As renowned nineteenth-century educator Charlotte Mason said in volume 1 of her Home Education series (now republished by Tyndale House and available from Charlotte Mason Research & Supply),

> *The problem before the educator is to give the child control over his own nature, to enable him to hold himself in hand as much in regard to the traits we call good, as to those we call evil. Many a man makes shipwreck on the rock of what he grew up to think his characteristic virtue—his open-handedness, for instance.*

For terrific insight into how we parents can help our children not only recognize but also rule their natural temperaments, I highly recommend Charlotte Mason's books.

Does Knowing Your Thinking Style Help?

Having said all that, it is worthwhile to understand one's basic tendencies, whether to cultivate them or fight them. Parents, in particular, can benefit enormously from the knowledge that their "difficult" child is just a different personality who doesn't necessarily respond to the same things in the same ways as the parents. You can then play to the audience—give the kiddies assignments they will really like—while fostering growth in the less-liked areas. One good example would be buying Junior a fishertechnik construction kit (Junior loves working with his hands) and teaching him to type (Junior hates to write, but you want him able to put creative thoughts on paper). A less savvy mother or father would be fighting it out every day with Junior over undone writing assignments, whereas you have successfully navigated to your real goal.

Children do owe their parents obedience and honor, and not every childish rejection of a task calls for negotiation. It's also important to recognize that such things as character flaws, weaknesses, and downright sins do

The "Four Temperaments"?

Professor David Keirsey has refashioned the "psychological types" of Carl Jung and Isabel Myers into "sociological types." Net result: two books about discovering your personality type—*Please Understand Me* and *Portraits of Temperament,* both published by Prometheus Nemesis Book Company.

Please Understand Me starts with a personality test. After scoring your answers, you end up as one of four types, each with four variants, for sixteen total possible combinations:

- *The Dionysians*—promoters, artisans, entertainers, artists
- *The Epimetheans*—administrators, trustees, sellers, conservators
- *The Prometheans*—field marshals, scientists, architects, inventors
- *The Apollonians*—pedagogues, authors, journalists, questers

These are based on four pairs of preferences: extrovert/introvert, sensation/intuition, thinking/feeling, perceiving/judging. The rest of the book first explains Dr. Keirsey's views on how temperament and character determine your behavior in marriage, child-training, learning, and business, illustrated with various literary excerpts featuring different temperament types.

Portraits of Temperament takes a more popular approach to the same subject. Here you get both the Person Classifier and the Temperament Sorter, but instead of personality types being named things like Promethean NJs, the four types presented earlier are now described as:

- *Artisans*—operators and players
- *Guardians*—monitors and conservators
- *Rationals*—organizers and engineers
- *Idealists*—mentors and advocates

Both books strongly stress the belief that even our beliefs are simply the reflection of our basic temperaments, and that we owe it to others to accept them exactly the way they are. This actually is an argument for the Dionysians/Apollonians being right in their basic outlook on life and the Epimethean/Prometheans being wrong. (Is that why the distributing company calls itself Prometheus *Nemesis?*)

Another book, by Dr. Keith Golay, entitled *Learning Patterns and Temperament Styles* presents four basic temperaments: the Dionysian (free spirit), Epimethean (dutiful citizen), Promethean (natural scholar), and Apollonian (crusader for self-actualization). I seriously question the use of these categories, mainly because the Bible says everyone should make the search for wisdom his top priority (the Promethean). The Bible also has some severe things to say about self-love and the consuming desire to be a self-actualized big shot (the Apollonian) and the rejection of absolute laws in the quest for personal autonomy (the Dionysian).

In fact, the four "temperaments" turn out not to be four equally valid personality types, but to be unbalanced to one degree or another. The Dionysian, for example, is like a baby that has never grown up. He lives only in the present and has no patience. The Bible would say this person needs to learn endurance and perseverance, and also needs to start putting others ahead of his own impulses. Golay, however, says that "to assign this type a paper-and-pencil task is deadly," ignoring the fact that millions of this type of boy could and did sit in rows in rural schools working with papers and pencils in the days before learning theory. This is not to say that some people are not validly more physical or action-oriented than others—just that we can and should grow to be more than our "natural" selves.

exist. In real life, I'm so-so and you're so-so and we both have things we need to work on. Still, wise moms and dads take care to understand each child's fundamental gifts and preferences.

So, what *is* your "thinking style"? It's not your preferred discovery channel(s), which we discussed in the last chapter. Discovery channels are the way you prefer to receive information. Your thinking style is the type of thinker you are: abstract or concrete, action-oriented or thoughtful, people-oriented or turned on by ideas, progress, or experiments. Each thinking style is motivated by a different "learning button." Find your child top learning buttons and you'll know which educational methods will literally "turn him on."

Temperament or Thinking Style?

Your thinking style is *not* your "temperament."

Personality is Good

In our eventual callings we may need enough courage to do what goes against the grain of our natural selves. But our education is not supposed to violate the personalities God gave us! Jesus, in the three and a half years He spent with His disciples, did not turn out twelve Peters or twelve Johns. Each of those men came out of his training period more of what he went in. Peter was more courageous, John more spiritual-minded, and Paul the Apostle, who received his teaching directly from the risen Lord, was more of an excellent arguer and scholar when Jesus had trained him.

If we can learn to think of students as people, each with his or her unique contribution to give the world—which may include being the one who does not fit in to society, but instead helps change society—then we will realize we have an obligation to treat each one differently. One moral rule fits all—e.g., "Thou shalt not smite thy classmate"—but one academic rule never will fit all. We must try to quench those little twinges of wishing Johnny were more like Suzy, who sits so nicely and quietly. Students are all different . . . but would you really want a classroom of robots?

Vive la différence!

—Schoolproof

This is important to stress. First, temperament theory is useless for helping children learn. Second, Jungian temperament theory has as its subtext that faithlessness and being willing to change your beliefs at a moment's notice is as much a valid "temperament" as faithfulness and belief in unchanging absolutes. To take this to its logical conclusion, atheism, New Age, the Nazi Party, hedonism, and Christianity are all just really the outworkings of equally valid temperament styles. Which is baloney.

A more fruitful approach has recently been developed, based on the ways people prefer to attack problems and the types of problems they prefer to attack. In the chart to the right, you'll see how four different authors and organizations identify these learning approaches. You'll also see my attempt to correlate these with characters from the popular "Star Trek" show of the 1960s. I threw that in to add some fun! (By the way, if you find it hard to think of Dr. McCoy, *aka* "Bones," as the sensitive, caring type because of how he verbally abuses Mr. Spock, just substitute Deanna Troi from the "Star Trek: Next Generation" show.)

Here's how it breaks down:

- **Spock is the Puzzle Solver.** He loves analyzing and coming up with theories. (I'm going here with Willis and Hodson, who combine these characteristics into one person. This makes more sense to me then separating them into "analytical" and "imaginative.") Names and terminology don't mean as much to this person as *how* and *why* things work. He loves to ponder.
- **Kirk is the Action Man.** He loves to face challenges head on and wants to do something "right now." He thinks "outside the box" and loves to discover new things—to "boldly go where no man has gone before."
- **Bones is the People Person.** On the show, his character is if anything too emotional, to form a foil to the impassive Mr. Spock. Concern for others is his hallmark, as is an ability to easily remember names and details about people and their actions. Again, if you have trouble with his abrasiveness (which only comes to the fore when he thinks Spock or Kirk are unconcerned about the needs of others), think of Deanna Troi instead.
- **Scotty is the Progress Person.** He is organized and can handle any job on time and under budget. However, he prefers *not* to have huge hairy challenges thrown at him. His idea of joy is cruising along sweetly with the ship running at greater than 100 percent efficiency.
- **Sulu is the Performer.** Several episodes brought out Sulu's underlying "swashbuckling" style, as have the books in which he is the main character. A razzle-dazzle pilot by training, and a swordfighting enthusiast, Sulu likes to impress others with his skills and flair.

You may legitimately question whether "Performing" is a thinking style, an out-of-balance personality, or anything to do with thinking styles at all. An extreme desire to draw attention to oneself would be labeled "sinful pride" by the Mennonite materials I have reviewed, for example. And three out of four learning-styles sources I referenced do not even list Performing as an option. The fact remains that some children just naturally love to entertain others, and you can either choose to work with this or against it.

Learning Approaches by Author/Organization

"Star Trek" Character	Alta Vista College *Learning Styles* packet by Cheryl Senecal	Marlene LeFever *Learning Styles*	Diana Waring *Beyond Survival*	Willis & Hodson *Discover Your Child's Learning Style*	What I Decided to Call That Thinking Style
Spock	Analytical	Analytical	Thinker	Thinking/Creating	PuzzleSolver
Kirk	Intuitive	Dynamic	Intuitor	Inventor	Action Man
Bones	Imaginative	Imaginative	Feeler	Relating/Inspiring	People Person
Scotty	Practical	Common Sense	Sensor	Producer	Progress Person
Sulu	n/a	n/a	n/a	Performer	Performer

"Star Trek" Character	Success Is	What They Say	What They Like
Spock	Figuring it out	"I see it now"	Finding the answer; puzzles; theories; new ideas; logic
Kirk	Completing a challenge	"This just might work!"	Action; experiments
Bones	Happy & healthy crew	"I know how you feel"	Harmony; working with others
Scotty	Perfectly functioning ship	"I built that"	Results & efficiency
Sulu	Doing it with style	"Look at me!"	Applause & attention; spontaneity

"Star Trek" Character	Favored Homeschool Methods
Spock	Classical Education/Great Books, Principle Approach (if allowed to figure out new applications of principles), Robinson Method
Kirk	Contests, Unit Studies, Unschooling
Bones	Charlotte Mason Method
Scotty	Basics, Contests, Unit Studies (heavy emphasis on projects & experiments), Unschooling
Sulu	Classical Education, Contests, Unschooling (with heavy emphasis on real-world activities that employ his talents)

Of greatest importance to us is the fact that

Today's schools do not push most children's learning buttons

Just the opposite occurs. Spock types are not encouraged to be absorbed in thought—they're supposed to pay attention to the teacher every minute. As a Spock type myself, I could relate to this line in *Discover Your Child's Learning Style*: "She might doodle or look out the window with a glazed stare while the teacher is talking." I have several old report cards that accuse me of exactly that! "Action Man" types may do great on the football team, but get easily frustrated by a schedule controlled by the ringing of bells. And don't even ask about what happens to Performers. These kids end up *living* in the principal's office. The charge? "Disrupting class" with their impromptu performances.

Today's schools were initially designed for the Progress Person. Grinding away at small, systematic steps towards a final goal is what this personality is good at. However, even the Progress Person might be double-crossed by educational fads which outrage his built-in sense of logic and order. Meanwhile, the People Person is happy as a clam as long as she has a few good friends. This does not mean she is *learning* anything, though.

Did you ever see or hear of a teacher doing this?

- Force a Puzzle Solver into a "cooperative learning" situation with a bunch of kids who refuse to do the work

- Make the Action Man do workbook pages for hours
- Tell the Performer to sit down and shut up
- Give the Progress Person an assignment where "it doesn't matter if the answer is right as long as you are thinking creatively"
- Punish the People Person for socializing during class time

I don't usually like to blame "the system" for what individuals do, but in this case, I really don't blame the teachers. If you had 30 strange kids staring at you, and you had to not only keep them from killing each other but try to teach them something, you'd do exactly the same thing (except, I hope, telling your students that right answers don't matter!).

Designing a classroom to accommodate all these thinking styles is just about impossible, and separating them into groups of like personalities would make school very strange. Imagine a classroom full of nothing but class clowns, and another full of people whose deepest desire is to socialize. Spock types would hide out in the library and never meet another soul, while Action Guys and Gals would be fighting over the lab equipment. Not a pretty sight.

The only solution that works, especially for those whose children don't fit the "I love to do worksheets" mold, is homeschooling.

Now, here are some tips.

For the Puzzle Solver

Give him lots of time alone. This personality will willingly learn, and even assign himself problems to solve, but does so best without distractions. Load up on strategy games (chess, checkers, Risk, Scrabble) and computer games of the "figure it out" variety. Go the the library frequently and bring a large plastic tote for all the books you'll be lugging home. Show him how much you expect him to complete during the school year, and don't be surprised if he gets all the math done in a month. Expect to spend extra time on drilling terminology, dates, and other "irrelevant facts" that the Puzzle Solver figures can just be looked up anytime in a reference book. *Some* names and dates are important!

Extra help with social skills may also be needed, particularly if the child has poor vision, which makes it harder to see people's facial expressions. I have a theory that the "nerd" personality, which seems to go along with thick glasses, has something to do with the fact that children who start out with fuzzy vision don't learn to "read" people's facial expressions, and thus grow up relating to people mainly by the words others say, and at best the tone with which they say them. Some instruction in reading facial expressions and body language might help, since college is a little late to be figuring all this out.

Some regular physical activity is a must, since the Puzzle Solver will happily sit all day with a book or a computer unless you get him in the habit of exercise. Preferably the exercise should have a definite goal, such as improving lap time or getting her next Karate belt.

For the Action Man

. . . who of course may also be an Action Grrrl! He or she likes ideas just as much as the Puzzle Solver. The difference is that the Action Man likes to solve *concrete* puzzles, while the Puzzle Solver lives for *abstract* puzzles.

Supply with: things to take apart and put together. Science lab kits. Construction kits. Lots of projects. Lots of physical activity. Remember, the word "hands-on" was invented for this kid!

For the People Person

Friends are all-important to the People Person, so make sure you sign him up for some clubs and activities where he can meet other kids. Since you, the parent, are a person too, encourage this child's natural desire to please you. Pick materials that focus on loving and serving God (another Very Important Person) and that teach about people around the world and people in history. Fiction of all kinds is good, especially historical fiction and biographies of people you'd like your child to emulate. See if you can team up this child with another of your children who is slightly older or younger, so they can study the same material together.

For the Progress Person

This kid needs to know where he is going. Show him the plan. Buy the workbooks. Hand out the assignments. Avoid nebulous, squishy, and time-wasting work, as this student will see right through it all and resent being stuck doing it. (Be sure to read Chapter 15 if you're not certain of your own abilities to spot this stuff!)

Don't let anyone put you down for being a "Workbook Mom" if this is in fact the way your child learns best.

For the Performer

You're going to have to cultivate some patience here. Your entire school training will have you reaching for the duct tape to strap this kid into his seat and cover up his motor mouth.

Fight those instincts. Try actually listening to what he is saying and watching what she wants to show you. Once you have filled up his or her "applause" bucket, you are more likely to get an audience for what *you* are trying to say or show.

If you can show this student how to do an assignment with flair and pizzazz, you have him. Don't just ask for a book report: have him pretend he is a radio announcer and "read" his book review "on the air." Don't just read a Bible chapter: act it out. A few props add verisimilitude. An old bathrobe can become an Israelite garment, topped off with a birdseye diaper wrapped around the head or hanging down for a veil. You can either use your imagination here, or just buy the KONOS curriculum (not KONOS-In-A-Box, but one or more of the original three volumes). These are just chock-full of great ideas tailored for the Performer personality.

Gregg Harris's *The Christian Home School* offers up some more neat ideas for a less-showy Performer personality. If you think your child would like to learn to do flip-chart presentations, for example, Gregg is your man. And you know he knows how to do it, because his oldest son Joshua is one of the most entertaining and inspiring speakers I have ever heard.

Remember These Hot Buttons

- The Puzzler's hot button is *ideas*
- The Action Man's hot button is *trying it out right now*—preferably something that involves making, fixing or experimenting
- The People Person wants to *meet, help, and inspire others.*
- The Progress Person *has to see progress* to stay motivated.
- The Performer yearns to be *noticed.* Try to give him attention (and lots of it!) for work done well—and let him pursue his own fierce interests as much as possible.

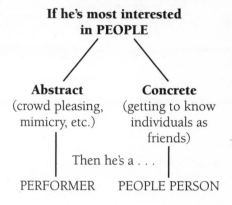

Here's a visual way to uncover your child's thinking style

If he's most interested in PEOPLE

Abstract (crowd pleasing, mimicry, etc.)

Concrete (getting to know individuals as friends)

Then he's a . . .

PERFORMER   PEOPLE PERSON

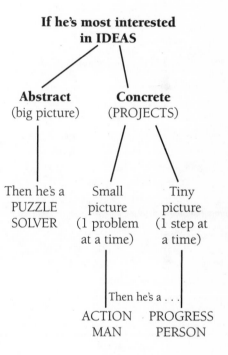

If he's most interested in IDEAS

Abstract (big picture)

Concrete (PROJECTS)

Then he's a PUZZLE SOLVER

Small picture (1 problem at a time)

Tiny picture (1 step at a time)

Then he's a . . .

ACTION MAN   PROGRESS PERSON

It's common to be strongest in one thinking style, and still score high in one or two more. This just gives you more buttons to push!

We understand, of course, that children are not machines. I came up with the "buttons" metaphor to make this discussion less confusing and more memorable, not to encourage untoward parental manipulation. You love your children and want to help them. Getting to know them better—their real needs and interests—is an important step towards homeschool success. I strongly urge you to get a copy of *Discover Your Child's Learning Style* and take that step.

If you're the slightest bit interested in learning styles, you need **Discover Your Child's Learning Style** by Mariaemma Willis and Victoria Kindle Hodson. Between them, these credentialed teachers (both of whom hold master's degrees) have been working over 50 years to develop their educational model, including many years helping a wide variety of students.

Their book is well-organized, easy to read, and personable, which right off the bat makes it better than most books on education written by educators. It's directed to parents, and though it stops short of recommending homeschooling, it does recognize that "parents are the most important teachers in a child's life."

Part I of *Discover Your Child's Learning Style* includes:

- An introduction to their philosophy that children are naturally eager learners and can succeed at learning
- Their "C.A.R.E.S." model of how parents should "coach" their children to academic success.

The C.A.R.E.S. model has these five suggestions:

- Celebrate your child's uniqueness rather than criticizing
- Accept your role as teacher

rather than avoid it,
- Respond to your child's feelings by following his lead as much as possible rather than reacting with blame or threats
- Expand your idea of where education can happen rather than excluding the home,
- Stop supporting labels based on a "bell curve" where some children *must* fail to make the curve look right.

You need this book

Part II, the heart of the book, introduces these five ways to unlock your child's learning personality:

- Dispositions: Performing, Producing, Inventing, Relating/Inspiring, and Thinking/Creating
- Talents
- Interests
- Modalities, which they subdivide as follows: Auditory (listening learners, verbal learners),

Visual (picture learners, print learners), and kinesthetic/tactile (hands-on learners, whole-body learners, sketching learners, writing learners)
- Environment: whether your child learns best when it's warm or cool, bright or subdued, noisy or not, etc.

There's a Learning Profile self-test for each of these, right there in the book.

Part III explains how to apply your new knowledge, including how to talk to your child's classroom teacher about accommodating his learning style. This part also includes a stunning chapter entitled "What About Learning Disabilities?" which totally debunks the testing-and-labeling model and the National Educational Goal, which defines coming to school "ready to learn" in terms that make it clear *only* children with the Producing Disposition will be recognized as "ready to learn"! They contrast this with their own Learning Style Model of education, show how the latter accommodates *all* children and pretty much does away with the ADD and "dyslexic" labels, and address special topics such as light sensitivity and food allergies. If your child has ever been labeled, this chapter alone is reason enough to buy this book.

I can't imagine how a single book could present this entire field of study more helpfully—and I can't imagine a book with greater potential to immediately improve your homeschool results than this one. Very highly recommended. *Mary Pride*

PART 4

A Quick Course in Teaching At Home

Terry Barhitte, a 17-year-old homeschooler from Vancouver, WA, recently earned a Saber Trophy when graduating from Royal Rangers Junior Leadership Training Academy. This is a four-year achievement with leadership training for teen boys in camping, trails, canoeing, survival, etc. The saber has his name and his favorite scripture reference (John 3:16) engraved on it. Terry also earned the Gold Medal of Achievement Award this year, the highest honor award that only a few Royal Ranger boys can claim.

Wonder what "hands-on learning" is all about? Here is an example! Arlene Hartley of Millington, TN, sent in this picture of her son, Kyle, investigating the heart and lungs of a pig (obtained from a slaughter house). As you can tell by the use of gloves, the Hartleys were hesitant to "feel" these parts. In the end, Kyle learned a lot about these body parts, a lesson long to be remembered.

CHAPTER 12

What Are Your Goals?

New homeschoolers often tell me that they feel "overwhelmed." I point out that every new teacher feels this way, and they don't have to face a class of 20 strange kids!

"But I never got a degree in education, and I'm not sure I can handle teaching my own kids," is a common reply. To which *my* common reply is that most education classes are about theories that don't work and classroom management strategies that you won't need at home.

Most of us have been trained to build education up in our minds until it's this huge task that can only be done by credentialed experts in multi-million-dollar buildings. As if nobody had ever learned to read in Grandma's lap, or in a little red schoolhouse presided over by a 16-year-old teacher! Yes, 16 years old. Read *The Long Winter* to find out about Laura Ingalls Wilder's first efforts as a teenaged teacher. You can bet *she* felt overwhelmed!

This section will help you see

- how to discover your educational goals, and use them to create a shortlist of homeschool methods that will help you meet them
- how to make a plan based on your true priorities and resources.
- how to trim away the overblown window dressing from what you previously may have thought of as "education"
- tips and tricks for making homeschool as easy and pleasant as possible for you and the kids

Go for the Goal!

The state's reasoning that children need to "learn skills for a possible goal" does not motivate learning. Students are told to learn algebra without ever being told when they may use algebra in real life. If the child doesn't know what the goal is, or if he will ever even be interested in such a goal, learning the skills is boring to the child. Adults learn the other way around —we choose a goal, then find out what skills are needed. When our eyes are on the goal, we are automatically motivated to learn the necessary skills.—*Robin Scarlata,* What Your Child Needs to Know When

The Many Goals of Homeschooling

The goal of homeschooling, oddly enough, is not to give your child a quality education.

It is *to meet your goals for your children and family*—including, but by no means limited to, your goals for your children's education.

The first step in choosing a curriculum that fits is to become aware of what your true goals really are. The same applies to choosing a homeschool method. Choose the one that best meets your goals, the deep-down wishes you may not even have dared express, and you're home free.

So what *are* your goals?

Here's how we're going to try to figure this out. I'll start by listing seven major goals. These, or a combination of them, probably include your own true goals. I'm then going to explain which types of curriculum and which methods are best suited to each goal. Finally, we will take a look together at which "seasons" of life are best for each goal. This process of thinking through each goal can be applied to any additional goals you might come up with.

The goals we will be looking at fall into four categories:

- Emotional
- Spiritual
- Vocational/success
- Academic

These categories sound pretty bloodless, so let's start fleshing them out right now.

Possible Goal One—A Happy Childhood

Giving your child a happy childhood is probably the most common, and least mentioned, homeschooling goal. People who have had miserable childhoods want to give their kids the childhood they never had. People who had wonderful childhoods want to share the best of their experiences with their children. This "emotional" goal feeds into the very heart of fatherhood and motherhood—the desire to protect and nurture.

Homeschooling is a powerful way—in fact, in our world the *only* way—to control the emotional quality of your children's life. As many of us have found, schools are cold places, where children do not learn to love each other and show kindness to others on a daily basis. At worst, a child can spend 13 years being persecuted for his appearance, brightness or dullness, race, ethnic background, social class, or even for something as foolish as a funny-sounding first or last name. (Sidenote: I remember reading that an extremely large percentage of chronic criminals have odd names.) At best, a schoolchild can form a small protective circle of like-minded friends. In either case, they will spend the bulk of their school years sitting still and listening to someone else talk. They will have their young shoulders loaded down with politically correct doom-and-gloom about endangered species, racism, sexism, overpopulation, pollution, world hunger, and the like, all the time being told that it's up to *them* to solve these problems *immediately*. They will be forced to engage in mindless group activities that actively assault their personal dignity. (I still vividly remember my kindergarten experience where the whole class was told, "Pretend you are a little tree waving its leaves in the breeze." Even as a five-year-old, I felt insulted.) They will be made to fear AIDS and nuclear holocaust. They will be expected to fixate on drugs, with (at best) whistle-in-the-dark campaigns with T-shirts and speeches against drug use and (at worst) curriculum that promotes the idea they should learn all about why drugs are so popular and then make their own decisions about whether to use them or not. If they are black, Native American, or any other significant racial minority, their textbooks will teach them to hate and fear whites. If they are girls, the stories they read and their history texts will teach them to resent men and boys. If they are white boys, they will be subtly taught to hate and fear themselves. Boy or girl, black or white, they will be warned that the end of the world is coming by ecological catastrophe—again, unless they *personally* take *immediate* political action *as children*.

Consider how you feel about the above paragraph. If you had a strong feeling of agreement with what I said, and a visceral desire to protect your children against all such negative influences, a "happy childhood" is likely one of your major, perhaps unstated, goals. If you feel neutral, or disagree, thinking perhaps that "we can't bury our heads in the sand" and therefore that even young children should be taught all about such things, I submit to you that, while you wouldn't want your children to have an *un*-happy childhood, you have other goals much higher on the list than a "happy childhood."

Please understand, I am not condemning anyone here. If close relatives of yours were Holocaust victims, for example, you might feel it is more important for your children to understand that such things can happen and to know their family history than for them to have a childhood untroubled by such thoughts. Arguments can be made on both sides: the "happy" side and the "tell them all about it" side. What I'm trying to do here is to get you to think *seriously* about your *real* goals. A knee-jerk reaction of, "Of course I want my children to have a happy childhood," defeats the purpose.

Assuming you have come down strongly on the "happy" side, here are the kinds of curriculum and resources that will most motivate and appeal to you:

- Educational and just-for-fun games of all kinds
- Shared experiences, such as field trips
- Shared projects, such as baking cookies or making a birdhouse
- Reading favorite books aloud to the children, and having them read to you
- Family pets
- Gardening and other outdoors activities
- Noncompetitive, or at least not wildly competitive, sports
- Co-oping with other homeschool families, so the kids can make likeminded friends
- Hands-on activities of all kinds (e.g., science kits)

Methods most suitable to a happy childhood:

- Unit studies
- One of the really good correspondence programs (these employ enough mental stimulation and hands-on work to keep kids interested, and many do grow up to look upon their childhood lessons very fondly)
- Charlotte Mason Method
- Delayed formal education
- Unschooling

What will realistically not appeal even if your friends talk you into it:

- Textbooks and workbooks for young kids. (Exception: the kind of workbooks that are full of cut-n-paste, coloring, and other hands-on activities.)
- Early formal education
- The Principle Approach
- Accelerated Education (unless your child is exceptionally brilliant and loves seatwork)
- Anything that involves forcing a reluctant writer to write a lot. It won't be a happy childhood if you spend all your time fighting over schoolwork!

Possible Goal Two—A Loving Family

In today's world of fractured families, the goal of a loving, together family is a deep "emotional" motivator. This differs from the "happy childhood" goal in that its main focus is on the child's bond with his parents and siblings, not on a medley of happy memories for the child to enjoy in later life.

It is important to note here that the "loving family" may not be present when homeschooling begins. You may have decided to homeschool because your children were turning into angry or cold strangers before your very eyes. You may be conscious of not having "been there" for them in the past, and be determined to rectify that error. You may have an unsupportive or missing spouse, and want desperately to give your children whatever family life you can in spite of it. Thus, you may not be sure you'll be able to provide a happy environment, but you're committed to forging the strong family links that will someday *result* in a happy home environment.

On the other hand, you may already have a great family life, and just not want to bust it up by sending the children off to an institution that believes peer group dependency is the pinnacle of socialization.

Either way, you plan to take positive action to make sure *your* family doesn't just drift away on the tide.

That being said, it's clear that *togetherness* is important to you. All forms of education that involve kids learning with minimal parental or sibling input will not work well for you. This means you should at first avoid:

- Traditional textbooks and workbooks (each kid is in a different grade, and while Mom can work with each kid individually, they are each isolated from their siblings by their studies. Exception: if the older children have already gone through the exact same books as the younger ones and if the older ones actively help the younger ones with their work.)
- Correspondence programs (same objections and exceptions as above)
- Video school (unless you all watch the videos together—not possible if you're using A Beka Video School for more than one grade at once)
- Early formal education
- Robinson Method and other forms of independent study
- Accelerated Education (unless all the kids are accelerated at once)

All the "happy childhood" activities will work for you. The list of most suitable methods, however, differs from the "happy childhood" list, because now

---

Safety First is Every Parent's Goal

Civilization began with the family, with children protected by mothers and fathers willing to sacrifice and even die for them.

If the family wasn't safe any more, if the government couldn't or wouldn't protect the family from the depredations of rapists and child molesters and killers, if homicidal sociopaths were released from prison after serving less time than fraudulent evangelists who embezzled from their churches and greedy hotel-rich millionairesses who underpaid their taxes, then civilization had ceased to exist. If children were fair game—as any issue of a daily paper would confirm they were—then the world had devolved into savagery. Civilization existed only in tiny units, within the walls of those houses where the members of a family shared a love strong enough to make them willing to put their lives on the line in the defense of one another.

—*Dean Koontz,* Mr. Murder *(G. P. Putnam's Sons, 1993)*

the essential question is whether or not several children, or the whole family, can participate in a given method. Consider choosing from:

- Unit studies (what could be more fun than making all kinds of projects and having Mom and Dad read lots of books with you?)
- Charlotte Mason Method
- Great Books (if you all read them together, or read them aloud to the whole family)
- Classical Education (again, learning what few people know today is a bonding experience of its own! The family that speaks Latin together is battin' together!)
- Principle Approach is somewhat dubious, due to the large amount of time spend individually researching and writing. If American history and government is a passion with you, though, this too can be a bonding experience.
- Online classes (if all the kids are enrolled as soon as they're old enough, and if the parents are computer lovers)
- Unschooling

One last thought to consider: While our society is fixated on the idea that each young adult should "start from scratch" and pick his own career without giving a thought to his father's vocation, carrying on the family business, or the family tradition of being involved in the military, or medicine, or teaching, forms a bond of its own. So does a daughter choosing to be a stay-at-home home-schooling mom like her mother. If a child is willing to follow in Dad or Mom's footsteps, then try hard to pick a method that lends itself to picking up that vo-cation in the teen and adult years. See Possible Goals Four, Five, and Six below.

Possible Goal Three—The Young Graduate

You may have good reasons for wanting your kids to be ahead of others their own age. You may have been a whiz kid yourself and enjoyed the ex-perience. You may have relatives and neighbors breathing down your neck and need some easy way to prove to them that your homeschool is not a stupid, irresponsible idea. You may just see no reason for wasting 13 years to cover what should only take six to nine years, if you leave out all the twaddle. You may have a medical condition that might cause your early death, and be anxious to get as many of your children as possible through college before you die.

Sometimes it's the kids who are anxious to get through school as quickly as possible. I was such a child myself. Some kids are just born wanting to go places and do things—in short, to *grow up*—in a hurry. The adult world may well appeal to such a child more than the "child's world" of school, where he or she doesn't fit in.

I say all this because some of us have the ingrained idea that accelerated education is the Little League of homeschool. Instead of parents screaming at their kids on the baseball field, we now have parents pushing their poor widdle kids to perform academically.

This may in fact be the case in some situations. There's nothing prevent-ing a "Little League Mom" type from homeschooling! But homeschooling tends to balance itself out. If children are really miserable, the homeschool parent can't avoid suffering the results of their misery right along with them. There is no coach, no teacher, no principal to take the heat off of you. All the complaints will go directly into your own ear.

On the other hand, it would take an awful lot of acceleration to really "push" a kid, in most cases. Without even trying, homeschooled kids are usually one or two years ahead of schooled kids academically. You'd have to be trying to rush a kid through all 12 grades in four years or so to really exceed most kids' ability to learn, assuming you were using streamlined curriculum.

Did I mention the word "streamlined"? This is *the* word to remember if you're thinking acceleration may be one of your primary goals. You won't have time for fooling around with silly, time-wasting projects or endless worksheets that simply test and retest what the student already knows. You need to cut to the chase.

That being so, you'll want to avoid:

- Video school—it moves too slowly
- Delayed formal education
- Classical education—while British prep schools were able to cover this material by age 14 or 16, it's a lot harder at home unless you already know Greek, Latin, rhetoric, formal logic, and philosophy. Besides, classical education requires lots of time for reflection, and rushing through school diminishes that time.
- Great Books—too much reading (save it for college)
- Principal Approach
- Unit studies

You'll want to consider:

- Traditional textbooks and workbooks. These are condensed, quantifiable, and it's easy to tell when you're done.
- Worktexts, for the same reasons
- Correspondence programs. The world's best-known advocate of accelerated education, Joyce Swann, has always used the Calvert School program, doing two lessons per child per day. It gets easier with each successive child, too.
- Early formal education—just for the reading, writing, and math
- The Robinson Method
- Online classes—for the more difficult or unique subjects, freeing the home teacher to concentrate on the basics
- Unschooling—I know for a fact that many unschooled children have entered college at relatively young ages. If done right, it breeds a habit of independent thinking and research that equips kids to move into the adult world well ahead of their peers.

Possible Goal Four—My Son, the Scholar

Although I refer for the sake of the famous phrase to "my *son*" in this headline, and the next three, we could also be talking about "my daughter, the scholar or whatever." The pertinent question here is (1) whether you consider yourself to be an intellectual, (2) whether you want your child to move in the world of ideas, and (3) whether your child seems to have any aptitude or desire for this.

If you answered a resounding, "Yes!" to all three questions, this has got to be one of your major goals. You don't just want to teach your child at home—you want him or her to achieve academic *excellence*. You don't just want your children to outshine public-school students—you want them to be able to hold their own in the society of educated people anywhere in the world.

If you are not an intellectual yourself, this becomes a more difficult goal. But who can tell if you're an intellectual? I'll make it easy, with a one-minute test.

Answer these three questions, and then ask your kids the same questions:

> (1) How many nonfiction books did you read in the past year?
> (2) How many substantive magazines do you subscribe to or regularly read? ("Substantive" in this context means "not focused on celebrities, fashion, sex, or ephemeral trends.")
> (3) How many fiction books, aside from romance novels, did you read in the past year?

Score your answers thusly:

> If your answer is, "Zero," you are not an intellectual.
> If your answer is, "I'm just too busy," you're not an intellectual.
> If your answer is, "I can't give an exact number, because I read all the time," you are definitely an intellectual.

We are not all intellectuals, so don't be embarrassed if you like to buy books and magazines with Fabio on the cover. The point of this exercise is to find out the truth about what your homeschool goals really are, remember? So why waste time struggling with Latin if you're honestly not interested?

It is, of course, possible for a non-intellectual parent to have a highly intellectual child. And there's even a way for this homeschooling situation to work out:

> • Online classes. Since the actual teacher is not the parent, all the parent has to know is how to make sure the student is getting his homework in on time.

For the more common situation where an intellectual parent is homeschooling an intellectual child, here are the methods that make most sense:

> • Great Books
> • Classical education
> • The Robinson Method
> • Unschooling, if the child is good at locating scholarly mentors

In this case, I won't bother listing the methods that won't work as well. Where *A* is the universe of all the methods mentioned in this book, and *A'* is the set of methods listed above, consider *A"* to be the set that results from subtracting *A'* from *A*, and you'll find that *A"* yields the set of indifferent or unsuccessful methods when it comes to the task of raising a young scholar. Proof: trivial.

Possible Goal Five—My Son, the President

The goal we're talking about here is "leadership." Many talk about it, but few think about what it really means. The Bible says, "He who would be greatest among you shall be servant of all." This has several implications for homeschoolers:

Advice From a College Professor

My father, Dr Stuart Martin, a professor of philosophy at Boston College, has been advising college students for many years.

His advice for students who want to pursue a scholarly career is as follows:

• Take Latin, Greek, German or the *most* difficult modern language in your field while still in high school, or even earlier. See if an ethnic organization in your city offers evening courses that teach that language. The Goethe Institute, for example, offers low-cost German courses in many cities.

• Spend your junior year abroad if at all possible. When choosing a college, make sure they offer this option and that the country you'll be living in is well-suited to your future specialty. Study the language *before* going.

• High scores on the SAT and ACT are essential—plan to spend extra time preparing for them. (For help, see resources in volume 3.)

• High scores on several AP exams are also important. (See chapter 42 for several online academies with AP courses, and Volume 3 for test-preparation resources.)

Patrick Henry College

PO Box 1776, Purcellville, VA 20134-1776. (540) 338-1776. Web: phc.edu.

Perhaps the ideal college for a homeschooled student whose goal is to work in a political office as an aide or a representative is the new Patrick Henry College, founded with the blessing of several people at Home School Legal Defense Association. Opening its doors in September, 2000, PHC has a very specific view of the type of education it plans to provide.

First, **PHC will initially only offer one major**—in government. If all goes well, a law school will be added next, for which the undergraduate courses will be a fine preparation.

Second, **PHC will be affordable.** Tuition plus room and board will be $15,000 per year. Compare that to $29,000 for a year at St. John's, a well-regarded classical liberal arts college. Work opportunities around campus will be available to defray part of that expense. Private scholarships will be encouraged. This is good, because as a matter of principle and conviction, PHC won't take any kind of government funding at all.

Third, **PHC will be rigorous.** Freshman and sophomore year will feature a very intensive classical liberal arts curriculum: American history and Western civilization, a lot of composition and literature, a little bit of math and science, and some foreign language, possibly Latin. This will all be delivered at a much higher level than you'll find in most colleges, because they're expecting their mostly-homeschool students to have a stronger liberal-arts background than most high-school graduates.

Fourth, **PHC will provide an unusual amount of real-world experience**, with the specific goal of providing "the nation's best training for young men and women to serve as legislative aides for the U.S. Congress or state legislative bodies, or in staff positions in executive or administrative agencies of federal, state, or local government." In the junior and senior year, students will study how government works, major issues in economics/social policy/foreign policy, research techniques, writing, and speech (including debate). They will also prepare actual legislative analysis for members of Congress, other government offices, or (as the opportunity arises) public policy organizations and think tanks This "directed research" work will be monitored and supervised by college faculty. Since the campus is based near Washington, D.C., students will have opportunities to meet and get to know personnel in government agencies and Congressional staffs, all of which spells e-m-p-l-o-y-a-b-i-l-i-t-y.

- We should not raise our kids to boss others around, but to try to find ways to help them. High-falutin' rhetoric about how homeschooled kids will be leaders someday needs to yield to a conscious desire to benefit others *whether our own contributions are ever recognized and rewarded or not.*
- You can't serve others without being around others.
- Kids imitate what their parents *do,* not what they *say.*
- The best way to learn to serve others is to do it, starting as young as possible.

So if you see your child as a future senator or church elder, start by involving your whole family now in church ministries and community service. For starters, you could volunteer to help out in your local food pantry or missionary clothes closet. For the bold, street evangelism is wonderful practice in public speaking. For the timid, bringing friendship baskets to the sick might be more your style. Older children can volunteer to help at the library or the museum. Little kids can "help" bake cookies for a church dinner or wrap presents for the needy at Christmas time.

Some homeschool methods lend themselves better than others to the skills needed for service to others. These include:

- Unit studies—you can almost always integrate your ministry into your academic program
- Unschooling—learning from real life is a natural fit with serving in real life

In the higher grades, kids can gain the knowledge needed by statesmen and church leaders through:

- Classical education—with its emphasis on knowing and learning from the past, as well as the entrance it provides into the society of the similarly educated upper class
- Great Books—ditto
- Principle Approach—for a detailed analysis of how government ought to work and what the real issues are.

Possible Goal Six—My Son, the Doctor

Or the plumber, or the farmer, or the graphics artist. Here we are looking at the "vocational" goal of a particular trade. You may not have the precise trade in mind, but you do know that it is extremely important to you that your child successfully hold a decent job. But the job you have in mind does not involve being a scholar steeped in the classics or a political or church leader.

What is needed here is:

- A good basic education, followed by
- A further education in the particular trade.

The winning methods here are:

- Traditional textbooks and workbooks. These are great in preparing you for the all-important standardized tests on which your high-school graduation and entrance into college or a vocation depend.
- Worktexts, ditto.

- Correspondence programs, ditto, with the additional advantage that in the high-school years you get a transcript signed by someone other than dear old Mom.
- Unit studies can be a natural way to discover and prepare for your vocation
- Unschooled kids have frequently shown great ingenuity in obtaining "adult" jobs while still quite young. This is a particularly good option if you are considering a traditional trade, such as auto mechanic or Hollywood cameraman. If your sights are set on the doctor/lawyer/dentist type of trade, you will be forced to interrupt your unschooling with a stint in college and graduate school. Impressive projects and experiences you have undertaken while unschooling will work in your favor when seeking admittance to a high-quality college, and if you read voraciously like most unschooled kids, the standardized college-entrance tests should pose no problem.

Possible Goal Seven—A Man After God's Own Heart

I saved this one for last, so you would have a chance to consider the other goals before getting all guilty over this one!

If you're a pious parent, you will be saying right now, "Of course this has to be our family's main educational goal!" But it's not quite that simple. The fact is that you can use *any* method and end up with a pious child, or use *any* method and end up with an irreligious child. It's not the method that counts now—it's how you live with your children and the books and resources you choose for your home school.

You can:

- Choose a curriculum that explicitly teaches religious history and doctrine
- Choose secular curriculum (because you believe this particular curriculum is academically or in some other way superior to the religious curriculum, or because you find the available religious curriculum lacking in truthfulness or depth) and teach religion "on the side"

Sincere Christian parents are bringing up pious kids with both options. So, I assume, are sincere Jewish parents, Muslim parents, and so on.

I would beware of anyone who insists there is only one "Christian" (or Jewish, or Muslim . . .) way to homeschool. "One-size-fits-all" education does not fit a universe in which God has made every snowflake and every child different.

There are universal facts and truths we can all agree on, such as the law of gravity and that two plus two equals four in base ten. There are also important universal facts and truths on which many of us disagree, such as the nature of God and whether there is a God. (The fact of disagreement doesn't mean there is no truth to be found; nor does it mean all religions are "true"; to believe this is to abandon all logic, even ultimately the logic that lets us know the law of gravity or that two plus two equals four in base ten.) But the *way* we teach and learn the facts and truths we know can differ from child to child, even within the same family, or be the same for two families that follow different religions.

Ultimately, godliness is knowing God and obeying Him out of love. If this is your goal for your children, you need to watch over your other

The Purpose of Education

The purpose of education is not to enable the student to earn a good income.

The purpose of education is not to preserve our American system of government and political freedom.

The purpose of education is not world unification.

The purpose of education is not to teach young people a trade.

The purpose of education is not to encourage the never-ending search for truth.

The purpose of education is not to put the student in harmony with the cosmos.

The purpose of education is not to raise the consciousness of students and train them for world revolution.

The purpose of education is not to prepare students for productive careers.

The purpose of education is not to integrate the races.

The purpose of education is not social adjustment of the child.

The purpose of education is not to stay ahead of the Russians (or the Japanese) in technology.

The purpose of education is not to create good citizens.

No, the purpose of education is far different, far more noble than any of these things. The purpose of education is to make Christian men [people], men transformed by the renewing of their minds after the image of Him who created them.

—*John Robbins,*
from the preface to Gordon Clark's
A Christian Philosophy of Education

King Solomon on the Purpose of Education

To know wisdom and instruction; to perceive the words of understanding;

To receive the instruction of wisdom, justice, and judgment, and equity;

To give subtlety to the simple, to the young man knowledge and discretion.

A wise man will hear, and will increase learning; and a man of understanding shall attain unto wise counsels;

To understand a proverb, and the interpretation; the words of the wise, and their dark sayings.

The fear of the Lord is the beginning of knowledge; but fools despise wisdom and instruction.

—*Proverbs 1:2–7*

goals. Happiness can turn into self-indulgence. A loving family can become clannish and selfish. Accelerated academics can lead to toplofty pride. So can scholarly studies. The desire for leadership roles can result in cut-throat ambition. An obsession with getting the kids a good job may reflect underlying materialism and lack of faith. Even the pursuit of godliness itself could be a mask for a spiritual form of showing off. That's one reason why we should all stop periodically and reevaluate our homeschooling goals. Another reason is that your goals will naturally change, over time, as your children get older and reveal new talents and interests. Make certain your curriculum and methods fit your present goals—and that those goals are worthy ones.

CHAPTER 13

What Is Your Plan?

Success in any endeavor can be approached step by step in this way:

- Step One: Identify your goals.
- Step Two: Make a plan.
- Step Three: Identify and eliminate obstacles to that plan.
- Step Four: Learn the tricks others have used who are successful in that area.

After reading the last chapter, you should have some idea of what your most important goals are for your children's education. The next two chapters will respectively deal with how to identify and eliminate "twaddle" from your curriculum and some very simple tricks you can use to immediately increase the educational value of simply living in your home.

This chapter is about Making Your Plan.

No Pain, Much Gain

Let me hasten to reassure you that this will be a painless process. You don't need to cringe in dread of dozens of worksheets to fill out. (If you *want* dozens of worksheets and planning forms, see Chapter 33, where planners and organizers are reviewed.) At the moment, let's just concentrate on a kinder, gentler plan . . . what you'll plan to do first each day, and which subjects and activities you will plan to spend most effort on.

The Preschool Plan

This is the one age at which One Size truly Fits All. No matter what homeschool method you have chosen, or are about to choose, and no matter what your goals are, everyone agrees that your preschool priorities should be the following:

A strategy is a specific way of organizing your resources in order to consistently produce a specific result.
—*Anthony Robbins,*
Unleash the Power Within
(1999, Nightingale-Conant)

(NOTE: The"power within" referred to on this CD seminar is not some New Age force,but your own native abilities.)

If Your Plan Isn't Working

If your child does not respond well to a particular learning opportunity, it's probably because you're pushing something for which he is not ready. Back off and try again in another week, month, or year. If he doesn't respond well to *any* learning opportunity, he either has a physical problem or a character problem. If he is uncooperative with chores you know he can do, it's likely a character problem, and your best way to overcome it is to work on getting him doing his chores with cheerful obedience rather than also battling him over supposedly "fun" learning experiences. Just one more reason for *always* doing chores *first!*

For help in recognizing and dealing with genuine physical problems (e.g., allergies, eye-tracking problems, slower brain speed), see Chapters 26 through 28.

- **Chores.** More about this later. Just remember, "For a homeschool that soars, always start with chores!" Even a preschooler can carry trash to the wastebasket, or put the spoons on the table. And if they're old enough to play with toys, they're old enough to put them *neatly* away.
- **Religious instruction.** This can be as simple as answering all the many questions your little one asks, or as elaborate as memorizing a catechism.
- **Prereading.** Read aloud to the munchkin . . . a *lot.* Tell stories. Help the little one develop the ability to "see" the story in his or her head, and to retell it in his or her own words.
- **Prewriting.** Making shapes with large arm motions, fingerplays, writing with your finger in the sand, and gripping and molding motions of all kinds help develop the fine motor skills needed for handwriting.
- **Hands-on activities of all kinds.** Preschools spend a fortune trying to duplicate your kitchen with its pots and pans to nest inside each other, your laundry room with its socks to sort and its laundry to fold, and your living room with its comfy rug to lie on. To this add puzzles (to teach spatial skills and logic), age-appropriate construction toys such as Duplo bricks and Dr. Drew's Blocks, washable paint and paintbrushes, modeling clay, and whatever other craft activities move you. These don't have to be expensive; whole books have been written about crafts you can do with paper plates!
- **The great outdoors.** Nature walks, chasing fireflies, and even lying with your nose in the grass watching all the little bugs scurry around are all invaluable experiences for the young child.
- **Science.** I heard this from Jane Hoffman, the Backyard Scientist, so it must be true. A study was done comparing two kindergarten classes. One class did nothing but science experiences and experiments all year. The other had a normal language-arts and math curriculum. By fourth grade, the all-science class averaged one grade level ahead of the other class in *every* subject area! I heartily recommend Jane's books and kits, reviewed in Volume 2. Janice VanCleave has written some excellent science experiment and experience books for young children as well: her books are also reviewed in that volume.
- **Love of learning.** Most of all, every homeschool should start off with a sense of wonder and fun. A kid who loves to learn is a kid you'll love to teach!

So, for your preschooler, your plan should be to do as much as possible of all of the above. This may involve scheduling biweekly library trips, or daily jaunts to the park, or supervised "backyard time" every morning. You may need to purchase some curriculum (such as the Jane Hoffman books) and supplies (arts and crafts goodies). You will know if you are meeting your plan if you can "tick" off many of the activities you planned to do, either on a list or in your head.

Remember, you can plan to *introduce* a skill, and give your child the *opportunity* to try it out, but it's not possible to force a child to be developmentally ready. With a preschooler, it is much better to plan to teach him a skill (let's call it X) than to plan to teach him X *by date Y.* Feel free to ignore the element of time; this is still the period when you are getting to know your child and his abilities.

The Kindergarten Plan

At this age, some methods advise early formal academics, while others say you should still concentrate on real-world experiences. Be certain of what you're aiming for, and then work out a schedule that lets it happen.

Even if you are using a formal kindergarten curriculum, these usually take only an hour or two of your time per day. The main thing to remember is

Back off from *any* academic activity for which your child is not ready!

Some signs your child is not yet ready for a particular academic activity (e.g., formal phonics instruction):

- Yawning a lot during lessons (a sure sign of comprehension overload)
- Fidgeting a lot during lessons (this may also be a kinesthetic learner who needs less seatwork and more ACTION!)
- Crying or seeming otherwise emotionally stressed by the work

Plan in advance to *drop* any activity which causes this kind of frustration until the child seems readier to face it . . . or until you locate a more appropriate curriculum directed at your child's emerging learning style.

The Early Reader Plan

You may also think of this as the "Grade 1 and 2 Plan" if you like. My suggestion for this group is, "Focus on character training, religious instruction, learning to read, and basic arithmetic."

While your child is learning to read, how much sense does it make to also load him down with history, geography, spelling, grammar, and on and on? Unless you want to read every instruction in the workbook to him, he can't even do most of those subjects in any traditional way.

So I say, "Plan to teach reading along with verbal counting, number identification, skip counting, simple addition and subtraction, and whatever additional *verbal* math you feel up to. Consider everything else a bonus." This avoids early burnout and gives you extra time to pick the curriculum you will be using when your child is ready for more. Too, keep in mind that most instruction in these other subjects at these grade levels is, to be kind, rinky-dink.

The Good Reader Plan (Grade 3 and up)

Now you're ready to really get serious! You're also ready to overload and burn out, if you don't plan to leave some things *out* of your homeschool program.

Your plan for this point on is to meet the educational priorities dictated by

- Your goals
- Your energy
- Your available time
- Your child's talents and interests
- Your child's learning style

First determine your goals (See the previous chapter if you haven't done that yet). Then select your ingredients (nature walks, books, etc.) and prioritize them. (This chapter is designed to help with that step.) Finally, pick the exact resources you'll use from the various *Big Book* volumes and make a schedule. It's a plan!

Some Subjects and Skills

- Anatomy
- Architecture
- Art how-tos (drawing, printing, etc.)
- Art Appreciation
- Bible Tools (use of concordance, Bible dictionary, etc.)
- Bible Memory
- Bike Riding
- Business Skills
- Car Mechanics
- Character Training
- Chores
- Cleaning
- Cooking
- Creative Writing
- Dance (ballet, ballroom, folk . . .)
- Driver's Ed
- Economics
- Electrical Wiring
- Electronics
- Engineering
- Etiquette
- Fabric Arts (sewing, knitting, etc.)
- Geography
- Government
- Handwriting
- History (U.S.)
- History (World)
- Horseback Riding
- Health
- [a] Keyboarding
- Languages
- Literature
- Logic
- Martial Arts
- Math
- Medical Skills
- Music (playing instruments)
- Music Appreciation
- Nutrition
- Performance Arts
- Physical Fitness Training
- Plumbing
- Safety Skills
- Science
- Skating (ice or rollerblade)
- Science
- Social Skills
- Solo Sport (golf, tennis . . .)
- Speech and Debate
- Spelling
- Swimming
- Teaching
- Team Sport (soccer, basketball, baseball . . .)
- Vocabulary
- Volunteering
- Woodshop

Obviously, this will differ from family to family, which is why we need all those different homeschool methods!

Let me suggest the following plan of attack for all those subjects and skills you want your child to learn.

First, list them. You'll find a suggested starting list in the sidebar. Then sort them into

- Necessary
- Essential
- Desirable
- Bonus

Necessary refers to topics and skills the child *must* learn, but that generally give neither you nor the child any bragging rights. Chief on the Necessary list are *chores* and *character training*. Necessary skills come first; never feel ashamed to say, "All we got done today was the chores." Days spent teaching your children lessons in meeting deadlines and getting work done before play are the most important teaching days you'll have.

Essential refers to the skills that make you feel comfortable about your homeschool. If your child is not learning these skills, you feel anxious and unsettled.

For most people, *reading* tops the Essential list, because it's what concerned relatives, friends, and neighbors want to see your child doing. It validates your homeschool in their eyes. If this is the first child you've homeschooled, it also validates your homeschool in *your* eyes. But beyond that, family priorities determine the Essential list. For a circus family, basic trapeze work may be on the Essential list, while for another it may be math, and for yet another it could be cooking, or Latin, or music, or art.

The key is to ruthlessly prune this list until it only contains the skills and subjects you can't live without for your child *at his current age*. Let me stress that *your* expectations are key here: you're not trying to keep up with the Joneses, and if you do, you'll end up overloading. You then prioritize your schedule so that these are the first academic subjects covered each day.

Desirable includes all those subjects and skills you want your children to learn before they leave home. "If we never get around to this subject or skill, I won't feel comfortable, but I can live with postponing it for a while until everything else is under control." Some typical subjects on this list might include French or Spanish, art, and music appreciation. While for some families these subjects are essential, or even necessary (picture a concert violinist whose family travels around Europe), for other families they are not.

Bonus skills and subjects are what you'd like to teach if you had the time, but your child could graduate from homeschool without them and you wouldn't go jump off a tall building. Good subjects to put on this list are those picked up in college and the working world, or that adults can teach themselves. An overview of classical music is important for general cultural literacy, for example, but a detailed study of opera can easily wait until the student decides to tackle it on his own in later life.

Now, sit down and make your own list of which subjects and skills fall into each area. Have your spouse and children do the same. Compare lists. It will be enlightening!

Don't Stagnate—Re-Evaluate

You don't just plan out your homeschool all at once and then stick to that plan for 13 years. At least, most of us don't! The most important part of your plan is remembering to re-evaluate your priorities on a regular basis. Beyond giving your children the basic tools of learning, don't let anyone shame or bully you into making *their* priorities *your* priorities. If learning to fly a kite or make a compost pile is more important to you than learning to diagram a sentence, go fly your kite. It's possible that next week or next year diagramming may loom larger on your mental horizon. Far better to share your passion for learning and life with your children than to waste years spooning instantly-forgotten facts into their heads.

It's About Time

Recognize the time-wasters in your home and plan how you're going to eliminate or control them. These include

- Lengthy phone calls with friends during the homeschool day (get CallNotes or an answering machine)
- The radio
- The TV
- The VCR
- The computer

One simple suggestion: no entertainment media whatever before 5:00, or until the day's work is done, whichever comes first. If a child is obsessive about a particular entertainment medium, lying and sneaking behind your back to use it constantly or during unapproved times, break the addiction by placing them on a "diet" where they are not allowed *any* access to that medium for a while. You may find out you can live without TV or rented videos altogether!

It's About You

Finally, plan what you're going to do to further *your* education. You need time to think and study, too. The best teacher is the one who knows the subject best and has learned to share his or her passion with others. Plan to go to the library and bookstore. Plan to read books and magazines on subjects that interest *you.* Plan to have or pick up a hobby and try to get good at it.

Just as it's true that the best gift a man can give his family is to love his wife . . .

> ## The best gift a homeschool parent can give his or her child is to love learning.

If you don't feel like you love learning now, I have good news for you; you were *born* loving to learn. School may have taught you to associate learning with various unpleasant experiences, but homeschool is going to reverse all that. You will learn that your instincts were correct; most "school" activities are a boring waste of time. You will learn to eliminate the "twaddle" and concentrate on what is fun, exciting, and effective. You will learn subjects and skills that totally eluded you in school. You will end up smarter and more confident than you started! (This applies even to those of you who went to M.I.T. or Harvard.)

The first step towards your homeschool Ph.D. is to take off your blinders and recognize another kind of PHD—Piled Hip Deep. Yes, it's time to grab your shovel and start removing the great wads of mental pocket lint that schoolkids are forced to waste so much time on. Like combat boots on a ballerina, twaddle drags down the joy of learning. Twaddle is your enemy. The next chapter will tell you how to identify and eliminate it.

CHAPTER 14

How to Slice & Dice

This is the chapter for Slasher Moms—those of us who recognize much curriculum is saturated with activities that fatten the teacher's manual but add no educational mass. In some cases, *super*saturated. You, too, can become a Slasher Mom or Dad. In fact, you'd better if you want to survive your homeschooling adventure. All that ugly twaddly fat will weigh you down and burn you out. So let's *slash* it!

Twaddle Happens

Curriculum authors are very creative people. Unfortunately, *their* creativity often does not take into account *your* need to get through the activities and projects in a reasonable amount of time.

Novice homeschoolers don't realize

(a) most activities are designed for enrichment and can be skipped without missing an educational beat
(b) how to recognize and slash all this unnecessary twaddle

That's why you need Pride's Top Ten Twaddle List. An activity is skippable twaddle if it is:

- Too big
- Too long
- Too silly
- Too unprepared
- Too unrealistic
- Too intrusive
- Too incomplete
- Too unimportant or trivial
- Too expensive
- Too time-consuming or too much effort

Let's take these one by one. I promise you'll never look at a teacher's manual the same way again!

When is a Learning Experience a Waste of Time?

Sometimes publishers of [twaddly] curriculum try to kid you along about all the "math experiences" and "language experiences" children are getting in their programs. What they are really doing is mushing isolated math and language fragments into totally unrelated activities. They are cluttering the curriculum with bits of math and language arts, and simultaneously obscuring math and language. Nobody needs to visit a carpet showroom to practice calculating area. This is curriculum clutter.

—Schoolproof

Too Big

Would you ask your five-year-old to paint a hundred-foot fence? Would you expect your eight-year-old to run for Congress?

I'm betting your answer is, "No." Yet curriculum authors often casually drop overblown and overresponsible assignments on kids. The worst offender is the guilt trip whereby kids are supposed to "save the planet" by becoming baby lobbyists and preteen political activists. Leaving aside for now the question as to whether the planet is really on its deathbed, surely a little common sense reveals that lobbying and activism is a job for mature, informed adults. Shoving this task onto kids is exploitative at best. So let me make it official:

Your kid does not have to save the planet.

"The planet" is too big. "Our city" is too big. "Our neighborhood" is too big. "Your bedroom" is just the right size. I fully support teaching kids to detrash their bedrooms.

In a similar vein, asking kids to create a mural, a tapestry, or a life-size statue is asking too much. So is asking them to complete a foot-by-foot graph of your backyard, a street map of your neighborhood, and so on. These activities qualify as twaddle for other reasons as well, but I wanted you to get the main idea here: too much is . . . too much.

Too Long

Some activities are stretched out over too long a period to mean much to the age group to which they are assigned. Making a graph of family members' heights over a year is *not* an efficient way to teach graphing skills.

Never measure anything that changes slowly over time for a school project.

Go ahead and measure the kids, just because *you* want to. Don't make it into schoolwork.

Planting a garden in order to emphasize certain character qualities and Bible verses is another example. Gardens are great, but by the time a kid has been pulling weeds for a few months you will have moved on to another unit. The example (what weeds are like) follows too far behind the instruction (parable of the sower and the seed) to make an impact unless you teach that lesson all over again each few weeks.

Never grow anything or get a pet for a school project.

Do it for its own sake or not at all. These long, slow lessons are really about gardens, animals, work, and love, not school assignments.

Too Silly

"Make up an imaginary animal/plant/alien. Then draw it/write a story about it/make a puppet of it." What *exactly* does this teach? My point exactly.

Again, if your student *wants* to do this, that's fine. But don't *assign* silly stuff like this.

More silly assignments: "Pretend you're a tree/a flower/a giraffe/anything else nonhuman. Then wave your little leaves in the breeze/sway your little petals/galumph around and eat stuff off the top of the refrigerator." Unless your child plans a future career as a mime or drama coach, pretend you never saw these assignments.

Too Unprepared

Curriculum authors *love* to include drawing assignments in the early grades. These vary from the specific ("Draw Puss in Boots") to the annoyingly nebulous ("Draw a picture that shows how you feel about summer"). Two things here:

- The kids are never taught to draw first
- Most kids *hate* these assignments because they were never taught to draw first.

One more point courtesy of the Slasher Mom:

- How much math, language arts, science, and history are they learning by making bad drawings? Or even good ones?

I believe every child can and should be taught to draw and paint. As an *art* course. For resources on how to do this, see the Art chapters in Volumes 2 and 3.

Your moral:

Slash every assignment for which kids have not yet been taught the skills to triumphantly complete the assignment.

Too Unrealistic

Asking kids to create simulations or models that do not in fact simulate or model the item being studied is just plain stupid. My personal favorite example: "Create a 3-D model of the human body out of toilet paper rolls." What are we trying to say here, people? That people are fat cylinders with scraps of T.P. attached?

Also popular among heavy caffeine users from the curriculum designer crowd: assignments that require kids to write or put on plays or skits about historical figures. Since we don't know exactly what they said, or their precise motivations, and kids are not about to put in the kind of serious research that writers of historical fiction and biographies sweat through, this teaches kids to *make up the facts*. A career in network news awaits!

Worst of all: the "interview" of a biblical character or other famous historical personage. "And just what did you think, Mr. Joshua, when the walls of Jericho came tumbling down?" "Why are your teeth wooden, President Washington?" Does anyone really think that any important person of the past would have put up for one second with this nonsense? The "interview" assignment chops great men and women down to the size of the stupid pet tricks on Letterman. (Which, amazingly, I know about even without owning a TV set.) Drop the phony nonsense and read another good book on the character you are studying instead.

Too Intrusive

"Write a paragraph about how much you love God." "Write about the worst fight you ever had with your parents." I cringe whenever I encounter this kind of assignment. All the more so since they usually occur in materials designed to be used in *classrooms*.

> Forcing kids to parrot piety they may not yet have achieved is a great way to teach hypocrisy.

> Making them reveal personal feelings or embarassments as an *assignment* is just plain evil.

Rule of thumb: if you curriculum designers want our kids to write about this stuff, *you* do the assignment too and let us all read what *you* wrote. Better yet, write out your answers and send a signed copy to your boss or some other authority figure in your life. This may provide a clue as to why kids' privacy should never be forced like this.

Too Incomplete

Don't you just love vocabulary lists with no pronunciation clues or definitions? How about huge lists of books to read that don't throw you a clue as to which are the *most important* books? Spelling word lists apparently picked at random (the words share no pattern or common topic)? Assignments that tell you, "Look up all the Bible verses on 'marriage' and 'family'"?

> Don't beat yourself to death trying to do the curriculum designer's work for him.

Nobody is paying you for this. Call, fax, phone, or email the company that put out these incomplete materials and *demand* updated, useful, *complete* information. In the meantime, skip all the incomplete assignments and replace them with complete materials from another publisher. Or just have the kids read more. Vocabulary building without pain!

Too Unimportant or Trivial

Always ask yourself,

> "Why am I teaching this? How much of my life and my student's life is it worth?"

An example: "Animals have fur." I figure that's worth about three seconds of my life. Yet I have seen a curriculum that orders parents to collect magazines with pictures of animals, then cut out those pictures and make a collage of animal furs. This swell creative idea has now expanded your time investment to somewhere between hours and days. Your child will also learn the valuable skill of chopping up magazines. All without ever *touching* a furry animal!

Another popular example: "Research and write about the history of your town." Since the average American family moves once every three years, this is less than a worthwhile assignment. It can, however, soak up unlimited amounts of your precious time.

For the technically minded among you, I offer this equation. Where T = minutes to complete a project, M = minutes it would take to just *tell* your child the facts or *show* him the skills, F = the "fun" value of the project on a scale of 1 to 10, and S = how much spare time you have on a scale of 1 to 10:

If T divided by M is greater than $\frac{FS}{10}$, forget it.

Too Expensive

Does the project or activity require expensive materials you don't already have on hand? Then either substitute less-expensive, more-available materials, or slash it. Comfort yourself with the thought that rich kids will be wasting time with this stuff while *your* student is zooming ahead in his workbook.

Too Much Effort

Some valuable educational activities may be more trouble than they are worth.

I am sure that visiting Cape Kennedy is wonderfully educational . . . for those who live or vacation in Florida. Making a seashell collection is great . . . if you live near a beach. Learning to rope and ride makes sense . . . if you live in Montana. Visiting the theater on a regular basis is fine . . . if you're a rich New Yorker.

When we lived in St. Louis, we were Zoo Members and regularly visited the museums, planetarium, and botanical garden. Here in Fenton, Missouri, a trip to Denny's is usually more than I can manage. Are my kids deprived? I think not. We have substituted activities that are near us (Tai Kwon Do and swim team) for the far-away stuff.

You can't do everything for your kids . . . but you can do enough. If an activity is a major strain on your family, in travel time, planning, or preparation, drop it. *You* are the teacher, not the curriculum designer. Slasher Moms everywhere are probably skipping that exact same activity!

So there you have it. Ten ways to identify twaddle—and now you know them all. Take out that chainsaw and hack out the undergrowth—your kids will love you for it!

CHAPTER 15

The Lazy Homeschooler's Five Top Success Secrets

After the first edition of *Big Book of Home Learning* came out, many mothers and fathers wrote to share about the fantastic time they were having teaching their children at home.

Meanwhile, I received a small but significant number of letters with sad stories to tell. Typically, a mother of one or two would tell me she tried home schooling or afterschooling and gave it up because it was "too hard" and "wasn't working out." This puzzled me because at the same time I was hearing from hundreds of large and small families that loved homeschooling. And when I say "large" families, I mean eight, nine, ten, or more children.

What amazing secret did these parents have? How were they able to do so much with so many children, while some with only one child found the task overwhelming?

It turned out their secret is the same as my secret. It's . . . laziness! Like other survival-oriented large families, for many years now we have been searching for easier, simpler ways of doing things. And surprise! There *are* easier, simpler ways to learn at home. Now let's take a look at some short-cuts.

Access

The best way to teach is to not have to teach at all. Ideally, our children should learn how to learn and begin to teach themselves.

How can we help our children reach this stage? In part, by giving them access to educational tools.

Let's define what we're talking about here.

Access does not mean simply having educational items available somewhere in the house. It means having them ready to hand, right where the child can get them when he wants them or when you want to direct his attention to them.

Maria Montessori, the famous Italian educator, called this "preparing the environment." She also stressed keeping items that would distract kids with "junk" activities *out* of their environment. Try sticking the Sega in the closet and getting a lock for the TV!

Children blessed with access to the tools of learning will tend to use them on their own much more frequently than those who have to climb stairs, navigate stacks of clutter, or ask you to get out the items in question. Here is how the access principle works.

- **FOR A BABY:** Alphabet letters, numerals, and educational pictures clutter our homes. *But* how often do you have the time to sit down with your little one and help him play with all his educational toys? Instead of all those fancy toys, try taping a simple sheet of paper with the ABC's on it on the wall next to your changing table. You have to spend what seems like hours there every day anyway, so why not give your baby something interesting to look at? You will have plenty of opportunities to point to and say each letter, and your youngster will have lots of time to become familiar with the shape of print. The same can be done with color and shape charts, "touch 'n feel" strips with different fabrics glued to them, numeral strips, and so on.

- **FOR A TODDLER:** Is the piano lid often left rolled back so he can plink away at the keys? Are there lots of hard-to-destroy books around that he can "read"? Even better, have you trained him how to handle *your* books properly so he doesn't have to be shooed away from them? Do you have special places for his toys so he can find one easily when he wants it, or are half of them lost and the rest scattered all over? Have you taught him how to put cassettes in the cassette player or just stuck them up high somewhere? Remember, if a child is taught how to use it, he won't abuse it.

- **FOR AN OLDER CHILD:** Do you leave that expensive pint-size violin out between scheduled practice sessions, or is it carefully put away in some hard-to-reach spot? Is art material a mere drawer pull away, or is it locked up in a cupboard somewhere? Is the encyclopedia in your family room (or whatever favorite reading spot your family has chosen) or displayed under glass in the den?

Human nature being what it is, you can be sure that if it is hard to find, hard to get out, or hard to put away, children will avoid it. But when parents make the materials of learning accessible, amazing things start to happen!

I once read the story of a Suzuki mother who decided to hint that her daughter should put her violin away by leaving it out in plain view. The daughter never did put the violin away that day. Instead she practiced for half an hour more than usual. Every time she saw the violin she picked it up and used it. You can imagine how this astonished the mother, who had been used to meeting resistance to music practice.

In exactly the same vein, Maire Mullarney, an Irish home school mother, tells in her book *Anything School Can Do You Can Do Better* how she used to let her children paint all over their ancient kitchen table and walls, serving dinner around the latest masterpieces before wiping them off. Several of her children won national art competitions. This interest in art continued unabated until the family received an inheritance. With the money they bought fancier furniture and redid the house. The unexpected side effect was that the children no longer felt free to paint all over the new, expensive walls and table, and consequently started spending far less time on their art.

In short, if you put it where they can get it and teach them how to use it properly, children will use it. Provided, of course, that you have a good relationship with them and they are not trying to prove something by upsetting you, and also that your home is not loaded with time-wasting distractions that divert them from better pursuits.

The principle of access applies to all subjects, not just art and music. My children are surrounded by math and science texts, thanks to all the companies that have let me review their wares. It's not at all uncommon to see one of the children browsing through these in an odd moment. All the Pride children have free access to crayons, pencils, pens, and paper, and in return we receive a never-ending stream of poems, stories, and art. A few more examples:

- When my daughter Sarah was only three, already she was writing great sentences like "HA HAL NAO PHH" (which of course I did *not* correct!). At the age of 10, she started playing with our computer, again on her own, and published several issues of a newsletter for homeschooled kids. She took an on-line class in journalism at age 13 (her request!) and has been a big help with our magazine.
- Although I never had time for formal piano lessons, my son Joseph picked up enough by fooling around with our easily accessible piano and the bargain electronic keyboard we bought one Christmas, and by spending hours on his own with the *Miracle Piano System* software so that people gather around to hear him play his original compositions!
- Here's one common "access" story: Surrounded by computers from an early age, my oldest son, Ted, taught himself all the necessary computer languages and is now a web designer. (It seems like half the homeschoolers I talk to on the phone have a kid who is doing this!)

The knowledge the children pick up entirely on their own by their free foraging through our books helps schoolwork zip along and makes for interesting mealtime discussions. I'll probably never have to teach them art appreciation because of our art books and art cards, and the same goes for laser technology and robotics.

So the secret of making learning accessible is really

- good resources that the children know how to use
- happy children, and
- getting rid of worthless distractions (more on this later).

Clone Yourself

Wouldn't it be wonderful if you could hire a private tutor for some minimal sum like, say, 5¢ an hour, to drill your children on all those memory facts and to tell them fascinating stories?

You want it, you have it. Introducing . . . the **Tape Recorder** and its cousin, the **CD Player**. Faster than a speeding mother! More powerful than a tired father! Able to leap tall buildings on either Fast Forward or Rewind! These remarkable visitors from our own planet have powers and abilities far beyond those of mortal men. Perfect recall of every story. Perfect patience. Perfect manners—they never complain about having to read the same story again (and again, and *again*)!

Yes, friends, the humble audiocassette recorder can teach you and your children how to sing or play a musical instrument, how to speak a foreign language, or how to win in business. It can give you math drill set to song in stereo or read you the entire Bible. Art instruction, phonics courses, great literature, even sports tips are all available direct from the famous people who invented them. It's like having an army of tutors! And the best part is that you and your children can learn together.

Virtually all the cassette products I reviewed in *The Big Book* were listened to at lunchtime. The children also like them at breakfast, suppertime, and in between. Adults can listen to cassettes while washing dishes, nursing the baby, driving to work, or exercising.

Audio lets you learn while you do other things—a classic example of time-sharing.

An increasing array of **video** curriculum is also available. These require more of your full attention, but allow you to see experiments demonstrated, rockets blasting off, flowers unfurling in extra speedy motion, and other sights you are unlikely to encounter in your neighborhood. Be aware that sitting in front of a video is *not* the same as "watching" it—we've had a few children who just wouldn't watch educational videos unless we sat right there with them.

Software is a third way to hire a tutor for an unbelievably low sum per hour. Can you say, "No more flashcards! Ever?"

Incremental Learning: The Hits Just Keep on Coming

I am indebted for this next suggestion to John Saxon, developer of the popular Saxon Algebra series (read all about it in Volume Three). Saxon's idea was brilliantly simple:

> Teach one skill at a time. And then *let students keep showing off that skill*.

Saxon called this "incremental learning"—learning one little thing at a time and then building on it.

Obvious, you say? Not in *practice*. In *practice*, once a student learns a new skill, do we ever reward him again for his achievement? Isn't the standard response a sigh of relief and "Now let's get on to the *next* subject"?

Whether in kindergarten or college, students spend their whole lives constantly struggling with the unfamiliar, only to be rewarded for their successes by *more* hoops to jump through. The constant pressure to learn *new* things never relaxes.

Math instruction has been an arid field when it comes to praising the student. Children are taught new skills, and then the skills are abandoned until final exam time, when they spring from the shadows on hapless test-takers. Saxon, seeing the fruitlessness of this "method," decided to *not* jump from skill to skill, but to include questions on previously learned concepts in *every* lesson. This is *not* the same thing as teaching the same old tired idea over and over again, that odious practice of unnecessary review. Saxon's students get to *use* their learning, and be praised for it.

How does this apply to other subjects? Here are some suggestions:

- Every multi-syllable word decoded is cause for rejoicing, not just the first one, until the student gets so good at reading that it would be insulting to praise him. (At this point, accepting his reading as just as good as yours, and asking him to read things for you, is praise enough.)

- Can Johnny color inside the lines? That doesn't mean he has just graduated from coloring books and never gets to color again. It does mean he can experiment with hard and soft coloring, with density, with different kinds of crayons and markers and coloring pencils, meanwhile being praised for his fine coloring.

- Just because Suzy is now in Book 3 of Suzuki piano, she shouldn't think she can never play her old Book 1 pieces again. Rather, encourage her to give them a whirl every now and then. She'll be able to see how much her expression and dynamics have improved, and see her progress.

Seeing how much you have improved is always great encouragement. So is feeling really competent at a task. Incremental learning makes kids *want* to learn!

Learn the Lingo

Shakespeare was wrong. A rose by any other name definitely does not smell as sweet. If you'd like a dash of quick encouragement, learn how to give fancy names to what you are doing with your children. A walk down the street can be a Science Excursion. Reading *Tintin Goes to Tibet* is Social Studies (your child is being exposed to the culture of Tibet, after all). That half-hour with the paint pot is Artistic Self-Expression. Weeding the walk is a Hands-On Nature Investigation. And don't forget all the time you spend answering their questions (stop thinking of those as "interruptions"—the official term is "teachable moments"). Write it all up in a daily journal and you'll be astonished at how much you are getting done.

The Teacher's Role—Teaching as "Putting In"

Lastly, here is how to make *teaching* more enjoyable.

You know, teachers are the most overworked and harassed bunch of people around—and that includes parents who try to teach their children. Why is that? In large part, it's because so much of their assigned job is *pulling facts out of people*.

I've never plowed with a mule, but I do believe that it's no harder to get an ornery mule to pull that plow than it is to get an ornery kid to divulge what's in his mind. Especially if *nothing* is in his mind. You can't pull out what isn't there—yet 90 percent of school time is spent on tests, quizzes, seatwork assignments, and verbal cross-examinations ("Who can tell us when Charlemagne was crowned Holy Roman Emperor?"), instead of on giving children information and giving them a chance to ask their *own* questions.

These demands for feedback are not teaching.

Teaching is *telling or showing people what they don't know*.

And it is so much easier to concentrate on input (telling) than on output (dragging feedback out of students)!

To make the most of your teaching time, and to make it easier on yourself, *tell your children what they need to know*. Don't be afraid to repeat yourself. Increase the proportion of input to output. A few simple oral questions will tell you whether your offspring are on track. Forget those piles of workbook exercises!

Read history to your children. *Read* science books together. *Read* the Bible at meals. Whatever the knowledge you want to impart, put it *in!* Don't wear yourself out checking whether they are learning. *After* they've received ample instruction is the time for a little low-pressured feedback.

Nobody tests your children on TV commercials. But if you still have a TV, you can see they have learned the ads. TV taught them. Unless your children are actively hostile, or so lazy that they won't even bother to listen, or so illiterate that they never read anything, you should be able to do at least as well as a TV set.

I don't mean that we should expect to play all the time. Learning can be hard work. But it should lead to the pleasure of success and be as pleasurable for our students as we can make it. If it's nothing but unalloyed drudgery for them and us, the fault is almost certainly to be found in the teaching materials or method.

When you find yourself working too hard, stop and ask

- **Am I overdoing it?** Am I making a simple subject too fancy? Am I trying to do *all* the suggested activities in the teacher's edition (this will kill any program)?

- **What can I eliminate?** What is essential in this course and what is extra?

- **Do I need to be doing this at all?** Is my child too young for this subject? Am I just trying to show off? Could I or my child live a worthy life in the world without mastering this material?

- **Should I give it a rest?** Are there other worthwhile things we would like to study or do instead of this until we can come back to it later?

Your goal should be to do the essential (teach Johnny to read, clean the kitchen before the Board of Health condemns it) and to get to the rest when you have time. Don't exhaust yourself trying to imitate all the success stories you read in homeschooling magazines (even mine!). Forget the fancy projects and the field trips that need two weeks to plan. You can always get to them later when your children have more enthusiasm for them and you have more time.

At various times I have had to give up piano lessons for the children (too young, not enough interest), art appreciation (overdoing it, neglecting more essential subjects), and Latin (not enough time, not needed at the moment). In the meantime I learned a lot more about teaching each of these subjects and located better materials. Art appreciation and piano are now being handled by the children themselves, and a few years ago we found an online academy that teaches Latin. The world did not end because we let some things slip that were giving us no joy for the present.

If it's something basic like reading or math that's giving you headaches you need to check out some of the other resources for these subjects. But even these subjects can be laid aside for a bit while you all recover.

Let's make learning as simple as we can, and learning will be fun!

PART 5

Homeschool Methods

If the method you choose involves a lot of memory work, your child may want to enter contests that recognize his efforts. One such contest is the Youth Evangelism Association National Bible Quizzing Tournament in Louisville, KY, in which nine homeschoolers from Columbia, MO, qualified to participate. The students worked hard throughout the year, each memorizing from 5 to 10 chapters of the book of Acts and representing homeschoolers well in Louisville.

Levi Dolan achieved the highest award of #1 Bible Quizzer in the nation! In addition to a large trophy, Levi received a $1,000 scholarship. In the picture we have, from left to right, in the back row: Levi Dolan, Luke Dolan, and Andrew Dolan. In the front: Rachel Algya, Kara Haithcoat, Angela Schweikert, Philip Swenson, Lori Plog, and Alissa Swenson.

Nathan Harter, a 12-year-old homeschooler from Madison, NY, has apparently been learning more than academics at home. His 4-H project, a Windsor Chair that he made in his father's shop, won a blue ribbon at the Madison County 4-H fair. It was then taken to the New York State Fair and put on display with items from around the state. The picture shows Nathan with his chair and poster at the state fair. Nathan spent about 20 hours working on his chair, starting right from the log!

CHAPTER 16

Methods or Madness?

Homeschooling is not just about a *place*—the home—it is about a *different way* to learn, and a *different way* to teach.

To be even more accurate, homeschooling is about a *number of different ways* to learn and teach. Because you are not only blessed with a huge number of resources to choose from, but a wide variety of popular home-school methods.

Each and every one of these methods is more successful than public school, both academically and in terms of building stronger character. But that is about all they have in common. They use different *materials* . . . reach for different *goals* . . . use different *teaching and learning styles* . . . require differing amounts of *time* and *preparation* . . . and much more.

We've already looked at how to determine which curriculum and teaching method best fits you. Now you need to know what's available. So in these next nine chapters, we'll discuss *all* the major homeschool methods, starting first with the methods used in past centuries and going right through to the high-tech methods of tomorrow.

But first, this quick overview.

Overview of Major Homeschool Methods

The best way to get a grip on the major homeschool methods in use today is to break them up into groups that share some common characteristics. Remember, we have an entire chapter on each of these methods, so just treat this as your handy guide to which chapters to read first.

Our first group is old-fashioned (mid-1800's) public schooling updated for today. If you are a fan of no-nonsense education, or don't have a lot of time to spare, these might be for you.

- **Accelerated Education.** This is not strictly a method, which is why our chapter on acceleration is not in the methods section, but it's often discussed as if it were, which is why we included it in this group. You pick a curriculum and do extra lessons each day or week so you finish more quickly. Typically, the curriculum is a "back to basics" or lite classical type (not heavy on Latin or reading hundreds of Great Books).
- **Back to Basics.** No-nonsense, authoritative instruction. Much emphasis on skills of reading, writing, and ciphering, plus traditional grammar, spelling word lists, and so on. Much drill and practice.

Our second group fits those of a more scholarly turn of mind. Each method calls upon a list of "great books" to study, and looks back further than the mid-1800s for its inspiration.

- **Classical Education.** Based on the medieval "trivium," children first are taught many facts by rote (including Latin vocabulary and grammar). They then learn to analyze and reason, using formal logic, and study many great works of Western literature (by which I do *not* mean Zane Grey!). We're talking Homer, Aristotle, Dante, Cervantes, and so forth. Finally they reach the "rhetoric" stage, in which the persuasive arts are taught.
- **Classical Education Lite.** No Latin. Fewer and easier books.
- **Great Books.** Similar curriculum to Classical Education, with even greater emphasis on the books themselves. The Socratic method of instruction is used, whereby the teacher challenges the student to form and defend his own opinions.
- **The Principle Approach.** Inspired by the character and achievements of America's Founding Fathers, this curriculum attempts to recreate the kind of education that formed these men. Much time is spent studying historical source documents from that period. Much time is also spent writing, analyzing, and applying the "seven principles" that the curriculum developers believe incorporate the keys to America's success.
- **The Robinson Method.** A hybrid of back-to-basics and classical education, this method concentrates on teaching the student to learn on his own as early as possible. Many Great Books are studied, as well as popular American and British fiction of the 1800s and early 1900s.

The next group catapults us into the modern age—or even farther into the past, depending on how you look at it. Learning what you need to know from the world around you is both a bold new educational theory and the way just about everyone learned before the modern university system was developed during the Middle Ages.

- **Guided Exploration.** This is typically used as a subset of the other methods in this group. The student is given assignments, and possibly even a list of sources to explore. He then completes the work on his own. In preschool, this can take the form of presenting the student with a set of objects to sort or manipulate in some structured way. In upper grades, projects and research assignments are common.

- **Unguided Exploration.** Also a subset of the other methods in this group, it is similar to Guided Exploration, except the student creates his own "assignments." These may be structured ("Build a model of the Starship Enterprise") or unstructured ("Find out everything I can about how to take professional-quality photos"). The parent has a low profile, either acting as a "facilitator" (who may volunteer useful hints and information) or "resource person" (who is *not* supposed to volunteer information unless asked first).
- **Unschooling.** Guided and/or Unguided Exploration, with an emphasis on real-world activities as opposed to contrived "assignments." In early years, children follow the parents around and learn skills mostly by having the skills demonstrated to them and by asking questions. In later years, the students develop their own interests and pursue them independently.
- **Unit Studies.** This combines exploration and projects with a "packaged" approach to education, in which the various explorations and projects both revolve around a central theme (the "unit") and cover as many school skills as possible (the "studies").

This next method stands on its own. Developed in the Victorian Era, it is the method best suited to People Persons and to auditory learners of the type that need to hear themselves saying something in order to really learn it.

- **The Charlotte Mason Method.** The emphasis here is on teaching children to love the beautiful and noble part of our civilization, to love God, and to love others. Training in good habits is central, as are some particular techniques (e.g., "narration" rather than workbook exercises). You will have to create your own curriculum, since no Charlotte Mason curriculum is yet available.

Finally, we have:

- **Contests.** These are not a method *per se*, but a great way to motivate kids in a particular subject area. Plus, many contests include their own "curriculum" in the sense of word lists to spell, geographical attributes to memorize, sets of math problems form old contests to solve, and so on.
- **The Eclectic Method.** This doesn't get a chapter, because it simply means you pick and choose your favorite bits from all the other methods!

Now, for further details on all these methods, just keep reading!

The most successful eclectic approach I have seen is that of Clay and Sally Clarkson in their book, **Educating the WholeHearted Child.** They divide school subjects into the "5 D's"—Discipleship Studies (Bible and Christian living), Disciplined Studies (the "basics"), Discussion Studies (the humanities), Discovery Studies (nature, science, the arts, and personal interests), and Discretionary Studies (real-life skills, field trips, etc.). They then explain how to complete these studies using the best techniques of the various methods.

Their oversized, 220-plus-page book includes much more than this: character training, whether you should homeschool, the practicalities of organization, realities of dealing with the spiritual blues, and sources of support. Much helpful advice and inspiration is included, as well as a hefty appendix of planning forms you can use in your homeschool.

For more details and insights, now there's *The WholeHearted Child* tape set and *The WholeHearted Mother* tape set. Each set is four audiocassettes in a protective slim case. Recommended.

Mary Pride and Charles & Betty Burger

CHAPTER 17

Back to Basics

The basics. The "3 R's". Reading, riting, and rithmetic. Most parents fervently agree that whatever "education" means, it surely must include these.

Until compulsory attendance laws were passed, which is a fairly recent development in our history, children were normally taught to read and count at home *before* attending school, and many well-educated people never went to school at all.

Even when children went to school, until partway through this century "school" was not at all like what we experience today. A typical school experience would last six years, with three semesters of 6–12 weeks each, scheduled so kids could take time off to help with planting and harvest on their family's farm. In that short amount of "school" time, they were expected to learn how to read material we would now consider "college level" fluently, handwrite beautifully, and solve complex word problems involving what we now deem "college level" consumer math. They were also familiar with the early history of American, its founding documents, and the principles set down in those documents—making them better-educated citizens than most of our current elected representatives and judges!

Our great-great-grandparents were expected to learn all this in one-room schoolhouses, whose accessories included pot-bellied stoves and outhouses, taught by a single teacher with no teacher's assistants except for the older children, no classroom TV, no audio-video equipment, no computers, no math manipulatives, no bulletin-board cutouts, and (very importantly) *no* teacher's unions and almost *no* Federal or state bureaucracy interfering with every step of her teaching.

Those who had their sights set on college, which at that time was a special experience achieved only by a relatively few, typically added more advanced math and science, Latin and perhaps Greek, and a European language or two to their studies, plus a reading course in the "Great Books." Following such a course, it was not unusual for students to be ready for college at age 14 or 16.

Back to Basics Curriculum

- A Beka Book (textbooks & workbooks, correspondence school option)
- A Beka Video School
- Alpha Omega Publications (worktexts, software option, and online academy option)
- Bob Jones University Press (textbooks & workbooks)
- Christian Liberty Academy (workbooks & textbooks, correspondence options)
- Christian Light Education (worktexts, correspondence school option)
- ESP Super Yearbooks
- How to Tutor Curriculum (step-by-step basics)
- Landmark's Freedom Baptist Curriculum (worktexts)
- Rod & Staff (textbooks & workbooks)
- School of Tomorrow (worktexts, associated correspondence school option)

Please note that most of these publishers also offer a variety of support and enrichment materials, plus curriculum for higher grade levels.

Why the Cry of "Back to Basics"?

The public schools have been experimenting for decades with methods
designed to bypass what progressive elements considered the "mindless
drill" and "rote learning" associated with the way these basics had been
successfully taught for centuries. Parents and many teachers watched in
dismay as Look-Say, the New Math, Whole Language, and other fads left
generations of kids in need of remedial reading courses in college and unprepared to make correct change at McDonalds.

The "Back to Basics" movement was a response to these falling academic
standards. A handful of curriculum companies, some secular and some
Christian, came out with workbook and textbooks that employed traditional teach-'em-and-drill-'em techniques. Some even reprinted classic
texts from the early days of public schooling, such as the famous McGuffey
Readers. The burgeoning Christian school movement snapped these up, as
did many in the emerging homeschool movement.

Since the skills at issue were those taught in the early grades, for the
purposes of this book we will consider "back to basics" to refer to materials
for grades K–6. However, publishers of "back to basics" materials often carry the same no-nonsense approach on through junior high and high
school.

Basics curricula have this in common:

- Authoritative instruction that tells students the facts and how
  to do the work (as opposed to encouraging them to guess or
  invent their own methods)
- Step-by-step approach to teaching new skills
- Lots of practice problems
- Lots of rote drill to ensure mastery

Where basics curricula differ from each other is not in their approach
(though there are minor differences). They differ in the amount and kind of
spiritual emphasis they include and in the medium they use to present the
basics.

You know what kind of spiritual emphasis you are looking for. So, for
the rest of this chapter let's look at the different ways—textbook, worktext,
audio, video, and software—you can purchase a peck of basics today!

Traditional Textbook

"Traditional Textbook" is what most people think of when they first
contemplate homeschooling—children setting at desks, reading textbooks
and writing answers down. Just like school. But at home.

Textbook learning follows this familiar school sequence:

- Give an assignment
- The child reads the lesson and you answer any questions
- The child does the "exercises" at the end of the section or
  chapter
- You grade the exercises and explain what the child missed
- The child takes quizzes and tests, and does some reports or
  projects, which you also grade

Textbook learning lends itself well to the "X pages a day method."
Simply stated, you take the textbook, divide its pages by the number of

days in which you desire to complete it (200 days for a 40-week school year, for example), and assign the child that many pages per day.

Advantages of textbook learning: Ease of assignments (X pages per day); only one study book (there many be additional exercise books, answer keys, teacher manuals, etc., though); lends itself somewhat to self-study; minimal teacher preparation; no shopping for additional resources or book; easy to provide a "grade" for each course; covers all material in the public-school sequence, so you're all set for standardized tests. Exception: Christian biology texts do *not* prepare you well for the heavily evolutionary CLEP, SAT II, or AP biology tests, and Christian literature courses leave out many politically correct/sexually oriented readings now included on the CLEP/SAT II/AP literature tests.

Christian publishers such as A Beka Book, Bob Jones University Press, and Rod and Staff are the most popular vendors of textbooks to the home-school market. You'll find complete reviews of their curricula in Chapter 35.

Many secular vendors offer a variety of individual texts of value in preparing for elementary and high-school level studies, but none of them offer an entire packaged curriculum targeted to homeschoolers. You'll find reviews of many of these individual texts in Volumes 2 and 3.

WHO IT'S BEST FOR: Puzzle Solvers, Progress People, and visual learners benefit most. The "wiggle worm" kinesthetic/tactile child may need some seatwork time to learn self-control, but an overdose of textbooks will kill his or her motivation, so keep it light. Auditory learners love to be read to, but most textbooks don't exactly cry out to be read aloud, and they don't provide the "people" connection that People Persons crave.

Traditional Worktext

A "worktext" is not exactly a textbook, and it's not exactly a workbook. It's a consumable booklet that includes both the instruction normally found in a textbook, and the exercises and quizzes normally found in a workbook. Many worktexts are "reproducible," meaning the publisher grants you the right to photocopy the pages for your own use. At home this is a mixed blessing, since few of us have home photocopy machines, and the price of photocopying an entire book can easily outweigh the cost of an additional copy. However, if you only need to photocopy a few pages (e.g., chapter exercises and tests), it can save you some money.

Worktext advantages include low initial cost and simplicity of storage—everything is in the one book. Since answer keys are either in the worktext itself, or available for sale separately, grading the child's answers is no problem. Except that there are *so many* answers to grade!

The worktext route is designed for more self-study and less parental involvement than the textbook route. You likely won't need a separate teacher's manual, except for the answer key. You will, however, have to do *lots* of grading. What you gain in lesson preparation time you lose in grading, filling out the umpteen record sheets that record the grade, and calculating final grades for every quiz, text, and the course itself.

WHO IT'S BEST FOR: Puzzle Solvers, Progress People, and visual learners benefit most. "Wiggle worm" Action People find worktexts less onerous than textbooks, since worktexts are usually thinner and it's easier to feel like you're getting somewhere. Plus, the "write on me" nature of textbooks is more appealing than having to do your work on separate paper. Auditory learners don't especially benefit. People Persons might enjoy a workbook that is written personably and illustrated charmingly (e.g., the *Simply Grammar* worktext, reviewed in volume 2).

The 7 "R"s

The basics are often defined as the minimum skills a child needs to learn in order to master *other* skills. Sometimes they are referred to as "the tools of learning," after a famous essay by British author Dorothy Sayers.

The original "back to basics" crusade contented itself with the goals of literacy and numeracy.

I would like to propose a stronger definition of the basics:

- Reading
- 'Riting
- 'Rithmetic
- Research
- Reasoning
- Religion
- Right & wrong (basic morality)

Where to Find Worktexts

Popular vendors of worktext curriculum include Alpha Omega Publications (now a part of Bridgestone Media), Christian Liberty Press, Christian Light Publications, and School of Tomorrow. ESP Publishers (the name is an acronym that has nothing to do with extrasensory perception) has what might be the ultimate worktext curriculum—its enormous "Super Yearbooks." Each of these includes an entire grade's worth of lesson sheets for all school subjects. For a quick "catch up," try the "summer skills" worktexts from a number of secular publishers, available in your local teacher's store.

Many vendors offer worktext curricula for a particular subject or grade. You'll find these individual product reviews in Volumes 2 and 3.

Video Teachers

To find educational videos for homeschoolers online, go to www.home-school.com/mall, click on "Curriculum Hall," and select the Educational Videos category. There you'll find links to sites that sell a wide selection of educational videos.

Go to class . . . without going to class. Yes, you can bring the teacher home. Just purchase his or her video series!

To date, phonics instruction on video has not been popular or successful. Phonics video instruction has worked best for showing parents how to do the teaching themselves. Math and science, however, both lend themselves well to the video format. A video teacher can demonstrate fractions with manipulatives, show you how to use a number line, demonstrate science experiments, and take you to the zoo.

You'll find math and science video series reviewed in Volumes 2 and 3. The "Standard Deviants" video review series for high school, which in spite of its MTV-like look actually utilizes a "basics" step-by-step approach, is reviewed in Chapter 41 of this volume.

WHO IT'S BEST FOR: If done right, a teaching video can hit everyone's buttons except the Action Man. The beauty of math is enough to enthrall the Puzzle Solver, while seeing it tidily organized step-by-step on screen appeals to the Progress Person. Be aware that both these types need to work out some problems on paper themselves to feel fully happy with the instruction; a videotape alone is not enough. If the video teacher is personable, the People Person will enjoy his company, while the Performer is naturally interested in the presentation's style. Videos are auditory *and* visual; and if you give the kinesthetic/tactile student the means of taking notes and stop the tape to "act out" new facts, you've got all the discovery channel bases covered.

Audio Drill Materials

To find educational audiocassettes for homeschoolers online, go to the Curriculum Hall as described above and click on "Audio."

Since now you're missing the picture, audio materials are good for topics you don't need to see demonstrated, and better for information you want the student to memorize and repeat. For the "basics," start with classics like the Alphabet Song, skip-count math drills, and so forth. Bible verses, the names of books of the Bible, and the catechism are great for audio drill. In fact, you can find audiocassettes and CDs for drilling facts in just about any school subject area. See Volume 2 for lots of examples.

WHO IT'S BEST FOR: Auditory learners. The type of auditory learner who needs to hear information can pick facts up easily this way, while the type who needs to hear himself say the information needs to "sing along" or "echo back" as well. Kinesthetic/tactile students can indulge their need for movement while learning. Visual learners should practice with at least some auditory materials, to strengthen important listening skills. As for thinking styles: Puzzle Solvers will not find a tape intriguing unless there's a mystery to be solved. Action People can't experiment much with a tape. Progress Persons may enjoy a logical organization of facts, while Performers enjoy mimicking the voices (simultaneously learning those facts!). A People Person may enjoy listening to a tape just because she likes the friendly voices.

Tutoring Software

Tutoring software may be text only. It may be mostly text plus some pictures and animations. Or it can basically be a teaching video plus advanced interactive drill and practice.

Everything I said about video teachers applies to even the text-only type of tutoring software. Many parents don't realize that kids react to the computer itself as a separate personality. Software that is text-only is like communicating with a teacher through email. Software that features video clips of a teacher is like videoconferencing with a teacher. This means that, contrary to what you might think, even People Persons can be found glued to a computer monitor from time to time.

Kids perceive even the dullest software to be more fun than all but the most exciting educational video. That's because you can hit a button and make things happen. In a kid's world, where almost all of his life is under adult control, the illusion of being in control of your computer is very compelling. (I say it's an illusion because the software programmers have limited your options to what they want you to do.)

While I still think phonics instruction belongs in Mama's lap, you can now purchase pretty good phonics tutoring software. Math tutoring, science tutoring, grammar lessons, history lessons, and much more are available on low-cost CD-ROMs.

WHO IT'S BEST FOR: Visual learners, Progress Persons. If the tutoring software makes the "patterns" of the subject clear, Puzzle Solvers will be interested.

Drill & Practice Software

This is basics at its most basic. Practice and drill those facts! If you don't feel like serving on permanent flashcard detail, grab a handful of drill and practice software. Instead of your kids groaning and moaning while you spend hours flipping cards, they will happily drill themselves on their phonics, math facts, science terminology, history dates, and lots more while you find something more fulfilling to do.

WHO IT'S BEST FOR: Visual learners (for visual drill), auditory learners (for spoken drills as in foreign-language software). Make sure the software type is geared to your child's thinking style. If the reward for completing a drill is to get another piece of the ongoing Hangman puzzle, for example, this will appeal most to a Puzzle Solver. If progress can be clearly seen (as in the "words per minute" and "words without errors" statistics in learn-to-type software), the Progress Person will be motivated.

Beyond the Basics

Yes, just about everyone agrees our children should learn the basics, and just about every homeschooled child will end up using some "basics" style curriculum, whether it be textbooks, worktexts, videos, audiocassettes or CDs, tutoring software, or drill-and-practice software.

These questions now remain:

- How far beyond the basics will he or she go?

- How many of the basics will the child be expected to discover through his or her own exploring, research, and experimentation?

The remaining methods in this section answer these questions in very different ways.

CHAPTER 18

Classical Education & Great Books

In this chapter you'll learn about classical education from some of its main proponents:

- **Fritz Hinrichs** is the founder of Escondido Tutorial Service and a pioneer of classical education via the Internet in the homeschool community. He is a graduate of St. John's College in Annapolis, MD, which is based on the classical model, and of Westminster Seminary, in Escondido, California.
- **Andrew Kern** is the Director of Classical Instruction at Foundations Academy, the founder of a research and consulting service for classical educators, and the co-author of *Classical Education: Towards the Revival of American Schooling.* He is a homeschooling father of five children.
- **Douglas Wilson** is a founder of Logos School in Moscow, Idaho, one of the few American day schools founded on classical learning principles. To promote these principles he has written *Recovering the Lost Tools of Learning* (Crossway Books, 1991), as well as texts on introductory logic and Latin grammar. A prolific author, with many other books in print, Douglas edits the monthly magazine *Credenda/Agenda* and is the father of three teenage children.

Fritz Hinrichs on Why Classical Education Is Undergoing a Revival

Most anyone familiar with history has come to the humbling realization that even our sharpest minds do not match the mental capabilities possessed by the shining lights of history. Many have found that the writings of our own nation's founding fathers show an eloquence and depth of thought that put us to shame. In the past, homeschoolers have desired to simply return to a wholesome "back to the basics" type of education—something like that had by Laura Ingalls Wilder. Today, many homeschoolers want to know how to raise an orator such as Patrick Henry or a man of the political insight and principle of George Washington. Increasingly, homeschoolers have been turning to classical Christian education for answers to these questions. Classical Christian education attempts to glean

Curriculum Based on the Principles of Classical Education

- Escondido Tutorial Service (online)
- Kolbe Academy (correspondence)
- Scholars Online Academy (online)

Curriculum with Some Classical Elements

- Calvert School (correspondence; combines classical principles and texts with modern educational theory and texts)
- Covenant Home Curriculum (correspondence; combines classical principles and texts with some modern texts)
- Seton Home Study School (correspondence; upper grades are somewhat classical in content)
- Our Lady of Victory (correspondence; upper grades are optionally classical in content)

"Great Books" Curriculum

- Great Books Academy (correspondence)

Christian Classical Education

Douglas Wilson

Pagan Classicalism

When people talk about classical education, they often are thinking of the classical world of ancient Greece and Rome, with special emphasis placed upon the "golden eras" of Athens under Pericles or Rome under Augustus.

While the art and literature produced in classical antiquity has great value and we ought to study it, Christians face one problem in using classical antiquity as the central point of reference in understanding classicism. The problem is, of course, the *paganism*. Many Christian parents rightly have a problem with an education that prominently features the gods and goddesses of the ancient world, pagan myths and heroes, etc. As a Christian classicist, I am not calling for a return to the paganism of the ancient world, or any attempt to revive a "kinder, gentler" paganism, as was partially seen in the Renaissance.

Mixed Classicalism

The second type of classical education is a compromise, so it is sometimes harder to see the problems it brings. Here we see the basic ideas, categories, and concepts of classical antiquity combined in assorted ways with Christian theology and terminology.

Obviously, given the nature of biblical truth, it is the integrity of Christian theology which suffers in the mix. An example of this would be Thomas Aquinas' attempt to combine the philosophy of Aristotle with the theology of Christianity, resulting in a theology called Thomism. In the field of education, a recent example of this would be the educational theory of Mortimer Adler, which is unabashedly Aristotelian. In his book *Reforming Education*, Dr. Adler makes the statement that the liberal arts are neither *pagan* or *Christian*, but rather *human*. This elevates the liberal arts into a religion of their own, midway between Christianity and paganism, and superior to both. Any consistent Christian educator must obviously reject Dr. Adler's statement, along with the worldview behind it.

Christian Classicalism

The third type of classical education—*Biblical* classical education—is what we are looking for. It attempts to provide a timeless introduction to knowledge, based not on the insights of great thinkers but on the Bible. Once the student's presuppositions have been formed and instructed by Bible study, he is then set free to consider the breadth and depth of human achievement—for example, what some call the "Great Books." The difference is that the student is trained to evaluate human insights by the yardstick of the Bible's teaching, not vice versa.

The classically trained Christian student doesn't have to hide from history. Without worshipping the past, he knows he can—and must—learn from it. In fact, without these studies in history, literature, rhetoric, and theology he will become a slave of the passing popular opinions of our day, incapable of leading others back to the timeless ways of God.

Modern Protestant educators, unhappily, have often tended to ignore the past. Many evangelicals mistakenly assume, for example, that to appreciate Latin you must be a Roman Catholic traditionalist. This indicates just how much of our Western heritage we have lost—and must recover. The Latin language is not the exclusive language of Catholics; it is the language of the West. John Calvin and Martin Luther wrote many works in Latin!

Because we have failed to educate our children properly, we have lost touch with our own Founding Fathers— the everyday Christians and church leaders of the past. While our culture has made much technological progress, in the liberal arts our culture is almost completely at sea. We have forgotten our heritage.

Our model for understanding culture—art, literature, history, etc.—will be the apostle Paul, who was the first biblical classicist. Thoroughly trained in classical languages, literature, and philosophy, he consistently refused to trim God's message to fit the classical pagan mold. Yet Paul was never a "fundamentalist know-nothing." We must remember that Paul demonstrated in his writings a thorough knowledge and use of classical culture. He knew classical poets (Acts 17:28), classical playwrights (Acts 26:14), the language (Acts 21:37), classical philosophy (1 Timothy 6:10), and so on. But as a consistent Christian, his intention in all of this was no secret—to bring every thought captive to the risen Christ.

What better time could we find for bringing our children to love and serve Christ than the time we spend teaching them? But because a large part of this work has been done before, it would be foolish to undertake the work "from scratch." Others have gone before us and already thought through how to accomplish these tasks. Is it not better to learn from almost 2,000 years of Christian civilizations—and learn to avoid copying the mistakes of the pagan civilizations—than to try to reinvent the wheel?

What's the Difference?

	"Modern"	Classical
Phonics	Emphasizes "creative" interaction with words—look/say & whole language.	Emphasizes a thorough mastery of the units of sound.
Reading	If literate, the student progresses to basal readers.	When literate, the student begins reading great books.
Maths	Emphasizes trying to get the student to understand the *concept*. Discourages rote learning of tables, rules, etc.	Emphasizes mastery of tables, rules, etc. as well as repetitive drills to make certain math processes *habitual*.
Bible	Bible? Are you crazy? Bible?	Emphasizes systematic Bible reading as soon as the students are literate.
Spelling	Concentrates on avoiding rules. The focus is to foster creativity and maintain the student's self-esteem.	Concentrates on being prescriptive, rule-guided autocratic, unforgiving, unyielding, rigid, puritanical, dictatorial, and harsh.
History	Debunks or ignores the achievements of western civilization. Uses history as a tool to support the ideological agenda currently in vogue.	Emphasizes the fact that history is under the providential hand of God, and that it therefore has a purpose. Holds that our heritage should be understood, and, unless at variance with Scripture, *appreciated*.
Rhetoric & Speech	As with many subjects, the "creativity" and self-expression, resulting in a stream of consciousness approach, as opposed to the more rigorous discipline of wordsmithing.	The point is to teach the student to recognize the structure of available means of persuasion, and avail himself of them.
Political Science	One of the largest liberal political organizations in the U.S. is the NEA. The students are the NEA auxiliary. Their grasp of politics is limited therefore to whatever the current "issues of the month" may be.	The emphasis is on the history of constitutionalism, and the application to current events.
Thinking Skills & Logic	Concentrates on getting the student to express an opinion, along with whatever reasons he may have for holding it. The key is self-expression.	Emphasizes the difference between truth and validity. Teaches the student to identify fallacies of form and distraction.
Languages	Modern foreign languages are not required for the non-native speaker. They are present, however, because a zeal for "multiculturalism" and "diversity" insists that non-English speakers shouldn't have to learn a foreign language either.	Foreign languages are taught to those who are not native speakers as a form of intellectual discipline, which has certain practical side-benefits.
Latin	Once fairly common in the government schools, Latin is now virtually extinct, as is viewed as a monstrous irrelevance.	Latin is seen as a foundation for precise thinking, English vocabulary study, appreciation of classical and English literature, study of the Romance languages, and, of course, *et cetera*.
Literature	The purpose is to bring books down to the level of the contemporary student—books that will not overwhelm a limited vocabulary, limited fluency, cultural isolation, and reluctance to read anything unfamiliar.	The object here is to bring the student to the level of great and classical literature, and to teach appreciation of challenging books from all ages.

Top Ten Tips for Classical Education

by Martin Detweiler, founder of Veritas Press

10 Don't believe everything is "classical" that says it is. A book or resource may be "classic," i.e., trusted by many people for a notable length of time, without being "classical"—part of the enduring tradition of centuries past.

9 Hard work is good.

8 Children are far more capable of hard work—and understanding—than we give them credit for today.

7 If you want your children to love learning, make sure they see your excitement when you learn something new. Emulate Archimedes in all but your choice of clothing.

6 A complete classical education won't happen in three hours a day.

5 Latin isn't really a dead language. And it didn't kill the ancient Romans, either.

4 Reading *Recovering the Lost Tools of Learning* is a must.

3 Books . . . good. Internet . . . good and bad. TV . . . bad.

2 When we talk about classical literature for your eighth grader, don't confuse the Boxcar Children and Nancy Drew with *The Epic of Gilgamesh* and Plato's *Republic*. Even Coke can be "Classic" without being classical.

1 Learning to distinguish between good and evil is only the first step. Learning to love the good is better. Learning to do the good is the whole point.

Digging Deeper

For more information on the use of the Trivium in a classical curriculum, Fritz invites you to peruse his Web page—**members.aol.com/ Fritztutor**. You might also be interested in obtaining a copy of Dorothy Sayer's "Lost Art of Learning" essay. This may be found in her book *Are Women Human?*, which can be ordered through your local bookstore.

Stages of the Trivium

A child begins a classical education by proceeding through the three stages of the trivium—*grammar*, *rhetoric*, and *dialectic*. Each of these stages is perfectly suited to a child's learning development. The *grammar* stage is appropriate for young children as it focuses on the memorization of facts. Young children are very quick at picking up facts, even though they are not yet capable of logically analyzing their significance. As children grow older, they gradually become aware of the logical relationship between facts and the potential for logical contradiction to arise. At this time, children can move into the *dialectical* period. During the dialectical period, children are taught logic in order to hone their developing natural abilities and equip them to analyze the information they have accumulated. After becoming proficient in logic a child moves into the *rhetoric* period and learns to present what he has learned in a manner that is not only logical, but also aesthetically pleasing and persuasive.
—*Fritz Hinrichs*

from the experience and wisdom found in the past in order to understand why are own contemporary attempts at education seem to fall so short.

Douglas Wilson on What Is Classical Education?

Classical learning is called "classical" because future leaders have been trained in its methods for centuries. In fact, some parts of the classical curriculum have been around for millennia.

Classical learning follows a particular pattern called the **Trivium**—which consists of grammar, dialectic, and rhetoric. The students learn the **grammar** of each subject (that subject's "particulars"). They then learn **dialectic**, or the relationships of these particulars to one another, and then go on to learn **rhetoric**. That is, they learn how to express what they have gained in an effective and coherent fashion. The purpose of following this pattern is not to teach the student everything there is to know, but rather to establish in the student a habit of mind which instinctively knows how to learn new material when the formal schooling process is only a faint memory. The student is not so much taught *what* to think, he is shown *how* to think.

As Dorothy Sayers, author of the "Lord Wimsy" mysteries and a friend of C.S. Lewis and J.R.R. Tolkien, points out in her famous essay, "The Lost Tools of Learning," the three stages of the Trivium match **the developmental stages of growing children** quite nicely. The very great value of this method is that it provides a rigorous education suited to basic human nature and tested over centuries, rather than one developed from the theories of educational faddists.

Another significant part of the value of classical instruction is that it teaches students the rigors of **logical analysis.** Our society abounds in buncombe; we desperately need to train people to recognize it, so that someone might take it away. In short, we need more epistemological garbage men. This requires training in logic and the apologetics of Christian worldview thinking. Classical education supplies this in a way not seen elsewhere.

Third, the student learns that **our culture and civilization is an outgrowth of the classical, medieval, and reformation world**. Modern students must learn that our culture was not purchased for them by their parents at the mall. As C.S. Lewis pointed out, by reading old books the student is protected against some of the sillier mistakes of modernity.

Fritz Hinrichs On How Classical Education Is Different

Classical education differs from most educational philosophies in that it attempts to step back from the parade of educational theories that seem to keep us in a state of continual bewilderment and asks,

- "What was education like in the past?"
- "What books were used?"
- "What goals were thought important?"

Dorothy Sayers, in her well-known essay "The Lost Tools of Learning," attempted to answer these questions, and in so doing gave us some very sage advice for education in our own day. She began by investigating the medieval model of education and found that it was composed of two parts: the first was called the Trivium and the second, the Quadrivium.

The Trivium contained three areas: Grammar, Dialectic, and Rhetoric. Each of these three areas were specifically suited to one of the stages in a child's mental development.

The Grammar Period. During his early years, a child studies the Grammar portion of the Trivium. The Grammar period (ages 9–11) includes learning a language—preferably an ancient language, such as Latin or Greek—that will require the child to spend a great deal of time learning and memorizing its grammatical structure.

During their younger years, children possess a great natural ability to memorize large amounts of material, even though they may not understand its significance. This is the time to fill them full of facts, such as the multiplication table, geography, dates, events, plant and animal classifications: anything that lends itself to easy repetition and assimilation by the mind.

The Dialectic Period. During the second period, the Dialectic period (ages 12–14), the child begins to understand that which he has learned and begins to use his reason to ask questions based on the information that he has gathered in the grammar stage.

The Rhetoric Period. The third period Sayers mentions is that of Rhetoric (ages 14–16). During this period the child moves from merely grasping the logical sequence of arguments to learning how to present them in an persuasive, aesthetically pleasing form.

Fritz Hinrichs on Learning to Learn

In modern education, we have put the proverbial cart before the horse by expecting students to master a great number of subjects before they have mastered the tools of learning. Even though the study of language and logic may seem dull in themselves, they are the tools that one needs to develop to be able to approach the task of mastering any particular subject whether it be Scottish political history or carburetor maintenance. Sayers ends her essay with this line: "The sole true end of education is simply this; to teach men how to learn for themselves; and whatever instruction fails to do this is effort spent in vain."

"Learning to learn for oneself" certainly well summarizes the pedagogical goal of classical education. However, once you can learn on your own, where do you go from there?

Fritz Hinrichs on Great Books of the Western World

Another educational truism is helpful: "Education is merely selling someone on books." To this end we must ask, "Which books are worthy teachers?" The answer to this question usually lies in what we are attempting to learn. If we merely ask in general "Which are the truly great books?" we find there is actually a fairly broad agreement on the answer to this question. Throughout history, certain books have generally come to be viewed as central to the development of Western culture and have had an unusually large impact due to the profundity and eloquence with which they have expressed their ideas. These books form the core of the Western intellectual tradition. The ideas contained in them have formed the saga that we know as Western History.

Anyone who has grown up in the West—by which I mean Greece, Rome, and Israel, and the cultures descended from them, which include America, the British Commonwealth nations, and Western Europe—and desires to understand the cultural milieu in which they have been raised, should read these books.

Andrew Kern on the Modern Classical Movement

The war for the soul of America, contested in the realm of educational theory, was fought fiercely around the time of World War I. The progres-

For more information on classical education:

- The Association of Christian and Classical Schools. 100 schools and some homeschool groups are associated with ACCS. *www.accsedu.org*.
- The Canon Press catalog (1-800-488-2034) carries most of the resources below, plus classical education resources such as elementary Latin and formal logic courses.
- *The Abolition of Man*, C.S. Lewis (New York: Macmillan, 1947). A classically-trained mind examines modern education. The book is readily available in Christian bookstores.
- *Classical Education and the Home School*, Douglas Jones & Douglas Wilson. This short booklet outlines the basic features of a classical education, and shows what parents should do if they want to provide this kind of education for their children at home. From Canon Press,
- *On Christian Doctrine* (Book IV), Augustine. This can best be found in volume 18 of the "Great Books" series. A good library should have it.
- *On Secular Education*, R.L. Dabney. A critique of the government school system, which was in its infancy when Dabney wrote. From Canon Press.
- *Recovering the Lost Tools of Learning* by Douglas Wilson. This book contains as an appendix Dorothy Sayers' seminal essay, "The Lost Tools of Learning." From Canon Press.
- *Repairing the Ruins*, a collection of 14 tapes from the first conference of the Association of Classical and Christian Schools. $50. From Canon Press.
- The Veritas Press catalog, 1250 Belle Meade Dr., Lancaster, PA 17601. (800) 922-5082. Inquiries: (717) 397-5082. Fax: (717) 397-6544. Email: Veritasprs@aol.com. Web: members.aol.com/Veritasprs.

What About Mythology?

by Rob & Cyndy Shearer

- Should Christians teach their children about Zeus?
- Should they know who Wodin, Loki, and Thor are?
- Would our children benefit by knowing anything about Heqet, the Egyptian goddess of birth? (Hint: She was usually depicted with the head of a frog.)

We are strong proponents of teaching more than just American history to our children. In fact, we advocate beginning with the Old Testament (as history) and teaching our children about western civilization in sequence, moving through ancient Egypt, ancient Greece, ancient Rome, the Middle Ages, the Renaissance, the Reformation, Explorers, etc. so that our children understand both the context and logical development of our culture.

There are a number of sound reasons for doing this. But attempting it does confront one with a different set of problems. If you begin with the cultures of Egypt, Greece, and Rome, you will immediately have to make some decisions about how you will (or won't) cover the topics of evolution and mythology with your students.

The "mythology" issue is one we have thought a lot about. Christian parents have legitimate concerns about teaching mythology. We don't want to teach falsehoods to our children, or lead them to confuse falsehoods with the truth; and we don't want to encourage any fascination with or inappropriate attention to the occult.

Having said that, we think that the study of mythology (Greek, Roman, Egyptian, and Norse) is still appropriate and profitable for our children when set in the proper Christian context for three reasons:

- It inoculates them against false religion.
- It gives them a deeper understanding of Greek and Roman culture (and Egyptian and European).
- And it builds a foundation for them to understand the great literature of western civilization.

What the Bible Says About the History of Religion

The key phrase in the paragraph above is "the proper Christian context." Whenever we approach the topic of mythology, we introduce it by reviewing with our children what God has to say about the history of religion.

Modern man spins a tale about primitive man beginning by worshipping anything and everything; trees, rocks, thunder, streams, grasshoppers, etc. Then (the wisdom/foolishness of the moderns speculates), man "progressed" to worshipping only a few specific deities. Then, as he began to walk completely upright, he moved from many gods to monotheism, the worship of only one god. The last step in this sequence you won't find spelled

What the Puritans Thought About Greek & Roman Myths

Tubal-cain, whom (as the learned conceive, and the agreement of the name and function makes probable) the heathens worshipped by the name of Vulcan, the god of smiths; and his sister Naamah, by the name of Venus. He first taught men how to make arms, and other instruments of iron. Naamah; so called from her beauty, which her name signifies.—Matthew Poole, Commentary on the Holy Bible, *commenting on Genesis 4:11*

Jabal was their Pan and Jubal their Apollo. Tubal Cain was a famous smith, who greatly improved the art of working in brass and iron, for the service both of war and husbandry. He was their Vulcan.—Matthew Henry's Commentary, *commenting on Genesis 4:11*

The Puritans believed the Greek myths were "tall tales," based on ancestor worship and a few notable exploits of living men, which were later magnified into tales of godlike prowess, with a few nature myths thrown in for good measure.

Whereas other cultures based their myths upon literal "doctrines of demons"—stories relayed to them by unclean supernatural messengers (as per the Aztecs and Babylonians)—the Greeks, and after them the Romans, seemed to have been content with "gods" who were just larger-than-life-sized human heroes.

By the time of Jesus many Greeks had come to look upon their myths the same way we look at our own American larger-than-life-sized heroes, Paul Bunyan and Pecos Bill. The myths were good stories that might include some character lessons, but should not be taken seriously. That's how the Puritans considered them, and how we should consider them today.—*Mary Pride*

out explicitly, but it is the logical completion of the "evolution of religion" and that is the step from monotheism to atheism, the worship of no god.

This progression, from many to few to one to none, is not found in Scripture anywhere. Beware of authors who present this as the way man's religions developed!

What the Bible says about the "development" of religion is quite different:

Since the creation of the world His invisible attributes, His eternal power and divine nature have been clearly seen, being understood through what has been made, so they are without excuse. For even though they knew God, they did not honor Him as God or give thanks; but they became futile in their speculations and their foolish heart was darkened. Professing to be wise, they became fools

Myths to Avoid

"LIVE" MYTHS believed today by substantial numbers of people. These should be studied under the category of "world religions," as a bare outline of those beliefs, *without* getting heavily into the actual stories and rituals behind the beliefs. Thus, we would not recommend making a detailed study of Hindu or Shinto myths. Native American myths might now fall in this category, as the public schools are making a mighty effort to get children to take them seriously, even requiring them in some cases to re-enact tribal religious rituals.

"SCANDALOUS" MYTHS. Some people's myths are graphically violent, anti-family, and sex-laden. Greek and Roman myths do *not* fall into this category, because the *details* of the sex and violence are unimportant to the stories. In fact, it's still easy to find editions of those myths that leave them out altogether. What counts is that Oedipus inadvertently married his mother, not how they conducted themselves as husband and wife. In contrast, sexual details are an integral part of Hindu mythology and of many African, South American, and South Seas tribal myths.

"FORBIDDEN" MYTHS. God specifically forbade the Jews to inquire too deeply into the religious practices of the Canaanites (Deuteronomy 18:9). The myths of Baal, Ashtoreth, Molech, and other Canaanite gods should therefore *not* be studied. It also seems to me that little is gained by studying Egyptian myths. Although it is quite true that knowing the titles of the Egyptian pantheon is helpful in understanding the plagues of Egypt, the stories themselves are depressing. They focus on death and actually *condone* incest and other gross sins.

In Greek and Roman myths, ill behavior and *hubris* (pride) lead to disaster. When Tantalus serves his guests with the flesh of their own children, he is condemned to eternal hunger and thirst. If Pandora had only kept her curiosity under control, the human race would have been spared countless ills. Because Zeus was unfaithful to his wife Hera with Hercules' mother, Hera brought many evils upon Hercules and his family. And so on. Thus, although the Greek gods and the humans in whom they interest themselves may not always act morally, moral results do follow their actions. This contrasts sharply with the myths of most other cultures, which often legitimize the grossest behavior.—*Mary Pride*

and exchanged the glory of the incorruptible God for an image in the form of corruptible man and of birds and four-footed animals and crawling creatures. (Romans 1:20–23)

The picture here is of the "devolution" of religion. The Bible says that men fall into false religion and the worship of idols when they reject the truth about God, refuse to honor him, exchange the truth for a lie and suppress the truth in unrighteousness. There's nothing here about "progressing" towards God by way of mythology.

Our recommendation then is **not to teach mythology until you have taught Genesis.** And begin your study of mythology by reviewing with your children what God says about man's religion in the book of Romans. Once set in proper context, there are valuable lessons to be learned while reading the Greek myths. Without setting it in context, you risk confusion and error. So by all means, include mythology in your history lesson plans about Egypt, Greece, and Rome but set it in context.

Moses, Paul, and Mythology

One last note about including mythology in your course of study: Moses clearly knew Egyptian religious stories and Paul clearly knew about Greek and Roman religion. This can be seen in the way each of them deals with the false religions of the culture they are dealing with. Paul even quotes from Greek poetry (a poem which discusses the pantheon of Greek mythological gods). To understand the conflict between Moses and Pharaoh, it is tremendously helpful if you understand the relationship between the plagues and the Egyptian pantheon. It turns out that each of the plagues is God's challenge to a specific Egyptian deity. If you don't know who the Egyptian deities are, you can't really understand what God is saying.

This does not mean that we need to dwell on detailed descriptions of immoral practices associated with the false religions. We use common sense . . . and rely for the most part on texts published before 1965. But a study of the themes and major characters of Egyptian, Greek, Roman, and Norse mythologies will have much to teach us and our children.

Three Reasons for Studying Mythology

To return to our three reasons for including mythology as a part of history:

(1) The best protection we can give our children from false religion is an early inoculation/exposure to it under controlled circumstances. Set in context as described above, we have an opportunity to discuss with our children the contrast between true and false religion. We can highlight the foolishness of the false gods. They will always remember the comparisons and will be much less likely to be taken in by "new age" repackaging when they are older.

(2) To understand the Greeks, Romans, Egyptians, or North Europeans, you need to understand what they believed about their gods. By including a study of the myths when you read biographies or study these cultures you can ask key questions about how the false religion affected the culture. You can ask, "If the Greeks believed the gods behaved this way, how do you think they would behave themselves?" With Greek religion you can discuss the reasons for Socrates' execution (one of the charges against him was that he taught the youth of Athens that there could be only one god and that the myths had many contradictions and couldn't be true). You can talk about why Paul went to Mars Hill and preached about the unknown god. You can talk about the background to the controversy in 1 Corinthians over eating meat that had been sacrificed to idols. These issues are much easier to understand if you have some knowledge of Greek religion.

With Roman culture as well, there are close links between morals, behavior, and religion. The Romans adopted the Greek gods, and then went further and began to deify the emperors. Christians who refused to sacrifice to the emperor found their lives in danger. Note well, it was not illegal to worship Jesus; it was illegal to worship only Jesus! The worship of the emperor fit Roman "statism" very neatly and meshed with the respect all Romans were taught towards "the fathers" (Latin *patria*, whence we get our English word *patriotism*). We cannot fully appreciate the issues facing early Christians unless we are familiar with Roman religion.

(3) The myths are an integral part of our literary heritage. One cannot fully appreciate any great writer (Shakespeare to name one) unless one is familiar with the stories from the myths. Knowing them does not mean we must accept them as true. But we should know them in order to intelligently converse with and present the Gospel to our culture. The great works of literature in the western tradition all use symbols and images drawn from the myths of the Greeks, Romans, and Scandinavians. We cannot appreciate the nuances or the ideas themselves unless we recognize the references.

An acquaintance with the myths of the Greeks, Romans, and Norsemen has seldom proven a snare to adult Christians or their children. Quite the opposite seems to be true. For scholars like C.S. Lewis and J.R.R. Tolkien the myths and legends (what Lewis called "northernness") aroused in them an appreciation for beauty and drama and a longing for "joy" that Lewis said was instrumental in his final conversion to Christianity.

Our conclusion then? Do not teach mythology as a separate subject or in a way that encourages or entices. But do teach mythology as a key part of the history and culture of the Egyptians, Greeks, Romans, and Europeans. And do teach it in the context of what God himself teaches about man and his turning aside to false religions. In this way you will make your children better able to serve God, to communicate to the pagan culture around us, and to stand as godly men and women in their own generation.

"Great Books" or Classical Education?

A classical education is more than reading great books, and a Great Books education is not exactly like other classical education programs. The "Great Books" movement promotes, not just a certain group of classics, but a Socratic method of teaching in which the professor leads the student to think out the answers for himself. For more information, see the Great Books Academy review. For a suggested list of Great Books, see that appendix in Volume 3.

Classical Homeschooling

Once upon a time, thousands of years ago, classical education happened at home. In fact, Cicero declared that state involvement in education was contrary to the Roman character. When the Renaissance brought about the renewal of ancient learning, children were frequently taught classically at home. Since then, many of the most important minds of western culture, such as Pascal, John Stuart Mill, and Abraham Lincoln, have been homeschooled.   —Andrew Kern

sives, led by John Dewey, and his school, believed that education was a forum for experience and training. The classicists believed that the goal was wisdom and virtue. The progressives won all the major battles, and, frankly, most Christians of the time, being practical Americans trained in favoring "a good job" over "fruit for eternity," were comfortable with the results.

A movement back to classical education began almost immediately. Its most important leader has been Mortimer Adler, who has written a number of brilliant books on education and founded a movement called The Paideia Program. In addition he edited and promoted the 52-volume Great Books of the Western World.

Dorothy Sayers fired a volley from England with her seminal article "The Lost Tools of Learning," in which she described the trivium as the key to an educational revival. Douglas Wilson's *Recovering the Lost Tools of Learning* propelled the ideas of Dorothy Sayers to the vanguard of popular reform theory.

As the classical ideas of Adler, Sayers, Wilson, et al., were filtering down from the theorists, homeschooling formed into a powerful movement. The two ideas joined hands in the pages of *The Teaching Home* magazine, which published the "Lost Tools" article by Dorothy Sayers some ten years ago. It sparked a tremendous interest among homeschoolers, but many felt frustrated because detailed curricula and methodology were not yet developed.

Nonetheless, in characteristic homeschooling fashion, a number of families stepped forward to pioneer the old path. The Bluedorns created Trivium Pursuit. In the early 90's Canon Press began making its materials available. Laura Behrquist published an excellent manual (*Designing Your Own Classical Curriculum*, Ignatius Press) specially written for the Catholic homeschooler, but eminently useful for any interested in classical education. Douglas Wilson, Doug Jones, and Wes Callihan wrote a handbook on the classical Christian homeschool (*Classical Education and the Home School*, from Canon Press). And homeschooling has always been well-represented at the Association of Classical and Christian Schools (ACCS) conferences.

Then classical homeschooling hit the Internet. Linda Robinson and others began Scholars Online Academy. Fritz Hinrichs, a graduate of St. John's College (another of Adler's great achievements) joined them with his Escondido Tutorial Service. Recently, David and Jennifer Hoos have published a weekly Internet newsletter for classical schoolers, called *CCS Digest*. Most of the readers are homeschoolers.

Meanwhile, Foundations Academy pioneered the classical school/home-school co-op. It makes seminars available to homeschooling high schoolers on such subjects as logic, Latin, classical history and literature, and composition. Finally, just this year, Veritas Press developed a full-fledged classical curriculum catalogue, a giant step further, presenting in its pages not only the books needed but an implicit scope and sequence as well.

Andrew Kern on Classical Education for All

Many homeschoolers are classical without knowing it because of their educational goals. In fact, most of the people who buy into the classical vision don't do so because it is new and exciting, but because it ties together and explains so many of the things they have long desired: virtue and wisdom, skill using words and numbers, and a heart to value and sustain their heritage (Christian, western, American, and family).

The classical curriculum gives a form to those desires. It does not exclude apprenticeship or training. It simply recognizes that everybody needs wisdom and virtue, skill at using words and numbers, and respect for their heritage while not everyone needs to be able to use a computer or fix a tractor. Classical education puts everything in its place and thus enables everything to fulfill its purpose.

Books on Classical Education

Judging by the size of the attendance at this past June's Association of Classical and Christian Schools convention (over 800!), classical education is here to stay. Like any educational movement, the philosophies continue to be refined and articulated by those from within. **Classical Education: Towards the Revival of American Schooling** is here to answer the question, "Just what *is* classical ed?" Co-authors Andrew Kern and Gene Edward Veith bring years of experience to this 99-page work, which serves as a much needed summary and concise explanation of where we currently stand in relation to classical ed.

Beginning with a brief explanation of the problems with modern and post-modern education, the book proceeds not only to define classical education, but to show how it looks in different forms.

For example: Christian Classical schools (Logos School in Moscow, Idaho), Democratic Classical schools (Mortimer Adler's Paideia Group), Moral Classical Schools (Renaissance Humanism), and finally classical education in the inner city (Marva Collins and Westside Prep) are all explained.

Taking things one step further, this book addresses the rise and fall of liberal-arts colleges as the authors explore the current state of higher education. Rounding out this brief volume is a list of current resources to further your own study into this subject. "We do well to avoid the fatal and arrogant conceit of jettisoning our heritage" say the authors, but they combine this with a reminder: "Heritage is not solely a gift of wisdom and virtue. It also contains cautions and forewarnings. Classical education reminds us of the bigger picture." And this book frames that picture quite nicely. *Renee Mathis*

If you think classics are stodgy, dusty tomes . . . think again. By the time you finish reading **Classics in the Classroom**, you will be motivated to reach for these treasures and share them with your children.

Michael Clay Thompson, the author, obviously enjoys what he's doing and imparts this excitement to you. He explains how to identify a classic, the "why's" of reading them, and practical ideas for encouraging your student to enjoy as well.

Classics in the Classroom
by Michael Clay Thompson
Royal Fireworks Press

NEW!
The Well-Trained Mind
Parents. $35 plus shipping.
W. W. Norton & Company, Inc., 800 Keystone Industrial Park, Scranton, PA 18512. (800) 223-2584. Fax: (800) 458-6515.

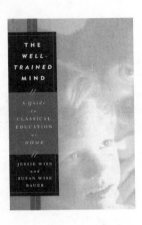

The first three chapters are the meat. The last is an amazingly long list of 1,300 classics that can be used as a reference point for your own lists.

Even though this was written for classrooms, the ideas can be adapted easily. There are some really wonderful ideas here, although I found myself disagreeing with some of his assertions. For example, he recommends the reading of "rascally" (i.e. censored) books and the suspension of disbelief when reading, so as to allow oneself to be enfolded into the story. Be aware the list of classics runs the gamut from *Malcolm X, The Oresteia,* and the *Koran* to *The Deerslayer, The Divine Comedy,* and the Bible. All the books are coded and tell you if the book is a Newbery winner, on the Great Books list, or has, in one way or other, received recognition. *Marla Perry*

It has been said that the real test of the modern homeschooling movement will come as the children of those pioneering families in the 1970's and 1980's have children of their own. Will those children continue to build on that foundation as they educate their own little ones?

Fortunately for all of us, in the case of classical educators Jessie Wise and Susan Wise Bauer, the answer is a resounding, "Yes!" A former public school teacher, Jessie Wise began crafting an educational plan for her own three children in the '70's. Laying aside the fluffy, mind-numbing contemporary educational philosophy in which she'd been steeped, she reached back for a set of tools proven over time to build solid, thinking adults. These tools, known as the trivium, have been popularized in the homeschool world by Dorothy Sayers' seminal essay on the subject, and by Douglas Wilson's 1991 book entitled *Recovering the Lost Tools of Learning.* Jessie Wise, nearly two decades earlier, did just what Wilson's book title suggests. The result was that her daughter Susan Wise Bauer now teaches literature at the College of William and Mary and yes, homeschools her own four children.

These two women have created the definitive guide to classical home education in **The Well-Trained Mind**. This 764-page hardcover book is a careful, detailed description of how to use the tools of the trivium (grammar, logic, and rhetoric) to prepare your child to think, read, and reason. The book not only tells you why (though it does that eloquently) but tells you how . . . specifically. The authors take each developmental stage and explain it, and offer a philosophical base for teaching each subject area within that stage, complete with detailed curriculum suggestions. This section of the book weighs in at over 500 pages alone. The remainder of the book is devoted to the nuts and bolts of home education, including scheduling, socialization, homeschooling with babies and toddlers, how to start home educating "mid-stream," and a terrific section on the college application process.

The Well-Trained Mind is a tremendous resource, and is a valuable read not only for those of you interested in using the classical model for your homeschool, but for most everyone who cares about learning well. The only weakness in this text is the very fleeting mention of faith. In discussions of teaching ethics or theology, the authors steer you back to your own religious traditions, and move off the subject quickly. Without anchoring education to transcendent Truth, a classical model of education will create a great big frontal lobe detached from a heart.

Even with that one weakness, this book is of incredible value, and comes highly recommended. *Michelle Van Loon*

CHAPTER 19

The Principle Approach

"What is The Principle Approach?" you ask. It is designed to make children "active producers rather than passive consumers of the educational process." It is also designed to steep them in the worldview of America's Founding Fathers (and Mothers), with an eye to raising a generation who will once again demand—and lead—a constitutional government, rather than our present "government" of whatever the media and the judges say is the law, is the law.

How is this done? Through:

- **Reading copiously in American source documents** (upper grades), **biographies of famous patriots** (lower grades), **and classic pro-liberty fiction** (all grades)
- **Looking up word definitions** in Noah Webster's 1828 dictionary, *The American Dictionary of the English Language*)
- **Learning the "principles" that make up the Principle Approach**, including principles for how each and every school subject should be taught and learned
- **Learning to use the "4 R's,"** otherwise known as the Notebook Method

Curriculum Based on the Principle Approach

- Judah Bible Curriculum
- The Noah Plan.

For reviews of these programs, see Chapter 38

The Notebook Method

The Principle Approach is based on "4 R's": *research, reasoning, relating,* and *recording*. **Research** means getting back to the real facts of "America's Christian history" and looking up word meanings in the 1828 Noah Webster dictionary. **Reasoning** means figuring out the basic biblical principles involved in what you just researched. **Relating** means using various ways to "echo back" the biblical principles in your studies and life. **Recording** means *writing* or *drawing* in a notebook: making a memorable record of what you have learned, in your own words or illustrations.

As you can imagine, this approach involves a *lot* of writing. "Wiggle worm" types actively resist all writing assignments. So if you just adore what this approach teaches, and your child is a Performer or Action Man personality, consider learning the material yourself and then adapting it to your child with activities that are more "hand on" and less "pencil on."

The Seven Principles

The Principle Approach is also based on seven principles:

1. **God's Principle of Individuality** Everyone is unique and special. This does not seem earth-shaking—in fact, it sounds kind of like the first principle of public education, "you are so special and deserve self-esteem." The difference here is that they are for individuality *as opposed to* socialist collectivism.

2. **The Christian Principle of Self-Government** In The Noah Plan's own words, "In order to have true liberty, man must be governed internally by the Spirit of God rather than by external forces."

3. **America's Heritage of Christian Character** "The model of American Christian character is the Pilgrim character, which demonstrates these qualities: *faith and steadfastness, brotherly love, Christian care, diligence and industry,* and *liberty of conscience.*"

4. **"Conscience is the Most Sacred of All Property" (James Madison)** This principle teaches the value of both property and conscience

5. **The Christian Form of Our Government** Teaches that separation of powers, checks and balances, and reservation of most power to the individual (as opposed to any level of government) are derived from the Bible.

6. **How the Seed of Local Self-Government is Planted** This principle teaches the necessity of salvation, "education in God's Law and Love," and the "Chain of Christianity," which traces the influence of the Bible from Israel to Europe to America.

7. **The Christian Principle of American Political Union** Standing together with others of like mind to form a "more perfect union"—starting with individuality and self-government you end up with a self-governed society of people who can work together well.

How it Works: Start with Words & Ideas

According to the Principle Approach, each school subject is approached in the same way.

First, the student looks up the name of the subject—e.g., History—in Noah Webster's 1828 dictionary, and copies down its definition.

Second, he looks up and records biblical passages related to the word and its definition. Sometimes these come right out of the *1828 Dictionary.* Sometimes the curriculum provides them. And sometimes the student is encouraged to look them up for himself in *Strong's Exhaustive Concordance,* a h-u-g-e book that lists every word in the Bible, its original

Principle Approach Principle	Biblical Principle	Opposing Principle
God's Principle of Individuality	Christian Individuality	Collectivism
The Christian Principle of Self-Government	Christian Self-Government	Anarchy (External Force)
America's Heritage of Christian Character	Christian Character	Degradation
Conscience is the Most Sacred of All Property	Biblical Stewardship	Communism
Our Christian Form of Government	God's Sovereignty	Autocracy
How the Seed of Local Self- Government is Planted	Sowing & Reaping	Centralization
The Christian Principle of American Political Union	Covenant	Social Engineering

Greek or Hebrew root and root meaning, and all the passages in which it occurs.

Third, he is given the basic vocabulary for the subject—its most important terms or "key words"—and asked to look them up in Noah Webster's 1828 dictionary. Key words associated with the subject Civics (also called American Government in many schools) may be *freedom, slavery, ruler, citizen, state, king, noble, law,* and *justice,* for example. Again, he copies down definitions and biblical passages related to these key words. This is intended to help him understand the "properties" of the subject.

All this is merely preliminary to the *real* point of the student's studies: determining how the "Seven Principles" govern each discipline. Then, the actual study of the discipline begins, ideally run along the lines of the principles, and with continual efforts to discern the cause/effect relationship between any application of or disobedience to biblical laws on the part of current or historical figures or theories. **The student also learns the "Christian history" of the subject:** its discoverers and chroniclers (even if they weren't Christians), how the subject has been used throughout history, and its place in the "Chain of Christianity." The methods used are research and outlining the major people and events.

Every subject, even math, has a history. *Someone* had to invent the Pythagorean Theorem, and I bet you know what his name was! The net effect is to learn the history of ideas, and to see how the ups and downs in human history relate to those ideas and their foundations. The student learns that, in the famous words of Richard Weaver, "Ideas have consequences."

Follow with Facts

When it comes to how to teach ideas and theories, Principle Approach advocates pretty much agree. But what about the *facts* of a subjects—e.g., addition and subtraction facts, states and capitals, etc.? Here, the consensus is that whatever was good enough for the Founding Fathers was good enough for us, with some slight modifications reflecting the fact that this *is* the 21st century.

Early American children learned phonics from a "horn book"—a thin piece of transparent animal horn with a one-page alphabet primer based on Bible characters. Example for the letter "A": "In Adam's fall we sinned all." Principle Approach students use more modern phonics materials, back-to-basics type math drill, diagramming, and traditional (but not Early American) penmanship.

So what you have here is an extremely defined, step-by-step, highly organized approach to learning, with a strongly American Christian worldview built in. Not surprisingly, history and government are emphasized as early as possible, from a this-is-how-the-world-*ought*-to-work perspective.

The chart above was created for *Practical Homeschooling* magazine by Principle Approach advocate and speaker Lori Harris. Her company, Landmark Distributors, can be reached at PO Box 849, Fillmore, CA 93016, email: landmark@jps.net.

Who Invented the Principle Approach?

It started with Verna M. Hall's study of U.S. history. In 1947 she founded a Constitutional study group. The group's studies revealed clearly that America had taken a 180-degree turn from its original Constitutional principles. But this study alone did not make it clear *why* this had happened or what could be done about it.

Provoked to deeper study, Miss Hall began unearthing original source documents that shed light on just where America came from.

During the 1960s, the Foundation for American Christian Education (FACE) began putting out large reference books containing the fruits of Miss Hall's research. The bottom line of her findings, which mostly consist of copious quotes from source documents written during the early years of the colonies and the republic: the United States of America was instituted as a Christian nation based on Christian character.

Rosalie J. Slater, a teacher who joined Miss Hall's study group, decided to dig deeper and try to find the common threads that tied America's Christian history together. It was Miss Slater who coined the phrase "The Principle Approach" and who rediscovered the methods used to educate America's Founding Fathers and the informed citizens who supported them. The "4R's" and the "Seven Principles" were first articulated in her book, *Teaching and Learning America's Christian History: The Principle Approach.* Since then, FACE has produced an entire K–12 curriculum, the Noah Plan, based on this method.

FACE, however, was not the only group that helped to implement and popularize the Principle Approach. As their own 1997 catalog says, "Today a number of ministries continue the work throughout the nation."

FACE is currently seeking to trademark the phrase "The Principle Approach." If they succeed, it will be harder for other materials based on this method to be recognized as such. Knowing the distinguishing characteristics of this method, as outlined in this chapter, will help you spot future materials in this vein.

What Is the "Chain of Christianity"?

FACE is currently attempting to trademark the phrase "Chain of Christianity," which could result in limiting its use to within their own curriculum and materials.

The "Chain of Christianity" is Verna Hall and Rosalie Slater's term for the spread of biblical civilization. In their view, it began in Palestine, was spread throughout the Roman Empire, and flowered in Britain, where a serious attempt at biblical law and government was launched. It then spread to America, which began as an entire political and legal system largely based on biblical principles. Presumably, the torch could be passed from America to another nation, but at present Principle Approach scholars prefer to concentrate on trying to revive biblical government, law, and lifestyles here.

Supplement with People Skills

A study of the Seven Principles, combined with an intense study of American history and its founding documents, will leave most of us with a burning desire to change the world around us. A lot. That burning desire, and the knowledge (if not the people skills) to back it up, are exactly what the Principle Approach offers.

But if you really want to change the world, it's not enough to be right, or smart, or informed. People have to want to follow you.

It's true that most other methods, with the notable exceptions of Charlotte Mason and character-trait-based unit studies, don't teach students

UPDATED!
FACE "America's Christian History" books

Parents. Christian History of the American Revolution, $42. Christian History of the Constitution, Volumes I and II, $40 each. Teaching & Learning America's Christian History, $35. American Dictionary of the English Language, $65. Rudiments of America's Christian History & Government, $15.
Foundation for American Christian Education (FACE), PO Box 9588, Chesapeake, VA 23321. Orders: (800) 352-FACE. Inquiries: (757) 488-6601. Fax: (757) 488-5593. E-mail: noahplan@pilot.infi.net. Web: www.face.net.

FACE is reviving the "Principle Approach" to government, an approach based on biblical law, on which they say the U.S.A. was founded. Their material traces America's roots through source documents. Political freedom begins with self-government, FACE says, and self-government begins in the home.

A complete curriculum based on the Principle Approach—the Noah Plan—is now available. See review in Chapter 38. However, you can also purchase individual books separately. Many of you who never plan to use the Principle Approach for your basic curriculum will nonetheless be interested in FACE's offerings on the subject of government and American history.

Before we proceed any farther, let me make it clear that these are not workbooks for young children. The theory is that you are going to work through this information yourself and then present it according to a set of complicated teaching suggestions that require you continually to flip back and forth between books.

The Christian History of the Constitution, Volume 1, formerly entitled "Christian Self-Government" (this is now the subtitle) documents that America is a Christian nation (that is, it was dedicated to Christ once upon a time) with a Christian Constitution (that is, one based on Christian principles). The "Chain of Christianity" is traced westward to America, as the gospel spread from Israel to the Roman Empire and thence to the uncouth white tribespeople who, once Christianized, spread it over the world. A large book, consisting almost entirely of quotes from source documents. Volume 2, previously titled "Christian Self-Government with Union" (again, this is now the subtitle) is more history from source documents, emphasizing the colonist's voluntary union that led to self-government.

Teaching and Learning America's Christian History is the original how-to manual of the Principle Approach. Each principle is spelled out, precept on precept, line on line.

Rudiments of America's Christian History and Government is a workbook for students filled with source quotes from distinguished American Christian leaders of the past and questions designed to develop both Christian thinking and an awareness of our Christian heritage. For teens and adults.

The Christian History of the American Revolution, previously titled "Consider and Ponder" (this is now the subtitle) covers the Constitutional Debate period of 1765–1775, during which Americans wrestled with the question of what an ideal government should look like. *Mary Pride*

how to be winsome. And only Classical Education includes training in the art of persuasiveness in its basic mission. But these other methods are not necessarily geared to producing graduates who are reformers, like the Principle Approach does. From what I have seen, it devotes little attention to helping students become persuasive and winsome. This is an area you should plan on "shoring up" with additional instruction and resources.

Final Thoughts

One last thing to remember about the Principle Approach: it is highly prescriptive. You'll find lots of "shoulds" peppering the pages of Principle Approach materials and a disinclination to let children skip any of the many steps or assignments, which they believe build character.

The Principle Approach excels in teaching kids to be systematic, methodical, logical thinkers and hard workers at desk work. It excels in preparing them to know a host of facts and skills. Visual learners, Puzzle Solvers, and especially Progress People may be drawn to this highly reading-and-writing, reasoning-and-logic based method.

CHAPTER 20

The Robinson Method

The "Robinson Method" is so called because it has been popularized among homeschoolers by Dr. Arthur Robinson, who has also produced a curriculum based on this method.

This method is designed to make children independent learners ASAP. It can be used with the curriculum designed for it—see the Robinson Curriculum review in chapter 38—or with any set of materials well suited to self study and individual reading.

What makes the Robinson Method unique is that it seeks to eliminate the teacher's role as soon as possible. This makes it perfect for parents who have motivated, well-disciplined children who are good visual learners and abstract thinkers, but the parents have little free time to actively teach their children.

At last report, about 32,000 children were being homeschooled with the Robinson Curriculum. Presumably some thousands more are being homeschooled according to this method, using other materials.

Since we have been fortunate enough to have Dr. Robinson as a regular *Practical Homeschooling* columnist in the past, we have his own "take" on his method. Thus the rest of this chapter is Dr. Robinson's own description of his method.

Dr. Robinson Explains His Method

There is a growing possibility that, if the homeschooling movement continues to expand, it may become the most important single force in American public life.

In order for this to occur, however, some current weaknesses in the homeschool movement need to be corrected. These include:

- **No full time homeschooling parent.** Homeschooling is very difficult for parents whose circumstances prevent at least one dedicated parent from giving a very large percentage of his or her time to the homeschool. While it is fine to argue that a family should always include one full-time parent in the home with time to teach the children, many families find themselves in circumstances which do not permit this.

Dr. Arthur Robinson is a scientist who works on various aspects of fundamental biochemistry, nutrition, and preventive medicine. He is President and Research Professor of the Oregon Institute of Science and Medicine. His wife Laurelee, who was also a scientist, homeschooled their children until her death in November 1988, when the children were 12, 10, 8, 6, 6, and 16 months. During the past eleven years, Dr. Robinson and the children have continued their homeschooling by developing a program entirely based upon self-teaching.

The Work of a Solitary Mind

A book is the permanent record of the work of a solitary human mind, to be read, marked, learned, and inwardly digested by another solitary human mind. A committee can no more make a book than it can play the violin, but almost every "book" used in schools—and in teacher-training academies—is written collectively and for collective purposes.

A magnificent education, as countless examples attest, can come from nothing more than reading and writing. In the one we behold the work of the solitary mind, in the other we do it, but we do it in such a way that we can behold again, and understand, and judge, the work of a solitary mind—our own. . . But the gimmickry of the schools . . . is an integral and large portion of a general program designed to prevent solitude. And while the children themselves are pestered with values clarification modules and relating sessions and group activities lest they fall into solitude, they are also protected from dangerous exposure to the fruits of solitary thinking in others.

—*Richard Mitchell*
The Graves of Academe
(1984, Little, Brown & Company)

- **Undereducated parents.** Many parents themselves lack the education that they so earnestly want for their children. As a consequence, homeschooled children have a difficult time rising above the level of academic achievement of their parents. This is true of many homes in which both parents are college trained and may even have advanced degrees. A large fraction of college graduates, for example, are not trained to do simple calculus—a level of academic achievement easily possible for most properly educated sixteen-year-old children. Even parents holding doctoral degrees in mathematics and science are often poorly educated in literature, history, and the foundations of our civilization.

- **Not reaching the child's full academic potential.** The average level of academic achievement in homeschools at present looks good only when compared with the disastrously poor results currently the norm in public schools. While it is true that SAT scores are a little higher for homeschools than for public schools, the average public school child comes from a generally poorer home environment and a school environment that is not conducive to learning.

We Need Higher Hopes

Some parents react to these difficulties with various forms of resignation. They hope that more families will find a way to rearrange their lives for homeschooling. In their homeschools, they emphasize subjects such as spelling and grammar and spend less time with difficult subjects such as mathematics and science. They hope that by the age of 18 their children will be strong enough to resist the evils that they encounter at the universities, or else they deny the children a higher education and direct them into occupations where that education is not required.

They are comforted by the fact that they have achieved slightly higher educational performance than the public schools while, at the same time, sparing their children the depravities of the secular world for at least part of their formative years. These are dedicated people who are doing their best for their children. I believe, however, that they should be thinking beyond the current homeschool situation.

In order to take our country back, we must do more in our homeschool movement than we are doing now. Our children must be not a little better educated when compared with those in the public schools—they must be so much better educated that they are entirely beyond such comparisons.

Our children must be able to think—and to think so much more effectively than their opponents that they are able, in one generation, to become a superior force in science and engineering and in industry and government.

Our children must be such shining examples for the homeschool movement that the majority of American families demand the same quality for their children.

Our children must be such superior performers in America's colleges and universities that they not only resist the corruption in those institutions—that they destroy, by their example, the corruption itself.

Interesting rhetoric, you may say, but how can this be done?

I respond, it MUST be done, and now I will describe an experiment that indicates the beginnings of a way in which it may possibly be done.

How It All Began

Like most successful experiments, this one reveals only part of the truth and suggests further experiments that may be worthwhile. Also, like a great many experiments that point in a different direction, this one was done by accident. If it ultimately proves to have been worthwhile, then the credit belongs to the Lord—not to the participants.

As our children reached school age, my wife Laurelee undertook their instruction. A highly educated scientist herself, she understood what they needed to learn, but she had no experience in teaching children. Moreover, she worked virtually full-time with me in our research work; she was still bearing new children and caring for infants; and she was carrying out a significant amount of farm work in addition to the usual household chores.

As an aid to her growing homeschool (all of our children have been entirely homeschooled), Laurelee purchased educational materials and curricula from a wide variety of sources. These she melded into a curriculum along with a large amount of Christian materials that she purchased. (She purchased so many Sunday school materials, that the people at the local Christian bookstore thought that we were operating a church.)

Not knowing whether or not these materials would be available to us in the future, she created an entire twelve-grade curriculum for each of the six children and obtained all of the necessary materials for that curriculum. These she organized meticulously in the order that they would be used. That curriculum occupies the equivalent of about five large filing cabinets and is in perfect order.

This effort, in degrees that vary according to the resources, education, abilities, and motivations of the parents, is one that is being undertaken today in tens of thousands of homeschools across America. It is being made increasingly effective by the growth of many excellent businesses that supply materials and curricula to homeschools.

Laurelee's effort was truly outstanding. It allowed for every academic eventuality and it utilized the very best materials available. It even included life insurance on me, so that she would be able to continue the homeschool in the event of my death. Her plan had only one flaw—a flaw that neither she nor I ever considered. The plan assumed that she would be alive to teach.

Six Children Who Teach Themselves

When Laurelee died suddenly years ago, after an illness that lasted less than 24 hours, her class contained Zachary, Noah, Arynne, Joshua, Bethany, and Matthew—ages 12, 10, 9, 7, 7, and 17 months—a class now without a teacher.

As I assumed her work, including cooking, laundry, and other household tasks, and continued the farm and professional work without her by my side, there was no possibility that I could even read the curriculum that she had so carefully created—much less have the time to teach it to the children. Friends tried to help, but the problem seemed to be intractable.

What happened then, with the Lord's help, was remarkable. Gradually, over the next two years and building upon the environment that their mother and I had already created for them and some rules of study that I provided, the children solved the problem themselves. Not only did they solve it themselves, they created a homeschool that, in many ways, points toward answers to some of the difficulties enumerated above.

Gradually, with occasional coaching and help from me, they created a homeschool that actually needs no teacher and is extraordinary in its effectiveness.

A Visit With the Robinsons

My husband and I were also intrigued by the article by Dr. Robinson in *Practical Homeschooling* #5 ("My Children Teach Themselves"), especially when Steve realized that he had been reading a book written by Dr. Robinson about civil defense.

We were going to be traveling through Oregon, so we called the Robinsons and asked if we could stop for a short visit. Dr. Robinson was very gracious and gave directions to his home.

When we arrived, the Robinson children were helping their father construct a building. The children were courteous with one another and all were working very hard. Steve and I visited with Dr. Robinson for 45 minutes in the building where their family has school. He told us about the literature project they are working on which will provide a systematic curriculum for reading for all grades. Many of the books in the program will be older books with no copyright, and they will be included on a CD-ROM. [This is the Henty Books on CD-ROM, reviewed in chapter 38 alongside the Robinson Curriculum review.]

As we were leaving, Dr. Robinson gave us copies of two newsletters he edits and publishes. One, called *Access to Energy*, used to be published by a famous physicist named Petr Beckmann. He asked Dr. Robinson to continue it after his death. It provides commentary on the anti-science being propagated in our society and provides real science with which to combat it. It is pro-science and pro-free market and well-written as well as easily understandable. It costs $35 for 12 issues to individuals and can be ordered from PO Box 1279, Cave Junction, OR 97523.

Dr. Robinson's methods may sound too streamlined to those always looking for newer and better curriculum or teaching styles, but it obviously works in his family!

—*Carmon Friedrich*

My favorite homeschooling philosophy is Dr. Arthur Robinson's (Robinson Curriculum). Let me warn you, this requires a lot of trust, but it doesn't need to be as formal or rigid. Dr. Robinson proposes two hours of math a day (which may be too much for a young child, but he's a mathematical person so he puts more emphasis in that area) and composing a one-page paper (the child's choice of topic) that will be corrected by you and returned for a possible rewrite. The remainder of the time is spent reading anything in your personal library (the books are there because they're good, right?).

Dr. Robinson proposes the right combination for education: reading, 'riting, and 'rithmetic. The three R's. There doesn't seem to be much exploration or hands-on activity in his style, right? Ah, but that's where you're wrong, because he lives on a farm that needs to be taken care of exclusively by him and the kids (he's a widower). This also means that the kids need to cook and clean. Do you see what I see?

He covers the basics, and all the life skills are part of their real world.

—*Kristina Sabalis Krulikas*
Homeschooling by Heart
(1999, Solomon's Secrets)

In judging its effectiveness, I have some experience for comparison.

I, myself, was fortunate to attend one of the finest public schools in Texas—Lamar in Houston—during the late 1950s when public schools in America still retained reasonable standards. I performed well and was admitted to every college to which I applied—including Harvard, M.I.T., Rice, and Caltech. After graduating from Caltech, I obtained a Ph.D. in chemistry from the University of California at San Diego and was immediately appointed to a faculty position at that University. There I taught introductory chemistry to 300 students each year and supervised a group of graduate students.

I can honestly say that the six Robinson children in our homeschool are, on average, at least two years ahead of my own abilities at their ages and have a far higher potential for the future than did I. Moreover, by the age of about 15, they are surpassing at least 98 percent of the college freshmen that I taught at the University of California at San Diego.

The oldest, Zachary, who is 16, is already completing a math and science curriculum that uses the actual freshman and sophomore texts from the best science universities in America. Last October he took the Scholastic Aptitude Tests for the first time (the PSAT). His scores of 750 in math and 730 in verbal for a sum of 1480 (and a NMSQT score of 221) were above the 99.9 percentile among the 1,600,000 students worldwide who took the test. The other children are, for their ages, performing at least as well.

During the past four years, I have spent less than 15 minutes per day (on average) engaged in working as the children's teacher. They are teaching themselves.

Moreover, each one of them has spontaneously, without suggestion or demand from me, taken over an essential aspect of our farm and personal lives. They do all the work with the cattle and sheep; they do all the laundry, cooking, and housework; and they are working beside me as Laurelee used to do in the scientific research and civil defense work that is our ministry and our professional life. One by one, my tasks just disappeared as the children assumed them.

In general, they prefer to work independently. They tend not to share tasks and have not divided them as one might expect. For example, 11-year-old Joshua is the cook—and already a better cook than I. Zachary does all the work with the cattle (about 30) and the chickens; Arynne cares for the sheep (about 100); Noah is in charge of all farm and laboratory repairs; and Bethany does the washing and teaches Matthew. Some tasks are shared, such as house cleaning, sheep shearing, and watching over Matthew.

This sort of extracurricular work is especially valuable as reinforcement for the homeschool. While self-confidence can be built somewhat in sports or other "activities," the confidence that comes to a child from the knowledge that he is independently carrying on an activity that is essential to the survival of the family is valuable indeed.

It is important, however, not to take advantage of this situation. The development of a young mind takes place in a few short years. A parent must always make certain that the children have more than enough time for their academic studies and for essential recreation. When children show an aptitude for productive work helpful to the parent, there can be a tendency for the parent to let them do too much. This can deprive the children of mental development necessary to their own futures.

I generally consider each child's time to be more valuable than my own. If I provide them the time for optimum development and direct them to the necessary tools, then each of them should be able to surpass my own abilities and accomplishments. If they do, then my goals for their academic work will have been fulfilled. Remarkably, they have spontaneously responded with efforts that provide me also with more time for productive work.

Our home is not as neat and clean as some, our spelling (including mine) is not all that could be desired, and our traditions have become somewhat unusual (they leave the Christmas tree and nativity scene up for six months each year—from December through June), but these children know how to work and they know how to think.

Their homeschool is a success. This school is entirely self-taught by each student working alone. It depends upon a set of rules that can be adopted within any home in America. As their parent, my sole essential contribution has been to set the rules under which they live and study.

How the Robinsons Do It

For those who consider adopting these procedures, I offer the opinion that they will work in any home and with any children, regardless of ability. Obviously children differ in innate ability. I believe, however, that these rules will achieve remarkable results with any child when compared with other alternatives.

These are not, however, "suggestions." They are rigorous requirements. I know what has happened here. I do not know what would happen in different experiments under different conditions. If, therefore, these suggestions are all followed in the same way, I expect the same result.

No TV. There is no television in our home. We do have a VCR. As a family we watch a video tape approximately once every six months. Television wastes time, promotes passive, vicarious brain development rather than active thought, and is a source of pernicious social contamination.

Most American children are addicted to TV. Their brains spend four hours or more each day learning bad, passive habits from the TV and another few hours (if they are fortunate to have good activities, too) unlearning the bad habits. Then, if there are any hours left, they can make positive progress.

Moreover, when TV is used as a tranquilizer, it can mask other problems that should be solved early in life. Children need to work out the ways in which they interact with other people. Even though their behavior while doing so may be more distracting than their behavior when pacified by a television set, the TV may be retarding this aspect of development which is then undesirably transferred to the classroom instead.

No Sweets. The children do not eat sugar or honey or foods made with these materials and have never done so at any time in their lives. Sugar alters the metabolism in such a way as to increase the probability of diabetes, hypoglycemia, and hyperglycemia, and immune deficiencies that can lead to cancer and other fatal illnesses at a later age. Most importantly to a homeschool, sugar diminishes mental function and increases irritability and mental instability. Most children are able to learn regardless of these effects, but why burden them with this disadvantage?

These points about sugar have been expanded upon in several texts that may be available in your library. I recommend these books: *Sweet and Dangerous* by John Yudkin, Peter D. Wyden, Inc., 750 Third Ave, New York, NY 10017 (1972); *Sugar Blues* by William Dufty, Chilton Book Company, Radnor, PA (1975); and *Food, Teens & Behavior* by Barbara Reed, Natural Press, PO Box 2107, Manitowoc, WI (1983). These books contain a substantial number of appropriate references to the scientific literature.

Though Laurelee and I (both sugar addicts) established this rule, it is now out of my control. Two years ago, when some visitors whom we greatly wished to please came for dinner, they brought sweet rolls and donuts. I suggested to the children that they should eat just one so as not to offend. They all refused.

I Found It in a Book

We sometimes talk of a student studying books on his own as "self-instruction." Nothing could be farther from the truth! The child or adult alone with a book is actually getting instruction from another human being—the book's author. Furthermore, this instruction is swifter than oral instruction, easier to review, and ideally suited to the disciplines of studying, thinking, comparing, and imagining.

—*Schoolproof*

Not a Team Sport

Learning is not a team sport. Learning is an activity that involves solely the student and the knowledge. Everything or everyone else that may become involved in this process is essentially superfluous—and is potentially harmful as a distraction from the fundamental process.

In the adult world this is, of course, self-evident. Adults ordinarily do not have special teaching aids and dedicated teachers available to hold their hands when they need to acquire new knowledge. Usually, they have only books. When the knowledge comes directly from other repositories such as computers, people, or other sources, that knowledge is seldom tailored for spoon-feeding to an unprepared mind.

—*Arthur Robinson*

Practical Advantages of Self-Study

Besides the great advantage of developing good study habits and thinking ability, self-teaching also has immediate practical advantages. Many children should be able, through Advanced Placement examinations, to skip over one or more years of college. The great saving in time and expense from this is self-evident. These and other comparable accomplishments await most children who learn to self-teach and then apply this skill to their home education.

Even children of lesser ability can, by means of self-teaching and good study habits, achieve far more than they otherwise would have accomplished by the more ordinary techniques.

—*Arthur Robinson*

Five Hours, Six Days, Ten Months. Formal school work occupies about five hours each day—six days per week—twelve months per year. Sometimes one of them skips his studies for the day as a result of some special activity, and we take an occasional automobile trip. With these diversions, their actual annual school time occupies about ten full months of six-day weeks.

School First. These five hours each day are the most productive hours—the morning and early afternoon. As soon as they wake—and with time out only for breakfast and milking the cows—they study. Each has a large desk in the school room. My desk is also in that room. I try to do my own desk work during the same time, since my presence keeps the school room quiet and avoids arguments about noise.

Phonics. The five older children were taught to read with the phonetic system—learning the individual sounds of our language. Laurelee taught them all. Matthew (five years old) is currently learning to read by phonics. The children are teaching him.

Lots of Good Books. The teacher-presented materials that Laurelee obtained are not used, but the history, science, and literature books that we accumulated, which include a good selection of classics, are essential to the curriculum.

Saxon Math. Each day, before beginning any other work, each child (except Matthew) works an entire lesson in the Saxon series of mathematics books. This usually involves working about 30 problems. If the 30 problems seem to be taking much less than two hours each day, we sometimes increase the assignment to two lessons or about 60 problems per day. If the lessons seem to be taking much more than two hours, then we reduce to one-half lesson or about 15 problems per day. This is an excellent series of texts. The children work their way through the entire series at a rate that finishes calculus, the last text in the series, when they are 15 years of age.

They grade their own problems and rework any missed problems. They must tell me if they miss a problem and show the correctly-worked solution to me. The younger children tend to make one or two errors each day. As they get older, the error rate drops. The older children make about one error each week. On very rare occasions, perhaps once each month, an older child will actually need help with a problem he or she feels unable to solve.

This emphasis on math with the help of the excellent Saxon series teaches them to think, builds confidence and ability to the point of almost error-free performance, and establishes a basis of knowledge that is essential to later progress in science and engineering.

It is also absolutely essential preparation for the non-quantitative subjects that do not require mathematics. The ability to distinguish the quantitative from the non-quantitative—the truth from error—fact from fiction—is an absolutely essential requirement for effective thinking. Otherwise one will tend to confuse independent, truthful thought with opinions based upon falsehoods and propaganda.

Our society is filled to the brim with public school graduates who imagine that they are independent thinkers when they actually are programmed to believe anything they perceive as fashionable. This cult-like behavior is not limited to graduates in "soft subjects." Many people supposedly educated in the sciences and engineering also practice this ritual of non-thought.

I believe that much of this difficulty stems from poor early education in mathematics and logical thought. It is essential to understand that physical truths are absolute and can be rigorously determined. This must be learned by actually determining absolutes. Mathematical problem solving is an excellent mechanism for doing this.

Grim examples of failures in this area are everywhere. Earlier today, for example, a local bureaucrat telephoned in an effort to get my help in fashioning a community compromise on environmental issues between the solid citizens of this valley and some pseudoenvironmentalist political agitators who have been disrupting the community recently.

During the discussion I mentioned that the agitators had filed a document with the federal government that contained a graph condemning the local lumber industry for destroying local game fish. Actually there was no correlation between fish population and timber harvest. The agitators had created a correlation by leaving out about half of the data for the last forty years—the half which proves that their premise is false.

"Oh well," the bureaucrat replied, "we all do that sort of thing."

An Essay a Day. After completing the mathematics work, each child writes a one-page essay about any subject that interests him and gives it to me. Some of the children enjoy writing these essays more than others. The remainder of the five hours is spent in reading history and science texts.

I read these pages and mark misspelled words and grammatical errors that the child must then correct. Sometimes I fall many weeks behind with these corrections, but the children just keep writing.

There is an unusual bonus in these short essays. Sometimes the student will write things that he or she would not (and sometimes should not) say to the parent otherwise. These essays have educational value, and they also open a new line of communication with the children.

College Level Science. Zachary (16 years old) has a more rigorous curriculum, since he finished calculus about a year ago. He is working his way through freshman and sophomore college physics and chemistry texts in the same way that he previously worked his way through Saxon math. After those years of self-taught math, he has simply gone on to self-taught science—and in the toughest college level texts that I was able to obtain. His mind has become used to the fact that there is nothing in the well-known sciences that he cannot understand and learn and no problem that, with a proper book, he cannot work correctly. His error rate is negligible.

No Computers. No child is allowed to use a computer until after he or she has completed mathematics all the way through calculus. (At one point Saxon calls for a little use of the hand-held calculator. I permit this, but only on a very few occasions.)

Constant Recreational Reading. Since they have no television, the children are prone to spend a substantial part of their non-school hours reading. They read whatever interests them from our library—which Laurelee purged of all books that she thought it best for them to avoid. By recreational reading, the children pick up most of their vocabulary and grammar and most of their knowledge about the world. Regarding current events, they do not listen to the radio, but it has become increasingly difficult to maintain control of my copy of the *Wall Street Journal*.

No Formal Bible Teaching. The Bible is not a required part of our formal curriculum. We have a family Bible reading before bed each evening, and we discuss elements of Christianity as they happen to arise in our everyday lives.

Like Isaac Newton, no one in our family ever questions the truth of the Lord's Word as provided to us in the Old and New Testaments of the King James Bible. We only seek to understand these truths by repeated reading. That reading is rarely accompanied by interpretive comment. Each of us must understand these things for himself and build his own relationship with God.

What We Leave Out. This curriculum is important for what it contains and also for what it does not contain. It contains about two hours of math

Good Study Habits

Since certain skills need to be acquired at an early age—particularly mathematics and reading, writing, and thinking in one's native language—it is sensible to arrange the homeschool so that learning these essential skills will automatically lead to the development of good study habits. This is one reason that self-teaching homeschools have a special value.

Consider, for example, the teaching of math and science. Many homeschools use Saxon Math. Although produced with teachers and classrooms in mind, this series of math books is so well-written that it can be mastered by most students entirely on their own without any teacher intervention whatever. This self-mastery usually does not happen automatically, but it can be learned by almost any student with correct study rules and a good study environment.

While the subject matter, can be mastered with or without a teacher, the student who masters it without a teacher learns something more. He learns to teach himself. Then, when he continues into physics, chemistry, and biology—which are studied in their own special language, the language of mathematics—he is able to teach these subjects to himself regardless of whether or not a teacher with the necessary specialized knowledge is present. Also, he is able to make use of much higher-quality texts—texts written for adults.

—*Arthur Robinson*

Mom & Dad as Living Books

To avoid misunderstanding, let me add that Dr. Robinson is not suggesting that parents should never answer their children's questions. Providing your children with information that is not "in the book" again reduces the educational equation to two participants: you (the source of this knowledge) and the child. You become the "living book" the child is studying!

What he is saying is that our children need to learn to ferret out new information and skills on their own. Obviously, this is easier if we give them excellent resources which provide the information in easy-to-understand, step-by-step fashion. So for those who choose to follow this method, choosing great resources is vital in the early years, to avoid discouragement. An older child who is trained in this method can squeeze juice out of even the driest resource, but let's not start our little ones with anything but the best!

—Mary Pride

or science problem-solving followed by about two hours of directed reading and a short essay each day—all self-taught by the student.

What it does not contain is also very important. Each additional subject that is added to the curriculum creates a demand upon the brain's 24 hours of time. If an unnecessary subject is added, it wastes not only the curricular school time, but also a fraction of the extracurricular time. It is therefore important to be very careful not to add unnecessary subjects.

Our public schools and also many of our homeschools have so many subjects in their curricula that the children's brains do not have time to give adequate attention to the fundamentally important subjects.

Although the children take piano lessons and engage in a rich variety of extracurricular activities oriented around our farm and laboratory, their formal curriculum consists of "reading, writing, and arithmetic" and *nothing more*. It also essentially has no teacher—a fact that I have come to realize can be an *advantage*.

Just Say Nothing

When your eight-year-old child is all alone at his large desk in a quiet room with his *Saxon 65* book and has been there three hours already—with most of that time spent in childhood daydreams—and says, "Mommy, I don't know how to work this problem," give him a wonderful gift. Simply reply, "Then you will need to keep studying until you can work the problem."

For a while, his progress may be slow. Speed will come with practice. Eventually, he will stop asking questions about how to do his assignments and will sail along through his lessons without help.

These study habits can then spill over into the other subjects—with astonishing results.

Learning to Think

In the formative years, it is absolutely essential that children learn how to think and how to learn independently. They have a lifetime to accumulate facts and will do so more effectively if they acquire a correct foundation—not of facts, but of ability to read, think, and evaluate for themselves.

The ability to think is the most important. A very large percentage of our public school graduates lack the ability to think. Most of them can, however, articulate acceptably. When we give the brain a small number of the most important tools to learn and use, we give it an opportunity to learn to think.

The Experiment Works

In this experiment, I have watched a group of children educate themselves in a far superior manner than I could have done for them if I had spent every waking hour teaching them in the usual manner. I am convinced that, had I done so, their progress would have been far less.

Although I have occasionally helped them with specific questions, that help has been so infrequent that they would have advanced almost as far if I had not helped. Moreover, the level of academic accomplishment that they have achieved is truly extraordinary.

Children learn by example and by doing. They do not learn effectively by being lectured to or by vicarious involvement as in television viewing. Our educational method works, and it involves almost no parental time once the school room and curriculum have been provided and the rules have been established.

CHAPTER 21

The Charlotte Mason Method

I f textbook methods and Principle Approach seem designed for the Progress Person . . . if classical education and Robinson Method appeal to the Puzzle Solver . . . if unit studies and unschooling appeal to the Action Man and Performer . . . then what kind of education is tailor-made for the People Person? Is there a homeschool method for the child who has a great heart and is most motivated by love and beauty?

Meet Charlotte Mason

Charlotte Mason was a Christian educator who lived and worked in Britain during the latter part of the 19th century. An idealist, she developed a Christian philosophy of education. When we speak of anyone being an idealist and/or philosopher we are usually implying that the person is preoccupied with high thinking but leaves the practical application to others. Unlike Dorothy Sayers, Charlotte did not do this. She was no armchair philosopher. She was one of those rare spirits who, having probed the depths of thought, could not rest content until she saw how it all worked out.

Today Charlotte's work is undergoing a revival in homeschool circles.

What's It All About, Charlotte?

For Charlotte Mason, education was not a list of skills or facts to be mastered. Education was **an atmosphere, a discipline, a life.** She saw education as a life process which is not confined to the classroom. Homeschoolers who follow her method do not attempt to duplicate the public school classroom regimen in their homes. They emphasize educating their children for life, not for achievement tests.

In the Charlotte Mason method, **whole books** and **first-hand sources** are used whenever possible, rather than textbooks.

Miss Mason advocated what she called **"living books."** Children, she thought, should read the best books, not graded readers or textbook comprehension paragraphs. Educators think they are doing children a favor by taking scissors to cut out pages of the best books. Charlotte called this putting literature in "snippet form." She felt children deserve to have more than just a nodding acquaintance with the best authors.

This chapter was written by Karen Andreola and Mary Pride, and is partly based on the following articles: *Parents' Review* 1923, "A Brief Account of the Life and Work of Charlotte Mason," by E.K. and *Parents' Review* 1910, "An Educational Union," by Mrs. Kirwain.

Karen Andreola

Karen Andreola is widely regarded as the world's foremost authority on Charlotte Mason education in the homeschool. She is the former publisher of *Parents' Review*, a newsletter dedicated to reviving the educational principles of Charlotte Mason. With her husband Dean she is the founder of Charlotte Mason Research & Supply Co., PO Box 1142, Rockland, ME 04841. Web: www.charlotte-mason.com.

What Drew Me to Charlotte Mason Education

by Karen Andreola

Living Books

One of the first things that impressed me about Charlotte was her method of using whole books and first-hand sources. . . . Textbooks compiled by a committee tend to be crammed with facts and information, at the expense of human emotion. This dryness is deadening to the imagination of the child. Miss Mason advocated what she called "living books." Whole books are living in a sense that they are written by a single author who shares his favorite subject with us and we pick up his enthusiasm. Textbooks written by one author might make this claim, too.

Narration

With living books a child gains knowledge through his own work, digging out facts and information. He then expresses what he has learned by clothing it in literary (conversational) language—in short, narrating it back to you.

Miss Mason believed that narration is the best way to acquire knowledge from books. Narration also provides opportunities for a child to form an opinion or make a judgment, no matter how crude. Because narration takes the place of questionnaires and multiple-choice tests, it enables the child to bring all the faculties of his mind into play. The child learns to call on the vocabulary and descriptive power of good writers as he tells his own version of the passage or chapter.

No Homework

Another attraction to Miss Mason's philosophy is that her schools never gave homework (under the age of 13). When a child follows her method there is no need for homework in the elementary years because the child immediately deals with the literature at hand and proves his mastery by narrating at the time of the reading.

Studies have proved homework to be less effective than this form of immediate feedback.

Instead of homework, my children enjoy an atmosphere of a cozy evening with a good book and parental attention.

No Grades—Short Lessons— Motivation of Lasting Value

Miss Mason was an idealist. Unlike some idealistic persons she worked out her scheme and saw it put into practice. She wanted children to be motivated by admiration, faith, and love instead of artificial stimulants such as prizes (stickers, candy, or money), competition, and grades.

Miss Mason managed to retain a child's curiosity and develop a love of knowledge in a child that he would carry on all through his life. The children took examinations where they narrated orally or on paper from "those lovely" books that they read that semester. Each child learned first to acquire the habit of attention by listening to and narrating short stories, and by accomplishing short lessons in the drills and skills. Short lessons discourage dawdling; they encourage the child to concentrate and make his best effort. Because the Charlotte Mason method employs whole books, narration, and short lessons, a child taught this way will try his best even though he will not be graded.

Free Afternoons

Bookish lessons in the Charlotte Mason scheme of things end at 1:00 P.M., or earlier if the children are quite young. High-school students will probably need some afternoon study time, but overall the afternoon is free for leisure. This is another aspect of her philosophy that so easily finds its way into the modern homeschool.

Leisure for children usually means running, climbing, yelling, and so forth—all out of doors. It has been observed that boys, particularly, cannot flourish without this opportunity. Handicrafts, practicing an instru-ment, chores, cooking, visiting lonely neighbors, observing and recording the wonders of nature may also be accomplished during this time.

Sadly, public-school children (young or old) must endure such long lessons and long hours that they are frequently tranquilized with drugs in order to pass through the system. They ride the bus home just in time to see the sun set and do homework.

Few Lectures

I was also drawn to Miss Mason's philosophy because it doesn't require me to give lectures. Charlotte pointed out that I need not be a certified teacher trained in the skill of giving lectures in order for my children to learn. This was a relief to me.

Through Charlotte's method, children gain the ability of educating themselves. Students do not depend upon notes they have taken from a teacher's lecture where most of the information has been predigested by the teacher. With Charlotte's superior method of narration from books, the carefully chosen words of an author are commented on by the child in essay form, either oral or written, starting at age 6 or 7. Too much explaining by the teacher can be a bore because, in actuality, the only true education is that of self-education.

Ideas and Culture

Inspiring children to love knowledge depends on how well ideas are presented to them. The mind feeds upon ideas. To quote Miss Mason, "Ideas must reach us directly from the mind of the thinker, and it is chiefly by the means of the books they have written that we get in touch with the best minds." This includes all forms of human expression. This is why Charlotte said the Bible and "varied human reading as well as the appreciation of the humanities (culture) is not a luxury, a tidbit, to be given to children now and then, but their very bread of life."

Charlotte's curriculum enabled children of all classes to experience books and culture in abundance when in Victorian days the arts and humanities seemed to belong only to the "well-to-do" classes.

Today, with so many pictures and art print books available, children can observe museum pieces and learn to recognize the works of dozens of artists over time just by changing what goes under the thumb tack once every two weeks or so. Our children can easily become familiar with the music of great composers by listening to cassettes and CDs, when years ago they would have needed to visit a concert hall. . . .

Education is a Discipline

What Charlotte meant by "discipline," in Victorian-day terms, is that proper education inculcates good habits. The mother who takes pains to endow her children with good habits secures for herself smooth and orderly days. On the other hand, she who lets habits take care of themselves has a weary life of endless friction.

The mother needs to acquire her own habit of training her children so that, by and by, it is not troublesome to her, but a pleasure, She devotes herself to the formation of one habit in her children at a time, doing no more than watch over those already formed. Remember, to instill habits:

- Be consistent. It's dangerous to let things go "just this once."
- Forming a habit is using perseverance to work against a contrary habit.
- Formation is easier than reformation. Nip each weed in the bud!

Sane Education

If the above ideas sound as sane and sensible to you as they have to me, perhaps it is because Charlotte Mason hasn't been the only one sharing these "open secrets." Other voices in homeschooling are now sharing conclusions similar to those that Charlotte Mason advocated so many years ago. Many of us have come to similar conclusions about what goes into a well-brought-up person— "great minds think alike." Happily, many children are benefiting from a Charlotte Mason-style education in homeschools across the nation.

From the article "What Drew Me to Charlotte Mason Education," originally published in Practical Homeschooling July/August 1996

Miss Mason said that **asking children to narrate back what they have learned** is the best way to acquire knowledge from books. Because narration takes the place of questionnaires and multiple choice tests, it enables the child to bring all the faculties of mind into play. The child learns to call on the vocabulary and descriptive power of good writers as he tells his own version of the story.

Miss Mason's schools never gave homework? Correct. If you follow her method there is **no need for homework** in the elementary years.

Charlotte Mason believed in **introducing the child to the humanities while he is still young,** while he is forming his personality. In her view education is for the spiritual and intellectual benefit of the child, not just to provide the skills needed for making a living. Short goody-goody stories are shunned for whole books that follow the life of an admirable character. Morals are painted for the child, not pointed at the child.

Miss Mason wanted children to be **motivated by admiration, faith, and love** instead of what she felt to be "artificial stimulants," such as prizes, competition and grades. There were no grades in her elementary schools. No As, Bs, Cs, or Fs. No happy-face stickers or gold stars.

Lessons in the Charlotte Mason scheme of things end at 1:00 P.M., and **the afternoon is free for leisure.**

Homeschoolers following Charlotte's philosophy and method try to give their children **abundant portions of the humanities** at regular periods. They don't allow themselves to get stuck in a routine which emphasizes skills alone. *"Oh, we only had time for math drill, spelling, and grammar, and a few pages from our history textbook today. Tomorrow we will hopefully have time for poetry, and maybe a little music appreciation."* Charlotte Mason-style educators believe that when fear of a poor showing on the achievement test allows skills to take precedence, humanities take a back seat. The result: lessons become wearisome, children become fed up, mom gets burned out.

In the Charlotte Mason method, **lessons are kept short,** enabling children to develop the habit of attention and preventing the contrary habit of dawdling over lessons. *"Oh, you're not finished with your one math page yet? Well, then there is no time for a short romp in the back yard. Perhaps you can finish your math page in less than 15 minutes tomorrow."*

Curriculum Suitable for Use with the Charlotte Mason Method

At this point, we have not seen any elementary curriculum yet developed according to the Charlotte Mason Method. However, thousands of families are using this method by following the suggestions in the books at the end of this chapter.

How Narration Works

When I tell new homeschoolers about Victorian-era British educator Charlotte Mason's technique of having children narrate what they have read or studied, instead of filling out endless workbook exercises, everyone asks the same question: "How do you do that?"

Here are some ways you can prompt your children to narrate what they have learned.

Charlotte's favorite—**"Tell me all you know about. . . ."**

- the habits of a shark.
- the landing of the Pilgrims.
- Heidi's visit to Peter's grandmother.

"Explain how . . ."

- a rose is pollinated.
- sedimentary rock is formed.
- Jesus healed the blind man.
- the U.S. Constitution came to be written.
- cheese is made.
- Robinson Crusoe settled on the lonely island.

"Describe our . . ."

- trip to the Oregon coast.
- nature walk.
- visit to the nursing home.
- planetarium experience.

"Tell about anything new you have just learned in this chapter."

"Tell the story (passage, episode) back in your own words."

"What four things have you learned about —— in this chapter?"

"Ask or write six questions covering the material of this chapter."

"Draw a picture, map, or likeness of —— ."

"What impressions have you on the life of (Abraham Lincoln, Queen Elizabeth I, Abigail Adams, William Tyndale, Frederick Banting [the inventor of insulin], Ebenezer Scrooge, Achilles, King Arthur, Black Beauty) in this chapter?"

—*Karen Andreola*

Charlotte didn't concern herself with **grammar lessons** until the children were well into the habit of narration. She thought it was more important that the child learn to express himself correctly. He should have daily opportunities to have an opinion, make a judgment, no matter how crude, develop a train of thought, and use his imagination. She felt that grammar lessons for first, second, third grade children should not replace this free use of expression.

How It All Began

Charlotte Maria Shaw Mason was born on January 1st, 1842. Her home was in Liverpool, where her father was a merchant. Just like her father and mother, she was an only child. When orphaned at the age of sixteen, her greatest desire was to help children. She decided to devote her whole life to them. After a short time training, and some experience in schools of various kinds and in a vocational college, she began to see a need for reform in the theory and practice of education. She told part of the story in the introduction of *Philosophy of Education*. In 1885, after twenty-five years' experience she proposed these theories and methods in a series of lectures about training and educating children at home. In 1886 her book *Home Education* was published. Mothers wanting something better for their children eagerly accepted the advice in this book. Friends gathered around Charlotte, and they decided to start a society to advance these principles "for the children's sake." Parents wrote letters requesting further lectures, and in 1887 Charlotte Mason was invited to speak before the British Association, held that year at Owens College, Manchester.

Lots of Letters

In 1887 Charlotte held a meeting in the living room of Mrs. Francis Steinthal to discuss starting a Parents' Educational Union, for Miss Mason always made her first appeal to parents. A further meeting and much correspondence with the educational leaders of the day led to meeting in London, at which the Union was made official, with a council and an executive committee. Miss Mason continued to lecture, and in 1890, with the help of her friends, launched the *Parents' Review,* a monthly magazine for home training and culture. The magazine was supported entirely by donations. She also set up a free lending library of books chosen to help parents and teachers.

A Training Center in the Country

Then came the question of how to further advance Charlotte's work. Miss Mason had for some years spent her vacation time in the Lake District, and she came to realize that this would be an excellent dwelling place for the center of her work — a spot full of beauty and literary associations, "an unwalled university," as she once called it. She founded the House of Education here in 1891. In the same year she sent out the first complete curriculum program to help parents or governesses teach children at home. In 1892 she opened a college to train of teachers. A mother's course gave mothers needed confidence to use her method in their homes. For a time Charlotte carried on her work from Ambleside, and she did much of the lecturing herself, but soon she needed an office in London from which the propaganda work of the Union could be carried out. The Union held an annual conference in various parts of England. Members of the Union began providing an ongoing series of free lectures to the public and formed support groups throughout the United Kingdom.

12 Quick Tips to Charlotte Mason Success

by Karen Andreola

1. Take courage and take the "real book plunge." The act of replacing a history, science or literature textbook with the many fabulous real books available in homeschool catalogs may be an experience similar to that of jumping into cool water on a hot day. Once you are in however, you are glad you had the courage because the water is wonderful.

2. Let your young children chatter. Charlotte Mason said that this was an amazing gift that every normal child is born with and that it should be taken advantage of in their education. Children of any age can start to narrate using an Aesop fable, for example. Over time a child's habit of narrating what he knows will carry over beautifully to his writing ability.

3. Pitch the worksheets. Develop the habit of narrating. Use it in place of so many worksheets.

4. Those who read twaddle may just as well twiddle their thumbs. Most children are bored by easy vocabulary found in "graded readers." Try reading aloud from a page or two of any well-written children's book. I recently finished reading aloud from the story, *Ginger Pye* by Newbery medalist Eleanor Estes. In it we read that the dog named "Ginger was a *purposeful* dog. When he found something he "thoughtfully and *earnestly* breathed in the *essence* of Jerry until it *permeated* his *entire* being . . ." Are the words I put in italics third grade vocabulary? fourth grade? fifth grade? sixth grade? I don't know. What I do know is that my eight-year-old son delighted in hearing it read aloud. He always looked forward to hearing the next chapter at bed time. Listening to vocabulary in context like this is the best way to become familiar with new or strange words.

5. Make a nature notebook. It's a pity when children can name all the Star Wars characters but do not know the names of the birds, trees, flowers and insects in their own neighborhood. My children's Nature Notebooks, filled with crayon drawings of the nature they have observed, are more precious than a pile of workbook pages could ever be.

6. Display at least six pictures of one artist's works over a period of a semester. This is all it takes for a student to become acquainted with some of the world's greatest works of art. Display six or more of Leonardo DaVinci, six of Jean Francois Millet, six of Michelangelo, or whomever you choose. Let the children look and look and look and then describe what they see.

7. Do the same for music. Just pop in a cassette of greatest hits of Mozart, Beethoven, Scott Joplin, or Gershwin. One composer at a time is suggested. Play that composer's music over and over again while you wash dishes, sweep the floor, ride in the car, draw, or give the little ones a bath. Music is the universal language and classical music is another part of a cultural heritage we can pass on to our children.

8. Hooray for the strong-willed child! My prayer is that all my children will be strong-willed children, that they develop the will-power to do what is right, to choose to follow God's will and to do it with all their might. My job as a parent is to guide and inspire. I place in the curriculum stories that invite "hero admiration." The Bible, biography and historical fiction can supply heroes with virtuous characters that children may choose to emulate.

9. Good habits need constant attention until they are formed. Faithfulness at a task involves consistency. To be consistent takes great effort until a habit is formed. Once a good habit is formed another can be added to the list of acquired attainments. And good habits can take the place of bad ones this way, too.

10. Keep lessons short in the early years of school so that a student can focus all his attention without being tempted to dawdle. Over time a habit of attention is formed that enables the students to do harder work without fretting.

11. Some twenty "habits of the good life" can be instilled in the lives of our children during their school years. A mother only needs to develop one habit in her children at a time, keeping watch over those already formed. Her homeschool days will go by more smoothly with some routine and good manners. Saying "thank you" and "please," sharing, taking turns, sitting up straight at the table, waiting patiently, and remembering daily prayer, can become habit. Speaking the truth in love, using determination, counting our blessings (to avoid self pity and depression) are virtuous actions that do not need strenuous moral effort once they have become habit.

12. You don't have to be perfect. I'll admit to you that I was not brought up by way of Charlotte Mason's guiding principles of education. I was an "all right kid" so I got through the system of public school okay with slightly above-average grades. But I graduated without reading more than one or two real books. I acquired little knowledge of literature, poetry, great art, classical music, history or science.

When my own children were small I was desperately in need of the wisdom and confidence to homeschool my children. So I asked God's help and searched for his answer to my prayers. This was the answer. I would learn along with my children. I cannot say I've never had a down, insecure or confused moment during my homeschool adventure. However, I can say that I am so glad I decided to homeschool fourteen years ago. We've been learning a lot together. And I am grateful Charlotte Mason's guidance was made available to me.

A Curriculum

The Parents' Union School (a correspondence school) arranged first for home schoolrooms and later extended membership to private schools. Soon thousands of British children from six to eighteen around the world were receiving a generous education under the Union's auspices. The Parents' Union School sent out a timetable and fresh syllabus of work each term, and examination papers at the end of the term in which children wrote narrations about what they learned. The hours were short; the youngest class only took two and a half hours per day. The children took delight in the work, which was varied and interesting. The chosen books were of great literary value, and worth keeping for a lifetime. There was no danger of "cramming." Students learned good habits (paying attention, doing their best without grades), Because their curiosity was protected, a love of learning carried them easily through their lessons. Through discipline, students gained wisdom and developed strength of character. Through the method of narration they learned to recall, reason, analyze, and finally evaluate what they read. The courses never used long lists of questions, true or false, multiple choice, fill in the blank, match the columns, and other sorts of "devices of the idle." Children were asked to tell, describe, and explain what they remembered from a book or an experience. The fee for a family of one or more children under ten was (in 1910) only one guinea a year, and two guineas for a child over ten (less than three to six dollars!). Much time was taken for activities like outdoor nature study, art and music appreciation, crafts, or an annual Shakespeare play for the older students.

In 1902 the Board of Education issued regulations enabling the head of any state school to use (with the approval of the local education authority) any method of teaching which seemed to benefit the children under his or her charge. Finally, Charlotte Mason's life-long vision of "A Generous Education for All" had come true. In 1913, the state school started in Yorkshire (setting of the story *The Secret Garden*) became the first to use Charlotte's method. From that time onwards examination papers came to Ambleside from children in every rank of life. Even poor children with illiterate parents in mining villages were learning to love knowledge and enjoy their "lovely books."

Retirement?

The Training College at The House of Education (nicknamed the House of the Holy Spirit) started with four students but very quickly increased to twenty-five. Here Miss Mason trained her students, speaking to them about her educational method, guiding her work in a small school in which the Parent's Union School's programs were carried out, and providing a quiet place for her students where for two years they might study nature and receive joy from simple life and high thinking. Everything needed for a generous education was shown in the college curriculum. As her prospectus said, "the aim of education presented to the students is to produce a human being at his best, physically, mentally, morally, and spiritually, quickened by religion and with some knowledge of nature, art, literature, and handicraft."

Miss Mason lived at The House of Education until her death. She remained in daily contact not only with the students and with the children in the practicing school, but in touch with the many thousands of children working in home schoolrooms all over the world. She passed away in 1923, still in active work at the age of 81. She left her students with work

Covering the Basics the Charlotte Mason Way

by Karen Andreola

From what Charlotte Mason wrote in her book *Home Education,* first published in England in the 1880's, I can give you a peek at how Charlotte taught children the basics—those fundamental areas of learning. Perhaps these few paragraphs will welcome you to explore her words further.

General Knowledge—Most of a child's knowledge will come from books. A very young student cannot read much for himself, so it must be read aloud to him. It used to be thought that the chief function of a teacher was to explain; with Charlotte Mason's emphasis it would be to read. She said a teacher's chief function is to distinguish information from knowledge.

If a child can put what he is learning in his own words, he has proved he is knowledgeable. The child who has only information can only fill in the blanks in the stereotyped phrases of his test-book.

To narrate is to know. Narration, retelling reading in one's own words, can be called "the art of knowing." But a child often finds it awkward to narrate from a dry, factual textbook. This is one reason real books on a variety of subjects are better to be used in acquiring knowledge.

An author of a real book is a person who decided to write on what strongly interested him. He shares his favorite subject, and any personal experience of it, with us. The writing is often touched with human emotion. And as we read, we pick up his enthusiasm for his subject.

Reading—Where there are no lovely little sentences there can be no reading.

"Lessons in word-making help the young student take intelligent interest in *words*; but his progress in the art of reading depends chiefly on the 'reading by sight' lessons. [Some of you may be gasping at this, but I successfully taught my children to read this way and they all *loved* learning to read. You start by teaching the sounds of the letters, and then . . .] The teacher must be content to proceed very slowly, reviewing as she goes. Say—

> *Twinkle, twinkle, little star,*
> *How I wonder what you are,*

is the first lesson . . . . Read the passage for the child, very slowly and sweetly. Point to each word as you read. Then point to *twinkle*, *wonder*, *star*, *what*, and expect the child to pronounce (sound-out) each word in the verse taken randomly; then, when he shows that he knows each word by itself, and not before, let him *read* the two lines with clear enunciation and expression. If these lines are written in a good size on paper, the words may be cut out to allow the child to piece them together. The cards can be kept for review.

"In this way the child accumulates a little capital; he knows eight or ten words so well that he will recognize them anywhere, and the lesson has occupied probably ten minutes. Lines can be taken from short tales, fables or poems. 'But what a snail's progress!' you are inclined to say. Not so slow, after all: a child will thus learn, without appreciable labour, from two to three thousand words in the course of a year . . . The master of this number of words will carry him with comfort through most of the books that fall in his way."

Some teachers keep their young students "in phonics" for a long, long time before anything interesting is given to them to *read*. "I should never put him into words of one syllable at all. The bigger the word, the more striking the look of it, and therefore, the easier it is to read, provided always that the idea it conveys is interesting to a child."

It is sad to see an intelligent child toiling over a reading lesson infinitely below his capacity—*ath, eth, ith, oth, uth*—or, at the very best, "The cat sat on the mat." "He ate cool noodles at noon with a spoon" is silly. How about: "He ate red lasagna at noon with spoon." This is reading, not just "sounding-out."

Reading lessons should not be twaddle.

Writing—Penmanship is a skill acquired by daily short lessons. After a child is somewhat fluent in it he can go on to gradually fill up his "copy book" with verse and prose that he has chosen. The old-fashioned black-and-white composition books are perfect for this activity. When a child narrates, a parent can take dictation. The child can then copy the dictation (or parts of it if it's a long one) into his copy book. He can tell about his trip to a museum, or tell back an Aesop fable, or tell about anything he is learning. These little narrations can be written in his copy book. Pictures and maps can be drawn and photographs added.

After a child is familiar with narrating orally, he can then begin written narration. This more independent skill should be started no younger than age ten. Instead of "telling aloud" he can "tell" on paper while the teacher makes herself available to any younger students. The teacher may assign a "narration question" such as, "Give a description of Columbus' first voyage to the new world," or "Tell how a honey bee makes honey," or "What four things did you learn from this chapter?" The student need not be overly concerned with spelling in his rough draft but should write freely. The following day attention can be given to the finer points of his writing. Through the regular use of oral narration a student's power to "tell" naturally carries over to his writing.

His written narration is his composition or essay.

Mathematics—Charlotte's book *Home Education* teaches us to begin teaching numbers through the evidence of the senses. Sets or groups of objects such as apples, beans, Lego bricks, buttons, or shells can be arranged in such a way to show addition, subtraction, multiplication, division or fractions.

But true mathematics is when a child begins to *think* in numbers and not in objects. At this point, the illustration should not occupy a more prominent place than the concept being illustrated.

For mathematics, "nothing can be more delightful than the careful analysis of numbers and the beautiful graduation of the work, only one difficulty at a time being presented the mind." The most delightful little word problems are those that have been invented by writers in sympathy with children.

Science—A young child strengthens his powers of observation in his young years by acting as a naturalist. Many children will be able to tell you the names of all the Star Wars characters, but do they know the names of the living things in their own backyards? To lie on his stomach beside a busy ant hill, to lie on his back to follow the drifting clouds, to dig in the soil for earthworms, to stare at a bumble bee, to take note of what time of day the petals of flowers open and close and to recognize their fragrance, to collect fallen leaves, acorns and seeds—these things and more can all be part of a child's "school."

When he is a little older, he can create his own nature notebook, filling it with drawings of his observations and a written record of his findings. These personal notebooks are priceless to their owners because they represent time spent in the glorious outdoors. Glorious it is because nature is one way in which God reveals himself to us. Poems and verses of hymns exclaiming the beauty and wonder of nature can be copied into these nature notebooks.

In a day and age when there is much concern for a child's attention span, the powers of attention and observation gained in the young years through nature study are valuable powers to be used later in any other of the higher sciences (filling out lab reports, etc.).

House Mouse

Wild Strawberry (Fragara Vesca)

April 26 I was glad we hadn't cut the grass yet because I found so many delicate flowering weeds and wild flowers. The girls came running to me calling, "Can we eat these?" They discovered an expansive patch of wild strawberries surrounding the oak tree.

April 29 There was a down pour of rain I was about to close the sliding glass door when a scurrying creature caught my eye. A gray mouse hid in the dry spot behind the drain pipe. With a loud whisper I waved the girls over. We stood staring. "It's the mouse from Peter Rabbit" giggled one sister. "No," argued the younger sister "There's no large pea in its mouth."

Karen Andreola

Pages From My Nature Diary-1989-Tennessee

March 30 Sophia and Yolanda spotted Wild Violets beside the driveway in the shadowy woods.

April 19 My son Nigel was born. The Red Bud trees were in full bloom.

April 22 The girls waded in the creek as the baby and I laid on a quilt. I made the girls wear their bonnets to keep the ticks out of their hair, and their old sneakers to keep the leaches off their toes. Sophia excitedy caught little crayfish with a pet store fish net. Yolanda piled up smooth stones from the creek bottom. Above our heads, high in the blue sky, a hawk circled. I wondered if it had its eye on my baby.

Crayfish

Wild Violet (Viola adunce)

History—Charlotte Mason strongly believed in focusing on the *story* part of history while children are developing their wonderful powers of imagination. Myths and legends have a place, too. This appeal to the imagination in history gives emphasis to its literary side.

According to Charlotte, no history should be read to young children unless it is in literary language. She dwelled on the pleasure derived from a study of former ages—the culture and refinement it affords, the enjoyment and mental profit that is gained through narrating it. She wrote that it is a fatal mistake to think young children must learn "outlines" or overviews of the whole of history of Rome or England [or America]. Isn't this what many history books do by including mostly names, and dates, and events with very little story aspect in between? Instead, Charlotte asserted,

"Let [the child] on the contrary, linger pleasantly over the history of a single man, a short period, until he thinks the thoughts of the man, is at home in the ways of that period. Though he is reading and thinking of the lifetime of a single man, he is really getting intimately acquainted with the history of a whole nation of a whole age . . . Let him know the great people and the common people, the ways of the court and of the crowd. Let him know what other nations were doing while we at home were doing thus and thus."

Books that are biographical in nature provide examples for imitation as well as for warning. The deeds of heroes give us the opportunity to admire and form higher ideals. If you venture to implement Charlotte's ideas in mid-stream, expect a period of transition. Take patience. You will start to recognize little accomplishments, and then bigger ones. Believe in God, believe in your children (and their natural-born curiosity), believe in Charlotte's principles for a gentle art of learning, and you will find joy.

Passages in this article have been taken and used with permission from the new book, A Charlotte Mason Companion—Personal Reflections on the Gentle Art of Learning *by Karen Andreola. All passages in quotes have been taken from Charlotte Mason's Original Homeschooling Series.*

so full of life from her principles that it has continued to be passed down from person to person since her death.

Times Changed

The training given in the House of Education was so famous that, at one time, it was impossible for them to supply the demand for governesses and teachers. However, over the years, especially after the Second World War, governesses and nannies and home-taught children were fast becoming a thing of the past. Parents sent their children to more competitive schools and then the government sanctioned a national curriculum. Today, there are little more than a handful of PNEU schools left. Of these, some have strayed from the original intent and style of program.

However, homeschoolers today have rediscovered Charlotte in a big way! Today's Charlotte Mason movement in home education traces its roots to the publication of Susan Schaeffer Macaulay's *For the Children's Sake*. Mrs. Macaulay had discovered Charlotte's works while living with her family at the L'Abri mission in England. Her book stirred in many the desire to try this warm-hearted and wise-headed form of education, and led ultimately to others making the effort to republish Charlotte's original works.

Charlotte Mason Materials

The slipcased six-volume **Original Charlotte Mason series** is the only series of how-to-teach books I know about that comes endorsed by Her Majesty Queen Elizabeth of England!

Charlotte Mason, as some of you might know, was a nineteenth-century British educator with some marvelous insights and ideas into how to teach children. Inspired by her philosophy, the Parents National Education Union of Great Britain and a number of schools were founded.

Charlotte Mason understood the need to respect the child while not worshipping him. She stressed the importance of the "fallow" first six years of life, when according to her children ought to spend much time out-of-doors playing and observing nature. Among her other contributions: geography taught the way adults like to learn it, through the medium of interesting travel stories; history centered around interesting people and their environments rather than as a list of dates to memorize; the importance of beauty in the child's life and the value of living with great art (in the form of inexpensive art prints); and how to train children in the habit of perfect obedience. This is only the tip of the iceberg, as Miss Mason had many fascinating things to say, all based on her personal experience of decades of teaching.

Having heard of Charlotte Mason, I went years ago in search of her books, only to find that they were not available anywhere, even in the entire St. Louis library system! Dean and Karen Andreola have solved this problem for us. While visiting England, they tracked down the books in the library of Charlotte Mason College and got an American publisher to put out this very nice facsimile edition of six Charlotte Mason books. The series includes *Home Education, Parents and Children, School Education, Ourselves, Formation of Character,* and *A Philosophy of Education*. All are easy reading—remember, British *parents* were inspired by these books! *Mary Pride*

After you've read *For the Children's Sake*, **A Charlotte Mason Companion** should be the next book on your Charlotte Mason reading list. In its 384 pages, Karen Andreola, the world's foremost expert on Charlotte Mason homeschooling (and a *Practical Homeschooling* columnist for several years!), has distilled, amplified, explained, and illustrated

The Original Charlotte Mason series
Parents. $58.95 plus $3 shipping.
*Charlotte Mason Research & Supply,
PO Box 1142, Rockland, ME 04841.
Web: www.charlotte-mason.com.*

NEW!
Charlotte Mason Companion
Parents. $18.99 plus $3 shipping.
*Charlotte Mason Research & Supply,
PO Box 1142, Rockland, ME 04841.
Web: www.charlotte-mason.com.*

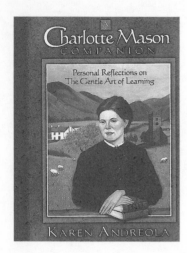

Charlotte's methods for today. Even if you've read—and reread—all six volumes of Charlotte's own "Home Education" series, you're sure to find much to treasure in this book's 49 chapters.

After years of editing her own Charlotte Mason method magazine, the *Parents' Review*, Karen knows the questions parents face when they try to rearrange their thinking and lives to fit this new way of living and learning. Where Charlotte's own writings scatter nuggets here and there, Karen has collected these insights together, rephrased them in more understandable language, and added numerous examples from her own experience and that of other Charlotte Mason families. Whether you want to understand more about how to train a child's will, how and why to use narration instead of written reports, what to do when a child doesn't want to narrate or does poor narrations, how to teach composition and grammar, why and how to study Greek mythology, the right and wrong way to handle picture study, or any of the other special features of Charlotte Mason education, *A Charlotte Mason Companion* will gently and thoroughly lead you like a good friend.

Unlike some other authors, Karen is not just *organizing* Charlotte's thoughts for us, but *explaining* and *applying* them, with many real-life illustrations.

I personally must admit that *A Charlotte Mason Companion* has clarified many things for me that I found obscure in Charlotte's books. But above all, you will enjoy the book's gentle, loving spirit. It's truly, as it is subtitled, "Personal Reflections on the Gentle Art of Learning." Highly recommended. *Mary Pride*

NEW!
Charlotte Mason Study Guide

Parents. $9.95 plus $2 shipping.
*Penny Gardner, P.O. Box 900983,
Sandy UT, 84090. (801) 943-3146.
Email: pennygar@aol.com.
Web: members.aol.com/CMSGpenny.*

In her **Charlotte Mason Study Guide: A Simplified Approach to a "Living Education,"** Penny Gardner has organized Miss Mason's ideas topically. The first of the twenty chapters (or "study topics") of this 166-page book is, appropriately, a study of Charlotte Mason herself. Following topics include Discipline, Geography, Nature Study, Narration, and more on philosophies, goals, and methods of education. Each study topic has brief quotes from the six-volume series, referenced for those who want to read further.

Penny Gardner weaves in just enough additional comments to be helpful and practical without detracting from the central focus of the book. Either as a tasty tidbit or the first course of a lengthy banquet, the *Charlotte Mason Study Guide* provides plenty of food for thought. *Renee Mathis*

For the Children's Sake

Parents. $10.99.
*Crossway Books, 1300 Crescent St.,
Wheaton, IL 60187. Orders: (800) 635-
7993. Inquiries: (630) 682-4300.
Fax: (630) 682-4785.*

For the Children's Sake: Foundations of Education for Home and School is not a "how to" book as much as a beautiful "why to" and "in what manner."

I have never read a book that was more full of joy. Addressing the relationship of Christianity and education, Susan Macaulay shares with us the insights of Charlotte Mason, a teacher extraordinaire from the last century. The sweeping freedom that a child raised God's way can know, and the depth of beauty he or she can enjoy, shines through on every page. The author includes many of her personal experiences as a homeschooled child, and the experiences of her own family as they searched for appropriate education for their children.

A historical note: this is the book that got Dean and Karen Andreola interested in Charlotte Mason's works, which led to Charlotte's books being reprinted, which led to "Charlotte Mason education" becoming one of the main homeschool methods! This is one powerful book. *Mary Pride*

CHAPTER 22

Unschooling

"Unschooling": what is it? Some people refer to the act of removing one's children from the schools, or refusing to enroll them, as "unschooling." This is actually not the right usage, as it confuses unschooling with homeschooling.

Rightly understood, "unschooling" describes both a very popular homeschooling *philosophy* and a popular homeschool *method*.

The Unschooling Philosophy

Let's start with the philosophy. While unschoolers like to argue among themselves as to the fine points of their philosophy, all subscribe to some extent to these main tenets:

1. Trust children
2. Learning happens best in the real world

Trust Children. Unschoolers may differ as to the degree of trust they offer their children, and at what age the children should be allowed to make what decisions, but in general unschooling is a philosophy that encourages children to take charge of their own education. The motto is,

"Back off! Let the kid do as much as possible on his own."

While this might sound like the Robinson philosophy, actually it's the opposite. In the Robinson Method, students follow a course of study designed by the parents or by Dr. Robinson and do the work on their own. In unschooling, the child defines the course of study as much as possible, and may enlist the help of a legion of people, if desired—friends, relatives, mentors, and outside experts.

Real-World Learning. You might, for example, teach writing the traditional way by assigning essays, poems, etc. which are then graded and filed away in a little folder. Alternatively, a child might learn to write the unschooling way by writing actual letters to Grandma, writing shopping lists, writing stories to be submitted to a children's magazine, and so on. A child can learn to read the traditional way by following a strictly tracked

John Holt and "Invited Learning"

John Holt can justly be called one of the fathers of the modern homeschooling movement, particularly its "unschooling" wing. While Holt, now sadly deceased, never married or had any children, he was a keen observer of children and a pioneer thinker in the field of alternative education. When his efforts to reform the schools failed, like all other such efforts, he turned his attention to homeschooling. The result was the first homeschool magazine, *Growing Without Schooling,* and a series of books outlining his theories and findings.

John Holt is the prophet of real-world learning. For years Mr. Holt quietly but insistently taught that children can learn *all by themselves,* without any well-intentioned adult interference. He sees the idea of programmed learning as positively evil. As he so tellingly put it in *How Children Learn,*

> *The difference between fond and delighted parents playing "This Little Piggy Went to Market" with their laughing baby's toes and two anxious home-based would-be clinicians giving "tactile stimulation" to those same toes, so that the child*

will one day be smarter than other children and thus get into the best colleges, may not on the face of it seem to be very much. But in fact it is the difference between night and day. Of two ways of looking at children now growing in fashion—seeing them as monsters of evil who must be beaten into submission, or as little two-legged walking computers whom we can program into geniuses, it is hard to know which is worse.

John Holt did not reject all of Montessori's thought, but he fiercely defended the right of children to tackle the *real* environment. Where Montessori would carefully create a lacing frame for children to practice on, Holt would let them mess with Daddy's shoes. Where Montessori would carefully exclude from her prepared environment all randomness and chance, Holt would be happier in the mess of normal living.

John Holt's motto was "Trust Children." Based on his own observations of children learning and not learning, garnered in real-life situations, Holt believed children really want to learn and that they will learn what they need to know if left entirely to themselves. In actual practice Holt advocated involving children in our adult activities rather than begging them constantly, "What do *you* want to do today?" His theory almost eliminates "teaching" as a profession, other than a master/apprentice type of relationship where the apprentice is eager to learn a particular difficult skill. What a person can learn on his own, Holt says, he should learn on his own—our teachers are not there to tyrannize us, but to offer the help we need.

The Montessori Method

(1) "Observation." According to Montessori "the teacher must refrain from interfering directly. . . . The child educates himself, and when the control and correction of error is yielded of the didactic material [she means when the stuff you hand the kid doesn't confuse him], there remains for the teacher nothing but to observe . . . the teacher teaches little and observes much." In "true" Montessori education, adults do not teach at all. Instead, they closely watch the children in order to see how the environment should be changed to meet their needs. The closest an adult comes to "teaching" a child is in showing him how to use Montessori's materials.

(2) "Individual Liberty." Children are turned loose and allowed to do whatever suits their fancy. This does not result in random play, however, because of the next principle.

(3) "Preparation of the Environment." In Montessori's thought it is very important to "control for error" by only presenting materials that logically relate to one another. Shapes must fit neatly into their allotted slots, graduated cylinders must go up by uniform sizes, color-coded items must logically follow the code, and so on. Thus children are not confused.

The point of this all, as is obvious, is to build a framework for the child. Montessori provides many experiences, and by concentrating deeply on the work provided, the child is able to build his own framework. Montessori called this process "normalization." A "normalized" child learns to look for patterns on his own and to try to fit reality into categories.

"primer" series; on the other hand, he might begin the unschooling way by reading books he picks out himself from the library.

The Unschooling Method

Unschooling is actually a constellation of methods. Among these, the four most significant are

- Preparation of the Environment
- Guided Exploration
- Unguided Exploration
- Constructivism

Preparation of the Environment. Based on the work of Italian doctor and educator Maria Montessori (see sidebar), in its most basic form preparation of the environment means *removing* items which contradict the orderly development of the mind and *including* those items that promote logical learning. It turns out that the home is full of such items, so classrooms that follow Montessori principles end up trying to emulate a well-ordered TV-free home environment! Socks come in matching pairs, cooking pots nest inside each other, cleaning implements have their proper storage places, and so forth. As a child gets older he discovers that mail is sorted into logical piles (bills, junk mail, letters), books in the home library go on appropriate shelves, the encyclopedia volumes are in A–Z order . . . It's no coincidence that the homes of successful homeschoolers are both rich in items to read and use, and that there is an order, understood by the entire family, underlying what may seem to be a riot of books, tapes, art supplies, carpentry tools, etc.

Guided Exploration. Think of guided exploration as "tours" or "field trips." A trusted older person, who knows his way around, takes the student to places he has never been before. Once at the "tour stop" or field-trip site, the student is free to explore, with a guiding eye upon him.

Unschoolers believe in adults sharing their real lives with their children, so in the beginning, the baby goes everywhere the parents can reasonably take her, rather than being left in daycare. As she gets older, the parents start planning special outings designed to expose her to options she might later like to pursue—e.g., symphony concerts, art museums, an architect's office, the United Nations. . . . Again, successful unschoolers try to add as much richness to their children's lives as possible, realizing that sticking only to what interests the parents may shortchange a child whose deepest interests may eventually lie elsewhere.

Unguided Exploration. Recognizing that children throughout history have taken on adult activities and responsibilities at what we today would consider a young age, unschoolers start training their children quite early to be independent. And yes, I said "train." Even though some unschoolers are philosophically opposed to the whole idea of child training, constant encouragement for the child to make his own decisions, and to recognize the consequences of his decisions, is certainly training in independence. Some of this training is in the area of life skills—e.g., a preteen child can learn to handle the stove properly and cook safely, rather than being told to stay away from the stove. Some of this training consists of encouraging the child to pursue ideas and projects that take him away from the home environment. Sometimes the child ventures into environments that have been made familiar through guided exploration, for example trying out for a role in a local theatre production. Teen children might take extended trips on their own or with friends, apprentice to an out-of-state mentor, or simply bike around the town or city to see what's there. I did plenty of this when I was 14 and 15! Eventually, this unguided exploration should result in the child discovering serious interests that result in serious projects that serendipitously develop academic skills.

The outstanding example of how this theory works in practice was given by the first homeschool speaker I ever heard. It was a small meeting, just a few of us, over 20 years ago, and I have forgotten her name, but I remember the story. Her eight-year-old son hated school so much that his behavior became more and more out of control. The final straw came when he dropped on his teacher from an overhanging tree limb, where he had been lurking, and bit her! The school was quick to agree (in a time when schools *never* agreed to this) that this particular child should be educated at home.

Needless to say, we're not talking about a child with huge academic motivation. The parents wisely did not bring out any textbooks, but gave him time to unwind and try out new interests.

One day, the boy told his dad that he wanted to build a raft to float on their pond. The dad asked him, "How many board feet of lumber will you need?" This led to a discussion of how area is length times width. Eventually the son had to learn to multiply, divide, add, and subtract, all in the context of building his raft. The use of tools was learned, and books about raft and boat design were dug out. Now the boy had to learn to read, which he did. By the time he had built his raft, he had learned all the math and reading the school was trying unsuccessfully to teach him, plus some.

Because of the many true stories like this, unschoolers tend to believe that *any* interest, faithfully followed, will lead to a child learning all the basics, plus of course the additional math, science, diplomatic skills, or whatever is involved in the particular area of interest.

Maria Montessori

Maria Montessori (1870–1952), Italian founder of the educational philosophy that has led among other things to a network of "Montessori Schools" worldwide, was a medical doctor, carefully observing children and making notes about what they liked and disliked. Asked to take over the education of some Italian slum children, she put her theories into practice and stunned the world by turning these children into adept scholars.

What did she do? She gave the children pieces of equipment carefully designed to help them learn adult skills: wooden frames with canvas attached and string for practicing lacing, frames for buttoning, frames for using the button-hook devices of that day. She gave them materials they could feel with their hands: textured blocks, letter stencils, number stencils. She gave them grown-up tools scaled down to child's size: pots and pans, brooms and mops. She gave them responsibility for doing as adult a job as possible. Children in Montessori's own school served themselves lunch and cleaned up afterwards, although they were only three to five years old.

Having prepared the environment as carefully as she could to be free of distractions, Montessori and her teachers sat back and watched. They might show a child how to use a piece of apparatus; then they would withdraw and let the children learn as much as they could totally unaided. The data was there—hands-on experiences by the roomful. The framework was there—carefully graduated exercises led the children almost imperceptibly to reading, writing, and figuring. The children learned.

Awed by Montessori's success, teachers all over the world descended on her. In time she ended up writing several books and teaching others to carry on her work. The "Montessori method" is now taught by several different societies and in hundreds of schools and preschools, as well as homeschools.

Constructivism

Constructivism. An educational method popularized by Dr. Seymour Papert, inventor of the LOGO programming language and author of several influential books, constructivism holds that children learn best when they discover facts for themselves.

Jean Piaget, the Swiss educator, and a name that unschoolers have been invoking for decades, came up with the slogan, "To understand is to invent." Papert puts it this way in his book *The Connected Family*: "The role of the teacher is to create the conditions for invention rather than to provide ready-made knowledge."

This sounds like our old friend John Dewey, who brought the Prussian educational system back to the United States, and his belief that all knowledge is based on personal experience—i.e., book-learning stinks. But actually constructivism is far more complex than that. Where Dewey espoused "learning by doing," constructivists espouse "learning by building."

As long as we're talking real-world projects based on an intense interest, learning by building is a good thing. I know of homeschool families that have built airplanes, cars, houses, rafts, playhouses, corrals, and museum exhibits. But of course, no one family can do *all* of this! It's also clear that the sum of human knowledge can not be achieved through hands-on real-world projects. It's also clear that lawyers, unions, and available space all conspire to make large-scale, permanent, meaningful projects of any kind impossible in today's classrooms.

Microworlds

Constructivists have risen to the challenge by inventing **microworlds**. These are specialized learning environments, usually in the form of computer software and/or construction kits such as Lego bricks. By playing with these materials, children are led to discover facts about school subjects on their own.

In the most famous example, the LOGO programming language teaches children not only the rudiments of programming, but also logic and strategy, as the children attempt to "tell" the LOGO turtle to draw various shapes on the computer screen. Other examples of microworlds are the Discovering Geometry software series from Key Curriculum Press, Interactive Physics from MSE Software, and KidPix from Mattel Interactive. In Discovering Geometry the student can manipulate geometric shapes and observe how his actions affect their properties. In Interactive Physics, the student can create his own virtual gizmos, assign them velocity and acceleration vectors, vary the gravity, and see what happens. In KidPix, the child is given a number of art tools, sounds, and effects, which he may combine in any way. One last, very familiar, example is the game of chess. Again, the board is a "microworld" upon which the student may apply his ideas about strategy and see how they literally play out.

Microworlds of this nature are **excellent** at teaching logic and strategy, which probably explains the huge improvements in school skills reported by those who use them with underprivileged children, whose real-world lives tend to be liven in the present moment without much concern or hope for the future consequences of present actions. A little training in logic and strategy can go a long way towards encouraging such children to take charge of their own lives, rather than to passively roll with the punches. However, homeschooled children have many other avenues to learn logic and strategy, starting with Dad's old chess set.

Software Company Addresses

- **Discovering Geometry software series:** Key Curriculum Press, (800) 995-MATH, www.keypress.com
- **Interactive Physics:** MSE Software, (800) 766-6615, www.msesoftware.com.
- **KidPix:** Learning Company, c/o Mattel Interactive, (800) 521-6263, www.shopmattel.com.

John Holt's Books

How Children Learn, $11. How Children Fail, $11. Teach Your Own, $11.95. Escape from Childhood, $9.95. What Do I Do Monday, $6.95. Instead of Education, $8.95. Shipping extra. *Holt Associates, 2269 Massachusetts Ave., Cambridge, MA 02140. (617) 864-3100. Fax: (617) 864-9235. Email: HoltGWS@aol.com. Web: www.holtgws.com.*

How Children Fail and **How Children Learn** are John Holt's firsthand observations of children doing both, along with some very penetrating analysis of why children learn, or fail to learn.

Teach Your Own is his book about home schooling: why and how to do it. It is an excellent introduction to the subject. Holt's chapter answering objections against homeschooling is particularly valuable.

What Do I Do Monday? comes from a period when Mr. Holt was still trying to reform the public school system. This brilliantly insightful book has long sections of suggestions on how to teach some difficult subjects, with the thoughts on math being especially helpful.

In **Instead of Education** Holt starts to look beyond the "school" system, whether public or private. He raises some serious questions in this book.

Holt's book on children's rights, **Escape from Childhood**, while provocative, is utopian in tone and therefore not as valuable. *Mary Pride*

Microworlds are **good** for getting deeply into some aspects of math and science, since these subjects are themselves simplifications of what we see in the real world around us. They are also suitable for computer art and music, which by their nature work with limited media and a limited number of musical notes and rhythms.

Microworlds are **lousy** for any non-mechanical, descriptive, or research-oriented discipline. As my husband Bill says, "You can't build history!"

Microworlds are an extreme example of preparation of the environment. They tap into our deep human urge to build and make sense of the universe, which is why some students become obsessed with them. The more chaotic and unstructured the child's environment, the more benefit he gains from a logic-based microworld.

In the unschooling world, children tend to create their own microworlds. One of the first homeschooling books, *Better Than School,* chronicled among many other things how the author's children spent weeks creating miniature worlds with small toys, using them to tell deeply involved stories. I have observed my own children doing the same thing with their Beanie Babies, and before that, with dolls they made from old-fashioned wooden clothes pins. They have also assembled furniture with a hammer and nails, sewed simple clothing, and created their own recipes. They have *not* made a puncheon floor, milled their own lumber, made their own cider, or done any of the other thousand things our ancestors did because they had to.

Which brings us to the reason constructivism can not be your *only* educational method—it takes too much time, too many resources, and too much money to discover how to do everything on your own (if you even could!). It's much quicker to read the "Little House" books and learn from them how to make a puncheon floor, or read the science book and find out how the water cycle works. Scientific theories can be deduced from a cleverly designed series of experiments, but if an adult designs the experiments to make sure the child learns everything he is supposed to, that defeats the purpose of having the child discover knowledge on his own, doesn't it?

Sim No More

As for the use of simulations for any subject involving human behavior, John Taylor Gatto handles that nicely:

Simulation games are a notorious example [of how behavioral theory is destructive] because they suggest through their operations that human affairs are only simple games, less complicated than chess, in which mathematical strategies always prevail. The destructive effect of simulations appears to be cumulative. As a teacher I stayed away from them as if they were toadstools.

"How do we know if our children are learning what school covers? How do we report unschooling/homeschooling to schools?"

Nancy Plent, the founder of the Unschoolers Network of NJ, compiled the curricular goals for each year of school and translated them into real-life situations unschoolers can relate to. Packed with suggestions for meeting and exceeding these guidelines, the **Living is Learning Curriculum Guides** double as record-keepers to help you organize your children's learning into an "after-the-fact" curriculum that schools can recognize. Compiled from national and state curricular guidelines, these book help you see what is going on in most schools for each grade level. A confidence builder for anyone wondering if they have what it takes to "cover" a year of learning without going to school.
Used by permission from the writeup in John Holt's Bookstore catalog

However, as a part of the unschooling educational mix, constructivism does provide an additional motivational and learning pathway.

The Top Ten

Unschoolers live or die by how well the learner is motivated. True motivation comes from *inside*, but it comes as a response to something *outside:* an interest, a person, a piece of the community that a child wants to be a part of. With that in mind, I humbly present this list of the top ten characteristics of successful unschooling families. They:

1. Go lots of interesting places and take the kids
2. Own lots of books and leave them where the children can handle them
3. Read a lot in front of their children
4. Talk to their children on an adult level from a very young age
5. Teach their children the rules of analysis, logic, and debate, through critical watching of videos, discussion of educational issues and political topics, drawing the child's attention to obvious hype in an ad, etc.
6. Are observant of their children's abilities and moods and like to journal them
7. Involve the children in necessary chores
8. Involve the children in meaningful family projects, not as a "schoolish" attempt to drag in education, but because the work is important, it has to be done, and the children are able to help
9. Have interesting adult friends to whom they introduce their children, encouraging them to become comfortable in the company of adults and to look upon adults as potential resources and mentors from an early age
10. Connect to other unschooling families online, through magazines, or in person

Unschooling is an adventure, for the adventurous. If all you do is sit at home and watch TV, you'd better skip this method. But if your life is filled with friends and activities, if you live where children are free to explore (here city or country both beat suburbs), or you simply feel it's time to break the mold and go boldly where you've never gone before, unschooling may be for you.

CHAPTER 23

Unit Studies

What is a unit study? If you are only beginning to think about homeschooling, you may have no idea. If you have friends who do unit studies, you may have a vague notion of lots of time spent sewing costumes, cooking ethnic meals, and acting out history and science lessons. Depending on your personality, this either sounds like a horrendous waste of time or scads of fun.

Despite the impression many people seem to have, unit studies are not undirected fun and games. They are a highly effective way to:

- Integrate school subjects—that is, you'll be using and learning skills and facts from many "subjects" all at once instead of in lessons separated into "math," "science," "history," and so on
- Include many family members in the same learning experience
- Liven your homeschool up
- Make a seemingly stuffy topic more memorable and enjoyable
- Prepare your child for real-world learning

Jessica Hulcy, whose wisdom adorns this chapter in several places, is perhaps the world's foremost expert on the use of unit studies in the homeschool. Jessica is co-author of the popular KONOS family of unit-study curriculum and products. You'll find our review of her curriculum in Chapter 37, along with reviews of other well-known and not-so-well-known unit studies programs.

How Units Work

A "unit" starts with a topic or theme. Theoretically, this could be anything. However, in homeschool curriculum circles, unit themes tend to be:

- **Character traits** (the ATII curriculum and KONOS curriculum)
- **Literature/authors** (the Calvert School units on Beatrix Potter and Laura Ingalls Wilder and the Five in a Row series, for example)
- **Science topics** (Kym Wright's units and the Media Angels Creation Science Units, for example)
- **Countries** (Teaching with God's Heart for the World)
- **Historical figures and events** (TRISMS, KONOS History of the World)
- **Fun topics** (Amanda Bennet's units on Baseball and Olympics, for example)

1. **More with Less Stress.** Teach all you can to everyone at one time.
2. **Fit, Not Fat.** Include as many academic subjects in each unit *that fit*, **BUT** do not force every subject into every unit.
3. **Read On!** Read deep and wide, from classic literature to reference books.
4. **First Things First.** Cover your basics in the morning.
5. **Write What You Know.** Teach language arts by writing from first-hand experience.
6. **Awe Them.** Teach multi-level by starting with a single hands-on activity that produces a sense of wonder.
7. **Efficiency Counts.** Choose only worthwhile, multi-purpose activities that kill more than one purpose with a stone.
8. **Handle With Care.** Use textbooks as a resource/information overview *only*.
9. **Dejunk.** Use only the workbook pages necessary for remedial use; throw the rest away.
10. **Teach Them to Learn and to Love to Learn.** Be obsessed with *process* not *product* in the younger years.
11. **Closure.** Wrap up each unit with a bang, such as show-and-tell at the dinner table, a medieval feast, a kid-created natural history museum, or a field trip.

Once you've picked your theme, you then come up with a number of activities designed to shed information on your theme topic.

This is where the confusion about unit studies arises. Some prepackaged unit studies have activities with little or no direct connection to the theme. Such units seem to be constructed like this:

"We're going to study trees.
"Trees are used to make cardboard.
"Cardboard is used in boxes.
"So we will do a bunch of crafts using cardboard boxes and we'll study the history of box-making."

Can anyone tell me what this has to do with our original theme of "trees"?

I call this "unit splatter." Someone drops the theme on the floor and you wind up studying the splatters that lands two yards away.

A *good* unit study will provide the following:

- **No splatter.** Activities and discussion questions are directly related to the theme.
- **Activities that include a variety of school subjects that *naturally* fit a study of the theme.** Typically, you'll read and do some research, do some writing, act out or dramatize persons or things studied, make models of things studied, do demonstrations or experiments that illustrate scientific principles studied, memorize some facts or famous sayings, build a working something-or-other, and play some educational games. Math problems may also be included, but beware, as this tends to be the fake and useless part of most unit studies. The most popular units curriculums all suggest you study math separately and systematically.
- **An excellent *annotated* reading list**—so you can tell which of the books you want to bother obtaining and studying
- **Lists of materials needed** lesson by lesson
- **Activities for both older and younger learners**

Let's see how this works in practice by going through a totally fictional unit I just made up: the Star Trek unit study.

In case you're wondering why I keep mentioning Star Trek, it's because research has shown that over 50 percent of the American public consider themselves Star Trek fans, and just about all of the other 50 percent have watched the show at least a few times. Plus, this is a topic you will *not* see in any curriculum package soon, so we can concentrate on how a unit works without worrying if you should do any of these activities.

The Purely Hypothetical Star Trek Unit Study

Let's hypothesize that you are obsessed with Star Trek. You want to learn all about the show and everything related to it.

This is the very definition of a unit study. In the real world, whenever you say,

"I want to learn everything I can about this,"

you are embarking on a unit study.

How to Spot & Avoid Mindless Unit Studies

Some units can verge on the ridiculous. Such units seem to be arduously contrived instead of flowing together naturally. Here are three red flags to beware of in units.

Beware of Units that Miss the Big Picture

If a unit revolves around American history, *The Witch of Blackbird Pond* is a natural book to read. If the unit launches off into pond life, for the sake of adding science to the unit, then the entire point of the book has been lost as well as the point of the unit. *The Witch of Blackbird Pond* is about Puritan history, tolerance and intolerance, obedience and disobedience, love and hate, not about pond life.

For a unit to be well constructed, each activity should contribute to the big picture rather than strain at minutia or incidentals. All activities should build on the same general theme, rounding out the unit.

Units should be as carefully woven as fabric is woven. It makes no sense to be weaving with yarn and then to insert a piece of barbed wire.

Beware of Units that Integrate Every Subject in Every Unit

Sometimes integrating every subject in every unit simply does not fit. A unit on air pressure should not "force" art into the unit just to check art off the list of subjects covered. While an art activity such as "paint or draw air" is a definite waste of time, another art activity to paint with a straw is not a waste of time. As the child sucks paint into the straw, places his finger over the end of the straw, and then releases his finger and slings paint on the paper, he is using the principle of air pressure he has just learned. This art activity reinforces the main theme of the unit.

Let's face it. Some units are heavy on science or history while other units are heavy on art or music. Many moms are frustrated, when they cannot have 30 minutes of each subject balanced perfectly in each unit. This attitude causes the natural flow of a unit to be lost.

Beware of Units that Have No Higher Purpose

Christians should teach children not only units of WHAT but also units of WHY. All knowledge should further our understanding of God as well as equip us to operate in the world. Units on simple machines, inventions, and the Industrial Revolution should emphasize the common character traits of the inventors such as resourcefulness and persistence. Children should focus on the character traits of those they study. While studying grains and bread, parents should point children to "the bread of life" which is in the Word of God and to the bread of communion which represents the body of Christ. As we study units on stars and planets, the goal for our children should be to crack open a door of wonderment revealing an incredible God of orderliness, creativity, and design.

Pointing to a higher purpose need not be contrived. Beyond all facts, figures and activities is the Creator of the universe whom we want our children to know personally. The more Christian parents study His Word, the more we will see it evidenced in everything from gardening to Beethoven, and the more we will pass this wonder on to our children.

—*Jessica Hulcy,* from her article in the first issue of *Practical Homeschooling*

Projects Are Not Enough

There are many new unit study curricula out on the homeschool market, yet a closer look reveals that all unit studies are not created equal.

Successful unit studies not only have a central theme and offer many related activities and projects based on that theme, they also encourage discovery learning.

Discovery learning is not merely the absence of instructions; it is the absence of instruction *plus* the presence of carefully constructed open-ended questions that lead children to the next thought, then the next thought, and finally to the big concept that connects their single activity to the larger issue being studied.

—*Jessica Hulcy*

Real Units Are Great!

Unit studies are great when done right. In fact, I believe *every* homeschool should include at least *some* unit studies, even if you choose another method for your core curriculum.

The warnings against "twaddly" and "mindless" unit studies in this chapter are meant to help you avoid bogus units so you can experience the joys of *real* units—unit studies that allow a child to get deeply into a beloved or much-needed theme, pulling it all together in the same way that adults do when we find a topic that fascinates us.

So, what would a serious Star Trek fan do?

- Watch every episode
- Learn all about the actors
- Purchase reference works, such as *Scotty's Guide to the Starship Enterprise,* and memorize the blueprints
- Engage in online or in-person discussion with other fans about the episodes, the ship design, the actors, the writers . . .
- Make a costume
- Play games based on the show
- Attend conventions
- Collect action figures and other "stuff" related to the show
- Learn Klingon

If you doubt any of this, see the video *Trekkies.* Real fans go a *lot* farther than this!

The Not-So-Hypothetical Charles Dickens Unit Study

Now, let's pick something a little closer educationally to what we really want our children to learn. Let's say your unit study will be on Charles Dickens. You'll . . .

- Read a few/some/many/all of his books (depending on time available)
- Read a biography of Dickens
- Maybe get distracted by the art in the Dickens book you read and read a biography of his most famous illustrator as well
- Discuss the stories in the books
- Make a costume so you can dress up like a Dickens character and/or act out scenes from a Dickens book
- Make crafts mentioned in the book you read
- Play games mentioned in the book you read
- Cook and eat a type of food mentioned in the book you read (Christmas goose and plum pudding are good!)
- Start slipping phrases from Dickens into your everyday conversation
- Study the culture of England during the time of Dickens
- Improve your vocabulary with words from the writing of Dickens

I could go on, but you get the point. You're immersing yourself in the world and work of Charles Dickens. Along the way you are practicing the following skills: reading, writing, analyzing, discussing, sewing, constructing, cooking, vocabulary improvement, and history. If you feel the need, you could add

- Science, by studying inventors who lived at the time of Dickens or whose inventions solved some of the problems people experienced in Dickens' books
- Geography of the British Isles
- Sociology, via the class structure of Dickens' England
- and so forth.

Of course, if what you really want to study is science, you're better of with the books of Jules Verne or David Macaulay!

Any attempt to drag in such topics as nuclear chemistry or genetic engineering would have to be grafted onto the topic of Dickens, as it does not flow naturally from the subject matter. This is one reason why it's important to either use a packaged curriculum that covers all school topics over time, or have a game plan of your own that ensures you won't miss any important topics.

The Match Game

It's also important to match the depth of your unit study to the interest of your students.

A "shallow" unit study is one that just introduces a theme. Taking Charles Dickens as our example again, you'd read *one* book, read a few paragraphs of facts about Dickens' life included in the unit study, and do a few simple activities that take no more than a hour or two combined. Just about any kid can suffer through this, even if he has no interest in Charles Dickens whatsoever.

A "medium" unit study adds more depth by including more books, possibly an entire biography, and more time-consuming activities (e.g., cooking and eating that Christmas goose!).

A "deep" unit study would take everything in the list on the left page and add to it. Perhaps you'd join an online Dickens newsgroup, or go to England and take a "Dickens tour." You'd study the court system and prison system at the time of Dickens—two important topics in his books. You might follow Mr. Micawber and study the Australian Emigration, or do a report on the plight of orphans in that time period and what reforms followed. All this requires a much deeper interest and commitment, or even the "fun" activities will be like pulling teeth.

Homeschool author and speaker Gregg Harris suggests the solution of what he calls "Delight Directed Studies." The student picks the unit topic, and the parent helps him develop activities related to the topic of interest. For more information on Gregg's approach, see his book *The Christian Home School*, reviewed in Chapter 6.

Teaching Many Kids at Once

A highly-touted advantage of unit studies is that the whole family can study the same unit at the same time, thus cutting down on Mom's workload.

This is partly true (students of all ages *can* study the same unit at the same time) and partly not (unit studies do not necessarily cut down on your workload). What you save in time that would be spent grading workbooks for different age levels will likely be soaked up in time spent shopping for and organizing materials needed for the clever unit projects, and in time spent doing those clever projects!

The main tricks to teaching children of different ages using the same unit study are:

- Let an older child read the books to the younger ones who can't read that well yet
- Give the older children more intense research and writing assignments

For example, if the whole family is studying Dickens' *A Christmas Carol,* the oldest child can read this aloud while the younger ones gather around. Then the twelfth-grader can research and write about the plight of workers

Take a "Unit Studies" Break

If you want to try unit studies, but aren't ready to make it your full curriculum, summertime and vacations are ideal. Units have a higher "fun factor" than any other method, so they fit well with the extra family time and fun feeling of these breaks from other methods.

I would suggest a shallow or medium unit study for starters, as you're just trying to get a taste of this method, not a full meal.

in Dickens' England, the tenth-grader can write a page of Dickensian dialogue, the fourth-grader can write an invitation to Tiny Tim's house, and the first-grader can practice printing simple vocabulary words from the story. Everyone can join in on the group projects: singing carols, cooking and eating a Christmas feast, making and wearing a nightcap like Scrooge's, and acting out the scenes where the Ghost of Christmas Past confronts our heroic villain (or is it our villainous hero?). The whole family can also join in on the discussion of why Scrooge started out so mean, how God feels about employers who fail to provide for their employees, why some people have no friends while others have plenty, and other fascinating topics that arise naturally from the story.

Now, for a more in-depth look at unit studies, I turn you over to *Practical Homeschooling*'s resident unit study expert, Jessica Hulcy.

Jessica Hulcy on the Difference Between Public School Units & Homeschool Unit Studies

Public education and homeschool have different goals for unit studies. While one may seek to camouflage the actual course of study, the other seeks to preserve children's sense of wonder.

In public schools, unit studies are usually called "study units."

More than the name is different, though. Although both "study units" (or just "units," as they are often called) and "unit studies" bring many subjects together under one main unit topic, the goals of most public school "units" is either to fill up the time with trivialities such as constructing a shoe box village to make holders for valentine cards (here the "subjects" employed are art and holidays) or to indoctrinate children in a politically correct worldview.

Such public school units often blur the lines of separation between the different academic subjects, so parents have difficulty determining what subjects are actually being studied and what material is actually being covered. Conscientious parents may become frustrated when their ability to oversee their child's education is nullified, because the all-in-one teaching of units obscures the fact that Johnny is really not learning science or history, but instead is studying politically correct ways to preserve the rain forest.

Units Are Naturals At Home

At home it is a different story. Here, integrating subjects allows subjects to be taught naturally in an unfragmented approach. Units preserve the unity, the interrelatedness and the wonder of God's creation. Unit studies work well for homeschooling, because the art teacher is the history teacher and the English teacher all rolled into one—Mom! The only faculty meeting necessary to correlate the subjects is in Mom's mind. An art project, say a papoose carrier, can fit right into a history demonstration and an English report on the Apache Indians. When students dramatize the Constitutional Convention, they are covering the subjects of history, drama, speech, debate, and even art through the making of their costumes. A unit on the classification of plants *must* be accomplished by reading *The Secret Garden* (at least, *I* think so!). Yes, the lines are blurred between the subjects, yet when subjects are meshed together, each is enhanced by the others.

Cynthia Pilling, the KONOS representative in Florida, recently trained a group of parents in How To Teach with Unit Studies. Instead of telling them how to integrate subjects and make learning hands-on and fun, she decided to teach them by giving an actual lesson. Her unit topic was "birds." Naturally, she would have included sketching birds as well as reading about John James Audubon, but her real goal was to have the parents participate in a hands-on activity. Laying out an assortment of tools that represented the birds' beaks as well as an assortment of birds' food, the parents were instructed to choose the best beak for the various foods. Nuts were cracked by pliers, a coffee filter was used to catch flying insects (mini marshmallows), while tongs were used to dig through peanut butter (mud) to pluck out a prized gummy worm.

For exercise, Cynthia had the parents stand up and flap their *wings* to see if their muscles tired easily. Then she told them how fast the humming-bird flapped its wings. They were amazed! As they talked about nests of birds, Cynthia passed out a milk carton cap to each parent. Placing one navy bean in each cap, she told them that the cap was the size of a hum-mingbird nest and the bean was the size of a hummingbird egg.

Although there had been much talking and bantering by the "students" during the other activities, as soon as the size of the hummingbird egg was revealed, all became quiet. The sense of wonder had overtaken them.

One mom put it so well when she said, "I knew it was small, but I never realized it was like this." Cynthia commented to the group of awestruck parents, "Isn't this what you want to give to your children?" A sense of wonder had been preserved.

Units Are More Than Projects

I encourage homeschooling parents who desire to raise thinkers to employ the methods of discovery *and* dialogue. Real thinkers cannot help but be educated. As my friend, Erin Blain, says, "Be obsessed with education, not graduation." Allow graduation to take its proper place as the icing on the cake of education.

Product-oriented education is obsessed with the answer, rather than the thought behind the answer. Dialogue, on the other hand, draws answers out of students, while demanding that students think in the process.

Anyone who has seen the movie *Shadowlands*, recounting the life of C. S. Lewis, has seen the art of dialogue at its best. At Oxford and Cambridge, young men came to class ready to dialogue with their mentor about what they had read. C. S. Lewis posed question after question to the students, each time insisting that the views they held be proved and supported.

> **While a workbook asks for a single word to be regurgitated, dialogue asks for an original thought to be articulated and supported.**

Because homeschool class sizes are small, homeschooling parents have the unique opportunity to use dialogue to stretch their child's reasoning and thinking ability by asking open-ended questions, such as, "What would happen if . . . ?", "Which solution do you think is best?", "Can you support your belief?"

Beware of unit activities that end with phrases such as, "tell your children . . ." or "read to your children . . ." as the consistent bottom line. Of course, as parents we are continually speaking and reading to our children, but if your curriculum ends there, you are merely teaching on the surface.

Only when you engage in dialogue with your children do you dig into the heart of learning, encouraging your children to think and understand.

Projects make your units memorable; research projects teach your children how to learn; dialogue makes your children wise. And wisdom, not a mere discovery and regurgitation of facts, is the real goal of all education, including unit studies.

CHAPTER 24

Contests

"Contests as a homeschool method? What possessed you to make this an entire chapter?"

Here's what happened. Over the years, I have been chronicling the achievements of homeschooled children in my magazine, *Practical Homeschooling*. I began to notice that some families frequently had "Show & Tell" pieces to submit about their children. It seemed that those families were using contests as a major part of their curriculum.

"Interesting," I thought. "I know my own children get really serious about a subject as a contest approaches." We're talking kids who *pressure* me into signing them up for the Spelling Bee, Art Fair, and every local math contest that comes down the pike. I knew from experience that most of these contests involve learning facts and skills above and beyond the regular curriculum. Plus, we have discovered that many of them have curriculum available to help you study for the contest—whether it's math problem sets from previous years, or spelling lists from the Spelling Sisters (reviewed in volume 2).

So, yes,

Contests are a *motivational* method

and if you so desired,

Contests could form an entire curriculum.

Homeschoolers have done well in many of them—taking first place at the National Geography Bee and first, second, and third place at one year's National Spelling Bee, for instance. The Richman kids alone must have won or placed in several dozen contests, judging from the reports in the Pennsylvania Homeschoolers newsletter, and I must admit I've had to designate a "ribbon drawer" for the smaller awards of my own kids!

See Appendix 4 . . .

for a huge list of contests your homeschooled children can enter.

Ugh! Contests!

I know some of you might be thinking, "Contests?! Ugh! Competition between children is something we wanted to get away from by homeschooling! Forget it, contests aren't for us." I'm sort of that way too—I don't feel comfortable with the kind of nastiness over rankings that can develop *at school* when kids compete. Worthwhile contests *at home* can be a whole different experience—something that you as parents can fully monitor, discuss, and assess. You can choose just what to encourage your child to participate in, and there is no peer group to taunt losers.

—*Sue Richman*

Laurie and Harvey Bluedorn are the founders of Trivium Pursuit, a provider of classical education products for homeschoolers. Laurie's insights on this page were taken from a column she wrote for *Practical Homeschooling*. You can find reviews of some of the Bluedorn's products in volumes 2 and 3. To request their catalog: Trivium Pursuit, 139 Colorado St., Suite 186, Muscatine, IA 52761. (309) 537-3641. Email: trivium@muscanet.com. Web: www.muscanet.com/~trivium.

Contests are an educational experience especially suited for home-schooled students. What can contests do for your child academically? Consider:

Laurie Bluedorn on Contests as Motivators

Envision a typical homeschool assignment. Mom asks Henry to write a composition on "What Valentine's Day Means to Me." Henry is not particularly interested in Valentine's Day and knows his finished composition will go no further than Mom's eyes and then into the three-ring binder on the schoolroom bookshelf. As a consequence, his motivation level is mediocre and his effort half-hearted.

But suppose Mom tells Henry she wants him to draw a scene from inter-galactic space and write a scientific narrative of that scene. Henry, who is the local expert on space exploration, lights up at this idea. When she tells him they will enter his drawing and narrative in the Intergalactic Art Competition (part of the Space Science Student Involvement Program), and he might win an all-expenses paid trip to the National Space Science Symposium in Washington, D.C. . . . well, the fire is lit; and look out world, Henry has a lot to say on that subject. It was a combination of good topic, competition, and reward that did the trick.

How Contests Develop Research Skills

To be sure, writing a scientific narrative on space exploration will take more than your 1952 *Encyclopædia Britannica*, so off to the library you go. Here is the perfect opportunity to teach the lad how to research. You will want to use a good college or university library along with your own local library. Arrange for personal interviews. And don't forget to tap into the Internet.

A contest can bring together all the skills you've taught your children into one exciting finalé. To write this paper on space exploration, numerous subjects will be covered: grammar, spelling, punctuation, science, penmanship or typing skills, logic (construction of arguments), and rhetoric (expressing your point in an eloquent manner). So this one essay contest is not just "another composition" to write, but an entire unit study in itself, with the final product bringing—as Jessica Hulcy says—"closure."

How Contests Develop Character Qualities

Many of these contests take a long time to complete. Some, such as a Science and Engineering Fair science project, will take an entire school year. It develops perseverance and diligence. Contests can seem overwhelming and unmanageable if you only look at the whole picture, but by planning and organization the process can be broken down into bite-size pieces. The student strives toward his goal, doing his best, and in the end can obtain the "satisfaction and pride of a job well done" (as Ranger Bill would say).

Some contests require teamwork. The national "Written & Illustrated By . . ." awards contest provided an opportunity for my oldest daughter Johannah to teach her younger sister Helena watercolor techniques.

Because of their flexible schedules, homeschooled students are at an advantage in contest participation. The first contest we ever entered was a local science fair. I learned about this competition only two weeks before it was held, so we devoted those two weeks full-time to the contest. What an exciting experience! That was back in 1989, but all the kids remember the fun of those days. Two weeks of pure science, not to be distracted by Latin declensions.

Sue Richman on Types of Contests

Here are a few things to keep in mind:

There are many types of contests. Some will be more suitable for your family and your children than others. I have a broad definition of a contest. Sending a piece of writing or artwork into a children's magazine for possible publication is like a contest in many ways, as is preparing for and passing an Advanced Placement (AP) exam in the late high school years.

Some contests have many winners. An art contest my daughters entered offers about 1,000 awards to the 4,000 U.S. entries. Last year both girls were thrilled to get silver and bronze medals and simple art supplies as prizes. Other contests have only a very few winners, which may be discouraging to some children.

Winners must sometime meet certain criteria, as in the AP program or the Presidential Sports Award program. Everyone who meets the established scale of excellence receives credit; you're not competing against others, you are competing against a clear standard.

Money rewards or trips, like to Washington, D.C. for final award ceremonies, are a part of some contests. Others offer plaques, certificates, or other formal recognition.

The "Written and Illustrated by . . ." contest publishes several wonderful books created by children each year. Each winning student also receives scholarship money and full royalties on his or her book. For the history buff, the *Concord Review* is a professional journal that publishes high school students' history research papers. Often college scholarships are offered, as in the National Merit Scholarship program for high school juniors who take the PSAT exam. Again, the thing to keep in perspective is that the better the prize, the fewer the winners. Prepare your kids accordingly!

Contests are local and national. Locally, our daily paper ran an editorial cartoon competition for high school students. Nationally, NewsCurrents sponsors an annual editorial cartoon contest for kids. It's up to you to decide which type of contest you want to encourage your kids to enter.

Sue Richman on Eight Benefits of Entering Contests

It's a Wednesday morning. A group of elementary-age kids are gathered around a table cluttered with test papers, math games, and manipulatives, all listening to another child explaining how she solved a tricky problem from this month's Math Olympiad set. She's diagramming her solution on the large chalkboard, and others are waving their hands to share how their ways of going about the problem were somewhat different.

Think this must be a school classroom? Wrong! It's our monthly homeschool Math Olympiad meeting. What's the Math Olympiad? It's a wonderful international competition for elementary age students that annually involves about 80,000 public and private school children in challenging math problem solving. We started the very first homeschool team 11 years ago, and now groups of homeschoolers all across the country are starting to take part.

The Math Olympiad is just one national program that our four homeschooled kids have taken part in over the years. Many team or group con-

Sue Richman is a Practical Homeschooling columnist and the co-founder of Pennsylvania Homeschoolers. Among many other things, they offer a terrific set of AP online courses. See their writeup in chapter 42.

Yet More Types of Contests

Don't forget local **sports contests.** Our children have participated in swim meets and martial arts tournaments so far, with soccer looming in the future. Such events provide goals that help kids measure their progress realistically against others and provide incentive for some extra workouts.

4-H and **state fairs** are another arena in which homeschooled children often compete—and succeed!

Outcome-Based Contests?

When it comes to the Olympic Games, everyone seems to understand that competition produces the winners and the record-breakers. It's unlikely that the athletes could reach such heights of achievement and endurance if they were not competing against other athletes who are closely matched in skills and putting forth their very best.

Some people, however, are at war against the whole concept of competition. They think it is undemocratic, unfair, and elitist. It's a sign of the times that, in Cecile County, Maryland, basketball is now played by some very unusual rules. If one basketball team is ten points ahead of the other, additional baskets don't count until the underdog team catches up. No record is kept of who scores how many baskets, so no player can ever be recognized as the star of the team.

This system should be called Outcome-Based Basketball because it's just like the Outcome-Based Education (OBE) that has spread through our public schools like a contagious disease. OBE is sometimes called Performance-Based Education.

OBE does not allow any student to progress faster or farther than the slowest child in the class. This system conceals the fact that some children aren't learning much of anything. What is the teacher to do with the faster learners after they complete the assigned material? They are required to do peer tutoring (trying to tutor the slower pupils) or "horizontal enrichment." The former is a frustration for all students, and the latter is just busywork.

"Self-esteem" is OBE's mantra. Since the lack of self-esteem is postulated to be the cause of all social ills (crime, illegal drugs, teenage pregnancies, AIDS, and low SAT scores), OBE's primary goal is to inculcate self-esteem. There is no evidence that lack of self-esteem causes

test programs welcome homeschoolers. Here are some of the benefits we've found in taking part in these types of activities:

1. **Learning to cooperate with others.** Cooperate while competing? Yes, that's actually the focus of many of the programs we've been in. A competition may be the culminating event, but the hours of working together with other kids and learning together is probably what carries much of the real value. The Math Olympiad wouldn't be nearly as much fun and so energizing for the kids if they were all doing these challenging math problems at home just on their own. At our meetings we encourage the kids to help one another, play math games together, share ideas with the group, and even present special projects they've done at home. It's positive socializing—and fun.

2. **Ease of organizing a group activity.** National team contests are already well-organized, making it possible for even this very busy mom of four to take part. For instance, the Math Olympiad program sends local teams all the needed materials for each monthly contest. I don't have to do a lot of last-minute planning or head-scratching about what to do on Wednesday when I'm faced with a dozen bouncing kids. And if we want to add extras, there are lots of ideas in the Olympiad newsletter.

3. **Provides focus for getting a group together.** Sometimes support groups want to provide kids' activities, but it can be hard to decide just what to offer. An agreed-upon group contest, such as the Geography Bee, can sometimes give that focus, and lets everyone know clearly what they are involved in. This can be especially important at the high school level.

4. **We get excellent, often free, guidelines** for developing an area of our curriculum that maybe we had been pushing to the background for too long. I think of the great materials from the National Geographic Geography Bee; they really got me realizing that we needed to focus more on this area. Or there's the MathCounts coaching books with all their sample problem sets and ideas for using calculators and advanced problem-solving techniques with junior-high-age kids. Many times these contest materials have spurred interests that last for years.

5. **We get an unusual chance to let our kids measure themselves** against kids who are traditionally schooled. Sometimes this is energizing—as when our Jesse at 16 came in third place for 11th graders in the national current events competition Global Challenge, and the same year our Jacob at 13 came in fifth place for 8th graders. This was out of thousands of kids in the country, and probably our team comprised the only homeschoolers. Sometimes competitions are humbling, and let us realize that there indeed are really bright and hardworking kids out there in the public and private schools. Good for keeping a bit of perspective! Our kids get an equal chance to reach high goals with other students and see how they measure up.

6. **Entering contests gives someone else the job** of setting parameters for a project, not just Mom. I can go over the contest guidelines for the American Statistical Association's annual project and poster contest with Jacob and his team partner and help them devise a plan to meet

the requirements. I become a coach and guide, not someone who is just dishing out assignments, or someone who is just weakly making watery suggestions. Proofreading is not Jacob's favorite thing, but we proofread his statistics paper with a fine tooth comb (it was on the demographics of homeschooling in PA!). That was our language arts work for a week. And it was authentic and needed, with no doubt about the purpose of it all.

7. **It doesn't hurt to have team contest accomplishments** listed on a homeschooler's high school records. Last year when Jesse applied to a special high school summer program on the workings of the free enterprise system, he had many recognizable things to list when asked about any special awards or honors he'd earned in his high school years. Many people might think that homeschoolers wouldn't have anything to put down—after all, aren't these types of activities only available through schools?

8. **Participating in contests can be good public relations work** on the value of homeschooling. People in my hometown come up to me all the time to say, "Oh, I see how well all you homeschoolers are doing—saw the article just last week in the paper about that math competition your group won!" Sometimes people outside of homeschooling really need to hear about these sorts of accomplishments before they can believe this "nutty" idea of ours is working. Impresses legislators too. And our PA Department of Education always notices how many homeschoolers make it each year to the state level Geography Bee. This year 6 out of the 100 state level kids were homeschoolers!

Later in this chapter is a list of some of the many contests for teams and groups of students that we've looked into over the years. Write for information on these programs, and see what might fit in with your group's interests. Just remember—when taking part in a national contest, your homeschool group must follow all the program rules. A few years back the Geography Bee threatened to disqualify all homeschoolers when one family had a child take the written test for the state level without actually having a local oral Bee with the required number of students. Let's show these national organizations that we can be trusted by being scrupulous about following all guidelines.

Laurie Bluedorn on Picking the Right Contest

A word of warning about contests. Avoid politically correct contests. If the registration form *requires* you to list your race, then it is possible that winners will be chosen on the basis of race, not simply merit. Some contests require you to travel long distances or cost large sums of money. MathCounts, a very popular math competition, recently started charging $40 per school. Avoid contests that just want to sell or promote a product (some of the poetry contests will do this) or build a mailing list. Some of the Internet "contests" are sweepstakes and not really contests at all.

Which contest should you pick for your child? If your child is extra good at math, then any of the numerous math competitions will stretch his skills, and there are plenty of art contests for the artistically inclined.

To integrate contests into your curriculum I suggest this plan. For the first year, pick one of the fun contests that coincide with that child's interests: Make It Yourself With Wool Contest, chess competitions, Tandy Leather Art Competition, Scripps Howard National Spelling Bee, Rocky Mountain Philatelic Exhibition, National Association of Rocketry contests,

those problems, nor is there any evidence that having self-esteem causes students to score better in academic subjects.

—*The Phyllis Schlafly Report*

Why Cooperation is Not Always Better Than Competition

Cooperative Learning, in which students receive a group grade, is another means of concealing who does the assignment accurately and who goofs off. The brighter students soon learn that their effort is not rewarded, and the slower students learn that there's no reason to try because someone will give them the answers.

—*The Phyllis Schlafly Report*

Want more?

If you really get hooked, and want to find out about even more group and individual contests, try this:

NASSP National Advisory List of Contests and Activities. National Association of Secondary School Principals, 1904 Association Dr., Reston VA 22091. An extensive listing of academic and arts contests that meet the criteria established by this organization. Price: $5 plus $2 S&H.

or one of the American Morgan Horse Association contests. Check out the deadline for the contest and make out a rough schedule for progress. For example, by October have the project topic decided, have outlines finished by November, rough drafts by December, etc. Break the process down into manageable bite-size pieces.

The next year, have the student enter one of the project contests (National History Day, science fairs, or invention projects). By the third year you will be considered a contest pro and can even make contests a major part of your curriculum. The student can enter a writing contest, a speech contest, and a project contest each year, making for a well-rounded curriculum. You can also use contests to help your student work on areas he is weak in.

Contests let the student bring together the skills he learns at home and apply them in his everyday schooling. This is the ultimate in practical homeschooling.

CHAPTER 25

What About Software?

There is no "Software Method" of home education. Some software is very authoritarian and drill-oriented; some is just bunches of organized data for you to peruse; some is set up to encourage exploration as you "click" on new discoveries.

In short, software, like print curriculum, is set up according to the educational philosophy of its designer.

Although software is not a *method,* it is a useful *tool.* Software gives you a quicker, more interactive way to present information, drill facts, and test retention. It also allows you to simulate experiences you are unlikely to have in real life: piloting an F-17 airplane, visiting the Rome of Julius Caesar, or touring the surface of Mars.

No matter what homeschool method you choose, software can help. The following software is most useful for each homeschool method.

- **Back to Basics.** Tutoring software, facts drills, and test prep
- **Charlotte Mason Method.** Very little tutoring or drill software is helpful in this very personal method, and real books are preferred.
- **Classical Education/Great Books.** CD-ROMs containing Great Books and historical source documents; foreign and classical language training.
- **Principle Approach.** Same as above, with emphasis on American historical documents
- **Robinson Method.** The Robinson Curriculum on CD-ROM, which includes Great Books, many popular children's books and texts of the 19th century and early 20th century, plus a fine collection of historical source documents
- **Unit Studies.** Software that specifically relates to the current unit study, plus math drill software and possibly math tutoring software.

NEW!
School's Out

Parents. $12.95 plus $2.50 shipping. *William Morrow and Company, 39 Plymouth St., Fairfield, NJ 07004. (800) 843-9389.*

In **School's Out**, Lewis Perelman claims that because of the technological revolution of the past several decades, schools as we have them today are as outmoded as the horse and buggy were becoming in 1900. All schools, through college level, are beyond any type of reform, and they along with the current educational establishment should be abolished. Classroom education, whatever the source, is done for.

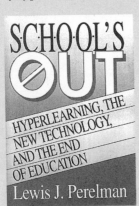

At the center of his argument is what he calls "hyperlearning"—the infusion of modern technology into the learning process. Network intelligence, he argues, is more valuable than the information that can be imparted by any one school teacher in a traditional classroom, whom he refers to as a "yak in the box." This is nothing new to homeschoolers, who are on the forefront of the use of videos and computers in education. Hence, many of us may not profit so much from this one, though traditionalists from all camps will be given good food for thought.

Technology is Perelman's all in all: "The good news is that science shows the way . . ." But we know science can't tell us *what* to do, only *how* to do it. In divorcing values from the learning process, he leaves open the problem of how the children of tomorrow will resist the ongoing cultural avalanche any more than they do today. A bit of Bible is needed among the bits and bytes.
Charles & Betty Burger

- **Guided Exploration.** "Discovery" and "construction kit" type software, plus strategy games and any tutoring software the child is motivated to study on his own
- **Unguided Exploration.** Reference tools of all kinds are a must, plus a wide selection of software on significant topics (science, math, etc.) that looks interesting enough for a kid to pick it up and explore it
- **Unschooling.** All the above!

Now, here are a few important points about software in the homeschool. **Every homeschooled kid needs these** (unless you have some political or religious objection to computers, that is!)

- Typing program
- Adult word processor (the kind people use in their businesses, not the cutesy kiddie kind.)
- Email program
- Web browser

Nix to non-educational games (and if you can make this stick, you're a better parent than I am!). This is even more important if you have chosen a method where the child is left unsupervised for long periods of time, as the typical child will *always* choose a mindless but "fun" game over one that requires learning real-world facts in order to solve the puzzles or get a high score. This can result in your kids turning into Doom Dave, Trekken Trevor, Nintendo Ned, and Starcraft Stephanie. If you're using a method that has you right there with the kids, then you can enforce rules such as, "No games until after 5 p.m.," but if they're on their own, it's better not to let these gravitational anomalies in the door at all, lest they suck in all your children's time.

To avoid excessive gaming, especially for boys, give them real-world challenges to master, preferably in the company of men they respect. I have a theory that the reason most boys fixate on violent action games just before and during puberty is that our society has cut off the normal ways boys are allowed to evaluate their success in turning into men. In the past, boys would learn to measure themselves against other boys and men by how long and hard they could plow, whether they could keep up with the men all day out on the range, how well they could hunt and fish, whether they could split a full cord of logs as quick as their older brother, and so forth. See the "Little Britches" series by Ralph Moody, or *Farmer Boy* by Laura Ingalls Wilder, for numerous examples of the kinds of real-world tests a boy could expect to face just 60 years ago. This built-in drive to compete with other young men and to test their courage is biological; but with no hands-on outlet, it degenerates into a pursuit of "high scores" in games that simulate "manly" challenges (mostly, killing evil virtual enemies). One obvious solution for those with no access to a rural lifestyle: **martial arts training.** At least the kid will get in shape, which I guarantee won't happen by playing computer games.

PART 6

Special Situations

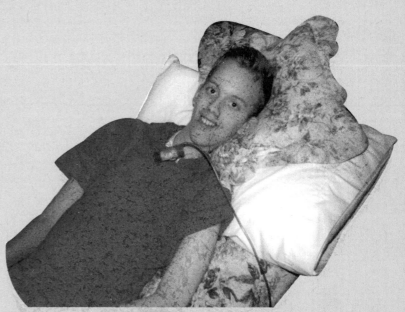

Our oldest son, Ted, almost died of pneumonia at the age of 14. He spent weeks in intensive care, and had to have a hole cut in his throat so a tracheotomy tube could be inserted. Even after he came home, he was on a respirator for months. In the next two years he had two major spinal operations, one of which required him to lay flat on his back for three months afterward. Homeschooling is a boon in special situations like this. It allowed Ted to keep up with his schoolwork even when he was in the hospital!

If your child is athletically gifted, she will thrive on athletic competition. Homeschooler Kayla Bingham, age 8, from Lake George, CO, won first place in her age division for her Acro-dance solo, "Hot-Hot-Hot," at Star Power National Dance Competition, held in Las Vegas in July. Acro-dance is a combination of gymnastics and dance. Kayla also brought home four gold medals in group (team) dances in pom-pom, lyrical, and acro. Kayla represents Robin's Danceworks of Colorado Springs. Way to go, Kayla!

CHAPTER 26

How Real Are Learning Disabilities?

Let's talk about the homeschool subject nobody wants to talk about: "What do we do when our kids don't learn what we're trying to teach them?"

In the public school world, an entire industry has been created out of "learning disabilities." Briefly, LD includes all the categories of children who have no discernible physical problems but who are slow learners or who don't behave the way their classroom teachers wish they did.

To date, the homeschool movement has been ambivalent to the concept of learning disabilities. On the one hand, some homeschoolers believe there really is no such thing as a "learning disability." On the other hand, people credentialed by the education establishment as learning disabilities experts have been popping up with increasing frequency as featured speakers at homeschool conventions.

After years of studying this issue—and years of raising nine children, two of whom at least would qualify for a public-school "LD" label—I have reached the following conclusions:

- **There is no reason**, except for getting government grants, **for using the term "learning disability."** The term exists to shift responsibility for a child's scholastic failures from the school and parents to the child's DNA.
- **By definition learning "disabilities" have no physical origin.** Real learning *problems* have actual medical names, such as "brain damage" or "Down's Syndrome."
- **What one person calls a "disability" could just as readily often be called a "gift."** Picture the difference between, "What an energetic little boy you have!" and, "Oh, that boy of yours is hyperactive." Or between, "Janie has Attention Deficit Disorder," and, "Janie is such a thinker!"
- **More important than labeling** is *what are you going to do about* your child's slowness or distractibility?
- **The first step towards solving a problem is getting a *correct* diagnosis**—as opposed to a responsibility-shifting "label." "Jimmy is disobedient" leads to entirely different parental responses than "Jimmy has ADHD." "Suzy has poor visual perception" requires a different line of treatment than "Suzy is an LD child."

Unreasonable Goals

. . . The National Education Goal . . . states that *all* children will start school prepared to learn. Unfortunately, because schools generally set things up so that only one type of learner [the Progress Person] can be recognized as "prepared to learn," this goal is basically impossible to meet. . . . Because the school traditionally decides *what* is supposed to be learned *when*, those kids who have natural abilities in those areas become the "gifted" ones and those who don't become the "learning disabled." Those who are unable to earn either of those distinctions are doomed to be "average," "below average," or "slow." . . .

If we continue to label students because their brains do not operate the way our educational system wants them to, we will continue to spread the idea that millions of brains are not as good as other brains, and perpetuate lifetime patterns of low self-worth, which affect future learning, career opportunities, and relationships.
—*Discover Your Child's Learning Style*

A School Principal on Learning Disabilities as Alibis

I have observed that in the last several decades there have been three classic "learning disabilities" promulgated by the educational community—or more properly, by the educational establishment. Each one has served its purpose for that time—namely, to get the responsibility off the back of the (public) schools and on to the back of "disabilities," with which everyone sympathizes.

The first of these classic three "disabilities" was **dyslexia**. This was a popular cause given for the inability of children to learn to read in the late 50s and 60s, when the educational establishment was reaping the grim fruits of their new, popular "Look-Say" or "Sight" reading system. Now, dyslexia is indeed a valid physical impairment. It is a specific disorder of the visual system, causing images to be perceived upside down, or reversed left to right. However, if one consults a reputable ophthalmologist, or a text book on the subject, he will find that the **incidence of dyslexia is about one in 10,000.**

In his 1970 book, *Classroom Countdown*, Dr. Max Rafferty addressed this "disability." Dr. Rafferty, who served as the Superintendent of Public Instruction of the state of California for many years, states on page 242:

> For any of you who are not of the Inner Sanctum of education, dyslexia is the tendency of certain children to see letters in reverse. Obviously, it would nicely explain inability to read, and equally obviously this makes it alluringly attractive to 'look-say' reading teachers, who are compelled now and then to explain why their pupils can't read.

> To ward off a Niagara of letters from parents of allegedly dyslexic children, let me hasten to state that I do indeed believe in dyslexia. During my thirty years in education, I have known precisely one case. But, of late, as reading difficulties have burgeoned despite our gloriously "modern" teaching methods, the learned estimate of persons affected by dyslexia has grown enormously, from practically none a few years back to as high as 30 percent of the population today!

> *Dyslexia neatly fits education's classic definition of the perfect alibi: It's scientific-sounding, it's mysterious, and it's something the teacher can't be expected to do much about.* (Emphasis added)

We may observe an interesting point here: if we substitute the term "Attention Deficit Disorder" for "dyslexia," the emphasized paragraph, now some 27 years old, makes perfect sense even today!

I will leave the subject of dyslexia with the final note that in my 15 years as school principal, during which time I interviewed every parent of children coming into the school, I found a high percentage of supposedly "dyslexic" children; the parents had been told that the reason for the child's difficulty in reading was some (mild?) form of dyslexia. **In no case was the "dyslexic" diagnosis accompanied by a note from a doctor;** it always seemed to be the "diagnosis" of someone connected with the school system, including the school psychologists. **But in every case, the child soon learned to read**, as we used a traditional, structured classroom, and traditional teaching methods, based largely on phonics.

The second of the three classic learning "disabilities" became popular in the early 70s; it was **Hyperactivity**. Again, neither the child nor the teacher was to blame. Just like dyslexia, or the now popular ADD, it was something that just happened to this particular child. The principal of one of the elementary public schools in a reasonably affluent section of the city of Columbus, Ohio, told me in 1973 that about 25 percent of the students there were on "Ritalin," which was then the drug of choice for "hyperactivity."

Again, as principal of the Christian school, I had parents bringing their children from the public school to ours, and cautioning us that their child was "hyperactive." Needless to say, in a structured classroom, and with proper discipline for any "hyperactivity" that disrupted the classroom, these students soon settled down and learned to read. To my knowledge, only a very few continued with their Ritalin. When I retired from the school, now 10 years ago, Hyperactivity had pretty much subsided as a problem.

The third of the three classic learning "disabilities" has now replaced Hyperactivity. That is the currently rampant **Attention Deficit Disorder**, or **ADD**. I heard one man, who had taught for some 40 years from the early 50s to the early 90s, ask where ADD had been for all these years. He simply didn't believe such a thing could have existed for the 40 years of his teaching, and he had not ever observed it. And there are many like him.

I submit that though, like dyslexia, ADD is a real disorder for a very few children, it simply has become the educational establishment's latest scientific-sounding excuse for the failure of the students to learn. Please note that I did not say the "inability." After ADD has run its course, I wonder what the educational establishment will think of next to excuse its failure?

I would submit that, when it comes to these learning disabilities, it was not doctors, but the psychologists and school administrators who "diagnosed" the condition. Again, in my 15 years as principal, though I consulted with doctors on many occasions, I never once heard a doctor say, "Little Johnny Jones is really hyperactive, and needs to be treated accordingly."

—*Jack E. Willer, Worthington, OH*

With all this in mind, we offer you the following diagnostic checklist designed to help you figure out what your child's problem, if any, really is, and what to do about it.

What to Do If Your Child Has Trouble Learning

If your child is having trouble with just one subject, try a fresh approach with that subject, or even leave it alone for a while in order to allow him to catch up to it developmentally.

But if your child doesn't seem able to do grade-level work on *any* subject, and you are not aware of any genuine physical problem, such as Tourette's Syndrome or head injuries, try the following:

1. **Check his eyesight.** This may seem almost too obvious to mention, but I personally, although blind as a bat, didn't get a single eye test until I was a teen, and didn't get contacts until I was 20 years old. If your child holds books close to his face, or rubs his eyes a lot, a vision test should be a priority. Even if he doesn't show signs of poor vision, it's a good idea to have vision checked as soon as your child can tell left from right and up from down.

2. **Check his visual perception.** This differs from a regular vision test in that you aren't looking at eye charts. Instead, you are checking such things as how evenly your child's eyes "track" from left to right. Again, red eyes and having trouble "seeing" the page are a sign of this problem. You may have to look around a bit to find someone in your area who does this kind of testing. However, if visual perception is the problem, eye exercises can make a huge difference in your child's ability to take in information visually.

3. **Check your child's hearing.** If he's had a lot of ear infections, he very well may have trouble hearing, especially in a noisy environment.

4. **Check his gross motor skills.** Children who are especially clumsy or delayed developmentally may have something physically wrong with them. This is not a learning *disability*, but an actual learning *problem* that needs remediation. Neurological patterning exercises, such as those offered by the National Academy for Child Development, can be helpful for children with neurological and other physical problems.

5. **Check him for allergies.** As you'll see in the next chapter, undiagnosed allergies to specific foods or environmental factors (e.g., new carpet fumes) can make children lethargic, hyper, confused, and/or highly irritable—all of which effectively prevent peaceful concentration on learning.

6. **Check his vocabulary level.** A reduced vocabulary level can be a sign of genuine physical problems, or of unresolved emotional problems which are affecting his learning.

7. **Check for interpersonal and environmental problems or trauma.** All these big words mean, "Has anyone betrayed, persecuted, or scared your child?" A divorce or the death of a relative or friend can cause a child to lose interest in learning. Or, if he has attended school in the past, he may well have emotional baggage left over from unpleasant school experiences. It's been said that a child needs as many years to *recover* from public school as he *spent* in public school. While that's not true in all

Labeling Fads

In 1990, when NATHHAN first started, we got thousands of calls from parents whose children were diagnosed with ADHD. This all but ceased and was replaced with autism and Pervasive Developmental Disorder. Presently we are getting lots of calls from families frustrated at the educational and medical field's new "rage diagnoses" Bipolar and Oppositional Defiance Disorder. What will it be next?

These diagnoses cheapen the help children with real LD, ADHD, true autism or PPD get. Parents whose children do have these problems are not faking it, and really do need help.

These "quick diagnoses" are being handed out like candy by the public school system and some medical professionals. Families may not realize that these labels follow children through life.

Thousands of these parents are excited about homeschooling. They are not accepting the label and "help" that does not fit their child, in exchange for being a school district's money making decoy. Special needs children bring in a school district anywhere from $10,000 to $19,000 and up, depending on the IEP signed by the parent.

—*Tom and Sherry Bushnell
NATHHAN*

Picture Learners & Dyslexia

Most people who are labeled dyslexic are Picture Learners. . . . Picture Learners are often mistakenly treated as Print Learners. I am convinced that this misconception is the cause of the majority of reading problems among our students.
—*Discover Your Child's Learning Style*

Obviously we couldn't cover every single situation with this checklist. But we hope this checklist, and the information that follows, will help make it clear that kids are never a set of walking "labels," but individuals with varying gifts and interests.

Furthermore, any "remediation" or "therapy" that doesn't actually *cure* the problem it addresses isn't worth our respect or attention. The public schools' "special education" doesn't produce kids who ultimately work at grade level. They don't even *pretend* to achieve these results. In fact, they make *more* money for each child who remains in special education. So why listen to them or use their failed methods?

Although homeschoolers are rightly wary of public education methods and philosophy, at this point we seem all too ready to let them in through the "back door" of special education. If we can be persuaded to label our kids, and call on a public-school-credentialed "expert" to tell us how to homeschool our labeled kids, we're right back in the public school's lap.

cases, giving your child some "time off" after a rough emotional experience won't ruin him for homeschool, especially if you provide lots of library books and interesting outings!

8. **Check his attention span *when he's doing something that interests him.*** If your child just "can't sit still" even for activities he favors, he likely has a chemical imbalance or allergies. In these cases, talking to a doctor *qualified in these areas* can yield excellent results. Beware of practitioners who prescribe Ritalin at the drop of a hat. Also beware of labeling a child "distractible" who is only distractible when he's doing what *you* want!

9. **If your child doesn't have any of the above problems**, but is always "zoning out" or daydreaming, consider the following options: (a) Pick more interesting and involving activities. (b) Check up on him frequently. (c) Encourage artistic, musical, and scientific pursuits. (d) Add more hands-on projects. Also consider that your child's "problem" may actually be a case of giftedness, in which case offering more demanding activities is the solution.

10. **If none of the above applies**, you may just have a child who is a slow learner. Throughout the history of the world, some have always been faster and some have been slower. This is really no big deal in homeschool, since there is no class to "keep up" with or "fall behind." We can afford to let our children learn at their own rates. The worst thing you can do is to keep harping on a child's failure by repeatedly pushing tasks at him that he isn't ready to do. In this case, the answer is to lose some of that parental anxiety, scale back on your expectations, pick only resources that break tasks down into simple steps, review a lot, and remember that you have 13 school years to teach this kid to read, write, and do basic arithmetic. If you succeed at these minimal tasks, your "slow learner" will actually be more advanced by high-school graduation time than 99 percent of public school graduates!

School Expectations

Traditionally, "prepared to learn" has meant that the child arrives at school ready and eager to:

- sit in a desk and work alone quietly for long periods of time
- follow the teacher's sequential directions
- focus and listen . . . even when there is the ongoing noise of construction outside
- do worksheets instead of playing with toys
- be quiet for long periods of time . . . [more examples follow]

The child who comes to school prepared to do the above is then labeled motivated, smart, eager to learn, and most probably, above average, maybe even gifted. Now let's look at some different children. These children arrive at school ready and eager to:

- play at recess
- draw or fingerpaint
- tell imaginative stories
- entertain the teacher and other students . . .
- tap on the desk with a pencil or any object, in the absence of musical instruments . . .
- play, act, and/or sing
- ask a lot of questions . . . [more examples follow]

Teachers become concerned about these students because they do not behave or perform according to school expectations. Many of these children are labeled slow, unmotivated, immature, distractible, disruptive, or lazy. If problems persist, someone usually suggests testing to find out if there is a learning disability.

—*Discover Your Child's Learning Style*

Screening Programs You Can Try at Home

This vision screening kit is a real breakthrough! No longer do pre-readers have to learn the letter "E" or the vocabulary of the picture chart in order to have their eyes examined. You can check all your young kids with this kit in the privacy of your home.

The **Blackbird Story Book Home Eye Test** starts with the story of a blackbird who flies in different directions, trying to find out what kind of bird he'd like to be. Kids follow the story with hand motions, meanwhile learning "up" from "down" and "left" from "right." When they have these down, you detach the included set of screening specs. Each lens has a pop-out circle, so you can cover either the left or right eye while testing. You then measure off 10 feet away from the child (you can use the included one-foot ruler), and hold up the Blackbird cards. Turn the card of the large blackbird and ask the child which direction the blackbird is flying. Do the same for the two smaller blackbirds. The included report sheet allows you to record the results for both eyes. If your 3–5-year-old child has difficulty seeing the second blackbird with each eye, or if your 6-year or older child has trouble seeing the smallest blackbird, he needs a full eye examination. Similarly, if your child can see well but tilts his head, squints his eye, moves closer in order to see, has crossed or wandering eyes, or if your family has a history of "lazy-eye" disease, you are urged to consult an eye doctor.

For schools, the **Preschool Vision Screening Kit** includes instructions, guidelines, and 50 pairs of screening specs. Extra packs of screening specs are also available separately, as is a Blackbird Wall Chart, with blackbirds of various sizes in various positions. The latter is recommended for older non-English speaking or non-reading students or adults.

Teachers everywhere are raving about how simple this kit is to use and how the kids now love having their eyes tested. Kudos to Blackbird for making it available for parents at home as well! *Mary Pride*

Blackbird Story Book Home Eye Test

Special needs children ages 3–7. $9.95. Preschool Vision Screening Kit, $104.95.
Blackbird Vision Screening System, PO Box 277424, Sacramento, CA 95827. (800) 363-6884. Fax: (916) 363-6438

Integrated Motor Activities Screening is a spiral-bound guide and test to help parents and teachers identify preschool and kindergarten age children who lag behind in motor skills development. Children with poor motor skill development are at-risk for learning disabilities, so early screening can be very beneficial to parents.

The test takes about 20 minutes and includes behavioral observations. Eye control, body awareness, behavior, and eye/hand/foot preference are included as unscored items. Auditory-visual motor skills, eye-hand coordination and gross motor development are all scored. Activities such as your child snapping his fingers to check eye-hand coordination or balancing on each foot with hands on head to check gross motor skills are some of the many testing criteria that are used during this screening. An interpretation guide helps you understand what areas you are testing, what the correct performance should be, problem indicators, classroom implications and severity rating.

The results from these test can help you identify weaknesses in certain areas, so that you can address the problem early. *Maryann Turner*

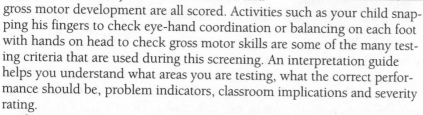

NEW!
Integrated Motor Activities Screening

Grades preK and K. $20 plus shipping.
Legendary Publishing Company, P.O. Box 7706, Boise, ID 83707-1706. (800)358-1929. Fax: (208)342-7929.

Labels v. Readiness

Perhaps kids are labeled because it is easier to attach the blame to a "learning problem" than to search for the teaching method, the setting, and the materials that fit each child. Many "learning problems" are actually created because an individual child's unique learning timetable is not taken into account. Who said they should all learn the alphabet in preschool, start reading in kindergarten and first grade, do fractions in third, and so on?
—*Discover Your Child's Learning Style*

What to Do If Your Child Doesn't Follow Your Instructions

If your child can see and hear just fine, has an OK vocabulary level and motor skills, has no allergies, is not suffering from any recent traumas, has an OK attention span when doing what he wants, is not a daydreamer, and *can* do the work "when he feels like it" (except that he rarely feels like it), what you likely have here is an old-fashioned case of disobedience. This is even more obvious in cases where the child explicitly refuses to do what you say, or shows disrespect in other ways.

It happens all the time, and the solution is the same as it has always been: consistent discipline, patience, and lots of prayer. Depending on the circumstances, discipline may mean a spanking, taking away distracting toys, or, "You don't eat supper until you finish your schoolwork."

The key here is not to get discouraged and give up prematurely. Contrary to what some child-training books make it sound like, rare is the child who responds with exemplary obedience to the very first time he is disciplined. Your job is to let him know that "school doesn't have to be fun, it just has to be done," in the deathless words of Luanne Shackelford (author of *A Survivor's Guide to Homeschooling*), and that he isn't going to get away with a thing. Once he is convinced of this, and you have *also* made sure that he realizes you are in sympathy with his aspirations and tribulations, most kids will settle down and (even if grudgingly) do the work.

Training in diligence is very helpful, since it's even rarer to find a rebellious child who isn't also lazy. Good old family chores are great for this training, which proves once again that it's always best to do chores *first*. It's also important for the parents to show a cheerful attitude about work. The lessons learned in chore time carry over to better work all through the homeschool day.

The one rare exception to the above is the case of a child who is so intensely focused on an interest that he keeps coming back to it in spite of all instructions to spend his time otherwise. In this case, you need to determine if the activity in question is bad—in which case you have a spiritual problem requiring even more prayer and discipline—or positive—in which case he may just be a genius who is following his vocation. Many famous musicians, scientists, and artists started this way!

Homeschool special education has the advantages of common sense, lots of time, one-on-one interaction, and a devotion to results. That is why it *gets* results. My "dyslexic" daughter now reads above grade level and her spelling has vastly improved. My "ADD" son was doing college work in ninth grade. Hundreds of other homeschool families have similar results. They are the true special education experts, not the guys with the Ed.D.'s and Ph.D.'s.

We don't need trendy buzzwords and theories, we need *results*. As long as we only listen to people who can demonstrate results, we'll be heading in the right direction—and special education at home will be *really* special.

More Reading

In this short (8 page) oversized booklet, pastor Alan J. Tabb examines the *medical* definitions of ADD and ADHD, and finds they are full of arbitrary terminology such as "often," "excessively," and "inappropriate." "What is the 'appropriate' level of fidgeting or talking?" **ADD: Does It Add Up** asks. The answer: the diagnostic manuals don't tell us! He also traces the change from strictly medical-physiological diagnosis to subjective "I know it when I see it" diagnosis. Did you know that, according to the *Diagnostic and Statistical Manual of Mental Disorders*, "8 out of 14" subjective criteria,

NEW!
ADD: Does It Add Up?
Parents. $7.50 plus $2 shipping.
EdifyCo, 1815 Paradise Blvd., Rockford, IL 61103-2918.

including such gems as "Often fidgets with hands and feet or squirms in seat," must be satisfied in order to produce a diagnosis of ADD? He quotes authorities who note that the subjective biases of the person doing the diagnosis are the major factor in labeling kids as ADD or ADHD. He points out that few researchers have paid any attention to the school environment itself as a possible *cause* of the set of behaviors labeled ADD. Finally, he points out how researchers in this field have neglected to separate children who *can* do a task from those that *cannot* do a task. Rather, the diagnostic industry seems to be headed farther and farther in the direction of assuming that all children who don't perform as expected *can't* perform, thus sidestepping the moral issues of the need for children to learn obedience and whether the tasks they are being asked to perform are worth doing. In a full eight pages he, of course, says a lot more than this, all with ample footnotes and graphs. It may seem pricey for 8 pages, but it still costs less than your first unnecessary Ritalin prescription. I would recommend this unique eye-opener to everyone whose child has been labeled. *Mary Pride*

In this follow-up booklet to *ADD: Does It Add Up?*, pastor Alan J. Tabb again examines the truth and motives behind the creation of the pseudo diseases ADD and ADHD. In **ADD & Psychopharmacology: An Unnecessary Evil?** he focuses on psychopharmacology: the combination of psychiatric/psychological therapy with the dispensing of dangerous medication. Has research on ADD and ADHD been economically compromised? He points out the prime encouragers of medication: the pharmaceutical companies. Through quotes from leading authorities, Tabb shows the vested interests that drug companies have in "inventing a disease." He discusses how the learning disabilities bonanza has become big business, not only for psychopharmacology, but for doctors, "specialists," researchers, schools, and even publishing companies. Perhaps the most disturbing fact is that doctors have chosen to ignore scientific research and prescribe potentially dangerous medication on a normal basis. Tabb describes in detail the primary classification of medications used to treat ADD and ADHD and discusses their effectiveness, or non-effectiveness, and associated risks. Once again, he uses a short (14 page) oversized booklet format and includes ample graphs and sources. Recommended. *Brad Kovach*

NEW!
ADD & Psychopharmacology: An Unnecessary Evil?
Parents. $7.50 plus $2 shipping.
EdifyCo, 1815 Paradise Blvd., Rockford, IL 61103-2918.

Square Pegs in Round Holes

Modern education generally does recognize that people are different. In fact, starting in preschool we get the "I am so special! I am wonderful!" treatment. Problem is, this encouraging litany does not mean what it says. It does not mean that children are unique human beings created in the image of God, each with his own personality, talents, and tendencies to sin. As we proceed through the grades we discover these same "special" and "wonderful" children forced into peer-group herds. The energetic are labeled "hyperactive" and sedated. The slow-and-steadies are labeled "learning disabled" and shunted into Special Ed. The mean and destructive are not told to shape up or ship out, but labeled "emotionally handicapped" and coddled. Solitary types who hate the group pressures and inanity of school schedules are labeled "school phobic" and granted no concessions to their sensitive natures.

The bottom line of all this, you will notice, is that children are forced to fit in to the school. Kids who don't fit in are forced in. Square pegs in round holes. Hard on the square pegs, and not too great on the round holes, either.

Could it be that highly critical people, and aggressive people, and slow methodical people, and humorous people all have a right to their own personalities? Can it be OK for students to be human not only in how they learn and are motivated, but in their different personalities as well? Could we perhaps get a nice big garbage can and place all those hundreds of little labels out on the curb for the trashman to take away?

—*Schoolproof*

Everyone Is Able—Exploding the Myth of Learning Disabilities

$3.95 plus shipping.
Holt Associates, 2269 Massachusetts Ave., Cambridge, MA 02140. (617) 864-3100. Fax: (617) 864-3100. Email: HoltGWS@aol.com. Web: www.holtgws.com

Guide to Learning Disabilities: What Do the Labels Really Mean?

Parents. Two-tape set, $18.
NACD, PO Box 380, Huntsville, UT 84317. (801) 621-8606.
Fax: (801) 621-8389.
Email: nacdinfo@nacd.org.
Web: www.nacd.org.

Learning In Spite of Labels

Parents. $9.95 plus $3.50 shipping.
Greenleaf Press, 1570 Old La Guardo Rd., Lebanon, TN 37087. Orders: (800) 311-1508. Fax: (615) 449-4018. Email: GreenleafP@aol.com. Web: www.green-leafpress.com.

If you would like to find out why intelligent people are questioning the whole premise of "learning disability," and why you should fiercely resist your child being branded with this label, this booklet from Holt Associates provides the ammo. In **Everyone is Able** you hear from the "other experts"—parents of labeled children (or whose children would be labeled if the mainstream experts got their hands on them) and specialists within the schools who see what the LD label does to children and education. These are real-life stories. Many articles were written especially for this booklet. The quality of the writing as a whole is thoughtful, but not dispassionate. Must reading. *Mary Pride*

Guide to Learning Disabilities: What Do the Labels Really Mean? challenges parents not to rest until they find out what is *really* wrong with their children. Robert Doman explores some common sources of children's problems (hearing/sight problems, memory problems, neurological imbalance and so on) and offers practical suggestions for unearthing and remedying these problems.

I really appreciate NACD's philosophy that labeling counts for nothing; it's solving the problem that counts. This is also the only remedial organization I know with the optimism to strive for bringing handicapped and labeled children up to or beyond *normal* (not handicapped) functional levels. *Mary Pride*

Get out the clear Contac paper and cover this book right away! It's destined to be dog-eared, so be prepared. Joyce Herzog has written a book on teaching strategies that will encourage, instruct, inspire, and revive you. By the way, did I mention that **Learning In Spite of Labels** was written for parents of children with learning difficulties? Doesn't matter! Anyone with a heart for helping children learn in whatever way is best for them will benefit from this book. Chapters cover:

- What it feels like to be learning-disabled: what learning is, how it works, typical behavioral characteristics, and strengths common to most of these children.
- 10 issues to consider (applies to all children): what Scripture has to say, where to school, discipline, success, priorities, goals, and more.
- 25 Teaching Techniques that Work.
- Teeny-tiny teaching tips: hints on specific subject areas, as well as structuring the environment for success.
- How to begin, learning styles, legal issues to consider.
- Famous historical figures, mini-biographies of those who overcame obstacles.
- ADD, normal speech development, vision problems.
- How to create an Individualized Education Plan.
- Resource list to help anyone locate expert help when needed.

After reading this book, you'll be firmly convinced that labels belong on clothing, not children. Highly recommended. *Renee Mathis*

CHAPTER 27

Help for Distractible Learners

First, let's all agree on this:

Some children are easily distractible.

Now that we have this out of the way, we can get to the *real* question:

How should we teach distractible learners?

We are not talking about "retarded" or brain-damaged children. The children in question *can* learn, but do not usually tackle their school studies with zest and success. Well, that's true of the average schooled child! But in this case, the teacher encounters additional difficulties. The child is just plain hard to teach.

This is not a new problem. What's new is the sheer *number* of children considered distractible today, and the number of labels invented to disguise the simple fact of what we're talking about, making it sound like a genuine disease.

Schools & Distractible Children

How do schools handle distractible children?

- **Drugs.** In the schools, the favored approach is to drug the child, usually with Ritalin.
- **Isolation.** Another favored school tactic is to place the distractible child in a cubicle where he is cut off from all stimulation from other children or the objects in the classroom.

Since you are reading this book, I assume you are looking for better ideas than these! Solitary confinement on drugs has got to be one of the most grotesque ways a supposedly civilized country has ever found to handle its young people. As Thomas Armstrong says in his book, *the Myth of the A.D.D. Child:*

Boring, Repetitive Tasks

The most interesting description of ADD I have ever read appeared in an ad for an organization that works with children. It reads, in part,

It [ADD] is is often present at birth, but may not be diagnosed until the elementary years because the symptoms go unnoticed at home. . . . But when sustained attention is required for boring, repetitive tasks in distracting settings like classrooms, the symptoms become easier to see. Sustained cartoon watching or video-game playing doesn't count. The behavioral symptoms are seen with boring, repetitive tasks in distracting settings.

It then goes on to describe the testing that is available and the treatment options, including medication.

I often think, Don't the people who read this ad see anything strange about it? In the first place, why would I want my child to spend most of the day in a place where she is required to do boring, repetitive tasks? And if that is what school is all about, why on earth would I medicate a child to ensure that he does those boring, repetitive tasks?
—*Discover Your Child's Learning Style*

Do Drugs Substitute for Discipline?

There is a medical, educational, and legal controversy raging over the issue of the drug Ritalin in dealing with "problem" children, children described as "hyperactive" or "inattentive." From Massachusetts to California indignant parents have filed suits against school systems and doctors seeking redress against the quasi-mandatory use of this drug. Sweden has outlawed its use. From Canada come warnings of what the epidemic use of Ritalin may ultimately do to society.

The controversy has attracted relatively little attention in our news media, even though it is estimated that over a million children in this country are routinely being required to take a drug that is listed in the Drug Enforcement Agency's "Drugs of Abuse" as a "Schedule Two" drug, along with cocaine and opium.

Last June, the controversy over the use of Ritalin attracted the attention of ABC's "Nightline." In a program aired on June 10, Ted Koppel promised to examine Ritalin's "effectiveness in controlling hyperactivity in children and its occasional negative side effects." He went on to say, "Nearly a million American children suffering from what is know as A.D.D., an acronym standing for Attention Deficit Disorder, take Ritalin or some similar drug." Since then an article in the *Journal of the American Medical Association* revealed that in the public schools in Baltimore County, MD, six percent of the elementary school students, four percent of the middle school students, and 0.4 percent of the high school students were taking Ritalin. The Baltimore figures indicate that the use of this drug has been doubled every four to seven years. If extrapolated to the country as a whole, they suggest that 1.6 million children may now be taking Ritalin to "cure" their hyperactivity and inattentiveness.

What exactly is this Attention Deficit Disorder mentioned by Koppel? It has been recognized only in the last 25 to 30 years, and psychiatrists have yet to agree on its exact characteristics and even its name. The last changes in the diagnostic criteria took place as recently as 1987, when it was renamed Attention-Deficit Hyperactivity Disorder.

Exactly how powerful and addictive is the drug Ritalin (methylphenidate hydrochloride), so freely given to grade school age children to treat the new "disease?" How exactly is the decision arrived at to give a child the drug?

Despite his reputation as an interviewer who is persistent in seeking answers to tough questions, Ted Koppel failed to get good answers to the hard questions that need to be asked about Ritalin. Indeed, many of the questions weren't even asked.

Drugs in Lieu of Discipline

Showing a boy at play, ABC reporter Gail Harris commented, "Shooting baskets in his backyard, Casey Jesson seems like any other energetic 9-year-old." But then she pointed out that Casey had been diagnosed as "hyperactive" and treated with Ritalin. What exactly are the indications that Casey suffers from an illness requiring treatment with a potent drug? David Brown, Superintendent of Schools in Casey's home town of Derry, New Hampshire, explained: "Always doing something, humming, movement of furniture, looking for attention, outward bursts, verbal bursts, refusal to do all kinds of things." Superintendent Brown was supported by Dr. Betsy Busch of the New England Medical Center who explained, "What Ritalin and other medications that are used for children who have attention-deficit seem to do is help children focus their attention."

No one pointed out that in other days, and even now in other countries, these are the kinds of problems that parents and teachers were expected to overcome with discipline. With the demise of discipline in our schools, a drug is becoming a disciplinary tool.

This may be easy for teachers, but it can be hard on children and families. Casey Jesson's mother, Valerie, strongly objected to the use of Ritalin to solve what the school though was Casey's problem. She said, "The child right from the beginning [of medication] complained of headaches, stomach cramps, he couldn't wind down, he couldn't fall asleep, so therefore he didn't want to go to bed." She said that getting him to eat was even starting to be a real problem.

When Casey went off the drug these side effects disappeared, but the school authorities wanted him back on it. His parents refused. His father said, "The child was sick from the drug. Why are they trying to force us to put drugs down our son's throat . . . ?"

Nightline brushed these objections aside. Gail Harris reassuringly declared, "Despite the Jesson's experience, the evidence is that Ritalin helps most hyperactive children cope with their condition."

Whose Evidence?

The 1988 edition of the authoritative *Physician's Desk Reference* states, "Sufficient data on safety and efficacy of long-term use of Ritalin in children are not yet available." The entry goes on to mention reports of stunted growth with long-term use on children. Ritalin's manufacturer, Ciba-Geigy, has included this same warning about the lack of data on long-term use on children in a product information release on the drug.

"It can have side effects, including loss of appetite and loss of sleep," reporter Gail Harris acknowledged, but she stopped short of mentioning even more serious adverse reactions among the 28 side effects to Ritalin listed in the *Physician's Desk Reference*. One of them is Tourette's Syndrome, whose sufferers display uncontrollable facial tics and sometimes bark like a dog as their nervous systems are affected by the drug.

A 1982 article in the *Journal of The American Medical Association* on Tourette's Syndrome says researchers "reported the development of motor tic symptoms in 1.3 percent of children receiving methylphenidate hydrochloride [Ritalin] for their attention-deficit disorder. Tics were said to disappear when therapy was discontinued, except in one child out of 1,520 studied." The article states, "The continuing appearance of Tourette's Syndrome in children after periods of stimulant pharmacotherapy remains a cause of concern for clinicians."

No mention was made on Nightline of dangers during withdrawal from Ritalin, but the *Physician's Desk Reference* warns, "Careful supervision is required during drug withdrawal." *The Diagnostic and Statistical Manual of Mental Disorders* (third edition, revised), published in 1987, the book known as the "bible" of psychiatry, discusses "complications" during withdrawal from Ritalin and drugs in its class. "Suicide," it states, "is the major complication."

Oblivious to such dire warnings, Nightline's Gail Harris reported, "The vast majority of doctors and psychiatrists say that for every failure there are many more success stories." She did not, of course, say how many cases of less active behavior it would take to offset a child's suicide.

In a Class with Cocaine

Gail Harris assured Nightline viewers that Ritalin is "strictly regulated by the Drug Enforcement Administration," and said that "doctors say in proper dosage it is not addictive in children." This implies that all doctors agree on this, but they don't. The doctors and medical scientists who compiled the Drug Enforcement Administration's list of "Drugs of Abuse" classed Ritalin together with cocaine and opium as a "Schedule Two" drug. The DEA describes these "Schedule Two" drugs as having a "high potential for abuse" and "may lead to severe psychological or physical dependence."

Less than a decade ago cocaine was considered a non-addictive drug. Today even laymen in the U.S. are familiar with the addictiveness of cocaine. In Canada, where cocaine is less readily available than in the U.S., Ritalin is used as one of the major street drugs, with addicts injecting it directly into their veins. In some areas in both Canada and the U.S., schools have been broken into by street drug addicts looking for Ritalin.

Nightline did not address the question of whether the U.S. is running the risk of making its already serious drug abuse problem worse by introducing millions of elementary school aged children to a Schedule Two drug like Ritalin. Apart from the imperfectly understood side effects, we have no way of knowing what the long-term effects of this will be in terms of influencing receptivity to the abuse of this and other Schedule Two drugs.

Schools Bullying Parents

Many parents object to being pressured by school authorities to put their children on Ritalin. Ted Koppel sided with the parents on this issue. When Superintendent Brown explained why his school system disagreed with Casey Jesson's parents and insisted that the boy go back on Ritalin, Koppel asked, "Doesn't the next stage belong to the parents to decide?" Brown said, "Not really." This prompted Koppel to ask, "Where does the school administration, or a superintendent, or a school board as a whole come off saying, 'Your child must take drugs?'" Brown retreated saying, "Well, indeed we didn't say that." Koppel persisted, "The decision has to be the parent's doesn't it?" Brown relied, "Uh, yes, it does."

But off camera, in conferences with parents called to discuss their "difficult" child, school authorities have tended to insist that unruly children be put on Ritalin, taking the attitude first expressed by Superintendent Brown, that this is "not really" a question for the parents to decide. A standard procedure is for school officials to gang up on a parent in a meeting with the teacher, the principal, the school counselor, a school nurse, or a psychologist. If the parent resists efforts to have the child placed on Ritalin, they threaten not to promote the child to the next grade. Two parents who fought school officials over Ritalin refused to be quoted for this article, saying they had endured enough trouble and didn't want to stir up any more for themselves and their child.

When confronted with lawsuits over Ritalin, school systems claim that they do not diagnose or directly suggest to parents that a child be given Ritalin. But the record shows otherwise.

Dr. Michael Levine, a San Antonio, Texas, psychiatrist and child development specialist, told the New York Times, "I know of instances in Texas where school districts specifically told parents that they thought their children needed Ritalin, and they gave them the names of physicians they knew would prescribe it."

Andrew Watry, executive director of the Composite State Board of Medical Examiners in Georgia, and head of a probe to determine the cause of a huge rise in the consumption of Ritalin in the state, found that teachers were pressuring parents to have their children placed on the drug. Watry commented, "The school systems are to blame if someone says, 'Your child needs Ritalin,' because they [the teachers] cannot make a medical judgment."

Commenting on the results of his probe, Watry said, "What we found was that there was a general notion that this drug was a panacea for a lot of behavior problems. People would seem to think it was a miracle drug and would suggest it for any kid who squirmed in his seat."

Diagnostic Difficulties

This brings up a basic question with regard to the use of Ritalin and the diagnosis of the conditions it is used to treat. What exactly are the criteria for determining that a child is suffering from A.D.D. or Attention-Deficit Hyperactivity Disorder, to use the name adopted in 1987? *The Diagnostic and Statistical Manual of Mental Disorders* (1987 edition) lists 14 indicators of this disorder, of which at least eight have to be present for at least six months. It cautions that each of the behavioral patterns listed must be "considerably more frequently than that of most people of the same mental age." Here are some of the indicators:

1. Fidgets or squirms in seat.
2. Talks excessively.
3. Has difficulty playing quietly.
4. Has difficulty waiting turn.
5. Shifts from one uncompleted activity to another.
6. Easily distracted by extraneous stimuli.
7. Fails to finish chores.
8. Loses things.

The ease with which the rules of diagnosis can be disregarded was shown on Nightline. Koppel introduced Dr. Jerry Wiener, president of the American Academy of Child and Adolescent Psychiatry and chairman of the Department of Psychiatry at George Washington University Medical Center. Speaking of Casey Jesson, seen earlier in the program, Dr. Wiener said, ". . . it is painful to see the film of that young boy, who is obviously even in the film so hyperactive and sort of so driven, and to hope that some effective treatment could be found."

Dr. Wiener made a diagnosis right on the air apparently based on the footage of Casey shown earlier in the program. He had seen the boy playing in his backyard, shooting a basket, doing gymnastic exercise while hanging on the basketball rim, and then playing inside, singing a song and yelling and laughing with his sister. ABC's Gail Harris had said that Casey "seems like any other energetic 9-year-old." But Dr. Wiener viewed his behavior as symptomatic of a disorder requiring drug therapy.

When Koppel asked if there weren't alternatives to Ritalin, Dr. Wiener immediately suggested another drug. When Koppel asked if there wasn't any other alternatives to the giving of drugs, Wiener replied that people do not object when certain other types of medication "they need" are prescribed for children. He said, "We don't have that reluctance after all with antibiotics . . ."

John Coale, attorney for several families suing school officials and physicians for damage to their children resulting from Ritalin, came on the program to criticize the criteria used to diagnose the disorder. He said, "These are little children—seven, eight-year-olds. Are we going to drug them because they don't behave, they don't stand in line?" Koppel asked Dr. Wiener, "Where is the line drawn? All children tend to fidget."

The question went to the heart of the controversy, but Dr. Wiener ducked it. He replied with an attack on Mr. Coale. The crucial question of precisely how the line is drawn between misbehavior that is so severe that it requires drugging the child and actions that should be handled in other ways went unanswered. Ted Koppel concluded his exploration of the Ritalin controversy saying, "I'm sure we'll be following this story in the months to come."

Teachers Play Doctor

In most cases the medical profession jealously guards its license to diagnose illness. Since the symptoms of Attention-Deficit Hyperactivity Disorder have to be observed for at least six months and often don't show up in a visit to the doctor, physicians are generally reduced to making diagnoses based on what teachers say. A child's being placed on Ritalin hinges on how a teacher chooses to interpret words such as "often" and "frequently."

Often the symptoms for which Ritalin is prescribed may be due to external circumstances including bad nutrition, problems at home or outside of school, boredom, or antagonism that may be caused by lack of skills on the part of the teacher. "Drugs should be the treatment of last resort," says child psychologist David Elkind of Tufts University. Yet the organization CHILD (Children with Hidden or Ignored Learning Disabilities) found that only two out of 102 children given Ritalin underwent the complete battery of tests that manufacturers recommend before a child is put on the drug.

While Ritalin definitely influences "social" behavior in the classroom, no study has ever shown that it improves academic achievement (such as reading skills or any other area). It is truly surprising to discover that much of the administration of drugs to young school children to deal with school problems is based on mere speculation, without any proven scientific basis.

Very Big Business

Another point not touched on the Nightline program is the question of how much money is being made on Ritalin. No exact figures are available from Ciba-Geigy, the drug's manufacturer, but in 1987 the Drug Enforcement Administration reported that a growing demand for the drug caused the agency to increase its proposed ceiling on Ritalin to twice the amount it had been two years earlier. "Its potency ranks right up there with cocaine," says the DEA's Gene Haislip. "I don't feel very comfortable about the production increases."

A state investigation took place in Utah, where the consumption of Ritalin was the highest in the country, four times the national norm. "The problem is, we really don't know why we use so much here," the New York Times quoted David E. Robinson, director of the State Division of Occupational and Professional Licensing. His division was trying to determine if the drug was being illegally diverted to street sales, or if Ritalin had become "trendy these days" because doctors were "over-diagnosing a problem."

A 1983 book put out by the American Academy of Child Psychiatry detailed ways of increasing business for psychiatrists through building up connections with school systems. The book, entitled *Child Psychiatry: A Plan for the Coming Decades*, lists Dr. Jerry Wiener as one of its contributors. At one point, the book suggests, "Service contracts can be developed between the schools and private child psychiatrists and with other groups such as medical centers" (page 67). Today Dr. Wiener is the most prominent and frequently quoted psychiatrist sponsoring use of Ritalin for school children.

Writing of the growing discussion developing over drug treatment for school children in an article appearing in the *Journal of Applied Behavior Analysis* back in 1980, K. Daniel O'Leary of State University of New York commented, "When the potential market for a medication is five percent of all elementary school children, that market is very big business."

Teachers asked about Ritalin often support its use, saying that it makes their daily job easier. There are many physicians who believe that when properly monitored, as any powerful drug should be, Ritalin can be of benefit to children who suffer learning disabilities that impair their ability to concentrate and perform assigned tasks. Many parents are also satisfied that the drug has helped improve the behavior of problem children, but many others are not only complaining but also suing because they were not informed about the possible side effects of the drug when they were urged to put their child on Ritalin.

For example, LaVerne Parker sued school officials and doctors in Georgia over harmful effects to her son resulting from taking Ritalin. Parker said teachers pressured her to put her son on Ritalin, insisting that he take it if he wanted to stay enrolled in public school. She says it stunted his growth, and he became violent and suicidal. Later she discovered that his original school difficulties stemmed from other problems than those which were earlier diagnosed and for which he was given Ritalin. As such suits go to trial, Ritalin controversy will become more visible in the news.

The news media may even be inspired to make an effort to alert the public to the dangers posed to our children by the excessive prescription of Ritalin. They showed how effectively they can do this kind of thing in publicizing charges that aspirin could cause Reyes Syndrome in children, sometimes with fatal results. This led to drug manufacturers being required to warn aspirin users of this possibility.

The *Journal of the American Medical Association* of October 21, 1988, acknowledged the possibility that Ritalin is being prescribed for children that don't need it. It said it was possible that the increased use of Ritalin reflects a "return to an antiquated simplistic approach that views all school and behavior problems as one." The Journal said, "In such a view, the diagnostic process is replaced by the reflex use of a particular treatment, in this case stimulants, prescribed for almost any child presenting with a behavioral or learning problem."

The *Journal* said this possibility should be of concern to physicians, educators, parents, and legislators interested in public policy. That amounted to a call for an investigation of the possible abuse of this potent drug. That is a call that the media have so far done little to amplify.

—*Ann Steinberg*

This excellent article is reprinted by permission from the AIM Report, ©1995 Accuracy in Media (AIM), 4455 Connecticut Ave NW, Ste. 330, Washington, DC 20008. (202) 364-4401. Fax: (202) 364-4098. Email: ar@aim.org. Web: www.aim.org. AIM fights to restore the "fairness, balance, and accuracy" that is so often lacking from today's news reporting. This non-profit, non-partisan service organization struggles to gain rights for American citizens who currently have no protection against media misinformation. The AIM Report is published twice monthly; subscriptions run $35 per year.

Just Say No to Drugs, Schools, and Labels

I am writing to comment on the recent article "Do Drugs Substitute for Discipline?" I read it with great interest . . . and a heavy heart.

We have been homeschooling four children (ages 16, 15, 13, and 7) for four years. It is a decision we have *never* regretted. They are a delight, and I cannot imagine spending my days alone with them in school.

However, we have five children. My oldest son is 21 and is currently in jail for parole violation after having spent four years incarcerated in a state prison. He began life as any other child, except he was very active. In 1982, when he was in the first grade, his teacher expressed concern that he may be hyperactive (ADD) and encouraged us to have him evaluated. We did. At that time we believed that teachers knew what our child needed better than us. The doctor felt that he may also be hyperactive and told us of a new drug being used with hyperactive children—Ritalin. Although admittedly stupid, we still didn't believe in "drugging" him, and we declined using Ritalin permanently. He struggled through school, and I sat up with him many nights to get him to finish schoolwork that he had not done that day at school. He hated it, and so did I.

When his impulsive behavior finally put him in the Juvenile Justice system at the age of 15, he was put on Ritalin, Lithium, Prozac, and who knows what else. He spent three weeks in a Psychiatric Unit for attempting suicide, and another six weeks at the Minirth Meyer Clinic in Chicago. When he was 16, he was finally kicked out of school for taking a .22 shell to school. I might also add that he was on Ritalin and under a counselor's care at the time he attempted suicide. This is the true story of a hyperactive child not disciplined correctly.

Our youngest child, Emily, displays many of the same symptoms of ADD. She has never been to school and has been taught to read at home by her "incompetent" mother. She currently reads at a fifth grade level. She did not learn until she was almost seven and had great difficulty sitting still and paying attention. She continues to blossom here at home, but I feel that she would quickly wither in a public school setting.

We had to go through some very deep waters before we were willing to let the Lord have his way. In looking back, I know that my son was not disciplined properly, and sometimes not at all. He was a constant source of irritation, and I frankly did not deal with him in a godly way. However, I do know that we are now on the right path. This child had put me into the depths of despair, but with that I have also reached a total commitment to the Lord.

I would not advise anyone to put their child on a drug. I would follow the suggestions given in the referred article and even more importantly, I would fall down on my face before the Lord. I would never, never send an ADD child into a public school setting. They must have a loving, godly home for shelter.

—*PHS reader "S.M." from MI*

Bouncing—that's what Tiggers do Best!

My young daughter would surely be labeled ADD if she were in public school. She was the only child of my four who threw temper tantrums. She had no attention span, and was always easily distracted. She was also very sickly.

I thank the Lord for a very perceptive pediatrician who had the foresight to pursue other avenues rather than slapping her with the "hyperactive" label. Because of her frequent illnesses, he suggested a blood test to see if something was wrong with her immune system. The test showed that her allergen count was abnormal. We took her to an allergist, where she was found to be allergic to wheat, corn, yeast, and other foods. Almost everything she ate had those three foods in them. Her immune system was so busy fighting the food allergies that there was nothing left to combat any virus or bacterial infection that entered her system.

We immediately changed her diet, and cleansed her system of everything she was allergic to. We gradually introduced the various foods to her, and she has out-

Children who were once seen as "bundles of energy," "daydreamers," or "fireballs" are now considered "hyperactive," "distractible," and "impulsive": the three classic warning signs of attention deficit disorder. Kids who in times past might have needed to "blow off a little steam" or "kick up a little dust" now have their medication dosages carefully measured out and monitored to control dysfunctional behavior. . . . I wonder whether there aren't hundreds of thousands of kids out there who may be done a disservice by having their uniqueness reduced to a disorder and by having their creative spirit controlled by a drug.

There's plenty of relevant information throughout this chapter to hopefully convince you that the drug/disease/isolation model is *not* the way to go when teaching distractible children.

Help for Distractible Children

Let's attack this from another angle. When do *you* get distracted? When you're:

- bored
- hungry
- worried
- out of control (we adults call this "losing it")
- overstimulated (too many decisions to make at once, too much to see)

"Bored" is a chronic state for schoolchildren, not for homeschooled kids. "Hungry" is again a state you can control at home by providing good food at regular intervals. "Worried"—there's a lot less to worry about at home. See Beverly Cleary's *Ramona* series for examples of how even nice suburban kids in a nice suburban school get emotionally overwrought about what their teachers and classmates think of them. How much more so in more dangerous school environments! "Out of control" is cured when the parents get *in* control

Drug It Down or Run It Out?

I propose we stop acting ashamed of little boys, and energetic little girls. There's nothing wrong with lots of energy and a desire to be the boss. Give it a place to go instead of stomping on it.

An example: We were looking at a house a while back. The owners, former foster parents, told us this story about two young fellows (call them John and Don) who came to live with them. The first two days, John and Don ran everywhere. Up the hill, down the hill, up the front steps, through the house, out the back, around the house. Nobody stopped them. The foster family was used to kids having strong reactions to a new placement. John and Don stopped running around wildly on the third day, and were subsequently enrolled in a local school.

Some time after this, the boys' caseworker came by to talk to the foster parents.

"Have you been giving John and Don their hyperactive medicine?" she inquired.

"Why, no," the foster mother replied. "Nobody told us they needed any medicine."

"Well, have you at least enrolled them in their Special Ed classes?"

"Special Ed? They're doing fine in regular classes!"

John and Don needed to run. They did not need counseling, Special Ed, or alligator tears of sympathy. Running made them feel better. When they felt better, they acted better and started learning.

Another example: our friend Jim helped found a private school. I asked him if he had ever had any trouble with "hyperactive" children. "Oh, you mean those wired-up boys?" he grinned. "Nope, never had any trouble. Whenever one of them started jumping around and acting wild, I took him out to the football field and had him run around it a couple of times. Settled 'em right down."

—*Schoolproof*

through simple, fair, consistent discipline (something you won't find in most schools, thanks to the Supreme Court). That leaves "overstimulated" as the last factor which can make *normal* kids hyper. Here, the answer is simple: dump the TV, eliminate sugar and caffeine, and get that kid some exercise!

Now that we've eliminated "false hyperactivity"—stuff that drives normal kids wild—let's take a look at some more productive approaches to educating *all* children, regardless of their averageness, slowness, genius, or distractibility.

- **I mentioned *exercise*.** This is a must. Cardiovascular exercise to the point of sweating, 20 minutes or more a time, three days a week, is necessary for general health. Highly energetic kids and couch potatoes both need *more*. Sometimes *much* more. See the box entitled "Drug it Down or Run it Out?" on the previous page for an example of how exercise alone instantly cured two foster kids of hyperactivity.
- **I also mentioned *good food*.** And let's stop kidding ourselves here: the mass-produced, packaged American diet does *not* include all the nutrients any of us need, especially growing children. Vitamins alone can't make the difference, so unless you grow your own food and grind your own grain, supplement drinks may be in order. See the *Crazy Makers* review later in this chapter for an example of how a once-a-day protein supplement noticeably improved mood, and slightly improved academics, in a reluctant group of teen testers.
- **Eliminating sources of allergies.** This is a big one. If exercise, good food, consistent and meaningful discipline for well-understood offenses, eliminating TV and video games, and interesting curriculum don't seem to make any difference, I suggest you have your child checked for allergies. Our chiropractor had a testing package we could send directly to the processing company for $75 per child. I found out my daughter had dairy and wheat allergies—not surprising, since dark circles under the eyes, pale skin, very fine hair that was lusterless and not growing, and unexplained rashes all are signs of allergies. Now she has beautiful hair, no dark circles, no rashes, and is *much* calmer. Thanks for asking!

grown all food allergies except for her allergy to wheat. When she eats wheat, she becomes hyperactive and does not concentrate well on her schoolwork. We call her our "bouncy Tigger" when she eats wheat. She knows that she "bounces" when she eats wheat, and is very responsible about eating only the special breads or cookies we have for her.

A friend of mine who is a teacher told me that my daughter would easily have been labeled ADD if she attended public school. Because we know how to "control" her, she is very "normal" in her behavior. I wonder how many children are being forced to take Ritalin, Prozac, Lithium, or other dangerous drugs to control their behavior, when it could be a simple food allergy. I have been able to share with friends whose children were very active and inattentive. Some were indeed allergic to certain foods: most commonly wheat, milk, or soy products.

I hope this letter may help some parents who may think that their children are "bouncy Tiggers." The Lord makes each child a unique individual, and who better to nurture and minister to that uniqueness than his/her parents?
—*Kathleen McC., Cool, CA*

Reading, Writing, and Ritalin

An estimated two million children (three times as many boys as girls, and four times as many as in 1990) have been labeled with Attention Deficit Disorder (ADD) or Attention Deficit Hyperactivity Disorder (ADHD). The most widely used drug to treat this condition is methylphenidate, known as Ritalin. A powerful stimulant, it juices up the central nervous system, takes effect in 30 minutes, and peters out in three to four hours. Ritalin is classified as a Schedule II controlled substance in the same category as cocaine, methadone, and methamphetamine.

In 1994, the U.S. Department of Education, Office of Special Education Programs, under contract HS92017001, gave the Chesapeake Institute of Washington, D.C., the funding to produce two slick videos: "Facing the Challenges of ADD" featuring actress Rita Moreno, and "One Child in Every Classroom" with Frank Sesno as moderator. Parts of the videos sound like an infomercial for Ritalin.

In a PBS documentary following eight months of investigation, a Department of Education spokesman was asked if he was aware that the parents who spoke so enthusiastically about Ritalin on the videos were board members of Children and Adult with Attention Deficit Disorder (CHADD), and if he knew that CHADD has received cash grants of $900,000 plus in-kind services from Ciba-Geigy, the manufacturer of Ritalin. Obviously embarrassed, the bureaucrat denied such knowledge. . . .

Parent of a child who is diagnosed, labeled, or treated by school-paid personnel would be well-advised to seek an independent, unbiased medical opinion.

—*Phyllis Schlafly Report*

The **Learning Style Model** developed by Mariaemma Willis and Victoria Kindle Hodson, and explained in their wonderful book *Discover Your Child's Learning Style,* reviewed in Chapter 11, provides a promising new approach. Instead of "labeling" and "remediating" children, they suggest the following. In their own words:

1. *All aspects of learning style are identified, including talents and interests.*
2. *A program is set up to work with those learning style needs.*
3. *The student's potential is seen as unlimited.*
4. *Excuses are replaced with problem solving and collaboration*
5. *Strengths are used to overcome weak areas.*
In other words, students are seen as capable rather than disabled.

Here are some other thoughts to consider for your distractible child:

- **Training.** At the Catholic private school I attended for four years, the nuns made us sit quietly in study hall for one hour a week. Being slightly hyper myself (normal for a strongly kinesthetic kid), I at first found this hard to take. But eventually, the practice in sitting still taught me to calm down and just *think* for an hour without any distractions, even schoolwork. You might not want to start with a whole hour, but for a Wild Child, working up to it might help.
- **Have you thought of thanking God** for your child's high energy level and hyperacute senses?
- **Maybe your child should be outdoors more.** Former generations of kids spent most of their out-of-school time outdoors, and nobody complained about their energy levels then!

Now I'll turn over the floor to special education expert Joyce Herzog, who has some more specific suggestions for you.

Joyce Herzog on How to Help

Joyce Herzog has been working with homeschoolers for almost 15 years. She is the author of the popular Scaredy-Cat Reading System, *Learning in Spite of Labels*, *Choosing & Using Curriculum: Including Special Needs*, and more. Her company, Simplified Learning Products, can be reached at 800-745-8212 or www.joyceherzog.com.

The following examples suggest that a child is poor at blocking out the variety of stimulus in his environment: he hears the curtains rustle, he sees the dust flecks floating, he feels the breeze lift the hairs on his arms. Many of these children who have been labeled hyperactive, hyperkinetic, ADD, or ADHD may not be able to shut out the overwhelming stimuli which confront their bodies and brains and, therefore, cannot concentrate on what is being said.

How Can I Help Him Listen?

- Allow him to hold and mold clay or Silly Putty as he listens.
- Save gum or hard candy as something he gets only when it is time to listen.
- Allow him to use crayons or markers with blank paper as he listens.
- As you read him a story, or in church, firmly rub his back.

How Can I Help Him Slow Down?

- Decrease the stimulus in his learning environment.
- Only ask for slow down when essential.

- Structure his learning time and always include something for his hands and/or mouth to be doing.
- He, above all children, needs to know what is expected, needs consistent discipline.
- Allow some kind of white background noise (ocean waves, very gentle and quite classical music, even quiet static) when he is to concentrate.
- Start with very small times of concentration interspersed with periods of total body involvement such as running, stretching, or somersaults. Gradually increase concentration time.
- Keep him out of situations that you know will over-stimulate him (unstructured situations, large numbers of people, loud concerts, etc.).

Other Helpful Hints

- Teach him early to jog, run, swim, and play ball and allow those activities as breaks between academics as often as possible. Start with two minutes of concentration followed by three minutes of controlled physical activity.
- Use a teaching style which allows him to get totally involved a controlled way. This means body, mind, and spirit, not just see, say, and write.
- Separate behavior from the person: "That behavior will not be tolerated." "You are always welcome, but that behavior is not." "Go to your bedroom (or a time-out area) until that behavior is under control." "I love you so much, but that behavior is . . . dangerous (disturbing me, distracting to others, etc.)." "We will have to leave . . . if you persist (until that is under control, until it stops, etc.)."
- As often as possible, he needs to understand the purpose of what he is doing and be motivated by his own agreement that it is important.
- It will be very important to keep the child from feeling worthless or inadequate. Praise him every **real** chance you get—not just for achievement, but for who he is or for trying his best. Believe in him and his potential to become a good person. Discover strengths and encourage their expression.
- Find something he is really interested in (cars, airplanes, horses, etc.) and try to associate anything you want him to learn with what he likes.
- He may rarely see a difficult project through to completion. Give him some very simple projects (one at a time) and see that they are finished. Then help him identify and enjoy the good feeling that comes from having finished the job.
- Encourage him to read aloud and use a marker to keep his place, but allow him not to if he becomes more distracted.
- Encourage him to make at least one good friend outside the family. This may be an older child who understands the need, an adult, or even a pet. He needs to have affirmation from someone other than Mom and Dad.
- The child will need to grow up and be involved in decisions about his learning as young as possible. He will succeed only with a great amount of effort on his own part, and he will be willing to put that forth only if he sees it is worth it.

What ADD and ADHD Really Stand For

In most instances, people who have been labeled "LD" are learning *deceived*—that is, they have grown up believing that they are deficient and their own natural abilities are not worth much. In my opinion, ADD more aptly refers to Attention to Dreams and Discoveries, and ADHD describes Alert to Daydreams and Humorous Diversions. . . I will admit there is some truth to ADD standing for attention deficit disorder—there is a definite *deficit* in the kind of *attention* that our young learners receive; therefore the *disorder* is with those schools who are labeling our children!
—*Discover Your Child's Learning Style*

- Give him a timer with a gentle count-down. Have him concentrate for a designated period of time, continually increasing the increments. When the timer signals, he may take a designated break, in continually decreasing increments. At first, he will need a signal to get back to work as well. The timer's signal should be gentle and unobtrusive.
- Don't give options. **It must be done now**. Be sure he understands in a firm but gentle way.
- You must always remain firm but gentle. Know what you expect, know what the limits are, and communicate them to him in a way that he understands. Do not allow him to break the rules until you are angry, and then yell and strike out. Any disobedience must be stopped early and consistently and redirected.
- Find times and ways to enjoy your child and your relationship with him. He won't find acceptance in many places or from many people. It is **essential** that he knows that you love him (always) and enjoy him.

More About Ritalin

The Ritalin-Free Child is an encouraging book that offers insight into the facts behind ADHD and drug therapy. It's easy to read, and filled with suggestions for helping you and your child manage his hyperactivity and attention deficit problems. This 155-page paperback offers many alternatives to medicating your ADHD child.

The ADHD diagnosis is examined in depth, along with many causes of the disorder. From that perspective, ways of improving your child's self-esteem, behavior, and education are suggested. Behavioral management and diet are discussed as acceptable replacements for drug therapy. There is even a chapter from the child's perspective about how drug therapy negatively affects his life. The different medications commonly prescribed to treat ADHD and a summary of what the drug was initially prescribed to treat (including side effects) enhance the usefulness of this book. This is a must-have book for parents and children struggling with the medication issue. *Maryann Turner*

Diet, Environment, and Your Distractible Child

The A.D.D. and A.D.H.D. Diet! is a small, concise paperback book that shares information about possible causes of ADD and ADHD, and suggestions about changes in your child's diet and living environment that can have positive effects on their ADD and ADHD behaviors.

The following questions are addressed in the book:

- Is there a connection between chemical fumes and learning ability?
- Can maldigestion contribute to behavior problems?
- What is commonly misdiagnosed as ADD or ADHD?
- Can diet contribute to fatigue and depression?
- What really is ADD/ADHD?
- Is the problem hereditary?

Nutrition, recipes, detoxifying methods, supplements and non-dietary approaches to ADD/ADHD are topics included in the book. A resource directory and bibliography make it easy to find the products and resources

NEW!
The Ritalin-Free Child
Parents. $12.95 plus shipping.
Consumer Press, 13326 Southwest 28th Street, Suite 102, Ft. Lauderdale, FL 33330. Orders: (800) 266-5752. Inquiries: (954) 370-9153. Fax: (954) 370-5722. Email: bookguest@aol.com. Web: www.consumerpress.com.

NEW!
The A.D.D. and A.D.H.D. Diet!
Parents $9.95 plus $2 shipping
Safe Goods, P.O. Box 36, East Canaan, CT 06024. Orders: (800) 903-3837. Inquiries: (860) 824-5301 or (941) 483-4518. Fax (860) 824-0309. E-mail: safe@snet.net

that the authors are discussing. There is a wealth of information about how foods affect behavior and nutrients necessary for optimum control of ADD symptoms. *Maryann Turner*

No drugs for my child! **ADD to Excellent Without Drugs** can help equip you with some necessary tools to rule out ADD triggers and find the root cause of your child's attention deficit disorder. Case studies are included in this 127-page, easy-to-read paperback.

Many cases of ADD are triggered by environmental factors, and if these triggers can be eliminated the need for drug therapy is eliminated as well! The book includes a list of the classic symptom of ADD, and 10 common causes of ADD behavior. The entire book addresses the 10 most common causes and how to take control of and prevent attention deficit disorder. *Maryann Turner*

This book could save your homeschool . . . or even your child's life.

We're used to thinking in terms of individual children having food sensitivities or allergies. But the problem may be much more widespread. **The Crazy Makers: How the Food Industry is Destroying Our Brains and Harming Our Children** demonstrates that a huge number of children today are having their academic performance and emotional stability undermined by what passes for food in our society.

Based on new research and a formal study the author, nutritionist Carol Simontacchi, conducted of American school children's eating habits, *The Crazy Makers* makes a compelling case that American food manufacturers are eroding our mental and emotional functions, all in the name of profit.

Consider these facts, drawn from the book:

- Twenty percent of teens contemplate suicide each year—and the rate of actual teen suicide increased nearly 30 percent from 1980 to 1992.
- The rate of mental depression has been soaring since World War II, especially among young men
- Up to 24 percent of adults experience a mental health crisis in any given year.
- Seven to 14 percent of children will experience an episode of major depression before the age of 15.

Now, we all know that modern life has its pressures, and that the downfall of the church and family has dramatically affected society. But in past centuries, people withstood greater pressures—wars, serfdom and slavery, death of family members at a young age, wholesale loss of babies due to unhygienic living conditions—without going nuts. So what's up?

Food used to be complete fruits and vegetables, brown grains with the bran intact, *un*homogenized milk and other dairy products not subjected to temperatures that kill all the enzymes needed to digest them, meat from animals who had never tasted an antibiotic, and fish. Now, our food mostly comes in packages and boxes, "enhanced" by substances with names like allyl antharnilate, methyl delat-ionone, and FD&C Blue No. 1. Carol Simontacchi claims—and demonstrates from research—that the effects of this daily chemical onslaught includes hyperactivity, depression, fatigue, confusion, and aggressive, even violent behavior. When it comes to our

children, the problem escalates, especially around puberty, when the body is subject to massive changes.

The typical teenager's diet is grossly inadequate in most vitamins and minerals, in particular the B complex vitamins. Simontacchi had children keep food diaries listing everything they ate, and found that, "It is not uncommon to see a seven-day food diary containing twenty-one meals with almost no vegetables, no fruit, no protein, and no water." When she had one group of teens from a Christian high school drink a protein supplement shake before school every day, even though they had not wanted to be part of the study, even though they did not change any of their other eating habits, and even though some were uncooperative to the point of washing the nutritional drink down with soft drinks, a mood test showed significant improvement in these teens' emotional state, as compared to the control group who received no supplement.

Food affects mood. As the book puts it,

> *Take a child and deprive his brain of adequate nutrition through his entire life, dump him into a hostile, unstable social scene [she's referring to school], and pull away the pillars of his support network (his family— he pulls away from them).*
>
> *Then load up his breakfast cereal with stimulants, feed him more stimulants at lunch, snack, and dinner, and at the same time, rob him of the very nutrients he needs to process the stimulants. Toxic chemicals from his food target his endocrine system and prevent his natural hormones from locking into place. Inject other toxic chemicals from his food into his nervous system that prevent neurotransmitters from relaying messages back and forth. This is a recipe guaranteed to make him or her crazy.*

Contributing to the problem are our schools, who make deals with vending machine companies, fast-food franchises, and others to provide low-quality, high-profit food to 51 million children and young adults. Over $750 million is spent annually on vending machines in schools alone, not counting the less-than-wonderful products parading through the cafeteria kitchens. The most chilling part of the book, to my mind, is where the author chronicles how school nutritionist after school nutritionist, knowing better, sells out their students for a few thousands in profit for the school.

What this all means is that perfectly normal children with excellent parents can still go nuts if their diets are deficient—and bad, but tasty, food drives out the good.

- Iron deficiency is markedly associated with overagression in young men; nearly twice as many incarcerated males are iron deficient as their nonincarcerated peers
- Magnesium deficiency causes chronic fatigue, twitching, constipation, anger, depression, frustration, agitation, and panic attacks. Weepiness, clinging, or secluding oneself are symptoms.
- Zinc deficiency leads to fuzzy-mindedness, confusion, depression, headaches, and bread cravings. Copper-toxic, zinc-deficient people may become verbally abusive.

It gets more serious. As the book explains, "Twenty-five percent of all teenagers will engage in activities so severe that if they even survive adolescence, some form of permanent damage will haunt them the rest of their lives." We're talking about anorexia, bulimia, suicide fixation, self-mutilation, violence towards others, drug abuse, and drunkenness, to name a few.

Bottom line: the more pre-packaged and fast food your children eat, even supposedly "good" packaged food, and the less they eat fresh fruit and vegetables, exercise, and supplement with proper protein, vitamins, and minerals, the more likely you are to see mild-to-severe emotional disturbances and academic problems, especially in the teen and young adult years, even from children who never before gave you a day's trouble in their lives. Even good home-cooked meals might not be enough, if you frequently cook the same things and they lack some essential nutrient. Conversely, if a child is experiencing emotional problems and is unhappy about it (e.g., not wilfully rebelling), following the author's advice and possibly following up with personalized nutritional therapy from a professional you can locate through her appendix could end the nightmare.

I hope we all know that evil behavior is sinful, not just an inevitable result of chemical programming and that a major reason today's kids "act out" is that society sends them the message that even kids who commit major crimes don't get punished. Given this situation, a kid under stress does not have social taboos and peer pressure as bulwarks against bad behavior. Indeed, today our media are avidly *selling* bad behavior, and peer pressure is a major *cause* of bad behavior. This leaves the child with just his inner character and parental support to offset any overwhelming emotional impulses he may be experiencing. The Lord's Prayer includes the prayer to be preserved from temptation—stresses that make it easy to fall into bad behavior. And Micah 6:14 also makes it clear that, when God judges a nation, "Thou shalt eat, but not be satisfied," which in our day may well include a food supply geared more to tastiness than to fulfilling our nutritional needs. Protecting our children from unnecessary temptation—in the form of chemicalized food and nutritional deficiencies that make them irritable, displeased, or confused—may become an increasingly important part of our role as parents.

So, what are we going to do? First step, read this book. Divided into chapters on how to nourish the unborn baby, babies and toddlers, young children, teens, and adults—each of which explains what can go wrong at each age as well as what is needed—*The Crazy Makers* can easily be used as an introductory nutrition course at the junior-high or high-school level, one way better than anything I've seen on the market. You will learn a ton about how food provides energy to your body, the ingredients of good and bad food, and food deficiencies, all far beyond the typical (and unhelpful) "food pyramid" taught in textbooks. The author is not into any form of food faddism, so you don't have to worry about her preaching that you should eat odd food, avoid all meat, etc. Meanwhile, you'll be getting an easy-reading education on the food industry, nutritional research, and why this all matters.

The Crazy Makers also includes recipes, a primer on how to create your own healthful menus, an appendix of resources, another appendix listing groups who can refer you to a trained nutritionist, and an index.

So now we have one more reason to homeschool—to protect our kids from the body-and-emotion-destroying school food. *Mary Pride*

The Feingold Association is a reputable organization that boasts of amazing results in helping parents of hyperactive children, with abundant proof to back up their claims. The material is easy to understand and well worth the money.

Starting from the premise that dietary allergies are a leading cause of hyperactivity, the Feingold diet was designed to eliminate the major dietary culprits. **Diet, Learning & Behavior** is a 13-page, spiral-bound introduction to the Feingold diet. It explains what membership in the Feingold Association provides. It lists symptoms of additive/salicylate sensitivity, and specifies the dangers of artificial colors, flavors, preservatives and environ-

NEW!
Diet, Learning & Behavior
Parents. Feingold Association membership & program materials, $75 plus shipping.
Feingold Association of the United States, 127 E. Main St., Riverhead, NY 11901. (800) 321-3287 or (516) 369-9340. Web: www.feingold.org.

mental chemicals. Salicylates are defined, and research studies are provided.

Included in your membership package is a list of acceptable foods from a varied assortment of items available in your supermarket. The list includes over a thousand brand name products which are free of unwanted additives. You also receive the Feingold Handbook which provides the most current information on the use of diet to help you or your child. A list of additive-free medications is also included. Recipes and a two-week menu make planning your first few weeks easier. A one-year subscription to their newsletter, *Pure Facts,* accompanies your membership. A "Dear Grandma" letter is included that explains the program to relatives, friends, teachers, etc. Program Assistant List and FAUS Counseling Line, staffed by parents who are experienced in the Program, are available to answer your questions and give support. *Maryann Turner*

The Impossible Child

Adult. $10.95 plus $2 shipping.
Still available at amazon.com or try used bookstores or the library.

"There is a subset of children who appear to learn well and easily on one day, but not on another. They seem unable to function consistently well in school. They often act appropriately but suddenly, for no apparent reason, their behavior can exasperate the most patient teacher or parent. Other children appear unable to learn or behave most of the time. Some are too active; others are too tired . . . Many have recurrent headaches, leg aches, or digestive complaints."

Any of this sound familiar? Then **The Impossible Child** might hold some answers for you. The purpose of this book is to show you how to detect if your youngster is experiencing an unsuspected allergic reaction, and what to do if he or she is. The book does not lay the blame for all bad behavior at the feet of allergies. It does, however, point out that some kids get high on some foods, or bummed out by molds and pollens, and that we all have a much harder time functioning properly under such circumstances.

This is not a superficial book, in spite of its easy-reading style. You are given specific facial or body clues to tip you off to a possible allergic reaction—e.g., red earlobes. The book also includes numerous before-and-after examples of children's work and considerable detail about specific allergies and how to spot and treat them.

Is behavior modification therapy the solution to non-allergy-caused behavior problems? Author Doris Rapp says yes. I say no. This fairly major disagreement aside, I think this is a good book. We do owe it to our kids to find out if they suffer when exposed to chemicals, pollen, pets, or dairy products. However, in no way can the vast increase in kids' rotten behavior today be blamed on allergies. Allergies may indeed provide extra pressure, but even a splitting migraine does not have the power to force any of us to bite, spit, and swear unless we let it. All this granted, before you give up on a child who is not responding normally to character training, it's worthwhile checking out whether he is suffering extra pressure from undetected allergies—and this book can help with that.

The Impossible Child is hard to find, but is still available through Amazon.com. *Mary Pride*

Help & Advice

NEW!
Managing Attention & Learning Disorders

Parents. $11.99.
Harold Shaw Publishers, Box 567, Wheaton, IL 60189.
Orders: (800) 742-9782.

Finally, a book that helps adults maximize their potential and organize their lives, in spite of attention deficit disorder or other learning difficulties! **Managing Attention & Learning Disorders** is filled with useful ideas from an author/educator who suffers and benefits from ADHD. From the ADHD checklist to the multitude of helpful hints in this book, cover to cover this book is a winner! Learn to organize your life, master your job, understand your personal struggles, get along at home and structure your household to make the most of your strengths. ADHD can be a blessing in disguise if you learn to use the positives and minimize the negatives.

The survival strategies in this book are terrific. Even people that don't suffer from ADHD can benefit from some of the ideas in this book.

Thousands of adults suffer from ADHD symptoms, but have never been diagnosed because ADHD recognition is a relatively new area of research. Regardless of a diagnosis, this book helps you recognize your symptoms and organize your life in order to eliminate the confusion and chaos that often accompanies attention deficit problems.

This is a 186-page paperback, written in a format that makes it possible to read topics of interest in any order. *Maryann Turner*

Inquiries: (630) 665-6700 ext. 223.
Fax: (630) 665-6793.
Email: shawpub@compuserve.com.
Web: www.shawpub.com.

The Caregivers' Skills Program is a unique method designed to help ADD and ADHD children behave correctly, pay attention, function independently, and solve problems without medication. This program was developed over 25 years by the author of this book, David B. Stein, Ph.D. **Ritalin Is Not the Answer** details a drug-free program for your ADHD child. The dangers of Ritalin are discussed, and an alternative method of teaching your children to handle his problems is explained in detail.

The 203-page paperback book is divided into the following chapters:

- What Are We Doing to Our Children?
- Understanding the Myths of Attentional Disorders
- The Importance of Effective Parenting
- Beginning the Caregivers' Skills Program
- Improving Behaviors
- Punishment
- Beginning to Learn Discipline
- Using Time Out Correctly for the IA or HM Child
- Reinforcement Removal for Very Difficult Behaviors
- Improving School Performance
- Helping the IA or HM Child to Feel Better
- Ten Ways to Stop Creating an Attentional Disorder Child

Appendices, reference lists, and an index are also included.

By learning the techniques explained in this book, you can equip yourself with the necessary ammunition to help your child succeed. The tools that Stein uses are ignoring, time-out, and reinforcement removal (taking away objects and activities that are most important to your child). He explains how to overcome the traps that can occur with these methods, so that you are able to be more consistent. The methods Stein suggests build your child's confidence and encourage him to think for himself. This book offers helpful advice and motivates you to seek appropriate discipline in order to bypass the use of Ritalin. *Maryann Turner*

Does your child have trouble keeping up with his school work? Are you wondering if he has a true learning disability? Do you need ideas to help reach your child? Both of Katherine Koonce's **Windows of Opportunity** audiocassette tape programs are filled with valuable insights into learning disabilities and attention deficit disorder.

The two programs are entitled **Helping Children Who Have Difficulties Learning** and **Helping Children Who Have Difficulty Paying Attention**. Each program includes two tapes: "Pinpointing the Problem"

NEW!
Ritalin Is Not the Answer

Parents. $15 plus shipping.
Jossey-Bass Publishers, 350 Sansome Street, San Francisco, CA 94104. Orders: (800) 956-7739. Inquiries: (415) 433-1740. Fax: (415) 433-0499. Email: webperson@jbp.com. Web: www.josseybass.com.

NEW!
The Windows of Opportunity Program:

Parents. $20 plus shipping.
Common Sense Press, P.O. Box 1365, Melrose FL 32666. Call (352)475-5757 for a retail store near you; they do not sell retail themselves.
Email: LearnCSP@aol.com.

and "Strategies for Success." The "Pinpointing the Problem" tape walks you step by step through the process of determining where your child struggles. The second tape, "Strategies for Success" enables you to find ways to encourage your child when he struggles. Katherine Koonce helps you create a learning environment that is unique to your child's learning challenges.

A record booklet that becomes your observations and plans for your child is also an important part of the program. The tapes and booklet are encased in an attractive plastic album to help you keep up with the components.

Unlike many programs on the market that address learning differences, Windows of Opportunity was originally designed for homeschooling parents. That makes this a user-friendly program for parents that are trying to decide if their child has a true learning or attention problem. *Maryann Turner*

Success Stories & Inspiration

NEW!
Every Child Can Succeed

Parents. $17 plus shipping.
Focus on the Family Publishing,
Colorado Springs, CO 80995.
(719)531-3400. Fax: (719)531-3424.
E-mail: mail@fotf.org.
Web: www.family.org.

Every Child Can Succeed contains practical tips meant to help your child achieve greater success. It's easy to become frustrated when you are trying to raise a seemingly difficult child. Tobias shows us how to maximize the benefits by using your child's particular learning style to master the areas that are causing stress in your life. She explains the different learning styles and how they affect the way your child learns and behaves. She shares ideas on motivating your child, making the teachers work with your child, discipline and conflict solving.

Celebrating your child's strengths and boosting his self-esteem works wonders in solving behavior problems. Using the gifts God gave your child as a springboard to self-appreciation is often all we need in order to overcome what appears to be learning problems. Tobias includes a chapter that helps determine if your child truly suffer from ADD or if you simply need to change the way you are presenting the information or instructions. By understanding why your child behaves the way he does, you can find effective ways to bring out the best in your child.

This 154-page, hardback book wasn't written from the home education viewpoint, but none the less the author's ideas are beneficial to those of us that homeschool. *Maryann Turner*

NEW!
Succeeding With LD

Parents. $14.95.
Free Spirit Publishing, Inc., 400 First
Avenue North, Suite 616, Minneapolis,
MN 55401. (800) 735-7323.
Fax: (612) 337-5050.
Email: help4kids@freespirit.com.
Web: www.freespirit.com.

Learning differences are real! The people in this book are real! **Succeeding with LD** is a heartwarming, inspiring compilation of 20 stories of real people with learning differences. The ages vary from 10 to 62, and each story is unique. The one thing they all have in common is that they all struggled with LD and they all are talented and successful. Some are even famous!

Also included in this inspirational book is a question and answer section, tips for succeeding, and resources for more information about learning differences. This is an easy to read, large print,147-page paperback book. The larger than average print makes it even easier for our LD teens to become inspired by the hurdles that these special people have overcome. *Maryann Turner*

Uncommon Gifts is the true story of one man's battle with multiple learning differences. James Evans shares his real-life struggles with hyperactivity, attention deficit disorder, and dyslexia. His learning difficulties plummeted him into depression and into having a poor self image.

In his 236-page account of his life story, Evans determination and faith emerges victorious time and again. From the early days when his parents first realized there was a problem until a time much later that it was finally diagnosed, James struggled to fit in. The story takes him through his teen years and into adulthood. You see him gain victory over his struggles as he becomes minister, husband and father. You celebrate with his successes!

This paperback book is a real inspiration for parents who has a child struggling with learning differences. *Maryann Turner*

Resources for Typical Treatment

The **Directory of Facilities and Services for the Learning Disabled** is now in its 17th edition. It contains scads of useful information about facilities serving these children: size of staff, services offered, types of problems handled, ages served, fee type, and year established, all listed by state for convenience. The body of the Directory is state-by-state listings of more than 500 facilities and services for these children.

If you are not terribly excited about the services of experts, the Directory also includes a comprehensive listing of companies offering specialized materials for labeled children and their teachers, national organizations and agencies serving this community, educational journals, college guide for LD students, and more. An alphabetical index and index by service provided finish off the book, which closes with an area code map so parents can easily call any interesting references. *Mary Pride*

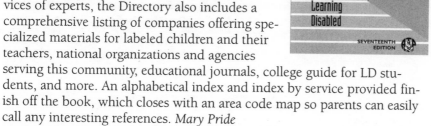

CHAPTER 28

Help for the Challenged

Families have many reasons for homeschooling. Perhaps one of the most compelling is that the school system either has already failed their child or does not offer the help they believe their child needs. This is often true in the case of children with challenges—among which we include both physical impediments and learning problems with an *organic* physical cause, such as a recognized birth defect or actual brain damage resulting from an accident.

True, today's schools have immense funding to help just such children, and laws compel them to do so. But often the results bear no resemblance to the amount of funding and good will invested. As with every other area of school operations, special education has its fads. The fad of the moment may involve lumping physically challenged kids with mentally challenged kids, or even with "emotionally challenged" kids—a euphemism that now includes the youthful assaulters, rapists, and murderers who the courts require to be kept *in* school. Maybe it's a craze for teaching all deaf kids sign language—and nothing *but* sign language—so they can form a separate language group incapable of communicating with others and as such press for more government funding. (I'm not making this up. The anti-lip-reading lobby is large and loud.) Maybe your school district mainstreams all physically challenged kids, and you have reason to fear for your frail or disabled child's physical safety at the hands of the school bullies. Maybe you just think your child is capable of a whole lot more than the school will admit, and you're starting to believe you can do a better job yourself.

Or perhaps you feel homeschooling really is your only option. Maybe your child is housebound, confined to the vicinity of life-support machines, like my oldest son. Perhaps you simply believe in an educational philosophy or rehabilitative method unavailable in your local school.

Whatever the cause, you want to homeschool.

But can you homeschool a child with physical or mental challenges—even serious physical challenges?

Can you homeschool your children even if *you* are the one with the challenges?

The answer to both questions is, "Yes!"

And the good news is, you don't have to do this all on your own.

In this chapter, you will find organizations and products geared especially to help you in your homeschooling endeavor.

Lateblooming, Laziness, and Deficiency

Kids, of course, will try to sucker you into going easy on them. In this, they are exactly like adults. You will need to be able to distinguish between lateblooming, laziness, and deficiency.

- **Lateblooming** is when a child needs more time to learn.
- **Laziness** is when he won't even do what he knows how to do. (Very little kids forget things easily— keep this in mind).
- **Deficiency** is when the poor kid actually has something organic wrong with him. "Mental retardation" is not deficiency. It's what doctors say when they don't know what's wrong with you. On the other hand, identifiable birth defects may cause a child to be slower across the board than other children.

You need more patience for lateblooming and deficiency, less for laziness. Remembering that human beings are more than organic brain cells, I would be inclined to treat "deficient" kids as latebloomers who possess all the spiritual equipment of other human beings. This includes the ability to understand a story, make jokes, and resent being treated like a machine or animal.

—*Schoolproof*

Organizations That Can Help

Many groups whose titles suggest they help children and parents of children with disabilities are less than helpful. Some of these groups promote erroneous beliefs about human nature and education. Others seem to exist mainly to demand huge legal settlements and huge amounts of taxpayer money for their agenda. Yet others have some helpful resources, along with others that are less helpful or downright unhelpful.

We suggest that you steer clear of materials and "experts" who encourage you to obsess about your child's problems. Rather, ask these people and groups what successes they have had. Use these groups and resources to meet other families who are contending with the same challenges and to find out about breakthrough technologies and methods that are not covered in the mainstream press.

Remember, your fellow homeschoolers are a goldmine of information. With the notable exception of a few special education "experts" who can be seen from time to time peddling the same old failed public-education strategies at homeschool conventions, your fellow parents have no axe to grind. They know what works for them and what doesn't.

ERIC CLEARINGHOUSE ON DISABILITIES AND GIFTED EDUCATION
1920 Association Drive
Reston, VA 20191
(800) 328-0272
www.ericec.org
Database of information, curriculum, software, etc., for disabled and gifted

FOUNDATION FOR TECHNOLOGY ACCESS
1128 Solano Avenue
Albany, CA 94706
(510) 528-0747
FTA works to provide assistive technologies to those who need it. If your child is physically disabled in some way (blind, deaf, paraplegic, etc.) these people can lead you to equipment that can help your child interact with a computer.

NATIONAL ASSOCIATION FOR CHILD DEVELOPMENT
PO Box 1639
Ogden, UT 84402
(801) 621-8606
www.nacd.org
NACD has books, tapes, seminars, and in-person consultations at local chapters around the country. Helps for the physically and neurologically challenged, the slow learner, and the gifted. Very compatible with homeschool philosophy. NACD trains parents to do the therapy themselves. They were a big help with our son, Ted.

NATHHAN
National Challenged Homeschoolers Associated Network
PO Box 39
Porthill, ID 83853
(208) 267-6246
Email: nathanews@aol.com
Web: nathhan.com
$25/year NATHHAN membership offers folks all of these services:
NATHHAN News, NATHHAN Family Directory, Lending Library, and HSLDA

Group discount. If you are unable to afford the fee, families who really need encouragement may still contact NATHHAN for further information.

THE ORTON DYSLEXIA SOCIETY
Chester Building, Suite 382
8600 LaSalle Rd.
Baltimore, MD 21286-2044
(410) 296-0232
www.interdys.org
Pioneering organization studying dyslexia. Promotes phonics methods for dyslexia reversals.

An Organization for Challenged Homeschoolers

The NATional cHallenged Homeschoolers Associated Network (NATHHAN) is a "national and international support network for families with special needs, who home educate." The network began in March of 1990, when Kathy Salars telephoned a friend asking for help with her special education homeschooling. Kathy's friend Diane, who was already writing to several families through a newsletter column titled "Dear Special Ed," decided to begin a network of parents helping one another. NATHHAN was born.

Since its humble beginning in 1990, the families in NATHHAN have received hundreds of letters and phone calls asking for resources, ideas, and encouragement. The exponential growth experienced by NATHHAN demanded the formation of a centralized office. In the fall of 1992, Tom Bushnell, his wife Sherry, and their children stepped into this rapidly growing ministry to write the newsletter and operate the support network. Tom came home to work in the NATHHAN office full time in January of 1995.

NATHHAN has always invited families to participate in the sharing of experiences in order to help and encourage one another, most of all through prayer. NATHHAN's goals and purposes speak for themselves: "To be spiritually and financially equipped to help others with their needs in home educating their children. To speak and share with families personally. To act as a support network, uplifting families. To have this ministry and all of its activities be forthright and consistent in giving honor and glory to the Lord Jesus Christ."

NATHHAN currently has four specific services to offer homeschoolers:

* **NATHHAN Support Network** is made up of 12,600 families throughout the world. The network provides an abundance of resources, encouragement, and friends. The service is free and can be joined by simply sending a letter or postcard describing the challenge or questions which need to be addressed.
* **NATHHAN NEWS** is a 56-page quarterly newsletter. It includes features on resource reviews, adoption of special needs children, and articles pertaining to raising and homeschooling a challenged child. It also includes a section devoted to finding help for individual families and many letters from challenged homeschooling families around the world.
* **NATHHAN Family Directory** is published once a year and includes families who graciously share encouragement and experiences with those in need. The trusting families who appear in this directory do so out of love and care, not monetary funds. "Only those who ask to be a part of this directory will receive their own to use. It is NATHHAN's sincere hope that many wonderful friendships will be formed."
* **NATHHAN Lending Library** is located at the NATHHAN office in Porthill, ID. However, it is available to all members through the mail. Postage is paid by the people who use it. Write NATHHAN for information on what books are available.

It is easy to feel confused and isolated when attempting to choose the right path. NATHHAN is full of love and enthusiasm for the task set out before us.

Presently disabilities represented in NATHHAN range all the way from children with dyslexia or learning disabilities to the multihandicapped, blind, cerebral palsy, and seizure-disordered children.

—*Tom and Sherry Bushnell, NATHHAN*
Tom and Sherry Bushnell live in Porthill, Idaho with their 9 children, 3 of whom are adopted and have special needs. Along with working in the office and writing the NATHHAN NEWS, the Bushnells give NATHHAN presentations to churches and attend a few homeschooling fairs.

Making Your Individualized Education Planner

An Individual Education Plan (IEP) may be required in your state, if your child has been labeled "special needs." Check with HSLDA for the law in your state. Below is the (as far as we know) only resource ever developed to help homeschool parents develop their own IEP.

IEP's made easy! This multi-grade level, **Individual Education Planning System for the Handicapped Student** is designed just for homeschoolers in an easy to use fill-in-the-blank format. You will create professional looking IEPs specific to the special needs of your home-educated student.

The fruit of author Deborah Mills' eight years of experience teaching workshops and creating IEPs for her disabled son, it is largely based on the use of a Functional Curriculum format. A Functional Curriculum is one that teaches skills through Daily Living Tasks. When using a non-traditional curriculum such as this, it is important to be able to document the learning process in a meaningful way. HSLDA recommends that a special needs student have quarterly evaluations. The IEP forms included in the manual provide you a way to credibly demonstrate that your student is indeed learning and making progress, even if you have a severely retarded child who is only learning personal grooming skills and daily chores.

The Manual explains how to develop your own IEP specific to your child's special needs. Its planning sheets and Activities Listing serve as a springboard of ideas for IEP goals. Also included: articles of encouragement and examples from the author's personal experiences with her son. There is even a section that explains how a regularly educated sibling can receive high-school credit for a four-year Special Education Course!

Topics included in the manual are:

- What is an IEP?
- Functional Curriculum vs. Traditional Curriculum
- How to design an IEP for Home Education
- How to set goals
- How to implement the plan
- How to evaluate progress
- Lesson planning and documentation
- High-school planning
- The ITP (Individual Transition Plan)
- Graduation requirements
- After high school services, programs, and options
- Resource listing

Reproducible Master IEP Forms, come with permission to copy for personal, in-home, family use. These are:

- Individual Education Program (Statistics)
- General Information Page
- Life Space Domain/Current Functioning Levels
- Basic Skill Infusion Grid
- Individual Education Plan (Forms for Each Domain)
- Activity Evaluation Sheet
- Summary of Achievement (Quarterly Assignment)
- Daily Activity Worksheet, Grid
- Daily Lesson Plan, Grid
- IEP Planning Sheets, Target Activities (3 pages)

NEW!
Individual Education Planning System for the Handicapped Student
Parents. $35.
Deborah Mills, 8266 Leucadia Ave., san Diego, CA 92114. (619) 469-5822.

The Chronological Age-Appropriate Activities Listing for students with severe handicaps offers a menu of ideas from which to draw when developing an IEP. You are encouraged to use this as a starting point for your own curriculum.

The curriculum information contained in this guide is organized according to four "life space domains"—*community, domestic, recreation/leisure,* and *vocational* domains. Each domain is addressed across six age groups: Ages 2–3, Preschool (ages 3–5), Elementary School/Primary (ages 6–8), Elementary School/Intermediate (ages 8–12), Middle School (ages 12–16), and High School (ages 16–18).

This 226-page manual comes 3-hole punched, ready to put into a binder for easy shelf reference. *Mary Pride*

How to Homeschool with Special Needs

Need help choosing material for your special needs child? Joyce Herzog is the expert. This book is filled with Joyce's wisdom and down-to-earth advice. **Choosing & Using Curriculum for Your Special Child** includes hundreds of reviews for programs in math, reading, language arts, handwriting, geography, history, and science. In this oversized, 76-page paperback Joyce discusses the different curriculum types and evaluates the advantages and disadvantages of each. She pulls no punches when pointing out the disadvantages to some of the more popular programs. Throughout the book are tips for teaching each subject. She covers spiritual, religious, and Bible training in her product reviews. Included are chapters on testing, special education resources, deaf education resources, legal information, support groups, and magazines. Joyce is very matter-of-fact with her reviews, making this a very valuable tool when choosing curriculum for your special needs child. *Maryann Turner*

Educational Care is based on the view that education should be "a system of care that provides for the specific needs of individual students." This 320-page textbook starts by identifying and describing 26 common behaviors that interfere with learning. These phenomena are grouped in chapters according to the following six themes: weak attention controls, reduced remembering, chronic misunderstanding, deficient output, delayed skill acquisition, and poor adaptation in school. Note that this list does *not* include dietary, emotional, or environmental problems—for that kind of help, check out the books we reviewed in the previous chapter. The book also includes information on "dysfunctions" such as ADD, gross-motor dysfunction, problems with short-term memory, and weak visual processing.

Following the analysis of each behavior are lists of suggestions about how to help students who are having difficulty with the particular area. In addition, these chapters provide ideas about how to help demystify disabilities by naming, explaining, and discussing them.

The author, Dr. Mel Levine, believes that many problems result from labeling and segregating impaired students. He states, "Without denying the existence of specific conditions, we will avoid the labels and explore in some depth the phenomenas."

The book concludes with descriptions of teaching methods, kinds of assessment, and by-pass strategies. The book also discusses available medical treatments, all of which will be helpful in letting you see what kinds of approaches you can expect a school to subject your child to.

The appendices contain a variety of handy forms. Some, such as the mathematics interview, can be used for diagnosis, while others, like the report and story organizers, help the student organize, carry out, and evaluate specific tasks. Numerous tables and graphs help the reader navigate and recognize important information.

Unfortunately, *Educational Care* asserts that children with learning problems should be educated through "collaborative management" of parents and teachers, and does not discuss home education.

My advice: don't skip the book because it is not specifically targeted towards homeschoolers. When applying the doctor's suggestions, just remember, you are the teacher and your home is the school. *Brad Kovach*

NEW!
Home Schooling Children with Special Needs

Parents. $12.95 plus shipping. *Noble Publishing Associates, PO Box 2250, Gresham, OR 97030. Orders: (800) 225-5259. Inquiries: (503) 667-5084. Fax: (503) 618-8866. Email: Noblebooks@aol.com. Web: www.noblepublishing.com.*

Written to meet the questions and needs of the Christian homeschooler, and subtitled "Turning challenges into opportunities," **Home Schooling Children with Special Needs** is intended to be a framework to aid you in teaching your special child.

This 180-page manual is broken down into three easy-to-understand sections: Section 1—Getting the Facts, Section 2—Tackling the Issues, and Section 3—Planning Your Program. Each section is further divided into short, authoritative lessons about every facet and emotion involved with teaching a special learner. The author, Sharon Hensley (M.A. Special Education), speaks from experience. She is a homeschooling mother of three, one of which is autistic.

Section 1 identifies and analyzes numerous behaviors that can disrupt learning. These are grouped in six segments: learning mismatches, learning disabilities, slow learners, language/communication disorders, mental retardation, and autism. Some of the behaviors discussed include auditory system disorders, motor sensory disorders, and attention disorders. After discussion of each phenomena, the author provides a list of judging criteria, suggested therapies, and resources.

Section 2 tackles two important issues in the home education of special learners: emotions and expectations. The author discusses, from experience, feelings of inadequacy, grief, anger, acceptance, and discouragement and how to deal with their appearance. She provides a loose schedule of expectations and talks about balancing the education of siblings. The author also uses this portion of the book to face the moral and ethical reasoning behind home education of the special learner: public v. home school, medication v. behavior modification, etc.

Section 3 help the reader plan their homeschool program. Developing a consistent and individualized plan with set goals and testing is discussed in detail. The author explains the importance of choosing the correct teaching method and curriculum. Teaching methods such as computer-assisted learning, interest-directed learning, therapies, textbooks, and unit studies are defined and analyzed. Curriculums are similarly broken down and discussed. The author even reviews of large list of curriculums and products designed for the special learner.

A final note promising the continuation of the book leaves the reader wanting more: more curricula, more resources, and more of the heart-felt writing. *Brad Kovach*

NEW!
The Special Artist's Handbook: Art Activities and Adaptive Aids for Handicapped Students

Every now and then you come across a resource so well done, and so obviously needed, that you wonder why nobody ever came up with something like it before. **The Special Artist's Handbook** is one such resource.

In this oversized quality paperback, author Susan Rodriguez provides:

- **A section on handicaps** that explains myths, prejudices, and misconceptions; characteristics of exceptionalities and how to respond to each of them in the art classroom; and a sign language guide covering the most-needed words for art instruction. Exceptionalities covered are mental retardation, socially and emotionally disturbed, learning disabled, physically handicapped, sensory losses, and gifted.
- **An A–Z section of craft activities,** from Apples and Oranges (working with clay) to You're a Doll! (making a paper doll that has your features). Not only are these activities exceptionally clever and well-designed for teaching special students lessons other than crafts (e.g., the I Can See Right Through You! craft based on X-rays of human anatomy), but each activity comes with adaptations spelled out for each exceptionality, in which the author explains what to do to make the activity more accessible or educational for each special-needs group. The activities themselves are described quite clearly, starting with a list of materials, teacher preparation necessary, basic directions, suggestions for further development, and photographs of final products produced by some of the author's special-ed students.
- **The section on adaptive aids and materials** is a Godsend for parents and teachers of special-needs children. Here you'll find easy-to-implement, clever ideas for overcoming difficulties. Does your child have trouble holding narrow objects? Try pushing a foam hair curler over pencils and brushes. No arm movement? Try tucking brushes into a headband and painting with head movements! Also included: aids to organization (especially needed by some students), resources that help in sewing and cutting, and adaptive aids for visually handicapped and blind students, and a recipe file of materials that appeal to the senses of smell, touch, or sight.
- Section 4, "The Art Classroom," explains **how to set up your art area** for safety and maximum educative potential and encourages visits to art museums.
- The whole book is topped off with a **glossary** of special-education terms and (very helpful) a **general index** to the entire book.

The layout of this book couldn't be any easier to use. Everything is just where you need it, with no need to flip back and forth. Any parent or teacher of a special-needs child can really benefit from the information, activities, and ideas tucked between the covers. Highly recommended. *Mary Pride*

Special Education: A Biblical Approach is a practical handbook for pastors, parents, Christian school officials, home educators, or anyone needing to deal with the gamut of special education problems.

The publisher of this book, Hidden Treasure School in Greenville, SC, established by the Rev. John Vaughn after his own daughter had been severely burned, is a school for children with physical, mental, and learning disabilities. The folks at Hidden Treasure have built their philosophy of education firmly on the Bible. They believe that every child is born fully equipped to do the job God has planned for him. It is the parents' and teachers' role to guide the child in developing his gifts. They repeatedly emphasize that special education is individualized education (which con-

Parents. $21.50 plus shipping.
Dale Seymour Publications, PO Box 5026, White Plains, NY 10602. (800) 872-1100. Fax: (800) 551-7637. Web: www.cuisenaire-dsp.com.

NEW!
Special Education: A Biblical Approach
Adult. $14.95.
Hidden Treasure Publications, 18 Hammett St., Greenville, SC 29609. (864) 235-6848. Fax: (864) 233-6366.

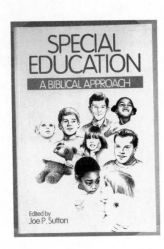

SPECIAL EDUCATION
A BIBLICAL APPROACH

Edited by
Joe P. Sutton

cept homeschoolers are already very familiar with). They are also right that the Church has in general failed miserably in ministering in any real way to the handicapped.

With these points established, they orient parents and teachers to special-ed concepts, major legislation, problems requiring special ed, and available resources. Then follow excellent chapters on physical disabilities, emotional disabilities, learning disabilities, educable mentally retarded and slow learners, and trainable and severely/profoundly mentally retarded.

The chapter on learning disabilities should be helpful even for those who object to that label. The chapter on emotional disabilities calls the Church back to its role of counselor of troubled families, thus practically eliminating this area of special education.

The book's only real drawback is that it is too friendly towards the state. It is pro-state certification of teachers and not wary of state evaluations and testing of prospective special-ed students.

This book should be a great asset in aiding the Christian community in fulfilling its responsibility to the disabled among us. *Betty Burger*

NEW!
Strategies for Struggling Learners

Parents. $18 plus shipping.
Exceptional Diagnostics, 220 Douglas Drive, Simpsonville, SC 29681. (864) 967-4729. Email: jpsutton@juno.com.

Maneuvering the maze presented to parents of special needs children can be frustrating. The challenges faced by your child can be further complicated by technical jargon and "expert" advice. **Strategies for Struggling Learners** by Joe Sutton, a professor of Special Education at Bob Jones University, helps you understand your options and offers unconventional methods to help your struggling learner. Practical advice is interspersed with professional explanations of the various testing available, individualized education plans and techniques that may be implemented with your child.

Included are chapters titled:

- Formula for Success
- Learners with Limitations
- Essential Teaching Beliefs
- Scriptural Model for Teaching
- Testing and Evaluation
- Blueprint for Instruction
- Consultant Services
- Modifying Instruction
- Generic Teaching Techniques
- Techniques for Specific Subjects
- Educational Procedures
- Managing Student Behavior

The Suttons offer their sound advice in a manner that educates you, as a parent, on the resources available for your special child. They help you wade through the jargon and counsel you in all areas of special education. This 212-page, paperback book is a valuable resource filled with information and suggestions. *Maryann Turner*

Miracles of Child Development

Parents. Six-hour cassette program with note outline, for home use, $50.
NACD, PO Box 380, Huntsville, UT 84317. (801) 621-8606.
Fax: (801) 621-8389.
Email: nacdinfo@nacd.org
Web: www.nacd.org

Neurological Therapy at Home

Founded by Robert Doman, NACD specializes in home therapy programs for the really hard cases. Children who have suffered severe brain damage, or who have neurological problems, or fits, or physical handicaps, are thoroughly diagnosed by NACD's staff and then presented with a home program tailor-made for them. NACD is expensive (hundreds of dollars a year per child) and many of their methods are severely criticized by the medical establishment. They do have some spectacular success stories, however, and their philosophy of optimism at least keeps them trying to achieve results, whereas medical experts seem to be getting more and more pessimistic these days. We were members of NACD for a while, and Ted just loved his program (all except the knee bends).

NACD programs are a lot of work for the parents and are highly patterned. You do exercise A for two minutes three times a day, and listen to tape B for three minutes twice a week, etc. NACD is also into the "dominance" theory of brain organization, whereby the goal is to be right-handed, right-footed, right-eyed, and right-eared, or conversely left-handed, -footed, -eyed, and -eared. Thus your child may end up wearing an eye patch or ear plug to assist him in "switching over" from right to left, or vice versa. NACD also believes strongly in the stages of development, and enrolled teenagers and even adults sometimes wind up crawling around like babies until they improve their coordination in that stage.

You can order NACD's introductory tape set, **The Miracles of Child Development**, for $50. The tapes are fascinating and inspirational, but take them with a grain of salt. B-mod is not the answer for *all* childhood discipline problems as Mr. Doman believes, though his suggestions for motivating children, and especially his stress on praise and encouragement, are well worth hearing. *Mary Pride*

Social Skills

Deal Me In, subtitled *The Use of Playing Cards in Teaching and Learning*, is more than directions for a slew of card games. The author, Dr. Margie Golick, contends that playing cards are high-interest educational tools as well as a means of social entry for children who lack physical prowess or social skill. Some skills she claims card games can develop: rhythm, motor skills, sequencing, sense of direction, visual skills, number concepts, verbal skills, intellectual skills, and social skills.

After a lengthy introduction presenting her case for card games, she gets down to cases with more than five dozen games, plus card tricks and logic games. Every card game is summarized, learning skills enhanced by the game are summarized, and then you get the rules: rank of cards, basic overview of the game, bidding (if appropriate), object of the game, rules of play and scoring, comments, and necessary vocabulary for play.

The book includes several indexes to help you find the game you want, and some psychotherapeutic moralizing by the author. She approves of gambling and swearing, and although her comments on these subjects do not take up any significant part of the book, I didn't want you to buy it and then accuse me of not warning you! By and large a helpful resource that could use some light editing in the next edition. *Mary Pride*

Betty B. Osman's pioneering book **No One to Play With** deals frankly with the problem of the "living disabilities" which affect many children with so-called "learning disabilities." For youngsters who lack confidence both in the classroom and on the playground, life may not be easy in any area.

No One to Play With is excellent on diagnosis, but spotty on cures. Christian parents, for example, may not appreciate the suggestion that LD children "may require far more concrete and graphic presentations [of sex] than many local school boards deem appropriate." I also can't share the author's faith in behavior modification as the cure for poor behavior. Where this book shines is (1) in its realistic appraisal of a problem too many of us

Deal Me In
Ages 6 and up. Price $9.95.
Audio-Forum, division of Jeffrey Norton Publishers, Inc. 96 Broadstreet, Guilford, CT 06437. (800) 243-1234. Fax: (203) 453-9774. Email: info@audioforum.com. Web: www.audioforum.com.

No One to Play With—Revised: Social Problems of LD and ADD Children
Parents. $12 plus $3 shipping.
Academic Therapy Publications, 20 Commercial Boulevard, Novato, CA 94949-6191. (800) 422-7249. Fax: (415) 883-3720. Email: atpub@aol.com. Web: www.atp.com.

ignore, and (2) in the compelling case histories which, if nothing else, create empathy for the victims of living disabilities. You may recognize your child, or yourself, in the story of Freddy, the withdrawn TV-watcher who avoided other children, or in the saga of Susan, whose own brother and sister called her names at home. Distractible George; Jimmy, who was never included in games; Jeff, whose parents were divorced; ornery Danny, who always "had to" pick fights; and a host of other children pass before your eyes, along with the tale of what the author did to help each of them and why it worked. She also covers the situation of gifted kids with learning disabilities and LD adults. *Mary Pride*

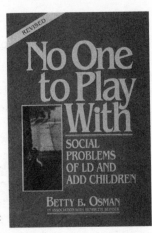

Speech Therapy at Home

"Help Me Talk Right" series

Ages 5 and up. Help Me Talk Right: How to Correct a Child's Lisp, Help Me Talk Right—"L" Sound, Help Me Talk Right—"R" Sound, $32 each plus shipping.
Gersten Whitz Publishers, 8356 East San Rafael, Scottsdale, AZ 85258. Credit Card Orders Only: Thinking Publications, (800) 225-GROW. Also available through Amazon.com, Barnes and Noble, and Borders online. Other orders & inquiries: (480) 951-9707. Email: mirlag@yahoo.com. Web: www.speechbooks.com.

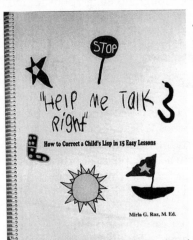

I wish I had known about **Help Me Talk Right: How to Correct a Child's Lisp in 15 Easy Lessons** *before* spending several hundred dollars on speech therapy for my daughter. Author Mirla G. Raz has done parents a great service in providing them with the information allowing them to help their own children. A speech therapist herself, she doesn't discount the need for calling on a professional if necessary.

The book contains instructions for carrying out 15 therapy sessions, practice requirements, worksheets, and trouble-shooting ideas for use when things aren't progressing. Children are motivated with a great deal of positive reinforcement, games, prizes, and contests. Directions are clearly and concisely spelled out. You won't need any additional materials other than some games and toys that you already have on hand.

Much of what I saw in this book we experienced personally with our speech therapist.

Helpful would have been some photographs or detailed illustrations of the correct and incorrect tongue placement, as well as a basic discussion of speech theory; the "why" to go along with the "how." *Renee Mathis*

It's a miwacle! Um, a miracle! At least that's what we hoped **Help Me Talk Right: How to Teach a Child to Say the "R" Sound in 15 Easy Lessons** would be.

Having a little one who can't say her "r"s was kind of cute. Until she passed age 6. And then when her little sisters imitated her. At one point we had *three* "wah wah" birds in the Pride family! It was time for help. Hence this book.

You've seen Renee Mathis' glowing recommendation of Mirla G. Raz's earlier book above. Now I see why Renee was so excited. With the very clear lessons, from tongue positioning with the "jelly spot" to practicing initial and final "r"s in single words, phrases, and sentences, any parent can use this book. With the built-in games, worksheets, and activities, any child will be happy to go along.

Mirla Raz believes you should consult a speech pathologist several times during these lessons, to make sure the child is in fact saying the "r" sound properly. She suggests that you request the free services of your local public-school speech pathologist. Having heard some horror stories about homeschooling parents whose encounter with the "free" therapists or pathologists at the school turned into intrusive attempts to force their child into the public school, I think you'd be smarter to go the "private practitioner" route, if you find it necessary.

Also available, but not reviewed by us in time for this edition, **Help Me Talk Right: How to Teach a Child to Say the "L" Sound in 15 Easy Lessons.** We also hear a book on preschool stuttering is in the works. *Mary Pride*

Special Equipment

Debra Evans, the author of several Crossway books on womanhood and mothering, sent me a very nice catalog called **Options**. It's "an exclusive selection of gifts for people with special needs," published by the Attainment Company. On the cover is an attractive picture of a young woman with Down's Syndrome sitting by a basket of apples. Inside are all sorts of products designed to help mentally-handicapped teens and adults gain independence in their shopping, cooking, eating out, grooming, housekeeping, and so on. Many of these products are also good for people who have trouble, for whatever reason, with communicating intelligibly. The catalog is uniformly respectful of the abilities and needs of those who can benefit from its products, and is targeted at their families and friends. *Mary Pride*

This 284-page book is an absolutely splendid resource! Inside **Computer Resources for People with Disabilities**, which was produced by the Foundation for Technology Access (see their organization listing earlier in this chapter), you'll find all the information you need to locate hardware and software options for people with disabilities. Lists of support groups, publications, professional associations, and training institutions are included, as well as personal stories and product reviews by type of product. For example, if the book is talking about touch screens, it will tell you how they work, who they benefit, features to consider, cost, and list "common vendors," i.e., companies known to regularly carry this type of product. An "additional information" section gives an insider's view of how a touch screen hooks up, whether you'll need special software, and so on.

With a Foreword by Stephen Hawking

Computer Resources for People with Disabilities

A Guide to Exploring Today's Assistive Technology

• what to do – who to ask – where to go
• personal stories and information networks
• product descriptions and funding sources

The Alliance for Technology Access

Why is this important? Because assistive devices make the difference between learning and not learning, working and not working, and communicating and not communicating, for many people. Legally blind? Try a Braille printer, or voice technology that lets the computer read to you. Physically impaired? Your choices range from voice entry, to special keyboards, to mouth sticks, and lots more. And the list goes on. Even carpal-tunnel sufferers can find help here!

The book is physically attractive and easy to use, packed with charts, graphs, lists, and photos. *Mary Pride*

NEW!
Attainment Company Options Catalog
Free catalog.
Attainment Company, 504 Commerce Parkway, Verona, WI 53593. (800) 327-4269.

NEW!
Computer Resources for People with Disabilities, 2nd Edition
$17.95 paperback, $22.95 spiral bound, plus shipping.
Hunter House, Inc., Publishers, PO Box 2914, Alameda, CA 94501. Orders: (800) 266-5592. Inquiries: (510) 865-5282. Fax: (510) 865-4295.

Rifton: Equipment for the Handicapped

All ages.
Rifton Equipment, PO Box 901 Route 213, Rifton, NY 12471-0901. (800) 777-4244. Fax: 800-777-4244. Email: cpwebmail@communityproducts.com. Web: www.rifton.com.

NEW!
Resources for People with Disabilities

High school to adult. Set of two library-bound volumes, $89.95 plus shipping.
Ferguson Publishing Company, 200 West Madison St.,Suite 300, Chicago, IL 60606. (800) 306-9941. Fax: (800) 306-9942. Email: fergpub@aol.com. Web: www.fergpubco.com.

NEW!
Special Needs Resource Guide

Parents. $18.95.
Great Books & Gifts, 9895 West Colfax Avenue, Lakewood, CO 80215. (303) 274-0680 Fax: (303) 274-0288.

As I said, school supply houses and firms that cater to preschoolers are good places to start, especially those that carry Montessori materials. For physical therapy, **Rifton Equipment** has the stuff. Exercise chairs, bolsters, wedges, play equipment, and so on—it's all here. Prices are acceptable for the quality, and it's possible that insurance may pay for some of it if you get a doctor's prescription. We've used similar equipment of our own manufacture, and it did Ted a lot of good. *Mary Pride*

Resource Guides

Resources for People with Disabilities is over 1,000 pages big. That's a lot of resources! In its two volumes, you'll discover

- where to find 17 categories of assistive technology: communications devices, mobility and transportation, and a lot more
- where people with disabilities can get scholarships, grants, and awards, with eligibility and deadline information
- publications, publishers, and conferences devoted to thee issues
- organizations and associations for people with disabilities—14 categories, from legal assistance to independent living centers and government agencies

Introductory essays cover topics such as teaching students with learning disabilities and understanding the basics of assistive technology. The books have three indexes, making it possible for you to search for information by state, by type of disability, or by name of organization. Be aware that, thanks to political pressure, "disabled" now includes all kinds of behavioral and lifestyle choices, as well as physical handicaps. *Mary Pride*

The **Special Needs Resource Guide** is aptly named. This 90-page manual by Pat Rendoff provides nearly 450 resource listings on topics which range from deaf/hearing disabled to Tourette's Syndrome. The guide is broken down into 12 sections, as follows: resource books, special education/gifted catalogs, Christian education catalogs, secular education catalogs, educational software catalogs, private special education providers and tutors, magazines and newsletters, special services and supplies, educational toys, state home school organizations, and special video/audio tapes.

Many of the sections are further divided by topic (i.e. home education, autism, etc.), making the information very easy to navigate through. The topical index provided will make finding specific information a snap. If you have a special learner and are in need of resource information, you must get this guide! *Brad Kovach*

CHAPTER 29

Help for the Gifted

In one sense, every child is gifted. God has given each of us special abilities and talents, so that what is easy and obvious for one person may be difficult or impossible for another. It's also true that every organically normal child has the ability to *appear* gifted if he or she homeschools.

However, not every child is "gifted" in the *technical* sense of precocity and strong internal drive to master a given subject area (or "domain" to use the technical term). Not every gifted child is equally gifted. And yes, children who are "gifted" in the technical sense *do* have special needs.

Is your child gifted in the technical sense? If so, how much? What kind of education and home support do such children need? Can they get what they need in school? How can you have your child recognized as gifted by a Talent Search program, and what opportunities does that open up?

This chapter will answer these questions.

Multiple Intelligences or Multiple Gifts?

Howard Gardner has gained much attention with his "multiple intelligences" theory. In his book *Frames of Mind: The Theory of Multiple Intelligences* he lists the following types of intelligence:

- Logical-Mathematical Intelligence
- Spatial Intelligence
- Musical Intelligence
- Bodily-Kinesthetic Intelligence
- Interpersonal Intelligence
- Intrapersonal Intelligence

Although these represent some of the natural forms of giftedness, I don't think it helps much to transmute the classic term "intelligence" to include all the above. "Intelligence" has traditionally meant "quickness in learning academic material." The term "giftedness" more accurately represents both the categories Gardner lists, and several more besides.

High IQ, Low Support

To be honest, it appears to more acceptable today to be athletically gifted, musically gifted, artistically gifted, or even socially gifted than intellectually gifted. Even within the homeschooling community, there is a definite sense of isolation among the parents [of gifted children] with whom we've spoken.

—*Janice Baker, Kathleen Julicher, and Maggie Hogan,*
Gifted Children at Home

Giftedness & IQ

"Giftedness" covers a wide range of ability levels as measured by IQ (Intelligence Quotient) tests. Here are some ways it is defined:

- **Moderately gifted.** IQ of 120–139. About 2 or 3 out of 100 children have IQs of 130 and up. A typical cutoff for entrance into gifted programs is an IQ of 130, although some Talent Search programs have now extended this downward to the 120 level.

- **Highly gifted.** IQ of 140–159. About one in 100 children has an IQ at this level.

- **Profoundly gifted.** IQ of 160 and up. About one in 10,000 to 30,000 has an IQ at this level.

- **IQ of 180 and up:** about one in a million. There is no special term for this level of giftedness, since the children exhibit the same characteristics as profoundly gifted children, and they are so rare as to be little studied.

- **Prodigy.** Regardless of IQ level, this is a child who can perform at an adult level in a given domain—e.g., Mozart.

What's more, as Ellen Winner's excellent book *Gifted Children: Myths and Realities* makes clear, an overview of the research on giftedness shows that , while children with the various gifts outlined below all share certain characteristics, they are *not* all equally good at schoolwork. So, while children who exhibit any of Gardner's "multiple intelligences" may be quick at learning the rules of their particular domain (music, socialization, sports, etc.) they are not necessarily quick at learning *in general,* as traditionally "intelligent" children are.

With that in mind, let's take a quick peek at some of the types of giftedness:

- **Academic giftedness.** This is normally called "intelligence," and is what IQ (Intelligence Quotient) tests are supposed to measure. Academic giftedness is usually divided into *mathematical* and *verbal* giftedness, with possibly the additional category, sometimes linked with mathematical giftedness, of *spatial* giftedness.
- **Artistic giftedness**
- **Musical giftedness**
- **Strategic giftedness** (e.g., chess and other strategy games)
- **Mechanical giftedness** (the ability to understand, fix, assemble, and invent items made of many parts)
- **Charismatic giftedness** (leadership and dramatic ability)
- **Emotional giftedness** (the ability to "read" people effortlessly and respond appropriately to their emotional needs)
- **Athletic giftedness**

Types of Academic Giftedness

In the sidebar you will see how levels of academic giftedness are defined by IQ scores. Now, we must consider two more categories of academic giftedness:

- **Global giftedness**—equal ability in both mathematical and verbal areas
- **Unbalanced giftedness**—the child scores high in verbal ability, but not in math, or vice versa. Such a child might even be labeled "learning disabled" in one area, while he is demonstrably gifted in the other.

Now here's an important point:

All these types of giftedness are normal.

As you go through the checklist below, you may find yourself shouting, "That's my kid!" Compared to the children around him, he may appear different. But compared to other gifted children, you'll see that he is "one of the gang."

Checklist for High Academic Giftedness

Wondering if your child is highly gifted? If so, Winner suggests you should have seen at least some of these signs before your child turned five:

- ☐ Recognizes and responds to you at a very early age
- ☐ Long attention span in infancy
- ☐ Easily bored, wants to see and do something new
- ☐ Early at crawling, rolling, and walking
- ☐ Early talker, often jumping right into sentences and complex vocabulary. My Hungarian mother was a great example of this. She was talking at six months, causing old ladies on the street to make the sign of the "evil eye" to protect themselves from this obviously strange child!
- ☐ Learns to read with very little help. Winner notes, "It is not unusual for such children to read at sixth-grade level in kindergarten."
- ☐ Oversensitive to noise, pain, and frustration

Is your child five years or older? Look for the following:
- ☐ Learns well with minimum instruction
- ☐ Persistently curious; asks tons of questions
- ☐ High concentration on topics that interest him
- ☐ High energy level that may come across as "hyperactivity" when he runs out of interesting things to do
- ☐ Highly aware of his own reasoning processes
- ☐ Obsessive interests, to the point of becoming an expert in one or more topics
- ☐ Loves to explore numbers and math topics—the kind of kid who considers a book of math puzzles a great gift
- ☐ Great memory
- ☐ Excels at logic and abstract thinking
- ☐ Prefers typing to handwriting—it's faster!
- ☐ Gets along better with older children and adults than with children her own age, mainly because agemates do not understand or share her interests
- ☐ Worries at a young age about the "big questions"—justice, world peace, the meaning of evil, the existence of God.
- ☐ Has an excellent, sharp sense of humor that may manifest itself in annoying puns and practical jokes

Testing for Giftedness

To confirm your child's academic giftedness, you can

- **Have him take an intelligence test**, which usually must be administered by a licensed professional. Two such are the Stanford Binet Intelligence Test and the Wechsler Intelligence Scale for Children. Other tests for various forms of giftedness are the Goodenough Draw-A-Person Test (originally designed as an IQ test, now mostly used to test for artistic giftedness), the Ravens Progressive Matrices Test (this uses picture symbols only and tests for logical thinking and spatial ability) and the Clark Drawing Abilities Test, which unsurprisingly tests for drawing ability.
- **Have him take a standardized test.** You can order several such tests from Bob Jones University Press Testing Service, Christian Liberty Academy, Summit Christian Academy, or Sycamore Tree, among other sources, and administer them yourself at home. See the BJUP writeup in the Evaluation & Testing chapter for details. If your child scores in the top two percentiles, he will be eligible for all of the regional Talent Search programs. If he scores in the top five percentiles, he will be eligible for some of them.

Some Cautions

Bear in mind that IQ tests may be administered in such a way as to make the results less meaningful. I well remember being tested at the age of 7 by a psychologist who made me wait the entire time prescribed for each section of the test, although I finished each in half the time. This exhausted me to no purpose (the entire process took over four hours of alternate intense anxiety and boredom, with nothing to eat or drink), and the final score did not reflect the fact that I was able to finish each section early. Test anxiety and "dumb errors," such as skipping a question and then forgetting to skip a line on the response form, or expecting a question to be more tricky than it was and answering it accordingly, can also lower scores.

In the long run, you will be able to determine where your child falls on the "giftedness" range quite accurately by his characteristic personality and behavior, and by his achievements, such as his scores on other tests and his performance in national contests.

Beware of the temptation to declare your child "profoundly gifted" if he is not. Remember, this giftedness level brings with it a host of social problems. If a child has that level of giftedness, he also has the fortitude to face the corresponding isolation from his agemates. But if he does not, persuading him that he is profoundly gifted may set negative social factors into play without any offsetting inner benefits.

Web Addresses

- **Goodenough Draw-A-Person Test.** www.ericae.net/eac/eac0103.htm.
- **Ravens Progressive Matrices Test.** Info: www.publinet.it/users/ad88/products/frames/ravens.htm. Orders: publinet.it/pol/products/noframes/order.htm.
- **Clark Drawing Abilities Test.** aspin.asu.edu/~rescomp/compilations/clark.html
- **Stanford Binet Intelligence Test.** edcen.ehhs.cmich.edu/~mnesset/binet.html
- **Wechsler Intelligence Scale for Children.** edcen.ehhs.cmich.edu/~mnesset/wisc2.html

What to Do If Your Child is Intellectually Advanced

First, thank God for this special gift!

Second, make plans to spend some time teaching your child basic social skills.

Gifted kids tend to be "project"-focused rather than "people"-focused. That's what helps them advance so rapidly in intellectual matters. This type of child is unlikely to pick up appropriate social behavior by osmosis, the way other, less focused, children do. However, this type of child also responds well to social skills taught as a "school" subject.

Beside the usual mall manners, restaurant manners, and library manners, you may need to teach your gifted child not to interrupt . . . to listen courteously to others . . . to not share *everything* he knows on a given subject . . . cues that tell him it's time to leave . . . how to introduce himself at a gathering . . . and so forth.

Such children also tend to be hypercritical, so time spent teaching him how to encourage others will be well spent.

These social skills will make the difference between raising a hyper-intelligent geek, who people tolerate but nobody likes, and raising a future leader, whose intellectual skills can be used to their maximum capacity and who has the respect of others.

What Is a Talent Search?

These are really "IQ searches." Four sponsoring universities have divided the country up by states. Schoolchildren in a sponsor's state have the opportunity, if their standardized test scores qualify, to apply to that Talent Search. If the student's score on a follow-up test is high enough, he can now attempt to enroll in a panoply of advanced courses—summer courses, weekend courses, correspondence and online courses, and CD-ROM courses, depending on what is available through that particular Talent Search program.

As a homeschooler, your child won't be offered the Talent Search information through his school. So we have told you all about them, and how to apply, below.

The main advantages of qualifying for a Talent Search program are (1) the excellent advanced courses, (2) the social opportunity to meet kids who can compete at your child's level, and (3) the entree these courses provide to top-tier colleges, which *love* Talent Search kids.

How to Apply for a Talent Search

You have never seen this written up before in a homeschool publication—at least not in any book or magazine that *I* have read! Here, after dozens of hours of phone calls and more dozens of hours spent poring through the literature from every Talent Search program in North America, are the steps you must follow to participate in a Talent Search if you are a homeschooler.

1. **Take a standardized test in the fall** (early fall is best) and achieve a score in the top 95 percent or 97 percent (depending on the Talent Search in question).

2. **Apply to the Talent Search of your choice.** Ideally, everyone would apply to the Talent Search that covers their state. However, in reality I found out that **you can apply to *any* Talent Search**. So you should pick one that (a) your child's scores will likely get him into and (b) offers the kinds of summer courses and distance learning opportunities you need. For example, in Missouri we fall under the Duke University TIPS program, but the Midwest Talent Search courses are offered across the creek in Illinois, whereas the Duke U courses are all the way across the country. On the other hand, the Rocky Mountain program is more likely to have available vacancies than either TIPS or MTS. See how it goes?

3. **Register with the SAT or the other follow-up test** your Talent Search requires, which usually must be taken in January through March. If you plan to take it at a Sylvan Learning Center, be warned that Sylvan will not sign your youngster up for the test without a referral from the Talent Search program, who of course you will list on your test form as one of those chosen to receive a copy of the results.

4. **If you qualify, you will be sent a packet** outlining the available summer, online, and computerized courses available through your Talent Search.

5. **You can then apply for the courses you want to take**, but again be warned—there is a pecking order for who gets accepted. Returning students have the first crack, and Talent Search registrants beat out those who merely have a qualifying SAT score. So if you are serious about such courses, you're better off having your student enter the program as young as possible, rather than gambling that he or she will be able to take their very first course in eighth grade. Again, sooner is

better when applying, as summer courses have a cutoff signup date.

6. **If you do all this correctly at the right time of year**, you may be awarded a certificate at the annual award ceremony. Then you can get a nice picture taken at the ceremony, write up your achievement, and send it in to *Practical Homeschooling*, where it may get printed on our "Show & Tell" page!

How to Pick a Talent Search Course

All the same warnings apply about Talent Search courses as are true of school gifted & talented courses: beware of political correctness, paganism, and values deprogramming. Some folks have the erroneous notion that gifted children should form the core of a new group of technocrats, managing the masses on behalf of elite leaders. The future these folks envision has nothing to do with Constitutional liberties or Christian families. While you are much more likely to encounter such courses through a Governor's School program or local G&T course, the possibility exists that whoever is in charge of a given Talent Search program or teaching a given course at the time your child is thinking of taking it might have bought in to this worldview. Hence, some sensible cautions are in order.

Courses that emphasize "open-ended thinking" and encourage children to reinvent the future typically are the most dubious. Math and science courses typically are just straight academics that will do your child's future academic career a lot of good, with the exception of highly evolutionary biology courses. History, foreign languages, and so forth can go either way, depending on the instructor. Ask for a syllabus or talk to the instructor if you're trying to figure out where a given course is coming from.

The EPGY CD-ROM math courses, available through many Talent Search programs, are widely reputed to be excellent. I hope to check them out for myself by the next edition of this book. I would expect the online writing courses to be savory, considering that parents can read the child's writings.

Talent Search Programs

Johns Hopkins University sponsors the oldest, most exclusive talent search. **CTY** absorbed the previous University of Arizona Talent Search a few years ago, making it also the largest talent search. Students must place in the top 3 percent on the qualifying test to be admitted.

The qualifying test for students 12 years and older is the SAT; the qualifying test for students 10 and 11 years of age is the PLUS (developed by ETS for Johns Hopkins), and the test for students 7 to 9 years of age is the School and College Abilities Test (SCAT).

The SAT and SCAT may be taken anywhere in the country. The SAT can be taken when it is normally offered to high-school students. Both the SAT and the SCAT are offered nationally through Sylvan Learning Centers. The PLUS is also available nationally through Sylvan.

Johns Hopkins offers advanced courses in math and writing online, and summer courses on science, computer science, and the humanities as well.

Center for Talented Youth
John Hopkins University
3400 N Charles St
Baltimore, MD 21218
410 516-0337 /
Fax: 410 516-0108
Email: CTYinfo@jhu.edu
Web: www.jhu.edu/~gifted/cty.html
States served:

Alaska	New Hampshire
Arizona	New Jersey
California	New York
Connecticut	Oregon
DC	Pennsylvania
Delaware	Rhode Island
Hawaii	Vermont
Maine	Virginia
Maryland	Washington
Massachusetts	West Virginia

Center for Talent Development
Northwestern University

617 Dartmouth Place
Evanston, Illinois 60208-4175
847-491-3782
Fax 847-467-4283
Web: www.tip.duke.edu/index.html
States served:

Illinois	North Dakota
Indiana	Ohio
Michigan	South Dakota
Minnesota	Wisconsin

Duke University Talent Identification Program

Box 90747
Durham, NC 27708-0747
(919) 684-3847
Fax: (919) 681-7921
info@tip.duke.edu
Web: tip.duke.edu/index.html
States served:

Alabama	Mississippi
Arkansas	Missouri
Florida	Nebraska
Georgia	North Carolina
Iowa	Oklahoma
Kansas	South Carolina
Kentucky	Tennessee
Louisiana	Texas

Rocky Mountain Talent Search
University of Denver

2135 E Wesley Ave
Denver, CO 80205
(303) 871-2983
Fax: (303) 871-3422
Email: ahurley@du.edu
Web:
www.du.edu/education/ces/rmts.html
States served:

Colorado	New Mexico
Idaho	Utah
Montana	Wyoming
Nevada	

Students who wish to enter the **Center for Talent Development** program must have scored in the top 5 percent on national standardized tests. The Midwest Talent Search, for grades 7 and 8, uses the SAT. The MTS for Young Students, grades 4, 5, and 6, uses the EXPLORE test.

When you qualify in this Talent Search, you can then take a huge variety of summer courses, from debate to chemistry, from social theory to recombinant DNA. They offer the Education Program for Gifted Youth (EPGY) courses on CD-ROM, with teacher assistance via email or phone. Finally, for $15, you can obtain their latest *Educational Program Guide* to *all* summer, commuter, residential, and overseas programs available to MTS and MTYS participants, including those offered by universities who are not among the four Talent Search sponsors.

Duke University's Talent Identification Program now has an addition, the Motivation for Academic Performance (MAP) program, available to students in the fourth or fifth grades who have scored in the top 10 percent or better on national standardized tests, the EXPLORE being TIP's preferred choice. TIP also accepts SAT scores from students through the 10th grade who score in the top 5 percent.

A satisfactory score on the tests and an accepted application entitle you to take many excellent advanced summer courses, including history, physical education, and even travel-related courses which involve trips to Europe. TIP also offers textbook-based correspondence courses in many subjects and EPGY computer-based math courses.

The **Rocky Mountain Talent Search** requires a score in the top 5 percent on national standardized tests, plus a score in the top 10 percent on the SAT or the ACT, and caters to ages 11–16.

A good score on the tests, or failing that by some insignificant margin, a good portfolio demonstrating academic skills, means you'll be eligible for the Rocky Mountain Talent Search Summer Institutes. These are advanced courses in math, science, and the humanities, with titles covering such topics as robotics, genetics, chemistry, physics, geometry, creative writing, mock trial, acting, and more along the same lines. The course catalog, pictured here, is fairly small compared to the other talent programs' catalogs, shown above. There are no distance courses, not even the EPGY computer-based courses, *yet*. In order to take advantage of the RMTS courses, you must show up physically at the Denver University campus at the correct time. Of course, some would say showing up and spending time with the other gifted kids is the most important part of the experience . . .

Books to Answer Your Questions

There are a multitude of resources to help parents who have children with learning difficulties. But the pickings can be pretty slim if you have a child (or children) who are academically gifted, and even slimmer if your gifted child also has learning or behavior disabilities.

The well-known homeschool authors of **Gifted Children at Home: A Practical Guide for Homeschooling Families** (Kathleen Julicher of Castle Heights Press, Maggie Hogan of GeoMatters, and writer Janice Baker) all have years of experience in teaching their own gifted children. Janice's oldest, Seth, is finishing his MBA at University of Delaware at age 20. Kathleen's highly gifted children are all out of the house now and excelling in the Air Force, at work, and in college. Maggie's oldest son, JB, graduated at 15 and was a National Merit Finalist.

These homeschool moms want you to know that your gifted child is just that . . . a gift. These children come with their own unique set of challenges, both academic and emotional. This information-packed 138-page manual will offer you encouragement, tools, and lots of great ideas that will help you tailor your homeschool to meet the needs of your gifted child.

The book starts with a wonderful discussion about evaluation: What makes a child gifted? Though the usual litmus test is IQ, testing alone will not present a complete picture. *Gifted Children at Home* gives a brief but specific analysis of the testing process for those that choose that route or have been in public school, as well as a discussion of characteristics of the gifted. They strongly encourage home education as the best alternative for these children, not only for the usual spiritual and academic reasons, but because you can tailor an educational program plus outside activities to best meet the needs of your child.

This guide tells you not only why, but how. After the introductory chapters on giftedness and homeschooling, chapter topics include parenting the intellectually gifted learner, what to teach when, curriculum considerations, usable techniques, acceleration and grade skipping, activities for gifted kids, computers, apprenticeship, preparing for high school and college, recordkeeping, mentors for parents, and the perspective of a homeschooled gifted child looking back over his education. Tons of resources, including useful web sites. The text is spiced with great first-person anecdotes, and fills a niche that is often overlooked in standard home education materials. Highly recommended! *Michelle Van Loon*

Gifted Children: Myths and Realities by Ellen Winner is the first book you should read about giftedness in children. This 450-page hardcover will quickly bring you up to speed on all the current theories about giftedness, the history of gifted education, the ways schools and families try to deal with gifted children, and more. Chapter titles are:

- Nine Myths About Giftedness
- Globally Gifted: the Children Behind the Myth
- Unevenly Gifted, Even Learning Disabled
- Artistic and Musical Children
- The IQ Myth
- The Biology of Giftedness
- Giftedness and the Family

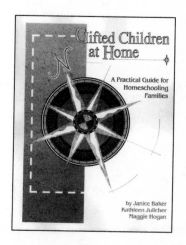

- So Different from Others: The Emotional Life of the Gifted Child
- Schools: How They Fail, How They Could Help
- What Happens to Gifted Children When They Grow Up?
- Sorting Myth from Reality

The author divides gifted children into two classes, the moderately gifted and the profoundly gifted. She points out that much that is written about gifted children—their superior social adjustment and leadership roles—only applies to the moderately gifted. The stereotype of the eccentric, socially isolated genius is still reality for many of the profoundly gifted—and this also applies just as much to those who are outstandingly gifted in the areas of athletics, art, and music.

Gifted Children is not just a stream of facts and figures. The author has thought about all this data and has plenty of opinions to share. She identifies and disproves nine myths about giftedness:

- Global giftedness, the notion that "gifted children have a general intellectual power that allows them to be gifted 'across the board.'" As she says, "The child with a combination of academic strengths and weaknesses turns out to be the rule, not the exception. Children can even be gifted in one academic area and learning-disabled in another."
- The distinction between "talented" (referring to children who are exceptional in the arts, music, dance, or athletic areas) and "gifted" (referring to children who are exceptional in academic areas.) She says, "Both classes of children exhibit the three characteristics of giftedness"—precocity, marching to their own drummer, and a rage to master.
- The myth that children "talented" in the areas of art and music must have high IQs, even though IQ tests only measure "a narrow range of human abilities, primarily facility with language and number."
- The myth that either genetics or environment is *solely* responsible for giftedness.
- The myth that giftedness is produced by an overzealous, driving parent. As Winner says, "It is true that parents of gifted children are highly involved in the nurturance of their children's gifts. But such an unusual degree of investment and involvement is not a destructive force. It is a necessary one if a child's gift is to be developed."
- The myth that gifted children are "popular, well-adjusted, exceptionally moral, and glowing with psychological and physical health." Winner goes into some detail to demonstrate this applies only to the moderately gifted child; profoundly gifted children often are socially inept, physically awkward, and unhappy.
- The myth that all children are gifted.
- The myth that gifted children become eminent adults. Actually, a child's personality and character is much more reliable predictor of future success than his IQ.

If I may put it this way, Winner has really done her research on the research. Her far-ranging book takes you from case studies of individual gifted children, to the classic large-group studies, to studies of gifted autistic children and savants which reveal some fascinating glimpses of how some types of giftedness work. She does not confine herself to the academically gifted, but spends plenty of time on the musically, artistically, and athletically gifted as well, and appears to know every study that is or has ever been done with gifted kids in any country around the world.

If you are gifted, if you have a gifted child, or if you have ever known a gifted person, you'll catch yourself saying, "Aha!" and "She got that right!" at frequent intervals. For further study, you can revel in the excellent bibliography, footnotes, and index.

My one and only gripe: the author obviously knows very little about homeschooling or the life of most homeschooling families. She speaks against homeschooling in one place as being an extreme last resort, because it cuts children off from other children their own age, which readers of this book know is not true. (Can we all spell Y-M-C-A, A-W-A-N-A, and S-c-o-u-t-i-n-g?) On the other hand she repeatedly mentions that homeschooling, sometimes with private tutors, had been the educational method of choice for gifted students until recently, and she tells about the excellent results, both emotionally and educationally of one homeschooling mom. (She does mention how "lucky" the young student was to have a sister being taught with him, to provide the necessary socialization, I assume.)

Perhaps the best service this book provides is, paradoxically, to assure gifted children and their parents that they are normal. Different from other kids, yes, but with characteristics in common with *other* mildly, highly, or profoundly gifted children, depending on into which category the child falls. Winner excels in her analysis of what giftedness is, how it affects children, and what families can do to maximize the beneficial aspects of extreme giftedness while overcoming its social and emotional pitfalls. Very highly recommended. *Mary Pride*

Over the years I have come to rely on the enormously helpful, down-to-earth guides published by Free Spirit Publishing for parents, children, and teachers. Whether your child (or you?) are gifted, talented, highly creative, or just a square peg in a round hole, you are sure to find a book to help from the thoughtful folks at Free Spirit.

These two books are aimed at the gifted traditionally-schooled child and written in an engaging style that invites the young reader to feel at home. Gifted kids are often puzzled by everyday life, so the authors of these guides provide sensitive and encouraging advice that can help such a child understand his strengths, and practical suggestions for overcoming weaknesses.

The Gifted Kids' Survival Guide, For Ages 10 & Under, is a slim volume that explains giftedness to children in terms that they can understand, alleviates fears adults may not realize they have ("Am I expected to be perfect just because I'm gifted?"), and guides them in responding to challenges they face at home and at school. Topics include The Six Great Gripes of Gifted Kids, Smart Ways to Make and Keep Good Friends, Coping With Teasing, Famous GTs Who Were First Pegged as Losers, and more. When You're Bored Silly would have helped my youngest child one Sunday when his teacher asked, "What are you thinking?" Surely, the advice in this book might have kept him from blurting out, "I'm so bored I could scream!"

The Gifted Kids Survival Guide, A Teen Handbook, disappeared into my teen daughter's room as soon as it arrived. She read it through that evening, and the next morning at breakfast she pronounced it, "Great!" Once again, giftedness is explained and topics of interest are covered in more detail, with references to other books and materials for the teen who wants more information. Teens face greater challenges than younger children, and gifted children are perhaps more at risk. Some have social skills

or common sense that are seriously lagging; others find that they are more bored than ever in school or that their giftedness is offset by areas of profound weakness; while others seek risks and stimulation that are extremely dangerous. This book provides essential advice for teens, and it pulls no punches in warning them of dangers and folly. Many teens will find the authors understand them as few others do, and parents will find that the authors present advice that is 99 percent pure and only occasionally politically correct. Teens are encouraged to be proactive in their education, and to create positive change in their schools.

If you and your children are looking for books that are easy to read, and show a sensitive understanding of giftedness, you would be hard-pressed to find books better than these. *Kristin Hernberg*

CHAPTER 30

What About Acceleration?

If you use a traditional textbook or worktext curriculum, it's possible to do *two* lessons each day, and complete a regular 13 years of school (kindergarten through high school) in just six years. That is the method followed by *Practical Homeschooling* columnist Joyce Swann. Each of her ten children completed high school at age 11, college at age 15, and received a Master's degree at age 16. All of their work was completed at home through correspondence schools and external degree programs offered by major western universities.

An accelerated education program of this type would be a lot harder to construct using unit studies, difficult to complete via online courses, and completely antithetical to someone favoring the Charlotte Mason method. With textbooks and worktexts, however, it's easy to see just how much progress you need to make each day.

While few homeschoolers have the Swann family's level of drive, many families enter homeschooling with one or more children needing to "catch up." For these children, accelerated education is a wonderful way to quickly meet—and surpass—the level of work expected of them in school. And for the increasing number of families willing to clip a year or two off the school schedule, workbooks and textbooks make it easy.

Ways to Accelerate

There are four basic ways to accelerate a child's education.

Compacting. Your child learns all the material, but skips unnecessary assignments. For example, you might assign every other question in the math book, or every other sentence in the Latin translation, instead of all of them. Every homeschool parent can apply this technique to some extent by merely writing "SKIP" next to every assignment that smacks of twaddle or that covers material the child has already demonstrated he knows. Profoundly gifted children can often move ahead amazingly fast using this method.

Telescoping. Your child completes all the normal school work, but in a shorter time frame. The Swann family uses this method; they do every single Calvert assignment, but at the rate of two a day instead of one a day. As Joyce Swann stresses, special giftedness is not required in order to telescope successfully, but hard work is.

Curriculum Suitable for Use with a Program of Accelerated Education

Grades K–8
- Calvert School (correspondence)
- ESP Super Yearbooks (one-book text)
- Escondido Tutorial Service (online)
- How to Tutor Curriculum (step-by-step basics)
- Robinson Curriculum (CD-ROM-based, child needs to be able to read)

High School
- American School (correspondence)
- Cambridge Academy (correspondence)
- Keystone National High School (correspondence)
- Newport/Pacific High School (correspondence)
- Robinson Curriculum

What Curriculum Did the Swanns Use?

Mrs. Swann chose the Calvert School curriculum for K–8; then, since Calvert has no high-school courses, she switched to American School for the high-school years. Her children then completed college through Brigham Young University, which only requires brief stays on campus, with most work completed at home. Mrs. Swann accompanied her still-quite-young children during their campus stays. Postgraduate work was via the external degree program of University of Southern California—Dominguez Hills.

EDITOR'S NOTE: *Joyce's children do move along more quickly than most—they have been "accelerated" up to a faster speed—but they are not "accelerating." Twice as fast is fast enough! :-D*

Skipping. Your child skips a grade entirely. Typically, skipping a grade or two works best for moderately gifted children. If your child can read, write, and cipher before age 6, skipping straight to second grade makes sense. Lewis Terman, author of possibly the most famous long-term study on moderately gifted children, opined that students who enter grade 1 with a mental age of 10 should be able to reach fourth-grade level by the end of that school year. This would mean a two-year skip, allowing the child to enter college at age 16. The junior-high years also work well for skipping, as they cover little that is not repeated in high school. If your older child is behind in school, once he does the work to catch up to the sixth grade level in basic writing, grammar, and math skills (via compacting), skipping seventh or eighth grade can work well. The prospect of finally being up to the proper grade level is often a great motivator for students of this age.

Radical Skipping. The child jumps three grade levels or more all at once. As Ellen Winner, author of *Gifted Children: Myths and Realities* points out, "No large-scale study of *radical* grade skipping has been conducted . . . ." She did mention that the available case studies of profoundly gifted children who were only skipped a grade or two showed them still bored, frustrated, and socially isolated. If your child has an IQ or 170 or above, and demonstrates the signs of profound giftedness outlined in Chapter 30, I'd say, "Go for it." If your six-year-old can do fifth-grade work, get her fifth-grade curriculum. If you have pulled your 11-year-old out of school, where he was bored out of his mind repeating work he had mastered four years ago, jump him straight to ninth grade. Bear in mind this advice applies only to *profoundly* gifted children, who will thank you for giving them a real challenge for once, and that once your child is working at the higher grade level, you may then choose to slow down once again and add more enrichment material. Five years of high-school level work leaves lots of time for sport, music, art, community service, and Advanced Placement courses; two years of middle school followed by three years of high school generally means a lot of unneeded repetition and much less opportunity for enrichment.

Joyce Swann on Accelerated Education

Webster defines "accelerate" as "to go faster; to make something go faster." From some of the letters I receive, I suspect there is an image among homeschoolers of me standing next to my children whispering, "Faster! Faster!" in their ears as they press forward to meet more and more demanding deadlines.

When John and I decided that I would teach our children at home, acceleration was never a consideration. We wanted what most homeschooling parents want for their children—a superior education delivered in a safe and moral environment. Our home, of course, provided what we considered to be the ideal environment, but it was the search for a superior educational experience which led to the early graduations.

In the true sense of the word, acceleration has never occurred in our homeschool. At no time have we gained speed as we move forward. In fact, I would describe us as faithful plodders who are able to accomplish quite a lot because we are *consistent*.

The key to our success is simple: When God told me to homeschool, I said, "Yes." And then I committed myself to the task. Any homeschooling mother can do the same if she is willing to make a long-term commitment to a disciplined lifestyle which centers around an unwavering homeschool schedule.

The first thing I did after making the decision to homeschool was to de-

NEW!
No Regrets

Teen–adult. $15.52 postpaid.
Cygnet Press, HC12, Box 7A, Anthony, NM 88021. (505) 874-3306.

Judging by the interest generated by Joyce Swann's columns in *Practical Homeschooling*, I'd say a lot of you would be interested in this book. **No Regrets: How Home Schooling Earned Me a Master's Degree at Age 16** is the personal story of Alexandra Swann's homeschooling. It recounts how she graduated eighth grade at age 10, high school at age eleven, college at age 15 (as the youngest graduate ever in

Brigham Young University's 111-year history), and received her accredited master's degree from California State University at age 16—all through home learning. More than this, it is the remarkable story of her mother Joyce Swann, and how she homeschooled—and is homeschooling—ten (as in T-E-N) children at once—all at this pace!

I wanted to read *No Regrets* as soon as it came out, but gave up the first time because of the truly awful sans-serif typeface the book is set in. Recently I ran across the book again and resolved this time to just plunge in regardless. Once I got past the first few pages and my jittering eyeballs had a chance to adjust, I was fascinated. The Swanns struggled bravely as homeschooling pioneers, going so far as to move to make sure their children could be taught legally at home. Those of us who are tempted so easily to give up because of "homeschool burnout" need to see how the Swanns faced heartbreaking—and undeserved—financial trials, social trials, and even health trials. How would you like to try continuing home-

schooling while your baby is dying in the hospital from surgical complications following removal of a bowel obstruction? Mr. and Mrs. Swann took turns for weeks by their little boy's side. He was never alone—and homeschooling went on! (Happy ending: this Baptist family's prayers were answered and the boy survived.)

Meeting the Swann family through the pages of this book was a delightful experience. From 16-year-old Francesca telling off the 30-year-old rowdies in the audience before presenting her "senior thesis," to Judah learning to crawl as a baby without the use of a left hand (which the doctors thought was impossible), all the Swanns demonstrate incredible drive and determination. Thus it is no surprise that they use a sequence of structured correspondence courses as the backbone of their home education program. While this teaching method would not fit every family situation, *No Regrets* does show what can happen when a dedicated family pushes structured home learning to its limits. Highly recommended. *Mary Pride*

cide on a teaching schedule. I planned from the beginning to have **a twelve-month school year** so that I would not have to constantly re-teach lessons that were forgotten over summer vacation. I also decided that I would give the children **short holidays**: Memorial Day, the Fourth of July, Labor Day, one day for Thanksgiving, Christmas Day (I later allowed them to take off Christmas Eve as well), and New Year's Day. In addition they had off every Saturday and Sunday. I then scheduled **a three-hour school day** and worked everything else I had to do to care for my rapidly growing brood (I had ten children in twelve years with no multiple births) around those hours.

I carried that same philosophy of commitment into the classroom. We have undergone some scheduling changes over the years. For instance, when I had lots of preschoolers, I scheduled half of the school day in the morning and the other half in the afternoon during the preschoolers' naps. As my number of preschoolers diminished, however, I changed the schedule to one three-hour session from 8:30 to 11:30 A.M. The rules that had always governed our homeschool stayed in effect:

1. **No talking about anything not pertaining to lessons.** Given the opportunity, nearly all children will attempt to distract the teacher so that they can escape their assignments. Frequently, that effort will take the form of pretending to be interested in something that has little if anything to do with the subject at hand. A simple, "I would love to talk about that, but we will have to do it after school," works wonders. Nine times out of ten the child has no interest in the subject and does not want to discuss it later.

Fast & Steady Wins the Race

Perhaps the whole topic of accelerated education can best be illustrated with a simple algebra problem.

Q: Car A leaves Smithtown traveling due south at 100 miles per hour. At the same time car B leaves Happyville traveling due north at 55 miles per hour. Smithtown and Happyville are 450 miles apart. How long will it take the cars to meet?

A: **The cars will never meet.** The car traveling at 100 miles per hour will crash and burn and the police will have cleared away the dead bodies and debris long before car B approaches the site of the accident!

If you would like to see your children move ahead in their educational experience, forget everything you have ever heard about accelerated education. Do not even consider skipping grades. Banish all thoughts of eight-hour school days. Never concentrate on how you can get your children to "go faster." Instead, set a steady pace that can be maintained over your children's academic lifetimes, and put your homeschool on a course that will allow your children to move forward naturally, while reaping the full benefits of their educational experiences.

—Joyce Swann

2. **No wasting time.** At times everyone is tempted to sit staring out the window or gazing into space. It is the teacher's responsibility to gently remind them to get their minds back on their work so that they will be free to act out those daydreams after school.

3. **No food or drinks.** Virtually anyone can go for three hours without eating. Students should get that drink of water *before* school.

4. **No breaks** unless a trip to the bathroom is absolutely essential. Students should also make it a habit to use the bathroom before school. It is then seldom necessary to interrupt for a bathroom break. All breaks should be avoided because they do exactly what their name implies—they *break up* the school day, *break apart* concentration, and *break down* order and discipline.

In a stable atmosphere there is really nothing to do *but* learn. I am always present in the classroom to answer questions and help with any difficulty a student may encounter.

Given the right reinforcement and encouragement, children are able to grasp a great many concepts that adults tend to think of as "too difficult" for youngsters—especially if no one tells them that they are difficult! I love discussing my student's assignments with them and helping them discover new insights into lessons in history, literature, philosophy, etc. For me, some of the most meaningful moments with my children have been spent in the quiet, undistracted atmosphere of that home classroom, and I feel that many of them would agree.

Now, the big question. Should *your* child be accelerated? And if so, how? Via "fast-and-steady" continual progress, as per Joyce Swann's insights in the sidebar, or would it ever be OK to skip a grade?

Sue Richman on To Skip or Not to Skip

Maybe your child was a **late bloomer**, getting off to a nice relaxed start with reading at age nine (that is, a nice, relaxed start in retrospect; you were a nervous wreck until he finally caught on). So you decide to call him a first-grader (or perhaps "non-graded primary") for longer than usual, and gradually he does fine, until he's now pushing 15, and only in 7th grade. Now he begins to complain about the lower grade placement—he wants to be up with his age-mates, and you begin to realize just how old he will be when he graduates from high school at home. Will he stick it out? Can you now boost him ahead and skip a grade or two? Did you make a big mistake to hold him back?

Or possibly you have **two children close in age** and you teach them together, using the older one's textbooks. The younger one takes part easily in all studies, and seems to be doing fine. Shouldn't he get credit for doing fifth-grade work like his sister? Shouldn't you call him a fifth-grader also? Maybe his test scores as a fifth-grader aren't so hot, and his handwriting is pretty atrocious, but, gee, he is doing that fifth-grade level work.

Or this: your child is a **very bright student**, always has been. Learned to read early and effortlessly, catches on to new ideas readily and quickly, is an eager learner in many fields. But you don't want to appear to be saying that your kid is better than anyone else, so you have always just kept your child at her age level grade-wise. On top of that, your child's birthday is in early November, which means that she is actually one of the very oldest at her grade level. She has always aced achievement tests, and has always been above grade level in the actual work being accomplished. Now that she's hit junior high you are wondering about skipping a grade. Can you? Should you? What about socialization questions, what about future chances of scholarships, what about other possibilities?

And then there is this variation: through a combination of compacting, telescoping, and skipping, **you now have a 13-year-old ready to graduate next year**. So far, so good. Then perhaps doubts start arising. Your daughter isn't so eager for this after all. She may not *want* to be faced at the young age of fourteen with the types of decisions kids need to make after graduation. She certainly doesn't want to leave home for college that early, and might not really be ready even for college-level correspondence work. She took the PSAT and earned only mediocre scores—are scholarships lost? Maybe this plan just won't work for you. You and your daughter realize there is still lots more to learn about, and after all she never was that hot in mathematics even though she'd always been a super reader. Can you slow down at this point without making your child feel she has been "failed?" And what will colleges think of a "5th" or "6th" year of high school?

Over the many years that I've been talking with and counseling homeschool parents, I've encountered all of these situations, and many other variations on the theme. I've also dealt with many of these questions in our own family, and made different decisions based on each child. Maybe I should start here, to give you all some perspective on where I'm coming from.

Some Examples

Slow Start, No Skipping. Jesse is now 23 and in grad school (married too, first baby due this coming winter). As a 6-year-old first grader, he scored in the lowest 2 percent on a standardized test of reading ability. I actually thought to myself that if I were putting him in a regular school, I might have held him back a year, in part because he had a late birthday . . . and that reading score. However, I realized that at home grade-level distinctions didn't really make much difference, and I strongly felt he'd do fine as he went along. He did do fine, and I was very glad that I hadn't kept him back. But as strong a student as he was all through his homeschooling (once he got the hang of how to read!), I was never tempted to skip a grade with him. By the end of high school he was clearly ready for college-level work, but instead of early admission we did a college correspondence course through Penn State University and also helped him prepare for taking four different Advanced Placement exams. He went into the University of Pittsburgh Honors College with 18 college credits. This cushion of extra credits enabled him to really broaden his studies in college—he was not eager to finish college early, just eager to try out as many fields as possible while he was there for four years. He ended up with a double major in history and political science, along with an honors degree for completing a major senior research project, and had time to travel around the world on the Semester at Sea program also.

Jacob, now 20 and heading into his junior year at Carnegie Mellon University studying computer science, also had a July birthday, and also got off to a bit of a slow start in reading. Again, I decided against holding him back, and again that panned out as a good decision. Jacob early on showed a marked ability in mathematics and computer programming, and by mid-fourth grade was working with his older brother Jesse on high school algebra. He completed high-school-level geometry in 7th grade, then went right on to calculus in 8th and 9th grade. He was a very bright kid, but not necessarily in all areas. Again, I was never tempted to skip grades with Jacob, and again I'm pleased with this decision. Jacob had the time to really develop his

Radical Skipping at Home

Seth Baker, son of Janice Baker, one of the authors of *Gifted Children at Home*, had the chance to experience acceleration through **radical skipping**. His school history is as follows: homeschooled in preschool and kindergarten, first school in a Christian school, second grade at a new school (the family moved), starting to get bored in third and fourth grade, homeschooled from fifth grade on. In his own words:

We had a great time [homeschooling] through the sixth grade. Then I started to get bored again. I convinced Mom that I already knew virtually all the material in the seventh grade textbooks, and she got me eighth grade books. I really think that this was the turning point in my schooling career. At the same time that we realized I was getting pretty good at this "student" thing, we realized that we didn't actually have to follow any kind of traditional grade system. So I skipped seventh grade altogether. I was ecstatic.

In much the same fashion, as we continued the high school experience, I skipped the ninth and eleventh grades. Like I said before, I don't think this was because I was "smart" or gifted," I just caught on to this stuff and didn't have to go over it time and time again. I have a sneaking suspicion that a whole lot of kids in the world could breeze through school a lot faster (and with far fewer headaches) if they were just given the chance.

As a 12-year-old, Seth took his first class at the University of Delaware, and got an A. The next semester, he took pre-calculus, and discovered he was the highest scoring student in the class. He graduated high school at age 14, and was accepted at Delaware State University with a full scholarship, graduating *summa cum laude* with a B.S. in Business Administration at the age of 18. Like Alexandra Swann, he has no regrets about his early graduation.

Pick a Grade Level and Stick With It

Jacob and Jesse every now and then used to point out that they thought that it was a mistake to have boosted Molly ahead though—thinking mainly of the various academic competitions our family enjoys taking part in. Being a grade ahead meant she lost out on being in Math Olympiad for one more year, or the Geography Bee for one more year, or MathCounts for one more year, and more, as most of these competitions have grade level guidelines.

I firmly believe that homeschoolers can't play it both ways—that is, can't be one grade for some purposes, but another grade for other purposes, especially when it comes to academic competitions. If there is a grade-level designation, you need to be consistent with what you've decided your child is—you can't waffle around and try to have your proverbial cake while eating it too.

Molly and I actually discussed this whole issue together quite a few times, and realized that because she's been a grade level ahead, that's how we've viewed her—our expectations were raised because of it. If she'd been at the lower grade level, most likely we would never have encouraged work at the level she was actually very able to meet.

It's hard to even explain why I feel so comfortable with skipping Molly ahead a year, when I never considered it with either of the boys, or with Hannah, our youngest. But I've also never considered skipping any more grades with Molly—she was after all just barely a teenager when officially entering high school at home, and she had plenty of growing up to do before being thrown in with much older students at college. One year of skipping was plenty.

—*Susan Richman*

strong interests, take part in many special accelerated academic programs in the summer and throughout the year, and build up his somewhat weaker areas. There really is a lot to be said for just plain growing a bit older. I felt he was ready to go on to college when he turned 18, and indeed he's done super. He also used the AP program to validate the college-level work he did in high school, and ended up taking a college-credit distance learning course in multi-variate calculus through Stanford University's EPGY program (Educational Program for Gifted Youth). And he also got to be my tech man in my online AP US History course, as well as a course participant—in short, there was plenty for him to do at home those last couple of years. I'm glad he had that time.

Early Start, Skipped a Grade. Molly, not quite 17, is another story. While riding in our car right before her fifth birthday (and she has an early August birthday, making her very young even for her proper grade level) she began reading aloud fluently from the loved book *Charlotte's Web*. She had started beginning reading very early, and caught on very quickly. She also seemed socially very mature and competent. She also did reasonably well in math understandings. It just didn't seem quite correct to call her a kindergartner at that point. Early on we let our local school district know that because she was advanced overall, she was boosted ahead a grade. She did third grade testing (required in PA) as a very young 7-year-old, and did very well (math computation was average, but concepts were at the top of the chart, and she had a perfect score in reading). I've never regretted my decision of skipping a grade with her. This is a kid who read *Jane Eyre* for the first time when in sixth grade (and remember, that meant young fifth-grade age for her), who picked up Shakespeare plays to read independently for fun, and who took on major challenges like entering the "Written and Illustrated by . . ." competition two times. She's also a pretty good pianist, is an incredible artist, has now taken eight AP exams, is a National Merit Finalist, went to France twice during her high school years, and more and more. She's heading off to the University of Pittsburgh Honors College this fall, with a full-ride academic scholarship—tuition plus room and board all paid for four years. Seems like the right decision for her to have skipped a grade—it's all worked out even better than we might have hoped.

Young for the Grade, No Skipping. Hannah is now 12, and properly just finished with seventh grade, although again with her very late summer birthday she is young for the grade. It seems perfect for her—she's excelling at this level, has plenty of fun challenges through her work with Mathcounts and the National French Exam and the Mythology Exam, but is not thrown in over her head. She's able to be a really nice bright 7th-grader. Skipping grades never entered my head with her.

Some More Options

So how can a family make these types of decisions regarding grade level? What questions do you need to ask yourself? What factors should be considered?

I think families need to look at this issue very carefully.

In many ways skipping a grade means very little in homeschooling, as we can always do whatever level of work we feel is appropriate for a given child, no matter what the grade level. A fourth-grader does not have to be stuck plodding through a fourth-grade reader when he's ready for meatier stuff.

At the far end of the scale, if a student does feel very ready for going on with college attendance early, but didn't skip a grade earlier on, he can still go to college ahead of time. He just goes right after 11th grade, using the college's early admission policy. If he can demonstrate a very strong record, strong SAT or ACT scores, and the maturity to handle college life, most colleges are more than happy to have a student who would otherwise be a senior in high school. Several students in the Pennsylvania Homeschoolers diploma program have done this with no problem. They then receive their diploma from PHAA after completing their freshman year in college, which is the standard procedure with most public or private high schools also.

Skip to Catch Up

In the scenario mentioned above, of the child who needed a longer starting-out time to gain basic academic abilities, though, I feel it's very reasonable and probably very desirable to skip the child ahead a grade at some point, even if the child would only be considered barely average according to test scores at the upper grade level. There is a wide variation found within any grade level, and sometimes it can be very motivating to a child to realize that now is the time to step on the gas and zoom ahead a bit to catch up with his age-mates. Some kids can get very discouraged by realizing they have been held back and now are significantly behind grade-wise—they feel no reason to even try to do their best, because after all, they must be pretty stupid since they were once kept back a year or two. You might set very concrete goals with a student in this situation: if you can complete this level math work, read this many books, and write this many compositions next year, and take the 8th grade level test and do at least OK on it, we'll consider next year as covering both 7th and 8th grades, putting you where you should be age-wise. This generally gets a very positive response from the student, encouraging hard work and effort and real concrete gains. The parents then have a real goal to help their kids meet. Everybody wins.

Skip if the Student is Superior at the Next Grade Level

It gets trickier for the me when I talk with families who want to skip ahead nice, normal bright kids. I often ask what the rush is; is there some specific plan ahead, some goal that requires double promotion? Test scores I think can be very useful here—if a kid takes an achievement test at the upper grade level and still scores in the superior range (that is, 90th percentile or above), I feel skipping a grade might be a good idea. If a student scores very well at the current grade level, but is only mildly above average when taking a test at the next grade level, I'd stop thinking about skipping grades, even if a child is officially using books from the upper grade level. There is frankly not that much difference between books at, say, the fourth- and the fifth-grade level—using the upper-level books does not really mean your child should be skipped. An elementary school principal once said to me, "What's the point in boosting a kid ahead to be average? Why not let him stay a nice bright kid at his grade level?" Much as some of us might not like to admit that any school principal knows anything, I think the man made a good point here.

Skip if the Student Craves It

Then there are some parents who are faced with a child who really feels it's important to get things moving along faster. Often this is a junior-high student, and he may have realized that at least in some diploma programs he might not be allowed to skip a grade during the high-school years. If it's going to be done, the time is now. These kids have plans, they have goals, they are ready for upper level work and they know it. Test scores are supe-

---

How to Graduate Early

1. **Prepare your students to take the Advanced Placement tests**. AP students are allowed to count their courses towards high-school credit, and depending on their AP test results, they can earn college credit as well. You can do the same with CLEP tests. See the chapters on AP and CLEP in volume 3 of *The Big Book*.

2. **Design your high-school plans to reflect an accelerated curriculum.** For example, you could create a curriculum of your own which includes in one semester a French course (for 3 credits), American literature (your own choice of books and assignments, for 3 credits), algebra (3 credits), a social studies unit-study course incorporating history, geography, art, and philosophy (6 credits), physical science (3 credits), music theory (3 credits), physical education (1 credit), and home economics (as an elective, for 3 credits). This would give you a total of 25 credits for that semester, as opposed to the usual 15 credits, enabling your student to meet graduation requirements much more quickly.

3. **Do as the Swanns do and take a correspondence course** which you complete according to an accelerated schedule.

4. **Pre-enroll in college.** One of our local Christian colleges has started recruiting 16-year-old homeschoolers to take some college science courses. Community colleges will often do this, too. You take the course while in high school, then it is counted towards college credit upon receipt of proof of high-school graduation. Just make sure that the college of your choice will accept transfer credits from the institutions in question.

If You Have To, Slow Down in High School

What if you did accelerate, and now part way through high school at home you want to cool things down and call your child a lower grade level? What will colleges think? It is in general easiest to just rewrite a transcript to reflect the new, and lower, grade levels and not tack on a fifth or sixth year of high school—unless you are ready for doing some real justifying. Not that it can't be explained well—in fact I know a couple of terrific homeschooling families in PA that opted for naming this extra year a fifth year of high school, and all went just fine with college admissions.

—*Sue Richman*

rior, the child is strong overall in many subject areas, and everyone is just beginning to feel that the current grade level description just isn't even, well, honest. Often, though not necessarily, these are kids with birthdays that put them at the older end of their current grade level. They are the kids who I always thought were a grade ahead of what was listed on paper. The homeschooling families I know who have had a child skip a grade for reasons like this are generally very pleased. The kids usually rise to the occasion, and really achieve strongly.

It's Your Decision

So, to skip or not to skip? To accelerate or not to accelerate? It depends on the child's birth date, the child's ambition, the parent's energy level and commitment, whether the child needs to catch up, and the child's ability to do superior work at a higher grade level. This decision should always be a family one, and I hope people don't feel that they should accelerate just because some others find it works for them. The Swann family's example shows it *can* be done; your family's needs will determine whether, in your case, it *should* be done.

Ideas for What to Do After High School When You're Too Young for College

Of course, you're only "too young" for college if *you* say so. With that in mind, here are some answers to the question, "What will I do with myself if I graduate high school at age 12, 13, or 14?"

- **Get a job.** Our outmoded child labor laws still allow some minimal kinds of employment outside the home. You can work for your parents' business, or start your own business, or volunteer to help a non-profit group. A year or more of full-time work, no matter how you can swing it, is a super preparation for college, and may even help you find the right major.
- **Travel.** If you're smart enough to graduate high school, you're smart enough to travel with a tour group. Most of us will never have the necessary free time to spend a month in Europe, or visit all the historic spots in the Old West, or spend a year living with a French family, or helping out with a cattle drive, or bike across the USA with a few good friends. If you look around, the

world is full of great enrichment opportunities.

- **Have some adventures.** Go on an Outward Bound survival adventure, learn to sail via Hocking College's inexpensive (and college-credit-bearing) summer course (*www.hocking.edu*), go on safari.
- **Indulge your sports and arts ambitions.** Join a band, take all the martial arts courses you want to, get a part in the local community theater's production, spend days in the museum sketching famous paintings.
- **Get your lifesaving and CPR certification.** Useful to have, and easy to manage while you're not trying to juggle school courses.
- **Get a mission.** Short-term missions assignments are available for teens through several missions organizations. You may be on the young side, but as a high-school grad you should be able to talk your way into the group. Again, months spent serving others in the inner city or overseas, under the protective umbrella of the group, can give you a sense of purpose and competence while enabling you

to perform useful service to others.

Ignore the myth that if you don't go straight from high school into college you'll lose your desire and ability to study and *never* complete college. That is the main reason people use to discourage teens from taking a year off after high school to pursue adventures they may never have again. If 40-year-old adults can go back to college to get a degree, a year off won't kill you.

Also ignore the myth that if you're "too young" for college, you're too young for any solo adventures or responsibility. The peer pressure and misbehavior on college campuses is generally not found to the same extent in the adult and professional world, unless you live in Hollywood!

Many of the options I have listed above allow for adult supervision, while others can be done while living at home. Those that involve "going solo" can usually be done with friends (so now you need to talk some friends into graduating early, too!). When you're done, you'll be *more* mature and experienced than the typical college freshman . . . and more interesting to colleges, as well.

CHAPTER 31

Study Skills for Everyone

Teaching is to learning as preparing the feast is to eating it. As each teacher needs the tools of teaching in order to prepare an inviting and digestible educational feast, so each student needs to master the tools of learning. He needs to learn how to chop up the lesson into smaller, more digestible parts. He needs to learn how to thoroughly "chew" new material until he has digested it. He needs to learn how to refresh his mind ("take a drink") in the midst of arduous study. Then, after all that, he needs to know how to turn around and prepare the same feast for someone else—since you don't really know a subject until you can teach it yourself.

Study skills don't come naturally to all of us. Although a child might spend hours poring over a book, unless he has been trained, or has trained himself, to study for meaning, he will most likely just remember the parts that especially interest him. Thanks to television, which has trained almost all modern children in the habits of inattentiveness, he may not even remember anything at all! Learning, for such a child, is the process of being entertained, and hardly any residue is left in his mind after the "educational experience" is over.

So, although this is a chapter of study skills resources, let me suggest that the first step to improved understanding and better grades for any child or adult, whether in school or out of it, is to **minimize or eliminate passive entertainment such as television**. The habit of attentiveness is the first study skill to cultivate. Try reading books aloud to your students to develop auditory attentiveness. Nature walks, in which you try to observe and identify the flowers, trees, birds, and so on along your way, are great for developing visual, tactile, and auditory powers of observation. Is the tree's skin *rough* or *smooth*? Does it have *pointed* leaves or *round*? Does that bird *warble,* or *chirrup,* or *screech*? By pointed attention to the real world and to real words, you can lay the framework for disciplined habits of mind that will benefit your family for the rest of their lives.

Listen & Learn

Listening to stories told without any commercial breaks—whether it's Mom and Dad reading aloud or a book on tape—builds your child's attention span. Listening may *seem* passive, but imagining the story in your mind requires active thought and concentration.

In contrast, frequent commercial breaks train kids to have short attention spans. In addition, watching TV or a video is completely passive, unless you are actively analyzing the plot, theme, cinematography, etc. That's why kids should be taught how to *actively* view a film, just as we teach them how to read a book.

Study Techniques

Perhaps the most familiar study method is SQ3R. As I recall from my elementary school days (the recollection is a bit fuzzy), SQ3R stands for Survey, Question, Read, Recite, and Review. First you *survey* the material, getting a feel for it, but not actually studying it. You scan the table of contents, read the blurbs on the back cover, browse through the book noting headings, if any, and so on. Next, you *question*. You decide what information you will look for in this material. For example, when reading a book on King Henry the Eighth, you might ask, "Why did Henry decide to break with the Catholic church . . . who were his wives . . . what were their names . . . was Henry a good king or a bad king?" As you study, you will be looking for answers to these questions. Now you *read* the material through carefully. You then *recite* your questions aloud. Finally, to tamp down what you learned, you *review*, skimming through the material and reminding yourself of the important facts you wish to remember.

The reason SQ3R is so popular is that . . . it works. Surprise! Look at SQ3R from the data-framework standpoint. First you play with the data, then you try to structure it (by means of preformed questions), then you assimilate data into your structure, then you modify your structure to include even more data, and finally you cement the connections by reviewing the newly-gained data. All very natural.

As you get better at asking questions, and come to your studies already loaded with relevant data from previous study, you will find the process easier and easier. I still find myself using SQ3R unconsciously when reading a particularly important book, taking my yellow highlighter to significant passages on the Revise and Review steps. There just seems to be no way to skip any step profitably, unless you are one of those rare people gifted with a photographic memory. (Or perhaps "cursed with a photographic memory," depending on how much network television you watch!)

Now here are some products especially designed to focus your listening skills, memory skills, note-taking skills, research skills, and general study skills.

Curriculum That Teaches Study Skills

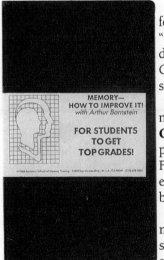

OK, I'll admit to sitting in church, looking for Galatians in my Bible and saying to myself "Go eat pop corn," so I can remember the order of Galatians, Ephesians, Philippians, and Colossians. We all have some tricks up our sleeve to help us remember things.

Memory expert Arthur Bornstein's technique, as presented in his **For Students to Get Top Grades** video, is to create "mental pictures" to use in remembering various facts. For example a moving van with the number eight on the side, carrying a bureau, to remember Martin Van Buren as the eighth president.

If you are serious about improving your memory and are willing to spend the necessary time and effort, this video might be of some use to you. I say "might" because this is just a bare-bones introduction to the Arthur Bornstein philosophy, although it is enough to determine if you want to invest any more money in his extensive line of visual-memory products, or if you want to further pursue this visual-memory technique. *Renee Mathis*

I had one college professor who refused to give extra credit assignments. After all, it was usually only the A students who turned in the extra work anyway. That's what I kept thinking while reading **How to Study** by Edward J. Shewan. The students who really need help with study skills are probably the least likely to pick up this book.

Chapters cover the basics of note-taking, report writing, memorization tricks, and test-taking skills. Subtitled "A Practical Approach from a Christian Perspective," the Christian content consists of exhortations to work hard, consider and evaluate an author's world view in light of Biblical doctrine, and a short reading list of classic Christian literature.

This 116-page paperback is not a detailed reference guide. For specifics you're referred to standbys such as *Strunk and White's Elements of Style.* Neither is it engaging enough to hook the struggling learner. Adam Robinson's *What Smart Students Know* does a much better job with its numerous "walk-you-through-the-process" examples and his attitude toward learning situations as a whole: it's a game, but it's a game you can learn to play and win. *Renee Mathis*

These eight 45-minute lectures, available only on videotape, have great things claimed for them in the Teaching Company catalog. According to the catalog description of **How to Become a SuperStar Student,**

> *This is surely one of the most remarkable classes taught anywhere in American high schools. Instead of teaching a specific subject area, Tim McGee teaches how to be a winner in EVERY subject. And from his high-school classes in a little town in Wyoming come a steady stream of honor students. They win scholarships, get into top universities, and even have their writings published while still in high school.*

Some of these students are shown on the tapes, demonstrating successful study and writing skills.

Topics covered in this series: Your attitude and learning philosophy, how to keep a "learning journal," how to develop effective study habits, annotation and active reading, notes and exam preparation, "jam" writing, informal writing, how to draft and edit a formal essay, setting up your master schedule, how to put together a top-notch research paper, what it means to be a well-rounded high-school student, and options available after high school. Two lectures for parents, on how children learn and how to help them academically, are also included. The 64-page booklet that comes with this course outlines each lecture in depth, gives suggested readings, and provides related websites to visit.

My one criticism: The author seems unaware of the different learning styles' environmental needs. He specifies silence, studying at a table, and good lighting, while some people need background "white noise," dim lighting, and study best seated on their bed or lying on the floor.

An impressive course that could make a difference for your high-school student. *Mary Pride*

If you find yourself wondering how to teach your children abstract lessons in following directions, The Learning Works has a workbook ready to fill the gap! **I'm Following Directions** is a wonderful workbook for primary age students on mastering the sometimes difficult area of following directions. The lessons are so fun your child won't realize he is actually developing skills to be used all his life. Each activity is one complete page, printed in bold black and white, and

includes such subjects as how to draw a turkey, how to solve a treasure hunt, how to read a map, and much more. There are lessons on marsupials and soccer, toucans and clowns. This is 31 pages of adventure and discovery that will leave your child wanting more. There is also a handy answer key provided for parents who want to attempt some of these activities . . . and forget to follow directions. *Lisa Mitchell*

Outlining, Note Taking and Report Writing Skills

Grades 4–8. $4.95. Shipping extra. *Hayes School Publishing Co., Inc., 321 Pennwood Ave., Pittsburgh, PA 15221-3398. (800) 245-6234. Fax: (412) 371-6408. Web: www.hayespub.com.*

This wonderful book starts with simple classifying exercises and takes your child right up through all the outlining and note-taking skills he will ever need.

Outlining promotes logical thinking, and helps us get so much more out of what we study and hear. It's absolutely fundamental to real progress in any intellectual endeavor. Knowing this, most textbook companies throw in a unit on outlining somewhere in their English courses. However, almost universally they don't take it slowly enough, explain it enough, or provide enough practice for children to really master this essential skill. The solution: this book.

Outlining, Note Taking and Report Writing Skills: A Step-by-Step Guide to Mastery is a public-school workbook, so some of its text selections have that flavor. Even so, it's the best, easiest-to-use resource on this subject I have yet found. Recommended. *Mary Pride*

The Overnight Student

Grades 5–adult. $6.95 postpaid. *Louis Publishing, 4016 N.W. 68, Oklahoma City, OK 73116. (404) 840-1284.*

The Overnight Student by Dr. Michael L. Jones is a small volume of 63 pages. Yet it has the potential to *revolutionize* your children's higher education. Why? Because it presents a study method that literally enables college and high-school students to go from straight F's to straight A's, *without* any faddy gimmickry.

The Overnight Student method has been tested for years. It worked for its author, who failed every college class he was taking for two semesters in a row before he discovered it. After using this method, he went on to earn a doctorate! It also has worked for hundreds of people he has taught. It works for students, teachers, businessmen . . . anyone who needs to quickly master *and retain* a large amount of information.

Did you know that "we remember 14 percent of what we hear, 22 percent of what we both see and hear, 70 percent of the movies in our mind, and 91 percent of what we teach others"? OK, so *how* do we put this knowledge to use? This is where Dr. Jones excels. In a winsome, easy-reading fashion he eliminates all the obstacles you place between yourself and successful study habits. If you can read and write, you can read this book and *instantly* begin to excel in your studies.

Dr. Jones' study method is not only easy to implement, but scripturally-based. It involves a special, simple system of note-taking, plus instruction in how to teach yourself the content of what you are studying. Along with this come tips and inspiration that can dramatically improve your study abilities.

As I said, the method was designed for college and high-school students. Dr. Jones assumes you are attending classes in which the teacher lectures and expects you to take notes. Home-schooled teens *will* need to learn these skills, even if at present their education consists of self-study from books and informal instruction from parents. Sooner or later, all of us end up taking some kind of class. Sunday school. Bible classes. On-the-job training classes. Even the weekly sermon at your church provides an excellent opportunity to practice the skills taught in this book.

The Overnight Student can help students studying from books, too, provided the students are good at outlining their textbooks' contents. I have already suggested to Dr. Jones that he include information about outlining books in a future edition. In the meantime, it can help anyone who has organized information before him that he needs to learn. *Mary Pride*

Right off the bat you can see a lot of overlap between all seven of these books: **How to Study**, **Ace Any Test**, **Improve Your Memory**, **Manage Your Time**, **Improve Your Reading**, **Write Papers**, and **Take Notes**. How can someone with poor note-taking skills write an effective paper? And aren't studying, acing a test, and managing time all necessary for success in each area? (In fact the memory book is probably the only one of the seven that could stand on its own.) It is frustrating to be reading one book, only to be constantly referred to another. That's where *What Smart Students Know* by Adam Robinson has it in spades over this series—all of the information is in one place.

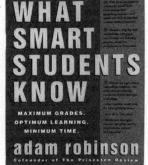

There's nothing wrong with the quality of Mr. Fry's information. It's all very sound advice in each category. However, I did have some problems with the way it was presented. Mr. Fry tries very hard to be "hip and lively." Consequently he assumes his readers are addicted to Madonna, try to evade their household chores, love watching Jay on the Tonight Show, and in general fit neatly into the mass-media picture of a typical teen. My hunch is, this isn't a fair description of most homeschoolers (let's hope not!). *Renee Mathis*

How's this for a bright idea: No one can teach you as well as you can teach yourself.

What Smart Students Know by Adam Robinson is dynamite reading if for nothing else than the chance to see the educational establishment turned on its ear. Are you ready for such revolutionary thoughts as, "Not everything you are assigned to read or asked to do is equally important." Or how about, "You're in school to learn to think for yourself, not to repeat what your textbooks and teachers tell you." One more: "If you're doing it for the grades or for the approval of others, you're missing the satisfaction of the process and putting your self-esteem at the mercy of things outside your control."

Mr. Robinson's CyberLearning method consists of 12 questions. Number one is "What is my purpose for reading this?" and number twelve is "How does this fit in with what I already know?" The questions in between are aimed at getting students to personalize and make relevant everything they need to learn. Everyone knows that's better than fighting it tooth and nail from start to finish. In other words, by changing your attitude about learning, you can become a better learner. Along the way you learn how to take good notes (both in class and from texts), how to rehearse for tests, how to manage your time and study efforts for maximum benefit, what professors really look for, and how to write a good paper. Just for fun there are various attitude quizzes, thought-provoking quotes, and sample exercises to test what you've learned.

The system for taking notes is one of the best I have ever seen. It involves continually refining and paring down your class notes over the course of the semester so that by the time finals roll around you don't need to reread every bit of material. The book includes plenty of illustrations showing exactly how this is to be done.

What do smart students know? That school is a game, but it's a very important game. This book shows you how to play to win. *Renee Mathis*

PART 7

Planning & Recordkeeping

If you keep really great homeschool records, will a Congressman want to shake your hand? Well, if your child enters the right competition, a Congressional handshake may indeed be on the agenda. Take, for instance, Joyce Watson of Kleinfeltersville, PA. At 16, Joyce won the grade 10–12 category of the National Student Zinc Essay Contest sponsored by the American Zinc Association and the U.S. Bureau of Mines. As part of her award, Joyce spent the day in Washington, D.C., where she met with her senator and congressman. "I am very pleased to have a student from my district selected as the winner," said Congressman Gekas, pictured here with Joyce. Joyce, along with her three younger sisters, is taught at home by her mother, Laura-Jean Watson.

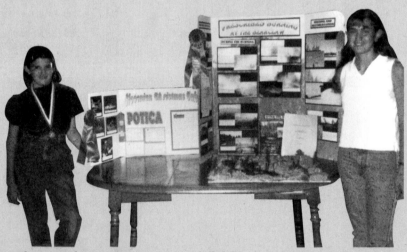

Taking good notes and writing up projects is a skill children can learn . . . and use to win prizes! Both Meredith Novak, age 15, and Pauli Novak, 12, homeschoolers from Embarrass, MN, won purple ribbons, the highest award possible, at the Minnesota State Fair. Meredith, on the right in this picture, won with her 4-H project about forestry's use of prescribed burns. Pauli, on the left, won her ribbon with a food and nutrition project titled Potica. Both girls went on to win the Grand Champion Awards in their respective project areas at the St. Louis County Fair.

CHAPTER 32

How to Get Organized

Books and magazine articles make it sound so easy . . . "To organize your life, start by labeling a set of boxes A–Z. Get file folders and label them as follows: Accounting, Aster seeds, Acts (book of), Articles . . . " With enough file folders, you can conquer the world!

Well, maybe *you* can conquer the world. As for me, I'll be in the middle of filing and inevitably start reminiscing. "Oh, I remember this article!" "Someday I'm going to try this craft." "Look at this college paper; I really did have a mind once." And I'll stop to read it.

I've avidly read books on organization since my first baby uncovered this hidden inadequacy in my life years ago. Over the years, six principles have emerged that have remained true friends in my struggle to conquer clutter and pursue beauty in my home. These are:

- Organize around themes
- Less is more
- Plan in blocks
- Prioritize space by time, money, and use
- Put it in plastic
- Weed consistently

This chapter originally appeared as a series of articles in *Practical Homeschooling* magazine. It is by organizing expert and all-around homeschooling ideas person Katherine von Duyke. Kathy is the mother of ten homeschooled children. She is the author of the *Home Education CopyBook*, reviewed in this chapter. For years she also published the excellent *KONOS Helps* newsletter.

Organize Around Themes

A theme directs your thinking, prayers, and creativity and helps turn them into reality. A theme should feel satisfying and whole. It weeds out the fuzzy decisions from the productive ones.

As I stood back and looked at the work produced in my kitchen, its own theme emerged: simple and natural. My children are allowed to use the kitchen for all kinds of messy food experimentation. Therefore, the kitchen is kept simple, with plenty of counter space and replacements for most of the important equipment. Places for things are clearly marked so the children can clean up without my help.

Our decorations usually consist of a bunch of drying herbs, a tray of recently planted seeds, an onion someone is sprouting, and rows of assorted grains and legumes in antique canning jars. I can easily see that stoneware, wood, and dried herbs will compliment the look, while fussy decorations

would be a source of tension. Decorative canisters that can't be knocked around or knick-knack shelves would work against my goals.

Some themes slowly develop as we stand back and look at the whole of the work we do, as in our kitchen, and some themes are decided at the outset. I'm currently working on building a western theme into my boys' room. I started by picking red, white, and blue, with touches of green, for my palette. My boys and I keep finding little ways to make the theme come alive: denim patchwork quilts, coiled rope lamps the boys can make, a collection of old horseshoes on the wall, stuffed fabric cacti, and tab curtains with bandanna tie backs.

A theme can also help to simplify. I use one for clothing decisions. I'm usually blessed with bags of outgrown children's clothes. Initially, I saved and catalogued everything. This job was tiring, and the results were disappointing. I'd find that this year's neon colors were a poor mix with last year's pastels. My children were dressed, but the result was an fashion nightmare. I took a lesson from the Amish and chose a palette of colors and styles for my children. Anything outside of that palette, with no match, goes to a local thrift store where patrons have a better chance of finding matches from a larger selection.

We picked jeans, turtlenecks, and sweat shirts in the primary colors for our everyday pattern. Winter dress outfits are in black, red, white, and gold. Summer outfits follow a sailor look. Some of my children look better in fall colors, while others look better in pastels, so we chose the colors that looked best on everybody (off-white, royal blues, and orange-reds). Though my choices are not unique, I'm thrilled with the time I save on Sunday mornings. Plus, since we seem to add a new baby to our family every two years, whatever clothes survive can be mixed and matched with new purchases or hand-me-downs.

Less Is More

I've always loved the way Japanese homes are decorated. They often use blank space to offset one exquisitely curved floral arrangement. I use this example to remember that "less is more." As I plan my theme I ask myself, "Which are the simplest choices?" I then rule out the rest. For example, if the children's drawers are stuffed with outfits, they won't be able to keep them neat. So I remove some of the clothes. They only need a week's worth of outfits in their drawers. A few extras can be kept in storage.

Picking themes limits the amount of crafts we will do, instruments we will play, businesses we will attempt, or units we will study. I'd like to do pottery, but don't have the time or space for it now. In the meantime, I'm not collecting pottery materials; they would clutter and detract from the themes I am faithful to now. The less themes I follow in the present, the more potential there is for developing new themes in the future. Less is more.

As our home schooling has progressed, our family learning style has developed a few themes. We love fun, unit-style activities that weave in practical skills along with history, science, literature, writing, and a basic survey of art and music. I love sharing these studies with my children, but I recognize that I would burn out fast if I tried to teach everything this way. We balance our schooling by teaching math, foreign languages, grammar and spelling, and a sequential art program (I confess, PHS has influenced me!). In addition, I want my children to have some time available to pursue their own interests. I make my purchase decisions while keeping in mind the aim of our homeschool. I won't be buying a complicated science textbook or an intricate, activity-based math program. They don't fit our scheme. I want to invoke the "less is more" principle so that I'm not saturating my children with more material than they can possibly absorb.

Plan In Blocks of Time

A study once noted that men are usually convinced that whatever they are doing is what they should be doing, while woman are almost always sure they should be doing something else. So we need to prioritize time as well as space.

A rigid clock-watching schedule doesn't work for me. I need time to initiate tasks, but I also desire the flexibility to respond to the people in my life. Schedules should follow a progression of priority, energy, and natural setting. My priorities begin with the Lord, then my husband, then my children, then my physical home, then business, etc. When I have time left over, I can dedicate it to items lower on my priority list.

I've learned that my family is most faithful to anything scheduled before lunch—probably because that's when we have the most energy. Therefore, we clean the house, have school, practice instruments, and write in our school journals early in the day.

I usually don't have a lot of energy in the afternoon, but I can accomplish mending and sewing and be available to answer questions as my children work on individual assignments.

Many tasks have natural settings and times. For example, we take an exercise break midday, because that seems to be what we all physically and mentally need. While I am cooking, I can do laundry because my washer is in the kitchen. Your environment will shape when you can accomplish some tasks. You can't fight your surroundings, so you have to figure out how to efficiently work within them.

Big Blocks or Little Plods?

Many women have enjoyed the benefits of grouping their cooking tasks into one block of time. They save on preparation work and clean-up. One clever woman simply re-thought a task normally done in little bits, and chunked it into one large block.

As you plan your schedule, try to visualize yourself maximizing performance while completing tasks in organized blocks of time. Should I clean one room every day or clean the entire house in an eight-hour period once a week? Can I remodel the kitchen over a period of days or should I set aside an entire concentrated week?

On a yearly basis, I may need to schedule a whole week for one task. For example, I like to map out the entire school year in the summer. I also enjoy taking a few major sewing and craft breaks throughout the year.

On a weekly basis, I need chunks of time to spend on organizing, cleaning, schoolwork, desk work, homemaking, and errands. All of these jobs need more than an hour to complete. While I could do a little bit every day, the time it takes me to gather my thoughts, locate the materials, and clean up afterwards is too costly. I save time by minimizing these steps and working at the task longer. The activities I perform within these blocks of time change throughout the year and involve some trade-offs. If I'm on a writing hiatus, I can use the extra time to paint. If I am gardening heavily in April, I won't sew much that month. My goals and duties may change, but I still know when the best time is to work on each block.

On a daily basis, I need bits of time to keep the small jobs from adding up. I write better if I work at an article over many days. Mending is less monstrous if it doesn't pile too high (though some prefer to mend all in a

day). The house needs to be picked up often or it looks like "eclectic clutter."

With my time blocked out, I now have the ability to tie up those nagging loose ends. I use business cards to list my tasks (you could also use ScanCards or sticky notes). I then file these in a card holder under the appropriate day/time heading (Monday—10:00, Tuesday—3:00, etc.). All of my business ideas get filed under Wednesday since that's when I establish my office hours. Each Wednesday, I scan down my list, decide which tasks take priority, and work my way through them. Any "leftovers" stay under the Wednesday heading until that block of time comes up again. The card holder saves me from having to re-write lists, and I don't have to look at a whole mess of different jobs to do, just those that apply to the current block of time.

Space, the Final Frontier

Once your time is blocked, you can decide how to store materials. You may only cook once a month, so a lot of your big pots and pans can be put in storage. If you sew only once a month, your supplies can be kept in the closet. However, if you sew every day, you'll want your supplies accessible. Your house may not readily lend itself to a sewing corner, but if you are an avid sewer, get creative. If experimentation is a big part of your homeschool, an extra bathroom could function as your lab.

My point: balance what you want to accomplish with the traits of your home. Leaving out lots of lab equipment isn't feasible, so we have a lab box that can be readily taken down and used in the kitchen.

Ask yourself three questions when deciding where to store an item:

- Will it be stored in the open or hidden?
- How frequently will the item get used?
- How much manhandling or hard use will the item receive?

Bookshelves, walls, and tables are easily accessible and open to public view. Frequently-used items are often stored there, because they make for interesting conversation and are not easily lost. Items that receive hard use, like dishes and utensils, should have the most stable storage. Items used only on a weekly basis can be stored in harder-to-reach areas, such as high cupboards, and seasonal items can go into deep storage.

We had a problem that demanded high priority in all three areas. Our house had no front closet, and coats are usually stored in the entrance hall (first point of public view). Coats are used frequently and the children are not always gentle in pulling them down. My husband spent time and money building an attractive, sturdy shelf and hook system so that each child would know exactly where to put his things.

We didn't need to expend the same amount of time and money to organize the children's drawers. Each top drawer has a homemade set of containers to hold, socks, belts, "treasures," etc. This helps to keep drawers neat and teaches categorization.

In a large family where everyone is responsible to help with the laundry, it is important that everyone knows where things go. I can remember spending many frustrating moments weeding through our children's drawers trying to find the baby's socks! Organization makes problems more clear and makes them easier to isolate and identify. We can also come up with creative solutions. We keep a bin on the back of the dryer labeled: "Personal: Lonely Crew seeks same for Mate" for all the single socks that turn up.

I also seek the minimum level of organization that yields the maximum time benefit. For instance, my spices are divided between savory and sweet. I know many people who alphabetize their spices, but since I don't alphabetize well, I'd have to sing the alphabet song every time I wanted the salt! I would use more time than I would save.

Now, I'll share some of the ways I store our materials.

How to Store for Success

When was the last time you went to the library and noticed all the books on the floor? When did you hit the grocery store and have to rummage through piles of boxes? I know storage containers are expensive, but by prioritizing your storage you know where to rely on homemade containers and where to invest your money.

I remember baby-sitting for a friend who had a very nice play area, with all the toys categorized and shelved in homemade containers. Unfortunately, the shelf and the containers were poorly made. When her little boy scrambled up to get an item, the whole system came tumbling down. We were looking at several hours of sorting!

My friend's carefully selected categories helped her child play in a purposeful way, unlike a child who is distracted from deep play by the mess (usually created when the toy box gets dumped to find that one special toy). However, her system wasn't up to the hard use under which it was required to perform. As a result, she bought sturdier shelving and clear containers with lids that snapped on securely. She hadn't felt she could afford the containers until she saw the valuable time it was costing her to not have them.

My favorite organizers are

- Velcro
- clear slip-in report covers
- large plastic containers with lids

Here's how I use each:

Velcro. This sticky-backed tape comes in three decorator colors: white, beige, and black. I keep some strips on the wall space designated for posters. The wall gets the fuzzy side, and the poster, which I laminate, gets the looped side. This makes it easy to rotate posters or maps according to our needs, without leaving lots of holes in the walls. Unfortunately, you can't take the Velcro off without removing the paint, so I use the color that best blends in. I also use Velcro on the back of a clipboard to attach notes to my work station. A piece of Velcro keeps the VCR remote stuck to the monitor, and pencils stuck to pads near the phone. Velcro is also wonderful on felt. I stick it on little timeline people to fit them on a large piece of felt. The figures come off, but don't constantly fall. In humid climates, where basement walls spit off tape like a baby spits spinach, posters stuck on with Velcro will stay.

Slip-in Report Cover. I originally began using these pocketed report covers to make up my children's school portfolios, and they work great. The younger children enjoy browsing through their older siblings' work, and we have no fear of damage. The artwork can also be beautifully displayed. One reader told me that she had used this idea and built an art portfolio dating back to the time when her child was scribbling. She keeps it on the coffee table with other display art books. What a way to motivate a child!

Since we keep a large supply of these plastic sheets handy, we've found other ways to use them. I organize my sewing patterns with them. The illustration on the pattern envelope goes in front of each plastic pocket. Each size I design goes into its own cover. When I want to make PJ's or sweats for several children, I can readily find the sizes I need. I keep women's dress patterns in one binder so I can easily flip through to the pattern I want. In another binder, I have collected iron-on appliqués with coordinating fabric in each pocket.

In the kitchen I use the covers to hold our favorite recipes. I told you about my themes; well, this works in cooking, too. Monday is Mexican night, Thursday is stir-fry night, Friday is always Dad's homemade pizza. Under my Monday tab I'll find several of our favorite Mexican dishes, plus whatever else I've planned to make that day of the week.

In my teaching binder, I keep my master chore sheets in one cover and our monthly timeline people in another. I've also been known to tape a report cover opposite the toilet and fill it with poetry or scripture we are attempting to memorize.

I generally buy report covers in bulk through Viking Office Supplies. They also carry Velcro and ship free to your door, usually by the next day.

Don't Put It Down, Put It Away

Once you've organized your materials, you need to teach yourself and your children to put things away. When a new area is established, I have difficulty getting in the habit of putting items in the right bins. My children may toss items anywhere. I will go through and rearrange misplaced items, until my children catch on. After a while, they know where things go and begin to put them there themselves.

When they neglect to follow through, I will remind them to "put the details away." If needed, I will ask a child to pull a whole section of drawers and put away each detail that they've allowed to pile up. I point out how much easier it is to maintain the system if they put things away directly after they use them.

I keep a little bin or basket for odds and ends that I pick up throughout the day, and designate one child to go find the homes for the items. This has helped keep us from losing scores of minuscule game pieces.

Believe it or not, the children really like to have things organized. They like to know where to get what they want, when they want it.

Staying organized is much easier if everything is in its proper place. I have found plastic to be a natural solution for many of my organizing woes.

Put It in Plastic (Bins, That Is)

How I love my plastic bins! Naturally, we use them to store toys. Most large families come to the conclusion that toys are best stored in a central location and not in bedrooms. This also works if you are a small family but your children are little. Most young children don't have the ability to keep their rooms neat if there is much in them. The central location also promotes shared use of toys and allows you to build on (here I go again) themes. The toys go in labeled bins, which go on a labeled shelf. By specifying for my children, I make it easy for them to help me clean up. Our shelves are metal, the kind used in workshops, so they can take some climbing. We have a huge open bin of Duplo blocks on the bottom, then smaller bins with lids for things like the castle set, plastic zoo animals, and math manipulatives. Exploration of manipulatives is an option at any time of day.

From the Big . . .

Caution! Some of these bins are large enough for a child to fit inside. Any large plastic container can form an electrostatic seal with carpeting and can suffocate your child. When we first purchased the large bins, I would wake up at night with nightmares of my children suffocating in them. During the day I would get busy, and it seemed too hard to ask Daddy, tired from work, to watch the kids. One day, while my children were playing, I came around the corner to find one child under a bin, with another child humming and sitting on top of it. I think I shook for a full hour while I dumped every bin we owned and stacked all 20 of them by the front door! My husband drilled holes in the sides and bottoms of all the bins and I started sleeping better at night.

Even with the holes, these large bins are very effective. My favorite use: **unit-study bins.** Over the years, we've collected a lot of homeschooling stuff, mostly in themes (of course!). A reader told me about a terrific storage solution and business idea. A woman in her area has organized 45 bins which she rents out on a monthly basis for a fee. Taking that idea home, I was able to ease the crunch on our bookshelves, our game closet, and our videos and tapes, and put them in unit bins. We never have time to use those items while on a different theme, because we are usually too en-

How to Avoid Interruptions
by Joyce Swann

Interruptions often steal many hours of our homeschool day. Robbing us of precious hours that should be spent teaching our children, these time thieves can keep us from accomplishing our goals and leave us feeling inadequate and guilty. Yet, by planning ahead, we can make provision for both internal and external interruptions.

Most external interruptions fall into one of several categories:

- phone calls from friends
- appointments with doctors, dentists, hairdressers, etc.
- appointments with plumbers, appliance repairmen, and other service personnel

External interruptions are easier to control since you usually can anticipate them ahead of time, and plan to make them less intrusive.

Phone Rules

When we began homeschooling, the first thing I did was let my friends know what we were doing and tell them our school hours. Most were considerate enough not to call while we were in school, but when one did, I talked to her for few seconds and then told her that we were in school. I then asked if I could return the call and set up a specific time to do so. This usually worked quite well. Some, of course, were displeased with the arrangement, but I soon discovered that they were not so much opposed to having their call returned as they were to the idea of homeschooling.

Now that my children are older, I try never to answer the phone during school hours. If someone calls, I have one of the children take the name and number, and I return the call as soon as we finish school.

Appointments

I also quickly discovered that a successful homeschool depends on strictly adhering to school hours and planning the rest of our lives around school—not vice versa. Appointments with doctors, dentists, hairdressers, etc., were set up so that they would not cut into school hours. I made it a rule to tell everyone that I could not take any appointment before 3:00 P.M. Of course, the receptionists tried to talk me into taking the appointments most convenient for them, but I always responded, "That is not possible. I cannot come in before 3:00 o'clock." After all, *I* was paying *them* and I felt that I had every right to insist on appointments that worked best for me.

I handled appointment for plumbers, appliance repairmen, and other service personnel a little differently. If I knew that all I had to do was open the door and point the way to the appropriate repair job, I allowed them to come during school hours. Since these kinds of appointments are not usually disruptive to school, I felt it best to accommodate the repairmen.

Ready to Teach

Internal interruptions require a little more effort since they are more difficult to control. Generally, internal interruptions stem from one of the following:

- lack of preparedness on the part of the home teacher
- lost or missing school materials
- breaks—bathroom breaks, recess, etc.
- general discipline problems

Coming to school prepared to teach prevents many major disruptions to your school day. This means you must know what you are going to be teaching before the school day begins.

If you do not use a curriculum which includes a daily lesson plan, make up a written plan in advance so that you will know how many pages each student will be covering in each subject. In my lectures I recommend that this daily lesson plan be made up several months before the school year begins.

You should also make certain that you have read the material your students will be covering that day and that you are prepared to answer questions and help them with math when problems arise. Having your students sit idly while you prepare to give them assignments, look for answers, or try to figure out how to solve a math problem, robs them of valuable study time and plays havoc with your school day.

School Materials In A Box

Lost or missing school materials can also be the source of major disruptions.

In our house, we assure that everyone has his materials on hand at all times by giving each child his own cardboard box in which he keeps his text books, syllabus, a pad of paper, pencils, erasers, a ruler, a compass, a protractor, a pocket-sized spelling dictionary, and any other materials, such as flash cards and art reproductions, that may be included with his course. When it is time for school, the children bring

their "school boxes" to the table, and we are ready to begin. When school is over, they return their materials to their boxes and store them in their closets. Thus, we NEVER waste time looking for materials.

Breaks & Recess

Breaks are planned interruptions which should either be eliminated or kept to a minimum.

In our home, we are in school for three straight hours with no breaks. While it is sometimes necessary for someone to use the bathroom, it is rare for any of my students to leave the school room until school has ended for the day. By having children use the bathroom and get a drink before they come to school, these kinds of interruptions can be largely eliminated.

Another major disruption for many homeschoolers is recess. Because most of us are products of the public school system, we tend to believe that recess is necessary. However, in my nineteen years of homeschooling I have never given a recess and do not believe that it serves any useful purpose. Homeschooling mothers who do give their children a recess tell me that these breaks frequently extend to twenty or twenty-five minutes since children often do not return to their seats on time. In addition, it takes a while for them to "settle down" and resume their studies. With thought processes interrupted, children often have a difficult time picking up where they left off. The homeschool teacher often finds that what was supposed to be a brief break to refresh her students has turned into a serious interruption which results in a longer school day for everyone.

The most obvious interruptions to the homeschool day are likely to stem from general discipline problems. Children sometimes try to manipulate the classroom by bringing up subjects unrelated to their school work.

Since we want our children to know that we value their ideas and think their questions are important, we may feel it is necessary to put aside lessons and discuss those subjects immediately. This approach will, however, probably result in everyone being distracted from his studies for an extended period.

I handle this problem by telling my students that I am "very interested" in what they have to say but that we will have to discuss it after school. Later that day I remind them that we were going to talk after school, and I then spend as much time on the subject as they like.

Classroom Rules

I discovered quite early that the key to a well-disciplined class lies in establishing a few simple rules to insure a quiet, orderly atmosphere in which little scholars can thrive. Here are my rules which have governed our homeschool for nineteen years:

- No talking about anything that does not pertain to the lessons being studied.
- No staring out the window.
- No food or drinks in the classroom.
- No talking to other students.
- No wasting time.

While no one can create a homeschool that is entirely free of interruptions, each of us can eliminate many of the predictable interruptions by planning ahead. Controlling the external interruptions and setting up guidelines to minimize the internal ones is the best way to provide your students with a quiet, stress-free atmosphere which encourages learning and promotes good scholarship.

Joyce Swann and her amazing family are featured in chapter 30.

grossed in our present topic. So, now we have bins for the 1700's, the War for Independence, the 1800's, the Middle Ages, and Creation.

One bin may combine several units until I find I need to split them up. To accommodate the flow of items from bin to bin, I've labeled each with an index card and black marker, which I put at the front of the bin on the inside. To change the contents I only need to mark or change the card, instead of trying to peel and stick on new labels. These unit bins can be made from cheap containers and stored in out of the way places.

Out-of-season clothing seems to store best under beds. This allows me to claim all under-bed areas for my own use, keeping the territory free of junk and dirty clothes. Containers may be of any sort, but they must fit snugly under the bed and have some sort of cover. Otherwise, the children may be overwhelmed by the temptation to stuff the containers with their own items. This system works beautifully: new or outgrown clothes are stored under the bed of the child who will next wear them. The bins can be pulled and riffled through whenever someone grows and changes size.

The quickest way to work through a seasonal change of clothing is to have each child bring their bins to the living room. Then, starting with the oldest, each shows the contents of their drawers in turn and leaves with outfits that fit and match. The oldest is first to "shop" for clothes, so he can have the broadest range of choices (you know how clothes can be mis-sized). Meanwhile, I set aside unmatched clothing and take notes on what each child needs from the store. One of my children loves to function as fashion coordinator, so this job gets easier all the time.

. . . To the Small

Smaller, clear bins organize craft items near their point of use, but high enough not to tempt the little children. My children don't get these down without permission, and we are careful about putting them back. This has saved us from loads of disasters.

These craft bins consist of paints (some toxic), glues, glitter, and assorted craft items. In my sewing area, I keep bins for elastics, thread, buttons, bias, and lace. I have a separate storage bin for tools that I don't use as often.

Rubbermaid makes cute little clear drawer bins which offer easy-access storage for daily homeschool supplies. We have one with colored pencils, another with office supplies (tape, stapler, glue sticks), another with math manipulatives, another with pattern blocks, another with cards and envelopes, and another with rubber-stamp stuff. We have a set for frequently used games, labeled "Bible games," "Math games," "Chess and checkers," and "Geography games." The game boards are stored on top. The preschoolers have a set of drawers on the floor that include cars, pegboards, snap cubes, inch blocks, and small puzzles. We can quickly locate the drawer we need for the task at hand. I'd much rather spend my energies helping my child understand a difficult math concept than hunting for pencils.

Being organized is like a bank account: I can draw from it in bad times and add to in good times. And with money in the bank, I no longer feel like I'm drowning.

Teach Yourself How to Organize

The following products are designed to help you organize your life so your homeschooling will be successful. Additional reviews of recordkeeping systems can be found in the next chapter.

Blueprints Organizer: A Planning Guide for Home-Schooling Parents

$9.95 plus shipping.
Hewitt Homeschooling Resources. PO Box 9, Washougal, WA 98671. (360) 835-8708. Fax: (360) 835-8697. Email: hewittths@aol.com.

NEW!
Help! I've Gotta Organize This Stuff!

Parents. $39.95 plus $4 shipping.
Valerie Royce Coughlin, 13428 Cedar St., Hesperia, CA 92345. Phone/fax: (760) 947-3982. Email: famfare@gte.net.

NEW!
The Home Education CopyBook and Planning Guide!

Parents. $25 plus shipping.
KONOS Helps, 1212 Ogletown Rd., Newark, DE 19711. (302) 737-3673. Fax: (302) 737-3651. Email: vonduyke@aol.com. Web: www.chesco.com/~vonduyke/ konoshelps/.

Blueprints Organizer: A Planning Guide for Home-Schooling Parents is a set of 116 reproducible sheets covering family goals and expectations, children's goal sheets, quarterly subject goals, sample schedules, daily planning sheets, yearly calendar of months, month-at-a-glance calendars, weekly planners, progress summaries for each month, yearly summary by subject with comment blocks on the back, grocery list with teaching suggestions for shopping trips, memo sheets, and certificates. It comes with a binder, instructions, and a cassette. *Mary Pride*

Are you sitting down? Here's a resource that contains over 250 pages of organizing help. The good news is that you aren't supposed to use all of them. The really good news is that with this resource at your fingertips you'll be able to customize planners that your family will be able to use for years.

Valerie Royce Coughlin has created what amounts to the Cadillac of "create your own" with her book **Help! I've Gotta Organize This Stuff!**

You aren't bound to a particular system, nor does Mrs. Coughlin give you advice on how to use her forms. And what about the forms themselves? Simply gorgeous. Superb printing quality, 70# paper, all clamped together in a sturdy plastic cover means these will last. Space prevents me from listing out each type of form. Broad categories include calendars, attendance records, progress reports, lesson plans, unit studies, family objectives, certificates and awards, household planning, health records, greeting cards, and "extras" for even more choices. Support groups can have forms for calendars, group activities, awards, certificates, posters, even greeting cards.

Let's compare this to a similar product. Personally, I love Kathy Von Duyke's *Home Education Copybook* almost more for her narrative than for the forms themselves. Kathy's book is comfy, cozy, and folksy-friendly. For someone who really doesn't know where to start organizing, I'd recommend Kathy's book. If that's not important to you, then this book offers a great value just for the sheer amount of forms you have to choose from. *Renee Mathis*

Information, inspiration and lots of practical advice! This latest version of **The Home Education CopyBook** is no longer just a book of reproducible forms—though it *does* include forms, forms, and more forms!

Using these forms you can customize your planner to meet your needs, regardless of the homeschool method you use. Forms for organizing and running your household help you to maximize your time. Then with all the extra time on your hands, you can use the wonderful homeschool planning forms. You get yearly forms, daily lesson plan grids, unit study plans and evaluation sheets, journal sheets, maps, book lists, resource lists—you name it and it's in here.

Katherine von Duyke, mother of ten children and long-time editor of the *KONOS Helps!* newsletter, explains in detail how to do the needed decision-making that goes into planning. Within each chapter are filled-in forms taken from her own teaching notebook. A magnifying glass ought to be included in each book, because you can squint out some great ideas from these samples!

"Planning 101" is for the new-to-homeschooling mom. Kathy cuts out all the glitz and clutter of the early school years and focuses on the most needed skills: reading, math, and housework! This chapter provides a detailed look at what a home with four young children can actually accomplish for school, plus helps moms focus on foundational habits needed for future years. She includes such nitty-gritty issues as when to do laundry, what to have for lunch, and when to take a potty break! You even get her own program for preschool math and phonics, which if followed, the author says, will prepare your child to tackle high school sciences well before high school.

"Setting Objectives" covers spreading units over the course of a year to make the most of each season, teaching units over a four year cycle, and includes a month-by-month discussion of typical homeschooling and home management activities. Next, grade-level objectives are broken down so that you decide the best method to teach each subject, your standard of excellence, your documentation method, and what will end up in your child's portfolio. Kathy shows you how to document loosely-taught subjects so they look official. These objectives are then translated into assignment sheets with several options for different styles of documentation. Her best advice? Plan out where you can double up on tasks, and don't assign out any work you can't "freelance."

"Unit Planning" takes the rest of the subjects you wish to teach as a unit and helps you unravel the unit for subject-by-subject documentation, without giving up any of the spontaneity of a unit study. Described in detail are how to plan a unit, the elements of a successful unit, and how to document your unit—not to please the state, but to get more mileage out of your teaching. Typically, you get several cute forms with lots of different ideas for using them.

"High School (and College)" gets very personal. There's a bit of a philosophical discussion about the purpose for the high school years and a discussion of inner versus outer motivation. High-school courses are evaluated according to what is required, the level of student interest, the level of pursuit, and the means and methods chosen per course. To illustrate this she discusses her own high schoolers and how she has coached them into being responsible for their own education. She tells her own story of struggling with her then 13-year-old son who no longer wanted to do school "Mom's way" but ended up graduating two years early! She concludes with some strategies for completing college work at home. The high-school log form allows for very fluid record keeping so that students can keep official records for everything from textbooks to lifestyle learning.

The *Home Education CopyBook* is a wonderful addition to any homeschool family's library of homeschool helpers. This book is especially suited to homeschooling veterans who are ready to take more control over their children's work and want to build a lifestyle around deep learning. Lots of information packed in this book! Recommended. *Mary Pride and Maryann Turner*

I really, really like this book! **Homeschooling by Heart** is just the juice disorganized types need to become successful homeschoolers. After all, the book's original title was going to be *So You Want to Quit Homeschooling?*

Yes, this book has charts, tables, and scheduling forms galore. What makes it stand out from the herd is that (1) this is *not* a book for those who naturally love to fill out forms and (2) the warm human touch author Kristina Sabalis Krulikas brings to the book. You're not exhorted to picture-perfect conformity. Rather, she takes you through first reex-

Organization is most of what the old *CopyBook* used to contain, but even this has been updated. Kathy tells you how she has changed over the years. She discusses when to do tasks (ie. daily schedules, chores), where to put stuff, and where to stuff papers (filing). Included are directions for setting up a teaching notebook and a purse-sized notebook. A little more philosophy comes through as the chapter ends with a discussion of life themes. In the appendix is a listing of her favorite tried and true products. Kathy states that her goal in organization is not a perfect home, but a prepared home fit to meet the needs of her family.

The book and planner sheets are bound together with a removable, slide binding making it easy to take the forms out to copy for your use. Then you can just put everything back together. If only all of life could be that simple!

NEW!
Homeschooling by Heart
Parents. $19.95 plus $3 shipping.
Solomon's Secrets, 1264 Alhambra Dr., Ft. Meyers, FL 33901.
Email: sudievu@aol.com.
Web: www.solomons-secrets.com.

amining your reasons for homeschooling and recognizing homeschooling is a lifestyle and motherhood is a job. She then encourages you to simplify, build community bonds without going crazy with activities, and *not* compare your family to others.

After this overview of your homeschooling "road map," Krulikas takes you step by step through goal setting, child training and discipline, a detailed step-by-step guide to organizing your entire house room by room, scheduling, menu planning, budgeting, and kids' allowances. The rest of the book is taken up with helping you plan a curriculum that focuses on wisdom first, the love of learning second, and having fun third, including an entire chapter on why you should homeschool through high school. I think I found one sentence I disagreed with in the entire book!

If you're looking for from-the-trenches advice and organizing helps that will make you feel better instead of guilty, get this book. *Mary Pride*

If you're like me, you probably need extra encouragement in the organization department. Where do you put the information on those little slips of paper that float all over the house? What's in that box out in the garage?

Here's your answer. **Let's Get Organized!** comes with over 60 reproducible cardstock forms decorated with cute pictures, 10 tabbed divider sheets, 2 pocket dividers, and 1 manila envelope. A binder is not included.

What do you do with all these sheets? Not to worry. There are 5 pages of organizing tips plus 13 pages of ideas on how to use the forms, personalize them to meet your needs and even a page entitled, "Confessions of a Disorganized Homemaker" lest you think the author is perfect. Here's a partial listing of what to expect: a master sheet, monthly and yearly calendars, exercise records, family illness record, gardening organizer, a co-op order sheet, shopping list, mom's daily checklist, menu for the week, freezer meals and preparation, camping/RV list, gift ideas and birthday reminders, Christmas shopping, and curriculum/book wish form. Even husbands have their own forms: spiritual update, financial budget guide, home maintenance, car maintenance, and calendar type forms among others.

There are probably more forms here than any one woman needs, but that's the beauty of it. Use what you like and ignore the rest. Now where do I put my organizer? *Marla Perry*

Do you need a book filled with copies of every form or chart imaginable? If so, **Organization with Ease** will register high on your "must buy" scale!

I was quite impressed with the variety of forms included in this book. They are all there for you to copy until your heart's content.

For us organizer "wanna-bes," the sky is the limit. There are forms for chores and responsibilities, grocery lists, meal planners, baby-sitter's instructions—and the list goes on and on! A checklist for your daily housecleaning is even included. You can copy what you need to make your household run more efficiently, and save the originals to copy again later.

Interspersed among the array of goal sheets and diet sheets is wonderful organizing advice on almost any topic. The author, a mother of 12, shares a wealth of information on making your household run more smoothly. She even includes a sheet to help you evaluate how you spend your time!

Although this book isn't specifically for homeschoolers, it is chock full of valuable information and encouragement. Recommended. *Maryann Turner*

NEW!
Let's Get Organized!
Ages 5–adult. $29.95 plus shipping.
Beall's Learning Games, 5220 Lone Jack Lane, Garden Valley, CA 95633. Phone/Fax: (530) 333-4589.

NEW!
Organization With Ease
Parents. $14 postpaid.
Carla Hofstee, PO Box 1342, Coeur d' Alene, ID 83816-1342.
(208) 687-7012.

Chore Systems

A neat new development (in more ways than one) is the chore record-keeping system. Realistically, homeschooling is half studying and half trying to keep the house clean. Thus no mere system for preserving academic records can do justice to your pressing need to have the kitchen floor mopped.

The best way to do your chores, of course, is to train the children to do them. However, this means you need some way of deciding which child does what and checking up on them. If you believe in rewarding your children for chores well done, you will also need some way of totting up their pay.

Here are some systems which do nothing but teach children how to do their chores and organize who does what when. If you have more than one or two children, such a system might be a worthwhile investment.

Author Patricia Sprinkle has tackled the topic of household chores and children in this chatty 198-page softcover book. "I'm convinced that we as parents do ourselves a disservice if we carry the full load of regular household chores and fail to share them with our children," she writes. Overflowing with quotes from parents and a plethora of other experts, **Children Who Do Too Little** examines why our children's need to work, as well as many parents' reasons for not making them work. The last two-thirds of the book are where you'll find the how-tos: how to have a family meeting, how to teach skills, not chores, how to teach by natural consequences, and more. The appendix section of the book profiles some of the parents who shared in the book (a nice touch), and also has a group discussion guide.

The tone of this book may remind you of that found in many mass-market women's magazines: tons of bite-sized quotes and thoughts advance Sprinkle's basic thesis that our children need to help shoulder the load in our families. You may find the wide variety of approaches and ideas helpful if you have children who don't have a sense of how to work, and you're not sure how to get them to start. But for many of you, this book may feel like too much information about a fairly straightforward topic. In order to function as a family, particularly if you have several children, each one in the family needs age-appropriate responsibilities and a patient and realistic parent to train them to do the job well. *Michelle Van Loon*

The **Choreganizers** package has been updated. You now get an 11 x 17" Chore Store and 48 colorful Picture Cards. Also included are a set of Dad Dollars and Mom Money to encourage children to do the job well and cheerfully. Set includes all materials for up to six children.

Instructions for how to complete each task are printed on the back of the cards. 48 Chore cards slip into 6 chore charts. Glue the Store Chore Chart to a box stacked with items children can redeem with Dad Dollars and Mom Money. *Mary Pride*

Do you need a way to encourage your little ones to do their chores each day? Do your older children want to know how much allowance a particular task will get them? If so, **Daily Duties** and **Allowance Chore Checks** were designed with them in mind. These tools are actually charts with various items listed. *Daily Duties* would include getting dressed, brushing

Sun Sales, Inc., P.O. Box 1315, Cardiff, CA 92007. (800) 392-9134. Fax: (760) 431-8928. Web: www.sunsalesinc.com.

teeth, making the bed, helping with dishes, etc. *Allowance Chore Checks* is a chart on which you write your child's chores for that week and what he will earn. At the bottom of the chart is a "chore check" that you make out at the end of the week and pay to your child. Of course, he'll only want the cash and not a pretend check!

If your child needs to see his/her progress on completing chores, *Daily Duties* is an excellent way to go. In most cases, the child wants to see all the spaces with check marks in them. On the other hand, some children will not care one way or the other. *Allowance Chore Checks* will help your older child see just what needs to be done to earn his "salary" for the week. It will also teach him that a paycheck never goes as far as you would like it to! *Barbara Buchanan*

NEW!
Organized Kids OK Cards Complete Set

Ages 4–6. $14.95 plus shipping. Items available separately. *Good Beginnings, 56 Marion Lane, Eugene, OR 97404. (541) 688-7103. Email: esmith@eugene.net. Web: ok.eugene.net.*

Do you have young children who just can't seem to remember to brush their teeth and make their bed? If so, **Organized Kids OK Cards** might be for you! Since OK Cards contain pictures and no words, non-readers can use them with little parental supervision. Each system includes

- a file-card holder, eight dividers plus a reward section for each day of the week
- 10 activity cards which illustrate each activity (e.g. making a bed)
- five Fun Day cards which picture rewards (e.g. going to the library, going out for ice-cream, etc.) for completing the weekly routine
- five blank cards which enable you to customize the system
- clock face stickers which can be used if you want the various activities to be scheduled
- and a marking pen for designing schedules or custom cards

Set #2 includes seven new activity cards geared to the older child, three Fun Day cards with different rewards and five additional blank cards which parents or children can use to create their own reminders.

Here's how the system works. The child draws out the various cards and then completes the activities on the card. After completing the activity, the card is then filed under the next day's tab, to be done again the next day. At the end of the week, a Fun Day card is drawn to reward the child for his or her hard work.

Although the system is designed with independence in mind, most young children will require some help in using the cards (e.g. refilling them). *Rebecca Livermore*

CHAPTER 33

How to Keep Great Homeschool Records

I'm going to tell you the truth—I don't especially enjoy reviewing record-keeping products for homeschoolers. Too often they consist of huge binders loaded with forms you could just as easily design for yourself. Then there's the difficulty of trying to figure out whether *this* system would meet a lot of people's needs, or if *that* system might be better. If Family A uses textbooks, and Family B relies on unit studies, how can anyone possibly compare the record-keeping systems they use?

Aha! A way out of this dilemma! Let's look at the different *types* of record-keeping systems, instead of at single products. Let's determine which kind of system fits which kind of home schooling. Then you will be able to decide which type of product you prefer, or whether you'd really rather invent your own.

Who Am I?

Are you a Portfolio Person, or a Diarist? A Daily Planner Dad or a Mondo Mom? Take this simple test to find out.

- **Do you create individual lists** for each member of the family, listing what they should do and what they should take, before you go on vacation? Does it make you feel more secure to have everything written down in advance? Then you are a Planner Person. Maybe even a Mondo Mom.
- **Do you have a completely filled-out baby book** for every one of your children? Do you truly enjoy taking the time to chronicle your children's achievements? Then you are a Diarist. Do the journal thing.
- **Do you love to collect** knick-knacks? Do you enjoy taking pictures? Videos? Audio taping the kids' cute sayings? Then you are a Portfolio Person.
- **Is your life a series of random disasters** that kill all your plans and leave you too exhausted at the end of the day to write down what each child actually did? You're a Mini-System Mom! Get some workbooks in the major subject areas, break them down into pages per day, write it on the workbooks, and you'll be able to ensure that *something* is getting done every day.

Keep the Results and Nothing But the Results

Those of us who teach our own children, or run our own schools, are in a strong position to make our record-keeping and grading useful rather than destructive. For starters, we can determine to throw away the steps and keep the results. This is what we do in the real world. No businessman saves the first drafts of his memos. No homeworker treasures up her botched dress seams. Instead, the businessman tosses the first drafts as soon as he has the final copy in his hands, and the homeworker rips out the botched seam and replaces it with one sewn properly. As adults, we quite rightly want to be judged on our final products, not on our missteps along the way.

—*Schoolproof*

If you can't decide, then remember that less is usually more (the more sheets, the more guilt). Try keeping your own records your own way for a while, and you'll find yourself falling into one of these categories. Big on To-Do lists? Get a daily planner. Like to write at length about your children's charms? You're a Diarist. Love checklists and filled-out forms? Get a mondo system. Always changing your plans on the fly? Try a card-based system. Too much work, too little time? Add a chore system. Children discouraged by their chores or work? Add an incentive system. No matter what, keep a portfolio of their best work—this is an encouragement in itself—and remember to take some time to smell the roses.

The Daily Planner

These are the familiar planning books used by executives. Each double-page spread has the weekdays across the top and hours across the left side. Each box on the page represents a specific day and hour.

You can use a daily planner two ways:

(1) As a lesson planner. You write the assignments in for each hour of each day.
(2) If you prefer to use the "journaling" method, you write in what you actually did after it is done.

The lesson planning method obviously works best if you use textbooks, while a journaling method is usually better for unit-study and project-oriented homeschools. The more unpredictable your daily schedule, the more likely you are a candidate for journaling.

One tip to help you fit many children and courses onto a daily planner: **assign each textbook a code.** You might want to write a list of all the texts you are using on one of the other forms in the planner, along with their codes. Then you can write, say, "ABM7 12, 13" instead of "A Beka Math Grade 7, pages 12–13."

If your children tend to work a lot on different assignments, you might want to consider getting a separate planner for each child. Then even if the children aren't all in the same location while they are doing their work, each child can follow his own assignments. This also is a good idea if you have many children, as it can be hard to write six assignments in one teeny-weeny planner box!

Daily planner systems usually also include monthly and yearly planning sheets. These are handy for writing in field trips, projects, and errands.

One drawback of the daily planner is that you can't both plan and record what you did without a lot of erasing or arrows pointing from one block to the next. If you don't do exactly what you thought you would exactly when you thought you would do it, the lesson plans fail to serve as a record of your actual homeschool hours. Conversely, just writing down what you did in a journal form means you miss out on the comfort of seeing your plans written out in advance.

"No school profits from disorder," say the folks at Christian Liberty Academy. They've come up with a professional-looking, quality planner to ensure this doesn't happen to you.

Designed for families who are members of the CLASS (Christian Liberty Academy Satellite School), the **CLASS Lesson Planner** will nevertheless benefit anyone using a traditional, structured curriculum. Sufficient record-keeping sheets are included in this spiral-bound book for one child anywhere from kindergarten up through high school. Requirements are

NEW!
CLASS Lesson Planner
Parents. $7.95.
Christian Liberty Press, 502 West Euclid Ave., Arlington Heights, IL 60004. (847) 259-4444. Fax: (847) 259-2941. Email: enquire@homeschools.org. Web: www.homeschools.org.

suggested for families with college-bound students as well, in order to help you map out their course of study.

Unlike most lesson planners, the CLASS planner groups subjects in weekly blocks. You're provided enough room to record the week's assignments, quizzes, and items still needing review. Report card forms, transcript form, and a quarterly evaluation form are all included. Even if you don't use all of the forms, the price makes this especially affordable for families with more than one student. *Renee Mathis*

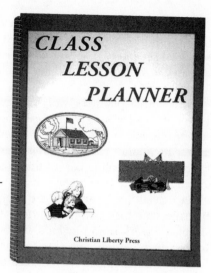

What the CLASS lesson planner does for those who mostly rely on textbooks, the **Harris Homeschool Planner** (not to be confused with the Noble Planner authored by seminar leader Gregg Harris, reviewed below) does for unit studies. Finally, a set of high quality planning forms you can put together yourself, plus an included clip-book! The print quality is outstanding, a definite plus considering you can use these for your whole family for the rest of your life. Armed with these sheets, you can create just the tool you need to benefit your family's needs. A notebook for Mom, an assignment book for older students, a journal for the younger ones—the possibilities are endless.

A well-organized unit study doesn't just happen by itself. But with Caryn Harris's planning sheets you can lay out the books you will use, the vocabulary words your will study, the projects you will complete, and the field trips you will enjoy. Especially handy is the independent-study contract form, as well as a planner for constructing and evaluating an end-of-the-unit presentation.

In addition to the sheets for you to copy, there is a clear, concise guide for using the planners. Just enough examples and a well-written invitation to explore unit studies for yourself.

"But I'm just not the unit-study type!" you say. Even so, the other features of this product make it a sound investment. *Renee Mathis*

Karen Toussaint designed her **Home School Helper** to help other busy families stay on target without an overload of work. It's an admirable effort.

You get a simple three-ring binder divided into tabbed sections, the sort you can find at your local office-supply store. There is a section to keep track of yearly hours spent, another with weekly planner sheets (subjects down the left-hand side, Monday–Friday across the top), a section for recording quarterly test scores, a yearly overview section to plan how many pages need to be covered each day, and a section for listing all curriculum used for each student during the year. Sample report cards are included, along with very simple field-trip planners, check-out slips for loaning out books and tapes, health forms, weekly job chart, and Mrs. Toussaint's rotating six-week menu system. Blank, tabbed sections are provided for your support-group mailing list and newsletters. In addition you get three large envelopes for storing awards, certificates, or projects.

Karen grants you permission to make copies for your family. Unfortunately, she has only included six sheets of each section—not enough weekly sheets for the year. Since you have to make your own copies anyway, I'd suggest buying the master pack and saving some money. *Renee Mathis*

NEW!
The Home School Lesson Planner

Parents. $25 plus shipping
*AlmaNichePublishing, LLC, 310
Williams St., Hattiesburg, MS 39401.
(800) 299-6974.
Inquiries/fax: (601) 584-8932.*

NEW!
The Homeschool Parent's Perfect Planbook

Parents. $15.95 plus shipping.
*Queen Homeschool Supplies, P.O. Box
245, McClellandtown, PA 15458.
(888) 695-2777.
Email: questions@queenhomeschool.com.
Web: www.queenhomeschool.com.*

The Homeschool Lesson Planner by Elizabeth Nicholson was designed with the busy mom in mind. It makes homeschool record keeping simple and painless. The simplicity of the system makes it require minimal time. Yet all your papers and lesson plans are organized into one spiral-bound book.

Unlike other planners, which are made up of pages, this planner consists of 36 10x13" sturdy *envelopes* spiral-bound together. On one side of each envelope is a full-page weekly lesson plan sheet. Spaces for comments, attendance records, and grades are printed on the reverse side.

The most appealing part of the system (at least for me) is the envelope. You can put next week's work, completed work, or mementoes that you wish to save into the appropriate envelope. Since there are 36 envelopes, the papers are filed in a neat, orderly fashion. It gives you quick access to completed work from previous weeks. It's especially useful when you need to keep documentation to show authorities.

Sample lesson plans are included to make it easy to adjust the planner to fit your needs. Ample room for large families makes it possible to use only one planner for your entire family.

At the end of the year, you can just file the completed planner away. You have the documentation you need to satisfy the authorities. The peace of mind from knowing that you can find what you might need for future reference is an added bonus. Recommended. *Maryann Turner*

I'm not sure if we'll ever see a perfect planbook, but this one has some nice features. The **Homeschool Parent's Perfect Planbook** is comb-bound with a plastic see-through cover. You get:

- Calendar squares—Cross off one each day you homeschool.
- Goals/Objectives—1 sheet/year. Enough for 8 students.
- Week at a Glance Planning Sheet—1 page/week, divided into 6 days.
- Quick Check Subject Logsheets—Sheet divided into small squares with space down the left-hand side to list day numbers and space across the top to list subjects. By using different colors of ink for each child, you can tell at a glance whether or not all the subjects have been done for the day. This is a great idea for those subjects (*Saxon Math* for example) where you just "do the next lesson." For the visual learners among us, it's also a good way to see if any subjects are being neglected. I'll bet we've all had days where we wonder, "Did I do math with everyone?"
- Unit Planning Worksheets—1 sheet to note Main Theme, Library List, Sub-Units, Activities/Field Trips, and Additional Resources. There are only 10 of these - I wish she'd included more.
- Booklist Sheets—Space to list "Books Read By" and "Books Read Together" (nice touch!)
- Student's Daily Logsheets—Reproducible form. Make enough copies for each child to have their own book. The 1 page/day format allows you room to note assignments or journal for 10 subjects. Spaces at the bottom track prayer requests, answers to prayer, and special activities per day.
- Happy Helper's Mall—Really just a chore sheet, but the kids might get a kick out of being assigned a "store" (a room in your house) to manage for the week. The "Weekly Special" is where you list the family reward to be earned.

This planner makes a lot of sense for families who tend to be more laid-back and just need to record somewhere that "school is getting done." On the other hand, it's also a great idea for tracking several children without sending you into "organizational overload mode." Flexible and family-friendly; can't ask for more than that! *Renee Mathis*

Sarah Crain, a 13-year-old in her fifth year of homeschooling, decided the best way to get a planner to suit the needs of her family was to design it herself. Five years later, she has come out with the **Fifth Edition** of **The Homeschool Planbook**.

This is a very nice effort that is designed to keep records for one student. As an individual assignment book it could work very well.

The author has included enough pages to keep track of school hours. She has a page each for yearly goals, curriculum used, weekly planning pages, field trips taken, projects completed, verses memorized, books read (you can fit 70 books here), and a four-year calendar. Also included is a section for keeping track of your goals, subjects, curriculum, and resources. The 52 weekly planning pages are very simple: 7 days of the week down one side and 9 subjects listed across the top. If you are in a state that, like Missouri, wants you to keep track of hours spent on academic goals, you'll find the 12 monthly "hours of instruction" pages in the back helpful. These are set up according to Missouri standards of "core" and "non-core" hours, and also includes space for separating hours spent away from home (e.g., on field trips, at the library) from hours spent at home. The pages are spiral-bound and the cover is now "jelly proof," so your copy should survive longer under ordinary use.

Starting with the **Fourth Edition** (which is still available), you can also tally your hours at the bottom of each weekly page. The Fourth Edition is only available in the three-hole-punched format. It comes pre-punched and shrink-wrapped.

The **Family Edition** has the same information as the Fifth Edition, with enough planning pages for four students doing separate assignments.

The **Unit Study Edition** can handle four students doing unit studies together, and language arts and math separately. Great idea!

The **Homeschool High School Planbook** is quite different. Sarah designed this one when she became aware that high school requires different recordkeeping from earlier grades. What you get: a two-year calendar, a four-year course planner with accompanying requirements checklist (important for college-bound and those who plan to earn a high school diploma), space for writing out course descriptions (room for 16 courses now—another improvement from the previous edition,) an official-looking grades/credits sheet, another official-looking report card sheet (suitable for photocopying and sending to college admissions officials), and 52 weekly planning spreads, with subjects left blank. This edition is currently under revision; you can email Sarah to obtain a list of proposed changes.

You will need a *High School Planbook* for each year of high school, just as you need one *Homeschool Planbook* per child—or one *Family Edition* or *Unit Study Edition* for every four children—for each earlier school grade. *Renee Mathis and Mary Pride*

The spiral-bound **School Scheduler** by Nancy Glick is meant as your complete homeschool planner. The author, who has won an award for organizing skills, starts her scheduler with several pages of scheduling suggestions.

This organizer uses a two-page-per-week spread for its main planning section, with one square per subject per day for the usual 52 weeks. The scheduler is set up for a five-day week: Monday through Friday. Subject

NEW!
The Homeschool Planbook
Fifth Anniversary Edition, $9.50. Family Edition, $15. Unit Studies Edition, $15. Fourth Edition, $8.50. High School Planbook, $8.50. Shipping extra.
The Homeschool Planbook, 164 Strack Farm Lane, Troy, MO 63379. (314) 338-9218. Fax: (314) 338-9917. Email: macrain@surfnet2000.com.

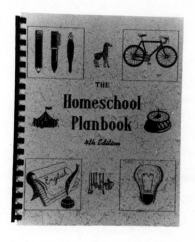

NEW!
School Scheduler
Parents. $10 plus $2 shipping. *Palm Tree Press, P.O. Box 290, Arlington, OH 45814. (419) 365-5994. Fax: (419) 424-1858.*

blocks are Bible/character, English/journal, math, reading, science or health, social studies, spelling/handwriting, and art/music/phys ed. A column on the right-hand page allows you to keep track of total hours spent homeschooling, while there is room at the bottom of each subject column to jot down a few ideas for next week's studies.

Pages are provided to log up to 86 books read, attendance (hours and days), curriculum used, grades (plus several suggested grading scales), plus suggested Bible verses to memorize and character traits to inculcate. You also get pages for setting up an individualized spelling word bank and keeping track of math facts drill results—two very important areas neglected in most planners.

This book is intended for use with only one child, which I personally think makes more sense than cramming lots of kids into one scheduler.

If you like your organizers simple and easy to use, this one may be for you. *Mary Pride*

Dear Diary

Once you get started journaling, you find that seldom do your projects divide themselves up neatly by hours. You might then prefer to keep more of a "daily diary" type of journal, in which you write down the events of the day all at once.

To give more structure to this approach, some record-keeping systems include sheets you can regularly fill out with weekly, monthly, and yearly objectives. The style and topics of these sheets seem only to be limited by the imagination of their publishers. I have seen spiritual objectives sheets, character-traits objectives sheets, marital relationship objectives sheets . . . you get the idea.

More useful to my mind than blank "objectives" sheets are checklists, out of which you can pick your objectives. At present you will have to invent your own checklists, as I haven't seen any published systems with such checklists. Ideally churches would have such checklists for their own members' spiritual and academic growth. The more specific the objective, the better—e.g., "Memorize Ten Commandments," is better than, "Do more Bible memory."

Daily-diary systems also often include sheets for you to record your impressions about your children's progress. If you like to do this sort of thing, you'll find it lots of fun, and you'll have it to read later when your children are grown.

Relaxed Record Keeping will be appreciated by you relaxed homeschoolers out there. (If you're like me and like to see neat little squares filled in, this is probably not the book for you.) The intended audience for this 26-page large-format booklet is those who adopt a very unstructured approach, yet are required to make an account of their year to the local authorities. If this applies to you, then heed her instructions on how to make your assessments sound "official." *Renee Mathis*

Card Systems

A switch on these approaches is to keep your plans and/or records on cards. The cards can then be filed by child, subject, project, date, or whatever.

I have seen two card-based systems that impressed me. One uses index cards and coded lesson assignments. The child gives you assignment cards as the assignments are finished. You then file them as a record of his work. The other uses special square cards and an executive-type binder with staggered panels, so the top line of each card is always displayed. This makes it much easier to see where all your cards are.

Card-based systems are more flexible than daily planner systems. If your plans change, just change the date on the card. You never have to scratch over a written page. Your child can complete assignments at his own pace without messing up your records. You lose the ability to see your week at a glance, but this only matters if you want to know exactly who is doing what each hour. If you prefer to start at the beginning of a study or project and continue on to the end without worrying about how long it takes, consider a card-based system.

Unlike other planning systems, the **ScanCard System** uses cards. You write the project name of top of a card, jot down whatever you want to remember to do, and stick it in one of the pockets of your organizer. Every day you quickly scan all your cards to see what ought to be done next.

Like most really useful inventions, the ScanCard system happened almost by accident. Founder Marvin Williams was fed up with project lists and overstructured time management systems. So he developed a system of filing project cards into staggered pockets, with the project name peeking out on top. Everywhere he went, his fellow businessmen wanted one. Getting the hint, Mr. Williams formed a product line featuring these organizers.

The ScanCard system's best feature is that it is not tied to particular dates and times. Instead of writing in the date and time you intend to do a project, you just write the project down on a card. Then, when interruptions inevitably mess up your schedule, you don't have to cross out boxes on your calendar, draw little lines back and forth between pages, and so on. No guilt, no pain, no projects forgotten because they weren't done on the right day and you forgot to write them in again on a later page. If you need to do something by a certain date, just say so on the card. The card format also makes it super-easy to add or subtract projects.

It would take too much space to list all the different styles, colors, and bindings in which ScanCard comes. So here are the most popular:

- **The Organizer** is made to fit the needs and budgets of most people—executives and professionals, homemakers, teachers, students, and the clergy." It is 9x12" and only about 3/4 inch thick. Inside its two covers you find on the left 24 ScanCard pockets and a small year-at-a-glance calendar that sits in a plastic pocket of its own just beneath those pockets. On the right is a yellow legal pad, a one-sheet phone/address index on thick stock with room for 100 names that becomes visible when you flip forward the legal pad, and a "TrapFile" vinyl pocket behind it all where you can hold important papers. In between is a narrow little pocket where you can keep your pen or pencil. It comes with 100 ScanCard project cards.
- **The Chairman** is the deluxe model. It comes with three ScanCard panels which handle up to 120 projects, and is expandable (with purchase of additional panels) to a total of 200 projects. It also has an appointment calendar, phone index, built-in multi-function calculator, business and credit card compartments, and concealed pocket files for important papers, plus everything included in the Organizer model. It comes with 500 ScanCard project cards.

ScanCard System
Organizer: vinyl, $39.95; leather, $89.95; top-grain calfskin, $119.95. Chairman: vinyl, $49.95; leather, $99.95; top-grain calfskin, $149.95. Soft Leather Zip-Around ScanCard Folio, $119.95. Other models available. Shipping extra.
Scancard Systems, LLC, 4660 Kenny Road, Suite C, Columbus, Ohio 43220, 1-800-848-2618. Fax: 614-457-8755. Email: eg@executivegallery.com. Web: www.executivegallery.com

ScanCard Organizer Model

ScanCard Chairman Model

- **The Soft Leather Zip-Around ScanCard Folio** is scan cards to go. Sized 9½" x 12¼" x 1¾", it comes only in drum-dyed, full-grain leather and includes an expandable, double file pocket, a removable 40-project ScanCard panel (more can be added), ruled notepad, double pen/pencil holder, outer back pocket, and more.

The beauty of this system is that you can keep your personal, business, home, and ministry projects all in the same place, and the ScanCard system can be adapted easily to homeschool lesson planning. One organizer per child is ideal, plenty of space for homeschool recordkeeping with room left over for Junior to do his own kid's business and chore planning. Then just save the completed project cards and you have a complete "paper trail" of your home-schooling activities for legal purposes.

We recommend the Chairman model for business owners and the Organizer model for children and most other uses. The Zip-Around model would be ideal for someone who has to carry his organizer out and around with him. *Mary Pride*

Mondo Systems

Mondo systems are very popular with the people who design homeschool record-keeping systems—although I'm not sure how many people actually use all those fancy features! Basically, a mondo system is designed to organize your entire life. One sheet will tell you which library books you have out. Another will list the Bible verses you are memorizing. A third will hold your personal address list. A fourth will tell your spouse, in the event of your unfortunate demise, where the insurance policy is hidden. And so on. In the middle of all this will also be found sheets for keeping your homeschool records. Lists of textbooks. Lists of objectives. Daily planning sheets. Monthly planning sheets. Yearly planning sheets. Auto repair checklists. Etc.

Mondo systems appeal because they promise to bring your helter-skelter life under control. Unfortunately, even the best mondo system won't work unless *you* take the time to fill in all the records! Only you know if you have the discipline to do this, or even really *want* to do it.

Most of us will find that we can live very nicely without some of the sheets in a mondo system. For example, we take out about 50 library books each time we visit the library, and there's no way I'm going to write those titles down every week or two. I already have a separate address book, so I don't need the address-list features. I prefer to write my appointments on a huge wall calendar, where I can't miss them, and I *never* write down objectives (too busy trying to achieve 'em!). Someone else might live and die by the library book list, but not me. Determine how many of those "extra" sheets you are really going to use before you pay the hefty price for one of these systems.

I confess. I've had flings with planners before. I've succumbed to the siren song of the supple leather covers. I've fallen for the tantalizing tapestry binders, the pristine pages waiting for the penciled notes that would bring joy and order to my life. Alas, these dalliances were all too brief and before long I was back to finding post-it notes stuck to the bottoms of my shoes. So much for organization.

Could **The Noble Planner** help someone like me? Or you? Yes, yes, and yes! Gregg Harris has come up with a planning system that far outshines the other big guys on the block. The difference is that he fully bases his method on the truths of Scripture. You'll learn how loving God with all

The Noble Planner by Gregg Harris

Starter package in 7-ring binder with 2-pages-per-day, $89.95. 2-pages-per-week starter package, $67.95. Starter package conversion kit (without binder) 2-pages-per-day, $59.95. 2-pages-per-week, $49.95. 2-pages-per-day daily planner pages, $24.95.

your heart, soul, mind, and strength can translate into specific purposes, goals, plans, and actions. You'll discover the ultimate in team management techniques as Gregg teaches from Genesis, Chapter 1. You'll understand how planning on Sunday afternoon, "in the afterglow of worship" can lead to a week that's focused and centered. This goes way beyond keeping track of dentist appointments.

Your starter kit contains the binder, 7-hole-punched like most day planners, and a supply of basic forms to set up your system. The 38 pages of instructions lead you through the process of setting up your system. You're given sample copies of all the basic forms. Some of these will be more or less useful to you depending on your situation. You get 2 months worth of 2-page-per-day and 2-page-per-week calendar pages. After using them, you'll need to choose your preferred style and then order a year's supply to fill out your binder. The gorgeous binder even has room to store your wallet and cash. Bet you won't be tempted to forget it now! If you already have a planner cover, you can ordering just the forms themselves. Some of what's available:

- Sermon notes
- Inductive Bible study
- Business expenses
- Detailed project and goal planning
- Relationship maintenance
- Communication log
- Household records
- Honey-do list
- A note keeping system that actually makes sense.

Although not specifically a homeschool planner, using this to organize the "non-school" part of life would put your homeschool miles ahead. As for me and my Noble Planner, well, I can already sense a long-term relationship in store for both of us. *Renee Mathis*

Portfolio Systems

One problem with "planner" systems is that they combine your personal requirements (keeping track of or deciding what your children should do) with other people's requirements (proving to family members and government officials that your homeschool program is legal, educationally sound, and fat-free). Generally, your rule of thumb should be

(1) **Do the planning or record-keeping *you* feel is necessary** to help you keep track of your educational program. Don't overdo it; your job is home teaching, not Administrator of Public Records.

(2) **Add anything impressive that pops up.** Did your fifth-grader get 700s on the SAT? Did she win the science fair grand prize? Is he Paper Carrier of the Month? Did she write a three-page report on how chocolate bars are made? Standardized test scores, contests, any lengthy written work, any major science or crafts projects, any outside jobs or volunteering— this is the stuff you should keep. Not just because it will im-

Week-in-view weekly planner pages, $14.95. Add shipping. *Noble Publishing Associates, PO Box 2250, Gresham, OR 97030. Orders: (800) 225-5259. Inquiries: (206) 587-6497. Fax: (206) 587-0443. Email: noblebooks@aol.com.*

press the neighbors, but because your child will enjoy sharing this with his or her own children some day.

Take one hanging file folder (or catalog-sized envelope, or artist's portfolio, or photo scrapbook, or box, or all the above). Place your child's dated work in this container. File away. It's done!

The portfolio system is one good way to document your child's work. Many states have dignified the portfolio system with the same status as a planner or journaling system. If you can show the authorities what your child did, plus perhaps some good test scores, they'll be satisfied.

The trick here is to not let the portfolio swallow your house. The problem is that your child's most creative work just won't fit in a few square feet. A few dinosaur dioramas and fishertechnik robotic creations will overflow any decent-sized portfolio.

The solution: take pictures or videos of sizable projects. Date them (announce the date on a video) and file in your portfolio. Then dispose of the masterwork itself in humane fashion when it has outlived its usefulness.

By homeschool author Joyce Herzog, **Simplified Homeschool Record Keeping** tells how to keep a notebook/portfolio for all ages. General divider headings, plus a sample list of topics for each grade from K–6. This scope and sequence makes a great guideline for unit studies as well. Junior high and up have a page for suggested topics to include in a Lifetime Notebook. 16 pages. *Mary Pride*

Memories Systems

What can turn your stash of photos into a creative, meaningful keepsake? **Fiskars Photo Memories Shop**! Fiskars, the company that makes durable, easy-to-use scissors has now created an entire line of photo album and scrapbook products. Here are some examples of the products you can purchase: a glue pen, useful for permanent or temporary bonding; adhesive photo stickers for mounting photographs; writing and drawing pens which are acid free, will not bleed through paper, and have archival quality ink; a swivel knife; acid-free page protectors; acid-free solid and print pages on which photos can be mounted; stencils in various shapes; reusable stickers, and pattern and instruction books.

You will need to provide the photos and the creativity. Fiskars will provide all of the other items needed to create beautiful scrapbooks and photo albums. If you long to preserve all of your priceless photos creatively, this line of products is for you. But be forewarned: Fiskars products can be addicting! *Rebecca Livermore*

Okay, so one of the drawbacks of homeschooling has been that your children don't get a yearbook with pictures of their school, teachers, friends, clubs, etc. in it. Some large support groups now band together to have yearbook pictures taken. If you don't live in an area with a large support group, or if your group isn't into yearbook mode yet, **My Homeschool Yearbook** is the solution to this problem.

The oversized book is printed on sturdy card stock and comb-bound so it will lie flat when open. The cover has a charming color

My Homeschool Year

As for me and my house, we will serve the Lord. Joshua 24:15

drawing of a home with several children and a cat peeking out of the windows, with the Bible verse Joshua 24:15 printed beneath it. The rest of the black and white pages have lots of space for you or your child to paste photos and other memorabilia. Each page has a title and some pen-and-ink drawings near the edge.

Topics include My Family, My Chores, Holidays, Things I Like To Do, Special Friends, Subjects I Studied, Books I Used For School, Sports, Field Trips, Favorite Bible Verses, Some of My Best Work, Photographs and Autographs.

The title page has blank lines for your child to fill in his or her name and the year, as well as a spot for a picture. Thus, the book is more suited to use by a single child rather than a family; families with more than one child will probably want a copy for each child.

My Homeschool Yearbook seems to be intended to be used more like a scrapbook than a portfolio, since at least half of the pages have non-academic topics. There are few totally blank pages, but titles could be altered or covered over if you find them limiting. *Melissa Worcester*

Mary's Mini System

The very simplest way to plan is to not use planners at all. For all courses involving workbooks, I do the following:

> **(1) Write the child's name** on the front of the book, or on the title page.
> **(2) Calculate how many pages** per school day he must do to finish the book in the allotted time. If it's to be completed in one school year, divide the pages by 160 school days.
> **(3) Write how many pages per day** are to be completed on the cover or title page.

You wind up with something that looks like this: "Franklin, 3 pages/day." Then all you have to do is figure out which day of the school year it is. "We're on the first day of the second week, so this is Day 6. He is supposed to do 3 pages a day, so he should have finished page 18 by the end of the school day."

Once you have written the daily page allotment on each workbook, all you have to do is keep track of which school week it is. Then when the child finishes the workbook, write the completion date on the cover and file the book on a shelf in the basement along with all the other completed school workbooks. If anyone ever wants to check out your homeschool, the sheer boredom of evaluating dozens of ratty workbooks will elicit the response you're looking for: "Never mind, I can see you've been doing a lot of schoolwork here." For better results, also make sure to give each child a bulletin board where he can pin up his ribbons from the math competition, science fair, art show, and whatever other homeschool events he enters. For best results, combine with yearly standardized testing, so you can also demonstrate the children's actual achievement levels, if asked. Easy!

Hourly Logs

Some states require you to log the hours each child spends on schoolwork. Missouri, the worst in this regard, requires you to log core academic subjects differently from non-core subjects, and hours spent at home separately from hours spent on field trips. If you're stuck with a situation like this, the best thing to do is ask your local support-group or state leader what forms (or ideally, software) they recommend homeschoolers use in your state.

Now, for the truly brave, creative, and inspired, I turn the rest of this chapter over to veteran homeschool leader, Renee Mathis. She will explain how to create your very own unique planning system.

Renee Mathis has served for years as a homeschool support group leader, online forum sysop, and *Practical Homeschooling* writer and reviewer.

Renee Mathis on Creating Your Own Planner

Depending on the legal requirements in your state, the number of children you are teaching, and your personal level of flexibility versus structure, here are several things to keep in mind when creating your own planner.

The Space Race

Your first decision: "To bind or not to bind?" Three-ring binders are great for adding your own materials (support group newsletters and mailing lists, for example) and customizing the number of pages. You are usually given permission to reproduce the forms within your family as well. Unfortunately they can also be bulky, and pages tend to rip out. Spiral-bound volumes, on the other hand, often aren't as durable (get out the "jelly-proof" contact paper) but they are more portable. If you go the spiral-bound route, you'll also need to re-invest every year in a new planner.

If you live in a state where it's necessary to keep track of days and hours, I wouldn't even consider a system that doesn't allow space for these records. Conversely, if your state is "loosey-goosey" you might be happy with a simple journal that you fill in as you go along.

Although it might not seem important now, especially for you novices, keep track of all books and materials used—even for the little ones. If the Lord should add to your quiver, you won't want to be racking your brain years down the road, trying to remember the name of that great kindergarten math game.

It is also important for you to consider the number of students you can accommodate in one planner. The planner needs to be big if you're tracking two or more. As they get older, consider getting an assignment book for each child. You fill it in, and they check off lessons as they are completed.

What about progress reports and evaluations you ask? Space to record letter grades? Sometimes they are included, sometimes they aren't. You decide how important this is.

Medical forms can be helpful as well. It makes sense to have them in a handy place.

Making Your Own

If you really want the ultimate in customized planners, don't overlook the option of making your own. It's not as hard as you might think. With the help of a computer and simple graphics program, you can become a creative genius. With a typewriter, felt-tip pen, and some clip art you can do a very nice job as well. Make the desired number of copies and you're in business. Once you've decided on the forms that best suit your family, you can decide whether you want to go the loose-leaf notebook approach or spiral bound.

Just a suggestion: If you're buying a notebook, splurge and make it one you really like! This is going to be your friend and constant companion day in and day out, so save the office rejects for the kids to play with.

While we may not be creating miniature classrooms in our dining rooms, there is no reason not to have the best tools available at our disposable. Nothing is more frustrating than having to search in umpteen different drawers and cabinets to find your teaching materials (or your HSLDA membership number, or the name of the person who's going to test your kids, or the address of that catalog you've been meaning to send away for . . .). The costs you pay for being organized in the present can pay off many times over in the future!

CHAPTER 34

Evaluating and Testing

W hy do we test our kids?

- To find out what they know . . . or don't know
- Because they have to perform in the top 3 to 10 percent on a standardized test to qualify for the various regional Talent Search programs
- As good practice for later tests they will have to take, such as the SAT and ACT
- Because the state we live in requires it

Some of these reasons may be more compelling to you than others. Nonetheless, the vast majority of homeschooled kids will take some kind of nationally standardized test during their years at home.

Standardized tests are not all they could be. As famed activist Phyllis Schlafly notes,

The testing system has been corrupted. Not only do all students score "above average" (a marvel of statistical fakery), but many tests are peppered with questions that ask for non-objective responses about feelings, attitudes, or predictions, or which have a built-in bias toward political correctness.

Other critics have pointed out flaws in test design ranging from overly high "guessability" to questions geared to mainstream middle-class kids that other kids will get wrong through not being familiar with that environment. None of these are a huge problem, as long as a number of competing tests are allowed to exist. That's why homeschoolers have always opposed any national testing standards, despite the fact that homeschooled kids have al-

What Good Are Standardized Tests?

I tend to view standardized tests the same way I do studio portraits: lovelier than a snap-shot but not always a realistic picture. It's usually been my experience that standardized tests don't tell me what I didn't already know in the first place.

So, am I saying that there's no place for testing homeschooled children? Absolutely not! Testing can be a wonderful tool to help us as teachers know whether or not we're doing our jobs well, or whether we need to work on an area or two. I'm all for comparing children to a standard and saying "How're we doing?" as opposed to comparing them to other children and saying "Where do we rank in the standings?"—*Renee Mathis*

Reading & Riting & Readiness for Tests

The public schools are actually pushed into being test-preparation organizations.
　　—*Robin Scarlata, author of* What Your Child Needs to Know When

States That Require Standardized Testing

Most states do not require homeschooled students to take standardized tests. Here are the states that do require testing:
- Alaska
- Arkansas
- Georgia
- Hawaii
- Minnesota
- Nevada
- New Mexico
- New York
- North Dakota
- Oregon
- Pennsylvania
- South Carolina
- South Dakota
- Tennessee
- Virginia

The Four Steps of Evaluation

Teresa Moon, in her book *Evaluating for Excellence*, lays out a four-step evaluation process. First, you **diagnose** the child's current abilities and skill levels. A diagnostic test works well at this stage. Second, you set academic goals and create a **plan** for achieving those goals. Third, you **guide** the student to reach those goals. This step involves determining what *you* have to do to help the student succeed. Fourth, you **evaluate** how the student has done. This step may involve achievement testing. From the results of the achievement test, you form a new diagnosis and begin the four steps again.

ways scored higher on standardized tests than public-school kids; the power to dictate the test is the power to dictate what must be taught.

Why Bother with Testing?

As I said in an earlier book, **Schoolproof**, people are always confusing *teaching* (putting information out where the student can get it) and *feedback* (finding out what the student knows).

"Teaching is telling or showing people what they don't know."

Asking students to show and tell you what they already know is feedback, not teaching!

You do have good reasons for wanting to know what your learner knows. For one thing, you can keep from wasting your time and his. I say this as a student who struggled through her entire academic career with schools that insisted I take courses on material I had already learned on my own. The excitement just leaks out of teaching and learning when the student already understands what you are trying to teach.

Another good reason for finding out what your learner knows is to locate gaps in his knowledge and understanding. Like little cracks in a house foundation, these are best found and mended before you build any further on them.

Finally, as many others have observed, showing what you know tends to reinforce your knowledge. The simple act of explaining or demonstrating knowledge to another cements it in your own mind. In this last sense, getting feedback from your learner tops off your teaching effort.

The Difference Between Diagnostic & Achievement Tests

Before we go further, it's important to distinguish between diagnostic and achievement tests.

Diagnostic tests are, in theory, a helpful tool to discover your student's grade level in the academic areas tested. In addition, some diagnostic tests pinpoint specific areas of weakness (e.g., punctuation skills, addition facts from 11-99, alphabetization) that need more work.

I said, "In theory," because today some "diagnostic" tests are actually probes designed to label as many children as possible. Tests of developmental readiness are particularly notorious in this respect.

At home, academic diagnostic tests are extremely helpful when you begin homeschooling, in order to determine your child's correct grade level in each subject.

Achievement tests show how well your child is performing in academic areas, as compared to other children in that grade. Typically, scores are expressed as percentiles. A score in the 51st percentile means your child did better than 51 percent of the children taking the test; a score in the 99th percentile (the highest possible) means he did better than 99 percent of test-takers.

When states require homeschoolers to take tests, the tests required are nationally-standardized achievement tests. Following are reviews of both diagnostic and achievement testing resources.

NEW!
A Parent's Guide to Standardized Tests in School

Parents. $14.95 plus shipping.
Educational Dept., LearningExpress, 900 Broadway, Suite 604, New York, NY 10003-1210. (800) 295-9556. Fax: (212) 995-5512. Email: Educate@learnx.com. Web: www.learnx.com.

Having trouble finding your way around the maze of nationally standardized tests? **A Parent's Guide to Standardized Tests in School** lays it all out for you. From a brief overview of the history of standardized testing, the book moves briskly to cover these topics:

- Can you really prepare for a standardized test? The answer is yes, and the authors (both PhD.s) tell you why.
- Rundown of the most popular standardized tests.
- Sample questions, with answers, from popular standardized tests
- How to interpret those impenetrable score sheets
- Does your child qualify for test exemption or special testing conditions? How exactly is a "learning disability" diagnosis—which may allow such exemption or special testing conditions—implemented? What about special testing accommodations for a child with physical disabilities? Nitty-gritty answers here, that may or may not apply to your homeschooling situation, depending on whether your state requires school-administered standardized testing.
- How schools use test scores, and what you should do about it if your child is in school

Some of the information isn't needed by homeschoolers, such as the chapters on working with your child's teacher and how schools use test scores. However, it's all interesting to know. This is the clearest, most parent-friendly introduction to the subject I have seen. Recommended. *Mary Pride*

Formal and Informal Tests and Evaluations

BJUP's Academic Skills Evaluation Program uses the Iowa Test of Basic Skills to test academic achievement for grades 1–8 and the Tests of Achievement and Proficiency for high schoolers. Also available for grades 3–12 only is the Cognitive Abilities test, "a test to appraise reasoning ability that yields verbal, non-verbal, and quantitative evaluation scores."

In order to administer the test you must either be (1) currently certified as a teacher by a national or state organization, (2) a graduate of a four-year college program, or (3) a current teacher in an operating conventional school. These requirements were established in conjunction with the test provider.

For test security reasons, the tests can only be mailed to the qualified tester, and all testing materials including answer sheets must be returned within 60 days of receipt to BJUP for scoring and interpretation. You get back an analysis of the results in four to six weeks.

We have personally used Bob Jones testing for several years now and are quite pleased with the results. Since these are the same tests used in many public and private schools, with the same fill-in-the-boxes-with-number-two-pencil interface, our children are learning test-taking skills they might need later on. They are also being evaluated against a huge group of public-school children, so we have a good idea where they stand relative to this group. The returned scores break down the children's results into specific enough areas that we can see exactly what areas are weak or strong—e.g. capitalization, punctuation, map-reading.

Hints: Be sure to follow ordering instructions carefully to insure you get the proper grade-level test for your child. Call Bob Jones University Press if you have questions about which test to order. You might also do better to plan on testing in the late spring and summer. During the months of April and August test scores returned will not only include grade placement and percentile rankings, but an "item analysis of test results" as well. This item analysis pinpoints your student's strong and weak areas and provides other useful information. *Mary Pride*

Covenant Home CHAT Tests

Grades K–12, $24.50 each grade. Indicate grade level just completed. *Covenant Home Curriculum, 17800 W. Capitol Dr., Brookfield, WI 53045. (414) 781-2171. Fax: (414) 781-0589. Email: educate@covenanthome.com. Web: covenanthome.com.*

NEW!
Evaluating for Excellence

Parents. $17.95 plus shipping. *Beautiful Feet Books, 139 Main Street, Sandwich, MA 02563. Orders: (800) 889-1978. Inquiries: (508) 833-8626 Fax: (508) 833-2770 Web: www.bfbooks.com*

NEW!
Evaluation of Basic Skills

Ages 3–18. Start-Up Kit, $49.95 plus shipping. *International Montessori Trust Tutoring, 912 Thayer Ave., Suite #205, Silver Spring, MD 20910. Phone/fax: (800)301-3131 or (301) 589-0733. Cannot accept credit-card orders.*

Covenant Home Curriculum sells self-test materials. They carry their own **C.H.A.T. Little Windows on Progress series** (Covenant Home Achievement Tests). These are meant to give you an accurate reading of your child's grade level equivalence in the two main academic areas of math and language. The tests are easy to administer, taking only thirty minutes for each of the two sections. Scoring by Covenant Home Curriculum staff is included.

The C.H.A.T. series is partially patterned after the sample SAT national standards and grade levels. Standards are also based on curriculum levels established in *Warriner's English Grammar and Composition,* a standard work. *Mary Pride*

Written just for homeschoolers, **Evaluating for Excellence** breaks new ground. The oversized, 200-page book first presents a four-step approach—Diagnose, Plan, Guide, and Evaluate—then breaks each step down.

Mostly this consists of showing you how to use the 66 pages of reproducible checklists and forms for every academic subject found at the end of the book. Some forms are "student inventories"—the student evaluates his own progress in various subskills on a scale of 1 to 10 and describes his interests and goals in his own words. Some are diagnostic checklists, objectives lists, assignment sheets, critiques, evaluation forms, guidelines, and notes pages for the parents to fill out. Four pages of forms are designed to help you develop an IEP (Individualized Education Plan) for your child, which author Teresa Moon believes you should do whether your child has official "special needs" or not. The body of the book includes sample filled-out examples of each form, often with comments explaining how and why to use it.

The method of portfolio assessment and how to create a portfolio are also covered, again with samples of student work showing how you can evaluate progress using this method.

A "Putting It All Together" section shows how to begin using this method with three different grade-level groups: preK–3, 4–6, and 7–12. This section also includes the Sample Forms Use Guide, a chart showing which forms correspond to which of the four steps. For example, the "Book Projects" form can be used for the Guide and Evaluate steps, while the Educator's Diagnostic Survey can be used to Diagnose, Plan, and Evaluate. Information on teaching and evaluating critical thinking is also found in this section, which is followed by a glossary of terms referring to education and evaluation, taken from the 1828 Noah Webster's *American Dictionary of the English Language.*

Nowhere will you find a list of norms against which to compare your student. The book's philosophy is that you need to chart the student's *progress*—how he is doing now compared to how he was doing before.

Studying this book will give you a lot of food for thought. It is certainly packed with ideas! As to whether you will use each and every form, that depends on how much time you want to spend getting comfortable with this level of grading, whether you have easy access to a photocopy machine, and just how "measurement-minded" you are. A folder of these filled-out forms certainly should impress school officials, relatives, and neighbors, but will be way more fun to produce if you are a Progress Person than if you are an Action Man, People Person, Puzzle Solver, or Performer. (If you don't know what these terms mean, see our chapter on Thinking Styles!) *Mary Pride*

Have you ever wished for a simple diagnostic test that you could use in your own home or home school group? The **Evaluation of Basic Skills** gives you a quick overview of your child's academic progress. Based on the Montessori theory of instruction, the tests are designed to be low-stress and low-hassle. Each test takes about 30 minutes and tests your child for basic reading, math, spelling, and writing skills. A parent can be certified to administer the test by purchasing the kit, listening to the two training tapes provided, and filling out the application. I used the test on my six school-age children and found them to be accurate and easy to use. I would like to see the training tapes redone in a more professional manner, however. *Marcella Burns*

This is as informal as testing gets! Unlike a typical trivia game, **The Game of Knowledge** mostly deals with actual education-related questions, and is designed so kids can compete on equal terms with adults. The enclosed 496 cards have two questions on each side of each card—one question for ages 10–15, and the other for ages 16 and up—for a total of 1,584 questions in all. Questions are worded in such a way that even if you are unfamiliar with the topic, you might be able to figure out the answer by drawing on your previous knowledge. Categories for questions are:

- Science—space, inventions, famous scientists, extinct animals, physics, biology, the human body, chemistry, and energy
- Sports—baseball, basketball, football, hockey, soccer, golf, fishing, tennis, car racing, and Olympic sports; most questions involve rules and facts related to each sport, although some do require knowledge about famous players and games
- Media—TV, movies, books and stories, music, comics
- Nature—plants, animals, land, oceans, weather, the environment, natural phenomena; a few questions are evolutionary
- Fame—entertainers and stars, U.S. Presidents, world leaders, heroes, myths and legends, Biblical characters, fictional characters, artists, authors, composers, and royalty
- Our World—U.S. history, world history, geography, politics, man-made structures, justice and the law, economics and currency, and food

Your aim, as one of the two to six competing players, is to collect one ring for each of these six topics. Gameboard play determines which topic questions you can be asked at any given move, adding an element of chance. My guess is that the travel version doesn't have a gameboard; the catalog says it does have 400 "all-new" questions. *Mary Pride*

The **Personalized Assessment Summary System (PASS)**, like other achievement tests, evaluates student achievement in reading, math, and language. Unlike the others, PASS was designed for you to give at home, and takes into account the type of individualized curriculum your child may have been studying; it is also untimed.

PASS was "normed" (that is, calibrated for accuracy) using a standardized item bank. The difficulty of each question on the test was figured using a method developed by Danish mathematician Yorg Rasch. All items on any given test fall within a limited difficulty range, which presumably makes it easier to find gaps in learning.

The student taking the PASS first takes a placement test designed to find his or her approximate achievement level. The computer-scored results from the PASS test itself include suggestions for reaching goals in each subject area. You can also compare results with homeschool and national norms for that grade level. *Mary Pride*

NEW!
How Well Does Your Child Read?
How Well Does Your Child Write?
How Well Does Your Child Do Math?

Grades K–6. $9.99 each plus shipping.
Career Press, PO Box 687, Franklin Lakes, NJ 07417-0687. (800) 227-3371. Fax: (201) 848-1727. Web: www.careerpress.com.

Ann Cook has developed a tool to help parents see how their child is doing in reading, writing, and math. Each of the 190-page paperback **How Well Does Your Child . . . series** books is structured along the same lines. A brief introduction explains the assessment procedures (very simple). Next comes a set of tests covering concepts usually taught in kindergarten through fifth grade. After that is a short glossary to familiarize you with the vocabulary of the subject. Finally comes a series of chapters with grade-level guidelines as well as teaching tips and hints for explaining them to your child. These aren't in-depth treatments, but they are a wonderful supplement to the curriculum you're already using. I found it extremely helpful to have a scope and sequence of concepts in one place so that I could see how my teaching materials stacked up.

The tests in each book are easiest at the kindergarten level and get progressively harder. Each one should only take your child 20 minutes to complete. If the answers are incorrect, you're instructed to stop there and retest at a later date after re-teaching the material. I like that. It minimizes the frustration level.

How Well Does Your Child Read? starts with basic alphabet recognition and covers letter sounds, blends, and sight words. Children are tested using nonsense words in order to minimize guessing (example: short vowel words include *weg* and *wog*). Older children are tested on context clues, finding main ideas, drawing conclusions, and fact finding.

How Well Does Your Child Write? covers printing, spelling, punctuation, grammar, vocabulary, structure, and idea flow. Upper grades children are tested on descriptive, informative, and persuasive writing. Since this can be a little harder to judge, the author provides you with a rubric to help you evaluate the results. By scoring the individual parts of a writing sample, you come up with a good idea of just where the strengths and weaknesses are.

How Well Does Your Child Do Math? starts with shapes and number recognition, ends up with geometry, fractions/decimals, and mixed word problems. The author writes from the point of view of a professional educator and concerned parent. She has a few sentences about the need for a nationalized curriculum (her opinion) and her online resource guide contains some sites you'll probably skip. (Unless, that is, you care to see what the NEA is up to!)

Like many homeschoolers, I'm not tied into a specific grade with my children. I'm more concerned about making sure they cover the material in a systematic order without leaving gaps. These books gave me the tool to do just that, at a fraction of the cost of a standardized test and without the waiting period for scores to be returned.

Just a hint: I found the type size to be a tad small for my kindergartner. Don't be afraid to rip out a page if needed and enlarge it on a photocopier. I also made copies of the scoring tables to keep in my kids' portfolios and record files. *Renee Mathis*

NEW!
Special Educator's Complete Guide to 109 Diagnostic Tests

Parents. $29.95.
Center for Applied Research in Education, W. Nyack, NY 10094. Web: www.phdirect.com.

Anything titled **Special Educator's Complete Guide to 109 Diagnostic Tests** can be expected to be huge, and it is. "Comprehensive" is just the word to describe this oversized 328-page book. It covers all the following:

- **Wechsler Scales of Intelligence.** What you need to know about the three most commonly used IQ tests
- **Intellectual Assessment Measures.** Facts on nine different tests that measure such things as perception, mental processing speed, and long- and short-term memory, including the Stanford-Binet Intelligence Scale, Kaufman Assessment Battery for Children, and more

- Achievement Assessment Measures. 31 tests that evaluate math, reading, spelling, and writing achievement are covered
- Perceptual Measures. 14 tests designed to diagnose thinking styles and discovery channels are covered.
- Language, Psychological & Social, and Adaptive Measures. 25 tests that evaluate a child's development in the areas of language, emotional and social growth, and behavior.
- Early Childhood, Hearing Impaired, Occupation & Physical Therapy, and Bilingual Tests. 29 tests designed to check for potential disabilities are covered in this section.
- How to understand the stages of evaluation, test interpretation, how tests are used to diagnose and prescribe educational and therapy strategies, and more
- How to write and develop an IEP
- How to put remediation techniques into practice in a classroom situation

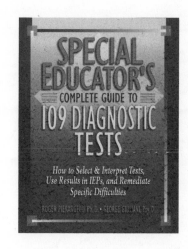

Each test has a one- or two-page description, including its author, the address/phone/fax of its publisher, its purpose, a brief description including administration time/type of test/who is allowed to administer it/appropriate grade levels, "subtest" information (what further details can be gleaned from test subscores), its strengths, and its weaknesses.

Appendices provide contact information for the test publishers, test reference guides by category and name, glossary of terms, and glossary of special education abbreviations.

Although naturally we don't agree with all of the theories behind some of these tests, or the labels they are used to confer, this book can be a huge help towards understanding the system as it currently works, why and how your child was labeled, and what tests you might want to use yourself to explore puzzling areas of your child's educational development. I would say this book is a "must" for a well-stocked support-group library. *Mary Pride*

Sycamore Tree offers a wide variety of diagnostic and achievement tests from other publishers.

The first nationally standardized test in their catalog, the **Comprehensive Test of Basic Skills**, is completed in your home. The CTBS is an achievement test covering reading, language arts, spelling, math, science, social studies, and reference skills. Twice a year batches of these tests are submitted by Sycamore Tree for machine scoring—on May 15 and August 15. At other times of the year, Sycamore Tree staff will hand-score the test for an extra $10. You need to provide your child's age and grade level when ordering the CTBS, and should allow 6–8 weeks for test results to be returned to you.

The **Gates-MacGinitie Reading Inventory**, another nationally standardized test, tests reading skills, vocabulary development, and comprehension. It may be administered at any time of the year, and will be hand-scored at no extra cost.

Each of the **Achievement Tests** series (available for grades 1–7) is a 32-page booklet covering both math and language arts. These inexpensive tests are designed for use by parents and may be helpful for your own peace of mind, but aren't accepted by outside authorities such as Talent Searches and state authorities, as the nationally standardized tests above are.

As opposed to these achievement tests, diagnostic tests help you find a child's proper grade level in a subject. The **Diagnostic Prescriptive Assessment** series, available for grades K–5, includes the test, an outline of material that should be learned at that grade level, and can be used as a yearly evaluation or as the basis of a portfolio or an Individual Education Plan (required in some states for special-needs students). Each 50-plus page test booklet is designed for use by parents. The "Prescriptive" part of the name means the booklet includes suggestions for dealing with problem areas uncovered by the test.

For an all-in-one language arts diagnosis you can use for grades K–5, the **Total Language Diagnostic Assessment with Remedial Strategies and Answer Key** is the real deal. This 101-page workbook covers all tested areas of reading and language, includes test items from criterion-referenced diagnostic tests, and includes 30 pages of strategies for remediating problem areas. All six grade levels are covered in the one fairly pricey product.

For grades 3–adult, the **Self-Administered Vocabulary Test** is just what it says. Find out if your seven-year-old already has a college-level vocabulary!

Sycamore Tree also carries test-prep materials. See the separate writeup later in this chapter. *Mary Pride*

Scope & Sequence

If you know what your child is supposed to know when, you can use your own preferred method to find out whether he or she *does* know it . . . and then fill in any gaps you find. That's the premise behind a "Scope & Sequence," a list of topics and skills arranged by grade level.

A number of books have been published that list such skills and facts, sometimes with instructional help included to teach the facts. Or you can simply request the Scope & Sequence from one of the major textbook publishers reviewed in the Traditional Curriculum chapter.

Can we judge **Culturescope** by its cover? You tell me. Billing itself as a "guide to an informed mind . . . a new approach to a complete education" the cover features rock music, the atom bomb, a red AIDS ribbon, a caricature of George Washington making the "peace" sign, Abraham Lincoln's face with a cartoon body, Martin Luther King, Jr., an Indian chief, basketball, and baseball. Where's mom and apple pie?

Mom's in another room blushing at all the sexual innuendo and nudity contained within the covers. Call me "priggish" (and *Culturescope* does!) but could someone please tell me why Picasso's painting of nude prostitutes belongs in a book for elementary aged children? Why it's OK to call Christopher Columbus "a jerk"? Why Christianity gets less coverage than film? Why the Aztecs are called "our ancestors" but the Puritans aren't? Why the Mayflower Compact, the Magna Carta, and Nero are missing? (Probably to make room for that film chapter.) It doesn't matter which level you look at (college/adult, high school, or elementary) there's enough to offend everyone.

If you're looking for a cultural literacy type of book for your younger children, stick with E.D. Hirsch's *What Every . . . Grader Needs to Know.* They're much more comprehensive since each grade gets its own volume. And for your middle and high schoolers? No worries. By that time they'll be smart enough to read the original documents and writings for themselves.

I've seen other Princeton Review books and they're pretty good. Their guides to standardized tests are very good. While a dose of sassiness makes them go down a little easier, this kind of politically correct, irreverent attempt at making history and culture easily digestible by the MTV generation just doesn't make the grade. Here it all adds up to one stupendous stomachache. Where's the antacid? *Renee Mathis*

NEW!
Culturescope

Grade School Edition, $18. High School Edition, $20. College/Adult Edition, $20.
Princeton Review, Random House, 400 Hahan Rd., Westminster, MD 21157. (800)733-3000. They prefer you to order from bookstores.

Okay, so **How Do You Know They Know What They Know?** doesn't have a title that just rolls off your tongue. Give it a chance anyway! Cathy Duffy's Grove Publishing is starting small, but with Teresa Moon on hand, they're off to a wonderful start. This author is that rare blend of professional educator (she knows her stuff!) mixed with sensitive, understanding homeschooling mom. I was hooked after the first chapter.

How many of us have had the same experience as Teresa: We tend to evaluate our children's education based on our precipitous feelings and circumstances, not on objective criteria. If the kids aren't fighting, if the toddler hasn't finger-painted with all the Crisco, and if you've managed to get dressed before 11:00 A.M., then hey—it's a good day! And what about this scenario? We assign little Ermintrude and Percival a research report. After a few days our enthusiasm fades, the kids aren't sure where they're supposed to be, and the assignment that started off under a full head of steam dwindles to a screeching halt.

Isn't there a better way? Yes, and here it is! With a writing style that manages to be encouraging and friendly without being overly familiar and chatty, the author walks you through these four steps of teaching and evaluating:

- Diagnose—Where you are now?
- Project—Where do you want to be?
- Guide—How to get there?
- Evaluate—Did it work?

At this point, you've either achieved your goal or else you go back to step one and keep working. It doesn't matter what your particular teaching style or preference, there is something in here for absolutely everyone! Along the way, you're given loads of forms and tools to help you through the steps. Here's a brief sampling of the forms and instructions included:

- Diagnose—scope and sequence, reading and writing inventories, how to diagnose writing skills, character qualities review, student inventory
- Project—creating an individualized education program, educator's objectives, using projecting tools, junior and senior high writing assignments
- Guide—oral presentation guidelines, how to critique writing, timelines for creating oral presentations and science projects, literature project ideas, book projects, math skills checklist, and reading comprehension
- Evaluate—creating a portfolio, writing mechanics and punctuation, evaluating research projects, unit study projects, math records, public speaking evaluations
- Pulling it all together—what the sample forms look like when used successfully, where to begin, and a good practical discussion on using critical thinking skills as a part of your everyday studies.

User's tip: Buy the book. Proceed to carefully cut out all the pages in the back marked "forms," put them in a clear page-protector, and store them in your planning notebook. That way they're close at hand for you to grab and copy as needed. *Renee Mathis*

NEW!
How Do You Know They Know What They Know?
Parents. $14.95 plus shipping. *Grove Publishing, 16172 Huxley Circle, Westminster, CA 92683. (714) 841-1220. Fax: (714) 841-5584. Web: www.grovepublishing.com.*

Teaching Children

Parents. $12.99.
Crossway Books, 1300 Crescent St., Wheaton, IL 60187. Orders: (800) 635-7993. Inquiries: (630) 682-4300. Fax: (630) 682-4785.

Teaching Children: A Curriculum Guide to What Children Need to Know at Each Level Through Sixth Grade by Diane Lopez is the third in the Child Light series published by Crossway Books. The first two books in the series, *For the Children's Sake* by Susan Schaeffer Macaulay and *Books Children Love* by Elizabeth Wilson were both enthusiastically received. This naturally created a lot of anticipation for *Teaching Children*.

The basic premise of *Teaching Children* is sound—to present a "Scope and Sequence" for each subject area based on the Charlotte Mason style of education. The Scope and Sequence you do get, with a tremendous amount of suggested topics of study, most following the standard public-school curriculum. However, *Teaching Children's* specifically Christian emphasis is not all I had hoped for. Apart from a brief rehash of the Charlotte Mason methodology and some Christian literature selections, the topics often sound quite secular—e.g., the study of Occupations, which the public schools use to thrust careerism on little girls. The way these topics are studied also is often secular. So under Substance Abuse Prevention (a topic most homeschoolers don't feel much need to meddle with), we find "Learn how to express feelings." Charlotte Mason never would have said that! Like the Bible, which says you conquer "drunkenness" (not "Substance Abuse"!) by being filled with the Holy Spirit, Charlotte Mason always stressed developing self-control, a love of the Lord, and habits of Christian character.

Those who expected the gentle approach of *For the Children's Sake* will be surprised at the tone of this book. Skills are rigidly divided into grade levels, parents and teachers are told to do this and do that, and we find the passive tense widely employed (e.g., "It is recommended that . . ."). Again, this is far from Charlotte Mason's own approach to education.

Another weakness: The "Developing a Christian Mind and Worldview" chapter is limited to resources put out by L'Abri workers. Yes, I know the Child Light people are all products in some way of L'Abri, the Christian fellowship founded in the Swiss Alps by Dr. and Mrs. Francis Schaeffer, but *Teaching Children* would have been a much stronger book if the author had been aware of the excellent work others not connected with L'Abri are doing in the area of Christian thinking and education. *Mary Pride*

Typical Course of Study

Grades K–12. 99¢ plus shipping.
The Sycamore Tree Center for Home Education, 2179 Meyer Place, Costa Mesa, CA 92627. Orders: (800) 779-6750. Information: (949) 650-4466. Fax: (800) 779-6750 or (949) 642-6750. Email: sycamoretree@compuserve.com. Web: www.sycamoretree.com.

The classic scope-and-sequence published for years by World Book, **Typical Course of Study** can probably be obtained most painlessly through homeschool cataloger Sycamore Tree, who actually answer their telephone. Based on studies of what topics are taught in each subject area in public schools around the country, *Typical Course of Study* should not be used as a slavish guide, but as essential "comfort reading" that lets you know you're doing as much or more than the schools and a starting point to your own set of objectives. After all, if you wanted to teach exactly what the public schools do, you could just send your kid to public school! Feel free to skip the transparently politically correct objectives, to forge ahead in math (kids don't need four years to work their way up to writing numbers in the millions, as just one example), and to rearrange the entire science curriculum. Should Life Science be taught before Earth Science, or vice versa? Who cares? *Mary Pride*

NEW!
What your 1st/ 2nd/ 3rd . . .
Grader Needs to Know: The
Core Knowledge Series
Grades K–6. $11.95 each, except kindergarten and 1st grade which are $12.95.
Bantam Doubleday Dell Publishing Group, Inc., 2451 S. Wolf Road, Des Plaines, IL 60018. Inquiries: (800)323-9872. Can order by mail only.

You probably know the **Core Knowledge Series** better by the names of its individual volumes. For instance, *What Your 1st Grader Needs to Know: Fundamentals of a Good First-Grade Education.* The titles for the other grade levels are similar: *What Your 2nd Grader Needs to Know, What Your 3rd Grader Needs to Know,* etc.

Edited by E.D. Hirsch, Jr., author of *Cultural Literacy,* these books were originally published by the Core Knowledge Foundation, whose mission is "improvement of education for all children." Consequently, this series is not just a list of what should be learned at what age, but contains actual reading selections and instructions for all major school subjects in each grade level covered.

For example, in the first-grade book, you get familiar nursery rhymes, classic children's stories, a number of Aesop's fables, explanations of famous sayings such as "If at first you don't succeed, try, try again," a quick tour of world geography, an introduction to world religions and civilizations, an introduction to American civilization that starts at the fabled crossing of the Bering strait, introductions to the fine arts, explanations of first-grade math concepts (math facts, geometry, time-telling, calendar, money, and more), and introductions to various sciences. The illustrations include classic engravings, photos, and maps.

The outlook behind these books is similar to that driving Bill Bennett's "virtue" books. Realizing that the public schools are failing to produce culturally and morally literate Americans, a number of people have taken it upon themselves to fill in what's missing. However, they are still operating from the same basic outlook as the schools: statist, evolutionary, multicultural, eco-socialist, and feminist, among other things. What these people want is, in Mr. Hirch's own words, to "create a *school-based* culture" (emphasis his) that is "fair and democratic." This means ignoring unpleasant realities, such as the fact that, while many Africans were captured for use as slaves, others were sold into slavery by their own greedy chieftains. It means that the only three scientists considered worthy of study in first grade are Nicholas Copernicus, Charles Drew (a black man who pioneered the use of blood plasma for transfusions), and the ecologist Rachel Carson. It means encouraging children to act out pagan religious ceremonies (e.g., a Chinese New Year celebration that "lets in the good spirits of the new year") and to consider all religions equally valid (except possibly the Aztecs, whose human sacrifices are correctly condemned). It means teaching a child to think of himself as "a very special animal," which though true from the point of view of physical anatomy, should have been balanced with some thoughts on people as spiritual beings.

The more I look at these books, the more frustrated I get. Such a good idea. Such a good design. So many useful facts. Presented as a conservative solution for America's academic ills, but larded throughout with politically-correct bias. What a waste. *Mary Pride*

If you are contemplating the return of your child to a traditional classroom, you must read **What Every Parent Needs to Know**. If your plans include continued home education, you might glean some insights and ideas here.

Written by a trio of professional educators with a combined 70 years of educational experience, this 166-page book guides parents through appropriate teaching practices for each primary grade subject. It gives parents a list of what to look for to evaluate the effectiveness of a teacher's approach. Parents are then given suggestions for activities to do at home to support the child's work in the classroom.

A good science program, for example, encourages children to think like a scientist and to apply this thinking to active investigations of the subject matter. In this area, parents should look for a good mixture of hands-on experiments and book learning.

This book is helpful because it can serve as a basis to evaluate your child's classroom. For home educators, it can help the parent to look at the components of their home program to determine if they really fit the way children in this age group learn.

There is a very helpful section on assessment which tells parents to look beyond their child's performance on standardized tests. A thoughtful evaluation of a child might include skills checklists, written observations of children at work, portfolios and student logs. This is a good reminder to all parents, whether homeschooling or not, to look at the whole picture of a child's experience as we evaluate our programs and methods in the home,

The authors support the implementation of national standards and are unmistakably in favor of quality public education. If I were returning my child to the school system, I would consider this a must-read. As a die-hard homeschooler, it is of limited value. *Christine Field*

What Your Child Needs to Know When is really two books in one. The second half of the book includes:

- One Year Through God's Word, a study plan using *The Narrated Bible,* a narration based on the NIV and published by Harvest House Publishers. Instead of just Bible reading assignments, you get a week-by-week outline of the point each passage makes, plus check boxes to track your progress.
- An alphabetical list of positive character traits, from *appreciative* to *virtuous,* with definitions and Scripture references.
- The most popular part of the book—119 pages of "Evaluation Check Lists." These are arranged by subject: language arts, mathematics, science, social sciences, and state history. Each subject is further divided into grade levels, and inside the grade levels, into subtopics. For example, under Language Arts, the second-grade listing is subdivided into Language Mechanics and Expression, Spelling, Study Skills, and Listening and Comprehension. Check boxes to the right of each listed skill are provided for up to five children. You assign each column of check boxes to a particular child, and there are five columns of check boxes. A typical skill to check off might be, "Identify correct use of singular and plural nouns."

NEW!
What Every Parent Needs to Know About 1st, 2nd & 3rd Grades

Parents. $12.95.
Sourcebooks, PO Box 372, Naperville, IL 60566. Orders: (800)727-8866. Inquiries: (630) 961-3900. Fax: (630) 961-2168.

NEW!
What Your Child Needs to Know When, New Expanded Edition

Parents: covers grades K–8. $19.95 plus shipping.
Heart of Wisdom Publishing, PO Box 1198, Springfield, TN 37172. Orders: (800) BOOK LOG. Inquiries: (615) 382-5500. Fax: (615) 382-4019. Web: www.heartofwisdom.com.

Unlike some other books of this type, each grade level's skills list does *not* include every single skill already checked off in the lower grades. Rather, you get skills needed at *that* grade level.

Did I say "other books of this type"? Actually, aside from the check lists, there *are* no other books of this type. The first half of this oversized 296-page paperback is devoted to exploring the differences between biblical-based education and secular education and the history of each, analyzing the pros and cons of standardized tests versus other feedback methods (such as evaluation check lists!), and introducing author Robin Scarlata's own "Heart of Wisdom," or H.O.W., teaching approach.

The H.O.W. approach is an attempt to make the Bible the core of the curriculum, by having students read through it in a year and create their own Bible portfolios. Along the way, they practice reading, handwriting, spelling, creative writing, critical thinking, phonics, grammar, vocabulary, map skills, and economics. This approach is based, as Robin tells us, on a combination of methods from the Judah Bible Curriculum, Ruth Beechick's books, Charlotte Mason's books, Marilyn Howshall's *Lifestyle of Learning,* David Mulligan's writings, and the write-to-learn philosophy of the Write Source books. History and science is added by reading aloud related books. For example, if your Bible reading for that day mentions the eye, you can read a library book about the eye. If it mentions a king of Persia, you can study Persia. Suggestion: *The Amazing Expedition Bible* (written up in Volume 2) would make finding these history tie-ins a piece of cake! *Mary Pride*

Test Preparation

More than just sample tests, the three **On Target for Tests** books for grades 2–3 (level A), 4–6 (level B), and 7–9 (level C) offer solid suggestions to make test day go a lot smoother for families that face that ritual on a regular basis. If you don't have to test, but are considering doing so, these 32-page workbooks can help you evaluate how your child would do before you make the commitment.

Test-taking tips include mechanics (like filling out bubbles), how to time yourself, types of questions, and guessing techniques. They grow more sophisticated at higher grade levels. Optionally available is a brief (eight page) teacher's guide to help you be sure your child "gets it." I'll bet you'll find at least one suggestion you hadn't thought of! Black-and-white, not reproducible. *Kim O'Hara*

Sycamore Tree not only carries tests, but books, workbooks, and software designed to help your children ace their tests.

I've covered SAT and GED test preparation thoroughly in Volume 3. Sycamore Tree does offer a small selection of preparation helps geared to these high-school-level tests. What we're concentrating on right now is what they have that can help your K–8 student face and ace the diagnostic and achievement tests they may be asked or required to take.

The **Scoring High** series is for people who take nationally standardized tests seriously. Available in separate series for the California Achievement Test, Iowa Test of Basic Skills, Stanford Achievement Test, and Comprehensive Test of Basic Skills, each grade level for each test has its own student edition and teacher's manual, except for the CTBS, which is divided into K–1, 1–3, 3–5, and 5–8. Basically, your child will be taught how to take the test, trained in the skills and facts covered in the test, and provided with problems strongly resembling those on the actual test. You need the teacher's manual to score the practice tests and to figure out how to use the student books. Software is also available in this series for some grade levels.

NEW!
On Target for Tests
Grades 2–9. Each book, $5.50. Pack of ten, $15.95. Teacher's Guide, $2.50, or free with 10-pack. Shipping extra.
The Continental Press, Inc., 520 East Bainbridge St., Elizabethtown, PA 17022. Orders: (800) 233-0759. Inquiries: (717)367-1836. Fax: (717) 367-5660. Web: www.continentalpress.com.

NEW!
Sycamore Tree Test Prep
Grades K–12. Scoring High series: student's editions, $3/grade except CTBS, $4/grade; teacher's manuals, $10/grade. Scoring High Test Prep software, grades 3–5 or 6–8, $19.95 each. Preparing Students to Raise Achievement Scores series, $8.95/workbook. Test Smart!, $29.95. A Parent's Guide to Standardized Tests in School, $14.95. Shipping extra.
The Sycamore Tree Center for Home Education, 2179 Meyer Place, Costa Mesa, CA 92627. Orders: (800) 779-6750. Information: (949) 650-4466.

Fax: (800) 779-6750 or (949) 642-6750.
Email: sycamoretree@compuserve.com.
Web: www.sycamoretree.com.

NEW!
Test Ready series
Grade 2–8. Student workbooks,
$6.95. Teacher guides, $3.50.
Curriculum Associates, P.O. Box 2001,
North Billerica, MA 01862-0901. (800)
225-0248. Fax: (800) 366-1158. Web:
www.curriculumassociates.com.

A more generic series, **Preparing Students to Raise Achievement Scores**, prepares kids for any of the above standardized tests, and more. These reproducible workbooks do not require or have separate teacher's manuals. Three workbooks are available for grades 1—2, 3–4, and 5–6.

Test Smart! Ready-to-Use Test-Taking Strategies and Activities for Grades 5–12 has over 100 worksheet activities to help students prepare for tests covering language arts and writing. *Mary Pride*

Does the idea of standardized testing stress you out? Curriculum Associates has a set of workbooks that prepare your child for testing. You can choose from a variety of test subjects in the **Test Ready** series, such as:

- OMNI Mathematics
- PLUS Reading
- Reading and Vocabulary
- PLUS Math
- Mathematics
- Language Arts
- Algebra I
- Social Studies
- Science
- Tips and Strategies

This program was designed to help ease test anxiety, identify skills and problem areas, familiarize students with test procedures, and indicate growth with a pre-test and a post-test. Curriculum Associates guarantees if your child spends 14 days with Test Ready his score will increase. He will learn the strategies needed to be successful. Some of the subjects have writing exercises to help prepare your child for test that require more than fill-in-the-bubble answers. This is a comprehensive test preparation program, allowing you to buy only the workbooks for subjects that your child needs to practice. Of course, you can buy the whole set and be ready for anything! *Maryann Turner*

PART 8

The Curriculum Buyer's Guide

Homeschooled girls like science . . . and so do boys!
Audrey Creighton, of Romoland, CA, took second
place at both her local science fair and the R.I.M.S.
County Science Fair. She also went on to the
California State Science Fair and won a $250
Special Cash Award from the American Heart
Association. Her project was a study on
cayenne's effects on the heart.
Audrey's brother, Courtney, also won a
Special Cash award of $500 from San
Bernardino College's Inland Empire
Energy Efficiency Project.

Abigail Rustad, a homeschooler in grade 7, won first place in the 7th–12th-grade third annual Adventure Safaris Homeschool Science Fair, sponsored by the Twin Cities Creation Science Association. She won with a variation on the classic "mice in the maze" experiment; mice listening to classical music ran observably short times, compared to those without music . . . and mice listening to Christian rock learned more slowly than if they hadn't been listening to anything at all. (And they can't even understand the words!) Abigail presented all this with graphs, photos, and samples of the music being tested. Conclusion: Abigail is a budding scientist . . . And Christian music needs better musicians.

CHAPTER 35

Traditional Curriculum

Textbooks. Workbooks. Worktexts. Here are some reasons why these are among the best-selling materials in the homeschool market:

- **Convenience.** Everything needed for the lesson is in one place . . . unless your child manages to lose his pencil!
- **Ease of assessment.** Grade the work using the provided answer key, and you know exactly what your student learned . . . and what parts of the lesson need to be reviewed, if any.
- **Cost.** Hardbound textbooks can be used for child after child. Workbooks and worktexts are inexpensive enough to purchase a set for each child as needed.

It is hard, although not totally impossible, to do math or grammar without textbooks or workbooks. And a history textbook or two can provide a chronological outline for your history studies. Other subjects, such as science and creative writing, can go either way. Innovative non-textbook curricula of all sorts exist for teaching these topics, while on the other hand, you can also teach them perfectly well using the kinds of textbooks and worktexts reviewed in this chapter.

Although classical education is certainly "traditional," for your convenience we decided to review programs with a classical flavor in the next chapter. Right now, we'll be looking at publishers of "back to basics" style curricula. If you're looking for something time-tested, solid, and simple to use, that sticks with the basics rather than delving into more elite topics, this is a good place to start.

Traditional Curriculum Reviews

An offshoot of one of America's largest Christian day schools, **A Beka's correspondence program** is a ministry of Pensacola Christian College, using the popular A Beka Book series of Christian texts that the college publishes. The Day School itself is recognized by both the State of Florida and the Florida Association of Christian Schools. (See also the entry under A Beka Video Home School for A Beka's home video program, and the entry under A Beka Book Curriculum for an overview of the curriculum itself.)

A Beka's rules are strict: no discounts, no payment plans, no refunds, no course alterations allowed. A Beka says, "Continued enrollment is contingent upon compliance with program guidelines."

What's In a Name?

- A **textbook** is a softbound or hardbound volume that includes instructional material for the course that the student is expected to read, plus lesson assignments, but does *not* provide space in the text to fill in the answers. Textbooks are reusable; since no answers are filled in, child after child can use the same book.
- A **workbook** is consumable (non-reusable). It is usually bound like a booklet, not perfect-bound with a spine, and consists of student exercises plus the necessary space to fill in the answers.
- A **worktext** combines the two. It includes the instructional content found in a textbook, plus the exercises (and space for the answers) you'd expect to find in a workbook. Worktexts are consumable. They often include quizzes and/or have a test covering all the material in the worktext bound in.

A Beka Correspondence School

Kindergarten to Grade 6, $655 each. Grades 7–12, $800 each. Discounts available for reuse.
A Beka School Services, Box 18000, Pensacola, FL 32523-9160.
(800) 874-3592.
Fax: (800) 874-3593.
Email: ABSSinfo@pcci.edu.

Homeschooling parents may purchase individual subject area curricula, textbooks, tests, and teacher aids in all subjects without enrolling in A Beka Correspondence School. Send for the free A Beka Books catalog—and be sure to read our separate review of the curriculum.

UPDATED!
A Beka Book Curriculum

Grades preK–12. Textbook prices vary.
A Beka Book, Box 19100, Pensacola, FL 32523-9160. (800) 874-2352.
Fax: (800) 874-3590.
Web: www.abeka.com

A Beka provides a Teacher's Manual identical to that used in Christian classrooms with their A Beka materials. A Beka also supplies all needed textbooks and materials; periodic grade reports; permanent school records; and advice and counseling as requested.

Lessons follow one another logically, so students should not become frustrated through lack of understanding. Though there is a lot of repetitive drill, the exercises are fairly interesting.

The amount of recordkeeping is average (returning work to school, grading daily work, keeping attendance records).

This entire program is available on video for grades K–12. See the A Beka Video Home School review in this section.

If you enroll in the Correspondence Program, prepare to move along at a brisk pace. A Beka expects you to administer weekly tests and keep right on top of things. Some people like being held to a schedule like this. But if you're the mellow type who dislikes tight schedules, or like to pick and choose workbook exercises instead of assigning them all, or need to move at the pace you set rather than having it set for you, you'd be better off bypassing A Beka's enrollment services and just buying the A Beka books you need direct from the catalog. *Mary Pride*

If you've spent any length of time in homeschooling circles, you're likely to have heard of **A Beka Book.** A curriculum supplier affiliated with Pensacola Christian College in Florida, A Beka Book offers conservative Christian curriculum and supplemental materials for prekindergarten through twelfth grade. You can buy individual items; you also have the option of enrolling in their regular correspondence program or their video correspondence program (see separate reviews of the latter).

A Beka books have lots of color and eye appeal. All are paperback worktexts with quality bindings.

A Beka favors a "back to basics" programmed approach, with the child drilled in correct responses, rather than a discovery approach. Kids are expected to memorize facts and repeat drilled responses instead of discovering them for themselves. A Beka Book books thus frequently use "I" sentences. Example: "I must ask God to help my hands do what is right." Expect to find a lot of questions with one right answer and not too many open-ended questions.

In keeping with their conservative Christian perspective, A Beka's approach to history is patriotic; to science, creationist; to economics, free-market; to government, mostly pro-liberty and Constitutional; to reading, phonetic; to math, factual and rule-based; to Bible, classically Protestant. The surprise here is the upper-grades literature, which is uncharacteristically grim and even dubious in spots. (See separate review in Literature chapter of Volume 3.)

A Beka's approach is traditional and textbook-oriented. Curriculum is based on a classroom model. If followed exactly, it would be a whole school day's work for both parents and students. Count on spending some time adapting the lessons to your home situation.

Lessons follow one another logically and step-by-step. Though there is a lot of repetitive drill, the exercises are fairly interesting.

Handwriting starts with manuscript in kindergarten. Cursive writing begins in grade 2. Writing and reading are taught together in kindergarten, which is a serious academic program also including fun stuff like art, music, and poetry.

A Beka's products are colorful and professional-looking. They have made an effort to upgrade the art where it was amateurish (early-grades history and science texts). Their upper-grades materials are very good looking and approachable.

In **grades 1–3**, A Beka is strongest in math, Bible, and health & safety. The updated worktext-based math program still flies along, compared to those from other publishers, but now includes more visual aids, games, and other "fun" stuff. There's still a ton of drill and repetition, though, so feel free to skip some pages. Their Bible materials are sweet and easy to use, and the health & safety books are charming. Less useful are the history and science books at these grade levels. In grades 1 and 2, history and science are accessories to the reading program. They are first introduced as academic subjects in grade 3. These books are mostly useful for introducing a conservative Christian view of these subjects, to be expanded on later in other grades.

In **grades 4–6**, creative writing begins to be included in the language-arts books. Math continues to fly along, with again a large amount of drill and review. Science and history at this level are quite good; in fact, I would suggest using them for *older* children as well, then skipping back up to the high-school texts, since middle-grades texts tend to drown the student in too many details. You can depend on A Beka to protect your child's modesty in their separate "health" texts. Unfortunately, these tend to be mainstream in their view of nutrition, first aid, "doctors know best," and so forth.

Junior high and **high school** are pretty much what you'd expect from normal classroom texts—with a few surprises. Lots and lots of grammar review, repeated from year to year. Lots and lots of math. The science offerings are uneven. *Science: Matter and Motion* (grade 7) and Science: *Order and Reality* (grade 8) are wonderful overall introductions to science from a Christian viewpoint. The biology text abandons the evolutionary "molecules to man" sequence in favor of a much more sensible "man to molecules" approach. Again, it contains so much detail students will have trouble remembering it all, but it's still an exciting book. Chemistry and physics fare less well: both are typical textbook treatments, meaning hard to follow and you'd better have all the teacher's manuals and answer keys.

The upper-grades literature texts include a surprising amount of stories related to death and loss, and some stories and poems that in my opinion don't belong in a Christian literature series at all. Why include ghosts and goblins when there are so many better stories available, and when bookstore shelves are lined with "Goosebumps" horror tales for teens? The next edition definitely could use more tales of courage, hope, and other virtues.

A Beka's junior and senior high history books are solidly Christian and easy to read, if not to memorize. Like most school texts, there's a tendency to overwhelm the student with details. This is definitely a course that would work better on CD-ROM, where you could stick to the main story and follow the people and events of lesser significance as interest beckons.

No record-keeping is required for nursery and K4. Beyond these grades the amount of record-keeping is average (grading daily work, keeping attendance records).

With the exception of the phonics course, from which we have seen mixed results, you can't really hurt anything by using A Beka. Since as a whole this is a curriculum that "works" rather than one that "excites," you may want to follow most people's example and cherry-pick the subjects and texts that most appeal to you. *Mary Pride*

Subjects we liked the least were lower-grades Language Arts and upper-grades Literature. I'd advise you to skip A Beka's phonics program entirely and substitute one of the standalone phonics programs reviewed in Volume 2. Subjects we liked the best: Math, History, and Geography.

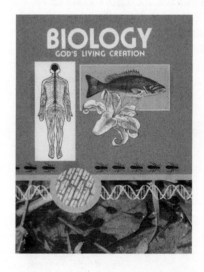

Will you need all the teacher curriculum guides, teacher's editions, and answer keys? Probably not. It depends on the course. As a general rule, **teacher's editions** (books that contain the entire student text, with answers filled in, and additional teaching information) are much more useful than the **curriculum guides** (these include lesson plans and lots of classroomy teaching suggestions).

A Beka Video Home School

Grades K–12. Grades vary, $790 to $1000 plus $90 refundable video deposit fee. Everything included. Discounts are available. Tapes must be returned via UPS Authorized Return Service (included in cost) every six or nine weeks depending on grade. Payment Plan: $300 down and $88 to $123 per month for 6 months. Option for grades 7–12 subjects: individual courses may be ordered for non-credit. Tapes returned every nine weeks, as per above. Courses $315 each plus $55 retainer; $50 additional per course for each additional student within the immediate family using the course, excluding student books. *A Beka School Services, Pensacola Christian College, Box 18000, Pensacola, FL 32523-9160. (800) 874-3592. Fax: (800) 874-3593. Email: ABSSinfo@pcci.edu. Web: www.abeka.org.*

You will need a VCR for each student enrolled, unless one watches the videos mornings and the other does so in the afternoons. This is not the program for large families.

UPDATED!
Alpha Omega LIFEPAC Gold

Grades K–12. Grade K: Math & Language Arts sets, $39.95 each. Grade 1, $354.25. Grade 2–6, $229.75. Grade 7, $241.70. Grade 8, $234.75. Grade 9, $246.65. Grade 10, $241.70. Grade 11, $252.70. Grade 12, $238.70. LIFEPAC Electives, Complete Boxed Sets: Art, $45.95;

You knew it was inevitable. We have video cooking classes, video fitness programs, and now . . . video homeschool! Launched in 1986, **A Beka's video program** sparked instant controversy. More on that later.

When you sign up for this program, you get instructional videocassettes and A Beka's very popular texts and teaching guides. The A Beka textbooks used in this program are widely used and generally well-regarded. See the A Beka Curriculum listing for further details.

The videos take you inside a real classroom, with a teacher lecturing and demonstrating and a class of students who ask and answer questions. The classroom content is not scripted, staged, or noticeably edited, and the tapes themselves are of the "slow-play" variety that don't work on some older video players.

Important point: **videos remain the property of A Beka Video Home School, and have to be returned at regular intervals.** This makes the course proportionally more expensive, since you have to re-rent the videos for each subsequent child to take the course.

Students also have homework assignments. You return completed work and tests at designated intervals of six to nine weeks, depending on grade level.

Kindergartners receive two and a half hours daily instruction from the videotape teacher, and children in grades 1–6 spend slightly more than three hours watching their tapes. High-schoolers will spend one and a half to two hours per course per day. To many of us, this seems like an excessive amount of time spent plopped in front of a video player—but then again, the average American child spends more time than that daily watching largely uneducational TV programming.

The real problem is the lack of pace and editing. You spend as much time waiting for something to happen and for the other kids in the videotaped classroom to "get it" as you would in a real classroom, plus you have to wait repeatedly while the microphone is passed around the classroom. Too, you don't get the visual aids (photos, video clips, reenactments) that would be so easy to edit in and would make the program so much more valuable educationally and so much more fun to watch. In today's homeschool market, with TV-quality video instruction becoming available from suppliers such as School of Tomorrow and just about every new phonics supplier, A Beka really should consider updating its videos and re-recording them on regular-play media instead of slow-play.

That being said, this program has three main benefits: (1) It allows parents who have little or no time or ability for teaching to homeschool, (2) at the junior-high and high-school level you can add just one or two video courses in subjects you otherwise might not feel capable or comfortable teaching, and (3) it provides as close to a "real" classroom experience as you can get at home. If you intend to send your homeschooled child to a well-organized private school at some time in the future, they will have a good idea what to expect. *Mary Pride*

Alpha Omega's conservative Christian curriculum has changed quite a bit since the last edition of this book. **LIFEPAC Gold**, their updated and greatly improved "worktext" curriculum, has now been completed. The original LIFEPACs are no longer available, unless you find them secondhand or through a catalog that has not yet sold out its stock.

Each LIFEPAC Gold grade level now is available attractively packaged in a sturdy, colorful cardboard box. Inside you'll find 10 color-coded worktexts apiece for each of five subjects—Bible, social studies, language arts, math, and science—plus a teacher's manual for each subject. Each spiral-bound teacher's manual includes a K–12 scope and sequence for that sub-

Consumer Math, $44.50; Home Economics, $45.95; New Testament Greek, $40.95; Spanish I, $100.95 (includes audiocassettes). LIFEPAC Select sets, $23.95 each. Additional learning items available for each grade. Parent Starter Kit, $19.95. Student Testing Kit, $19.95. Student Placement Service, $45. Shipping extra.
Alpha Omega Publications, 300 N. McKemy, Chandler, AZ 85226. Orders and inquiries: (800) 622-3070. Fax: (602) 785-8034. Web: www.home-schooling.com.

ject, schedules and lesson planner forms, grading forms, a course outline, lesson-by-lesson teaching instructions, alternate tests (to supplement the test in the worktexts, if needed), materials needed for each LIFEPAC, and answer keys for all the worktext exercises and quizzes.

One difference you'll notice right away is that the LIFEPAC Gold worktexts are printed in full color. Other changes: Social studies is now "history & geography." The political correctness that crept into previous editions has now been edited out. The worktexts themselves are printed on whiter, stronger paper, with more durable and attractive covers.

One of the strengths of the single-subject worktext approach is that a child can take subjects at different grade levels. This is still possible with LIFEPAC Gold, though those cute boxes with all the subjects for a year of homeschooling are tempting!

LIFEPAC Gold follows the format of "read the information, do the activities, answer the questions." The questions are not just simple fill-in-the-blank; students are encouraged to think and analyze, not just remember. Periodic quizzes enable parents and students to see if a student is ready to move on to the next section. Note that parents *should* expect to be involved. Not only do you need to do a boatload of grading (not necessary if you're using their Switched-On Schoolhouse software, which grades answers automatically—see review in chapter 42), but you'll want and need to discuss the "thought" questions with your children and help them with some of the activities. In other words, don't expect the kids to go off in a corner with these worktexts and emerge years later fully educated.

For **kindergarten**, they offer a Kindergarten LIFEPAC Gold set with two units: one for language arts and one for math. The kindergarten offering for math comes with two large, colorful, student books and a spiral-bound teacher's guide. So does the language arts.

Nine **high-school electives** are available in LIFEPAC Gold format: Spanish, Accounting, American Literature, British Literature, Health Quest, Consumer Math, Home Economics, Art, and New Testament Greek. The Spanish course comes with cassettes, to help you learn pronunciation. Additional study helps are available for some of these courses, from Greek lexicons and Bibles, to foreign-language vocabulary cards and activity books.

Can't figure out where to start? The Parent Starter Kit and Student Testing Kit may help. Alpha Omega's **Parent Starter Kit** is designed for first-time homeschool parents, and includes *A Parent' Guide to Mastering LIFEPAC Management,* the newly revised *LIFEPAC Curriculum Scope & Sequence,* a sample LIFEPAC, and Ray Ballman's book, *The How and Why of Home Schooling.* The **Student Testing Kit** is a set of diagnostic tests for all

Here's an unusual option. Want some high school electives, though you're not using the LIFEPAC curriculum? Then there's **LIFEPAC Select**. Each of these units is made up of five LIFEPAC Gold worktexts selected from grades 7 through 9, plus a teacher' manual. This way, you can cover a subject in depth all at once. LIFEPAC Select units include Astronomy, Christian Perspectives, Civics, Composition, General Health, Geography, Geology, Life of Christ, Life Science, and Mankind: Anthropology & Sociology. Each of these may be considered as ½ a Carnegie unit, e.g., a one-semester high-school course.

five subjects, helping you determine the correct LIFEPAC grade level at which your student should start in each subject, plus a set of student record books for recording grades and progress and a parent' cumulative file with more forms to help organize your homeschool. If you'd like even more placement help, a new Student Placement Service allows you to send in the diagnostic tests to be graded by testing specialists, who will return a complete one-year "prescription."

A lot of work has gone into the new edition of this program. It is very well-organized, thorough, and attractive. If you could use the structure this meticulously-planned Christian curriculum offers, give it a look! *Mary Pride*

Alpha Omega, publisher of the LIFEPAC Gold curriculum reviewed above, also publishes a second curriculum line, called **Horizons**, which is designed to be a bit meatier. So far the Horizons line includes a kindergarten program called *Phonics and Reading,* two grades of penmanship, and grades K–6 of math.

The least expensive way to purchase **Horizons Phonics and Reading** is an attractively packaged boxed set. This includes four full-color workbooks with corresponding spiral-bound teacher's guides with answer keys, four readers, an alphabet floor puzzle, and a wipe-off tablet for practicing handwriting. It introduces basic reading, phonics, and spelling skills and is quite streamlined and easy to use.

Horizons Penmanship is another colorful program that is meeting with much acceptance. The Grade 1 book teaches manuscript handwriting; grade 2 introduces traditional cursive. Each book has 32 weeks of daily lessons, with the fifth day a "picture page" on which the student can copy the indicated Bible verse and draw a picture.

Horizons Math is a solid curriculum that presents math according to the typical public-school scope and sequence. Once presented, a concept is reviewed in future lessons. Each level has two colorful student books and a spiral-bound teacher's guide with complete daily lesson plans and answer keys. Kids are tested once every 10 lessons. (For an in-depth review of Horizons math, see Volume 2.)

Compared to LIFEPAC Gold, Horizons is more teacher-directed and a better choice for kids who grasp new concepts quickly. *Mary Pride*

NEW!
Alpha Omega Horizons Curriculum
Grades K–6. Phonics and Reading Boxed Set, $132.60. Penmanship Grade 1 and 2, $27.45 each grade. Math: Grade K, $65; Grades 1–6, $75 each. Shipping extra.
*Alpha Omega Publications, 300 N. McKemy, Chandler, AZ 85226. Orders and inquiries: (800) 622-3070. Fax: (602) 785-8034.
Web: www.home-schooling.com.*

UPDATED!
Bob Jones University Press
Foundations Home School Kit (K4), $96. Beginnings Home School Kit (K5), $169. Math K5 Home School Kit, $49. Music Home School Kit: $119 each grades 1–2; $125 each grades 3–6. Science Home School Kit: grade 1–3, $51 each; grades 4–6, $63 each. Math Home School Kit, grades 1–4, $44 each; grades 5–6, $64 each. Grade 1 English Skills Home Kit, $149. Other subjects and items available separately only, prices vary.
*Bob Jones University Press, Greenville, SC 29614. (800) 845-5731. Fax: (800) 525-8398. From other countries: Call (864) 242-5100, x3349.
Email: bjup@bjup.com.
Web: www.bjup.com*

Now here's a big-time company that's *really* friendly to home schoolers! **Bob Jones University Press** has a toll-free number for questions about their curriculum and a gorgeous catalog loaded with everything you need from preschool through high school. Not only that, BJUP's line of (often hardback) texts is widely conceded to be the overall best in Christian publishing. The university's more controversial positions appear nowhere in their homeschool materials, which are strictly mainstream fundamentalist.

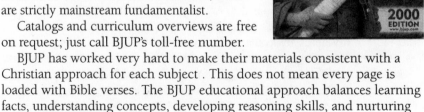

Catalogs and curriculum overviews are free on request; just call BJUP's toll-free number.

BJUP has worked very hard to make their materials consistent with a Christian approach for each subject . This does not mean every page is loaded with Bible verses. The BJUP educational approach balances learning facts, understanding concepts, developing reasoning skills, and nurturing Christian character, all for use in a real-world context.

This curriculum offers Bible from grades K4–12; reading, K–6; handwriting, K–6; spelling, 2–6; grammar and composition, 2–12; literature,

7–12; vocabulary, 7–12; history, 1–7 and 9–12; math, K–12 (includes geometry and two years of algebra); science, 1–12, including chemistry and physics.

The biggest change in BJUP curriculum since the last edition of *The Big Book* is the tremendous effort they have put into updating their teacher materials for homeschoolers. Home teacher's guides (as opposed to classroom-style teacher's manuals) are now available for

- Foundations (the Bible program) in grades K–4
- First-grade English
- Spelling, grades 1–6
- Math, grades K–6
- Science, grades 1–6

The home teacher's guides are inexpensive and much easier to use than the classroom manuals.

Just as before, you may still buy classroom-oriented teacher's manuals for any subject. Most of the teacher's editions include a complete student text. This could eliminate the need for a student book in some subjects. Check first whether the teacher's edition includes answers printed in the student text—some do.

Now, let's take a look at the curriculum itself. Keep in mind that more detailed reviews of many of the courses are found in Volumes 2 and 3.

BJUP has two **kindergarten** programs. "Foundations," designed for four-year-olds, is a "readiness" program comparable to Calvert's. "Beginnings," for five-year-olds, is an academic language-arts program. You'll find reviews of both in Volume 2. Phonics instruction is completed in their new First Grade English Skills program. This course exhaustively covers all aspects of language skills—phonics, listening, reading, structural analysis, handwriting, composition, and oral communication—while using songs, games, listening practice, and much more.

BJUP is currently revising their **Bible** curriculum for grades 1–4. I hear that *Bible Truths for Christian Schools 1* is out, but I haven't seen it. In grade 4, the life of Christ and early church history is covered. Grade 6 is a survey of the Old Testament. For some reason known only to the curriculum designers, in grade 7 the series shifts confusingly to "levels." The seventh-grade *Bible Truths for Christian Schools* book is "level A." Eighth grade is "level B," and so on. Here's what you get: Level A: *Learning from the Life of Christ.* Level B: *Portraits from the Old Testament.* Level C: *Lessons from the Early Church.* Level D: *Themes from the Old Testament.* Level E: *Directions for Early Christians.* Level F: *Patterns for Christian Living.* The outlook of the series is fundamentalist, premillenial, Baptist, and evangelistic.

BJUP offers textbooks and teacher's editions for all the subjects and grade levels they carry. In addition, they offer texts in a number of special areas—computer science, speech, family living— where Christian materials are not generally available.

BJUP's policy of printing most upper-grade texts as hardbacks (students do assignments in separate notebooks) means you buy the book only once and can use it again and again with all your children.

Now, language arts. For **handwriting**, BJUP has their own precursive that's a cross between D'Nealian and cursive italic. It's quite functional and pretty. Somewhat less useful are the "Practi-Slates" you can buy for handwriting practice. These are our old friends that we used to carry on long car trips— "magic" slates with a top sheet that lifts up so you can keep writing on the same surface. They have never held up well for me, and I suggest you skip them.

Spelling is a course of its own, and BJUP has made the massive effort to produce Home Teacher edition's of the teacher manuals for grades 1–6. Their program includes a number of innovative features, from the exploits of detective Dick Shanary (read his name out loud!) to humorous word studies. The catalog description will tell you all you need to know to determine if you want to order it.

Writing and Grammar is a course for grades 1–12. This is a fairly painless way to teach and test your student in what he needs to know in these areas. Beware the deadly "topic sentence" concept: it's included in the grade 4 book.

Reading is another separate course for grades 1–6. Frankly, if you have a library card you don't need it. You might, however, want to pick up some of the assigned novels, especially the delightful *Derwood, Inc.*

The grade 1 books for handwriting, spelling, reading, and writing & grammar are all included, along with many other things, in the First Grade English Skills kit.

Turning to **math**, we find that BJUP uses hardbound student books in grades 5 and up. This is supposed to save you money, but I personally find it a real pain when trying to grade student work. At all grade levels, BJUP moves at a normal classroom pace, and intersperses "calculation" type math (e.g., arithmetic facts and math problems) with other activities such as measuring, graphing, time, temperature, and many word problems. They are trying to teach students to think analytically, but again I find it works better for student to go straight through from beginning math facts to calculus, then it does to keep jumping out with other activities. (I keep waiting for someone to make time, temperature, and so on into a separate course—*that* would make sense!)

In high school, you have your choice of Algebra I, Algebra II, Geometry, Consumer Math, Advanced Math (algebra review, trigonometry, and introduction to calculus), and the brand-new Logic course. The latter covers both mathematical logic (Venn diagrams and the like) and verbal logic (syllogisms, fallacies, and all that good stuff).

BJUP takes **music** extremely seriously. It's one of the relatively few subjects you can purchase as an entire kit, by grade level. The thrust is on developing singing and sight-reading abilities, plus some basics of familiar instruments. By grade 6, the student is working on two- and three-part songs in English and foreign languages, learning basic composition (write your own opera, anyone?), and exploring the evangelistic and worshipful uses of music. He will also have had some experience with the recorder, guitar, autoharp, and keyboard.

The **science** courses for grades 1–6 have been recently revised to include more activities. As usual at this level, you can do as well with library books, and get better experiments in books written for that purpose, such as the Jane Hoffman "Backyard Scientist" and Janice VanCleave "Science for Every Kid" series. However, if you feel more comfortable having regular tests to assign and grade (so you actually know what your child is learning), BJUP has some extra helps for you, above and beyond the quizzes in the books. Their new Ask•It Test Bank software lets the computer quiz and grade your kids. Or, if you prefer, you can buy regular paper TestBanks (for grades 4–6 of science), and whip up new tests whenever you want them.

Among the hundreds of specialty items from BJUP— their Summer Skills Readers Program! It comes packaged in a cute decorative shopping bag, as shown above.

Speaking of **Ask•It**, it's time for BJUP to upgrade its software. It's nice that you can use your PC or Mac to select groups of questions, create your own tests, and even have the computer quiz the student (as long as all you ask are true/false and multiple-choice questions) in the subjects of Heritage Studies (grades 4–12), science (grades 4–6), literature (grades 7–12), life science, earth science, biology, health, family living, and economics. But with competitors such as Calvert and Alpha Omega coming out with jazzy multimedia courses that both present the subject and do the grading, it's about time for BJUP to pick up its socks and show what they can *really* do.

Upper-grades science is all of high quality, but varies quite a bit in ease of use. The sequence is typical of that offered college-bound students: life science in grade 7, earth science in grade 8, physical science (called "Basic Science") in grade 9, biology in grade 10, chemistry in grade 11, and physics in grade 12. You'll find the biology, chemistry, and physics courses emphasize lab work. Although it is *possible* to order lab equipment and materials from BJUP, it is expensive and difficult to do. There are no handy "Biology Home School Kits," for example. You have to first order the *order form* (science lab material is not included on the regular homeschool order form), and then select and add up literally dozens of items. The science order form is designed to tempt you to try to substitute common household items, but the problem is that you probably don't have most of these items on hand. Still, it's tempting to make yourself huge shopping lists of wire, charcoal briquettes, and the like, when you see how much the actual lab items cost. I found the whole process paralyzing. You'd be better off signing up for Science Labs-In-A-Box (reviewed in volume 2) for your lab equipment and ingredients, doing *their* experiments, and just using BJUP's science texts to teach the concepts.

Heritage Studies, a BJUP specialty, has been upgraded to add maps and timelines to grades 1 and 2. Also new is something called *Current Events*. This annual publication updates your Heritage Studies and science textbooks, kind of like a yearbook updates an encyclopedia. New maps, statistics, feature articles, and a walk through the current year are included. The teaching sequence remains the same. Grade 1, from pre-European America through the colonial era. Grade 2, from Jamestown to the War for Independence (BJUP prefers this to calling it the "American Revolution.") Grade 3, life in early America. Grade 4, from the Constitution to the building of the republic. Grade 5, the geography and culture of the Western nations. Grade 6, dittos for the Eastern nations. Grade 7: World Studies, a look at the cultures of the world's people. Grade 8: A survey of U.S. history. Grade 9: world geography. Grade 10: world history. Grade 11: U.S. history, again. Grade 12, you have a choice of two courses: American Government or Economics. All Heritage Studies courses are well-written and well-organized, and feature a conservative, free-market perspective.

Vocabulary, another BJUP specialty, is taught as a separate course in grades 7–12. If this sounds like it's a follow-up to their lower-grades Spelling sequence, you're right. You'll study word roots from Latin, Greek, and French, as well as how language develops and the precise use of words.

Literature becomes a separate subject in grade 7. In grades 7 and 8, the emphasis in on exploring literary themes, such as courage. The grade 9

Worthy of note is that videos are now available for the Chemistry course, through HomeSAT. This company, reviewed separately in chapter 42, collects and rebroadcasts the BJUP "Linc" live video classroom courses over satellite. You can sign up for most courses via satellite or video: your choice. They comes with additional student handouts geared to the video lectures. I would pick the videos myself, having too often missed recording the satellite downloads due to forgetfulness, equipment failure, or bad weather.

course, *Fundamentals of Literature,* and grade 10 course, *Elements of Literature,* introduce literary analysis. You wind up with American literature in grade 11, and British literature in grade 12. Both could easily pass for college courses: see full review in Volume 3.

Spanish, German, and French are available at the high-school level, as are a number of secondary music courses. Other electives include Family Living, Health, Speech, and Logic.

Motivated older students *can* teach themselves with BJUP materials, but it won't be easy. If this is the way you choose to go, plan on reading ahead through the teacher's manuals and sitting right there with the kids to answer their questions. They will be getting a good education—you can be sure of it. *Mary Pride*

UPDATED!
Christian Liberty Academy Satellite Schools
Grades K–12. CLASS Administration Plan tuition: K, $195; grades 1–8, $325; grades 9–12, $375. Family Administration Plan tuition: K, $165; grades 1–8, $255; grades 9–12, $295. Curriculum Kit prices: K, $105; Grade 1, $115; grade 2, $126; grades 3-5, $120 each; grade 6, 141; grade 7, $170; grade 8, $163; grade 9, $165; grade 10, $205; grade 11, $110; grade 12, $108. Adventures in Phonics kit, $49.95. Advanced Reading kit, $40. High-school electives: $10–$90 each. Book credit (only in CLASS or Family Plan) when younger student reuses materials. No discounts. Partial refund within 30 days of books shipped. School Starter Kit (for Christian schools), $125.
Christian Liberty Press, 502 West Euclid Ave., Arlington Heights, IL 60004-5495. To request their free information packet: (800) 348-0899. Enrollment: (847) 259-1297. To request free CLP catalog: (800) 832-2741. Inquiries and customer service: (847) 259-4444. Fax: (847) 259-2941. Email: webmaster@homeschools.org. Web: www.homeschools.org.

With over 26,000 students enrolled, **Christian Liberty Academy,** also known as CLASS, is one of the most popular packaged curriculum providers. As its name might indicate, CLASS (it stands for "Christian Liberty Academy Satellite Schools") is strongly pro-freedom, anti-statism, and pro-historical Christianity and traditional teaching methods. CLASS operates its own large day school (on a lovely campus purchased from the local public school district!) where courses are originated and evaluated by its staff of well-educated professionals.

CLASS has been around for the entire modern homeschool movement. Only four years after founding their day school (in 1968), CLASS Superintendent of Schools Dr. Paul Lindstrom was already putting together what developed into an entire homeschool curriculum.

Dr. Lindstrom is a colorful character with strong views. Do you remember the Pueblo? This American ship was held by the Koreans for two months. The sailors were only released when they confessed to being spies. Dr. Lindstrom was chairman of the Remember the Pueblo Committee, and also instrumental in efforts to release missionaries, POWs, and MIAs who were left behind in Southeast Asia at the close of the Vietnam War. Forged in the crucible of the Cold War, the program he helped develop is strong on comparing Constitutional government to socialism, free-enterprise economics to planned economies, and traditional Christian morality to the fruits of the sexual and ethical revolutions. The goal throughout is to develop a strong biblical worldview in the student and to build up the student's family.

The CLASS program began its life as an eclectic mixture of books from other publishers, accompanied with a large manual packed with information on how to homeschool. CLASS offered "satellite school" services, including recordkeeping, grading, transcripts, and they promised to intervene if the authorities challenged your homeschool program. As the years have gone by, the legal climate has improved, and any remaining battles are mostly fought by Home School Legal Defense Association. This being so, CLASS has had the time to bring out their own books in many subject areas—books that more exactly reflect their outlook and educational philosophy. Christian Liberty Press (CLP), their publishing arm, now has its own large catalog. However, they still use books from many publishers, including the following: A Beka Book (language arts, literature, and science), American Vision (God and Government series and *War of the Worldviews*), Bob Jones University Press (mostly books on how to teach various subjects from a Christian point of view), Baker Book House, Banner of Truth, Crossway Books, Home School Legal Defense Association (Mike Farris' Constitutional Law book), Judy Rogers Recording Company, Modern Curriculum Press (elementary math and phonics), Saxon Publishers (*Math 76* through *Algebra 2*), Steck-Vaughn, and Wordsmiths (Jensen's Grammar series and *Format Writing*). The Christian biographies, Bible study, and doctrinal materials include a few titles each from stalwart biblical publishers such as Presbyterian & Reformed, Banner of Truth, Baker, Eerdmans, and Great Commission Publications. In many cases, CLP has produced its own answer keys and teacher materials to accompany the books from other publishers. For example, CLP created answer keys and test packets for the A Beka science textbooks, and both video and audio tapes to accompany Jensen's Grammar.

The CLASS approach is to provide some generalized support materials (legal backgrounders, Christian educational philosophy). You get answer keys, course instructions, and tests, and an occasional teacher's manual to accompany a particular textbook, but no day-by-day lesson plans. You, the parent, are supposed to figure how long you want to take to cover the material. Then divide the number of pages in each book by the number of days and do that many pages each day. It's up to you to figure out how to deal with any learning difficulties as they arise. If this becomes too difficult, you can contact CLASS directly with your questions by mail, email, or phone.

You can either buy individual books from the Christian Liberty Press catalog or an entire grade-level Curriculum Kit. In addition, you have your choice of two recordkeeping options.

If you choose the full-service **CLASS Administration Plan**, CLASS will issue you annual achievement tests, grade your student's tests, issue quarterly report cards, keep a transcript on file, provide assistance if necessary with school officials, and issue diplomas. You no longer have to submit the student's daily work to CLASS—just the tests. Instead, parents now fill out a signed Report & Identification sheet, showing the percentage score assigned to the student's daily work. This counts for 20 percent of the grade, lowers your mail costs, and means you'll get your quarterly report cards sooner.

Under the **Family Administration Plan**, you still get achievement tests, curriculum design assistance, and customer service assistance, but you save some money by doing all the grading and recordkeeping yourself.

Both plans include not only these services, but all the books, textbooks, answer keys, and so on included in that grade's curriculum.

If you prefer just to buy the kits, the testing service and curriculum recommendation service are now available separately for $20 each.

The main complaint about CLASS used to be the amount of work it required of younger students. CLASS has redesigned their entire program to be more friendly to the younger student. They have two kindergarten options, Standard Kindergarten and Advanced Kindergarten. The old Rod & Staff readers have been replaced with CLP's own phonics books and readers. Modern Curriculum Press math is now used in the younger grades, instead of the more accelerated A Beka books they used to use. In this more streamlined program, you get a CLASS Lesson Planner the first time you enroll. And here's what else you get.

For phonics, the **kindergarten** program includes a set of "Adventures in Phonics: Level A" materials (workbook, teacher's manual, and phonics flashcards), a book about teaching reading, plus CLP's own Kindergarten Phonics Readers —*It Is Fun to Read, Pals and Pets, A Time at Home, It Is a Joy to Learn*. The kindergarten program also includes an American history book and teacher's manual (it includes a chapter on beginning geography as well), a Modern Curriculum Press math workbook and teacher's manual, arithmetic flashcards, an art workbook, a Bible workbook, a handwriting workbook with writing pad and teacher's instructions, CLP's *Hearts and Hands* kindergarten workbook, and A Beka's kindergarten science text with teacher' manual.

Now you can order books online, and registered CLASS families can also use the online message boards at the CLASS web site to connect with other parents and students, or get tutorial help. The web site also has a nice set of links to other educational sites of interest—this free educational assistance is always appreciated!

A new **Composition Evaluation service** is now offered. For $18 you receive composition evaluation materials, which are then returned to CLASS with the student's work to be evaluated. CLASS will then send you the evaluation, with suggestions for improvement.

One unexpected note: though CLASS is situated in the North, and Dr. Lindstrom is a Northerner, their current curriculum features not only the life of George Washington (grade 9) and Union general George McClellan (grade 10), but also the lives of Southern soldiers J.E.B. Stuart (in grade 7), Stonewall Jackson (grade 8), and Robert E. Lee (grade 11). Some of their readers also are sympathetic to the lost Southern cause: not restoration of slavery, of course, but the restoration of Constitutional limits on government, which was widely presented to the South's own people as a major reason for fighting.

Of particular note: CLP has revised the previously-liberal *Streams of Civilization* series, and added historical charts, answer keys, and test packets. The resulting courses, used in grades 9 and 10, are about the strongest world history courses currently available from a Christian viewpoint. Their civics text, *The Land of Fair Play*, is another unique, quality resource.

Streams of Civilization Volume 1

Streams of Civilization Volume 2

UPDATED!
Christian Light Education

Grades K–12. Homeschool Plus Program tuition: first year, $100 (U.S.) $115 (outside U.S.) plus $5 for each student; subsequent years, $75 plus $5 for each student. Incentives: $10 off for completing training, $10 off if reports are in office by the 10th of each month and $10 off if you renew

Note: an **Adventures in Phonics kit** and an **Advanced Reading program** are both available separately. The first includes all the phonics components of the grade K kit, plus a few extra books for the parents, while the second is a remedial program intended for those who need help filling in the gaps.

Grades 1–3 continue phonics instruction. In first grade, it's Level B of CLP's Adventures in Phonics. Grades 2 and 3 switch to Modern Curriculum Press phonics workbooks.

In math, it's Modern Curriculum Press for grades 1–6, switching to Saxon Math in grade 7. CLP's own Bible series is used in grades K–7; CLP's spelling series is used in grades 1–8; CLP's handwriting series is used in grades K–4; and CLP's Nature Reader series is used in grades 1–5. Language arts other than handwriting and phonics are covered via A Beka texts from grades 2–6, and CLP's new Applications of Grammar series in grades 7–12. Science is mostly taught with A Beka texts, plus CLP answer keys and test packets. The exceptions: CLP's *Exploring God's Creation* is the science text for grade 2 and BJUP's physics book is the text for grade 12. CLP materials are used for history, except for grades 6, 7, and 10. A Beka texts are used for those years.

The **junior- and senior-high years** feature the science, math, and history courses already mentioned, plus a literature course each year and a historical biography each year. In addition, there is a large emphasis on Bible study, catechism, economics, Constitutional government, art, and music in the upper grades.

Please note that grade 11 and 12 students will need to add math and science courses. CLP does carry the A Beka chemistry text, and BJUP Physics text and teacher's manual, but from my experience you'll also want the answer keys and lab books (which CLP doesn't offer) to teach these courses properly.

High-school electives are Consumer Math, Algebra II, Geometry, Trigonometry, Advanced Math, Pre-Calculus, Calculus, Physical Science, Chemistry, Physics, Creation Science, German I, French I and II, Latin I and II, Spanish I and II, Advanced Theology, Christian Conduct, Family Life, Philosophy, Sewing, Cooking, Auto Mechanics, Typing I and II, Personal Typing, Shorthand, Basic Computer Studies, Woodworking, College Vocabulary, Creative Writing, Speech, and Constitutional Law. For some reason these are not listed in the catalog; I found them on the web site.

CLASS doesn't have tons of "living books" for your student to read, like Sonlight. They don't include all the school supplies, like Calvert. Their science courses don't include lab supplies, like University of Nebraska-Lincoln. But considering that their *most* expensive option costs about half of what the average homeschool family spends per child per year, you could easily take some of those savings, hop down to the bookstore and teacher's store, and add enough supplemental material to wow all the other parents. Or you could just hang onto the extra money, and use these courses for what they are: one of the most streamlined, inexpensive ways available to train your child up in a biblical worldview. *Mary Pride*

Christian Light Education was established in 1979 as a part of the ministry of Christian Light Publications, a provider of school materials to the conservative wing of the Mennonite community. Their materials emphasize a literal understanding and practical application of the Scriptures. Their "Lightunit" worktexts are based on their own revision of Alpha Omega's original worktexts. Like Alpha Omega's, these come in sets of 10 worktexts per subject per grade. The Christian Light worktexts have sturdy kivar-like paper covers and colored ink within. As revised, their curriculum is more down-to-earth.

Mennonites are followers of Menno Simons, a sixteenth-century religious leader who practiced believers' baptism, nonresistance, and unworldliness. The main differences you will note are (1) Mennonite dress—little girls in pigtails and women with head coverings (they call these "veilings"), (2) an emphasis on diligence and obedience, as opposed to "you are so special" self-esteem teaching, and (3) real-world outlook: no fantasy elements.

Your ordering options:

- **Homeschool Plus Program**—pay a fee every year and you get training by mail or at a CLE training center for one parent, plus phone and mail assistance, diagnostic testing, record-keeping, transcripts, California Achievement Test, and diplomas on completion of grade 8 and high school. To maintain the full program, you have to pay a fee each subsequent year. Curriculum costs are extra. Over 1,000 families are currently enrolled with this option.
- **Training Without Services**—just what the name implies; pay a smaller fee to get training program by mail or at a CLE center for one parent, and nothing else. Curriculum costs are extra. Relatively few sign up with this option.
- **Curriculum and materials**—you may buy full grades, full subjects, or individual books—everything except the CAT tests. This used to be the most popular option, but more and more families are switching to the Full Program option.

Grades 1–8 have as their major subjects Bible, language arts, math, science, and social studies. First grade starts off gently with Learning to Read, math, and Bible. Once the child has made a start on reading, the language arts, social studies, and science Lightunits are introduced. Grade 2 has an additional Reading course, to tamp down this area.

Christian Light's reading program

Answer keys, including teaching instructions, are available for every Lightunit. They are easy to follow, as are the worktexts. Students who can read well can do most work without much adult intervention.

Christian Light's own textbooks include the new first-grade reader, *I Wonder,* second grade readers, *Helping Hands* and *Happy Hearts,* the third-

next year within 10 business days of your school year end. Curriculum is additional as follows: Lightunit subject sets, $22.90 each (4 or 5 sets/grade); answer keys: $5.95 if answers are in the teacher key; $22.90 for grades 1–3 or $11.95 for other grades if not. Supplementary items, language arts textbook-based courses for grades 9/10/12, and high school electives are extra.Shipping extra. *Christian Light Education, PO Box 1212, Harrisonburg, VA 22801. (540) 434-1003. Fax: (540) 433-8896. Email: orders@clp.org. Web: www.clp.org.*

With the Homeschool Plus Program, you can now define your own school year! Start anytime, not just in September.

One unusual feature: like other Mennonite publishers, Christian Light puts a good deal of emphasis in the early grades on learning diacritical markings (those funny little symbols you see above vowels in the dictionary). This stems from their roots in the Mennonite community, where traditionally many children spoke German at home and only learned English in school. Hence, the emphasis on proper pronunciation of English words. In the past, they used a non-standard diacritical marking. Their newly revised Learning to Read and language arts courses will employ a diacritical marking system almost identical to the Merriam Webster system.

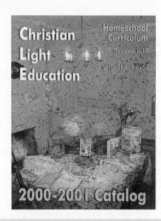

The large CLE catalog also includes Bible study helps galore, books on Anabaptist doctrine, Christian biographies, church history, children's true-to-life fiction, poetry, music, tracts, maps, Sunday school supplies, dozens of teacher's helps, preschool workbooks, handwriting materials, materials for teaching music, foreign-language materials, and much, much more, including science supplies to accompany their science curriculum.

Coming soon: a series of readers for grades 1–8. As of this writing, grades 1–3 are available. One new reader should be added per year, starting with grade 4 in fall 2000.

Also under development: CLE's own new curriculum, the "Sunrise Edition." This brand new program, written from scratch, will replace the current Alpha Omega-based curriculum. The new materials will still be called "Lightunits," but their content will be different. Levels 100 and 200 (grades 1 and 2) are available now. The production schedule calls for adding a grade level per year after that. It will include beefed-up language arts, with a strong creative-writing emphasis. Continuous review will reinforce skills taught in earlier lessons. A separate teacher's guidebook will contain the answer keys. The student worktexts will be two-color and graphically inviting. Your overall curriculum costs will actually be a little lower, and you won't have to keep track of all those slippery little answer keys.

grade social-studies text *Living Together,* the fourth-grade social-studies text *Into All the World* (recently revised to reflect the break-up of the Soviet Union and other geopolitical changes), fifth-grade science (*God's Marvelous Gifts*) and social studies (*North America is the Lord's*), sixth-grade social studies (*God's World—His Story*) and the hardbound *Perspectives of Life in Literature* and *Perspectives of Truth in Literature* (intended for grade 9/10 and 12, respectively). All these reflect CLE's nonresistant and pietistic outlook.

Christian Light has two types of **high-school electives**: Lightunit electives, and textbook-based electives. The latter mostly employ texts from other publishers. Lightunit electives are Home Ec I (follow-up units on making a veiling and a cape dress are available), Spanish I, Consumer Math, Greek I, Art, and the new Computer Literacy course. We were impressed by the Computer Literacy elective, which costs only $13.50, *including* the answer key. The price is especially low because it only has five Lightunits; the others have 10 each. The Computer Literacy course introduces computer history and design, binary and hex, basic programming techniques, and does a fine job of introducing the student to word processing, spreadsheets, and databases.

Textbook-based electives are Accounting, Agriculture, Basic Automotive Service and Systems, Beginning Woodworking, Carpentry, Christian Ethics, Computer Applications, Electricity, English Literature, English half-credit courses covering grammar and usage for use in grades 7/8, 9/10, and 11/12, Keyboarding/Formatting/Document Processing, Music in Biblical Perspective, Practical Math, Home Repair and Maintenance, Practical Recordkeeping, and Small Gasoline Engines.

CLE's **high-school program** is highly regarded. Many students report high grades on the SAT and ACT college exams. A number have won scholarships. Among the many colleges that have accepted CLE graduates are Vincennes University, Victory Valley College, Southeastern College of

Lakeland, Fl, Liberty University, Anderson College, Asbury College, Ball State University, University of Louisville (KY), University of Southwestern Louisiana, Muskingham College, Kent State University, William Penn College, Pensacola Christian College, University of Indiana (Ft. Wayne), University of Texas (El Paso), Taylor University, John Wesley College, Indiana University, Masters College, Ohio State University, Perdue University, Virginia Military Academy, and the University of Beijing.

Many non-Mennonite families looking for a wholesome, inexpensive curriculum report enjoying Christian Light. More than 80 percent of their current users are non-Mennonites, representing a cross-section of over 40 denominations and even a few non-Christians as well. *Mary Pride*

Established originally in 1909 as "Fireside Correspondence School," a service to Seventh-day Adventists, **Home Study International** has served more than 300,000 students from over 60 countries with their home study programs for preschool through high school. In academic year 1999-2000, about 3,000 students were enrolled. The staff consists entirely of certified teachers, many of whom have a Master's or Ph.D. The program is accredited or approved by a number of organizations, including the Distance Education and Training Council, the International Council for Distance Education, and the Maryland State Department of Education.

Materials used include a number of Seventh-day Adventist (S.D.A.) texts as well as some standard public school texts. Most books are up-to-date. In early grades, HSI has its own adapted version of the Ginn 720-Rainbow readers. All the S.D.A. texts I saw were professionally done and colorful.

HSI's own materials are conservative and pro-family, as are the materials they employ from S.D.A. publishing houses such as Pacific Press Publishing Association and Reform & Herald. Some of the public school texts HSI uses are less so. These include books from Addison Wesley, D. C. Heath, Glencoe Publishing, Harcourt Brace Jovanovich, Merrill, Prentice Hall, Silver Burdett & Ginn, Scott Foresman, and Simon & Schuster.

Religiously, HSI is creationist and evangelistic. Some Christian books are used and the Bible is taught. Seventh-day Adventists believe that their founder, Ellen White, was a prophet of God, and her writings are quoted in some Bible and Health sections of the curriculum, as well as occasionally in the Parents' Guides.

I'd better explain how the pricing options work before I go any further. Basically, for grades K–6, you have your choice of an "accredited" or "non-accredited" program. The **"accredited" option** requires both tuition and supplies, and includes interaction with HSI staff. They will answer your questions, grade some student work, keep records, issue report cards and diplomas, and verify upon request that your child is enrolled in a Maryland state-approved and accredited curriculum. The **"non-accredited" option** provides you with the "supplies" (HSI lingo for the curriculum materials), and you do all the record-keeping and grading yourself. However, since the course syllabi and parent's materials are included in the tuition, the additional supply cost for the accredited program is *less* than the supply cost of the non-accredited program. So, for example, the grade 2 tuition of $349 plus the accredited supplies cost of $360 = $709 total cost for the accredited second grade program. Compare this to the "supplies only" cost of $509 for the non-accredited program, and you see that the total cost to you of HSI's advisory and record-keeping services is $200 for grade 2.

You don't need to purchase an entire grade, though. You can purchase just the individual subjects you want, and for each subject choose "accredited" or "non-accredited." For that matter, you can even purchase just the individual *books* you want. Talk about flexible!

UPDATED!
Home Study International
Grades preK–12. Preschool, $53. Tuition prices (only apply to accredited programs): K, $120; grade 1, $340; grades 2–6, $360/year; grades 7 and 8, $68/semester course; grades 9–12, $145/semester course. Supplies cost by grade: K, $194 for accredited/$265 for non-accredited; grade 1, $390/$576; grade 2, $349/$509; grade 3, $323/$522; grade 4, $332/$504; grade 5, $357/$535 or $573 (depending on whether student purchases microscope); grade 6, $341/$510; grade 7, $342/$865; grade 8, $320/$836. Grades 7–12 enrollment fee, $60. High school supplies vary by course, from $19–$229. Excellent catalog lists all materials used in each grade. Parents only purchase items they lack. Used books can be sold back to HSI for up to 50% of purchase price. Interest-free installment plan available. Shipping extra. *Home Study International, PO Box 4437, Silver Spring, MD 20914-4437. (800) 782-4769. Fax: (301) 680-6577. Email. 74617.74@compuserve.com. Web: www.hsi.edu.*

This is a standard, structured, school-at-home program. Young students are taught by their parents; older students are expected to work directly with the HSI staff under their parents' guidance. This means that the "non-accredited" option is *not* available for high schoolers, although it has recently become available for junior-high students in grades 7 and 8.

The HSI **preschool** readiness program includes music (three *Wee Sing* book/cassette combos come with it), lots of simple arts and crafts activities, nature awareness, physical education, math readiness, and more. Laid out as a series of eight four-week units, with daily lessons, its notable features include an emphasis on teaching manners and empathy, the usage of correct scientific terminology (e.g., *thorax, mammals,* and *veterinarian* rather than *middle section, hairy animals,* and *animal doctor*). Unlike other preschool programs, this one doesn't have extensive weekly library suggestions—just a book or two at a time. The accompanying *Preschool Handbook for Parents* includes general information about teaching and child development. Like all HSI's programs, this includes optional Christian and Adventist teaching.

Elementary students are graded beginning in kindergarten. Subjects include art and music, health/science, language arts, math, physical education (grades 3-6), reading, social studies, spelling, and handwriting. To accommodate their non-SDA and non-Christian customers, Bible is an optional, separate subject. It is included in the basic grade-level price, but you can order a grade without it.

HSI's grades 1 and 2 emphasizes on back-to-basics problem-solving, using Harcourt Brace Jovanovich's *Mathematics Today.* Grades 3-6 math is the "new math" and reading is only partly phonetic.

The handwriting curriculum is Concerned Communications', and is Christian in tone. Health/science, language arts, and social studies use secular texts, while the reading program is from an S.D.A. publisher. The spelling curriculum is HSI's own, as are the art/music/P.E. modules.

HSI's **upper grades** cover fewer subjects and use fewer books, but still require a lot of work. Students of high-school chemistry, for example, are expected to spend seven to ten hours a week on that one subject.

Art, music, grammar, spelling, and handwriting are no longer included in the grade-level packets for grade 7 and up. An additional Elementary Keyboarding course is recommended for junior-high students.

There are no high-school grade-level packets at all. Rather, you select the units desired from the following list: Bookkeeping and Accounting, Typing, Word Processing for DOS (using WordPerfect 5.0/5.1), Word Processing for Windows (using WordPerfect 8.0), English I and II, American Literature, English Literature, Structure of Writing, Adventist Literature, Art History, Music Appreciation, Health, Home Planning, Clothing Construction, Foods, World History, American History, American Government, Geography, French I, Spanish I–III, Consumer Math, Pre-Algebra, Algebra I and II, Geometry, The Bridge: Bible for High School Students, Bible I–IV, Biology, Chemistry, Earth Science, and Physics. The catalog offers suggested courses of study for a basic diploma and a college-preparatory diploma.

HSI has some terrific ideas that others would do well to emulate. Example: Professionally-drawn Bible Activity Sheets printed on card stock enable young learners to make projects like an Ark (with animals!) that look great and will really hold together. Example: The health curriculum teaches survival and first aid skills. Example: Like University of Nebraska-Lincoln, HSI provides a lab kit so upper-grades science students can do *real* experiments (although you do have to purchase the chemicals somewhere else).

What's more, they offer distance-education college courses too. I don't know much about this option of theirs yet, but it certainly can't hurt to request their college brochure.

HSI will appeal most to families who prefer modern educational methods and who appreciate HSI's professional materials and consistent Adventist flavor. *Mary Pride*

HSI's Parents' Guides are *great.* Most lessons include stated objectives and list materials needed to do the assignment. Upper-grades lessons consist of a "commentary" section intended to substitute for the normal classroom lecture followed by assigned exercises. Guides directed to the student himself are written in a breezy style, while those addressed to parents are more serious in tone.

Samuel Blumenfeld fans, wake up! Now you can get an entire basics curriculum built on Sam's years of tutoring experience.

Mr. Blumenfeld, whose book *Is Public Education Necessary?* has been a homeschool classic for years, and whose Blumenfeld Alpha-Phonics Kit is a homeschool staple, is also very popular as the author of *How to Tutor*, a book which explains in streamlined detail how to teach the 3 Rs.

The **How to Tutor Curriculum** includes the book (reviewed in Volume 2), plus all the following:

- *Extra Large Type Student Lesson Book.* Created in response to popular demand, this 175-page, spiral-bound book accompanies the textbook lesson by lesson.
- *How to Tutor Reading Pronunciation Audio Tape* with 60 minutes of training on the precise phonics sounds for each alphabet letter and phonogram. If you have not been trained in phonics yourself, or if English is your second language, this tape is invaluable.
- *Mrs. Barbara's How to Tutor Phonics Reading Companion Workbook.* Extra exercises in writing words and sentences. Designed to complement the How to Tutor lessons.
- *How to Tutor Companion Readers.* A set of 10 little phonetic readers. Simple art. Designed to follow a typical intensive phonics instruction sequence (as taught in *How to Tutor*), so you start with the *Short A Vowel Reader*, followed by the *Short E Vowel Reader*, etc.
- *Mrs. Barbara's How to Tutor Cursive Writing Practice Book.* 40 pages of traditional cursive instruction, again paralleling the instructions in *How to Tutor*.
- *How to Tutor Arithmetic Workbooks.* These include all the math exercises in *How to Tutor*, plus timed tests for arithmetic facts, with suggested times for completion, and a few new exercises for beginning fractions. Inexpensive comb-bound workbook format. *Addition/Subtraction Workbook* is 89 pages; *Multiplication/Division/Fractions/Decimal Workbook* is 110 pages.
- *PhonicsTutor CD-ROM.* Rated five hearts in *Practical Homeschooling* magazine, our highest rating, this no-frills program includes all the lessons found in Sam Blumenfeld's Alpha-Phonics book, plus human-voice reading of letters and sounds and student exercises that ensure understanding. Teaches and tests over 3,500 words. Available for Win or Mac systems—your choice. Also sold directly by its publisher, 4:20 Communications, 888-420-7323, www.phonicstutor.com. For the skeptical, a demo disk is available, or you can download a demo from the Web.

This is probably the most simplified back-to-basics no-fooling-around curriculum you can get. It will teach your child to read, to write in cursive (Mr. Blumenfeld believes in skipping manuscript writing altogether), and math up through the sixth-grade level. It doesn't include any history, geog-

NEW!
How to Tutor Curriculum

Grades K–6 and remedial students. Complete set, includes all items following except demo disk, $199.95. How to Tutor book, $24.95. Extra Large Size Type Student Lesson Book, $19.95. Reading Pronunciation Audio Tape, $5. Phonics Reading Companion Workbook, $14.95. Companion Readers, $19.95. PhonicsTutor CD-ROM (specify Win or Mac), $90. Cursive Writing Practice Book, $11.95. Math Workbooks, $19.95 each. PhonicsTutor demo disk, not included in complete set, $5 (specify Win or Mac). Add $3 shipping for 1st item, $1 each additional item.
Paradigm Company, Box 45161, Boise, ID 83711. (208) 322-4440 (24-hour, 7-day answering machine). Fax: (208) 322-7781. Web: www.howtotutor.com.

raphy, art, or science. What you *do* get are the tools a child can use to learn all those other subjects . . . and without which, he won't learn a thing.
Mary Pride

Originally launched in 1979 as the Associated Christian Schools curriculum, the renamed and redesigned **Landmark's Freedom Baptist Curriculum** (LFBC) is the most inexpensive Christian worktext curriculum available for homeschoolers today. LFBC uses the King James Version Bible throughout, and is heavier on the Christian doctrine and lighter on the secular academics than other Christian publishers.

Associated Christian Schools was founded by well-known Baptist author Dr. Donald Boys to provide an "educationally sound and biblically true" curriculum for Christian schools. With the help of 54 writers, almost all of whom hold Masters or Doctorates, he produced a complete K–12 program. In 1989 Dr. Boys selected Landmark Baptist Church and College in Haines City, Florida—a church with a day school, college, and radio station—to carry on the curriculum under the Landmark's Freedom Baptist Curriculum label.

Preschool is a K3 program consisting of a teacher's manual and student kit of activities and worksheets. The **Champion program** for five-year-old **kindergartners** uses a strong phonics approach. The teacher kit includes daily lesson plans, their own phonics reader, *McGuffey's Eclectic Primer*, 31 alphabet flash cards, 20 numbers flashcards, a Hundred Chart, 36 Bible memory verse cards (KJV), five phonics chart, 19 "phonogram towers" (large charts showing a "ladder letter" progression for each consonant, e.g., *ba, be, bi, bo, bu*, with the phonograms pictured on a stack of alphabet blocks), and a phonics audiocassette. The student kit includes another copy of their phonics reader and the McGuffey primer, five pads of worksheets (over 700 in all), an ABC Bible Memory Verse chart, 10 number flash cards, a report card, and a diploma.

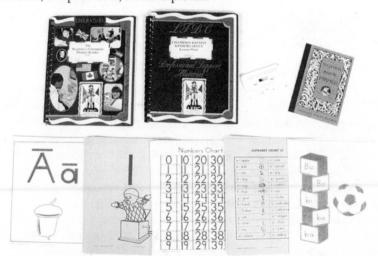

Landmark Freedom Baptist Reading Teacher's Kit

The LFBC program for **grades 1–12** is packaged as "subject sets." Each subject set arrives as a shrink-wrapped package including a a "Studyguide" (a large comb-bound worktext with 36 weeks of daily lessons), an answer key for the Studyguide, weekly quizzes, and answer keys for the quizzes. Subjects sets for grades 4–12 also include quarterly tests with answer keys. There are no "teacher" materials as such, other than the Teacherguide, a single 66-page guide to using LFBC: how to set it up, schedule it, and grade it, plus a set of reusable timed arithmetic tests and sample forms. The

UPDATED!
Landmark's Freedom Baptist Curriculum

K–12. K3/K4 Teacher's Curriculum Manual, $75. K3/K4 Student Kit, $25. Champion Baptist Kindergarten Kit: teacher's kit, $125; student's kit, $75. Options for grades 1–12 follow. Plan A (full services including curriculum): $360 for the first child, $325 each for the second through fourth, $300 for each child thereafter. Plan B (placement testing): $25/student, maximum of $100/family. Plan C (single subject set): $35. Elective subject sets, $25 each except Principles of Music, $35 and Spanish I, $45. Solution guides for Algebra I, Geometry, Algebra II, and Business Math, $25 each. "Teacherguide," $5; free with purchase of four or more subject sets. Sample Pac includes Scope and Sequence plus your choice of samples from two subject sets of your choice (specify subjects and grade levels), $5; add additional subject/grade level samples for $1 each. All options include free continental U.S. shipping.
Landmark's Freedom Baptist Curriculum, 2222 E. Hinson Ave., Haines City, FL 33844. (800) 700-LFBC. Fax: (863) 422-0188. Email: LFBC@juno.com. Web: www.landmarkbaptistchurch.org/lfbc.

LFBC's ordering options are a little complicated, so let me explain. Plan A provides you with recordkeeping services. They will issue report cards, transcripts, and a high-school diploma (when earned). They also provide annual achievement testing They do *not* provide advisory services, grading of papers, and so on. If all you want is *placement* testing (as distinct from *achievement* testing), you need "Plan B." Plan A includes one year's worth of curriculum; Plan B does not. Plan C just means "I order the curriculum I want."

Teacherguide is free when you purchase four or more subject sets, and only $5 otherwise; you definitely should get it if you plan to use this curriculum.

Landmark Freedom Baptist Grade 12

Subjects available are Bible, English, Math, Science, History/Geography (LFBC proudly notes that they do *not* do "social studies"!), and Literature. At a cost of $35 per subject set, and with free shipping included, this comes to $210 for an entire grade level of curriculum.

As a "back to basics" program, LFBC employs a lot of drill, diagramming, and Scripture memory work. Every area is approached from an explicitly Christian perspective. Literature studied is classical and Christian. Composition skills are emphasized.

LFBC curriculum is designed to be as easy as possible for the teacher to use. All the lessons for one week appear in one chapter of the subject's large worktext. This eliminates the need for setting goals or drawing up lesson plans. Everything you study is right there in the workbook; there are no lists of suggested books to read, videos to watch, or web sites to visit. Also, LFBC is "the only publisher of school material that provides weekly quizzes."

The LFBC material is user-friendly. Texts are addressed directly to the student and marked with good humor and wit. Lessons are straightforward and follow each other logically. Although there is some fill-in-the-blank and multiple-choice, especially in the earlier grades, the curriculum is designed to teach students to reason, research, and write out their conclusions. This is not overdone; the length of written answers required is appropriate for each grade level.

The **Bible** sequence is robust. Starting in grade 1, here's what you study year by year: Old Testament Characters, Stories of Israel, New Testament Characters, Miracles of Christ, The Book of Acts, Book-by-Book Bible Survey, Bible Doctrines (from a fundamentalist Baptist viewpoint), The Book of Genesis, The Book of Proverbs, The Local Church, Romans/Corinthians/ Galatians, and The Inspiration of the Scriptures. I particularly appreciate this last course (typically covered in seminary), as this is the kind of worldview preparation Christian kids should be able to expect *before* they go to college.

English is pretty standard, covering grammar, usage, composition, vocabulary, and spelling in grades 1–6. The approach is to teach a different concept every week—e.g., nouns, alphabetizing, abbreviation. There is no incremental review. The last weeks of the course are devoted to a review of all material taught in that course. Weekly spelling lists are in the back of each student worktext. Spelling is no longer taught as a separate subject in grades 7 and 8, which basically cover what you normally learn in those years. The high-school sequence is four years of English Grammar and Composition. Each year requires a formal term paper, plus continuing grammar review and lots of instruction in research and composition.

The **History/Geography** sequence differs from most. Year by year, you get (starting in grade 2), The U.S. Presidents, Great American Heroes, Our Fifty United States, The Beginner's American History, U.S. Geography, World Geography, Introduction to World History, U.S. History, Baptist History (a course you won't find from other publishers), and Culture War/Current Events. In grade 12, the course is one semester each in U.S. Government and Economics. So through grade 6, the student is exclusively studying the United States, while

Landmark Freedom Baptist U.S. Geography

the last three years are devoted to worldview issues from a Baptist point of view.

Math is adequate from a college-prep standpoint, as long as you're not planning to try for a top-tier college or a career (other than business) that requires a lot of science or math. The high-school math sequence is Algebra I, Geometry, Algebra II, and Business Math. Complete subject sets include answer keys. Additionally, each of these courses has a "Solutionguide" that can be purchased separately in which the problems are worked out in detail.

Science again concentrates more on developing a Christian worldview than on passing secular standardized tests. The elementary-school sequence is devotional, but generic; many Christian publishers cover creation, nature, and facts about the earth. Unusual is the grade 5 course, Beginner's Physiology and Health. The middle-school science covers the normal topics. However, after the expected first two high-school years of Physical Science and Biology, grade 11 features one semester each in Health and Dynamic Biblical Living, while grade 12 is devoted to a study of scientific creationism. The only course that has suggested lab experiments is Physical Science in grade 9 (you'll have to purchase the equipment and supplies separately). All other middle and upper grades require you to write weekly reports on the subject studied that week.

Landmark Freedom Baptist Health

The **Literature** sequence is the least appealing. Children read and study selections embedded in the worktext, rather than entire separate books. While the stories, poems, and essays selected are classics, this falls far short of the amount of reading you can expect from a homeschooled child. The grade 12 literature course, for example, would be more appropriately titled "Source Readings in American History." Also, the practice of having children write out definitions of vocabulary words and answer comprehension questions about the material is often a waste of time. This can all be done verbally. On the positive side, the essay ques-

Here's something to think about. Even if you plan to use another curriculum, you might want to consider LFBC's Bible courses. They are inexpensive, ultra easy to use, and easy to add onto any other program you might be using. This might be a particularly helpful option if you are a Christian who shares LFBC's views, but who has chosen a secular curriculum.

tions are generally good, requiring the student to think about a topic raised by the literature selection.

Electives available are Penmanship, Principles of Music (2 semesters), Home Economics (2 semesters), Shop, and Personal Development for Young Ladies. All of these are designed to take two semesters, except Shop and Personal Development, which each take one semester.

Brand new or revised by LFBC since the last edition of this book:

- The K5 Champion Baptist Kindergarten mentioned above
- Bible grade 1 (Old Testament Characters), grade 10 (The Local Church), and grade 12 (The Inspiration of the Scriptures)
- History grade 2 (The U.S. Presidents), grade 6 (U.S. Geography), grade 8 (World History), grade 9 (U.S. History), Culture Wars/Current Issues, and Government/Economics
- Science grade 1 (God's Wonderful Creation), grade 2 (Nature Science), and grade 11 (Health/Dynamic Biblical Living)
- English grade 1
- Elementary elective: Penmanship (cursive handwriting)
- High-school elective: Principles of Music

Dr. Don Boys says "If you are not a Fundamentalist and a political conservative, you probably will not be satisfied with the LFBC Curriculum." If you *are* the above and are looking for a fully-integrated, easy-to-use Christian curriculum that emphasizes straight-arrow morality and Baptist doctrine, check out LFBC. *Mary Pride*

Do you *care* what your child learns? **Rod and Staff**, a large, serious publisher of Mennonite schoolbooks, says, "We do!" This company has been printing Christ-centered textbooks for more than thirty years. As one might expect, their books are very traditional and are filled with pictures of people in Mennonite dress. Home schoolers of all faiths enjoy them—Rod and Staff is one of the most popular homeschool sources.

Rod and Staff strives to incorporate Bible teaching in all subject areas. To them, this means extreme modesty, pacifism of the nonresistant rather than militant sort, and noninvolvement in government. In keeping with Rod and Staff's unworldly outlook, their materials are amazingly inexpensive—all the more impressive because many of their books are hardbound.

Rod and Staff textbooks are academically sound and character-building. No iffy stuff whatever. Subjects include reading, English, math, penmanship, science, spelling, health, social studies, history, and of course, Bible. Supplementary materials are also available for most of the elementary grades.

Rod and Staff describes their educational philosophy as "traditional classroom." This is supposed to include "listening to a teacher and taking oral direction and instruction," "properly directed class discussion," and "subjective-type exercises." By the latter they mean work that is not all multiple-choice,

One other point of note: LFBC promises to ship all orders on the *next business day*. Compared to providers such as Christian Liberty Academy and Calvert, who at busy times of the year can take up to two months and one month respectively to ship your order, this is definitely a point in their favor.

UPDATED!
Rod and Staff Publishers
Grades K–8. K, about $20. Grade 1, $236.30. Grade 2, $221.25. Grade 3, $188.15. Grade 4, $212.60. Grade 5, $204.45. Grade 6, $222.35. Grade 7, $220.80. Grade 8, $183.15.
Rod and Staff Publishers, PO Box 3, Highway 17 2, Crockett, KY 41413-0003. (606) 522-4348. Fax: (800) 643-1244.

Here's a unique feature: Rod and Staff has **Spanish editions** of their readers, phonics materials, and math curriculum for grade 1–3. Many storybooks are also available in Spanish, as are dozens of wholesome, inexpensive, hardbound "life on the farm" type storybooks in English.

but involves some creativity and/or give-and-take between teacher and student. They are not aiming for a Socratic dialog; the picture you should be getting instead is of a wise authority gently guiding a submissive student.

Straight-arrow seriousness does not deprive the Rod and Staffers of wit. My son and I had a happy five minutes giggling over this exercise from one of their books:

> Q: You have to work after school and do not have much time to play. (pick one)
> a. Be thankful you can work and help at home.
> b. Be thankful you do not like to work.
> c. Be thankful you know how to grumble a lot and show your mother how much you hate to work. (!!!!)

Rod and Staff is a publisher, not a correspondence school. However, their teacher's manuals are designed to assist the inexperienced. Thousands of homeschool families across the country are using these books successfully—even more so when they are smart enough to skip the occasional busywork and group activities. (After all, the books *were* originally written for classroom use!)

About those teacher's manuals. Many contain reduced copies of the student text, with answers shown. This is very handy for following along with your child while he works. Full teaching instructions, based on years of classroom experience, are also included.

For preschool, Rod and Staff offers their **Preschool A-B-C** series. This set of workbooks is reviewed in Volume 2.

Rod and Staff's "Readers" are a treat. Their **Bible Nurture readers** for grades 1–4, which consist solely of Bible stories told in simple language with no added flights of fancy, are great. Readers for grades 5–8 contain more broad-based, though still very pious, literature. A ninth-grade reader is also in the works. Workbooks and phonics workbooks are also available, correlated with the readers, for grades 1 and 2. You will be better off, in my opinion, with a regular standalone phonics program, using the readers for reading practice and also for the Bible teaching and character lessons they include.

Grades 1–7 of Rod and Staff's **Mathematics for Christian Living** series have received major revisions since the last edition of *The Big Book*. Whereas the old books were hard for many young children, requiring intense memory work and long periods of concentration, the new versions are much more child-friendly. Grade 1, for example, now comes with flash cards and a small tablet of 72 speed drills. Each lesson is on a single tear-out sheet and the work goes at a much more realistic pace. Math is also available for grades 7 and 8, from a much more real-world perspective than other publishers' math courses.

Grades 3–8 of their **Building Christian English** series has also been revised for easier teaching, and there are new books for grade 8 and (soon) 9. This is a classic grammar and composition curriculum, with concepts continually reviewed and chapter tests built in.

Penmanship is intended to be practiced at all grade levels; however, you'll only find actual teaching materials for grades 1–4. In grade 1, instruction in printing moves from the basic strokes, to letters and numerals formed by similar strokes, to capital letters. Grade 2 reviews manuscript printing and then introduces cursive. Grades 3 and 4 then provide review and practice. The cursive studied is traditional, with capital letters that often differ significantly from manuscript capitals.

The new **Spelling by Sound and Structure program** for grades 2–7 includes phonics rules (the "sound" part in the name) and word roots from

One Rod and Staff distinctive which causes some trouble is their somewhat unique choice of diacritical marks. Unlike typical curricula, which mainly stress short and long vowel sounds, Rod and Staff spends a lot of time teaching a complete set of diacritical marks covering even slight variations in sound. This approach is common to many Amish and Mennonite groups in which children speak German at home and learn English at school. The typical American child does not need to learn this material, which I recommend you skip.

Latin, Greek, French, and other languages (this is the "structure" part). Each book has 34 weekly lessons.

The **Christian Music** series for grades 1–8 teaches sight reading and *a capella* singing. You will definitely need the teacher's guides and flash cards for this program. Currently the eighth-grade text is under development.

The **Science and Nature** series for grades 2–9 is particularly nice. Wisely beginning with learning to identify natural objects such as trees and mammals, it progresses to basic science facts and simple experiments. There is not a separate text for every grade: instead, rather confusingly, the work entitled *God's Marvelous Works* is split into two books, one each for grade 4 and 5, and *Investigating God's Orderly World*, again split into two books, is suggested for use as a general science course in grades 7–10. *Discovering God's Stars,* a book on basic stars and constellations, can be slipped into grade 7 or 8 (or really, just about anywhere). In the meantime, there is no grade 6 science text, although one is being developed.

Health is a separate course, with one workbook for grade 2 and another to be used in both grades 4 and 5.

Social Studies starts very simply. In grade 2, the workbook *Our Father's World* introduces basic geography lingo—*lake, river, city*—and basic geographical features, as well as globes and maps. Also included are stories about children around the world. Grade 3, *Understanding Our Community,* introduces community organizations, from the church and hospital to the police and library. This is not quite the same "community helpers" approach you see in secular texts, as the context here is not exploring future careers and the doctrine is that Christians should not *be* politicians or policemen! Grade 4, *Homelands Around the World,* covers "the world's geography, cultures, and wildlife." For map work, students fill out blank outline maps, found in the back of their textbook. Grade 5, *Homelands of North America,* covers the history of the USA and Canada, plus more map activities. Grade 6, *Understanding Latin America: A Christian Perspective,* covers the geography and history of that region of the world. Grade 7, *Creation to Canaan,* is a history of the ancient world. Additional history/geography texts are being written as well.

For **art**, Rod and Staff now offers the popular Art with a Purpose program. See review in Volume 2.

Additional teacher helps, from weekly lesson plan books, to books about teaching, to maps of all kinds, are also available.

What you get is solid educational value with a very different outlook from the fun, games, and freneticism common in educational materials today. If any curriculum can teach kids patience, gentleness, and all-around goodness, this is the one. *Mary Pride*

NEW!
School of Tomorrow

Grades K–12. Complete curriculum kits (price with answer keys/price without keys): Preschool with Ace and Christi Kit, $325.60; PACEs for additional student, $117.60. ABCs with Ace and Christi: complete kit, $244.50; 11-week program kit, $145.60; PACEs for additional student, $43.20; other items for additional student, $10. Videophonics Kit, $260. Speaking English with

Ace and Christi, $199.95. English as Your Second Language kit, $250. Grade 1, $384 for complete kit with keys/$192 for complete kit with no teacher keys; Grade 2, $435.20/$230.40; Grade 3, $435.20/$230.40; Grade 4, $307.20/$230.40; Grade 5, $288/$216; Grade 6, $288, $216; Grade 7, $259.20/$194.40; Grade 8, $320/$240; Grade 9, $352/$240; Grade 10, $243.20/$182.40; Grade 11, $243.20/$182.40; Grade 12, $179.20/$134.40. Video series, $450 or $550 each. Videos can be rented for about 1/2 the purchase price. Most high school electives, $48 each plus $8–$16 for keys. Most college courses, $40 each plus $8 for keys. Enhancements, resource books, and literature available separately. Significant discounts available for complete grade level purchases. Shipping extra.
School of Tomorrow, PO Box 299000, Lewisville, TX 75029-9000. (800) 925-7777. Fax: (972) 315-2862.
Email: info@schooloftomorrow.com.
Web: www.schooloftomorrow.com.

Ease of use. Patriotic and creationist Christian content. Inexpensive. Many courses also available in Spanish. If this is what you're looking for, this is what you've got.

School of Tomorrow materials were originally invented to make it possible for parents to quickly and simply set up a church-sponsored school. Realizing that most parents are not professionally trained educators, from the beginning this K–12 curriculum was designed for children to work independently, with little to no lesson preparation or presentation by the parents. What resulted was originally called the "Accelerated Christian Education" curriculum. Each course was designed as a sequence of 12 black-and-white worktexts, called PACES, which children would complete in a school year. Parent volunteers and paid staff would act as monitors and supervisors, making sure that children, who worked in individual "carrels," did their work.

As originally conceived, the ACE curriculum was heavily criticized. Critics claimed students could just skim the reading sections of the worktexts to answer the quiz questions, without ever actually learning anything. They also objected to the image of children sitting alone all day filling out worksheets, and to the lack of rich and varied instruction material.

The people at ACE took all these criticisms to heart, and have worked very hard over the last decade at upgrading and improving their curriculum. Their name change to "School of Tomorrow" was not just a marketing maneuver; it reflected an underlying change in the entire educational philosophy of this curriculum. Rising from its humble roots, School of Tomorrow now has some of the most cutting-edge, high-quality materials available for homeschoolers today.

Today, almost all School of Tomorrow curriculum is printed in full color. While the PACE worktext format is still used, the content is a lot richer, and a variety of videos and computer software is available to supplement many of their courses. Literature and creative writing has been added to the curriculum; many courses now come with reference books, literature, audiocassettes, or other helps; and a wide variety of high-school and college electives are available.

Let's start at the beginning. Readiness is introduced via a kit called **Preschool with Ace and Christi**. This comes with four manuals of daily lesson plans, 60 PACEs loaded with typical readiness activities, a coordination development test, flashcards, progress reports, stars and stickers, and a song tape. This is followed by **ABCs with Ace and Christi**, where the cartoon "Ace" and "Christi" characters introduce your child to animal friends whose name begins with each alphabet sound. The ABCs course comes with 12 "Word Building" PACEs and three Math PACEs, plus flashcards, 36 tactile/kinetic cards (for "feeling" alphabet letter and numbers), two lesson-plan manuals, a song tape, and more. Supplemental materials available for the ABCs course include a math kit with flashcards and manipulatives; play money; coloring book and worksheets; and more.

Another way to learn reading is School of Tomorrow's **Videophonics** reading program. This is primarily a "second chance" reading program targeted at older teens and adults, who have been unsuccessful with other methods. It comes with a video introducing the program, 12 Videophonics lesson videos, 12 Skill-Pack workbooks, and six audiocassettes.

The **elementary** courses are still about the easiest available, for both parent and student. They start off slowly, and correct answers can still often be found by scanning the text. However, questions that require the student to think, rather than just "regurgitate" the answer, are employed frequently in the upper elementary grades and up.

School of Tomorrow's elementary and junior-high courses are set up just a bit differently than the typical school's. The subjects are

- **Math**: traditional although rather slow-starting coverage of math fact normally taught at each school grade
- **English**: mostly grammar and usage, plus some creative writing, alphabetizing, dictionary work, and other traditional language-arts topics
- **Social Studies**: mostly "social" studies plus church and Bible history, rather than traditional history and geography. School of Tomorrow is adding a new program, Map Mania, to fifth grade social studies.
- **Science**: creationist in outlook, with some simple experiments and activities built in, covering topics typical for each grade level
- **Word Building**: spelling, vocabulary, and etymology; School of Tomorrow's CD-ROMs featuring human voices reading the spelling and vocabulary words can be used for effective testing in this subject

Many courses require additional reference books or literature, all of which are available from School of Tomorrow. These books are well chosen to complement their subjects, and add a lot to the educational value of the courses.

Bible content and character development are integrated into every course School of Tomorrow offers, with one specific character trait presented in every PACE and the same 60 positive character traits studied every year.

Separate courses in Bible Reading are also available for grades 1–4. Literature and Creative Writing is available for grades 2–4. A separate Animal Science course is also available for grade 2. Finally, the entire Choose Art program is available for grades 2–7.

At the **high-school** level, you'll find the following:

- **Math.** Algebra I, Geometry, Algebra II. For more advanced math study, you can take School of Tomorrow's college course Mathematics II (precalculus).
- **English.** A typical four-year sequence, culminating in one year each of American and English literature

Extremely important note: Grades 1–6 of Math, Social Studies, and Science are available in **Spanish editions**, as are grades 1 and 2 of Word Building, the ABCs with Ace and Christi, and the Cursive Handwriting program. I have received a *lot* of requests for Spanish homeschooling materials over the years. Hopefully, these courses will help to fill that gap. An English as a Second Language course is also available.

In case you're interested, the character traits studied are *appreciative, attentive, available, committed, compassionate, concerned, confident, considerate, consistent, content, cooperative, courageous, creative, decisive, deferential, dependable, determined, diligent, discerning, discreet, efficient, equitable, fair, faithful, fearless, flexible, forgiving, friendly, generous, gentle, honest, humble, joyful, kind, loyal, meek, merciful, observant, optimistic, patient, peaceful, persevering, punctual, purposeful, resourceful, respectful, responsible, secure, self-controlled, sincere, submissive, tactful, temperate, thorough, thrifty, tolerant, truthful,* and *virtuous.*

College-level courses available for three credits each through the Calvary College extension school are Greek I and II, Old Testament Survey, Biographies of Christians, Introduction to Christian Counseling, English Composition I and II, Math II (precalculus), Bible and Science, Introduction to Physical Science, Introduction to Geography, and History of Civilization I and II. I imagine there would be no objection to qualified high-school students taking one or more of these courses. The School of Tomorrow catalog says you can earn a Liberal Arts Studies Certificate for 64 credits (about 2 years of study), or an Associate in Christian Education Certificate or Associate in Biblical Studies Certificate for 90 credits. My guess is that these credits would not transfer well to much of anywhere except a Bible college, but they would do fine as advanced high-school electives if your student has a particular interest in one of these subject areas.

- **Social Studies.** World Geography, World History, American History, and one semester each of U.S. Civics and Economics
- **Science.** Physical Science, Biology, Chemistry, and Physics. These courses all have excellent accompanying video series (24 videos each). Each of these courses includes a lot of science history as well as the concepts, nomenclature, and math. Labs are included on the videos.
- **Word Building.**
- **Bible electives.** Christian Growth, Introduction to Missions (this one is particularly good, with a fine mix of books, work-texts, and videos), Life of Christ, New Testament Church History, New Testament Survey, Old Testament Survey, Soulwinning
- **Business electives.** Accounting, Business Math, Computer Literacy, Economics, General Business, Typing
- **Fine Arts electives.** Beginning Art, Advanced Art, Brush Art, Basic Literature 9, Literature I and II, Music, Speech
- **Government electives.** American Government, Collectivism, The Constitution
- **Health elective.**
- **Language electives.** French I (you'll need the required cassettes), and Spanish I (videos are required)

Typically, a student will start by taking School of Tomorrow's diagnostic tests—one per subject. Diagnostic tests are available on paper or on CD-ROM. The program on the CD-ROM automatically grades and evaluates the tests. The test will tell you what grade level to start at, as well as identifying "gaps" in previous grade levels. You then start by filling in the gaps, if any, before progressing to a regular grade level. For achievement testing, the California Achievement Tests are available

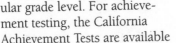
School of Tomorrow Missions elective

for grades K–12, as are the combined California Achievement Test/Test of Cognitive Skills (grades 2–12 only).

Online ordering and customer service is available. We'd like to see on-line message boards for School of Tomorrow students and parents. Since other homeschool curriculum companies offer this service, School of Tomorrow should eventually follow suit.

With all the free time this curriculum provides parents, you'll have plenty of time to think of library books, field trips, hands-on projects, software, and videos to supplement your child's studies. Consider purchasing a quality print or software encyclopedia to follow up on subjects the curriculum introduces. Or check out what the Web has to offer—there's a lot out there, and it's free!

School of Tomorrow Physical Science video course

School of Tomorrow Biology workbooks and videos

Video series are available for Spanish I, Geometry, Algebra I and II, Physical Science, Biology, Chemistry, and Physics. These are extremely well done, with TV-quality presentations of the subject matter and lots of visual pizzazz.

Overall, School of Tomorrow gets our pick as Most Improved Curriculum since the last edition of this book. We like the road they're traveling, and hope they continue the excellent work they're doing in the video and software areas. *Mary Pride*

Computer Video Interactive Courses

You can purchase a number of School of Tomorrow's high-school science and math courses in video format, or as what they call **"computer video interactive" (CVI)**. The CVI courses require a special computer with a built-in video player, or you can add the player unit and video board they sell to your existing computer. The problem here is that the card only works on a 286, 386, 486, or Pentium IBM-compatible computer. Owners of Macs are out of luck.

When you use a CVI course, it plays the appropriate video segment for you, and you can complete the quizzes on-screen with instant grading. You still have to wait for the video to be rewound or fast-forwarded to the right place, which seems a bit clunky.

CVI courses currently available are Algebra I, Algebra II, Biology, Chemistry, Physical Science, and Physics.

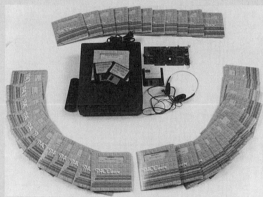

School of Tomorrow CVI courses and equipment

The Algebra 1 and Biology CVI courses are currently being remastered for the CD-ROM format and the others will soon follow. This is a step forward—no more strange hardware configurations needed!—but it remains to be seen how well the video will play on this medium.

What we'd really like to see are these School of Tomorrow courses on DVD, but this will probably have to wait until people massively adopt the DVD standard.

School of Tomorrow also offers their own non-video-related software for spelling (Word Builder), math (Math Builder), reading (Readmaster), and typing (Typemaster I and II). Integrated educational software and record-keeping software for schools is also available.

Classical Curriculum

The curriculum in this chapter is not all classical in the same way. Some of the programs reviewed, such as Calvert and Covenant Home Curriculum, have a classical flavor in their high academic standards and the emphasis they place on languages, classic literature, and the fine arts. You could also call the Hillsdale Academy program a "classical American" curriculum. Of these all, the one wholly classical program, in the sense most people mean, is the brand-new Great Books Academy.

You have quite a range of choices here, so let's get started looking at them!

In chapter 39 you'll find reviews of Catholic homeschool programs. They all follow the classical model: some more, some less.

Calvert School's building in Maryland

Calvert School, a private academy in the Baltimore area founded in 1897, has been providing a superior college-prep education for over 100 years now. For almost that long the school has also had a state-approved correspondence-school program, in which all lessons have been classroom tested in the day school before being released as part of the correspondence curriculum. Over 400,000 children have used Calvert's program over the years; over 15,000 are currently enrolled.

UPDATED!
Calvert School

Grades K–8. Pre-Kindergarten, $285. Kindergarten, $325. Grade 1, $520. Grade 2, $535. Grade 3, $550. Grade 4, $565. Grade 5, $580. Grade 6, $595. Grade 7, $610. Grade 8, $625. Math excluded option for grades 1–8 available for a lower cost. Re-use course, $100 less. ATS option for grades K–8, $225–$305 (it goes up $10/grade). ATS Online: Grades 5–8, $275–$305. Algebra 1, $151, $155 for optional ATS. All other Grade 8 subjects also available individually: $130 each plus $90 for optional ATS. Optional Video Lessons for First Grade, $50, available only with Grade 1 enrollment. Normal UPS domestic shipping included.
Calvert School, 105 Tuscany Rd., Baltimore, MD 21210. (410) 243-6030. Fax: (410) 366-0674. Email: inquiry@calvertschool.org. Web: www.calvertschool.org.

Calvert is not a Bible-based program, although it is extensively used by missionaries. The program includes positive references to Christianity, a suggested opening school prayer, and some Christian poems. Some of the textbooks and workbooks from other suppliers contain modern public-school values and teaching (e.g., evolution), but this material is never emphasized in the teacher's materials. Calvert's own self-published materials all have a pro-Christian flavor.

Over the years many missionary families have used Calvert, as well as hundreds of thousands of entertainers, ambassadors, rural families, and others. With all that experience, Calvert has a definite edge when it comes to the heart of their curriculum: the excellent lesson manuals. These lead the parent (in grades K–5) and the student (in grades 6–8) step by step through all the daily assignments, explaining exactly what to do and what pitfalls to avoid. Calvert's Advisory Teaching Service (ATS) stands ready to take you the rest of the way, providing personal input to your child via comments on his test papers, which they grade if you select this option. Be aware that **the Teacher's Manual(s) for each course are only leased from Calvert, and must be destroyed or returned when the course is complete.** This applies only to the grade-level courses, not to supplementary courses such as art or French.

Tests are bound into the manual(s) after every 20 lessons, so the student can see where he is heading and what progress he is making. Unfortunately, the test pages are not numbered and do not begin with a list of the lesson assignments to send, so in the years we've used Calvert I frequently ended up leaving out some essential papers and having to send them with the next Test Lesson. This problem can be solved by signing up for the new **Advisory Teaching Service (ATS) Online.** Now students in grades 5–8 can fill out the tests online and submit them via email. The tests are corrected and returned the same way along with teacher comments, for much faster response. Great if you're taking a grade of Calvert curriculum, especially if you're overseas or on the road.

You have to take a free placement test as part of the enrollment process in grades 4–8, unless your child has completed the previous Calvert grade, so allow some extra time to receive, complete, and send in this test.

The materials Calvert provides include a mix of textbooks from mainstream publishers, classic children's literature, and Calvert-written materials. The latter are by far more popular among homeschoolers, especially the books written by Calvert's first headmaster, Virgil M. Hillyer. You will frequently see ads in support-group newsletters offering to buy used editions of the Hillyer books *A Child's History of the World* (used in the grade 4 course), *A Child's History of Art: Painting* (used in grade 5), *A Child's History of Art: Sculpture* (used in grade 6), and *A Child's History of Art: Architecture* (used in grade 7). While the paperback editions of these books are only available by purchasing the grade levels that include them, as part of their centennial celebration Calvert has published a lovely leatherbound 618-page edition of *A Child's History of the World*, complete with full-color frontispiece and gold placemark ribbon, available for $35 plus $6 shipping. Also of interest is the lovely hardbound *Calvert School: The First Century,* at the same price. If you order both books at once, the cost is only $60.

Other Calvert-written materials (besides those reviewed separately in the Calvert Enrichment and Calvert Software writeups in this chapter) include spelling and vocabulary lessons in some grades, books of poetry and read-aloud selections for grades K–5, the new math texts, and lessons in diagramming. The latter are included in the sixth-grade lesson manual, and also as a separate book that comes with the eighth-grade course. All Calvert-written materials for the grade-level courses, including the lesson manuals, are spiral-bound, except for the Hillyer books.

Calvert School: The First Century
This lavish coffee-table book was released during Calvert's centennial celebration.

Calvert courses are constantly revised, to keep them in sync with their textbooks as the textbooks are revised to meet new standards. This sometimes is good and sometimes not. Their current first-grade readers, for example, are pretty bad—political correctness, self-esteem, driveling poetry, the lot. The seventh-grade science books, however, are an improvement over the last batch. You never can tell. What this means is that reviews of Calvert you may have read in the past will not necessarily apply in the future.

What I can tell you is this:

• **Each grade is purchased as a complete whole**, with the exception of eighth grade, which can be purchased as individual subject modules, and their new math program, in which you can purchase a different grade level than the rest of your child's course. The lessons for a few topics, e.g., grammar and handwriting for a few grade levels, are available as separate packages without purchase of curriculum. See Calvert Enrichment Courses writeup in this chapter.

• **Calvert's Pre-Kindergarten program is great.** Grab it if you want a truly fun "readiness" (as opposed to "early reading") style preschool. Lots of songs, poems, games, stories to read aloud, cut-'n-paste, arts-'n-crafts, holiday activities, kindergarten math from Macmillan, pre-reading, and pre-writing. The optional supplies kit comes with *all* materials needed, even the paper (large amounts of five kinds), scissors, wool, tapestry needle, crayons, clay, paper, watercolor, pipe cleaners, paper clips, and Elmer's glue, for $36.

Calvert Pre-Kindergarten, previously called Kindergarten

• **Calvert's new Kindergarten course** (previously named Kindergarten II) **is sure to be popular**. It's an academic kindergarten designed to bridge between Calvert's traditional "readiness" Kindergarten (now renamed Pre-Kindergarten) and their highly academic grade 1. Think of this one as the "real" kindergarten and the original Kindergarten course as a preschool course for four-year-olds. This incredibly fun and solid course includes Calvert's own phonics readers, plus math manipulatives, poems, music, and science. The optional Supplies kit ($63) includes tons of crafts materials and activities.

• **First grade I'd skip.** Use Calvert's new Kindergarten program, then follow it up with a good math course and a good phonics program instead of the first grade program. If you do decide to get the first-grade program, you definitely should look into purchasing the **first-grade video enrichment program**. These engaging tapes have a "Mr. Rogers" flavor, with snippets featuring different Calvert teachers giving show-and-tell style lessons in language arts, science, music, physical education, math, and fine art. They appear made for TV, with a lead-in and sign-off for each episode (not necessary on a home video!) along with very professionally-done shooting and staging. You might get a mellow piano player dressed in a rakish top hat introducing his "friends," the stringed instruments, or meet some animal babies, or practice hopping, skipping, and galloping. These lessons were designed to demon-

Calvert's new Kindergarten course

Calvert's First Grade Video Enrichment Program

strate concepts and activities that are hard to convey to young children in words alone. The set of three tapes is only available to families enrolled in Calvert's first-grade program. As for the first-grade course itself, it has decent math and science texts from mainstream publishers, less-enjoyable readers from more mainstream publishers, lots of Calvert-written "Reading Work Pages" a Calvert *Stories and Longer Verses* booklet, and a more businesslike set of supplies than the kindergarten course. No more clay, watercolors, yarn, or pipe cleaners are in the optional Supplies kit. We are now looking at pencils, paper of various sorts, eraser, ruler, scissors, 3x5 card, crayons, and connecting cubes for math manipulations, all for $17.

- **Second grade has no review lessons** at the beginning of the course—a big minus for children this age who have just had all summer to forget their lessons. You are also tossed into Calvert's simplified cursive right from the start. If that doesn't faze you, the rest of the course (with the exception of the readers, which once again are too classroomy) is fine. Again, there are Reading Work Pages and a poetry/reading selections book, this time titled *Rhymes and Verses*. Critical thinking exercises are introduced at this grade level, as is Calvert's own "Royalroad" device for practicing phonics. This is a piece of masonite with rectangular holes cut out of it in such a way that two tapes with phonograms on them can be pulled into position to spell many words. For example, you can add the ending *ad* to all the consonants, blends, and digraphs to spell dozens of real and nonsense words such as *bad, cad, dad, flad, glad,* and *shad.* Art pictures are included, along with the regular supplies of crayons, ruler, pencils, eraser, pads, drawing paper, and writing pads found at all grade levels. A Calvert "handsheet," for resting your hand while writing so as not to smudge the paper, is part of the supplies for this and all more advanced grades. Lastly, a new item not found in past years: an inflatable globe.

- **Third grade and up are excellent.** Lots of writing and composition activities. Solid science, including experiments. Good arts and crafts emphasis. Art history in grades 6–8, using the Hillyer books. The best secular history textbooks around (which still means you will have to straighten the kids out about a few things). Decent math courses with lots of drill built in, including a fine Algebra I course in eighth grade. Excellent spelling, vocabulary, and grammar instruction.

- **Greek mythology** is taught in third grade, using Calvert's own book, *Gods of Greece.* The study of the ancient world is continued in fourth grade, both with Hillyer's *A Child's History of the World* and Calvert's *Famous Legends* and *Mighty Men* books, both about the Greco-Roman world. In fifth grade, King Arthur, the Arabian world, and U.S. history are all introduced. In sixth grade, Old World history and world geography. In seventh, more world history and geography. In eighth, a complete review of U.S. history.

- **Literature, as opposed to "readers"** full of public-school short selections, is included with the courses from grade 3 and up. In grade 3, the book is *Smiling Hill Farm.* In grade 4, *Robinson Crusoe.* In grade 5, *American Tall Tale, Call It Courage, King Arthur and His Knights,* and *The Sign of the Beaver.* In grade 6, *Theras and His Town, Lorna Doone,* and *Swiss Family Robinson.* In grade 7, *Johnny Tremain, Kidnapped, Around the World in 80 Days,* and *The Story of a Bad Boy.* In grade 8, *The Prince and the Pauper, Hound of the Baskervilles, David Copperfield,* and *King Solomon's Mines.*

- **An annoying something called *Reading for Meaning*** is found in grades 5 through 8. In my opinion, these reading comprehension exercises are totally unnecessary in the home. Every child of mine has gotten 100 percent on every one of these exercises, with the exception of an occasional silly mistake. For kids who are good readers—meaning all homeschooled kids capable of doing the Calvert courses—such exercises are a waste of time. Calvert probably threw this one to provide extra help for children who are just starting home education. I'd just skip these exercises altogether, if I were you.

- **My one other pet peeve about Calvert is their geography material**, all taken from secular textbook and workbooks. Yes, it teaches you everything the public schools want you to know. But it's b-o-r-i-n-g. This is one subject for which Calvert should create its own materials pronto or pick up some more homeschool-friendly books.

Calvert's Fourth Grade

- **You can order an optional additional supplies package** with *all* needed supplies for each course (formerly, all supplies were included with the course purchase). Your basic course cost still includes the pencils and paper needed for completing lesson work. If you're living out in the bush, or even in the middle of a Third World city, the supplies package is a life-saver, as it may not be all that easy to find construction paper for your collage project!

- **All Calvert parents can take advantage of the Education Counselors**, even if you haven't signed up for the Advisory Teaching Service. You can call the special non-toll-free number from 8–5 EST to ask your questions, or email them any time. All Calvert counselors are certified teachers who have been trained in the Calvert educational philosophy.

- **Be aware that kids have to *work* with Calvert.** This is not a fill-in-the-blank program. They are learning to think, analyze, and write well, which takes time.

- **Calvert makes more effort than most to create a school spirit** among their homeschooled students. Your Calvert student will receive a regular newsletter that includes school news and examples of outstanding student work from other homeschooled children. You will also get a Calvert decal for your car window, and can purchase other Calvert gear (pennants, clothing, etc.) from the school.

- **Calvert's newly updated web site** now offers the "Learning Links" program, for an inexpensive $9.95 per year. The website includes a virtual student council and chat center for students, plus users can earn points towards discount on Calvert goodies.

- **Calvert's new pen pal program** allows your child, with your consent, to be matched with other Calvert students based on age, interests, and preferred gender. Over 500 Calvert students are currently enrolled in this program.

- **The new Re-Use option** allows you to save a significant sum ($100) when a second or third child takes the same Calvert course within three years after the course was first ordered. You get new copies of all the consumable course parts, plus a new lesson manual.

- **Many students have gone straight from Calvert grade 8 to college**, which says something both about Calvert and about American high schools.
- **If you want your children to finish eighth grade at age 9 or 10**, it can be done using Calvert. *Practical Homeschooling* columnist Joyce Swann's 10 children all have gone this route. But I personally haven't tried it!

In spite of their history as one of the oldest correspondence programs, the folks at Calvert are not resting on their laurels. See the following reviews of Calvert's new enrichment and software courses. As far as the basic curriculum, not only have they produced the totally new Kindergarten course I mentioned above, and optional video lessons to accompany the first grade curriculum, but a complete new series of math textbooks. Grades 1–4 of the new math program are currently available, with the kindergarten and grades 5–8 books due out in Spring 2001. At the moment, parents are encouraged to purchase the math program separately from the rest of the curriculum, so children can be accurately placed into the correct grade levels. This is important, since it is common for a child to be at different grade levels in math and language arts.

Calvert Eighth Grade

I had the privilege of visiting the Calvert day school, and was highly impressed. This is one school whose educational philosophy shines through in everything they do. From the main building, which was originally laid out to look like an "E" for "Education," to the chapel, to the planetarium at the end of a hallway decorated and painted by Calvert students, to the separate boys' and girls' wings (they study in separate classes, to improve student concentration), to the excellent student work posted on the walls, to Calvert's own in-house TV studio run by students that broadcasts daily to all their classrooms, to the care the headmaster takes in even such details as cafeteria seating to make sure no child is ostracized or mistreated, to the creativity shown in student artwork, to the well-furnished library, to Calvert teachers reporting back on their travel/study experiences abroad (funded by Calvert grants), to the beehive of multimedia programmers busily at work on cutting-edge projects for the years to come, the visit was an education in itself. I can't praise what they're doing any more highly than this: if we lived in the Baltimore area, I'd be strongly tempted to send my child to the Calvert day school. Assuming they could get in: only one child is accepted for every three that apply.

Calvert deserves an A+ academic rating. A child can graduate from Calvert's eighth grade course, take a few achievement tests, and go straight to the college of his choice. In fact, many have!

Not everyone enjoys Calvert's strict lesson plans. This curriculum also requires quite a bit of daily parental involvement, and getting all the papers ready to send in with each test is no joke. But for first-timers unaccustomed to teaching, and unsure of exactly what they want, or for families with little time to teach and older children capable of self-study, you can't go wrong with Calvert. *Mary Pride*

For the past few years, **Calvert** has been in a creative ferment, inventing new **enrichment courses** at an astonishing rate. Let's take a look at these, one by one.

Come Read With Me is Calvert's unusual pre-reading course. It doesn't teach phonics per se. Instead it introduces story readiness, alphabet sounds, context clues, and picture clues in the setting of a video saga about little creatures in a fantasy land. The muppet-like creatures, including the "wise creature," an iguana with red eyes, are trying to find out about the past history of their country, Zigzat, with the help of a friendly archaeologist. The importance of reading is stressed, as is the interconnectedness of all things and a story in the first person about talking to, listening to, singing to, and dancing for the Earth (!). Many ancillary activities are provided. Finger puppets and yarn are just a few of the kiddie-friendly supplies that accompany the eight videos, guide book, and activity book.

Reading Video Book Collection includes a dozen of the books quoted from in *Come Read With Me*.

Calvert Melody Lane

Their **Melody Lane** music appreciation video course for K–3 students is excellent. Thirty-two friendly "Sesame Street/Misterogers" style video lessons introduce kids to the instrument families, musical principles such as rhythm/beat/tempo/duration/melody, American and foreign folk music, how instruments are made, and five famous composers—Bach, Handel, Mozart, Beethoven, and Aaron Copland—among other things. The included guidebook provides detailed lesson plans, including hands-on activities, songs, and games.

The **Discovering Art** video course is also 32 lessons on six videos—convenient for giving a lesson per week in a standard school year. The story line features both child actors and professional artists, including a computer animator, a paper artist, a sculptor, and an artist who assisted "Peanuts" creator Charles Schulz. Lessons are TV-quality and cover both art appreciation (works from all eras are shown) and all the important artistic techniques—line, shading, perspective, color, light, positive/negative space—as applied to dozens of art forms, from drawing and painting to sculpture and fabric arts. A guidebook and project instructions, as well as a

Calvert Discovering Art

tremendous amount of art materials, are included in the basic program. A complete art kit and project booklet can be purchased for an additional student for $60—good deal!

Calvert's foreign-language courses are **French I and II** and **Spanish I and II**. These courses, while not as fun as Powerglide or the BBC's Muzzy courses, are more complete, including detailed pronunciation instruction, examples and practice, dialogs, spelling, vocabulary, grammar, and (in the Level II courses) a children's book in the language. You listen to the audio-cassettes, act out such commands as "Go to the table and touch the eraser," make your own Pronunciation Notebook, and do workbook exercises that drill vocabulary and grammar in a fun, visual way. Workbook, lesson manual, tape script (with every word on the cassettes), answer key to everything except the tests (which you can easily grade on your own if you know the language), and supplies are all included. Sign up an extra child for only $35 (Level I) or $45 (Level II) and save!

Calvert has also begun producing **Reading Enrichment courses**:

Calvert Beginning Spanish

- Their first, based on the **"Little House"** books of Laura Ingalls Wilder, won the highest accolades from our toughest reviewer, Renee Mathis. (Check our website, *www.home-school.com*, for her complete review.) As Renee says, the reading guides are "rich in background information . . . organized into lessons, each covering about 50 pages of reading from the books themselves . . . these would make wonderful additions to your family read-aloud time." Volume 1, for ages 6–8, covers *Big Woods* through *Farmer Boy*. Volume 2, for preteens, covers the rest. You can purchase the reading guides separately, or with a picture book, *Laura Ingalls Wilder Country,* or with a complete package that includes the guides, picture book, and all the Little House books.

Calvert Little House guides

- **Beatrix Potter: Her Life and Her Little Books**, based on the life and work of the author of *The Tale of Peter Rabbit* and other popular children's classics. This comes with a background book on Beatrix Potter, a set of 10 of her most popular little books, a reading guide, and more adorable supplies (Mrs. Tiggy-Winkle eraser? Peter Rabbit pencil sharpener?) than you can shake a glue stick at. The reading guide covers the background book chapter by chapter, then has a lesson apiece on each little book, with tons of activities and discussion questions.

Calvert Beatrix Potter: Her Life and Her Little Books

- **Drifter** is a course for first or second grade, based on the collection of 10 short real-life stories about a dog written in controlled vocabulary. Related activities and games are included. Calvert suggests this one for phonics reinforcement.
- **Robert McCloskey: Favorite Story Books** is a way for you to get more out of some of my very favorite children's books: *Blueberries for Sal, One Morning in Maine, Time of Wonder, Make Way for Ducklings,* and *Lentil.* The teacher guidebook provides further insights into the text, helps you teach your child to "see" what Mr. McCloskey is doing with his wonderful illustrations, and provides related activities.
- **Famous Americans: 52 Stories to Read With a Child** is a part of the third-grade course. The book has short bios of famous Americans from all walks of life, and the package includes follow-up questions and drawings to color.
- **Gods of Greece** is Calvert's third-grade mythology instruction, now presented as a separate package, You get the myths, plus a lesson manual with brief introductions to each myth, a pronunciation guide for those Greek names, and pictures to color based on the myths.

For older children (grades six and up), the **Guided Literature series** includes:

- *Bridge to Terbithia*
- *A Midsummer Night's Dream*
- *Anne Frank: The Diary of a Young Girl* (this is included in the seventh-grade curriculum)
- *The Giver*

These all come with lesson helps—the "guided lessons" referred to in the series title. Questions to think about and discuss, key themes, the author's use of image and setting, and so forth are part of these helps. The Anne Frank unit also includes an audiocassette and video featuring a Holocaust survivor.

Coming in Spring 2001, these additions to the Guided Literature series:

- *The Secret Garden* (included in the grade 5 course)
- *Sing Down the Moon* (included in the grade 5 course)
- *Shiloh* (included in the grade 5 course)
- *Number the Stars* (included in the grade 5 course)
- *The Phantom Tollbooth* (included in the grade 6 course)
- *King Arthur and His Knights* (included in the grade 6 course)
- *Lorna Doone* (included in the grade 6 course)
- *The Story of a Bad Boy* (included in the grade 7 course)

Another new trend: creating packages for separate sale that include portions of the Calvert curriculum. The handwriting lessons found in Calvert first grade are now available as **Writing Fun Kit**, while **Fourth Grade Grammar** and **Fifth Grade Grammar** are just what their names imply—the grammar lessons and workbook from the standard Calvert fourth and fifth grade curriculum.

For those students who already know cursive other than Calvert's unique cursive script, and who need extra handwriting practice, **Beginning Connected Cursive Writing** teaches a somewhat more typical cursive.

The message seems clear: you no longer need to invest in a year of curriculum to try a taste of Calvert. *Mary Pride*

NEW!
Calvert School Software

Grades K–8. King Arthur Through the Ages CD-ROM, $40. Ancient Greece CD-ROM, $40. A Child's History of the World CD-ROM, $40. Spelling and Vocabulary CD-ROMs for grades 3–7, $20 each. 8th Grade Spelling CD-ROM, $20. Vocabulary for Life CD-ROM, $45. 4th Grade Grammar CD-ROM, $40. Normal UPS domestic shipping included. *Calvert School, 105 Tuscany Rd., Baltimore, MD 21210. (410) 243-6030. Fax: (410) 366-0674. Email: inquiry@calvertschool.org. Web: www.calvertschool.org.*

Calvert Spelling/Vocabulary CD-ROMs

UPDATED!
Covenant Home Curriculum

Grades K–12. Standard Course Enrollment: Grade K, $369; Grade 1, $419; Grade 2, $421; Grade 3, $495; Grade 4, $507; Grade 5, $478; Grade 6, $459; Grade 7, $419; Grade 8, $430; Grade 9, $569; Grade 10, $549; Grade 11, $529; Grade 12, $500. Optional Tailoring Fee, $45. Optional Grade Auditing & Tutorial Service: Grade K, $145; Grades 1-8, $175; Grades 9–12, $200. Shipping extra. *Covenant Home Curriculum, N 63 W 23421 Main St, Sussex, WI 53089. (800) 578-2421. Fax: (262) 246-7066. E-mail: educate@covenanthome.com. Web: www.covenanthome.com.*

Calvert's first venture into the world of **software**, **King Arthur Through the Ages**, won a Parent's Choice Award in 1996. Designed to teach the literature, vocabulary, history, and art of the age of knighthood, it also includes an interactive game to test what you learned.

Calvert's second tutorial/drill multimedia program is entitled **Calvert School Spelling & Vocabulary**. This product employs all the "gee, whiz!" look and feel you expect from a mass-market software product, along with lessons based on Calvert's own theories of how best to teach spelling. Designed to accompany the lessons in Calvert's curriculum, each grade level includes 1,600 words, plus you can add your own. The program "talks" to you, pretests you, drills you, quizzes you, and also includes vocabulary lessons and (in grades 6 and 7) a grammar game. If you're already using Calvert grade 3–7, you definitely want this program. Even if you aren't using Calvert, it's an inexpensive *and* educationally superior alternative to mass-market spelling software. See detailed review in Volume 2.

In early 2000, a multimedia version of **A Child's History of the World** and a multimedia history of **Ancient Greece** were released, as were the **Vocabulary for Life**, **4th Grade Grammar,** and **8th Grade Spelling** CD-ROMs. The history products show you the art and culture of the time, plus provide audio pronunciation of difficult names, review questions, and games. In addition, *Ancient Greece* has web links, for further research. The language-arts products basically put those lessons in the Calvert curriculum in software form, with some nifty innovations peculiar to the software medium. *4th Grade Grammar,* for example, has a storyline children follow to collect clues, as well as exercises and games the computer grades interactively. *Vocabulary for Life* connects the lessons to passages from famous books and poems, to show words in context and build writing skills.

By the time you read this, **5th Grade Grammar** is likely available as well. Does this mean Calvert's programmers will take a well-earned rest? I bet it doesn't! *Mary Pride*

Covenant Home Curriculum wants you to consider them as "the Christian alternative to Calvert." Developed over a fifteen-year period in a K–12 Christian day school in suburban Milwaukee, this eclectic curriculum strongly emphasizes a Reformed Protestant worldview, classical literature (third- to fifth-graders get abridged versions of works like *A Tale of Two Cities* and *Pride and Prejudice*, upper-graders get full-length classics), writing and speaking skills, a reverently scientific outlook on life, and in-depth biblical knowledge. The curriculum includes the Covenant Home Preceptor, a manual for parents that explains how to administer the program; study guides especially prepared for homeschoolers; simple diagnostic tests; and study helps, such as Covenant's own *Guide to Writing Book Reports*, and *Day-By-Day Scheduling*, a calendar/lesson planner for each grade that tells what to do and when to do it. All texts and workbooks include answer keys and teaching guides.

Like Calvert, Covenant publishes some of their own materials, and obtains the rest from a variety of publishers. Also like Calvert, Covenant's own materials—including Classic Critiques, Art Masters, and Doré Pictorial Bible Briefings—are excellent. Those from other publishers are chosen for academic value and (where possible) beauty of presentation

Covenant Home Curriculum's Dore Pictorial Bible Briefings

and content. In this, I feel they actually beat Calvert, who, because their program is state-accredited, are forced to use contemporary secular texts and workbooks in subjects for which they have not published their own materials.

For fourth grade and up, Calvert requires your child take a diagnostic test before ordering curriculum. Covenant Home Curriculum also carries their own **C.H.A.T. series (Covenant Home Achievement Tests)**, but does not require them as a condition of purchasing curriculum. These diagnostic tests are meant to give you an accurate reading of your child's grade-level equivalence in the two main academic areas of math and language, so you can choose the appropriate grade level. The tests are easy to administer, taking only thirty minutes for each of the two sections. Scoring by Covenant Home Curriculum staff is included.

Covenant has recently added a **Kindergarten Readiness Test**, available either online or by mail. This test will tell parents how ready their child is for Covenant's Kindergarten course in language skills, social skills, motor skills, listening skills and interest.

Continuing the Calvert comparison, Covenant's outline-type *Day-by-Day Scheduling* guides are simpler to use than Calvert's full lesson plans; on the other hand, you might miss the extra teaching tips and friendly "we're talking to you" tone for which Calvert is justly noted. Given Covenant's academic rigor, I appreciate that they now include a *Day-by-Day* guide with each purchase of a full grade of curriculum. If you order a subject module, a daily scheduling guide is provided for that subject only.

About those **modules**. In the past, you could only order Covenant Home Curriculum as a full grade level at a time. Realizing that many homeschool families now follow the "eclectic" approach of picking favorite resources subject by subject, Covenant recently redesigned their catalog to offer individual subject "modules" as well as full grades. So, if you like the Covenant approach but have another Bible course in mind (for example), you can order everything except Bible; or if you just want to try a taste of one of Covenant's best fifth-grade subjects, you can order their wonderful Grade 5 History module. This makes the Covenant curriculum much more accessible, and provides a reason for many of you to send for their catalog who would have not considered it before.

Another new feature: **Covenant's wonderful Test Sets.** Designed to accompany most courses, including those using history texts from Bob Jones University Press and Greenleaf Press, these easy-to-use sets each come as a pad of tear-off sheets. Each set includes one-page weekly quizzes, midterms, and final exams. If you've ever considered using the Greenleaf Press "Famous Men" series, I can tell you it's about 100 times easier to find

Modules Prices

Kindergarten:
- Language module, $265.
- Bible module, $63.
- Math module, $47.

Grades 1–6
- **Language modules.** Grade 1, $265. Grade 2, $269. Grade 3, $319. Grade 4, $268. Grade 5, $249. Grade 6, $234.
- **Grammar alone.** 3, $89. 4–5, $105 each.
- **Science.** 1–2, $46. 3, $53. 4, $55. 5–6, $68 each.
- **Optional science Home Educator Kit.** 1, $39. 2–3, $33.50 each. 4-6, $36.50 each.
- **Bible.** 1, $45. 2–3, $49 each. 4–5, $64 each. 6, $49.
- **MCP Math.** 1, $51. 2–4, $52 each. 5–6, $54 each.
- **Saxon Math.** 4, $59. 5, $61. 6, $62.
- **History.** 2, $31. 3, $59. 4, $94. 5, $63. 6, $73.

Grades 7–9:
- **Language.** 7–8, $182 each. 9, $184.
- **Vocabulary alone.** 7–9, $41 each.
- **Science.** 7, $81. 8, $91. 9, $175. Optional Student Activity Kit 7–8, $31.95 each. Teacher Edition 7–9, $42.50 each.
- **Bible.** 7–8, $44 each. 9, $56.
- **AMSCO Math.** $39/grade.
- **Saxon Math.** 7, $62. 8–9, $64.
- **History.** 7, $96. 8, $92. 9, $99.

Grades 10–12:
- **Language.** 10, $164. 11, $129. 12, $115.
- **Science.** 10, $185. 11–12, $175 each.
- **Bible.** 10, $55. 11–12, $70.
- **AMSCO Math.** Geometry, $25. Algebra II/Trigonometry, $31. Calculus, $32. College Boards, $18.
- **Saxon Math.** Algebra II, $64. Advanced Math, $69. Calculus, $79.
- **History.** 10–11, $99 each. 12, $89.

Christian Doctrine
- Westminster Shorter Catechism Modules: part 1 and 2, $39 each or $55 for both.
- Institutes of Biblical Law module, $70.
- Summary of Christian Doctrine module, $49.
- Kingdom of God module, Parts I & II, $64.
- Ministry of Christ module, Parts I and II, $81.

Supplementary materials also available.

out what your children did or did not learn with the help of these test sets! I even found them easier to use than BJUP's own test materials.

Covenant's names for their materials are somewhat unusual. The parent's manual is called *The Preceptor*; the overview of their history curriculum is called *History Overlay*; the syllabus/scope and sequence/weekly assignments/teaching tips/discussion questions and answers/etc. for each course and grade is called a "Blueprint"; even the *Day-by-Day Scheduling Guide* is actually a set of weekly schedule charts with daily assignments filled into the chart grid. Where Calvert provides all teaching materials in a single lesson manual per subject or (in the early grades) per grade, with Covenant you need to flip back and forth between the *Day-by-Day* guide and Blueprint to figure out what's going on in each day's lessons.

Grading your student's work is an important part of the Covenant curriculum. Rev. Dale Dykema, Covenant's president, once wrote an article for *Practical Homeschooling* presenting their grading philosophy. Briefly stated, they believe in absolute standards (100 percent is perfect, anything less should be graded accordingly). Covenant has recently revised their grading sheets to make them easier for parents to use.

Covenant Home Curriculum Kindergarten

What does Covenant offer academically? Covenant's **kindergarten** is a phonics and discovery curriculum. **History** books are read to children in grades K–2, working up to grade 3, where history finally becomes a full-credit course. The Greenleaf Press "Famous Men" guides to Greece, Rome, and the Middle Ages are used in grades 4–6. Upper-grades history uses some BJUP texts and concentrates on presenting a biblical (pro-free enterprise and freedom) worldview, and covers government and economics as well as history. This culminates in grade 12's study of the *God and Government* series.

Science at most grade levels includes not only a basic science text, but appealing science readers that might tell the story of weather or follow the life cycle of an elephant or oak tree. Upper-grades science work covers natural science, biology, physics, and chemistry (one subject per grade), along with hands-on investigations and a solid grounding in creation science. Students electing the alternative high-school program can take either Science of the Physical Creation or Biology for two years.

The **math** courses continue Covenant's strong college prep emphasis. Modern Curriculum Press math is used in the earlier grades, with Saxon as an alternative in grades 4–8. Algebra starts in grade 8 and proceeds to more algebra (grades 9 and 10), trig and geometry (10 and 11), calculus (12th grade), and prepping for the College Boards (grade 12). Saxon math is included in the

cost of high-school materials with other options available, especially in geometry. Students can spread Algebra I or Plane Geometry over two years, but college-bound students should plan to take both Algebra and Geometry.

The **language arts** curriculum is Covenant's pride and joy. Earlier grades start with intensive phonics, and then focus on developing basic punctuation and grammar skills and developing a love of reading, with many short classics included in the standard curriculum as well as phonics readers and McGuffeys. Upper-grade students study grammar (including diagramming), spelling, poetry, vocabulary, composition, etymology (grades 5–11), and serious classics (books are included with the program). To accompany these, Covenant now offers an excellent series of Classic Critiques. Designed for parents, these brief write-ups point out the reasons the book is considered a classic and provide discussion questions and biblical analysis of the book. Covenant also offers a wide range of high-school literature and composition electives, plus elective Latin. A two-year course on the Westminster Shorter Catechism is also available.

Assorted Covenant Home Curriculum early grades materials

You get a *lot* of materials when you order from Covenant. The grade 6 language-arts module, for example, includes

- the text *Essentials of English* with answer key, quarterly tests, and Blueprint
- a booklet, *Fundamentals of Diagramming*, with answer key and Blueprint
- the workbook *RSVP with Etymology* with achievement tests, answer key, and Blueprint
- the reading-comprehension/vocabulary development workbook *Curious Reader, Book 5*, with answer key and Blueprint
- *Writing Skills, Book 1*, with Blueprint
- the Christian biography of William Tyndale, *God's Outlaw*, with study guide, Covenant Test Set, and Blueprint
- the unabridged Rudyard Kipling classic *Captains Courageous* with Covenant Classic Critique and Blueprint
- *Cathedral* by David Macaulay with quizzes and Blueprint
- *Castle* by David Macaulay with quizzes and Blueprint
- Covenant's own booklet, *A Guide to Writing Book Reports*
- *Day-by-Day Scheduling Guide* for sixth-grade language arts

Latin is now available through Covenant, using the programs *Matin Latin* and *Latina Christiana.*

Even if you choose to order a full grade level, Covenant Home Curriculum provides individualized curriculum (each subject may be at a different grade level). Additional help, in the form of reading comprehension books and test preparation materials, is available. If you sign up for the **Grade Auditing option**, you also are entitled to phone counseling, short turn-around grading time, and report cards. You will have an assigned telephone Auditor whom you may call during specified hours for a quick response.

Covenant Home Curriculum has enhanced support for their homeschool through their new **web site**. Homeschoolers can order courses through their on-line catalog. Covenant also will lead discussions online on various topics using internet chat. The web site is constantly being updated with news, articles, grading helps, book reviews, etc. Covenant's new Kindergarten readiness test is available online as well.

So, is this a "Christian alternative to Calvert" or not? Overall, I'd say Covenant has done a terrific job of improving their curriculum and making it more user-friendly. Their new catalog spells out exactly what you get in every module and grade level, along with photos of the books and sample workbook pages. You get the same solid academics and emphasis on classic literature and art as Calvert, with somewhat more cumbersome teacher materials. I have not had the opportunity to compare Covenant's "Grade Auditing" option with Calvert's excellent "Advisory Teaching Service," but it sounds like they offer similar services. Keeping all this in mind, I would have to say that yes, Covenant provides a similar academic style and content to what parents are looking for in a Calvert course. Your child will learn the same basics in the same thorough fashion. In other ways, it's apples and oranges. Calvert, though supportive of Christianity, teaches evolution; Covenant *is* Christian. Calvert offers school supplies packages; Covenant does not. Calvert has developed many supplemental programs; Covenant is developing lots of new modules and they have a Supplemental Catalog with select items from other, compatible publishers. And so on.

Covenant Home Curriculum Grade 6

What I can tell you is that, if you are looking for an excellent, thorough education for your children that involves a lot of reading, writing, and discussion, and that is solidly biblical, send for Covenant's catalog. It may surprise you! *Mary Pride*

NEW!
The Great Books Academy

PreK (Nursery)–12. $595–$695/year, includes textbooks and 12–15 reading books per year in grades N–8. Grades 9–12 may also purchase Britannica's Great Books of the Western World 60-volume set at discount, if desired. Discounts available for multiple children in same family.
The Great Books Academy, 1213 N. Piedmont Rd., Box 360, Piedmont, OK 73078. (800) 521-4004. Inquiries: (405) 373-0600. Fax: (800) 515-5565 or (405) 373-0700.
Web: www.greatbooksacademy.org.

As Classical Education becomes more and more popular among homeschoolers, people keep asking, "Why isn't there a classical curriculum?" **Great Books Academy**, which launched in fall 2000, wants to be that curriculum. Although it is designed to educate students in the 3,000-year-old Western tradition, the program is not antiquarian, or devoted only to the past, but goes right up to the present day. In fact, six of the 60 Great Books volumes your high-school student will study consist solely of works written in the 20th century.

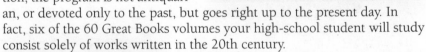

Based on the three Paideia program methods expounded by Dr. Mortimer J. Adler (more on that in the sidebar), GBA is a serious attempt to make the upper-class "prep" school style education of previous centuries available to all—not to foster elitism, as the prep academies do, but to build those qualities of incisive thinking, deep knowledge of our civilization, and leadership for which schools such as Eton and Harrow are famous. It does this via a combination of textbooks (mostly for the science and math "labs"), "Good Books" for the younger children (worthy, time-tested readings that aren't as heavy-duty as what we normally call the "classics"), Great Books, and "Socratic seminars."

Literature studied on the Nursery through Grade Eight level comes from the famous "1,000 Good Books" list compiled by Dr. John Senior who taught the Great Books program at Kansas University in the 1970s. Dr. Senior's contention was that, in order to understand the Great Books, a child first had to read 1,000 "good" books. Here, "good" doesn't mean just fun fluff like the Hardy Boys, sentimental bosh like so many Christian kiddy books, or a swim in sociopathic attitudes and dysfunction like so many "realistic" modern books. A "good" book has to be good literature *and* ethically worthy, introducing children to Great Ideas and preparing them to reject Bad Ideas, without cant or gush.

In grades 9–12, GBA literature consists of selections from the Great Books themselves, chosen by Dr. Adler, Robert M. Hutchins of Yale, and a host of prominent experts in many fields. We're talking about **Britannica's "Great Books of the Western World" series** that took eight years, millions of dollars, and hundreds of people to develop during the 1940s and 50s. Within a few years of its publication it was selling 40,000 sets a year, until the decline in study of the classics began in the 1960s. The 1990 set, revised under Dr. Adler as Editor-in-Chief for Britannica, in association with the University of Chicago, is 517 works by 130 authors bound into 60 volumes. From this, the high-school student will study a core reading list.

You will not have to purchase the Britannica set, since most of the books in it can be found in other editions at your library or bookstore. However, GBA is making the set available to its students for $795, a notable savings off the regular retail price of $999. In addition, each GBA student gets free access to Britannica On-line.

Here's what the curriculum includes:

- **Language Arts.** Nursery level, A Beka *Letters and Sounds*. Preschool–3: Sing, Spell, Read & Write. Grades 1–8: Shurley Grammar. Grades 1–3: *English from the Roots Up*. Grades 4–8: *Vocabu-Lit*.
- **Foreign Language.** Each student in grades 1–8 will be required to study at least one foreign language. Latin and Greek are particularly encouraged, but any language other than English will fulfill the requirement. Proficiency and fluency will be tested at the end of eighth grade; a satisfactory standard must be achieved before passing into the Great Books program in ninth grade. GBA will make resources available for a number of languages, including Latin, Greek, Hebrew, Spanish, French, and Russian. *Latin's Not So Tough* will be used for the first three grades, followed by *The Latin Road to English Grammar*. For Greek, *Hey, Andrew! Teach Me Some Greek* will be used for grades 1–6. For Hebrew, the Learnables program will be used. For other languages, the Power-glide courses will be used.
- **Math.** Nursery level, *Learning Numbers with Button Bear*. Preschool: *Numbers and Skills with Button Bear*. Grades K–8: Developmental Math series. As new levels are added to the Developmental Math program (it presently includes 16 worktexts, covering counting through pre-algebra), they will be incorporated in the program. Levels 17–22, Algebra and Geometry, should be ready in late 2000. Dr. Saad also plans to create a Calculus level. While waiting for these new worktexts, GBA will use Jacobs' algebra and geometry texts, *Mathematics: A Human Endeavor*, and Anton's calculus text.
- **Science.** Grades 1–6, Harcourt Brace science textbooks. These are typical secular school texts. Grades 7 and 8, the Glenco series (published by a division of Harcourt Brace). In grades

What Is the Paideia Program?

The Paideia Program, as popularized by Dr. Mortimer Adler, includes three main teaching methods:

- **Didactic** via lectures and books
- **Coaching** (in this case, by parents) in the seven liberal arts: grammar, logic, rhetoric, arithmetic, geometry, astronomy, and music. This includes the skills of Reading, Writing, Speaking, Listening, and Thinking.
- **Socratic seminars** to develop an understanding of the great ideas of Western civilization contained in the classics. The study of the classics is often referred to as the "Great Conversation," as the student mentally engages the greatest thinkers of previous ages and hopefully someday contributes his own thoughts to the world. Socrates was the Greek philosopher who originated the method of teaching by asking the student questions and challenging the student's answers until the student could demonstrate his ideas were correct and logical.

9–12, biology, chemistry, physics, and astronomy will be studied. At press time, the texts had not been selected.

- **Philosophy** will be studied starting in grades 1–6; critical thinking in grades 7–8. *Touchpebbles*, a collection of moral tales and dilemmas, is used in the early grades. A unit on "How to Read a Difficult Book" is planned for the end of eighth grade.
- **Music.** Nursery, *Classical Baby*. Preschool, *The Mozart Effect*. Kindergarten, *Color the Classics*. Grades 4–6, *Strike Up the Orchestra!* Grades 7–8, *The Enjoyment of Music*.
- **Art** will include mostly art appreciation, starting in nursery level. The following historical periods and types of arts are studied at these grade levels: grade 2, Bible history; grade 3, Egyptian; grade 4, Grecian; grade 5, Roman; grade 6, medieval. *The History of Art* by Janson will be studied in grades 7 and 8.
- **History** and **Geography** studies will correlate with the art studies, as above, with Modern and American history following medieval. Reading and study selections will include, among other resources, portions from the complete back issues of *National Geographic*, now available on CD-ROM. These are being screened carefully to avoid any objectionable content.
- **Religion.** GBA respects the right of parents to select the religion and the means of instruction in it. In keeping with their Western Civilization emphasis, they point out that "nearly every sage who writes on the subject notes that no education is complete without the study of God and one's relationship to God." The Bible is one of the Great Books studied. Additionally, to receive a GBA diploma, the student must present evidence of a serious study of the religion selected by the parents, or of comparative religion. This may take the form of an essay.

Comprehensive tests will be available, in addition to the regular course tests, at the fourth, sixth, eighth, and twelfth grade level. These will be essay tests and oral (via the Internet) tests, not true/false or multiple choice like most standardized tests.

The sample schedule they suggest is:

- **Monday, Tuesday, Thursday, Friday:** language arts, foreign language, science, math.
- **Wednesday:** history, geography, philosophy, art, music, units, and (from third grade on) Socratic Discussion Group.

Religion can be scheduled with either grouping.

The lesson plans I saw were minimalist. Each textbook or workbook is introduced via an overview of its content and presentation. Then you get either assignments broken down by week and day, or a general plan for attacking the material. E.g., for *English from the Roots Up*, "There are 50 words to cover in 36 weeks. Combine two root words during some classes in order to teach all 50 words." Don't look for extensive teaching tips or background information.

To make up for the lack of in-depth help in the lesson plans, tutors will be available for personal tutoring, educational counseling, and grading. The Academy will handle recordkeeping, transcripts, and diplomas. GBA will also communicate with students and their families via newsletter and email.

In another year or so, Socratic seminars discussing the classics will be conducted weekly over the Internet using the latest multi-conferencing technology, and in person periodically in major cities. In the meantime, Socratic discussion groups will be available through live audio online chats, weekly for grades 3–8 and biweekly for grades 9 and up. GBA is looking into the possibility of "moderator-controlled access," in which only one person may speak at a time.

GBA is concerned that the student *retain* and *understand* information, rather than passively listening to lectures and cramming for tests. Thus, their Socratic "questioning" rather than "answering" approach. Thus also, outlining of readings will be a major part of their program. This requires analysis and judgment of the work, and will be required in progressively greater depth as the grade levels increase. Dr. Redpath, the developer of their Philosophy for Children program, is perhaps the nation's foremost expert on this subject.

Upon completion of the 12th grade level, a high-school diploma will be awarded. At that point, further options will include:

What is "Great Books" Education?

The Great Books movement was initiated by John Erskine, an Elizabethan literature teacher at Columbia University who began a series of discussion seminars on the great classics of the West in 1921. Mortimer J. Adler and other students participated in this class, which read directly from the original source (rather than a commentary) and then engaged in a lively discussion moderated by the teacher, but not in a lecture or didactic manner. To their surprise, the participants, including the teacher, all were stimulated intellectually and gained new understanding in the lofty ideas the great writers of the classics tended to focus upon. The participants went their various ways.

Mortimer, later Dr., Adler went to the University of Chicago where he taught Great Books seminars with the President there, Robert Hutchins. Together, in cooperation with Encyclopaedia Britannica, they published the 1952, 54-volume set of classics entitled *The Great Books of the Western World.* This series was later republished in 1990 as 60 volumes containing the greatest works of 130 of the greatest minds of the West. This began a serious revival of classical education in the U.S. which grew until the late 1960s, when it came under severe attack from the growing ranks of the logical positivists and from the cultural relativists (i.e., there is no good or bad; cultural values vary from place to place, none are better in themselves, respectively). Classical education, whose core notion is simply that since we cannot study all books, we ought to study the best—the perennial classics—then went into a tailspin from which it has yet to recover.

When they discovered over time that high school graduates entering college were no longer prepared for study of classic works, the colleges resorted to introducing remedial courses and watered-down electives (*a la* basket weaving) akin to vocational schools. This degraded the resulting education and the value of diplomas, and so we are here today where college grads can barely read and write and many high school grads cannot.

Adler addressed this with the Paideia Reform program, which promotes three modalities of teaching (didactic, coaching, and Socratic). The essence of the Paideia reform is to abolish the remedial programs in the colleges by turning out well-educated grads from the high school level, already skilled in the liberal arts and familiar with the Great Books. In effect, this would push the B.A. programs back into the high school level (12/14–16/18-year-olds), so that young people would be schooled in the humanities upon graduation from high school and ready to pursue specialization at that time, rather than endlessly delaying it by remedial and elective course work.

The primary function of the Great Books program is to discover and develop an understanding of the Great Ideas contained therein. It is therefore necessary to develop thinking, independent, critical-realists, which are necessary to a free society and to a democratic one, such as we aspire to be. The alternative is, ultimately, slavery (the "liberal" arts in this context have the meaning of "liberal" as "free" or "freeman").

—*Patrick Carnack, President of Great Books Academy*

- Taking the Advanced Placement exams in areas covered in depth by the curriculum (e.g., English Literature and Composition, Calculus, sciences). GBA plans to "incorporate an orientation" toward the AP exams from the beginning, so their graduates can avoid remedial and repetitive courses in college.
- Receiving a B.A. from GBA's University division. Right now, GBA has affiliate status with the American Academy of Liberal Education, which may eventually enable them to award accredited college degrees.
- Attempting to gain advanced standing at university via tests designed by GBA as well as by the above.

GBA would like to award a B.A. degree, via its Great Books University College, to those who do well enough in its high-school program. This fits in with Dr. Adler's long-time advocacy of pushing the B.A. program back to the secondary (high school) level where it was in the Middle Ages and Renaissance, when it indicated successful completion of the liberal arts portions of the trivium, quadrivium, and some humanities. Further specialization would then be pursued via college or graduate degree.

These options will likely only be available to those who have attended GBA from grades 8–12.

The GBA curriculum was still in its final developmental phase as I wrote this, so I can't give a definitive verdict based on having seen each and every lesson plan and having attended online chats, etc. What I can tell you is that the GBA approach has a lot of potential. For the most part, the products from other publishers that they have chosen to use are streamlined and easy to use for home education. The science curriculum is unexciting but thorough. The literature reading list is way beyond what any other program offers, with the exception of the Sonlight curriculum, which has an entirely different emphasis (multicultural v. GBA's Western Civilization focus). The addition of real-time Socratic discussion groups enables GBA to fold in the best of what online courses have to offer, to what is otherwise a heavily reading-based curriculum. Their standards are high, and their future plans are ambitious. If you're sold on the "great books" approach, this might be what you have been waiting for. *Mary Pride*

NEW!
Hillsdale Academy Reference Guide

Grades K–8. Grades 9–12 guide will be available shortly. K–8 and 9–12 guides, $175 postpaid each; $295 for both.
Hillsdale Academy, 33 E. College St., Hillsdale, MI 49242 (800) 989-7323. Fax: (517) 437-4347. Email: stephanie.umphress@ac.hillsdale.edu. Web: www.hillsdale.edu/academy.

Hillsdale College, known for its conservative principles and adherence to Judeo-Christian values, is one of the most popular choices for homeschool graduates. Since 1990, the College has operated a day school, Hillsdale Academy, as a service to the local community, a demonstration of their educational principles in action, and a hands-on training ground for their college students majoring in education. Based on the principles of traditional education, and following a classical model, the Academy is quite up-front about its commitment to the traditional values of faith, self-reliance, accountability, courage, and honesty.

Small surprise, then, that there was quite a flurry of excitement in the homeschool community when it was announced that the **Hillsdale Academy Reference Guide** would be available for purchase by homeschoolers. To date, over 1,200 copies of the Guide have been sold to homeschool families and about 250 schools, many of which are changing their educational approach to reflect the Hillsdale model.

The Reference Guide is just that—a reference guide. You don't get weekly lesson plans or a big box of books. What you do get is a big, attractive ring binder with tabbed sections devoted to Introduction, School Culture, K–8 Curriculum, Reading List, Bibliography, Additional Titles List, Publishers List, Parents Handbook, Faculty Handbook, and Curriculum Outlines. The high-school guide will be sold separately. You also get a video about Hillsdale Academy. From the raising of the flag, the Pledge of Allegiance, the patriotic song, and the Bible or poem recitation that opens the day, to the weekly prayer meeting led by the college chaplain, to the teachers

greeting students at the beginning of class, to the numerous classroom shots of well-groomed children in uniforms, to the field trips and swimming classes, to the flag lowering ceremony at the end of the day, you get a good view of what education used to be like for many of us only 30 or 40 years ago.

The Hillsdale philosophy is, "If it ain't broke, don't fix it." Of course, they express this in more elegant language. Their idea is simply that we already know what kind of education is successful, so let's just do it, already. (Again, they express this much more elegantly.) So phonics is used to teach reading, students are taught and drilled in the math facts, history lessons are patriotic instead of filled with liberal angst, there is a well-understood code of conduct with penalties for misbehavior, and so on.

By purchasing the Reference Guide you have the information you need to offer a Hillsdale Academy-style education at home. You are given the school's philosophy, its code of conduct, and even its rules for parents and faculty (not that you'll need the last two). More importantly, you are given, by grade level, the library books and textbooks used, and who publishes each. The Publishers List gives you the contact information to order any books you can't find in your local bookstore or favorite homeschool catalog. Finally, the Curriculum Outline gives you weekly assignments or study topics by grade level and subject.

This bare-bones approach is great if you already know how to teach. Week 16 in kindergarten, for example, covers "Identifying and Writing Final *f*, Recognizing Initial *f*, Identifying Initial Consonant *L*, Writing Initial and Final *l*" from the SRA Phonics Readiness books, reading aloud *If You Give a Mouse a Cookie,* studying "The English in Michigan" (you have to figure out how to teach that one on your own, though you are encouraged to "supplement instruction" with two history texts used for the course), studying Lake Superior (again, you figure out how to do this), three units in the science text, and part of a Saxon Math K unit. No teaching tips of any kind are supplied. Generally, major publishers such as SRA and Saxon are careful to incorporate teaching strategies and suggestions in their materials, so this really just leaves you with two assignments to research on your own: Lake Superior and "The English in Michigan." The encyclopedia and atlas will tell you all you need to know about the former, and unless you live in Michigan, who cares about the latter?

And that's pretty much how it works. The beauty of a bare-bones approach is that you can see at a glance which assignments fit into your own plans, and modify any that don't meet your needs. The whole year is laid out for you in just a few pages. Hailing from Massachusetts, as I do, I probably would have substituted lessons on the New England colonies for the less historically important history of pre-Revolutionary War Michigan. Or perhaps, since we now live in Missouri, I'd substitute some Missouri state history. Again, if you have favorite books you'd rather read than the read-aloud books recommended by the school, you can make your substitutions in just a few minutes at the beginning of the school year. On the other hand, you'll likely follow the sequence of lessons that use the basic texts, because why buy the books if you're not planning on using them?

The value of this Reference Guide comes down to the question, "How good are their book recommendations?" I'd say, "Pretty good." Neither conservatives nor liberals should be offended at the basic reading selections, a blend of children's classics (including fairy tales and mythology) and Newbery Award books. Famous women are represented, as well as famous men. I'd have to say William Bennett would be comfortable with this reading list.

For math, Hillsdale Academy relies on Saxon math. For phonics, studied only in grades K–2, SRA. For history, A Beka texts and lots of historical

One real annoyance is that the publishers aren't listed in the K–8 Curriculum lists. You have to search for the grade in question in the Curriculum Outlines, look for the subject taught using the book, and *then* you can find the publisher's name—but not the address or phone number. For that, you have to switch over to the Publishers List. Worse, only the textbooks are identified by publisher. For all the "library" type books, no publisher is listed—with the exception of the separate "Reading List" section, that *does* list the publishers. Confusion! Granted, your local library or bookstore should have a copy of *Curious George* and *The Courage of Sarah Noble*. But I've too often been stymied in my attempts to find a book locally to trust that the more obscure literary recommendations will always be available locally. For the next edition of this guide, it would be great if publishers for every book were listed in the Curriculum Lists, and if a separate index of books *by publisher* were available. You could then at a glance see what books could be ordered from Scholastic, say, or Little & Brown.

Another annoyance is that the lengthy Curriculum Outlines only list the grade level once per grade. You can spend quite a bit of time flipping through the outline trying to find where "your" grade level starts. Running heads listing the grade level at the top of each page would be nice.

fiction, plus some source documents, including patriotic songs, in grades 1–4. In grade 5, Greenleaf Press and Longman materials are used to study Egypt and Greece. In grade 6, a study of U.S. history, autobiographies and biographies of famous Americans are used. In grade 7, studying Rome and the Middle Ages, again Greenleaf Press and Longman materials are used. In grade 8, something called *Review Text in American History* (no publisher listed). Penmanship is Palmer Method. Homeschool classics, such as ESP Publishers' *Jumbo English Yearbook* and Educators Publishing Service's *Vocabulary from Classical Roots,* are well represented, as are major textbook publishers such as Steck-Vaughn.

Oddly missing are lessons in French and/or Latin, art, and music, generally considered essential for a traditional private-school education. These will be added in the K–8 guide next edition and will be included in the 9–12 guide.

The most unexpected part of the Hillsdale curriculum is its science sequence. In this area, Hillsdale has decided that today's education beats yesterday's. They have chosen to use the SCIIS (Science Curriculum Improvement Study) series from Delta Education, Inc., Box M, Nashua, NH 03061-6012, 1-800-258-1302, www.delta-ed.com. Not having seen this series, we can't really comment on it, but you can certainly send for one of their brochures and check it out for yourself.

I saw the first draft of the high-school curriculum. It uses wonderful books, but not always in an immediately visible logical sequence. In tenth grade, for example, the student will study, among many other books, *The Iliad* (from ancient Greece), Plutarch's *Lives of the Noble Grecians and Romans, Christopher Columbus*, Shakespeare's *Henry V* (medieval times), Dumas' *Three Musketeers* (about 17th century France), *The Song of Roland,* a life of Marie Curie (20th century, and *A Sand County Almanac* (modern American). This chronological spread—from the beginning of history to yesterday—appears in every year's literature and Western Heritage selections. Equally puzzling, Plutarch is studied throughout high school, but why? What is gained by spreading the study of famous Greeks and Romans over four years?

Aside from the puzzling sequences in the Literature courses, and Foundations of Western Heritage courses (both taken for all four years), what you will get is:

- Grade 9: Grammar and Rhetoric, Latin, Geography, Algebra II, and Biology I and II
- Grade 10: Grammar and Rhetoric, Latin, World History, Advanced Mathematics I, Chemistry I and II, and Art and Music for electives
- Grade 11: Grammar and Rhetoric, Latin, U.S. History, Advanced Math II, Chemistry III and Biology III. Again, Art and Music are the electives.
- Grammar and Rhetoric, Latin, a clearly conservative course in Economics and Civics that uses all my favorite books, Calculus, Physics, and our old friends Art and Music

The science courses use mainstream texts, with the exception of physics, which uses Saxon. Summer reading suggestions are also provided. *Mary Pride*

CHAPTER 37

Unit Study Curriculum

I n this chapter we will look at:

- Complete unit-study packages.
- Individual units on specific topics
- Holiday units

We'll mostly be looking at elementary and middle-school programs. The high-school versions of some of these curricula are reviewed in more detail in the chapter on High School with a Difference.

Unit Study Curriculum

"Please Mommy, read it again!." Have you ever noticed that when young children love a certain book, it becomes "theirs"? They eat with it, sleep with it, carry it, and give it a place on the shelf next to their most treasured teddy? **Five In a Row** inspires just that kind of devotion.

So, why are about 50,000 children in 45 countries and all 50 states using these books? The concept is unique: Read the same picture book for five days. Each day choose a different activity that not only highlights a different part of the story, but focuses on a different academic area as well.

Here are just a few topics covered:

- **Social Studies**—geography, character building, relationships, and history
- **Art**—style, medium, elements, symbolism, viewpoint, and line
- **Language Arts**—vocabulary, literature devices, humor, hyperbole, and descriptive writing
- **Math**—counting, calendars, graphing, grouping, fractions, and patterns
- **Science**—animals, astronomy, seasons, senses, water cycles, wind, and navigation

NEW!
Five In A Row
Ages 2–4, Before Five In A Row, $24.95. Ages 4–8, Five In A Row: Volume 1, $19.95; Volume 2, $24.95; Volume 3, $19.95; set of all 3, $58.50; Bible Supplement, $17.95. Ages 8–12, Beyond Five In A Row: Volumes 1–3, $24.95 each; Bible Supplement for each volume, $9.95 each. Laminated full-color story disks, $15. Add $5 shipping per order.
Five in a Row Publishing, PO Box 707, Grandview, MO 64030-0707 (816) 331-5769. Fax: (816) 322-8150. Email: lamberts@sprynet.com. Web: www.fiveinarow.com.

When Renee and her four-year-old read *Mirette on the High Wire* by E. A. McCully (covered in *Five in a Row* Volume 2) they found Paris on their map. They talked about using bright colors in painting. They found all the blue and orange in the pictures. For an older child, you would discuss the color wheel the fact that blue and orange are complementary. Renee and her little one also pretended to be high wire walkers, and acted out several of the more dramatic verbs. These are just some of the 20 activities possible for this one particular book.

Five subject areas—one for each day. Several exercises are given under each subject heading so you are free to choose the ones most suitable for your child. You are also free to read the books in any order; this is not a week-by-week scheduled curriculum! Lessons can take as little as 30 minutes daily, including time spent reading the book, or up to several hours daily if you do every single thing and that day includes a suggested field trip. The main point, as author Jane Claire Lambert makes plain, is to "rediscover the joy of learning" and "build a special bond between you and your student." With your purposeful guidance, through the Five in a Row activities your child will begin to see much more in every book you read.

Each of the three volumes includes everything but the books themselves, most of which are easily available at your local library. Titles range from classics to award-winners, each chosen especially for its unique artistic style and its timeless story: *Peter Rabbit, Make Way for Ducklings,* and *Madeline,* to name a few. The geography lessons are enhanced by the use of a Story Disk for each book as well: small circles with a picture for you to color, cut out and place on a map. Laminated, full-color Story Disk sheets are also now available; the set has disks for all three Five in a Row volumes. Each volume also includes a few other handy charts and patterns used with some of the stories, as well as a bibliography, literary glossary, calendar and planning sheets (unnecessary if you teach "right out of the book"), suggestions for integrating Five in a Row with additional curriculum, and a Master Index subdivided into Social Studies, Language Arts, Art, Math, and Science. The index is further subdivided into topics (e.g., "Social Sciences: Geography"), with individual entries in alphabetical order beneath. This is helpful, but not quite as useful as a Scope and Sequence would be. Since the geographical entries are not in geographical order, and the history entries are not in historical order, etc., it's not easy to see what was covered and what was not. It would be helpful if the publisher would produce a separate Scope and Sequence covering all three volumes, so parents could see what they might want to fill in on their own.

Five in a Row Volume I delves into the following 19 books: *The Story About Ping, Lentil, Madeline, A Pair of Red Clogs, The Rag Coat, Who Owns the Sun?, Mike Mulligan and His Steam Shovel, The Glorious Flight, How to Make an Apple Pie and See the World, Grandfather's Journey, Cranberry Thanksgiving, Another Celebrated Dancing Bear, Papa Piccolo, Very Last First Time, Clown of God, Storm in the Night, Katy and the Big Snow, Night of the Moonjellies,* and *Stopping by Woods on a Snowy Evening.* Of these, the *Clown of God* book, an award winner which tells the Catholic legend of an old juggler whose gift is accepted by a statue of the Christ child, is the only one some homeschooling parents might have qualms about studying.

Five in a Row Volume 2 presents the following 21 books: *The Giraffe that Walked to Paris, Three Names, Wee Gillis, Owl Moon, A New Coat for Anna, Mr. Katz and Tush, Mirette on the High Wire, They Were Strong and Good, Babar: To Duet or Not to Duet; The Story of Ferdinand, Down Down the Mountain, Make Way for Ducklings, The Tale of Peter Rabbit, Mr. Gumpy's Motor Car, All Those Secrets of the World, Miss Rumphius, The Little Red Lighthouse and the Great Gray Bridge, Follow the Drinking Gourd, Harold and the Purple Crayon, When I Was Young in the Mountains,* and *Gramma's Walk.* This volume also includes a year-end review of what was learned in volumes 1 and 2, a dictionary of art terms, and suggestions for supplemental books, music, and videos.

Five in a Row Volume 3 wraps it up with 15 more titles: *The Bee Tree, Andy and the Circus, The Wild Horses of Sweetbriar, Paul Revere's Ride, Henry* the Castaway, *The Finest Horse in Town, Truman's Aunt Farm, The Duchess Bakes a Cake, Andy and the Lion, Warm as Wool, The Salamander Room, Climbing Kansas Mountains, Amber on the Mountain,* and *Little Nino's Pizzeria.*

While not overtly Christian in nature, i.e. you won't find Bible verses accompanying the character discussions, the author (a pastor's wife and homeschool mom with many years' experience) has permeated the book with a love for truth, beauty, and the wonders of God's world. You won't have any trouble discerning just where she is coming from! And if you want more directly Christian teaching, the **Five in a Row Christian Character and Bible Study Supplement** offers several devotional thoughts, with Bible verses, for each book in the Five in a Row series.

Two more products are now available in the Five in a Row series: *Before Five in a Row* and Beyond Five in a Row. For a detailed writeup of **Before Five in a Row**, see the "Readiness" chapter in Volume 2. Briefly, it's a readiness program based on 24 short picture books, with lots of information on how to teach this age level as well. *Beyond Five in a Row*, a literature-based unit study for ages 8–12, is a whole 'nuther animal.

Whereas *Five in a Row* uses "picture books" as its basis, *Beyond Five in a Row* uses chapter books. **Beyond Five in a Row Volume 1** explores two fiction selections, *The Boxcar Children* and *Homer Price*, as well as two non-fiction titles taken form the Childhood of Famous American Series by Aladdin—*Thomas Edison* and *Betsy Ross*. **Beyond Five in a Row Volume 2** again has two fiction selections—*Sarah Plain and Tall* and its sequel *Skylark*—and two nonfiction selections—*The Story of George Washington* and *Hellen Keller*. The two fiction selections in **Beyond Five In a Row, Volume 3** are *A Cricket in Times Square* and *The Saturdays*, while the two nonfiction selections are *Neil Armstrong, Young Flyer* and *Marie Curie and the Discovery of Radium*. Each volume covers one semester with activities including creative writing, history, science, human relationships, geography, fine arts, vocabulary, career paths, and much more. It does not cover arithmetic, spelling, grammar or penmanship.

Beyond Five in a Row is well-organized, winsome, and lots of fun if you have the time to pull together the additional resources and ingredients for the activities. Besides the activities themselves, each chapter includes a parent summary (helpful if you don't have the time to read the books), a list of learning objectives, tons of background information on each topic, and an essay question. Occasional illustrations and symbols (e.g., the Canadian flag, a telegraph machine) help amplify the background information. Internet links are provided, to sites related to lesson topics—a great 21st century touch!

Like *Five in a Row, Beyond Five in a Row* has a Christian point of view but no outright Christian teaching. The optional *Christian Character Bible Study Supplements* provide specific, explicit Christian teaching for Christian homeschool parents.

It's safe to say that children will learn—and remember—more with *Beyond Five in a Row* than with most traditional curriculum.

Five in a Row is the perfect unit study curriculum for busy moms, especially those new to homeschooling. It's flexible: except for a few seasonal selections, you can teach the books in any order; even within a week, the order of the activities is up to you. It's wonderful to use with the little ones while your older students are busy. For preschoolers and non-readers, this program is all you need for a gentle introduction to "school." For the early elementary students who already have a language arts and math program, *Five in a Row* does the rest. *Renee Mathis and Mary Pride*

For *Mirette on the High Wire*, to continue our example, the devotional lessons in the *Christian Character and Bible Study Supplement* to Volume 2 bring out that God has a plan for each of us, we should use our talents in His service (parable of the talents), determination is needed to master the art of wire walking or any other field (the determination Nehemiah showed rebuilding the wall of Jerusalem and the determination the apostles showed in continuing to preach despite persecution), compassion means offering help (the story of the Good Samaritan and the life of Jesus show compassion), and how encouragement can help others go on when they think they can't (God encouraging Elijah, and why the apostle Barnabas was called "Son of Encouragement"). Each of these mini lessons is only a paragraph in length, and uses incidents in the book (e.g., Mirette having compassion on Bellini when he freezes on the high wire) to introduce, illustrate, and interest children in the Bible concept.

Beyond Five in a Row is written by Becky Lambert, the daughter of *Five in a Row*'s author. Becky is homeschooled and began college at age 16. At age 21 she began working full-time as a curriculum designer for her folks' business, Five in a Row Publishing. Her work has the same warm, helpful tone as her mother's, *and* Becky certainly knows her stuff. The amount of background information she provides for each subject is impressive.

UPDATED!
KONOS Character Curriculum

Grades K–8. Volume 1, Volume 2, and Volume 3, $95 each. Colorful laminated timeline figures for each volume, $59.95 each. The dated lines on which to place time line figures are included in Volume 1 timeline or can be purchased separately for $9.95. Any volume plus its corresponding timeline, $144.95. KONOS Compass, $25. KONOS Index, $25. Seminar "How to Use KONOS Curriculum," 6 one-hour cassettes, $25. Writing Tapes, 2 one-hour cassettes teaching composition, $10. Starter kit includes Volume 1 plus its time line, KONOS Compass, seminar tapes, and writing tapes, all for $175. Video Version Starter Kit includes Volume 1, its timeline, KONOS Compass, and 6½ hour video, "Creating the Balance," $290. Shipping extra.
KONOS, Inc., PO Box 250, Anna, TX 75409. (972) 924-2712. Fax: (972) 924-2733. Email: konos@konos.com. Web: www.konos.com.

Each month's KONOS activities follow the theme for that month. The themes for Volume 1 include Attentiveness, Obedience, Orderliness, Honor, Trust, Stewardship, and Patience. Under the theme of Attentiveness, for example, children study how eyes and ears work (science), tell and retell the Bible story of Samuel (Bible, reading comprehension, creative expression), make a straw oboe and paper kazoo (music, art), read Davy Crockett's biography (history, reading), practice tracking (nature study), learn Indian sign language (language), and study Indian customs (social studies)—among many other things!

Every activity has the corresponding subjects listed next to it in the margin. Examples: "Hammer a nail into wood. The next time rub the nail with soap and see if there is a difference." This activity has "Science" listed in the margin. "How old was Noah when he started building the ark?" = Math. "Make your own sandpaper" (instructions follow) = Art and Science. "Learn Indian sign language and picture writing" (directs you to a book on the subject) = Language.

The popular **KONOS** unit-study curriculum for preschool through middle grades is a cross between a lesson plan book, super textbooks covering dozens of subjects, and an encyclopedia. Each volume features character traits—e.g., obedience, attentiveness, loyalty—as unit topics.

Each volume of KONOS can be used for two years. Subjects included are history (primarily American history), Bible, social studies, science, art, music, some language, and some math. All are taught from a Christian perspective. You will need to purchase separate math and phonics curriculum.

Because the authors believe that children learn best by "doing," this program is strong on activities—an ideal program for Action Man learners.

Most of you will want to start with Volume 1, which was originally designed for children in grades K–3. However, one volume is not a prerequisite for the next. Activities are not broken down by specific grade levels as in The Weaver, but you can easily select those that meet your children's abilities and needs. Use the included lesson plans if you need help in making these decisions. These list materials needed and tell you how to prepare for the activity, then break each lesson into suggested activity for younger children, middlers, and older children.

KONOS provides you with a vast array of activities. There are many, many more ideas than you could possibly use. Some people are overwhelmed at the choices, but so many alternatives allow you to choose how much time you spend, the amount of hands-on activity, field trips, books, etc. that fit your situation. The percentage of listed hands-on activities is probably greater in KONOS than in any other unit study, so there are plenty of ideas for very active learners. And the activities themselves are . . . well . . . more *active*. Example: You make a model of the digestive system using cardboard boxes, spray bottles, and your basement stairs. To try it out your child gets to slide down the stairs (he's pretending he's food going down the throat), get spritzed with water (simulating stomach enzymes), and crawl through a cardboard tunnel (the intestines). Compare this to typical textbook "activities" such as filling out crossword puzzles or cutting and pasting and guess which your child would rather do!

In KONOS **Volume 1**, you study a lot of interesting things, but not in any readily discernible order. In **Volume 2**, material is presented in a more chronological order. You'll study famous scientists and inventors by reading biographies and thinking through their experiments. What experiment would *you* concoct to determine whether the earth was flat or round? Hmmm . . . You'll also study colonial history through the eyes of the ethnic groups who settled here. Build a fire using tinder, flint, and steel. Try dressing like a Dutch housewife. Play Puritan games (I kid you not!). All this, plus practical living skills, astronomy, paper designs, a study of ants, model sailboat building, knot tying . . . is there *anything* interesting, useful, or fun that this curriculum doesn't cover? Everything is in a Christian context, with Bible verses to memorize and serious questions to discuss (like, why was it wrong for the Aztecs to sacrifice children to their gods?). All is logically laid out, easy to follow, and most of the materials and books you will use are free, thanks to the KONOS practice of using library books.

Even though all three volumes are multi-level K–8, **Volume 3** is definitely heavy on activities for older children. Under the character trait of Resourcefulness, for example (a trait every teenager should have!), your child studies inventors and their inventions, covering the Industrial Revolution as well as ninth-grade physical science. Under Cooperation (another vital teen virtue!) you study the normal fourth-grade states-and-regions, as well as the "body systems" portion of tenth-grade biology. For this reason, the authors recommend using the books chronologically even though they do not build on each other.

You will need the **KONOS Compass**, so called because it "orients" you to the program. Another great new help is the new **KONOS Index**. Using it you can look up a topic in the general index—say, the digestive system or the Declaration of Independence—and find all KONOS activities associated with that activity. Or you can use the subject index, which groups activities by topics (e.g., Animals) and subtopics (Eagles). This is great for designing lesson plans of your own that do not have to follow the KONOS character traits. With this index and the three KONOS volumes, *any* homeschool family can find activities in a flash that fit with the subjects they are studying, no matter what curriculum they are using.

KONOS does not cover history in chronological order. That's why they sell beautifully laminated **timelines** that coordinate with each volume of the curriculum, plus a Bible Timeline and an Artist and Composers Timeline. KONOS Timelines could also be used with any other curriculum.

If you use all three volumes of KONOS, you will cover material typically covered in history and science programs in school, with the exception of world history. This is covered in the new **KONOS high-school series**, *History of the World*, reviewed separately in chapter 41.

Like other unit-study programs, KONOS works best for well-organized families, especially if you have friends with whom you can share the burden of collecting materials and setting up each activity, such as the famous KONOS "medieval banquet." Even if you are *not* organized, the new Index makes it possible for you to pick and choose activities to fit any curriculum. The activities are great fun, and can put the joy back into homeschools that are beginning to sag. If you need more help in making up your mind about KONOS, check out their *Creating the Balance* video. *Mary Pride*

It's new! It's cool! It's well organized! It's completely rewritten! It's . . . **KONOS-In-A-Box**!

Picture a cardboard suitcase complete with travel stickers. Inside, nestled in a cloud of packing peanuts, is

- **an impressive unit-study curriculum** with complete teacher instructions, newly written writing and literature analysis lessons, and background information galore, all in a daily lessons format
- **timeline figures** and instructions for creating your KONOS timeline

Need a visual example of how to teach the KONOS way? KONOS has created a six-hour video, **Creating the Balance**, in which KONOS co-author Jessica Hulcy demonstrates how to organize school, home, and family while planning and using KONOS. Settings include two hours of "live" teaching footage of Jessica Hulcy teaching her own kids as well as a small co-op group in her front yard, around the kitchen table, and at the zoo. You also are treated to portions of Jessica's workshop presentations. Jessica has such great ideas and covers so much territory that even those using other curricula will learn much from this video.

KONOS provides detailed background information on some activities, but not all. You will need library books and other sources to round out the lessons. Detailed lists of resources and activities are under each heading. It is necessary to plan ahead to get books and other resources that will be needed. For those who have difficulty getting books at the library, KONOS has arranged with Lifetime Books and Gifts (see their catalog writeup in Chapter 7) to carry a line of books specifically correlated to KONOS units. With many, many titles to choose from, you can be sure you'll have plenty of convenient resource material!

NEW!
KONOS-In-A-Box
- Grades K–8. Obedience Kit, $175.
- Obedience Curriculum only, $60.
- Orderliness Kit, $175. Orderliness Curriculum only, $60.
- KONOS, Inc., PO Box 250, Anna, TX 75409. (972) 924-2712. Fax: (972) 924-2733. Email: konos@konos.com. Web: www.konos.com.

- **a to-drool-for collection** of literature and resource books—everything you need for the unit
- **complete craft kits** for about a dozen of the projects you'll be making

Experienced homeschool moms and dads are clutching each other in ecstacy as they read this. "At last!" they are crying. "Everything I need for a KONOS unit study all in one place! No more scrounging around for hard-to-find items and already-checked-out library books! This is so great! I can hardly believe it!"

The first KONOS-In-A-Box unit is right here in my hot little hands. It's the **Obedience** unit from the Classic KONOS Curriculum, rewritten as daily lessons with a complete literature analysis and writing program built right in. Divided neatly into sub-units of Authority and Light, Kings and Queens (a KONOS favorite!), and Horses, the curriculum takes nine weeks to complete.

The curriculum guide itself (a perfect-bound 191-page oversized book) is full of neat features. Some weeks open with the picture and testimony of a mom who has used KONOS successfully. A page is provided each week for lesson plans for three age groups: 5–7, 8–10, and 11–13. Weekly objectives, people you'll be studying, vocabulary words, and materials needed are listed at the beginning of the week. Lists of additional books and videos (for those of you who just can't resist adding more) are also provided. The lessons themselves tell you everything you need to know for each assignment. Subjects (Bible, history, etc.) are listed in the margin next to each assignment, so you'll know how to log them if your state requires this kind of recordkeeping. Pen-and-ink illustrations and diagrams add extra clarity to the instructions. Answers to discussion questions and assignments are provided in small print right below the questions. This is as easy to use as unit studies get.

Orderliness, the second KONOS-In-A-Box kit, which I also have sitting right in front of me, teaches sequencing, counting/measuring, animal/plant/rock classifications, planets/moon, and calendars/seasons.

This unit study guide comes packaged with all the reading books needed for the plan:

- *Usborne Field Guide to Trees of North America*
- *Favorite Book of Poems Old and New*
- *The Secret Garden*
- *The Starry Sky*
- *A Tree is Nice*
- *Frog and Toad are Friends*
- *Peterson's First Guide to Insects*
- *DK Eyewitness Explorer Flowers*

Like the first kit, this one comes with necessary craft materials for three children (including a quality flower-and-leaf press), eight weeks more of sub-units, a very attractive (and thick) perfect-bound teacher's manual with complete instructions, timeline figures, and a carrying case so you have somewhere to put it all.

Coming soon are the following units: **Attentiveness** (Indians, ears/sound/music, eyes/other senses/birds), **Trust** (deception/illusion, sheep/weaving, floating and ships, flight and airplanes), and a completely new unit, **Endurance** (history, geography, culture, people, animals, etc. of Russia).

At this rate, it won't take long until at least the first volume of KONOS is all available "to go"! *Mary Pride*

Let's do the math on this. A school year is typically 36 weeks long. It would take four KONOS-In-A-Box units, of nine weeks each, to fill up a school year. At $175 each, that would be $700 for a full year of school (excluding math and phonics) for all the children in your family between the ages of 5 and 13. Not bad at all! Plus, it's like Christmas every time one of these boxes arrives, which is more than you can say for most curriculum packages.

Teaching With God's Heart For The World is a unit-study curriculum written by a homeschooling mother, designed to bring the spiritual needs of the world into your living room.

The spiral-bound texts give you lots of help to get you started (224 pages in Volume I and 297 pages in Volume II), including a look at the scriptural "whys and hows" for world outreach, a historical overview of missions, blackline masters, and tons of teaching tips. There are sixteen weeks of daily lesson plans per volume, for two semester's worth of material. You'll need to add your own math and science. Beginning with a study of prayer and moving through history beginning with the Old Testament, your study will take you all over the globe, viewing familiar places and events through an evangelical missions lens.

Each week, you'll focus on a different country or region. A typical day's lesson always begins with family devotions and links a passage of scripture up with the prayer need of the place you're studying. Reading and language arts work focuses on gathering factual information about the spiritual condition of each country and depends on extensive use of missionary biographies and library books.

Writing assignments stem from the reading. Example: "In many countries of the world, it is forbidden to speak of Jesus . . . Imagine that you are a missionary in a 'closed' country in Asia. If you were needing prayer, and had to relay important information to your prayer partners back in America, what would you say? Practice writing a letter without saying anything that could possibly endanger your family." Lesson plans also include music (sampling music and learning songs of each culture), craft projects, math and science enrichment, cooking (lots of fun meal ideas!), and family video ideas.

The publisher of this curriculum, Family Mission/Vision Enterprises, carries much of the reading and resource materials you'll need, for easy one-stop shopping. Complete descriptions and prices are listed in the back of Volume II, along with an index of other suppliers. This is a terrific help that other unit-study writers should consider adding to their programs.
Michelle Van Loon

NEW!
Teaching With God's Heart For The World
Grades K–12. Single volume, $49.95. Both volumes, $89.95. Free catalog. *Family Mission/Vision Enterprises, PO Box 1483, Chesapeake, VA 23327-1483.* (757) 547-4605. Fax: (757) 547-2645. *Email: fmve@hotmail.com.* *Web: www.strategicnetwork.org.*

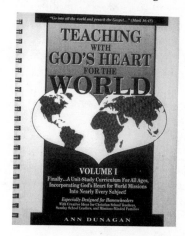

TRISMS Volume I is, to my knowledge, the only homeschool curriculum designed just for the junior-high level. TRISMS stands for "Time Related Integrated Studies for Mastering Skills," which being interpreted means it provides a chronological and geographical

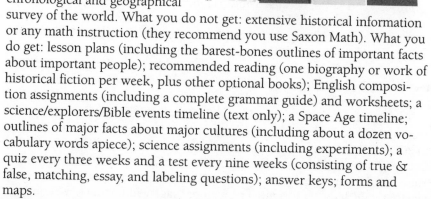

survey of the world. What you do not get: extensive historical information or any math instruction (they recommend you use Saxon Math). What you do get: lesson plans (including the barest-bones outlines of important facts about important people); recommended reading (one biography or work of historical fiction per week, plus other optional books); English composition assignments (including a complete grammar guide) and worksheets; a science/explorers/Bible events timeline (text only); a Space Age timeline; outlines of major facts about major cultures (including about a dozen vocabulary words apiece); science assignments (including experiments); a quiz every three weeks and a test every nine weeks (consisting of true & false, matching, essay, and labeling questions); answer keys; forms and maps.

Now perfect-bound, TRISMS Volume 1 comes with 37 lesson plans, in a week-at-a-glance format. A 22-page orientation to the program, a huge 35-

NEW!
TRISMS Volume 1
Grades 6–8 (volume I) and 9–12 (volume II). TRISMS volume I, $100. Student Pack, $25. Timeline book, $10. Add 10% shipping. *TRISMS, 1203 S. Delaware Pl., Tulsa, OK 74104.* (918) 585-2778. Fax: (918) 491-6826 *Email: linda@trisms.* *Web: www.trisms.com.*

Book packages to accompany TRISMS volumes are available from In His Steps, 1618 Kendolph, Denton, TX 76205. 800-583-1336. Email: inhissteps@juno.com. Web: www.trisms.com.

Your success with Volume 1 will entirely depend on how many of the recommended books or suitable substitutes you can lay your hands on and how much you, the parent, already know about the historical events and personages being studied. A good encyclopedia will also be a tremendous help. Presented with a day's lesson that reads, "1848 Sewing Machine; Vocabulary: abolitionist, missionary; News stories (English assignment C-19d); Historical Events: 1837–1901 Victoria, Queen of England; 1848 February Revolution—Louis overthrown; 1851 Louis Napoleon becomes dictator of France; 1852–70 Louis reigned as Emperor Napoleon III; 1853 Admiral Perry opens Japan," you had better have some way of finding out more about these tantalizing tidbits.

UPDATED!
The Weaver

PreK–K, $110. Grades K–6: Volumes 1–5, $145/volume. Grades 7–12: supplements, $30–$50/volume. Shipping extra.
Weaver Curriculum Company, 300 N. McKemy Ave., Chandler, AZ 85226. (888) 367-9871. Fax: (480) 785-8034. Email: weaver@aopub.com. Web: www.weaverinc.com.

You can still purchase the original editions, since the final editions are unlikely to come out during the fall 2000 school season.

page annotated reading list, and separate sections for science assignments, language assignments, poetry/literature helps, worksheet answer keys, timelines, culture outlines, and test and quiz answer keys round out this one-book curriculum. All sections are thumb-indexed—a helpful feature.

Students make their own timeline and fill out forms to answer questions about the people studied: Who? Motivation? Changes they caused? Consequences of the changes? Dates? New vocabulary? The questions are always the same, so eventually the student learns to ask himself these questions automatically as he reads. Students also write mini-reports on 3x5 note cards for every biography and work of historical fiction they read. Parents are supposed to read one recommended book aloud each month to the student (or have him read it to them), and watch one recommended historical/mythological movie a month.

Good news: TRISMS now offers a package of all the historical fiction and biographies needed with Volume 1—ask In His Steps for a price sheet!

TRISMS Volume 2 switches the emphasis from social studies to humanities. See separate writeup in Chapter 41.

You are allowed to photocopy the forms included with either volume for your family's use only, or if you prefer you can purchase a Student Pack, which includes all the forms needed for TRISMS, namely worksheets, tests, quizzes, and maps. At the low price of this curriculum, and considering each volume really covers two years of everything except math, I'd spring for a Student Pack for each student. It makes a handy record of student learning when filed away with sample assignments. *Mary Pride*

The **Weaver** unit-studies program has been purchased by Bridgestone Multimedia (publishers of the Alpha Omega curriculum) and set up as a new subsidiary company. The curriculum, whose units are based on chronological Bible history, is currently being revised and updated. The updated *Success in Spelling* volume is available now. Its new much-requested feature: master spelling lists for the teacher with diacritical marks included.

Additional supplemental teaching materials of many kinds were originally developed to accompany The Weaver. All of these either have been or will be reissued in updated editions. These include phonics (*1-2-3 Read!*), grammar and composition based on the book of Romans (*The High Way to English Grammar*), Bible-based language arts (*Wisdom Words*), *Teaching Tips, Penmanship to Praise,* and more.

Updated editions of Weaver volumes 1–3 with their accompanying Day-by-Day volumes are currently under development, as is a new edition of The Interlock preschool curriculum.

This is good news, because while the ideas behind the original Weaver curriculum were wonderful, frankly the grammar and writing needed some professional editing. Nicer graphics were also needed, as will making sure the activities are doable in a reasonable time frame. The original Weaver, for example, asked you to research the history of your town. This might be OK as an ongoing year-long study, but does not work well in the framework of a week-long unit on cities.

The final revision will have that professional editing I mentioned, the graphics will be updated, skimpy areas will be fleshed out (e.g., upgrading the Civil War coverage from one page to an entire unit), and overly ambitious activities will be pruned. Best of all, the questions will have answers! You won't have to spend all day with the encyclopedia to figure out whether your kids got it right! The final package will be much more user-friendly and eye-appealing, with the same creative touch that initially endeared The Weaver to thousands of homeschool families.

The original edition of the preschool-kindergarten manual, called **The Interlock**, starts at Genesis 1 and continues through Genesis 10. Volume 1 covers Genesis 11-50, Volume 2 does the same for Exodus and the Books of Law, and Volume III covers Joshua, Judges, and Ruth. All these are cross-referenced to other Bible verses, so you cover more of the Bible than you initially expected.

Teaching materials include:

- *Teaching Tips and Techniques,* a hefty book full of how-tos for all subjects, motivation techniques, developmental stages, and general teaching how-tos
- *Skills Evaluation for the Home School*
- Lesson plan guidebooks, with daily lesson plans for each chapter of The Weaver Curriculum

Volume I of the Weaver starts with Genesis and includes these topics: City, Architecture, Language, History, Transportation, Famine—Water, Plants, Animals, Stewardship of Money, Solar System and Stars, Covenant/Character Sketch, Family (life cycle and reproduction), Character Sketch of Isaac and Rebekah, Character Sketch of Jacob (focusing on deceit and its consequences), Character Sketch of Joseph (including a study of slavery).

Volume II goes through Exodus, Numbers, and Deuteronomy, with topics such as Desert and Royalty.

Volume III tours Joshua, Judges, Ruth, and part of I Samuel. By Volume III you are getting into topics like Exploration, Espionage and Communications, How History Is Recorded, Fortifications, Music, Thinking Skills, Time, Conquest of the Land (correlated with U.S. history 1790–1861), Idolatry, and Judicial Systems.

Volume IV deals with the history of the kings and prophets of Israel and Judah.

Volume V studies the life of Christ. It covers Matthew, Mark, Luke, and John.

Each volume also covers some aspect of world history.

It will be interesting to see what a large company can do with the ideas created in a small family. Will this be the unit-study curriculum of the future? Tune in later and see for yourself! *Mary Pride*

Individual Units

A well-planned unit study is like an educational banquet. While it seems that almost everybody has used at least one unit study in their homeschool, not everyone enjoys the work involved in planning one.

Amanda Bennett, mechanical engineer turned homeschooling mother, has written a new **Unit Study Adventure Series** series that makes planning a unit study as much fun as teaching one. When I opened the **Oceans** unit study guide, I could hardly wait to use it!

Each unit study guide is divided into seventeen sections: Introduction (overview of the unit), Outline (scope and sequence), Job Opportunities, Curriculum Resources, Reference Resources, Reading and Activity Resources, Suggested Spelling and Vocabulary lists for upper and lower grades, Room Decoration Resources (a section which gives addresses where students can write for free information and classroom decorations), Software and Games Resources, Video Suggestions, Subject Word List, Writing Ideas, Field Trip Suggestions, Trivia Quiz, Internet Resources, and a Worksheet Research Outline and Teaching Notes. There's also lots of

Volumes are color-coded to indicate which activities should be used with which age group. Kindergarten is gold, first grade is hot pink, second grade is pale pink, third grade is blue, fourth grade is yellow, fifth grade is green, and sixth grade is orange. This saves lots of time, as you can easily flip to the exact pages you need for each child.

While written for grades K–6, each individual volume can be upgraded to a junior/senior high curriculum by purchasing the appropriate volume supplement. These add grade-appropriate social studies and science assignments, divided up into three levels: grades 7/8, 9/10, and 11/12.

NEW!
Amanda Bennett Unit Study Adventure Series
Grades preK–12. $13.99 each. Journal, $7.99. Shipping extra. *Homeschool Press. Doing business through their website only,* *www.unitstudy.com*

space for you to write your own notes and discoveries. All you need to supply are students, time, a library card, and (optionally) an Internet connection!

The tone of these guides is so refreshing! Amanda Bennett states in the Introduction to the **Oceans** unit, "It's so important to understand our surroundings and learn all that we can about them, in order to maintain the wonderful natural balance that God had in mind."

The resource lists in these guides are varied and are meant to provide parents with a handy starting point for scouting out resources to "flesh out" the unit study. If you follow the guidelines, you can be assured that you haven't left out anything of importance. This gives parents peace of mind while allowing for flexibility in selecting materials. The resources you use can be selected to complement your child's age and reading proficiency levels.

These Adventure Series topics are currently available—**Baseball** (history, softball, and legends of the game), **Gardens** (history, gardening, and plant science), **Olympics** (history, geography, and sports), **Elections** (presidents, campaigns, and government), **Pioneers** (nature, life & times, American geography), **Computers** (technology, electronics, Internet), **Homes** (construction, architecture, and home economics), **Oceans** (sea life, exploration, world geography), and the record-keeping **Journal** (use one per unit study to collect your records of field trips, books read, daily activities, etc.). **Thanksgiving** and **Christmas** are also available. Look for more in this series to be available each year. *Teresa May*

NEW!
Kym Wright's Unit Studies

Grades preK–12: Birds, $17.95, Goats, $13.95. Grades 4–9, Microscope, $17.95. Postpaid. *AlWright! Publishing, PO Box 225, Middlefield, CT 06455. Email: KymWright@openarmsmagazine.com. Web: www.openarmsmagazine.com.*

If you have wanted to try your hand at **unit studies**, these are a great place to start! **Kym Wright** has brought her energy and enthusiasm to her well-designed units. These comb-bound study guides include fascinating activities, carefully-designed worksheets, resource listings, and Kym's adventurous projects. There are activities to please all learning styles, a wide variety of ages, and a range of climates. Also included are Scripture references, reading lists, supplier addresses, vocabulary lists, and ideas and instructions for writing projects or research papers. Worksheets can be copied for your family's use. Novices will find the unit planning and record-keeping sheets especially helpful.

Are your children fascinated by birds? If so, they will enjoy the 90-page comb-bound **Bird Unit Study** a well-designed 6–8 week introduction to the world of ornithology. "Bird Feeders," for example, includes simple feeder ideas that a very young child would enjoy and more complex ideas for older students, scripture verses for study and memorization, writing ideas, drawing practice, field study instructions, vocabulary, readings from Usborne's *Ornithology*, and even practice learning bird calls!

The first two-thirds of the book includes unit goals/objectives, record-keeping sheets, and clear instructions for each topic, from hatching chicks (optional) and building bird feeders, to identifying bird characteristics and learning to sketch birds in the field. The last third of the book gives Scripture references, a reading list, supplier addresses, more detailed instructions for "Eggsperiments," vocabulary lists, ideas and instructions for a research paper, and various worksheets that can be copied for your family's use.

The Bird Unit Study would be a delightful way to develop an appreciation and knowledge of birds, and the excellent directions make this a good choice for the unit study novice.

Next . . . goats? Yes, goats. From my own experience raising goats for Heifer Project International, I found that these animals are wonderful to raise, and far more economically important than most Americans realize.

The **Goat Unit Study** provides a wealth of fascinating information, intriguing projects, lists of goat-related books, and even a goat-less milking project! Also included are superb business-planning worksheets for those who are interested in pursuing this project further.

If you have been looking for a good introduction to microscopes, **Microscopes** will be a delight for the young naturalist or the novice biologist . History of the microscope, purchasing advice, microscope use and care, sources for materials, as well as numerous projects, are all included. The excellent lab sheets provide careful instructions, and are nicely laid out.

These are delightful units, and the excellent directions make them a good choice for the unit study novice or time-pressed veteran. *Kristin Hernberg*

The **Media Angels Creation Science Unit Studies** (*Creation Science, Geology, Astronomy,* and *Anatomy*) by Felice Gerwitz and Jill Whitlock each include activities divided into levels for grades K–3, 4–8, and 9–12. Each level includes a teaching outline, subject area division, games and activities. Plus excellent book lists and resource lists. Plan on a minimum of 4–8 weeks for each unit study, or more if you have the time. *The Science Fair Project Handbook* answers all your nitty-gritty questions about picking a topic, exhibiting, the rules of judging, etc.—I'd recommend it

to anyone who wants to enter a fair. *Teaching Science* is 91 spiral-bound pages that answer homeschool moms' questions, plus some great resource lists and recommendations for books and supplies. *Mary Pride*

Holiday Units

If your knowledge of the biblical feast days consists primarily of what you've seen in *Fiddler on the Roof*, then take heart! Authors Robin Sampson and Linda Pierce have done a commendable job in putting together a resource that will be appreciated by everyone from Old Testament scholars to those who aren't sure of the difference between a Torah and a Menorah. Thoroughly and systematically, they offer a treatment not only of the major biblical feasts, but also the Sabbath traditions, Purim, and Hannukah.

The first section of **A Family Guide to the Biblical Holidays** is a detailed overview of the importance of the holidays, our Hebrew roots, and how to understand the Hebrew calendar. This section is followed by a Preliminary Activities and Crafts section that will help you prepare for your family's celebrations. Instructions and patterns are given for centerpieces, wall-hangings, flags, and games. Following this are the sections devoted to the feasts themselves. Each section is laid out the same way:

- The purpose of the feast or holiday
- The feast in Bible times
- Jewish customs of the feast today
- Messianic significance of the feast
- Suggestions for celebrating the feast

Next come ideas for recipes, crafts, and games pertinent to each celebration. Each unit includes a coloring page as well as an activity suitable for older children, usually a word search or crossword puzzle.

Since this review was written, Kym Wright has produced four more units: Sheep, Poultry, Botany, and Victorian Sewing & Quilting.

The authors bend over backward not to give preferential treatment to any one particular denomination or doctrine. In cases where controversy is present (eschatology for example), they attempt to give equal time to all the major views.

NEW!
Holidays & Celebrations with Lasting Lessons

Grades K–3. $26.95 plus shipping. *Lasting Lessons, 1209 Avenue 'N', Suite 11, Plano, TX 75074. (800) 820-LAST. Inquiries: (972) 398-1834. Fax: (214) 821-5483. Email: lastinglessons@msn.com. Web: www.lastinglessons.com.*

The last section will be greatly appreciated by unit-study enthusiasts. "Holidays Across the Curriculum" features detailed suggestions and resources for implementing a year-long or seasonal study of the holidays in your homeschool. The correlation between feasts (units) are: Passover (Lamb), Unleavened Bread (Bread), Firstfruits (Plants), Weeks (Law), Trumpets (Praise and Worship), Day of Atonement (Grace), Tabernacles (Trees), Hannukah (Oil), Purim (Fruits).

Extensive appendices help round out this hefty volume. You get more resource lists, Internet sites to check out, further discussions of symbols and numbers, as well as answer keys for all the puzzles.

My only quibble is a minor one. I wish they had included a few more traditional recipes (What? Challah bread with nary an egg? And no latkes for Hannukah!) as well as a pronunciation guide for some of the more difficult words. Even so, at 583 pages they didn't leave out much. Shalom! *Renee Mathis*

If you are looking for new and different activities to go along with holiday units, this book might interest you. Each of the literature-based units in **Holidays & Celebrations with Lasting Lessons** contains ideas for a display table, a wall display, original poems, many hands-on activities and party ideas. Each unit features one core literature selection (books which should be available in public libraries) and a list of related literature. Though the book is written primarily for the classroom, there are some items throughout specifically for homeschoolers, denoted with a little home symbol. All the units are designed to be used over a one- to two-week period.

What's different about this book is that many of the activities are not the typical holiday fare. Each holiday unit centers around a theme, usually something gleaned from the core literature selection. For example, the core literature for Halloween is *Stellaluna* by Janell Cannon. The theme is bats and most of the activities deal with bats in one way or another. The activities are creative and hands-on and incorporate all subject areas.

If you are a Christian and are looking for activities which celebrate the religious aspect of many of these holidays, you will be disappointed. However, with the possible exception of a reference to magic in the Valentine's Day core literature (everything the boy touches turns to chocolate), you will find nothing offensive in this book either.

The following holidays are covered, with an average of 19 pages per holiday: Columbus Day, Halloween, Thanksgiving, Christmas, Valentine's Day, St. Patrick's Day, Easter, Mother's Day, Father's Day and Independence Day. In addition there are 7 pages of general instructions and hints, 13 pages on various ways to celebrate birthdays and 9 pages devoted to celebrating the 100th day of school (these last 2 have no core literature selection). There is also a 47-page appendix containing reproducible items that go with the activities throughout the book. The book overall is illustrated with simple, attractive line drawings. *Melissa Worcester*

CHAPTER 38

Very Different Curriculum

We had to make some judgment calls while designing this book. Here are some of the questions we were asking ourselves:

- "Where do you put a program that includes *both* unit studies *and* textbook studies?"
- "You *could* describe the Noah Plan as 'classical American" curriculum, but it has an unusual structure, unlike any other program . . . so where does it go?"
- "I guess you'd have to say the ESP Super Yearbooks are 'back to basics' in content, but they're unlike all the other worktext programs available, so do they *really* belong in that chapter?"
- "Advanced Training Institute curriculum includes unit studies, but it has a lot of other unique features . . . does it go in this chapter, or that one?"

We finally decided to put all the most provocative, innovative, unusual, and unique curriculum in a chapter by itself. This one.

So if you're a pioneer . . . if you march to the sound of a different drummer . . . if you're looking for something very different . . . check these options out!

Very Different Curriculum Reviews

A project of Bill Gothard's Institute in Basic Life Principles, the **Advanced Training Institute International** (ATI) program reflects Gothard's message. ATI materials use the Bible as the core of all learning and from that core are intended to lead students to master all areas of study. The program stresses the father's leadership role and the mother's homemaking role. Enrollment is limited to qualifying families: a preliminary qualification is that both parents have attended the Basic Life Principles Seminar and the Advanced Seminar.

Parents must also attend an intensive one-week training seminar, which fills them in on the program's philosophy and instructs them in how to operate it.

**UPDATED!
Advanced Training Institute International**
Grades preK–12. Post-high-school training is apprenticeship format. Telos college level online learning program and Oak Brook College of Law and Government Policy home based program are also available. $675/family, includes training seminar and materials. Food and lodging while attending seminar not included.

Institute in Basic Life Principles, Box One, Oak Brook, IL 60522-3001. (630) 323-9800. Fax: (630) 323-6746. Email: info@atiiblp.org Web: www.iblp.org.

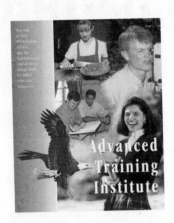

Another unique feature of ATI is its apprenticeship program. This program emphasizes that any vocation will be more significant if it is related to the goal of strengthening families, since the family is the foundation of both church and nation.

To be effective in their vocation, ATI believes that students need specialized training in four areas: counseling, medicine, law, and business. Rather than going to college, where students must major in a designated field, ATI apprenticeship students train under specialists in each of these fields. This is the focus of the Telos program. The address of the Telos program is The Telos Institute International, 2820 N Meridian Street, Indianapolis, IN 46208, 630-323-7073.

The program itself is heavily Scriptural. Much stress is placed on character development and application of Biblical principles in daily living. Parents evaluate their children regularly using ATI's computerized reports.

The ATI curriculum includes both *Wisdom Booklets* and *Wisdom Applications*. These unit studies start with a Scripture verse—e.g., "And seeing the multitudes . . . he went up into a mountain." The theme for this unit would be Seeing and Sight, and it would be studied from several perspectives: Linguistics (language, grammar, vocabulary, communication), History (archaeology, geography, prophecy, music, art, literature), Science (including math), Law (government, economics, logic), and Medicine (health, nutrition, behavior, counseling). Under the topic of Medicine, for example, ATI's study asks the question, "How do the things we see affect our physical strength?" Then follows a description of the way adrenaline affects the bodily organs, along with exciting stories of the amazing things people have done when moved by adrenaline, pictures of the organs involved, etc. Topics picked for the *Wisdom Booklets* are meant to demonstrate the applications of the Scripture passage.

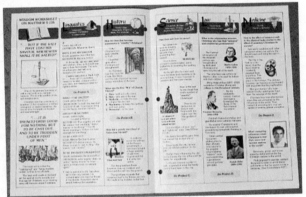

Alternatively, verses chosen are meant to illuminate the subject area.

A *Parent Guide* accompanies each *Wisdom Booklet*. This guide includes introductory ideas, bibliography, cross-references in the required resource library (for further study), an answer key for projects and quizzes, extra unit study ideas, and creative ideas for teaching concepts to younger children.

Scripture itself is studied intensively through "Wisdom Searches." These are Dad's responsibility, and consist of the whole family together searching out what the Bible says about important topics. Each *Parent Guide* includes suggestions for doing this effectively and correlating it with its *Wisdom Booklet*.

The curriculum includes many other unique materials, such as the *Parts of Speech* guide which provides activities for teaching the parts of speech, and (for older children) the 18-lesson *Sentence Analysis* course, and ATI's 24 x 36" illustrated *Time Line Chart*.

I should mention somewhere in here that all the materials are absolutely beautiful and intellectually intriguing. You won't find any fill-in-the-blanks here! Along with the strong Scriptural emphasis, the high quality and organization of the materials are probably why everyone I have talked to who has tried this program raves about it.

Hospitality and ministry are important parts of the program. ATI wants children to be involved in their parents' ministry, not to be an excuse for not having any ministry. Also, ATI believes in Biblical roles for boys and girls.

The "ALERT" program, which has been in operation for six years and as of fall 2000 had served over 600 young men, is an example of this apprenticeship approach for high-school graduates. This 68-week program is divided into three phases: a military-style "boot camp" that features discipline and fitness without the weapons training common to military programs; medical and rescue training that equips young men to help in a variety of crisis and service settings; and advanced training in a specialty of

choice, ranging from aircraft maintenance to National Academy of Police Diving certification. After completion of all three phases, actual ministry service related to the training rounds out the program. To apply, you must have attended the Basic seminar and have a high-school diploma. For more information, see the review in Volume 3 or contact ALERT's new headquarters in Texas (they've moved since I wrote the review in volume 3). It's at RR2, Box 6000, Big Sandy, TX 75755, (903) 636-2000, fax (903) 636-2013, alert@nwcc.iblp.org. An application package is $10; a brochure describing the program is available at no charge.

ATI's application booklet provides excellent information about the seminars and the ATI curriculum, along with sample sheets from the curriculum. Send for it if you have the time to spend a week away from home as a couple and if you're interested in this program. *Mary Pride*

Clonlara School is a program for the progressive, do-it-yourself type.

You get a curriculum to use as a starting point for a program you tailor yourself, a *Math Skills Guidebook*, and a *Communication Skills Guidebook*, plus Clonlara's menu of support services.

You create your own individualized program with the help of Clonlara's curriculum listing and as much guidance from your assigned contact teacher as you desire. The listing tells you what subjects to study and what the objectives are in each area. Some families take it just as it stands, some don't bother with it at all, and some change it around to suit themselves. This latter is the option Clonlara recommends most: to use it as a working paper.

Clonlara's *Skills Guidebooks* are diagnostic tools that cover the basics. You can find out where your children stand by checking off their accomplishments on the chart in the *Math Skills Guidebook* and seeing if they are on track for their ages in the *Communications Skills Guidebook*.

The choice of textbooks and other materials is left entirely to the family. Clonlara suggests you go beyond texts by making wide use of the public library and building up your home library.

Each month you send in a credit report form (for high school) to Clonlara, or a daily or monthly log (for levels 1–8). Clonlara teachers review these, and respond when necessary. A cumulative file folder (student record) is kept for each student. Clonlara provides report cards, transcripts, and a private school diploma on graduation. Graduation occurs when a student has completed his credits and exit examinations, regardless of his age. A Clonlara diploma is widely accepted.

Parents and students are not pressured into completing a particular amount of work and mailing it to Clonlara. Neither do you have to wait for Clonlara's judgment upon your work. Passage to another grade or subject does not hinge on Clonlara's approval. You decide what you are ready for and when you are ready for it.

The Clonlara staff bristles with official credentials, up to and including the Ph.D. Dr. Pat Montgomery, Clonlara's director, is very active in the alternative school movement, and has served as President of the National

Clonlara School

Grades K–12, US residents, Mexico, or Canada. $550 for families with one student enrolled, $575 for families with two to three students enrolled, $600 for families with four or more students enrolled. First-time juniors, $650. First-time seniors, $1150. Books and supplies extra. Standardized achievement testing extra. Refunds: $75 fee for cancellation within ten days after families receive enrollment materials. Clonlara must be notified in writing. *Clonlara School, 1289 Jewett, Ann Arbor, MI 48104. (734) 769-4511. Fax: (734) 769-9629. Email: clonlara@wash.k12.mi.us Web: www.clonlara.org.*

Clonlara stresses manipulative learning tools and real-life experiences in place of endless workbookery. You choose the texts you do use based on the student's achieved grade level in each subject, not his age. You can order texts from any school publisher through Clonlara.

Coalition of Alternative Community Schools. She has addressed education conferences in over 41 states and six foreign countries.

For online mavens, Clonlara has added a "Compu-High" program. See details in Chapter 42.

Families who follow John Holt's lead rank high on the list of those who find Clonlara compatible. This includes those who can "do it themselves" but want a friendly school's guidance and backup and those who want to try the structure of a traditional program without the pressure of deadlines and punishments (such as withholding grades). Progressive types looking for a relaxed program will probably be most comfortable with Clonlara. *Mary Pride*

NEW!
ESP Golden Edition Super Yearbooks

Grades K–7. $32.95 each plus $5.05 shipping.
ESP Publishers, Inc., 7100 123rd Circle N., Largo, FL 38773. Orders: (800) 643-0280. Inquiries: (727) 532-9100. Fax: (727) 539-6071.
Web: www.espbooks.com

The handiest curriculum solution around for busy parents may be ESP's **Golden Edition Super Yearbooks** for grades K–7. (The "ESP" name, by the way, has nothing to do with extra-sensory perception—this is a *very* traditional company!) Each of these monster workbooks is between 608 and 984 pages, getting bigger as the kids using them get older. The idea is that you get this one book, go through it from beginning to end, and thereby cover *every* basic subject in the *same order* they are usually taught in public and private schools.

Complete parent/teacher instructions are included, but are hardly needed, as each page explains itself, and answers can be found in the back of the book. You can see the curriculum areas covered at a glance by the color-coded boxes on the inside front and back covers. Finally, each book now ends with a lengthy Achievement Test and one or more bonus units on such topics as nutrition, Spanish, or the U.S. Constitution.

The Super Yearbooks are straightforward about matters of right and wrong behavior, including how we should treat others, and unambiguously opposed to alcohol and drug abuse. These are secular, but strongly moral, worktexts.

We have used these Yearbooks, and can testify to their usefulness and friendliness. Let's look at them grade by grade:

Kindergarten (608 pages). This starts out smartly with page after page of alphabet letters. The child traces the letter three times, colors the letter, and colors a picture of an object beginning with that letter. Then comes more tracing of smaller-sized letters, combined with recognizing similarities and differences; dot-to-dot work with numbers and letters, including some interesting exercises in tracing geometric shapes on a dotted grid; number recognition; vocabulary words (again with large letters to trace, plus pictures to color); all intermixed with typical preschool exercises on following directions, right and left, up and down, etc. Every page is inviting, with only a few words to trace, pictures to color, or whatnot per page.

I've described the majority of the first half of the book. In all, you get reading readiness (letter recognition and handwriting), vocabulary and spelling, hand/eye coordination, counting and number recognition, and lots of visual discrimination exercises, all organized so each day's work will build on the next. In addition, there is a bonus "families and neighborhood" social studies unit at the end (this includes a page entitled "Mother

In my experience, little kids love this book. For best results, I'd suggest supplementing with phonics flashcards (to drill letter/sound recognition) and some work counting real-world objects. For a complete kindergarten program, you'll also want to read aloud from library books, sing nursery rhymes, do a variety of art projects, play simple games, and practice basic motor skills such as hopping, skipping, and balancing.

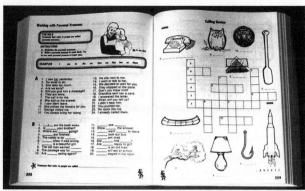

Works at Home," something you will *not* see in almost any other secular curriculum), plus a 30-page "Alphabet Testing" post-test to be given upon completion of the book, so you can gauge your child's progress.

Grade 1 (688 pages). In an attempt to make the course attractive to children, this book starts with an awful lot of coloring and nursery rhymes (with words, but no tunes, supplied). Our little girls enjoyed it, but our son definitely didn't. In contrast to the Kindergarten book, there is no handwriting in the beginning of the book—instead, the student colors page after page of large letters. Personally, I would rather have had the nursery rhymes in the Kindergarten volume, and I'd gladly trade handwriting practice for all the extra coloring. A review of the manuscript alphabet finally start on page 70. You then proceed to number recognition, tracing words that begin with a given alphabet letter (pages and pages of this), counting sets of dots, simple addition (illustrated by pictures of hands showing a given number of fingers), same and different, and so on. Phonics is introduced in the form of short-vowel words and long-vowel words. More addition exercises continue, with various objects being added, and some word problems. Missing-consonant and missing-vowel exercises are common.

Again, I've described about half the book so far. Keep in mind that a given number of pages will usually have a variety of different exercises, so the child won't be bored by doing the same thing for page after page.

In all, you'll cover phonics exercises with short words (though you need to know how to teach the vowel and consonant sounds yourself), counting through 50, simple addition and subtraction, an introduction to grammar, reading exercises that often teach science or social-studies lessons, vocabulary, spelling, handwriting, and health. You also get a bonus 94-page Health unit at the end of the book, as well as an achievement test with answers and a score conversion table to show your child's approximate grade level of achievement.

Grade 2 (816 pages). This starts right out with writing (not tracing) letters and words. At this level, the books start resembling a very traditional, thorough, public-school sequence, minus any hint of political correctness. Exercises cover phonics (a review of short and long vowels, plus diphthongs and digraphs not covered in first grade); all the addition, subtraction, word problems, coin problems, and so on normally covered in second grade; oodles of vocabulary and spelling pages; simple grammar; lots of reading exercises (each loaded with educational nuggets—no stories about rock stars); visual discrimination exercises; social studies; for science, an introduction to many topics covered in more depth in the coming years; health; and nutrition. There is also a separate 93-page Health and Nutrition section, and a 31-page Spanish/English Bilingual Picture Word Study. This consists of words with translations in a box at the top of the page, with a picture below that the student labels with the Spanish words appropriate to each part of the picture.

Given that you have phonics pretty much under control at this point (which you should by the end of first grade), you will only need to supplement with library books, art projects, music training, and phys ed. You can count on the Super Yearbook itself to cover everything academic needed at this age level.

To supplement this volume, again you'll want library books, art projects, simple music training, and phys ed activities. If you know how to teach phonics, you'll probably be able to work in enough lessons using this book—otherwise, it would be smart to invest in a separate phonics curriculum, mainly in order to teach you how to teach this subject.

At level 3, and subsequent levels, you will begin to notice that the reading selections at the tops of the science pages do not necessarily provide all the information needed to answer the questions below. Your general knowledge, an encyclopedia, and a good set of Usborne or Dorling-Kindersley books will be very helpful in "filling in the blanks." If all else fails, answers are of course available in the back of the book. This is actually beneficial, since you'll get more out of looking up "cotton" in an encyclopedia than from just reading a short paragraph or two about it. Even so, the science reading excerpts still contain more actual facts than you usually find in curriculum for this age group.

However, the history and social science reading excerpts *do* contain all the information necessary to answer the questions below them.

Grade 3 (872 pages). A student has to be able to read well to handle this book. It starts right in with reading exercises, fill-in-the-missing-vowel exercises, writing numerals for words, fill-in-the-blanks, true/false questions, and lots more. One thing you won't have to worry about after using this book will be having your child know how to do well on tests! Cursive handwriting training begins on page 9, with sentence models for the child to copy. The handwriting used features ornate capital letters. In my opinion, it's good for children to know how to *read* these types of capitals, but a mix of manuscript capitals and cursive or cursive italic letters is more efficient and legible.

Writing assignments in this book mostly consist of adding a sentence or two to an existing story. A few longer assignments are also included.

At this level, you'll also discover that the pictures on each page often contain valuable information about the topic. For example, a page on looms will include pictures of a simple loom, machine thread bobbins, and a machine spool. It is up to you to explain how these work, though.

For third grade, the bonus unit is on the U.S. Constitution, and includes the full text of the Constitution itself. You will definitely need to work through this *with* your child—don't count on an eight-year-old handling this as a self-study project!

Grade 4 (944 pages). The amount of sheer information presented in this and subsequent grades is impressive. From detailed information on a large number of animals, to the correct terminology for the parts of a flower, from Roman numerals to how to respect personal property, from the different types of Indian dwellings to what you can expect to find in a museum, there's way more here than you'll find in just about any other curriculum. In what other fourth-grade program can you expect to find how a jet engine works, right next to a page on how germs multiply?

Social studies in fourth grade is relatively slim, covering some very basic Americana (Thanksgiving Day, the national anthem, etc.) and some info on community institutions, such as clubs, church camps, fire stations, and the like.

Again, you get all the basic math, spelling, grammar, vocabulary, and so on you'd expect at this grade level, plus health, nutrition, science, life science (a separate topic in this grade, covering basic body systems with an emphasis on how to keep them healthy), plus the same unit on the U.S. Constitution as found in third grade, a vocabulary pre- and post- test, and achievement tests in math and English.

Supplement with a wide variety of library books, art, music, phys ed, and lots of time outdoors.

Grade 5 (952 pages). This picks up where fourth grade left off. Presented this year only are the topics of Reference Skills and Listening Skills. For social studies, you get U.S. history of colonial days, a quickie tour of the U.S.A. and major regions of the world, and a one-page look apiece at a large number of ethnic groups, including (amazingly) Hungarians. Being partly of Hungarian descent, I am naturally charmed!

Life Science in fifth grade is an excellent study of anatomy, teaching the correct terminology right along with how each body system works. Science (a separate topic) covers classes of animals and plants, weather, geology, and some simple chemistry. The Reading selections are interesting and educational, with a preponderance of selections about individual animals, but also some on ethnic groups and famous people. Vocabulary, spelling, math, and English are all thoroughly covered as well. You get the same bonus U.S. Constitution unit as found in the third grade book (the publisher is obviously determined that each child should have a chance to study it *sometime!*), a vocabulary test you are supposed to give both at the beginning and end of the course, and language arts and math achievement tests.

Now is a good time for your student to begin keeping a journal, for extra writing practice. Pen-pals are also fun. Add art, music, and phys ed as you are able. And don't forget the library!

Grade 6 (952 pages). Science, in this grade, includes mostly some chemistry terms, physics of light, astronomy, a smidgin of biology, and some paleontology (just a few pages) with evolution not specifically mentioned. "Life Science" is anatomy again. Reading selections are mostly about animals and plants. Social studies is world history and geography. Health includes etiquette, some first aid, hygiene, and some exercises. Nutrition is mostly basic food groups and dietary needs. English is mostly grammar. Math, vocabulary, and spelling topics all cover what is needed for this grade level. Exercises often require multiple-sentence written answers. Again, the book ends with the same U.S. Constitution unit, vocabulary test, and language arts and math achievement tests.

Grade 7 (984 pages). English for this grade level includes a complete grammar review, plus lots of training in how to write well. Science is topics in biology, chemistry, and physics. Reading selections are about half-and-half divided between real-world information—on topics from how to get a job to various types of housing and insurance—and the usual mixture of selections about animals, people groups, and other miscellaneous topics. Health covers anatomy and some diseases. You also get a U.S. Government topic, with dozens of pages covering everything from individual government agencies to the Bill of Rights. Math includes a complete review of arithmetic up through fractions and decimals, ratio and proportion, money and measurement , practical math problems, and geometry. Again, you get the U.S. Constitution unit, a vocabulary test, and language arts and math achievement tests.

The best way to use a Super Yearbook is to assign a definite number of pages to be done each day. Depending on whether you homeschool year-round, are trying to accelerate your child, or are just following a typical school-year schedule, you can plan the number of pages accordingly. In most cases, this will amount to only 3 or 4 pages per day. It's up to you whether you'd rather have your student struggle with the work on his own—and then explain the answers to any mistakes when you grade his work —or whether you'd rather read through each day's assignment in advance and explain any tough parts to him. In many cases, you'll find a day's work can lead to interesting discussions and opportunities for further research, if desired. That's why I find this program most useful for busy families who could use the totally prepared lessons, and who also have lots of reference books and materials on hand, or visit the library frequently. *Mary Pride*

You might have heard that **Hewitt** is known for its "delayed schooling" approach to education. This is no longer true. Since Dr. Raymond Moore, the foremost proponent of delayed schooling, parted ways with Hewitt, Hewitt now emphasizes informal learning in the early years, *not* delayed schooling. By "informal learning" they mean hands-on (as opposed to workbook-based) activities presented in a natural setting. They are also strongly committed to the idea of "readiness"—letting the child's interests and learning style dictate how and when the instruction will be offered. One look at their program will convince anyone that they're certainly not into delayed *learning!*

Another thing you should know: Hewitt is no longer Seventh-Day Adventist in flavor. What you get from them are wholesome, nondenominational Christian materials, many from other publishers. Hewitt provides its own teacher materials, its own PASS tests, many types of recordkeeping and educational counseling to help you succeed, and some courses they have developed for the early grades.

For kindergarten through grade two, Hewitt offers a set of their own excellent unit-study courses which provide daily lesson plans and a variety of

If your student reads as well as most homeschoolers, he is ready for some real literature. *Tom Sawyer, The Swiss Family Robinson, Robinson Crusoe, Robin Hood & His Merry Men,* and *Anne of Green Gables* are some titles that spring to mind. You may also want to supplement with art projects, music training, phys ed, and science experiences and experiments.

At this age level, you'll need to supplement with literature, art, music, and physical education. A research project each month would also be a good idea, as would some science experiments.

UPDATED!
Hewitt Homeschooling Resources
Grades preK–12. Home Education Guide (for new enrollees—updated for 2000), $25. Elementary individualized curriculum guide (grades 1–8, does not include books), $40. Preschool Plus (preK), $129.95. Training Wheels (K), $79.95. Here I Grow (grade 1), $59.95. A Bee Sees (alternative grade 1 program), $109.95. Across America grade 1, $69.95; grade 2, $129.95; grade 3 and 4 supplement, $29.95. American Tales reader (grade 3 and 4), $14.95. Unit Program Service Package (grades K–2), $80. Elementary

Service Package (grades 3–6), $175; Junior High Service Package (grades 7–8), $295. High School Credit in Escrow for grades 7–8, $115 per course. Special Needs Package (does not include books), $375 or $37/month. High School Full-Year Package (does not include books), $475 or $45/month. Hundreds of products available. Shipping extra.

Hewitt Homeschooling Resources, PO Box 9, Washougal, WA 98671. Free catalog: (800) 348-1750. Orders and Inquiries: (360) 835-8708. Fax: (360) 835-8697. Email: info@hewitthomeschooling.com. Web: www.hewitthomeschooling.com (in progress).

presentation methods that work with all learning styles. The lessons are low-stress, informal, hands-on rather than "workbooky," and create many opportunities for the child to interact with the natural world. These one-year courses include:

- **Training Wheels,** a 40-week nondenominational Bible-based kindergarten that starts at Genesis and goes as far as Paul's missionary journeys, hitting the usual preschool high spots (e.g., don't expect to meet obscure judges, prophets, or kings). This very complete program is reviewed in detail in the "Readiness" chapter of Volume 2.
- **Here I Grow** for grade 1 covers the same basic 40 stories found in *Training Wheels*, but at a first-grade level. Extra-challenge activities are included for advanced students. Math worksheets and manipulatives are included, as is a coloring book and reader, but the heart of the course is the teacher's manual itself, with its daily list of hands-on activities.
- **A Bee Sees**, an alternative grade 1 course with an "animals" theme. Its 36 weekly units, with daily lesson plans, study 20 animals. You'll study character traits based on each animal plus a Bible event or person associated with each animal, similar to Bill Gothard's *Character Sketches*. Aesop's fables, a wide variety of hands-on activities and work/service projects, language worksheets, and a math course complete with manipulatives are all included as well.
- **Across America,** an especially clever course that takes your student on a journey across the 50 states in both time and space. You start at the east coast in colonial times, and travel to new states as the country expands, discovering new inventions and ways of life as they were introduced in history. Designed for grade 2, this course is also usable for grades 3 or 4 with purchase of the third-and-fourth-grade supplement; a first-grade version has also just been published. See complete review in the "Geography" chapter of Volume 2.

Each unit-study course covers all core subjects. The complete packages include everything you need to teach each course; you can also buy teacher's manuals and course ingredients separately. Parents who are just beginning to educate their children at home will find these to be very user-friendly.

Hewitt's offerings for grade 3–8 are quite different. Basically, the curriculum gets more structured as the child gets older. Based on a questionnaire you fill out and send in, Hewitt will plan you an individualized curriculum, using selections from the hundreds of educational products they also offer for sale individually in their catalog. Veteran homeschoolers will recognize most or all of the products they recommend most frequently. The curriculum guide Hewitt sends you includes not only book recommendations, but teaching suggestions as well. This is similar to the service offered by Sycamore Tree (see review in this chapter).

Even as you head up to the high-school level, Hewitt's approach is still focused on "read, discuss, act" rather than "read, study, test." They encourage exploration, creativity, and community involvement. Service to others and work are frequently emphasized, as Hewitt considers the home educator's job is not just to provide academics, but to educate a student to maturity.

Hewitt's high-school course plan is based on "Carnegie units," the standard method of assigning credit for high-school courses used to show you have met state and college requirements. It follows a standard college-prep sequence, but is flexible enough to allow the student to tailor his program to meet his own goals and the requirements of his own state. Guidance counseling is available throughout high school, with a certified teacher who you can contact via letter, phone, fax, or email. For most high-school courses, a syllabus is included. This guides the student through the course, giving specific assignments and telling him which assignment should be submitted quarterly by mail to be evaluated and given letter grades. A diploma and transcript are offered.

Probably the simplest way to use Hewitt's services is to sign up for one of their special packages. Their **Unit Program Service Package** for grades K–2 includes one hour of toll-free phone counseling, a written evaluation of the child's work once a year, and a certificate of completion. If you feel the need for more frequent evaluations, you can order additional service packages. This package is for those families who choose to use one of the unit-study courses we mentioned above: *Training Wheels, Here I Go, A Bee Sees,* or *Across America.*

The **Elementary Service Package** for grades 1 through 8 is for those families who want Hewitt to plan a curriculum just for them, and *don't* plan to use one of the unit-study courses. It includes an individualized curriculum guide, two hours of toll-free phone counseling, written evaluations once a year, a certificate of completion, and two PASS tests, one at the beginning of the year and one at the end. PASS tests, available only for grades 3–8, are achievement tests designed specifically for homeschoolers. See the review of PASS tests in chapter 34.

If you have a child, ages 3 through adult ,who has been labeled ADD, autistic, Down's Syndrome, dyscalculistic, dysgraphic, dyslexic, EMR, TMR, hearing impaired or deaf, language disordered, learning disabled, visually impaired, or who has other physical or learning disabilities, you may be interested in the following option. **Hewitt's Special Needs Program** has the approval of HSLDA and offers assistance in developing an Individual Home Education Program (required by some states), as well as evaluating the progress of each student.

For gifted kids, Hewitt suggests "broadening" the academic program rather than "accelerating." Again, families enrolled in one of the service packages will get individualized help in preparing such a program.

Services may be purchased either in packages, or individually. For high school and special needs programs, payment plans are available for enrollment. Further services may be added at any time during the enrollment year.

If you would like a less "workbooky" approach to education, and could use the kind of help Hewitt offers (testing, evaluations, phone counseling, curriculum selection), you will find Hewitt very friendly and accommodating. *Mary Pride*

The Principle Approach is popping up everywhere these days. The **Judah Bible Curriculum**, created in 1992, was the first Bible curriculum for school-age children to use this approach.

For the benefit of the uninitiated, the Principle Approach is a method of study applicable to any subject, based on what some modern researchers consider the way Americans used to study in the early days of the colonies and Republic. It emphasizes a providential view of history (God as the agent making things happen), a "dominion" emphasis (God's purposes shall prevail on this earth), and the development of student character, especially self-discipline, through a rigorous program of study and creating notebooks. For Principle Approach teachers, there are "4 R's": research, reason, relate, and record.

Coming soon: *The Third Alternative: Christian Self-Government.* Designed for use as a government course for high-school-age kids, this course did not yet have a price or shipping date when I wrote this. Check with Hewitt for details.

UPDATED!
Judah Bible Curriculum
Grades K–12. $69.95 plus $5 per student in the first year only. Shipping 10%.
*Judah Bible Curriculum, PO Box 122, Urbana, IL 61803. (217) 344-5672
Fax: (217) 398-9889.
Email: info@judahbible.com.
Web: www.judahbible.com.*

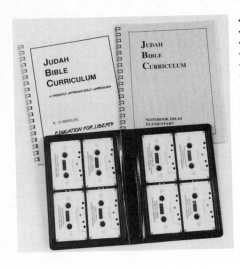

As this applies to Bible study, Judah Bible Curriculum students are supposed to *research* by reading the Bible and making use of Bible study tools. They *reason* out a series of conclusions about the nature of God, man, and the world based on their research and on the questions the curriculum asks them to answer. They *relate* these conclusions to the question of "government," which in Judah Bible Curriculum terms covers everything from personal ethics to how to run a world empire (and if there should even *be* a world empire). They *record* in a notebook all the findings they have researched. This finished notebook is supposed to be a model of neatness and organization, not to mention deep thinking. Students are given questions to answer and a way of recording information that forces them to think through Bible principles for themselves.

Bill Burtness, the curriculum's author, believes that liberty is the main theme of the Bible. He put it in the title of his curriculum—"Judah Bible Curriculum: Education for Liberty." Heaven is shown as a situation in which everyone is perfectly self-governed under God. Hell is just the opposite; everyone is totally governed from the outside. Here on earth, society wavers between self-government and outside government, depending strictly on how well we govern ourselves. People and nations who refuse to exercise self-control succumb to tyranny. The history of the Jews and the church is seen to be one of moving towards or away from liberty, depending on whether they (we) were (are) following God or not. All the character emphasis of the course is directed towards helping the student become a self-governing individual who then will be empowered to expand his sphere of influence as a godly servant, like Joseph, the curriculum's hero, who ended up ruling the largest empire of his age.

The original edition consisted of the "Curriculum Document" and a set of eight "Teacher Training Audio Cassettes" in a cassette binder. The cassettes included a curriculum overview (pretty much the same thing said in the Document), a cassette on "How God Changes Nations," another on "Internal Government: Creation–Flood," one on "Internal Government: Abraham–Malachi," one on "Internal Government: Matthew–Revelation," one on "Internal Government: Pentecost–Present," a cassette on the unique methods used in the curriculum, and one entitled "Personal Destiny—Studying the Life of Joseph."

The tapes featured an Armenian, as opposed to Calvinist, outlook. The speaker stressed that God has "overall superintendency" over what happens rather than actually causing everything directly to happen. The author tells me that the revised material will take a stronger approach to God's sovereignty.

I was not able to make it through all the tapes, mainly because all the material is covered so slowly. The speaker repeats a lot of the material in the Document, speaks slowly, has long pauses, and spends a lot of time retelling Bible history, often quoting great chunks straight out of the Bible.

The good news is that you don't have to listen to the tapes, unless you prefer to do so. The curriculum is now available in two spiralbound manuals that replace the old "Curriculum Document."

The *K–12 Manual* breaks the Bible down into five historical periods, called "themes." Each theme is broken down into "Biblical Keys." Bible portions are studied in terms of key individuals, key events, key institutions, and key documents. Each of these keys has a different "Key Sheet" on which the student writes all that he could find about that person, place, or thing. For example, the Key Sheet for Key Institutions has three sections: Doctrinal Base, Character of the People, and Government. Under Doctrinal Base are the words *foundations, concepts taught as foundational truths,* and *controlling ideas.* Under Character of the People you find *physical-energy activity, moral disposition,* and

Each week of study is grouped around a Weekly Theme Focus. Students read the Scripture passage themselves and analyze the Weekly Theme Focus using the appropriate Key Sheets. It's up to the teacher to explain how the key people, places, and things fit into God's plan. It's also up to him to come up with assignments like map-making, time lines, art and craft projects, and so on that can further bring out the weekly theme. The student puts one or two of these projects in his notebook each week

A course overview (scope and sequence) and Suggested Weekly Themes Guide for all seven years of the course and suggested weekly themes guide for the first year are included in the *K–12 Manual.*

mental disposition. Under Government are the phrases *manner of controlling men (internal/external), form of civil government, constitution/laws, how men are directed/controlled,* and *conduct.* Using these topics and subtopics as a guideline, the student researches and fills out his Key Sheet. If the institution was "Egypt", for example, he might write down, "Idolatry and the worship of Pharaoh as God" as a controlling idea in the Doctrinal Basis column.

The course contents are repeated twice between kindergarten and twelfth grade. All five major "themes" (Bible periods) are covered each year, but different individuals and events are studied each time. Sample blank key sheets are also included that you can photocopy in quantity for your students' use. Appendix I of this manual includes visuals illustrating the concepts outlined on the teacher tapes and a Bible time line. A new Appendix II explains the course principles outlined in four of the cassette tapes.

As promised, the author has also come out with a *Notebook Ideas: Elementary* manual. This includes samples of student work from both Christian schools and homeschools, showing how Key Sheets, quizzes, and notebook pages can be completed. The manual includes examples in Bible book order, from Genesis through Revelation. I think you'd be wise to get this manual as well if you plan to use the curriculum, because it really helps to see some examples of what kind of student work you are aiming for.

The Judah Bible Curriculum is a teacher-directed program. You will be using the Bible as your textbook. It requires a scholarly mindset and a lot of commitment on the part of both student and teacher. If you are good at teaching and enjoy coming up with creative ways to present things, and creative assignments for your students, you might very well find this a fascinating program. *Mary Pride*

Learning at Home: A Christian Parent's Guide with Day-by-Day Lesson Plans Using the Library as a Resource is just what it sounds like.

The **preschool and kindergarten** curriculum now has been combined into one oversized, 267-page, perfect-bound volume. No more spiral bindings, separate volumes for preschool and kindergarten, or rubber-stamp graphics. Now that Noble Publishing, Gregg Harris's company, has taken it over, it's all been neatened up into one slick, easy-to-use book. First and second grade are still in their original spiral-bound format, as of this writing.

For preschool you get a really rich program of learning activities, including: Bible concepts (four times a week), reading readiness (four times), arithmetic readiness (four times), God's world (social studies—twice), character building (once), health, safety, manners (once), art (twice), music (twice), physical education skills (four times), Bible memory verses (four times), and stories (four times). This schedule should take you an hour and a half four days a week. Friday is set aside just for field trips.

The lesson plans don't actually start until page 41. Before that, you're led through answers to questions such as "Why Teach at Home?" and "When Do I Teach?" Ann Ward explains how to motivate, how to plan and schedule, how to organize a successful field trip, what to expect developmentally from your three/four/five-year-old, and how to make the "matching grids" she has you use throughout the course. In addition, you get planning forms to photocopy, a list of basic/recommended equipment (most of which you already own), an annotated resource list of books/cassettes/videos on how to teach and other topics, an overview of what you will be teaching in each subject area, capital letters/numbers/symbols to copy on heavier paper and cut out, and even a section on 37 ways to use rubber stamps as a teaching aid!

New from the people at Judah Bible Curriculum:

George Washington: The Character and Influence of One Man, $42, a biography of George Washington.

UPDATED!
Learning at Home curriculum
PreK–2. Each volume, $49.95 plus shipping.
Noble Publishing Associates, PO Box 2250, Gresham, OR 97030. Orders: (800) 225-5259. Inquiries: (503) 667-5084. Fax: (503) 618-8866. Email: Noblebooks@aol.com. Web: www.noblepublishing.com.

As is typical with rich curricula, Learning at Home requires considerably more work than just opening a manual and turning to the proper page. You have to collect materials for the activities, find books at the library, schedule field trips if desired, and so on. Resources are listed on the day they are used, so it really pays to plan ahead a couple of weeks at a time—or even more, if your library is unlikely to have most of the books you need. Author Ann Ward has made this somewhat easier by providing card catalog numbers for the books she recommends. This means you can find another book on the same topic easily if the one you're looking for isn't there, and you won't have to spend hours flipping through cards or microfiche. Also, for people with less time and more money, she has arranged with Home School Books and Supplies to have them carry *all* the resource materials recommended in this program. Not all these materials appear in their catalog, due to space considerations; however, you can request them just the same.

The kindergarten program included in the preschool/kindergarten volume has a kindergarten arithmetic section and a reading section based on Bonnie Dettmer's *Phonics for Reading and Spelling* (available from Small Ventures—see review in Phonics chapter of volume 2). To this you can add the preschool activities, but that means you will be flipping back and forth between three sections of the book. However, this may be worth the effort to you, especially if you are teaching both a preschooler and kindergartner together.

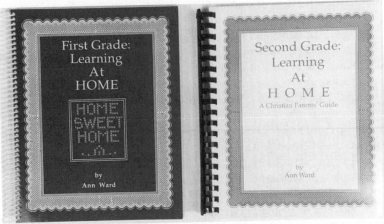

First grade and **second grade** continue to build on this approach. Each volume starts with an overview by subject of the entire year's program. Each day's work is broken down into calendar time (including praying and adding to the Thankfulness List), a short Bible unit study (example: looking at plants/poem about plants for the Third Day of Creation), language arts (reading phonograms, writing, grammar, spelling), music, art, arithmetic, health/manners/responsibility, physical education, history/geography/science (first grade covers American history from 1600–1700; second grade covers American history from 1700–1800), and Bible memory. Some of these subjects are covered on all days; others are not. Friday is left open, as in the preschool-kindergarten program, for field trips and service projects.

Children need a three-ring notebook in which they can keep their Thankfulness List, a journal, a calendar (many activities are based on this calendar), a list of books read, and notes from each subject. Daily calendar activities may include saying the Pledge to the Bible, saying the days of the week and months of the year, counting from 1–31 while pointing at the calendar square, counting the ordinals from first to thirty-first, saying today's day and date, recording today's temperature and weather, and various number-line counting activities.

For practical application in learning to write, instead of completing book lessons, every week first- and second-graders write a short letter to grandparents or an older person or shut-in, write a journal entry, and copy a short passage into the notebook. First-grade art takes a similarly functional approach, with art projects focused on preparing puppets and backdrops for the three puppet shows presented through the year (Pilgrims, Christmas story, Easter story). Second-graders do a variety of art projects. Second-graders also work on exercises to prepare them for (possibly) obtaining the President's Council on Physical Fitness Award.

Both the first- and second-grade programs coordinate with the preschool-kindergarten program in terms of what is studied when, making it easier to teach several children at once.

Every volume is very professionally-done, easy to use, and covers the territory with enough activities and questions to draw out real thinking but not so much that you or your children will be overwhelmed. Christian families that like structure and that can manage to locate or purchase the needed resources will like this program. *Mary Pride*

The **Noah Plan** curriculum is based on 20 years of experience with StoneBridge School, a model Principle Approach day school in Virginia. You may be interested to know that, in a class of high-school seniors taught using The Noah Plan, their average SAT score was 1305, with one student achieving a perfect verbal score of 800 and another achieving 790.

Years in the making, The Noah Plan is the first full-scale Principle Approach curriculum available for homeschoolers. The Noah Plan is made up of three elements:

1. **The Noah Plan Program Notebooks.** These notebooks include the "master plan" for the program. There are two: the K–8 Program Notebook, in a red binder, and the 9th–12th grade Program Notebook, in a blue binder. Each includes a Self-Directed Seminar (to teach you what The Principle Approach is all about) of 9 lessons illustrated copiously with charts, graphs, and timelines, with further teaching from Noah Plan master teachers on two included audiocassettes. Each huge three-ring binder also includes step-by-step guidelines and weekly schedules for each grade level, and within grade levels, for each subject. These are not weekly lesson plans. Rather, you get definitions, principles, purposes, concepts taught, goals, content (what exactly should be covered), additional resource recommendations, and so on. Most subjects are outlined quarter by quarter. The recommended daily schedule for K–8 runs from 8:30 to 3:00, with a 15-minute snack and half-hour for lunch.

2. **Individual subject guides.** At present, subject guides are available for art, history and geography, literature, English language, and reading. Currently under development are the guides for math and science, classical and modern languages, fine and performing arts, and Bible. You don't really need to wait for the Bible curriculum guide, though, since Judah Bible Curriculum already offers a Principle Approach Bible curriculum (see review in this chapter).

3. **The International Apprenticeship Program.** Despite its name, this does not have anything to do with finding appren-

NEW!
The Noah Plan

Grades K–12. Noah Plan Program Notebook for K–8, $125. Noah Plan Program Notebook for 9th–12th grades, $125. Curriculum Guides: StoneBridge Art Guide, $25; Literature, $40; English Grammar & Composition, $40; Reading, $25; History & Geography, $40. Christian History of the American Revolution, $42. Christian History of the Constitution, Volumes I and II, $40 each. Teaching & Learning America's Christian History, $35. Noah Webster's 1828 American Dictionary of the English Language, $65. Rudiments of America's Christian History & Government, $15. Noah Webster's Value of the Bible, $22. Teacher Guide & Poem for the Courtship of Miles Standish, $15. Plimoth Plantation Day Packet, $12. Family Program for Reading Aloud, $18. Syllabi for Key Classics, $8.50 each. Key Classics also available.

Foundation for American Christian Education (FACE), PO Box 9588, Chesapeake, VA 23321-9588. Orders: (800) 352-3223. Inquiries: (757) 488-6601. Fax: (757) 488-5593. E-mail: info@face.net. Web: www.face.net.

ticeships for homeschooled students or studying abroad. Rather, it is an opportunity for homeschooled parents, Christian school teachers, and others to get in-person instruction in The Principle Approach. Two sessions are currently offered: a 10-day session at the FACE demonstration school established in 1980, StoneBridge School, and eight days of formal instruction at Regent University. Both sessions are designed as graduate courses of study, and you can earn a total of six graduate credits by attending. Unlike Bill Gothard's Advanced Training Institute of America, which also offers in-person training to homeschool parents, FACE does *not* require you to attend these seminars before you can purchase their materials. Nonetheless, many homeschool parents have chosen to attend for their own edification (and possibly for those graduate credits as well!).

For **kindergarten**, the subjects to be taught are Bible, Writing Road to Reading (a phonics program often referred to as the "Spalding Method"), reading readiness/oral language development, penmanship, physical education, arithmetic, and literature. Music, French, art, science, and crafts each get one-half hour per week as well.

In **grade 1**, you have all the same subjects, plus English grammar and composition. Reading readiness/oral language development becomes reading. Science and French get two sessions each per week, instead of one. Literature and history are introduced as major subjects. And 40 minutes per week is now devoted to geography.

Grade 2 and **3** then have the same subjects as grade 1, except that in grade 3 separate phys ed classes (with the very same objectives) are set up for boys and girls. The latter likely will not apply in the home setting.

In **grade 4**, Latin is introduced. For schools using the Noah Plan, chorus is also a new subject, as is something called "The Scholars Reading Lesson" based on a method invented in France for integrating reading with all the other language arts. This is described in detail in the Reading Curriculum Guide, but *not* in the Noah Plan Program Manual—which can be quite confusing to the new user.

In **grade 5**, geography has more time allocated to it, and English grammar and composition shares its hour every day with Latin.

In **grade 6**, a full hour every day is given for the combined study of history and geography.

In **grade 7**, Latin gets 45 minutes a day to itself, as does literature. Two days a week literature is studied as "literature and drama." One hour a week is now set aside for computer literacy.

In **grade 8**, instead of history/geography you spend a daily period studying *Rudiments of America's Christian History*.

The high-school program is different. Let's take it grade by grade.

All grades of high school include Bible/Logic (a combined course), mathematics, classical or modern language, fine and performing arts (choose from drama, orchestra, chorus, and fine art), and physical education.

In **grade 9**, the additional courses are English Literature & Composition I (includes a research paper), Universal History, and Earth Science (includes a science project). The earth science course includes a resource list number of 18 books, including titles from both the young-earth and old-earth creationist viewpoints. I don't know which position, if any, FACE takes, because as of this writing *The Noah Plan Mathematics and Science Curriculum Guide* is not yet available.

No grade-level curriculum packages are available for the Noah Plan. Instead, you purchase the individual manuals, texts, classics, and syllabi necessary for the grade level. A handy chart (which would be even handier if prices were printed on it) shows which books are needed when. This chart is part of the free Homeschool Package, which also includes a catalog, a sign-up sheet for the sessions, and other helpful information.

In **grade 10**, you progress to English Literature & Composition II, Modern History, and a lab-based biology course with a science project.

In **grade 11**, you switch to American Literature & Composition I, American History, and a lab-based chemistry course with science project.. At campus-based Principle Approach schools, the physical education credit at this grade level is now based on *after-school* participation in team sports, as a player or cheerleader.

In **grade 12**, it's American Literature & Composition II, Government & Economics, and a lab-based physics course with, you guessed it, a year-long science project.

Mathematics courses for which course overviews are available include Algebra ½, Algebra 1, and Algebra 2 (all based on the Saxon Math texts, along with *Ray's Algebra*), Plane Geometry (a terrific but very expensive course, because you must purchase 10 well-chosen resources, including Key Curriculum Press's *Geometer's Sketchpad* software), Pre-Calculus (another expensive course, using 2 texts and 9 supplements), and AP Calculus (this uses a lot of materials, but most of them are already on the list for the pre-calc course, so it won't cost that much extra if you've already used their pre-calculus course).

We added up the prices, and found that Noah Plan kindergarten would cost you $500+. If you did their kindergarten and continued on to first grade, you would only need to purchase $20 of additional books for first grade. This seems to be the rule throughout: you spend more money the first year, and subsequent years are relatively inexpensive. This is because some very expensive books are required for all grade levels. These books, which are mostly to be used by the parent, are expensive because they are huge, hardbound volumes. These include, among others:

- **American Dictionary of the English Language** A reprint of the classic 1828 Webster's dictionary, prized for its erudite word definitions drawn from classical literature and the Bible, the way it traces word roots to 26 languages, and its Christian outlook
- **The Christian History of the American Revolution** Verna Hall's massive compilation of American source documents concerning the pre-war debates about what government founded on biblical principles should look like, along with her thoughts on the subject of the relationship between spiritual and political liberty
- **The Christian History of the Constitution** A two-volume work; Volume 1 is necessary for all grades, while Volume 2 is used in grades 5–12. Loaded with source quotes, this is Verna Hall's "classic compilation of America's establishment as the world's first Christian constitutional republic," used to teach the Providential (God is in charge) approach to American history and government
- **Teaching and Learning America's Christian History: The Principle Approach** by Rosalie Slater presents the principles and educational methodology that make up the Principle Approach, along with many references to Verna Hall's work

Other books you will need vary from grade to grade. These include "Key Classics" such as *Heidi* and *Carry On, Mr. Bowditch,* each with their own study syllabus, various books about the Bible and Christianity, and a few books about Pilgrim culture. You will also need a number of 3-ring binders for the student's own notebooks, of course!

I am impressed with the amount of work FACE has lavished on this curriculum. The new books are far more attractive than previous editions, with lots of illustrations and other graphics to enliven and explain the material. Having to hop back and forth between a number of Curriculum Guides, the Program Manual, and the large reference books is a bit cumbersome for those of us who have been spoiled by the weekly lesson plans now available for many homeschool curricula. Still, what you get is way more organized than any Principle Approach material previously available.

At the high-school level, your financial outlay will rise substantially. FACE has chosen excellent resources for each of their courses; these run into some serious money.

This is a curriculum for the reflective mind. If you or your children are "hyper," or if your major desire is to do lots of fun projects and get out of the house a lot, this is not the curriculum for you. Serious-minded Christian families who are not afraid to do a lot of reading, analyzing, and writing, and who are deeply concerned about the world we will leave to our grandchildren, will likely find the Noah Plan highly attractive.

And they offer a 14-day money-back guarantee! This is enough time for you to look over the books, listen to the tapes, and work your way through the Self-Directed Seminar. By that time, you'll know for sure if the Noah Plan appeals to you. *Mary Pride*

Oak Meadow curriculum has changed a lot in the last few years. Based in the early grades on the educational teachings of Rudolf Steiner (called "anthroposophy" or "Waldorf education"), it continues in the later grades with a strong emphasis on self-awareness and closeness to the earth. Following Mr. Steiner's theories, Oak Meadow places more importance on art and "right brain" learning, including the use of fantasy, than any other program.

Oak Meadow offers four purchasing options. **Option A**, the family enrollment, provides you with basic recordkeeping services, including Home Teacher training and a newsletter, and communication with school officials. In addition, every enrolled child has a Class Teacher. For grades K–4 the parents correspond with the Class Teacher; in grades 5 and up the student works directly with the Class Teacher, and the parents move into the background. The Teacher Fee is paid directly to the teacher. Curriculum costs are on top of the enrollment and teacher fees, making this one of the more costly homeschool programs.

If your child has special needs and requires an Individualized Education Plan (IEP), Oak Meadow can accommodate you under their **Option B**. You pay an IEP fee, and the curriculum cost will vary depending on what materials are selected. Enrollment and teacher fees remain the same as in the family enrollment option.

Option C is enrollment with a portfolio evaluation. The evaluation takes the place of the teacher support. You still pay the enrollment fee, and IEP fee if that applies, as well as your curriculum costs. The charges are based on a certain number of lessons completed during each evaluation period. Since Oak Meadow has a 36-week schedule, you end up paying $90 total for this option in grades K–4, $135 in grades 5–8, or $80/subject in the high-school years.

Option D allows you to purchase the curriculum without enrolling or taking advantage of the teacher services.

Oak Meadow curriculum used to have a somewhat radical flavor. This still can be seen in the areas of the upper-grade curriculum that deal with ecology and our relationship with animals. However, their choice of reading material has become more traditional and Christian-friendly over the years, stressing timeless classics. In fact, you'll find many of the same books in the Sonlight curriculum catalog! In addition, the syllabi for each grade level suggest many more books you can read.

How this came about makes an interesting story. It turns out that public-school students often have to spend some time at home, due to chronic illness, disability, or bad behavior. The school has to provide them with curriculum while at home. Some public schools have begun using Oak Meadow curriculum in these cases. In order to appeal to school personnel,

UPDATED!
Oak Meadow School Curriculum

Grades K–12. Enrollment fee, $425/year/family. Teacher fee (paid directly to teacher): grades K–4, $290/student for 36 lessons or 10 months; grades 5–8, $400/student; grades 9–12, $310/student/subject. IEP fee, $150. Portfolio evaluation fee: grades K–4, $30/12 lessons completed; grades 5–8, $45/12 lessons completed; grades 9–12, $40/subject/18 lessons completed. Curriculum packages: Grade K, $200; Grade 1, $235; Grade 2, $250; Grade 3, $245; Grade 4, $325; Grade 5, $330; Grade 6, $325; Grade 7, $340; Grade 8, $340; Grades 9–12, usually $50–$100 per subject. Shipping extra.
Oak Meadow School, PO Box 740, Putney, VT 05346. (802) 387-2021. Fax: (802) 387-5108. Email: oms@oakmeadow.com. Web: www.oakmeadow.com.

Oak Meadow decided to revamp their materials, toning down what many would perceive as the weirder features of Waldorf education and coming more in line with the public-school scope and sequence. They also buttressed the academic rigor of their upper-grades material, making it much more suitable for use by the typical college-bound homeschooler.

Yet Oak Meadow's distinctive personality remains. In the early grades, the stress is on developing qualities of imagination and perception in the child. Thus math is still the story of four little gnomes named Add, Subtract, Multiply, and Divide; the alphabet is taught through fairy tales that associate each letter with a real or fantasy object; science is first approached through nature experiences; and so on.

Art, music, and crafts all play an important part in the elementary curriculum. Children learn many classic children's songs, work with clay and nature crafts, learn to play the recorder, and learn basic carpentry.

Science in the early grades is mainly the study of nature and animals.

Math is downplayed (except for basic introductions to concepts) until grade 4, when Oak Meadow provides their own math book, switching over at grade 5 to the Saxon Math program.

As much as possible, **"learning by doing" is built into the curriculum.** Thus sixth-grade children study other countries by cooking their food, making their clothes, doing their crafts, learning conversational French, and so on. Science follows a hands-on discovery approach. Much attention is given to self-awareness, including many personal writing assignments with the student disclosing his feelings about a variety of situations.

Oak Meadow children learn how to forecast their local weather, how to track animals, how to paint meaningful pictures, and a number of other things that do not find their way into standard school texts. On the other hand, students get less practice and drill in the basics than those enrolled in more traditional programs.

Also of note: Oak Meadow has a drawing course (based on the very popular *Drawing with Children*) and an art course (based on *The Study of Art*), on top of what is offered in their regular courses.

Oak Meadow does use textbooks—many from from major publishers— in the upper grades. Examples include Addison Wesley, Holt, McDougal Littell, and Saxon.

Students in **grades K–4** "play" more than "work." Most assignments are informal and can be done anytime, and there is no pressure to meet deadlines. Once students reach grade 5, the parents are considered support and resource people and the Class Teacher takes over most teaching work.

Upper-grade students do have to work, although the amount of paperwork is less than many traditional programs require.

In **grades 5–8** Oak Meadow curriculum strongly emphasizes "human values and ideals." Subjects are approached from the angle of how they affect people (subjectively) rather than as collections of objective facts.

Grades 9–12 concentrate more on facts and the intellectual approach. Here you'll find your traditional college-prep math sequence: Saxon Algebra I and II, Geometry, Advanced Math, and Calculus. For those who prefer a gentler pace, Oak Meadow offers Key Curriculum Press's Algebra and General Math courses. Courses in consumer math and bookkeeping are also available, for those with a business turn of mind.

The science sequence is a bit more unusual. There's a biology course that uses a standard evolutionary public-school text . . . plus the book *The Tracker,* about a young man who lived in the woods and learned to track like a Native American. The chemistry course is lab-based, with a lab kit you can buy. This is more-or-less mainstream. Less so are the Environmental Science course and the Health course, both of which include books that

Oak Meadow's **online courses** are now becoming more popular. The Oak Meadow website now features chat rooms, a threaded message center, and more.

With its emphasis on feeling and doing, Oak Meadow will appeal most strongly to the Action Man and People Person type of learner.

wax evangelistic about the ecology agenda and the dangers of sugar. Physics is not offered.

Those not used to thinking of Oak Meadow as a "classical" program will be pleasantly surprised to discover they now offer Latin I and II, in addition to Spanish I and II. These are high-school courses. The Latin courses are built upon Oxford University Press's Latin texts, while the Spanish courses use *Spanish All the Way*.

High-school social studies options are U.S. History, World History, U.S. Government, and Psychology.

For literature and composition, there are English grade 9, English grade 10, American Literature, and World Literature. All these courses come with only a few literature books each and emphasize the angst (Franz Kafka, here we come!).

Oak Meadow is currently seeking accreditation for their program through the New England Association of Schools and Colleges. *Mary Pride*

NEW!
The Robinson Curriculum

Ages 7–21. Curriculum, $195. Henty Books, $99. Both purchased at the same time, $275. Free shipping in the USA. Requires computer as follows. PC: 486SX/33, Win3.1/95/98, 8 MB RAM, CD-ROM player, Mouse. Mac: 68030 and up, 8 MB RAM, CD-ROM player.
Oregon Institute of Science and Medicine, 2251 Dick George Rd., Cave Junction, OR 97523.
Phone: (541) 592-4142.
Email: art@oism.org.
Web: www.oism.org.

Dr. Arthur Robinson, whose homeschool method you read about earlier in chapter 20, developed the **Robinson Curriculum** to allow his six children to teach themselves when their mother suddenly died. The three components of his daily curriculum are: two hours of Saxon Math starting with Saxon 5/4 (Saxon is *not* included on the CD-ROMs in this set, it must be purchased separately, but you do get a 20 percent discount with the Robinson Curriculum), one page of writing on any topic, and then reading from good literature to fill in the rest of the five- to six-hour school day, six days a week, 10–11 months a year.

To fulfill the reading and science portion of the curriculum, you use this set of 22 CD-ROMs. They arrive encased in a sturdy storage case, with rigid flip pages holding each CD. You will be grateful again and again for this well-organized way to store your discs!

To fill these discs, Dr. Robinson compiled 120,000 pages of scanned-in text from more than 250 carefully selected, very high quality books: selections from diaries, literature, and other writings; the complete 30,000-page 1911 *Encyclopedia Britannica*; the complete 400,000-word 1913 *Noah Webster's Dictionary*; high-school level science text books and answer keys; and more—both in print and out of print. The books are generally sequenced by grade level starting with first grade. Either print out each book or read it on screen. Note: you can not search on topics, keywords, or author—it is just one long list of books. The Dictionary and Encyclopedia, however, have the entry words listed along side the text. Click on an entry and the program presents you with that scanned-in page. Each page in either the books or the reference material looks like a "picture" of the book, not like text in a word processor that you can copy, paste, and edit.

What everyone wonders about is what you actually get on these CD-ROMs. I've already mentioned the reference books and science texts. Here is a smattering of other selections to give you an idea of what the Robinson Curriculum includes.

Literature King James Version Bible, *The Bible for Young People,* Nursery Rhymes, McGuffey's Readers, Shakespeare, and dozens of children's classics, from *Aesop's Fables* to *Ivanhoe,* plus high-school and adult classics from *Don Quixote* and *Cicero's Orations* to *Pilgrim's Progress* and *Paradise Lost.*

Robinson Curriculum 2.0			
Encyclopedia			
Order	Title	Author	CD#
I	A to ANDROPHAGI	Encyclopædia Britannica	Disk 01
II	ANDROS to AUSTRIA	Encyclopædia Britannica	Disk 01
III	AUSTRIA LOWER to BISECTRIX	Encyclopædia Britannica	Disk 01
IV	BISHARIN to CALGARY	Encyclopædia Britannica	Disk 02
V	CALHOUN to CHATELAINE	Encyclopædia Britannica	Disk 02
VI	CHATELET to CONSTANTINE	Encyclopædia Britannica	Disk 02
VII	CONSTANTINE PAVLOVICH to DEMIDOV	Encyclopædia Britannica	Disk 03
VIII	DEMIJOHN to EDVARD	Encyclopædia Britannica	Disk 03
IX	EDWARDES to EVANGELICAL ASSOCIATION	Encyclopædia Britannica	Disk 03
X	EVANGELICAL CHURCH to FRANCIS JOSEPH	Encyclopædia Britannica	Disk 04
XI	FRANSICANS to GIBSON	Encyclopædia Britannica	Disk 04
XII	GICHTEL to HARMONIUM	Encyclopædia Britannica	Disk 04
XIII	HARMONY to HURSTMONCEAUX	Encyclopædia Britannica	Disk 05
XIV	HUSBAND to ITALIC	Encyclopædia Britannica	Disk 05
XV	ITALY to KYSHTYM	Encyclopædia Britannica	Disk 05
XVI	L to LORD ADVOCATE	Encyclopædia Britannica	Disk 06
XVII	LORD CHAMBERLAIN to MECKLENBURG	Encyclopædia Britannica	Disk 06
XVIII	MEDAL to MUMPS	Encyclopædia Britannica	Disk 06
XIX	MUN to ODDFELLOWS	Encyclopædia Britannica	Disk 07
XX	ODE to PAYMENT OF MEMBERS	Encyclopædia Britannica	Disk 07
XXI	PAYN to POLKA	Encyclopædia Britannica	Disk 07
XXII	POLL to REEVES	Encyclopædia Britannica	Disk 08
XXIII	REFECTORY to SAINTE-BEUVE	Encyclopædia Britannica	Disk 08
XXIV	SAINTE-CLAIRE DEVILLE to SHUTTLE	Encyclopædia Britannica	Disk 08
XXV	SHUVALOV to SUBLIMINAL SELF	Encyclopædia Britannica	Disk 09
XXVI	SUBMARINE MINES to TOM-TOM	Encyclopædia Britannica	Disk 09
XXVII	TONALITE to VESUVIUS	Encyclopædia Britannica	Disk 09
XXVIII	VETCH to ZYMOTIC DISEASES	Encyclopædia Britannica	Disk 10
XXIX	INDEX	Encyclopædia Britannica	Disk 10

The Encyclopedia Britannica (1911 "pre-politically-correct" edition) takes up 10 CD-ROMs all by itself!

Many of these books are out-of-print children's classics: e.g., the Elsie Dinsmore books, the Five Little Peppers series, the old Bobbsey Twins, the Uncle Remus tales, the Rover Boys series, the Ruth Fielding books, Tom Swift books, the Border Boys books, the Pony Rider Boys books, a slew of other old-fashioned books for boys, and even such forgotten treasures as *Little Prudy's Dotty Dimple* (there's an entire series of Prudy and Dotty books, believe it or not) and *The Tale of Patty Muskrat*. Even so, I've only listed a fraction of the literature.

History Books Caesar's *Gallic War, The Life of George Washington, Diaries of George Washington, Our Hero General Grant, The Autobiography of Benjamin Franklin, Christopher Columbus and the Discovery of the New World, Four Naval Heroes, Boy Knight: A Tale of the Crusades, The Soldier in Our Civil War, The Life of Stonewall Jackson, The Rise and Fall of the Confederate Government, The Autobiography of Theodore Roosevelt, The Life of Lafayette, The Life of Lincoln, David Crockett: Scout, Up From Slavery, Personal Memoirs of U.S. Grant, King Henry V, Fifty Years in the Royal Navy,* and much more.

Geography Books *The Heart of the Antarctic, Life on the Mississippi, My African Journey, The Friendly Arctic,* and more.

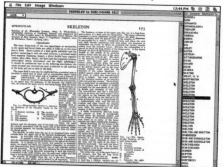

Here is a dictionary page. Notice that you were able to "click" on the keyword to select this page.

Economics Books *The Wealth of Nations* by Adam Smith, *The Law* and *Economic Sophistries* by Frederic Bastiat, *What Has Government Done to Our Money?* by Murray Rothbard, *Economics in One Lesson* by Henry Hazlitt, and much more, all from a free-market perspective.

Some Other Authors John Locke, Horatio Alger, Jr. (tons of his "lift yourself by your bootstraps" books that inspired a generation of American boys), Isaac Newton, Winston Churchill, Henry Wadsworth Longfellow, Washington Irving, Mark Twain, Louisa May Alcott, Jules Verne, David Crockett, James Fenimore Cooper, Rudyard Kipling, and many more.

Other topics covered include theology and political science (from Machiavelli to George Washington and beyond!). Many of the titles are old familiar friends from the Harvard Classics and Great Books of the Western World series, either of which costs far more than this curriculum.

For the college-bound student, you'll find about five science textbooks with answer keys, covering physics, chemistry, and thermodynamics. Also included is an economics textbook, an un-politically correct but rational and scientifically-based environment book, and a "be ready for nuclear war" book. Keep in mind however, these are not interactive textbooks but are meant to be printed out and used the old-fashioned way. No teacher's manuals are included.

Overall, the reading choices contain about 70 percent fictional literature, 10 percent autobiographies, 10 percent textbooks, and about 10 percent various other writings.

How do you read all this wealth of material? First, get lots of paper and ink for your ink-jet printer. Then, be ready to spend some money. To print the entire 120,000 page collection would cost approximately $6,000 if you figure about 5¢ a page. However, if you have a laser printer, it can be closer to 1¢ a page, and laser printers are becoming very common. Second, start your printer!

Keep in mind that these books are to be printed and read over a 12-year period of time. Printing it yourself is cheaper than buying a book, and

Henty Books on CD-ROM

I just got a sample of the Robinson Curriculum's newest release—*all* the G.A. Henty books on a set of six CD-ROMs, all packaged together in an attractive hardshell disc binder. This set includes 99 books and 59 stories by Henty and 216 other Henty era stories, is priced at $99 postpaid, runs under Mac or Windows 3.1/95/98/NT, and can be ordered from Oregon Institute of Science and Medicine.

For those of you few who haven't heard of Henty, last century he was revered as "The Boy's Own Historian." His books, set in a variety of historical eras, are well-researched action epics and were immensely popular for decades.

We haven't had a chance to review this new CD-ROM set yet, but I thought you'd like to know about it. Once again, the technology of the future is opening up the door to the past.

I personally recommend supplementing with some science and social studies materials for grades 1–8. In addition, Dr. Robinson states that the program has all the phonics and math flash cards you need to use and master to read and start *Saxon 5/4*. Personally, I feel a great deal more teaching must take place before your child is reading proficiently and able to start *Saxon 5/4*.

BEST FEATURES: A prescreened, ready-to-print library of exceptional literature and autobiographies.

WORST FEATURES: Not enough testing and application of learned principles. You must trust that your child will learn enough spelling, grammar, writing skills, science, history, and geography all on their own from reading. Some homeschool moms love this type of freedom from structure, but it would drive me crazy. If you enjoy this type of schooling, you can use this set of CD-ROMs as a full-fledged curriculum.

NEW!
Sonlight Curriculum, 2000 edition

Grades preK–9; upper-level courses can be used at grade levels up to grade 12. Preschool (no teacher's manual available), $175. Kindergarten Basic: Regular readers, $190; Advanced readers, $270. First Grade Basic: Regular and Advanced readers, $280 each. Second Grade Basic: Regular readers, $295; Advanced readers, $330. Third Grade Basic: Regular readers, $310; Advanced readers, $370. Fourth Grade Basic, $365. Fourth Grade for First-Time Users Basic, $330. Fifth Year Basic, $470. Sixth Year Basic: Boys, $410; Girls, $410. Seventh Year Ba-

some of the titles are out of print; so unless you find it at a used bookstore, being able to print these types of books to add to your own home library can be invaluable! There is a handy option to print the odd pages first and then flip the stack of paper over and print the even numbered pages on the opposite side, cutting your printing costs substantially.

As *Practical Homeschooling* reader Belinda Bowman pointed out, if you can find any of these books at a used bookstore or library sale for less than about $5, it will be cheaper than printing out the book. You might want to tuck a list of the book titles into your purse or glove compartment, to have it handy when you visit such places. Remember, the main value of this curriculum is not in "free books" but in the choice of books, the teaching material, and knowing that you have every title readily available to you whether you can find them for sale at a reasonable price or not.

Additional features include vocabulary flash cards keyed to the books, phonics flash cards you print out to teach reading, and some multiple-choice and essay-based exams. Only about 45 of the books have corresponding exams. The questions on the exams are designed to make you think about what you have read, not just regurgitate the plot and main characters. I had fun reading the questions. Some are far from politically correct. A question from the *Five Little Peppers* asked how Mrs. Pepper supported herself and one of the answer choices was she had food stamps and welfare. Obviously this was not the correct answer! You must correct these exams yourself, somewhat negating the idea of a complete self-teaching program. However, correcting 42 exams over a course of 12 years doesn't sound too tough.

I use the Robinson Curriculum in our homeschool on a fairly limited basis. However, I must stress that though I use and recommend this material, we use it more as a reference and research library—not as a full "this is all you need" curriculum. You can use it that way, and we know most families who use it do, but we use it as a supplement to our existing curriculum.

My future upgrade wish list includes more quizzes on reading material and perhaps more direction in the actual course of study. It wasn't clear to me what and when a child should be reading, and what and if any pre-requisite study was required before tackling any of the textbooks or more challenging reading selections. Nevertheless, I feel that any homeschool can greatly benefit from Dr. Robinson's educational ideas and this wonderful library of books. *Tammy Kihlstadius*

There's no doubt about it: **Sonlight Curriculum** is the fastest-growing homeschool curriculum around. This "literature-based curriculum with an international perspective" is *so* different from other homeschool programs it takes a full four pages just to *start* to describe it!

Its success is even more astounding when you discover that Sonlight was *not* invented for you and me. Far from trying to make a splash in the American homeschool market, the founders of Sonlight (John and Sarita Holzmann and Rebecca Lewis) set out to design a curriculum for, in their own words, "the peculiar needs of expatriate Americans." In other words, for American citizens who were living anywhere in the world *except* right here.

As back-fence neighbors at the U.S. Center for World Mission, Sarita and Rebecca discovered they shared a similar philosophy of homeschooling. The curriculum they began to envision would offer an international, Christian missionary-oriented perspective . . . and a whole different style of education as well.

What came into being in 1990 was a program with *many* distinctive features:

- **Oodles of books**. Boxes of books. Shelves of books. For example, the seventh-grade level comes with 55 real or "living" books including high quality historical fiction, Christian fiction, Newbery books, missionary books, biographies and non-fiction, all correlated with a Bob Jones history text. Even the science curriculum for seventh grade includes seven non-textbook science and experiment books.

- **Real books, not textbooks.** Kids who use Sonlight mostly read "bookstore and library" books, not textbooks. Many are biographies and historical fiction, chosen to *teach* history, character, the viewpoints of people in other cultures and religions, and more The selections also include quite a few Usborne, Dorling Kindersley, and Eyewitness books as well (mostly in the area of science). Homeschool kids are readers; the large number of "real" books they read in this program is one reason many families report increased enthusiasm and motivation when they switch to Sonlight.

- **About that "international missionary perspective"**: Sonlight's international perspective is hard to miss. The curriculum includes missionary biographies at each level. Students in upper grades are assigned a weekly international current event report. Fifth and sixth graders have World Studies. Fifth grade uses the World Book Encyclopedia. Sixth grade uses Bob Jones *Heritage Studies* 7. Of course, fifth and sixth graders also use the many real books that come with the Sonlight course. Eighth grade delves into church history. The emphasis is not so much "America first" as it is "God's Kingdom first." Sonlight believes that we can only reach other cultures with the Gospel if we truly understand their point of view, empathize with it, and then *still* are committed to the Bible's teaching. Not everyone agrees with this approach of course, which is why the thick Sonlight catalog actually includes a section entitled, "27 Good Reasons <u>Not</u> to Purchase Sonlight Curriculum"!

- **The "Basic" Sonlight curriculum** for each grade level includes Bible, history, readers, *and* "read-alouds." These last are books the parents will read to the kids, thus enabling the kids to encounter ideas and vocabulary way above their current reading level.

- **"Regular readers" and "advanced readers" versions** of the Basic curriculum are available for the earlier grades.

- **Complete science, language arts, and math courses** are available by grade level. These can be mixed and matched with the Basic program, making it easy to, for instance, pro-

sic, $435. Eighth Year Basic: Boys, $305; Girls, $300; Advanced Boys, $335; Advanced Girls, $330. Ninth Year Basic, $440. Tenth Year Basic, $470. Science, language arts, and math materials not included in Basic curriculum price. All materials also available by subject or individually. Add $5 shipping (waived if order over $100). No phone orders. *Sonlight Curriculum, 8121 South Grant Way, Littleton, CO 80122-2701. Inquiries only, no orders: (303) 730-6292. Fax: (303) 795-8668. Email: main@sonlight.com Web: www.sonlight.com.*

Sonlight has recently made lots of changes to their teachers' manuals for K–2. They have added phonics and grammar instruction based on dictation. Plus Narration, Geography, Comprehension, and Cultural Literacy questions, and vocabulary for read-alouds. Language arts manuals for all grades are also being revised to use Ruth Beechick's methods.

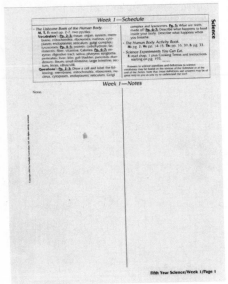

Vocabulary words, questions, and assignments are on the front of each Science schedule page

Definitions and answers are on the back, as are any special teacher's notes

vide a third-grader with fourth-grade math and second-grade language arts.

- **You have your choice** of Scott-Foresman or Saxon math programs for each grade. The early elementary programs use lots of inexpensive manipulatives. Kindergarten math, for example, comes with three sheets of patterns printed on brightly colored cardstock for you to cut out your own manipulatives, plus three sheets of Bingo squares and five sheets of domino cutouts for math games.

- **You have your choice** of Concerned Communications "Reason for Writing" cursive or the Portland State University "Getty-Dubay" cursive italic handwriting programs for each grade.

- **Dictation** is regularly required, for practicing handwriting, punctuation, and listening skills.

- **Sonlight is set up for a 36-week school year.** The teacher's manuals are designed so each week fits on a single page, with room for your notes. (Sonlight's own notes on a given topic may run to some additional pages.) If you purchase a Basic course, plus Science, plus Language Arts, plus Math, you'd end up with four schedule pages per week.

- **All teacher's manuals are three-hole-punched** and come with prepunched tabbed pages for weeks 1–36.

- **The design of these schedule pages is very handy**. You have plenty of room to note attendance, quiz results, etc., making your Sonlight manual your attendance record to show school officials if needed.

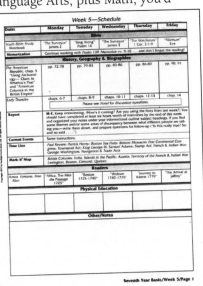

- **History** is studied not only with biographies and historical fiction, but with the aid of a timeline you create (available from Sonlight) and a mark-and-wipe map (also available from Sonlight).

- **Science** includes vocabulary and questions on the front of the schedule page, and definitions and answers on the back. (See the sidebar.) This really makes teaching science a lot easier—and I have to say that Sonlight teaches more science vocabulary (which is at least 50 percent of what learning science is all about) than any other curriculum I've seen.

- **Science also frequently includes extensive notes** amplifying; or in some cases correcting, material found in the books. These notes are fascinating reading, and add significantly to the quality of Sonlight's science instruction.

- **No one-sided ecological doom and gloom**. Both sides of the scientific arguments about such things as acid rain and the ozone layer are presented.

- **Language arts** includes handwriting, dictation, spelling, grammar, vocabulary, memorization/public speaking and (in the earliest grades) phonics

- **Math** in grades K–3 includes much work with manipulatives—"bean sticks" made from popsicle sticks and beans, for example. You can make some yourself, but if you are using the Saxon Math program for grades K–3 you also need to purchase a $55 manipulatives kit.
- **All the science and art supplies** can be purchased from Sonlight.
- **Supplemental courses** available include typing, art, music, physical education, critical thinking, and foreign languages.
- **The teacher's manuals** give you general teaching tips in the front along with some helpful appendices and notes in the back. If you're used to using textbooks that tell you when to breathe in and out, you'll be disappointed. Other than assigning specific pages each day, the teacher's manual offers little help beyond, "read this and talk about it." (For more on how to teach, you're referred to Ruth Beechick's excellent books.) For example, the beginning of the manual contains a section on developing thinking skills using Bloom's taxonomy, but you won't find questions given for every book you study. While the teacher's manual gives you a day-by-day subject breakdown, you are free to adapt the schedule to meet your needs. Good thing since there is a *lot* of reading material to cover each day.
- **Almost no busy work.** Projects, field trips, and other hands on experiences are up to you to plan and provide. For some this comes as a relief! Except for the science experiments, there is not a project emphasis in Sonlight. While the subjects are intertwined as much as possible, you wouldn't describe this as a unit-study curriculum per se.
- **Starting with the "Year 5" Basic course**, Sonlight courses can be used for a variety of age levels. Year 5, for instance, is suggested for grade levels 5–9.
- **Samples of all the basic manuals** can now be seen online.
- **Each basic manual has a book list,** for people who use the library, that tells what weeks what books will be used.
- **Now available: color stickers to color-code books** for different grades.
- **Sonlight provides an "8-week risk-free trial."** Try it for eight weeks, and if you don't like it you can return it for a full refund.
- **For books purchased individually,** Sonlight offers a six-month money-back guarantee if the book is returned in resalable condition, less a 10 percent restocking fee.
- **Did I mention** that every book in the entire catalog, including the teacher's manuals, can be purchased separately? You do *not* have to purchase an entire curriculum. However, be warned that trying to find all, or even most, of the books in this program at the library is likely doomed to failure. I tested this by searching at our St. Louis County Library for an extensive list of Sonlight books. The library didn't carry half of them in *any* of its branches. Of the remainder, three-quarters weren't on the shelves when I looked for them. (Other Sonlight families at work, no doubt!) For these reasons, **I strongly recommend actually buying the books you don't own**, with the possible exception of major Newbery Award books the library is sure to have.

For more info on what's included at each grade level, see the detailed info in the Sonlight catalog. This is a very brief list:

Caveats: Not all of the material is from Christian sources. Many of the Newbery award winners will need to be discussed. Fantasy and fairy tales are used in early grades. Some material from Usborne and Dorling Kindersley contains partial nudity (get the stickers out!). When covering some other cultures (specifically, India, Inca, Aztec, and Maya) the material is downright gruesome—parental guidance is definitely needed here!

Finally, in a move that offended and alarmed some customers, curriculum author John Holtzmann recently announced his conversion to an "old earth" creation model. This has, however, not yet affected the curriculum directly, although the catalog does refer to it and offers some books written from that perspective.

Sonlight Kindergarten

- **Kindergarten**. World geography. Bible stories. An introduction to world cultures and people. An intro to natural sciences. Phonics through three-letter blends. Numbers, sequencing, time-telling, money, place value. Handwriting.
- **Grade 1**. Four civilizations (ancient Egypt, Rome, medieval Europe, the Vikings). Beginning science experiments. Addition/subtraction through 18, time, money. Start dictation exercises. Handwriting. Spelling. Vocabulary. Grammar. (These last four continue up through grade 7). Creative writing starts—continues in all grades.
- **Grade 2**. World history to 1914. Bible facts. Earth science, creation science. Addition/subtraction of 2- and 3-digit numbers, estimating, simple "pizza" fractions, simple "coin flipping" statistics. Cursive starts halfway through Grade 2 if you are using the Reason for Writing program.
- **Grade 3**. U.S. history to 1850s. Bible overview. Biology. All basic math facts for addition/subtraction/multiplication/division, adding fractions with common denominators, graphing, etc.
- **Grade 4**. U.S. history to early 20th century, or a slightly more advanced version of Grade 3 history for the first-time Sonlight user. Bible study methods and a study of the attributes of God. Physics, microscopy, electricity. Math basics plus emphasis on ratios and fractions with Cuisenaire rods. Vocabulary lessons start. Grammar lessons start.
- **Year 5**. World's major non-Christian cultures, some seen through missionaries' eyes, others as cultural introductions, with particular attention to the Pacific Rim and Asia. *Remembering God's Awesome Acts*. Human body, survival, fitness, geology. Regular Saxon math sequence or Exploring Math program, supplemented with lessons on area, perimeter, and volume using Cuisenaire rods.
- **Year 6**. World history in depth. Bible overview. Chemistry, biology, physics, creation science. Math is supplemented with spatial problems with Cuisenaire rods.
- **Year 7**. U.S. history in depth. 14 methods of Bible study. Astronomy, oceanography, earth science, meteorology. Pre-algebra.
- **Year 8**. God's kingdom worldwide (church history including Orthodox, Roman Catholic, and Protestant). Apologetics and study of the Westminster Catechism. Research projects. Analogies. Algebra 1.
- **Year 9** is designed to shake kids up and get them thinking. 20th century world history and literature. Apologetics. Analogies. Dr. Jay Wile's "Exploring Creation" series for science. Algebra 2 and geometry. The literature selections for this grade include many dealing with human nature and social issues and should definitely be discussed with parents.
- **Year 10** deals with the relationship between God's law and man's laws. Biblical law. American government. American literature. Biographies and historical fiction. *Dating With Integrity. Exploring Creation with Chemistry*. Advanced algebra. Literature selections again deal with social issues that students should discuss with their parents.

Whew! Maybe now you see why Sonlight needs a 116-page (and growing) catalog, complete with charts and questions and answers, to provide you more information than we can in our humble little review.

If you are leaving a highly structured homeschooling program behind, or if you are looking for an impressive all-in-one program that incorporates all the goodies you'd probably pick and choose yourself, then you might want to let the Sonlight in. *Crystal Anderson, Renee Mathis, and Mary Pride*

Sycamore Tree is an alternative, individualized Christian program established in 1982 by Bill and Sandy Gogel, who between them hold about every teaching credential imaginable and who have put a lot of energy into making their homeschool programs feel like you're part of a community, not just drudging away at lessons on your own. You can start your program any time, year-round, with an amazing degree of flexibility in materials. Sycamore Tree also sells a wide variety of nifty Christian (and other) educational materials. Send for their catalog!

Sycamore Tree offers three programs:

Traditional Program. For grades K–8 you can use their handy grade-level curriculum packages, which come with all needed textbooks, workbooks, and readers, and are available with complete daily lesson plans. This is probably the best option for beginners. Or you can design your own curriculum with their help, either using materials from their catalog of over 3,000 homeschool products or even using materials Sycamore Tree does not normally carry.

High school students must enroll at the beginning of a semester, if using the Traditional Program. Community college classes and a certain amount of work experience can count towards high-school graduation requirements. To graduate, students must pass a proficiency exam in language arts, math, and writing.

For the traditional program, you pay tuition on a per-family basis, payable monthly on a ten-month basis, usually September through June, or with a $50 discount if paid in advance in one lump sum.

Books and supplies are extra, but families are not required to get their materials from Sycamore Tree, although in most cases they would be wise to do so, and Sycamore Tree offers a 10 percent discount to enrolled families on all items whose code begins with a letter. All materials may be returned for a refund within fifteen days after receipt.

Online School. Sycamore Tree's online school is one of two online academies Alpha Omega/Bridgestone has licensed to use their popular Switched-On Schoolhouse software. For each grade level, you get five CD-ROMS: one each for English, Math, Science, Social Studies, and Bible. The software interacts automatically with Sycamore Tree's site, allowing your child to email his daily lessons to be graded and tracked by Sycamore Tree teachers. High-school students may enroll in the online school any time of the year. For more details about Switched-On Schoolhouse, see the Alpha Omega Academy write-up in the Online Academies chapter.

Combination Program. Realizing that families may want to do some courses online, without committing to a totally computerized education, Sycamore Tree is unique in allowing you to combine their online courses with traditional courses. This can give you the best of both worlds, as the computer software teaches courses the parent is weak is, does not have time for, or simply lacks the energy to grade. Meanwhile, many kids are more motivated by computer software than by traditional learning materials, so an online course in a subject the child is reluctant to tackle may just add the pep you need, while you still can use traditional materials for other subjects.

UPDATED!
Sycamore Tree Individualized Christian Program

Grades K–12. Traditional Program: Enrollment fee, $50/child; re-enrollment, $25/child; tuition, $45/month/family (10-month basis); books and supplies extra (around $250 per child). Online School: Enrollment fee, $100/child; re-enrollment, $50/child; tuition, $1,000 for all 5 subjects or $200/subject (first student), $900 all 5 subjects or $180/subject (second student), $800 for all 5 subjects or $160/subject (third student); English taken as a subject rather than with full enrollment, add $50; online classes include Switched-On Schoolhouse CD-ROM curriculum. Combination Program: Enrollment fee, $125/child; re-enrollment, $65/child; tuition for 5 online subjects plus traditional classes, $1,200 first student, $1,000 second student, $900 third student; payment plan available; if taking fewer than five online subjects, same tuition as Traditional Program, add $200/$280/ $260 per online subject for first/second/third student. Optional HSLDA membership, $85/family, make check out to HSLDA. High school graduation fee, $50. 10% discount on all catalog items for enrolled families.
The Sycamore Tree Center for Home Education, 2179 Meyer Place, Costa Mesa, CA 92627. Orders: (800) 779-6750. Information: (949) 650-4466. Fax: (800) 779-6750 or (949) 642-6750. Email: sycamoretree@compuserve.com. Web: www.sycamoretree.com.

Sycamore Tree offers a **Composition Evaluation Service**. Parents can send in five compositions and one research paper to be evaluated. Cost is $70, or $50 if in the school program.

Homeschool groups or other group organizations can place orders as a group and get 10% discount. Minimum of ten orders, with each person attaching payment information to own order form. Orders shipped to the individual person, not to the organization.

Whatever your child's grade level or program type, you get more than curriculum: every lesson is checked by credentialed teachers and every month K–8 students get a 60–80 page enrichment packet in the mail that's chock-full of fun activities, ideas, and web sites. High-school students get their own monthly enrichment packets, which include information about scholarships, deadlines for high-school testing and college applications, scholarships, recommended web sites, humor, riddles, activities, and oddments such as a comic book from Merrill Lynch entitled *Savin' Dave and the Compounders,* on the merits of savings and compound interest. If you live in an area with one or more Sycamore Tree families, they will help you set up a local Sycamore Tree support group. Finally, Sycamore Tree is in the process of setting up an area on their message board where Sycamore Tree high-school students can interact and make friends with each other.

With all enrollment options, you get standardized testing in the spring using the California Test of Basic Skills, student body ID cards, a copy of World Book's *Typical Course of Study* to help you keep on top of grade-level objectives, a teacher's lesson plan/assignment book, and a three-ring binder loaded with information on how to teach, keep records, and use their curriculum. Upon completion of the necessary course work, you receive quarterly progress reports from the teacher assigned to your child, a yearly grade-level completion certificate and a Junior High or High School diploma. In addition, Sycamore Tree maintains records, provides official transcripts, helps high-school students obtain work permits, and offers professional educational guidance by phone and email. Plus, there's a partial money-back guarantee: if after following their program for one year, you are not satisfied, they will refund your enrollment fees.

The student's workload will reflect his and his parents' desires, since each Traditional and Combination program is totally individualized.

Sycamore Tree's catalog will make any true-blue home schooler drool with desire, especially if you have read Volumes 2 and 3 of *The Big Book of Home Learning* and thus have a better idea of what the offered products are all about than the brief catalog listings can provide. The range of materials they have chosen to offer reflects sound taste and judgment. You may order from the catalog without enrolling. See chapter 7 for more details.

Sycamore Tree materials are educationally sound and interesting. Here's just a sample of what they offer. The Alpha Omega curriculum, Saxon Math, Cuisenaire, Miquon Math, Key Curriculum, Horizons Math, Calcu-Ladder, Pathway Readers, Modern Curriculum Press, Hayes, Steck-Vaughn, Geo-Safari, KONOS, Amanda Bennett's Unit Studies, A Reason for Writing, Christian Liberty Press, Bob Books, Prairie Primer, and much more. Sticker books. Manipulatives galore for every subject. Activity packs. The largest selection of *Little House on the Prairie*-related resources I have seen anywhere. A wide variety of neat science and art equipment, including the best drawing text I have ever seen for young children. Foreign language materials. A whole host of Christian teaching aids that are hard to find elsewhere. I have not even begun to list the topics their catalog covers. You will just have to request one and see for yourself.

With all this variety of excellent materials to choose from, a family should have no trouble setting up an "A+" individualized program. *Mary Pride*

CHAPTER 39

Traditional Catholic Curriculum

Did you know your local Catholic school might not even be using Catholic texts? Yep, it's true. As the Our Lady of the Rosary catalog truthfully notes:

> For many years Catholic authors have not written Catholic textbooks. Catholic books are no longer required in Catholic schools and are no longer permitted where state or federal funds are provided.

That's why so many Catholic parents have turned to homeschooling and why you now you have a choice of *four* (count 'em!) Catholic home-school programs.

Catholic Curriculum

Founded in 1980, but only recently making a splash in the homeschool community, **Kolbe Academy** is a classical-education program from an orthodox Catholic point of view. Named after the Catholic saint Father Maximilian Kolbe, and enrolling nearly 2,700 students as of Spring 2000, Kolbe's program at first blush seems to resemble Seton's. Both programs offer textbooks, week-by-week lesson plans, quarterly tests, quarterly reports on work and exams submitted to the school, counseling and assistance from the staff, high-school diplomas, recordkeeping (including report cards and transcripts), a "thoroughly Catholic" outlook, and even the same Stanford Achievement Tests! But obviously there are some differences, or nobody would have felt a need to establish an entire new program.

One major difference is that Seton grades your child's work and keeps a record of the grades. Kolbe's position is that parents are the educators, and Kolbe's staff is there to provide assistance. So Kolbe parents do all the grading of their children's work. Answer keys are provided on some of the materials. On a quarterly basis, parent send in reports of their children' grade, along with samples of student work. A Kolbe proctor then examines the student work and the grades submitted, to basically double-check the parents, before adding the grade record to the student's transcript.

The second major difference is the teacher materials. While Seton prides itself on its detailed daily lesson plans, Kolbe's teacher materials—syllabi, course plans, and quarterly exams—are short and sweet. A Kolbe syllabus

NEW!
Kolbe Academy
K–12. Registration/Tuition: Grade K: 1st student, $75; Additional student, $50. 1–8: 1st student, $200; 9–12, $225; Additional student $125. Maximum book costs by grade: K, $100; 1, $119; 2, $117.50; 3, $144; 4, $243; 5, $241; 6, $246.50; 7, $230; 8, $236; 9, $303.50; 10, $412; 11, $443; 12, $374.50. Ignatian Education in the Home, $8.50. Classical Education in the Contemporary World, $4. Kolbe Academy Recommended Reading List, $3.50. Parent As Counselor, $5. Tenets for Readers and Reviewers, $5. Kolbe Academy Prayer Book, $4.50. Laudate! Kolbe Academy Listening Guide, $5. Shipping extra. *Kolbe Academy, 2501 Oak St., CA 94559. (707) 255-6499 or (707) 255-6412. Fax: (707) 255-1581. Email: kolbeacad@earthlink.net. Web: www.kolbe.org/.*

Kolbe's new **Parent as Counselor** guidebook helps parents of high-school students make sure their children complete all the requirements. It includes information on various standardized tests as well.

outlines a course: its goals and the topics studied. Kolbe course plans range from simply dividing a text in readings by week (e.g., Week 1, read such and such page in this book) to plans that provide brief descriptions of the pages studied, plus well-thought-out questions that students are expected to answer in essay form. An example of the latter: "Explain the theological assumptions of St. Gregory's statements against civil war. Are they all true, or not? Explain." If you're going to give your children assignments like this, you'd better plan on reading the books yourself!

Another difference is that, while Seton's program includes some aspects of classical education, Kolbe's program is classical education, Jesuit style. Ignatius Loyola, founder of the Jesuits, had definite ideas about education; Kolbe considers their course of study "Ignatian-directed," as it says on their web site.

The following descriptions of Kolbe Academy's primary (grades K–8) curriculum are adapted from their brochure and web site.

Religion. Knowledge of the Catholic faith; memorization of common prayers (Kolbe publishes their own *Ancilla Domini Kolbe Academy Prayer Book*); attendance at some and knowledge of all the Catholic sacraments; preparation for reception of the sacraments; study of the history of the Church, the Councils, Church law, doctrine; understanding the primacy of St. Peter; encyclicals; patristics; Vatican I and II documents; lives and writings of the Catholic saints, etc.

NEW!
Designing Your Own Classical Curriculum
Catholic Education: Homeward Bound
A Catholic Homeschool Treasury

Grades K–12. $14.95 each book. Add $5 shipping. *Ignatius Press, PO Box 1339, Fort Collins, CO 80522. (800) 651-1531. Fax: (800) 278-3566. Web: www.ignatius.com.*

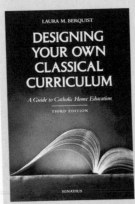

Designing Your Own Classical Curriculum: A Guide to Catholic Home Education provides a practical way of expanding the homeschool options for Catholics.

In *Designing Your Own Classical Curriculum,* you'll see how to combine the Trivium with a variety of the traditional (math, science, history) and the Catholic (the catechism, Latin, and the lives of the saints) to get a thorough and sound education.

A 160-page softcover book may seem too short to cover kindergarten through twelfth grade. However, you will find it contains:

- guidelines for what should be accomplished in each grade,
- an explanation of the importance of each subject,
- a bibliography which includes how to get the books mentioned, and
- a schedule for how often each subject should be taught at each grade.

Although *Designing Your Own Classical Curriculum* doesn't pretend to be a curriculum, it provides enough information that you *could* follow it to the letter and have a complete curriculum. It doesn't spend too much time explaining how you would design your own (aside from giving the author's example of the curriculum she designed). You can adapt it to suit your own needs and benefit from the mini-reviews of why each subject and book(s) were chosen for a particular level.

What I particularly like about *Designing Your Own Classical Curriculum* is that the recommended books include many homeschool favorites such as *Mommy, It's a Renoir, Saxon* and *A Beka.* Many of the history, poetry and literature books are available through the library. You will also find many books selected from Catholic suppliers such as Seton Hall and the Mother of Divine Grace. *Teresa Schultz-Jones*

A Catholic Homeschool Treasury is the cooperative effort of over 20 Catholic homeschool writers. The 196-page, handy-sized book includes sections on getting started, homeschool philosophies, simple suggestions for teaching some curriculum areas, enrichment ideas, "how we do it," and some short viewpoint articles. Appendixes include Catholic homeschool providers, other Catholic organizations/magazines/books/catalogs/etc., Catholic web sites, and a short math resource guide. No in-depth material here, just enough to supplement what you'll find in other homeschool books and resource guides. *Mary Pride*

Catholic Education: Homeward Bound is an all-in-one homeschool book that gets deeper into the underlying questions of how to make home education Catholic than *Catholic Homeschool Treasury.* Lots of appendices. 400 pages. *Mary Pride*

Texts used for the K–8 religion courses are the Faith & Life series from Catholics United for the Faith, Hardon's *Catechism* and *Catholic Dictionary*, St. Joseph's Baltimore Catechism series, Mary Fabyan Windeatt's Stories of Saints for Young People series, St. Joseph picture books, *Leading the Little Ones to Mary*, and Catholic source documents.

History. The Incarnation is the central event in the course of Christian history. Memory is broadened and perfected through the retention of the four facts of history: places, dates, people, and events. Emphasis is placed on the great civilizations of Greece and Rome, the study of which is introduced in the third and fourth grades.

Texts used are Greenleaf Press's series on Egypt, Greece, and Rome; *The Old World and America*, a Catholic text originally published in 1937; *Christ the King, Lord of History*, a Catholic text that covers world history from ancient times to the 1970's; *Quest of a Hemisphere*; *Christ and the Americas*, a Catholic introduction to U.S. history; *The Story of Canada*; Newton & Horan Bible history series; and original source documents. The works of Warren Carroll, John Mulloy, and Christopher Dawson are used for reference purposes.

Literature. In grades 1–8, the child is introduced to great literature through readers and independent book reports.

Texts include great books (Kolbe Academy publishes its own *Recommended Reading List*); Catholic National Readers (Kolbe publishes its own guides to these readers for grades 1–3); McGuffey Readers (Kolbe publishes it own guides to these as well); Open Court Readers; American and English literature; children's classics, e.g., *D'Aulaire's Book of Greek Myths* (the source text used for the annual National Mythology Competition) and *The Children's Homer* by Padraic Colum.

English. Critical reading of children's literature; book reports and literary analysis; writing, vocabulary; rules of grammar; penmanship; spelling; composition, and research skills. Reading for the Kolbe student involves capacity in four skills: *assimilative, recreational, vocational,* and *critical*.

Texts used include *Voyages in English* (Kolbe Academy now has the classic 1962 editions of these Catholic texts available for grades 3–8; the 1988 and 1995 editions are available for grades 1–2); Sadlier-Oxford Composition series (grades 6–8); *Learning Grammar Through Writing*; the Writing Strands program; and *Easy Grammar Plus*. For handwriting, the Bowmar/Noble Handwriting series, and/or (in grades 7 and 8) the Spencerian Handwriting Complete Course

Languages. Students can begin classical language study of Greek and Latin in the fourth grade or even earlier.

Texts used: the Latin is Fun! series, the Lingua Latina series, Latina Christiana, and *Basic Greek in 30 Minutes a Day*.

Phonics & Vocabulary. The study of phonics continues through the fourth grade, or through the sixth if the parent deems it necessary.

Texts used include the Modern Curriculum Press phonics series, *English from the Roots Up*, and the Sadlier Vocabulary series.

Mathematics. Basic operations, measurements, functions, decimals, estimation, negative numbers, percentages, line graphs, exponents, probability, geometric shapes & logic. MCP Math is used in grades K–3 with Cuisenaire rods. In grades 4–8, Holt Arithmetic series is available, as is the Saxon Math series (Kolbe recommends Saxon for grades 4 on up). Pre-algebra and elementary geometry (Euclidean approach) are offered in the seventh and eighth grades.

Science. Concentration on plants and animals, the food chain, rocks and minerals, weather, the solar system, energy and motion, earth, life, and physical science. Like the other Catholic homeschool academies, Kolbe takes a creationist point of view, which is brought out in the lesson plans when the textbooks present evolution.

When Kolbe says they are "classical," they *mean* "classical." Kolbe introduces the history of Greece and Rome in the third and fourth grades, and reprises it in grades 9 and 10. Medieval history is studied in grade 11, with American and the modern world winding up in grade 12. In grades 1–8, Kolbe students read great literature selections in their readers and do book reports on selected books. In high school, they read classics such as Homer's *Iliad* and *Odyssey*, Virgil's *Aeneid*, Dante's *Divine Comedy*, and works of Shakespeare. Greek and Latin are taught, starting in the fourth grade; modern languages are added in high school. There is a lot of emphasis on writing, the arts of persuasion, and literary analysis and logic. Primary sources are emphasized in high-school history studies. Music, visual arts, and performing arts are given prominence as well. Students at Kolbe's day school put on an annual performance of a classical drama. Obviously, this last is not practical in most home settings!

Probably the best way to tell if you're a Kolbe prospect is whether you and your children are excited by this kind of content—and of course, if you want a curriculum steeped in traditional Catholicism! You should then consider whether you need the extra accountability of having a school grade your children's work or whether you'd just as soon do it yourself, and whether you want detailed daily lesson plans or just a general outline with good essay questions. Remember, with Kolbe you will *have* to read the kids' books and study them enough to figure out if the kids' answers to the weekly essay questions are good or clueless. This only becomes a major commitment at the high-school level.

Kolbe sends its families a regular monthly newsletter, with updates on what's happening at the school, new materials available, teaching tips, and words of wisdom.

Texts used: Modern Curriculum Press science series (grades 1–5/6), Cambridge Science Series (grades 6–8), Janice VanCleave's Science for Every Kid series, and some books of experiments.

Geography. The study of geography begins with the mastery of map reading. It continues to be studied as a part of the history lessons. In fourth grade, students write a report on their state. In fifth grade, they write a country report. Rand McNally atlases and a Map Skills series are used.

A few resources are also available for art, civics, and music at these grade levels.

Kolbe's high-school years are divided according to the historical periods studied:

- Grade 9: Athens and Jerusalem—ancient Greece and Israel
- Grade 10: Rome
- Grade 11: London, Paris, and the medieval world
- Grade 12: The opposing forces of American constitutional republicanism and Soviet communism, representing the great political conflict of the modern world

The religion, literature, and history studies in each high-school year follow this historical sequence. Thus, in ninth grade, in religion class Kolbe students study the Old Testament, the sacraments, and prayer. In history, they study Greece and Hellenistic culture, including Herodotus's *Histories,* Thucydides *History of the Peloponnesian War,* and Xenophon's *Persian Expedition.* In literature, the *Iliad* and *Odyssey,* plus the Oresteian Trilogy, Sophocles' *Three Theban Plays,* the great dialogues of Plato, and Aristotle's *Poetics.* As you can see, this is similar to what you might expect from one year of a college course in the Great Books.

High-school science follows the usual biology/chemistry/physics sequence, with astronomy as the twelfth-grade science offering. High-school math is the usual college-prep sequence: Algebra I and Geometry I in ninth grade, Algebra II and Geometry II in tenth grade, Advanced Math consisting of Algebra III/Geometry III/Trigonometry in eleventh grade, and more Advanced Math, including introductory calculus, in twelfth.

Latin and Greek are available throughout high school. Students with an aptitude for these languages, who have studied them in earlier grades, are encouraged to read the Greek and Latin classics in their original languages. Four years of Spanish are also available.

Kolbe's booklet *Classical Education in the Contemporary World* does a fine job of presenting their philosophy. It's worth reading even if you don't plan to use this program. If you plan to send away for the Kolbe catalog, I would advise you to pick up this booklet as well. *Mary Pride*

UPDATED!
Our Lady of the Rosary School

Grades K–12. Registration: $25 per family per year. Full enrollment: preK, $99; K, $199; Grades 1–8, $459, plus $50 Saxon book fee for grades 5–8; Grades 9–12, $539 plus $40 Saxon book fee. Hardcover books must be returned. "Kindergarten for Catholics" religion program, $39 plus shipping. Grades 1–8 religion only, $65 plus shipping. Grades 9–12

Established in 1983, **Our Lady of the Rosary School** now serves 7,000 families in some capacity or other—whether they have signed up for the full curriculum, the "co-op" program in which parents grade the quarterly exams and OLRS reviews them, the "consumables" (useful when you have already purchased a grade level and just need new workbooks), or whether they have just purchased one of the wide variety of Catholic items (missals, scapulars, etc.) from OLRS's extensive catalog.

Our Lady of the Rosary Faith and Freedom Series

And boy, is Our Lady of the Rosary *Catholic!* The whole catalog will recall memories of Sister Monica in her long, black habit. Starting with materials for parents on how to teach Catholicism to their children, you have here a complete pre-kindergarten through high school old-timey Catholic curriculum. Stories of saints for all grade levels. Communion and Confirmation preparation. Latin. Home Economics courses with Catholic patterns (even altar cloths and vestments!). All this plus traditional math and grammar, Catholic science texts, penmanship, Catholic history, geography, and (in high school) a course intriguingly titled "Christian Culture and World Civilization." You also get high school electives—e.g., typing and computer intro; "Philosophy of History" in grade 12; and a catalog of Catholic gift items. Some of these materials were produced by OLRS; others are out-of-print texts they unearthed; some are still in print. The out-of-print material has to be returned when you are finished with it.

I don't have space here to review all of OLRS's unique materials, so let's just look at a few:

- **OLRS offers religion-only programs** for all grades, for those who want to supplement regular school or another program with Catholic education. Their "Kindergarten for Catholics" program has lessons, Bible stories, art and creative activities and resource books. A 22 x 23" "My Jesus and I" full-color wall chart with forty large pictures and text outlining basic Catholic devotional beliefs is also available.
- **OLRS's "Kindergarten Music" course** is exceptionally well-designed for home schools. It starts with a nice overview of the whole course that lists songs, instruments (you will be making several simple instruments during the year), listening selections (classics available at most libraries), and a glossary of terms. The program, like other OLRS courses, is divided by months and weeks, and the songs are (naturally) Catholic.
- **OLRS's "Math Kit for Home Schoolers"** starts at counting (with manipulatives provided) and goes right up to the eighth grade level. In one book you get the equivalent of curriculum and teacher guides for K–8. The kit comes with a set of linking cubes (for counting and arithmetic operations) and a fractions board. A very nice, simple approach that anyone can use.
- **Beginning readers** will be using *This Is Our Family: Faith and Freedom Reader,* a black-and-white reissue of the 1950s and 60s text from Ginn. The sweet Dick-and-Jane-style stories starring Timothy, Ann, David, and (eventually) Baby Mary were hugely popular in Catholic schools of those decades. The dog's name is Zip and the family is observant Catholics who attend church and send their older children to Catholic school.
- **Latin studies** begin in grade 5.
- **ID Digital math texts** are used in grades K–4, switching to Saxon Math in grade 5.
- **History is not really emphasized until sixth grade**, when OLRS introduces its own history and geography series. These books are black-and-white reprints of classic Catholic texts from Follett and Silver Burdett, first issued in the 1960s. The charming illustrations and friendly text will bring back fond memories from many who attended Catholic school in that period.
- **Secular texts** from Scott Foresman or Modern Curriculum Press are used for science.

religion only, $85 plus shipping. High school electives, some materials extra. Discount on second and other children. Extensive selection of materials. Many can be purchased individually.
Our Lady of the Rosary School, 116-1/2 North 3rd Street, Bardstown, KY 40004. (502) 348-1338. Toll-free fax (continental USA): (888) FAX-OLRS. Fax: (502) 348-1943. Email: information@olrs.com. Web: www.olrs.com.

New since the last edition of *The Big Book:* OLRS is now reprinting a number of classic Catholic texts, to which they have been able to obtain the copyright. Also new are their web site, their online support group, and the ability to email your OLRS teacher.

OLRS's web site is a treasure trove for Catholic parents. You'll find an "FAQ" (Frequently Asked Questions) list about Roman Catholic homeschooling . . . church documents related to homeschooling and the inalienable right and duty of Catholic parents to control their children' education . . . articles about homeschooling . . . online newsletters . . . electronic pen pals . . . the entire OLRS catalog . . . the OLRS course listings, and more. Students can even take tests in a password-protected area of this web site!

OLRS now also has a newsletter ($12/year for a subscription). Annual seminars ($55/family), combined with graduation ceremonies, are the last weekend in July. Of particular interest to homeschool families whose local priests refuse to give their children the Catholic sacraments unless said children complete the parish religious education program—complete with sex education—at the annual seminar a priest is available for First Communion, First Confession, and Confirmation.

- **High-school electives available:** Latin (2 years), home economics (four years), typing (two years), Using Windows 3.1, Using Windows 95, World History III (Christianity and Eastern Religions). Chemistry, physics, advanced mathematics, and calculus are also listed as electives, but really should be part of any serious pre-college program.

As you can see, OLRS is more activity-oriented than similar programs, and (with no disparagement intended) not quite as intellectual. It is well suited to the average, as opposed to outstanding, student, and consequently less demanding for both student and parent than Seton's or Kolbe's programs. *Mary Pride*

Our Lady of Victory School (motto: "Teaching Reading, 'Riting, 'Rithmetic, plus Religion and Respect") is a very traditional provider of homeschool curriculum to the Catholic community. Their perspective is that the past 35 years have been a disaster for the Catholic faith in America; their materials and teaching perspective attempt to revive the Catholic education common before that period. Thus, they have a dress code for during homeschool hours; they use classic Catholic materials when possible; they recommend you set up a consistent schedule; and you'll be doing a *lot* of grading. This is not as onerous as it seems. The "dress code" for girls consists of a below-the-knee dress or skirt and classic opaque blouse. For boys, regular (not slim) cut slacks or cords, and a long or short sleeve dress shirt. No ties, jackets, blazers, knee socks, or other classic Catholic-school accouterments are required. They even recommend some flexibility in your weekly scheduling, to accommodate holidays that shift days from year to year. And their curriculum materials include an E-Z Grader, to simplify averaging all those daily grades.

Our Lady of Victory Catholic History

OLV's teaching materials are patriotic and creationist. They employ daily lesson plans in grades 1A (kindergarten) through 6, and weekly lesson plans for grades 7–12. The K–6 lesson plans are mainly just assignments laid out by subject and day, in a kind of grid with space for you to write down the daily grade. The lesson plans for grades 7–12 are considerably more detailed, as befits the more difficult assignments for these grade levels. All lesson plans are based on a 38-week school year. The OLV school year starts at the end of August and runs through mid-June.

Your enrollment options are:

- **Full tuition.** This includes the lesson plans, plus tutorial services, quarterly progress report, report cards, and diplomas for eighth and twelfth grade graduates. Books are not included in

UPDATED!
Our Lady of Victory School

Tuition: Grades 1A (kindergarten)–6, $200/student. Grades 7–12, $250. Enrollment fee: first year, $25; subsequent years, $10. Satellite program (Grades 1A–12) lesson plans, $85/grade. Books by grade: 1A (K), $138.50; 1B (grade 1), $217; 2, $253.75; 3, $233.75; 4, $223.25; 5, $238.75; 6, $264.75; 7, $247.50; 8, $227.75; 9, $256.25 (with Saxon Algebra I option) or $226.25 (with AMSCO Algebra I option); 10, $239.75 (with Saxon Algebra II option) or $226.25 (with AMSCO Algebra II option); 11, $246 (with Saxon Advanced Math), $208 (with AMSCO Geometry option) or $204 (with Schaum's Geometry option); 12, $176.25 (with AMSCO Algebra II/Trig option) or $210.25 (Saxon Advanced Math). All grade prices include E-Z Grader, $4.50. Shipping extra.
Our Lady of Victory School, PO Box 819, Post Falls, ID 83877 or 103 E. 10th Ave., Post Falls, ID 83854. (208) 773-7265. Fax: (208) 773-1951. Email: lepanto@olvs.org. Web: www.olvs.org.

the tuition fee. About 1,200 students are currently enrolled with this option,

- **Satellite program.** You get the lesson plans for your grade level, but no tutorial or record-keeping services. Books must be purchased separately.
- **Book purchasing.** You can purchase an entire grade level, or just one book. About 2,500 students are using their materials using either the satellite or book-purchase-only options.
- **OLV also offers** a 13-year catechism course, entitled Traditional Catholicism at Home.

Some books from Protestant (BJUP, Rod & Staff) and secular (Saxon, AMSCO, Schaum) publishers are used, but these will be phased out soon. Most OLV materials are solidly Catholic. For example, grades K–2 now use the Little Angel Catholic phonics reader series of texts, workbooks, teacher manuals, and answer keys.

Our Lady of Victory Little Angel Readers

For kindergarten, the subjects are art (lots of Catholic coloring books), music (Catholic and patriotic songs), religion (six Catholic books), math, phonics (Little Angel and Phonics Is Fun), Science (Catholic), and handwriting (a Catholic text, believe it or not!). Grade 1 has a different set of Catholic coloring books, the same music materials, more Little Angel and Phonics is Fun materials, some Catholic readers, a Hayes history text, math, a grade 1 Catholic science text, and Catholic spelling and writing workbooks. Grade 2 uses some of the same books as grade 1, and otherwise uses a grade 2 book in the same series. The coloring books continue up through grade 4, after which Art is dropped as a subject. The science books in grades 1A–8 are generally updated older Catholic texts. Voyages in English picks up in grade 3 and continues to grade 8. The same song materials for music are used at every grade level from K through 6. A wide variety of Catholic readers are used, changing at each grade level. The Traditional Catholic

Our Lady of Victory Catholic Religion

Speller series is used for grades 1–12. Math and upper-grades science use standard secular texts. A sequence of primarily Catholic texts is used for history and social studies.

The readers (in grades 1–6) and literature books (grades 8–12) are chosen more with an eye to instilling Catholicism than to college entrance exams. Titles such as *St Louis de Montfort* and *Stories of Don Bosco* do not appear in standard literature lists, but are representative of the novels and biographies your student will be reading. The religion, philosophy, and theology materials are well chosen to cover all traditional Catholic doctrines. The literature assignments are being upgraded to include material tested on standard achievement tests and the SAT/ACT tests.

Our Lady of Victory Science

OLV has been revising and reprinting (not just photocopying) classic Catholic texts from previous decades, under their imprint, Lepanto Press. These hardbound, cloth-covered editions include the Voyages in English series (grades 1–8; grades 3 and up have hardcover student text, photocopied teacher's manual, exercises workbook, and answer key), the Catholic National Readers (hardbound in maroon with gold lettering on the covers: primer through book six, plus the *Catholic Speller*), the Science & Living in God's World series (grade K–8), the Our Quest for Happiness high-school religion series (four hardbound volumes), three history texts (*How our Nation Began* for grades 3 or 4, *American History* for grade 5, and *Our Old World Background* for grades 5 or 6), *The Holy Sacrifice of the Mass* (text, lesson plans, and answer key), *My First Holy Communion* (full-color), *Chats with God's Little Ones* catechism lessons, plus two Catholic song books, a historic novel (*Fabiola*), and some high-school grammar and composition books.

In addition, OLV provides a "Suggested Classic Literature" reading list for grades 9–12 of additional titles usually found in the library or in "Great Books" collections, but not primarily written by Catholic authors. Authors include Homer, Virgil, Austen, Bronte, Dickens, Dumas, Hardy, Hemingway, Kipling, C.S. Lewis, Crane, James Fenimore Cooper, Robert Louis Stephenson, Twain, and other familiar names. A few books in this collection are morally ambiguous or perverse, Darwinian, or fatalistic, in the "old" manner, that is, without any graphic description of sinful acts (e.g., *The Portrait of Dorian Gray, Call of the Wild,* and *Far from the Madding Crowd*). Such a book can be excellent for showing the bankruptcy of faithlessness, provided either the school or parents takes the time to lead the student through it. In any case, students are only expected to pick a book or two per year from the list. Even if students read every book on the list, they still will need to supplement with at least the Cliff's Notes for several dozen more modern works that are now widely studied in public-school English classes, if they want to take any college-prep exams with a literature component.

High-school electives mostly use inexpensive materials. Lesson plan cost is $40 if you're taking an elective in addition to the regular six subjects. Electives include Accounting/Bookkeeping, Business Math, Clerical Skills, Earth Science, French I and II, Home Economics, Latin I–III (using the Henle books), Music Theory, Physical Education, Spanish I–III, and Typing.

OLV's web site includes information about all the books and courses available from them, answers to frequently asked questions, general homeschooling information, and more. *Mary Pride*

UPDATED!
Seton Home Study School

Grades K–12. New family fee, $25. Tuition: $20/year/student enrolled in grades 4-5, $40/year/student for grades 6-8; and high school fee $100/year/student enrolled in high school. Full enrollment: K, $150; grades 1–12, $470/first student, $905/2 students, $1300/3 students, $1670/4 students, $1970/5 students, $300/child additional students. Payment plan: for one student, $200 down, $55/month for 6 months; two students, $400 down, $105/month; three students, $600 down, $150/month; four students, $800 down, $190/month; five students, $1000 down, $220/month; additional students, add $200 each down, $30 each/month. Some flexibility available in amount down, number and size of monthly installments. Single elementary course, $85. Single high school course: Half-credit course, $85; One-credit course, $125. Enrollment in Special Services (children with learning disabilities): customized curriculum, $75; monitoring, $125 extra.

Seton Home Study School is named after the Catholic saint Elizabeth Ann Seton. Initially established in 1980 as an outgrowth of Seton Junior/Senior High School, located in Manassas, Virginia, the home-study department now enrolls over 10,000 students, with many thousands more families buying Seton materials *a la carte,* and has taken on a life of its own.

Seton Young Catholics Series

Seton Home Study School is accredited by the Northwest Association of Schools and Colleges, and by the Commission on International and Trans-Regional Accreditation.

Seton's program is textbook-oriented with some classical elements, flexibly structured, aimed at preparing students for college, and—to nobody's surprise—very Catholic. "On all levels," Seton says, "it is important to remember that the primary purpose of home school is to teach proper Catholic attitudes about life, Catholic values, and the ability to see the integration of Catholic truth in all areas of knowledge and of daily living." Thus Seton emphasizes traditional Catholic distinctives: the Mass, the Rosary, prayers to Mary and the saints, and so on. The curriculum is also creationist and patriotic.

Seton's program is very thorough in all areas. Books come from a variety of publishers—some Catholic, some evangelical, some secular. From an academic standpoint, their choices are good.

A major development since the last Big Book edition was published: in response to the limited availability of classic Catholic textbooks, and the increasing worldly content of texts published for Catholic schools, Seton now publishes many of its own textbooks, all bearing the tag line "For Young Catholics." Currently available, or soon to become available, are:

- *Art for Young Catholics:* Grades 1, 4, 7, and 8
- *Art of Writing for Young Catholics:* (handwriting) Grades 1–5
- *English for Young Catholics:* Grades 1–4
- *History for Young Catholics:* Grades 1, 2, 7, 8, 10, and 11
- *Phonics for Young Catholics:* Grades K, 4, and 5
- *Reading for Young Catholics:* (reading comprehension) Grades 4–8
- *Religion for Young Catholics:* Grades K–4 and 12
- *Science for Young Catholics:* Grades 1, 2, 4, and 7
- *Spelling for Young Catholics:* Grades 1–8

Other Seton-written titles, such as **Catholic World Culture** and **Great Saints in World History**, are available only at one grade level.

Most people order Seton courses by grade level. You want grade 1, you order grade 1. You'll get a lot of books and workbooks, often several in one subject. In kindergarten, for example, the math books include Modern Curriculum Press's kindergarten arithmetic workbook and a 1-2-3 coloring book. Kindergarten religion books include a catechism, the book *My Jesus and I*, three Catholic coloring books, three St. Joseph Picture Books, and *Leading Little Ones to Mary*. And that's just two subjects! Kindergarten students also get two art books, two handwriting workbooks, a Catholic music tape, a science book, and lesson plans for Mom and Dad. As you can see, Seton's kindergarten is a readiness and phonics program which includes handwriting. Each kindergarten lesson tells you what materials are needed and the objectives for the lesson (this is a good feature).

Seton Kindergarten

The list of subjects is even longer in other grades. Starting in grade 1, English, history, reading comprehension, health, and spelling are added to the curriculum. Vocabulary is added in grade 3. Besides the lesson plan book, in grade 1 and up you also get a lesson plan folder, and a plastic bag full of tests and quarterly report forms. Answer keys are made available starting in grade 2.

A huge number of single courses are available at the high-school level. These include:

- **Business Education** Accounting 1, Bookkeeping, Business Communication, Business Math, General Office, Introduction to Business, Keyboarding, and Marketing
- **Computer** Basic, Word Processing
- **English** English courses for grades 9–12, Catholic American Literature, Catholic World Literature, Shakespeare, a ninth-grade Grammar course, Composition, and Vocabulary
- **Languages** Three years each of Latin, French, and Spanish, and two years of German
- **Math** Algebra 1 and 2 (using Saxon books), Advanced Math 1 and 2 (using Saxon), Geometry, Logic, and Pre-Calculus
- **Religion** Four years
- **Science and Health** Christian Biology (uses the excellent A Beka text, along with the papal encyclical *Humani Generis* and

Seton Home Study School, 1350 Progress Drive, Front Royal, VA 22630-3332. (540)636-9990. Fax: (540) 636-1602. Web: www.setonhome.org. Email: for a printed copy of their information pack, infopack@setonhome.org. For curriculum questions, courseinfo@ setonhome.org. For other questions and correspondence, info@setonhome.org.

Important note: unlike almost all other textbook series used by homeschoolers, Seton's texts are deliberately written for family use. Nowhere will you find references to classrooms. Instead, the texts make it clear that the parent is the teacher and the student is learning at home. They mention homeschooling in places, and even refer to homeschool support groups!

Another important note: since these are new books, not reprints of out-of-print books, they include information on recent people and events not covered in the older Catholic texts, such as Pope John Paul II and Mother Teresa.

Seton used to require you to return all materials except workbooks at the end of the course. Now that they no longer depend so heavily on out-of-print material, 90 percent of the books are available for outright purchase. **The lesson manuals still have to be returned when you have finished with the course.** Seton's rationale for this is that they continually revise their materials and publish new books, so they want to make sure new students get the best new materials.

However, many parents prefer to rent the more expensive textbooks, to save money. That's why even such homeschool standards as the Saxon math texts Seton uses are available for rental. The rule is that if the catalog says a book is "rental," you may choose to rent or buy it. If it says "rental only," the book can only be rented and must be returned at the end of the course. Be sure to check the course descriptions before ordering.

Seton Web Page

If you visit Seton's web site—a good idea—you'll see that Seton has not been napping during the Information Revolution. Among homeschool curriculum providers, their web site is easily the most impressive. You can see what books are used for each grade level, an outline of each high-school course, background on Seton staff, descriptions of Seton's special services for special students, upcoming events of interest to Catholic home educators, articles and comments about Catholic homeschooling, message boards for Seton students and parents, and more. You can even sign up for courses or order individual books online.

Everywhere on the Seton web site you'll see the influence of Seton's director, Mary Kay Clark. Mrs. Clark is not only the possessor of a Ph.D. but a homeschooler, as well as having served as the president of the Virginia homeschool state organization, and the curriculum reflects her understanding of the special advantages of homeschooling, as well as her passion for reviving a more full-flavored variety of Catholicism than you can find in most American parishes today. Prominently displayed on the web site you'll find a photo of Mrs. Clark meeting the Pope, along with information on the struggles many conservative Catholic homeschoolers are facing, such as the desire to have their children receive communion without having to go through the sex education now integrated into parish CCD classes.

some other Catholic materials), Chemistry, Christian Earth Science (uses the Bob Jones text and some creationist materials), Health 1 and 2, Christian Physical Science, and Physics

- **Social Sciences** Christian American Government, Catholic American History, Economics, Geography, and Catholic World History
- **"Secular High School Courses"** (this is Seton's own way of defining them): Four years of literature, three years of grammar and composition, Earth Science, Physical Science, American Government, World History, American History, and Retail Merchandising

Placement is by the California Achievement Test at no extra charge. Seton gives its students the California Achievement Test at the end of their school year.

Educationally, Seton has a more relaxed attitude than other programs. The Seton staff believes in mastering a concept and then moving on, rather than continuing to fill out unnecessary workbook pages. They also believe strongly in individualized instruction and make special provisions for accelerated and slow students.

Seton's staff bends over backwards to help parents. Their very detailed and constantly updated teaching aids are excellent, in my opinion. Curriculum is constantly revised and improved. Also, Seton maintains a small bank of educational software some produced inhouse available to parents at a nominal fee.

Seton is very involved with its families. Each new Seton family receives a mini study skills course, Dr. Clark's book *Catholic Home Schooling*, placement tests, and transcript release forms. If necessary, the staff will call you after evaluating the placement test to discuss the best course options for your child. Counseling is available by phone or email.

For students with learning disabilities, Downs Syndrome, mental retardation, and other challenges, two learning disabilities specialists are on staff. There is an additional fee for enrolling in the Special Services Department.

You already know about the placement and achievement tests and quarterly exams. Seton also offers periodic progress reports, permanent records on file, transcripts if necessary, and advice and counsel from the Seton staff. Graduates who meet Seton's high-school requirements are awarded a diploma. Parents are provided with course materials, lesson plans, teaching aids, and tests (which Seton grades).

Parents receive a suggested lesson plan and a blank lesson plan notebook. They then devise a schedule that meets their own needs. Each subject has its own teaching aids and enrichment suggestions. Parents fill out attendance forms and grade daily assignments. Quarterly tests and completed daily work are sent to Seton, for Seton to grade the tests and assign quarterly grades.

Parents using the Seton program can expect to work hard, but to find their work interesting. Students are given a great deal of material to cover, but unnecessary repetition of mastered exercises is not required, thus eliminating much school drudgery.

Seton has a full-time lawyer on staff and is in close touch with legislative realities. If problems arise, Seton deals directly with school officials, providing not only lesson plans but their objectives and curriculum guidelines.

Academically, overall Seton rates an A.

Families looking for a traditional Catholic program which emphasizes individuality and flexibility and provides tons of help and accountability for its families will find Seton very attractive. *Mary Pride*

CHAPTER 40

High School Like You're Used To

In this chapter, you'll find two kinds of correspondence programs. I call them:

- Easy High School
- State University-Based Distance Learning

Here's the difference. The "easy" high-school programs were originally designed for drop-outs and kids who had to take summer school. American School, for example, has been known for decades as "The School of the Second Chance," whereas the Keystone National High School program grew organically from a few summer-school courses for kids who needed to "make up" a course into a full curriculum.

With this clientele originally in mind, the "easy" programs have been designed to make high school at home . . . well, easy! Lesson content is as clear as the writers can make it, the exercises are designed to lead the student step by step, and the tests are easy to comprehend and pass.

This does *not* mean these courses are inferior. Actually, they are superior to those many kids get at their local high school. They are fine if you want to get an accredited diploma that will help get you into a state school or community college, and great if a high-school degree is as far as you want to go.

However, if you are firmly committed to a college-prep program and have your sights set on one of the more elite colleges or universities, the state university-based programs are a better bet. On the whole, they have higher academic standards and more course content. While the material may not always be explained as carefully as that in the "easy" programs, it should pose no difficulty for the normal bright high schooler. These programs, developed and accredited as they are through the independent study high school departments of major state universities, are blessed with government funding and connections unavailable to their private-sector competitors. Thus they are able to offer options not found in the "easy" programs, such as dual credit courses and Honors courses.

I called this chapter "High School Like You're Used To," because this is as close as you can come to public high school at home. Since parents are the market, all these programs are fairly conservative in their outlook— meaning free of political correctness, paganism, sexually oriented material, and the like. Any exceptions have been noted in the reviews. So, this is high school like you, the parent, are used to.

Other High School Programs

Traditional (see chapter 35)
- A Beka Book
- A Beka Video School
- Alpha Omega Publications
- Bob Jones University Press
- Christian Liberty Academy
- Christian Light Education
- Home Study International
- Landmark's Freedom Baptist Curriculum
- School of Tomorrow

Classical (see chapter 36)
- Covenant Home Curriculum
- Great Books Academy

Different (see chapter 38)
- Advanced Training Institute International
- Clonlara CompuHigh
- Hewitt Homeschooling Resources
- Judah Bible Curriculum
- The Noah Plan
- Oak Meadow
- Robinson Curriculum
- Sonlight Curriculum
- Sycamore Tree

All the Catholic programs in chapter 39 include high school.

Additional Christian high-school-only programs are reviewed and listed in chapter 41.

Online programs, most of which include the high-school years, are reviewed in chapter 42.

The How's and Why's of High School at Home

NEW!
The High School Handbook

Parents. $19.97 plus shipping.
*Christian Home Educators Press, CHEA of California,
P.O. Box 2009, Norwalk, CA 90651. (562)864-2432. Fax:
(562)864-3747.. Email: cheaofca@aol.com. Web:
www.cheaofca.org. Don't mail or fax without order form.*

There are a few "must-have" books for homeschoolers and this is one of them. Whether you are looking at
teaching a junior-high-schooler next year or a high-
schooler in five years, **The High School Handbook**
will make your job easier. Navigating the high-school
waters can be difficult, but Mary Schofield has made the
task as simple as possible with her well-written guide.
This large-format, 224-page paperback has 11 chapters
that are detailed but not overwhelming. Here's a list of
topics:

- Planning to Teach
- Teaching Junior High
- Teaching Senior High
- Setting Requirements and Planning Your Year
- Course Descriptions
- Designing Courses
- Scheduling and Lesson Planning
- Evaluating Progress and Setting Standards
- Transcripts
- Resources
- After High School (discussions on college, mis-
  sions, and apprenticeship)

As you can see, this book is for the parents. Mrs.
Schofield doesn't adopt a "one size fits all" approach as
she allows for plenty of flexibility in course design and
administration. However, she is always mindful of the
need to be above reproach in our recordkeeping and
planning. Her advice is sound, friendly, and accompanied by plenty of examples. She gives you a variety of
sample forms for things such as transcripts and lesson
plans.

Whether you're timidly testing the waters or bravely
forging ahead, keep *The High School Handbook* handy.
Renee Mathis

NEW!
Home School, High School, and Beyond

Teens and parents. $17.95 plus $5 shipping.
*Castlemoyle Books, 6701 - 180th St. SW, Lynnwood, WA
98037. Orders: (888) 773-5586. Inquiries: (425) 787-
2714. Fax: (425) 787-0631. Email: info@castlemoyle.com.
Web: www.castlemoyle.com.*

If the thought of continuing to homeschool your
child through his high-school years is enough to send
you running off to the guidance counselor, take heart.
Beverly Adams-Gordon (author of the popular Spelling
Power program) has written a short course designed to
make the transition into high school as painless as possible. Intended as a 9-week study for incoming ninth

graders, **Home School, High School, and Beyond**
could be used by any student wanting to polish skills in
time management, goal setting, recordkeeping, and organization.

The book is divided into one-week sections:
- Establishing Goals and Setting Priorities (basic
  goal-setting info)
- Create Your Tentative High School Plan (what to
  study for all four years)
- Working Out This Year's Plan
- Planning Individual Courses (including creating
  your own syllabus and establishing evaluation crite-
  ria)
- Completing Assignments and Projects
- Making Weekly and Daily Schedules
- Keep Records of Your Accomplishments (making
  portfolios, transcripts, and diplomas)
- Making Decisions About Post-High-School
  Education
- Paying For College

While the book is written especially for teens, it's
nevertheless a good idea for parents to read through the
book beforehand. Gather the necessary supplies (some
binders, envelopes, tabbed dividers, and copies of the
forms included in the book. When your child has completed the course you can award him ½ semester credit
in Occupational Education. (Note: For a really knock-
out one-two punch, I combined this book with Adam
Robinson's *What Smart Students Know* and awarded 1 semester credit in Study Skills!)

At 91 pages (not including forms) this book is not
intended to be an exhaustive resource. The author includes a resource list for getting into greater detail.
What I found extra helpful was her list of course ideas.
She takes traditional subjects and shows you where you
can go with them. For example, under English alone
there are 62 choices! (Script writing, Newswriting,
Allegory, etc.) Her explanation of calculating credits and
GPAs is easily understood.

Mrs. Gordon recognizes that not all students will attend college, nor do all students approach high school
at home the same way. But they do have one thing in
common: All need to be good stewards of the time and
talents given them by God. This book does an excellent
job of helping them do that.
Highly recommended. *Renee
Mathis*

NEW!
HotHouse Transplants

Teen & adult. $11.95 plus ship-
ping.
*Grove Publishing, 16172 Huxley
Circle, Westminster, CA 92683. (714)
841-1220. Fax: (714) 841-5584. Web:
www.grovepublishing.com.*

Ever wonder how your teenagers will do when they graduate? Will they find a job? Will they be able to do well in college? Will they be able to cope? Will their faith remain strong?

HotHouse Transplants was compiled by Matthew Duffy, Cathy Duffy's son. In this book are the stories of sixteen young homeschool graduates and how they are faring in the "real world." Some were interns for HSLDA, some do computer work, some have their own businesses, and some publish their own magazines.

The most impressive thing is that these young men and women were thankful to God and their parents for the opportunity to be homeschooled. They appreciated the hard work and dedication of their parents. These young people are an impressive group.

This is quite a lot of encouragement for both parents and their students. It gives a little view into the world of the homeschool graduate. They really do function! And they really do well for themselves . . . just like any other grad who desires to do well. *Barb Meade*

NEW!
Why Homeschool Through High School?
Grades 7–adult. $20 plus shipping.
Noble Publishing Associates, PO Box 2250, Gresham, OR 97080. (800) 225-5259. (503) 667-3942. Fax: (503) 618-

8866. Email: Noblebooks@aol.com.

You can't go wrong with Joshua Harris, son of famed homeschool speaker Gregg Harris, and this video is just another example. The first recorded appearance of young Mr. Harris, at the age of 17, it's a speech he gave at a Christian homeschool conference on the topic **Why Homeschool Through High School?** Josh, now the author of one of the top 10 best-selling Christian nonfiction books for adults, *I Kissed Dating Goodbye,* shows in his very first recorded speech that all those years his dad had him practice giving presentations to family and neighbors weren't wasted. With humor and aplomb he shares his own experiences being homeschooled from age 5 to 17, including the period when he begged his parents to let him go to public school to "have fun" like all his friends. He provides reasons, from a Christian perspective, for homeschooling through high school, and encourages viewers to make the most of this time to prepare for the rest of their lives. If you don't like paying this much for a video tape you might watch once or twice, get your homeschool support group to buy it. Recommended. *Mary Pride*

Easy High School

American School, widely known as "The School of the Second Chance," is a private school founded in 1897, the same year Calvert School offered its first correspondence course. Unlike Calvert, American School offers high-school courses. Over 3 million students have taken its correspondence courses over the years, with a reported 98 percent satisfaction rate.

American School is accredited by the North Central Association of Colleges and Schools and by the Accrediting Commission of the Distance Education Training Council. It is recognized as a private secondary school by the State of Illinois.

The school's ads are aimed mostly at adults. However, students of compulsory attendance age may enroll by attaching a note from their parents or guardians "explaining why this enrollment is necessary" and/or obtaining an exemption from local school authorities.

Usually the first course the American School will send you is Psychology Today (unless you have already taken it somewhere else). This may be waived by students who would rather take another course or by those who, for religious reasons, may not feel comfortable with psychology.

American School offers an immense array of job-related and enrichment courses.

Since American School was the only curriculum provider who refused to send me their courses for review, I have added a "hands-on opinion" below from a mother whose daughter has completed this program. It's also worth noting that "Accelerated Education" pioneer Joyce Swann uses American School for her 10 children's high-school program. The Swann children, as you may or may not know, so far have all completed high school by age 11, a Bachelor's degree by age 15, and a Master's by age 16. American School's streamlined approach lends itself to accelerated educa-

UPDATED!
American School
Grades 9–12. $379/year; $579 for 2 years; $779 for 3 years, or $979 for all 4 years of high school.
American School, 2200 E. 170th St., Lansing, IL 60438. (800) 531-9268 or (708) 418-2800.

American School lets you buy with confidence, allowing a ten-day free inspection of your courses and a generous refund policy for uncompleted courses. Also, take note of this! *American School will either refund your money or provide you with free additional training if you are required to take a qualifying exam within six months of completing their course and fail to pass it.*

Each year, American School's Scholarship Committee awards 15 scholarships totaling $18,000 to its top graduates.

One Family's Opinion of American School

American School is a good basic way to accomplish high school academics. The parents I have talked to that have used it for their kids say that if a child spends two hours per school day on American School, they can finish the four years in about two years. I can believe it. Our Katrina spends about two hours a day, three days a week on it at the most, and she has completed two courses. Four courses would be one-fourth of the four years.

We usually have school year-round and take vacations during the year. To round out her program, Katrina volunteers at the hospital one morning a week for four hours. She spends time doing educational stuff on the computer also.

The first course American School sends is Psychology. It was a good start. It was not too hard and helped the student focus on how he learns. Then, U.S. History was sent. My husband really liked the textbook.

How it works: you read the text, do some open-book self tests, then complete an exam which is sent back to be hand graded and returned. Katrina works on one subject until she sends the exam in, then goes to another subject. She usually does not work on two subjects at one time. The exams are open book. Each one has true-false, multiple-choice, fill-in-the-blank, and essay questions.

The essay questions have been a very good experience for us. Katrina has had to learn how to relate to another adult and put her thoughts together. American School teachers are picky about correct grammar and spelling. So, for the essay, Katrina usually prints the answer out on the computer.

On Prodigy, I talked with a person who has been one of the teachers at American School. She said that most of the teachers are people who are going back for advanced degrees at the University in Chicago (either Masters or Ph.D.). They grade the papers in their free time.

She said that some of the students send in all their exams at once for a subject and that frustrated the teachers because then they could not help the student along. So, we do try to send in one exam at a time and wait.

One time, Katrina totally missed a page on the exam. They sent it back telling her to finish it. This pleased me. This showed me that they were interested in the student really learning the material.

One word of caution—American School is not automated. They provide basics—not all the extras. They grade the tests by hand (which I like) and they don't have telephone support. Asking questions is handled by mail.

My friend using American School said the biology is about the same as hers was when she was in college. Her son had a question, and she had to read 80 pages to get to the point of being able to help him. Maybe it would be better if they offered a option, an extra fee for telephone support.

Overall, I am pleased. I expected basic academics and that is what I am getting. I expect to send Katrina to a community college when she turns sixteen to take some courses since they are free at that time. So, American School is just a baseline education for her. For $979 for all four years, it is a bargain. *Kathy Goebel*

tion for those who wish it. However, ICS Newport/Pacific now offers much the same type of program, with quicker grading options, toll-free telephone support, and at about two-thirds the price. *Mary Pride*

Cambridge Academy is a new (well, not actually *that* new) competitor to the likes of ICS Newport/Pacific, Keystone National High School, and American School. Like the others, Cambridge Academy offers an accredited high-school diploma. All the courses meet the "180 Carnegie hour requirements"—which means you should expect to spend 180 hours per course on coursework, not counting time spent reading the books.

Cambridge is slightly less expensive than Keystone, but more expensive than American School and ICS Newport/Pacific. Like these others, its clientele until recently was mostly the "remedial" student: kids who dropped out of high school but later decided to finish their degrees. This also means Cambridge Academy can't afford to monkey around with the student; if this kind of student doesn't "get it" fairly quickly, he tends to quit. So the school provides excellent step-by-step study guides for each course. These guides not only explain and amplify the course material, they also urge you to call the toll-free tutoring hotline if you have any trouble along the way.

I personally previewed 16 Cambridge Academy courses. They ranged from just fine (the Accounting course is excellent) to mildly evolutionary (Global Studies) to fascinating (Civil and Criminal Justice) to politically correct (American Government). The Literature courses are fine academi-

DIPLOMA PROGRAMS FOR HOMESCHOOLERS IN PENNSYLVANIA

When Pennsylvania passed a home education law in December 1988, it included requirements for high school graduation from a home education program, but didn't say who should give the diplomas.

At first, the Pennsylvania Department of Education was very negative. They told the school districts that they didn't have to give the diplomas, they said they didn't want parents to give the diplomas, and they were unwilling to award the diplomas themselves.

When homeschoolers finally cornered the PA Department of Education they said that homeschool organizations should give the diplomas because homeschoolers would have an interest in maintaining the quality of their own diplomas.

The first homeschool organization to award the diplomas was Pennsylvania Homeschoolers Accreditation Agency (PHAA) which was established during the 1990–91 school year.

Two sister organizations have since been started. These organizations allow homeschoolers much flexibility in the way they approach high school subjects at home. Their diplomas are accepted by the Pennsylvania Department of Education as the equivalent of a school diploma for such purposes as state sponsored scholarship grants (Pell Grants) and admission to state-related colleges and Universities. Partly as a result of these programs Pennsylvania has enjoyed a big boom in the number of homeschoolers continuing all the way through high school.

For information about these programs which can only serve homeschoolers in Pennsylvania contact:

1. **Buxmont Christian Educational Institute** Terry L. Johns, 146 West Broad St., Telford, PA 18969, 215-723-7226. A diploma program that is expanding from its base in Bucks and Montgomery Counties.
2. **Erie Area Homeschoolers.** Director: Edi Thomas, 9651 Old Route 99, McKean PA 16426, 814-476-1355. A program serving Erie County and extending into Northwest Pennsylvania. Transcripts must be filed by February 1st of the student's senior year.
3. **Pennsylvania Homeschoolers Accreditation Agency (PHAA)** Executive Director: Dr. Howard Richman, RD 2—Box 117, Kittanning PA 16201, 412-783-6512. A non-profit corporation which serves all of Pennsylvania. Diploma guide is $5. Bylaws and other info about the program is available on the PA Homeschoolers web site: pahomeschoolers.com.

—*Howard Richman*

cally but suffer from the usual death-doom-disaster emphasis. All the courses were more interesting and memorable than you would typically expect of a high-school course.

I mentioned my concerns to Cambridge Academy director Tanzee Nahas, and she told me they want their courses to appeal to Christian homeschoolers. This may mean changing some books, or allowing the student to skip certain assignments. In the meantime, you aren't doomed if you pick a less-than-satisfactory course: if you return it promptly, you'll get most of your money back, or you can switch it for another course.

To enroll in Cambridge Academy, you have to (1) take a placement test, (2) have a transcript of previous work sent to them (or send a signed and notarized "home verification form"), and (3) send in at least half of the yearly tuition. The remainder can be paid in interest-free $25 monthly payments. This entitles you to evaluation and placement, testing, grading, toll-free tutoring, recordkeeping, and all the consumable materials.

Cambridge high school students are required to complete four electives each year (two per semester) they are enrolled at the school. For each external elective, students must submit a proposal to Cambridge, outlining five learning objectives and how they plan to attain them. Students may also satisfy their elective credits with work-study projects or with courses that Cambridge offers.

External elective studies may be in an area in which the student has already demonstrated an interest, such as piano lessons or horseback riding. Or it may be in an area that he would like to learn about.

Once an external elective subject has been chosen, students must figure out just what and how they are going to learn, as well as providing a tangible way to document that they *are* learning. Journals, reports, video and audio tapes, photographs, lesson plans, games, computer programs, or any combination, are examples of documentary evidence of learning that might be accepted. Final approval must come from Cambridge. If they feel a proposal lacks enough development and detail, the staff will make suggestions and ask that the student submit a revised proposal.

I think Cambridge Academy's external elective option is probably their most intriguing feature. Unlike their competitors, it allows you to individualize your program "the homeschool way." However, it's only a benefit if you have a strong desire to design some courses yourself, which may not be the case for most college-bound students looking to fill up an academically impressive transcript.

To find out more about Cambridge Academy, request their free promotional video. It shows you their facility and explains their philosophy. *Mary Pride*

NEW!
ICS Newport/ Pacific High School

High school. Complete three-year program, $499. Standard payment plan: $29 down and $29/month for 16 months plus a final payment of $6.
ICS Learning Systems/Harcourt Learning Direct, 925 Oak St., Scranton, PA 18515-0002. (570) 342-7701. Email: info@harcourt-learn.com. Web: www.harcourt-learn.com.

Want to complete high school in two years or less? Want to spend as little money as possible? Planning to attend community college, junior college, a state university, or maybe just stop at high-school graduation? Interested in a traditional, secular course of study that recognizes your right to your own opinion on controversial issues such as evolution v. creation? Then read on . . .

You've heard of **ICS** (it stands for International Correspondence Schools). They've been around for over 100 years, offering correspondence programs in a wide variety of vocational and academic subjects. Now ICS is reaching out to the homeschool community with their **Newport/Pacific High School**, which is accredited by the Distance Education and Training Council and licensed by the Pennsylvania State Board of Private Licensed Schools.

With all those years of experience, ICS knows how to provide affordable, friendly, and complete materials. For their diploma program, you get not only the curriculum, but also toll-free educational support, record-keeping services, transcript forwarding, a diploma, and even a class ring!

The course materials are easy to use and include numerous self-check tests, so you can track your progress. Many of the subjects use Holt, Reinhart and Winston hardbound textbooks, and other subjects come with worktexts that contain the entire course. The study guides that accompany textbooks contain lesson objectives and summaries, pages to read in the textbooks, and the self-tests (with answers in the back of the book).

ICS has some unique options for submitting exams. You can either select the Exam Express testing option (fill in the correct circles on a computer card) or the Tel-Test option (use your touch-tone telephone to submit your test answers by pressing buttons to register your student number, test number, and answers). Both provide speedy grading, but without the benefit of essay questions and teacher interaction with your exams.

Diploma requirements include 16 core subjects and 5 electives.

The 16 core subjects are:

- **English** (4 courses)—Basic English, Practical English, Written Communication, Literature
- **Math** (3 courses)—General Math I, Consumer Math, General Math II
- **Social Studies** (3 courses)—American History, Civics, World History
- **Science** (3 courses)—Biology, Earth and Space Science, Physical Science
- **Arts & Humanities** (2 courses)—Reading Skills, Human Relations
- **Health & Physical Education** (1 course)—Fitness and Nutrition

A wide variety of electives are also available—46 in all, at the time I wrote this. These run the gamut from college-prep courses to a variety of vocational courses, as you can see below:

- **Math electives**—Business Math, Algebra I, Algebra II, Geometry, Trigonometry & Analytic Geometry, Calculus: Function & Use
- **Science electives**—Chemistry, General Science
- **Technical/Mechanical electives**—Appliance Repair, Auto Repair Technician, Small Engine Repair, Electronics
- **Building Trades electives**—Carpenter, Home Remodeling and Repair, Home Inspector
- **Language arts electives**—English Communications, American Literature, Spanish
- **Computer electives**—PC Specialist, Desktop Publishing and Design, Programming in Basic
- **Legal/Medical electives**—Dental Assistant, Legal Assistant, Medical Transcriptionist, Pharmacy Technician
- **Social science electives**—Psychology, World Geography
- **Miscellaneous vocational electives**—Bookkeeping/Accounting, Professional Secretary, Interior Decorator, Teacher Aide, Child Day Care Management
- **Self-improvement electives**—Catering/Gourmet Cooking, Art, Dressmaking and Design, Floral Design

After having seen all—and I mean *all*—of these courses, I would say this is not the program for those of you who hope to get into Harvard, but it will do quite well for those with moderate academic aspirations. In fact, thanks to the total lack of twaddle, you may even retain more than if you had chosen to struggle with a more challenging program. *Mary Pride*

This secular high-school program may be new to homeschoolers, but the company behind it, NLKK Inc., has been providing distance education for high-school students for over 24 years. Their Learning and Evaluation Center, founded in 1974 to provide students who had failed courses with a way to take them over again with greater success, has served over 95,000 students. Now the people who put together the "Home Study Summer School" have organized an entire high-school program which provides each enrolled student the opportunity to earn a recognized high-school diploma, since the **Keystone National High School** program is licensed by the Pennsylvania State Board of Private Licensed Schools and is also accredited by the Distance Education Training Council (formerly known as the National Home Study Council) and the Northwest Association of Schools and Colleges.

Like other successful correspondence programs, Keystone provides textbooks from other publishers, plus its own teaching manuals for its courses, called "Learning Guides." These lead students step-by-step through the course material, and include self-check tests so you can see if you're really understanding what you're studying.

Now, here's what makes Keystone different:

- **Keystone's Learning Guides** are exceptionally clear and easy to follow, as you'd expect from a company whose past success has been built on helping kids who didn't "get it" the first time around. The people who wrote these guides know all the ways

New Courses in 2000: Pre-Calculus. Business Law. Physical Education. Revised Psychology, Spanish I & II, and Geography courses. Advanced Placement courses now offered. Other new features include an online BioLab and student bookstore.

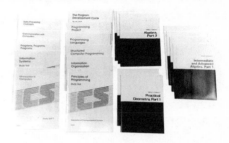

NEW!
Keystone National High School

High school. Diploma Program Enrollment (includes all courses for the year), $825 per grade. Selected Course Enrollment, $165 per course.
Keystone National High School, School House Station, 420 West 5th St., Boomsburg, PA 17815. 800-255-4937. Fax: (570) 784-2129. Web: www.keystonehighschool.com.

students can mess up, and go out of their way to deal with learning difficulties *before* they arise.

- **Examinations are graded by hand.** This may be important to those who are unhappy with the multiple-choice, computer-graded approach.
- **Exams may be returned three ways**—by mail, in the mailback envelopes provided, or by fax—at no extra charge.
- **The Advisory Teaching Service**, which includes instructor support by phone or mail, is included at no extra charge. This can be very helpful when a student is taking an advanced subject that the parent is not completely comfortable with teaching alone. Even when you are only taking one or two courses, the Advisory Teaching Service is still available.

Content-wise, this program is a bit of a mixed bag. Liberals will be much happier than conservatives with the Civics, Government, and Health courses. The history courses are "easy reading" that any sixth-grader could handle. On the other hand, the English courses are robust, covering all the writers and literature you'd need for the SAT II Literature test, while quite restrained for a modern textbook series (you get a synopsis of *Lord of the Flies,* for example, but do not actually have to read any excerpts from that ode to nihilism) and actually weighted more towards classic readings than "in your face" contemporary readings.

Like most correspondence programs, the science courses do not include lab materials or experiments.

Required courses for graduation include Skills for Success, 4 English courses, 4 Social Science courses, 3 Math courses, 3 Science courses, 1 Art/Music course, 1 Health course, and 4 electives. If you've already completed some of this work elsewhere, you just arrange for an official transcript or portfolio of work—including any courses entirely designed by you or your parents—to Keystone. In turn, they will tell you how many credits they have accepted towards their diploma program.

Courses for the diploma program are shown below. Keystone offers both an Academic and Career course of study for the Diploma program. The courses corresponding to each of these tracks are indicated by a (C) or an (A) following the course name.

Grade 9

- **Skills for Success.** This required course is the first course you'll receive upon enrollment, regardless of what other courses you may have taken elsewhere.
- **English 1.** Complete review of grammar, plus composition and appreciation of the following literary forms: non-fiction, short stories, poetry, drama, and novels. All the English courses use textbooks from Holt, Rinehart, Winston's *Elements of Literature* series. These include *lots* of reading.
- **Refresher Math** (C) or **Algebra** (A)
- **Earth Science** (C)
- **Civics.** An introduction to government on the local, state, and national level, with emphasis on personal rights and responsibilities. The textbook takes the position that it's OK to change the Constitution by "reinterpreting" it; presents the gun control issue in a way that clearly favors the elimination of personal firearms; presents the drafting of girls into the military in Israel (and by extension, the USA) in glowing terms; and so forth. While the book appears to present both sides of most issues, in crucial cases (such as strict constructionism *v.* judicial activism) only one side—the liberal one—appears, while in many other cases, the best arguments for the conservative viewpoint are strangely missing. Rush Limbaugh fans will not like this course.

Grade 10

- **English 2.** More composition skills, short literature, and grammar with a focus on correct usage.

	Grade 11	

- **Consumer Math** (C) or **Geometry** (A)
- **Life Science** (C) or **Biology** (A). These are both evolutionary in outlook.
- **World History.** The Globe-Fearon text for this course is written with a lower-grades vocabulary and big type. This means you get less detail, but students are more likely to remember the relatively few facts presented. Think of it as World History Lite.
- **Health.** "Responsible" sexuality with people of either gender (as opposed to marriage). Dysfunctional families of all kinds. Drugs. Suicide. Death. Sexual diseases of all kinds (for chapters and chapters). Mental health problems. Abuse of all kinds. All the wonderful topics that probably caused you to consider homeschooling in the first place are all packed into this Holt book.

Grade 11

- **English 3.** American Literature.
- **Pre-Algebra** (C) or **Algebra 2** (A)
- **Physical Science** (C) or **Chemistry** (A)
- **American History.** A fairly straightforward presentation without overt bias.
- **Geography**
- **Art & Music Appreciation**

Grade 12

- **English 4.** British Literature from ancient to modern times, using another massive book in the *Elements of Literature* series.
- **Sociology**
- **Physics** (A)
- **American Government.** The Federal system of government is studied.
- **Economics**
- **Psychology**

For a detailed review of Keystone's Driver Ed course, check out what we said about it in Volume 3 of the *Big Book. Mary Pride*

State University-Based High School Distance Learning

As you'll see in this section, not all state university high-school correspondence programs are alike. This particular state university is known for its award-winning high-school courses, and also offers a complete college degree program, unlike many others which only offer individual courses. Clearly, these people take distance learning seriously. They have no figures for actual numbers of students enrolled, but currently thousands of students take courses from **Indiana University Office of Academic Programs High School.**

Here are some of this program's features:

- **More than 100 courses** are available, including a number of Classical Studies courses; German, Italian, French, Spanish, and Latin; the "classroom" portion of Driver's Ed, including the inescapable video of road accidents; quite a few Business Education courses; several Philosophy courses; all the other typical college-bound high-school courses, with the exception of Chemistry; and a smattering of vocational courses.
- **Quite a few of the courses have won awards** from the University Continuing Education Association (UCEA)—in fact, the Indiana University program has won more of these awards than any other college or university.
- **No diploma option** is currently available—instead, you apply courses towards a diploma from your school or state. However, Indiana University is working to make a state-accredited diploma available in the near future, so you might want to check on whether this has become an option at the time you contact them.
- **Honors courses** are available, enabling you to perhaps achieve an honors diploma (check your state requirements). The courses offered meet requirement for an Indiana honors diploma.

NEW!
Indiana University Office of Academic Programs High School Course

High school. Usually $85 tuition. $96.25 per credit hour for dual-credit course tuition (each dual credit course runs one semester and is from 2 to 4 credits). Required learning guide, $11–$21/course. Textbooks, $0–$115/course. Shipping (only if ordering textbooks), $8/course in U.S./Canada/Mexico, $50/elsewhere. Air-mail lesson return postage (overseas addresses only), $35/course.
Indiana University, Office of Academic Programs, Owen Hall 001, E. Kirkwood Ave., Bloomington, IN 47405-5201. (800) 334-1011 or (812) 855-2292. Fax: (812) 855-8680. Email: bulletin@indiana.edu. Web: scs.indiana.edu.

- **Dual-credit course option** allows you to earn credit for both high school and college at the same time—if the college of your choice accepts these credits
- **Science** courses are not lab courses, and, oddly, there is no Chemistry course
- **A sophisticated "fax-on-demand" system** enables you to check on the status of lessons you have submitted (has your lesson been received? has it been graded?) and get more information about individual courses via fax
- **Voice mail phone support available,** with most questions answered within one business day
- **Some course assignments can be emailed** in, and some lesson guides are available via email.
- **Take up to one year** to finish your course, or 18 months if you live outside the U.S. and Canada. Request up to two six-month extensions per course, if needed, at a fee of $20 per extension per course.
- **Some textbooks** are hardbound, some are softbound.
- **Lessons are graded by instructors;** these are not just computerized multiple-choice courses.
- **"Used textbook" option**—difference between new and used price is refunded if used textbooks are available to fill your order. After completing a course, you can sell your textbooks back.
- **Generous** transfer, withdrawal, and refund policy.
- **Friendly** to homeschooled students—homeschooling is specifically mentioned in their catalog, and they advertise in homeschool publications
- **One high-school course**, Art History and Appreciation, **is available online.** All the lessons are out on the web. When you sign up, you are given a password to access the lessons. Assignments are emailed to the instructor, and grade and comments emailed back. Other online courses are in development. Message boards are not available at this time.
- **Advanced Placement** courses are under development.
- **Online Student Study Guides** now available for $35 each.

Each course contains about eight lessons, each the equivalent of one or two weeks of an in-school high-school course. After completing a lesson, you mail it in. Your instructor grades it and returns it with comments. Most courses also have mid-term and final exams, which must be requested separately on completion of the last lesson before the exam, and must be proctored. Indiana students may take exams at Indiana University Examination Centers—there are nine throughout the state. Out-of-state public-school students must arrange for a high-school principal or counselor to proctor; overseas students may take exams at a U.S. embassy or military base. Relatives may not proctor exams, and exams are only sent to institutions, not private residences. Homeschooled students can be proctored by a librarian who has an administrative position, who in turn can allow a "floor" librarian to do the actual oversight of test-taking, or they can make arrangements with a local college or university testing center.

Courses come with learning guides, textbooks (in most cases), and possibly other materials, such as cassettes, maps, CD-ROMs, and computer diskettes, depending on the course. The comb-bound learning guide provides your assignments, lesson summaries, study tips, and information on how to send away for the exams.

The courses we reviewed would all do the job of preparing students to do well on college entrance and achievement exams, such as the SAT IIs. They cover the material that these tests require. The lesson guides are easy to use, with lots of white space, and visually not very exciting. (But then, who has visually excellent learning guides? I sense an employment opportunity here for some graphics artists.) The textbooks are solid, as public-school textbooks go. Toll-free telephone support that reaches a live person, as some other programs offer, would be better than the voice mail phone support Indiana University's high-school program offers, and having to request each exam separately is a pain. It would be better if they mailed all the exams at once to your course proctor, as University of Nebraska-Lincoln does. So there is some room for improvement. However, all in all, this is a program well worth your consideration. *Mary Pride*

Five thousand students from all over the USA and 35 countries are currently enrolled in 10,000 courses from the **North Dakota State Department of Public Instruction Division of Independent Study** program. This one of the few *state- and regionally-accredited high school programs* available. That means that you can get a *real live diploma* through NDIS. From the public school's perspective, you would now be a NDIS student, so the approval of your local school administrator is not necessary.

NDIS prefers that a certified teacher, librarian, or university testing center oversee your courses, but they are flexible about this. In some cases, the homeschool parent has been allowed to be the course overseer. Lessons can be sent to the proctor or the parent—your choice.

NDIS's prices are extremely low. Book and supply charges are also slight (the program uses standard public school texts), and many textbooks can be returned afterwards for a one-half refund of the purchase price.

Major upgrades since the last edition of *Big Book*:

- **The Student Guides** have improved amazingly in appearance since the last edition of *The Big Book*. Most courses' content has been revised and improved. Science courses now come with lab supplies.
- **"Tool Skills" versions** of many courses are now available for students with learning difficulties. These courses are broken down into smaller segments, and come with accompanying audiocassettes, so the lessons can be played aloud, to reinforce the reading in the text. Ten semesters of Tool Skills are currently available, and more are under development in conjunction with the North Dakota Special Education Unit.
- **Middle-school courses** are now available, for grades 6–8.
- **Elementary-age courses** are being developed. In 1999, the first semester of fifth grade was finished. Eventually, NDIS plans to offer an entire K–12 curriculum.
- **NDIS is now placing its courses in multimedia format on the World Wide Web.** They have been pioneers in this area, as the first high-school distance education program to offer for-credit high-school courses online, starting way back in 1995. Forty courses are now available online. The entire study guide, including lesson instructions and assignments, are online, as are video and audio segments for most courses and many full-color photographs. This is a big advantage over the traditional print-only study guides! These courses are also interactive—you type your answers into the online forms and email them to your instructor. Message boards, for comment-

UPDATED!
North Dakota State Department of Public Instruction Division of Independent Study
Grades 5–12. Semester course, $63 for North Dakota residents, $75 for non-residents. Books and supplies extra (about $65 for most courses). $21 handling fee on all course registrations. Wide range of video supplements priced at about $10 total per video tape, for a total price ranging from $30 for Local History (9 lessons on 3 tapes) to $180 for Russian I (36 lessons on 18 tapes). Current video selection includes Child Development, North Dakota History, Russian I and II, Spanish I–IV, French I and II, Fitness for Life, and Psychology. All tapes 60-minute VHS. You may preview a one-part video for each course free if returned within 30 days.
North Dakota State Dept. of Public Instruction, Division of Independent Study, State University Station, Box 5036, Fargo, ND 58105-5036. (701) 231-6000. Fax: (701) 231-6052. Web: www.dis.dpi.state.nd.us.

ing on course topics or asking questions, are available for each course. The World Geography online course won a 1997 University Continuing Education Association Meritorious Course Award. It was the first online course in the country to win such an award. The U.S. History online course won the 1998 University Continuing Education Association Distinguished Course Award.

- **Whether you're taking the online course** version or not, you now can email questions and assignments to your instructor, for a much quicker response.

This is definitely the program for lots and lots of nifty electives: stuff like creative writing, and journalism. NDIS offers *six* languages: Latin, German, Spanish, French, Norwegian, and Russian (these courses include cassettes). They also have quite a variety of useful-looking art, business education, agriculture, home economics, and practical/mechanical courses. In all, 173 courses are offered.

NDIS courses are rather easy, as far as the assignments go. If you can understand the texts and syllabi you can breeze right along. Science might be an exception to this rule, though the experiments are also easy to do.

NDIS correspondence courses includes lesson wrappers in which you return the assignments (you pay the postage). You don't have to keep attendance records or grade anything.

Some of the study topics are quite interesting, such as a section on regional dialects in the Language and Composition course. The old-fashioned flavor of some of the courses is (to me, anyway) quite endearing. No courses in political correctness are required for graduation—another plus.

The most recent selection of NDIS correspondence courses I saw, although the directions were still couched in somewhat-difficult school vocabulary, looked more promising. *Developmental English*, for example, a basic grammar course, was well laid-out and easy to follow. *Personal Management for Independent Living* also covered much essential territory for a student facing life on his or her own: insurance, taxes, employment policies, choosing quality clothing, nutrition, how to make out a check, dealing with banks and credit agencies, even some necessary social graces! Once you got past the somewhat languid introduction with its unnecessary stress on personal autonomy and free-floating values, this course covers a lot of ground. And NDIS is now developing video supplements for selected courses. Again, these are more of a lecture format: the Russian teacher says the words, but does not act out the sentences. Thus, you get part of the educational benefit of a video (hearing a foreign language), but not all (no connection of words to images).

If you want a secular high school diploma at a low, low cost, or if you are interested in some of NDIS's unusual courses, or you like the look of their online courses, check out this program. *Mary Pride*

NEW!
Texas Tech University Extended Studies
High School. Tuition is $79 + $25 administrative fee per ½ unit credit. Credit by Examination or Examination for Acceleration, $28. College Credit, $189 per course. Supplementary books available.

Texas Tech's high-school program is an option to consider seriously if you are a college-bound student intent on admission to a highly-ranked college or university. About 57,000 students are currently enrolled in one or more of their high-school or Credit by Examination courses. You can not only obtain challenging courses, you can take a number of college-level courses for dual credit (i.e., you will get both high-school *and* college credit upon satisfactory completion of the course). A middle-school (grade 6–8) curriculum has just become available, and elementary school (K–5) is in development. Word is out that they may also be developing Advanced Placement courses in the next few years—write, call, and pester them until they do it!

All exams must be proctored. This is a nuisance, but does add some additional integrity to your course grade in the eyes of college admissions officials. The list of approved proctors includes school principals, counselors, or superintendents; proctors at university or college testing centers; armed forces education officers; certified librarians (the course catalog says they can only be proctors for students taking exams for Continuing Education Units, but since most homeschoolers live in the library, these would seem to be the most accessible proctors); or "other proctors approved by the Texas Tech University Extended Studies Office." In other words, call and ask who they will approve as a proctor in your situation.

Local testing facilities can proctor your exams. These services are often available at a local library or community college. Some students have made arrangements to be proctored at their local high school.

You have six months to complete each course. If circumstances prevent you completing a course in that time period, you may pay an additional fee and apply for an extension of from three to six months. The fee is $36 for three months and $12 for each additional month. There is only one extension per course, so be careful not to bite off more courses than you can realistically complete in a normal school year.

What are some of the subject areas in which high school courses are offered? First, you've got the basics: English/Language Arts, Mathematics, Science, Social Studies and U.S. History, and Languages. Courses are also offered in the areas of Economics, Health, Business Education, Health Occupations, Agriculture, Career and Technology Education, and Peer Counseling.

As far as course content goes, Texas Tech is definitely more conservative than many of its competitors. The Health course, for example, includes a fairly strong pitch for sexual abstinence until marriage, as well as unambiguous anti-drug-abuse and anti-drunk-driving messages. The bulk of the Health text is taken up with studies of anatomy, emergency first aid, and nutrition—instead of endless pages on mental disorders, dysfunctional families, socialist parenting, and diseases, as is unfortunately common in Health texts these days. Another example: the Government course actually includes as one of its lesson objectives, "Distinguish between judicial activism and judicial restraint," as opposed to the many Government courses from other schools we've seen that don't even admit the possibility of judicial restraint. Also, the Government course includes many more facts on how the Supreme Court handled major cases—including minority opinions—than I've seen in other schools' courses.

So far, Texas Tech is not making much use of the Internet to add value to its courses. Syllabi and course descriptions are online, and you can register online, but there are no message boards or other goodies. Webmaster Leslie tells me interactive courses, with forms you can fill out online for instant grading, are planned for sometime in the future, but so far no actual courses have been chosen for development. This is one area that really should be explored, especially when your institution is named Texas *Tech*.

Coming back to what's available right now: in keeping with its general conservatism, Texas Tech courses are no-nonsense, methodical, and well organized. Even the catalog is a visual treat, with icons indicating course options, and a pleasing layout. Everything from this program shouts, "Quality!" I give it an "A." *Mary Pride*

Extended Studies, Texas Tech University, Box 42191, Lubbock, TX 79409-2191. (800) MY-COURS. (806) 742-2352. Fax: (806) 742-2222. Email: enroll@ttu.edu. Web: www.dce.ttu.edu.

The enrollment form says you must have the signature of a local school official in order to enroll. The telephone sales lady told me that if you're homeschooling, you can just write "homeschooled" in that space.

Homeschooled students "must demonstrate mastery of any course completed through [homeschooling]" prior to entry, via passing a Credit by Examination. These exams are available for over 100 subjects, and cost $28 each. Credit by Acceleration is pretty much the same thing, and the exams cost the same, except that the latter seem designed for schoolkids who have managed to get ahead of their class on their own, and the former would be more suitable for homeschoolers, who always get ahead on their own.

In order to graduate from Texas Tech University High School, you must pass the Texas Assessment of Academic Skills (TAAS), even if you don't live in Texas. You will have to call the school to make arrangements for taking the test.

UPDATED!
University of Nebraska/Lincoln Independent Study

Grades 9–12. Nonresident, $170-$204/course. Resident, $4 less/course. Web-based courses, around $275/course. Possible handling fee, $23 per course. *University of Nebraska-Lincoln, Independent Study High School, 269 Clifford-Hardin, NCCE, Lincoln, NE 68583-9800. (402) 472-4321. Fax: (402) 472-1901. Email: unlishs@unl-notes.unl.edu. Web: www.class.com.*

UNL science courses include lab equipment and supplies!

UNL was the very first state university to create supervised correspondence courses for the high-school level. We're talking 1929, as in the year they began working on this. They have been accredited by the state of Nebraska, and able to issue state-recognized diplomas, since 1968. Further accreditation, from the North Central Association of Colleges and Schools, followed in 1978.

Traditionally a favorite for college-bound homeschoolers who want an accredited high-school diploma, **University of Nebraska-Lincoln Independent Study High School** is having to work harder to maintain this position. For one thing, other state universities are becoming more aggressive at reaching out to and serving the homeschool community with high-school courses of similar or better quality. For another thing, UNL courses have begun to suffer from a tang of public-school humanism that ranges from hardly there (most math courses) to mild (literature courses) to strong (a first-year Latin course seemingly fixated on pagan religions). Balancing this, UNL's new web-based courses and online services show their commitment to staying on the cutting edge of distance learning.

At present, about 5,000 students are enrolled in UNL's Independent Study High School. Of these, a majority are taking just a few courses, while 2,500 students are enrolled in the full diploma program. In all, there were over 16,000 course enrollments as of summer 2000.

The UNL program is one of the priciest high-school options, running about $800 per semester for a full load of five courses. The mix of courses is wide and challenging, with everything you could want for college prep from a wide variety of literature courses to four years of Latin, plus a wide variety of electives. They also offer courses suitable for the vo-tech student, and the student whose academic ambitions run no farther than a general high-school diploma.

These are true correspondence courses. You send in papers and tests, which are graded and returned to your "local supervisor." This person can not be a family member without special permission. He is responsible for proctoring closed-book tests and receiving correspondence from UNL. He is also supposed to supervise the coursework and make sure you stay on track. If you are not interested in the correspondence option, in other words you just want the course materials, you don't need a local supervisor. However, there is at present no way to get the benefit of personal interaction with a UNL teacher without having a local supervisor. This is a flaw we would like to see fixed, perhaps with an option for teacher interaction that does not include UNL giving course credit. As a compromise, UNL will send course materials directly to the student, only requiring that tests be proctored by an "approved person," which can include a librarian (we all go the library, don't we?).

In the past, UNL courses were hand-graded. The instructor often included lengthy comments and suggestions. Many UNL courses are now partially computer-graded. They have attempted to substitute for personal comments with computer-generated comments. You get back not just a grade for your test, but explanations of what you did wrong and what you need to restudy. From what I hear, most of us still prefer the human touch, however. This move to computer grading may be cost-effective, but in some people's opinion, it has removed one of UNL's major strengths. Two or three written assignments per course are still hand-graded with personal comments, which, in UNL's words, "allows the teacher and student to focus on well developed projects." Also students can contact teachers at any time if they have questions.

Students find their assignments in the course syllabus. They then read the assigned textbook pages, write the answers and essays in the syllabus, do the projects (science courses come with complete lab supplies), and take the pretests. There is a lot of study and writing; these are not Mickey Mouse courses. Although you are allowed to finish a course fairly swiftly (in as little as three weeks, with special permission), in real life a semester course takes about a semester to finish. I doubt even the incredible Swann family could zip through four years of UNL high school in a year!

UNL's lab science courses are still homeschool favorites, since unlike most other high-school correspondence programs, they include actual lab equipment and materials for experiments. They have recently added an on-line bulletin board and options for submitting homework via fax and email. Currently 20 courses courses are available via the Web. They started with four courses in 1997, then added sixteen more courses during the summer of 1998 and another ten in 1999. Their eventual goal is to offer a complete diploma program via the Web by 2001. Currently available Web courses include Global Perspectives: Bosnia, Advanced Composition, Basic Geometry, Basic Chemistry, Beginning Composition, Reading Comprehension Skills, English as a Second Language, Personal Economics and Finance, Macroeconomics, Introduction to Technology, Math Skills Review, Oceanography, Learning Fundamentals, and one semester each of U.S. History, American Literature, American Government, General Mathematics, Health Science, Chemistry, and Multicultural Studies.

In all, 159 high-school courses are available through UNL, in the following areas: Agriculture (4 courses, including two in horticulture). Art (7 courses in fine arts and art appreciation, including Drawing & Composition, Watercolor Studies, and Acrylic Painting). Business (5 semesters of Typing, plus Business English & Communication, Office Systems, 2 semesters of Shorthand, Consumer Education, Introduction to Business, 2 semesters of Accounting, Business Law, Business and Personal Protocol, and your choice of Personal Finance or Economics—one of them is required if you're in the diploma program). Career Planning (total ugh—see below). Driver Education. English (8 semesters of courses required for the diploma program, plus 17 others that cover the gamut of remedial reading, composition, grammar, and literature). Family and Consumer Science (6 courses in etiquette, home management, nutrition, interior design and something called Personal Adjustment & Family Living that is described as teaching students about "family-related social issues" and how to "analyze the development of healthy interpersonal relationships"). Industrial Education (2 shop courses, and 2 Small Engines courses for which you have to provide your own small engines and tools). Languages (4 semesters each of French, German, Latin, and Spanish). Math (2 semesters each of Basic Math, General Math, Business & Consumer Math, Beginning Algebra, Geometry, Advanced Algebra, and Pre-Calculus). Music (2 semesters each of Beginning, Intermediate, and Advanced Piano; Music Theory; and Harmony). Photography (1 introductory course). Science (2 semesters each of Health Science, Physical Science, Chemistry, and Physics; 3 semesters of Biology; 1 semester of a fun course entitled Basic Electricity and Electronics; all with lab kits available for doing experiments). Social Studies (one semester each of Civics, Sociology, Psychology, and Ethnic Studies & Human Relations; two semesters each of American History, American Government, World History, and World Geography). Study Skills (2 courses, Effective Methods of Study, and Learning Fundamentals).

Two diploma programs are available: College Prep and General. Each program requires the usual number of English, math, history, science, and foreign language courses, with the following notable exception. Reacting to new state requirements, UNL has now added not just one, but two new non-academic requirements to both of their diploma programs. (Students can meet these requirements in a wide variety of ways, including specific courses, development of their own curriculum, etc.)

Career Planning "guides you toward discovering your own potential for entering various fields of work," a task for which we feel parents are fully competent. Surely those who feel the need of a course in this subject would sign up for it on their own without the threat of a diploma being

Plans are currently underway to create some Advanced Placement courses. Till then, UNL's feeling is that you might as well take actual college courses, if you want to get college credit for work done in high school. After all, they do offer a college course catalog, too!

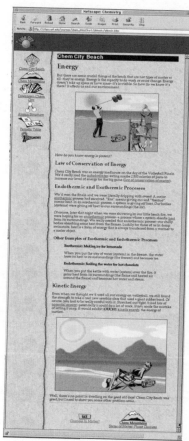

UN-L's web courses are lots more than text and graphics. See detailed review of new chemistry web courses in volume 3

withheld. For many of us with our own family businesses, this kind of course is a waste of time, as we have already spent years analyzing our children's abilities and presenting them with varied opportunities for careers.

Ethnic Studies and Human Relations "provides background information that helps you understand the attitudes towards ethnicity that exist today in the United States." The course "follows guidelines established by the Nebraska legislature for high school multicultural education." It does this in an surprisingly pugnacious style—the author's first words in Chapter One are "My commitment in this course is to *attacking prejudice*" (emphasis mine).

The very first essay question in the Ethnic Studies course is, "Why is cultural pluralism a more desirable goal than tolerance?" In other words, this course is not about knowledge but about bad attitudes all students are assumed to have and supposedly superior beliefs the course is intended to impart—the main belief being relativism, the notion that all cultures are just as good as each other in all of their ways, with the sole exception that white and Western cultures are soaked through and through with evil biased attitudes.

The historical fact, of course, is that all cultures are soaked through and through with the bias that their people are best (African tribal cultures being some of the most biased—against neighboring tribes), and some aspects of each culture are decidedly better or worse than aspects of competing cultures. Take, for example, the Aztecs' habit of torturing children to make it rain. For a more recent example, in pre-World War II Japan some young wives killed themselves and their children in order to show their support for their husbands going to war (the idea was that the husband would fight better if he didn't have to worry about his family), and this was considered quite noble. In modern China, women are coerced into aborting their wanted babies. On the other hand, Austrians show considerably less affection towards their children than Americans, who in turn show less affection than Africans (affection being, in our opinion, a highly desirable value!). There is no "perfect" culture out there, including yours or mine, whatever they may happen to be.

From an academic viewpoint alone, this course is solely lacking in accuracy, and doesn't deal with the real issue in comparative cultures, namely discerning what is good and bad about each culture, with the object being to amend our own where it falls short. This applies just as much to American ethnic and racial segments as to foreign cultures—not everything everyone does is admirable, and not everything everyone does is horrible. Nor does everyone of a particular race or ethnic group live according to that race or ethnic group's supposed "culture"—another point the course fails to raise. Its sole burden appears to be that the attitudes today prevalent in the U.S. are (evil white) bias and (enlightened non-white) pluralism, without ever telling us what the different cultures do (what is African-American culture? Korean-American culture? Hispanic-American culture? Swedish-American culture?), or how we as a nation can achieve any kind of common identity on the basis of "pluralism."

Academic merits or demerits aside, we object strongly to requiring students to go through any attitude adjustment before being allowed to graduate, let alone an attitude adjustment designed to make students of a particular race feel confused and guilty. And we are talking "attitude adjustment" here. One of the requirements in the Ethnic Studies course is that you keep a journal, in which you are assigned to write about your perceptions of your own cultural identity and how you feel about others. "These exercises give you an opportunity . . . to share your viewpoints with your teacher." You betcha. Isn't it a comfort to know that "Race, ethnicity, religion, gender, and alternative lifestyles are but a few of the major issues that may enter into a discussion in a course in multicultural education" (emphasis mine)?

Many UNL courses, such as Accounting, are still a fine choice. We would explore substitutes for the non-academic requirements before considering a degree program. *Mary Pride*

The first thing you need to know about the **University of Wisconsin-Extension** program is how to read the catalog. It's large—170 pages—and can be confusing at first. Notice the sections into which it's divided: How Independent Learning Works, Credit Courses (these are university courses), CEU Courses ("CEU" stands for Continuing Education Unit; these units can be applied towards a certain certificate or license), High School Courses (these are the ones you probably want), and WTCS Courses ("WTCS" stands for Wisconsin Technical College System; these are vocational courses).

To give us an idea of what they have to offer, the people at UWEX sent us a mix of their high-school and college learning guides. Unfortunately, they did *not* include any of the course textbooks, although we requested them. Here's what we gleaned from the material available to us:

- **The Learning Guides are not terribly beautiful.** A few showed the influence of desktop publishing, but most have a typewritten and photocopied appearance.
- **Some Lesson Guides** introduce you to the course author; others lack this personal touch.
- **Some textbooks** are hardbound, some are softbound.
- **Some courses are politically correct.** The American Literature course #H350-H31, which calls early 20th century America "sick at the core" while lauding the "liberals and radicals" of the day because of their supposed "opposition to fascism, or political dictatorship" (I guess Stalin, who they all supported, wasn't a dictator?), is one glaring example. In general, the history, literature, English, and health courses fall into this category.
- **My favorite** of all the courses we received, the college News Writing course (#U512-203), is excellent! Replete with "insider" information, it leads you from the difference between copy editing and proofreading to the ins and outs of libel laws, from common usage errors to style guidelines, from how to write a feature story to the inner workings of a newsroom. I heartily recommend that you substitute this course, for which you likely can obtain college credit, in place of a typical lackluster high-school English course.
- **75 high-school courses are available,** in the following subject areas: Art and Art History (3 courses in all; the Basic Drawing course uses *Drawing on the Right Side of the Brain* for its text) courses; Astronomy (1 course); Biology (2 courses); Business and Economics (4 courses); English (7 courses, including one quaintly titled "Attack on Grammar," 4 semesters of high-school English, and 2 semesters of American Literature); French (8 semester courses, plus Introduction to French Literature of 17th & 18th Century); Geography (2 semesters of physical geography); German (6 semester courses, plus 2 semesters of Intro to German Literature and a one-semester Intermediate Composition course); Personal & Family Health (this is one to skip); History (2 semesters of U.S.

NEW!
University of Wisconsin-Extension
High school. From $95-$286/semester unit for basic courses (most around the $95 price), plus $50 administrative fee/semester unit. Advanced Standing courses, $126/college credit hour. Materials are additional.
UW Learning Innovations, 505 S. Rosa Rd., Madison, WI 53719. Phone: (800) 442-6460. Fax: (608) 262-4096. Email: info@learn.uwsa.edu. Web: www.learn.wisconsin.edu.

History); Latin (sadly, only two semesters—these are good courses, with lots of good background information not found in the text and good exercises; they use the Cambridge Latin books); Math (5 courses: two semesters of Algebra I, two semesters of Geometry, and Trigonometry; no Advanced Math or Calculus courses available); Meteorology (1 course); Music ("Understanding Music" and two semesters of Beginning Music Theory); Physics (they suggest you take their two General Physics university courses for deferred credit); Polish (two semesters of "Reading Polish"); Political Science (one course, "American Government Today"); Russian (8 semester courses, plus Russian for Reading Knowledge, Reading Russian for Fun, and Beginning Conversation & Composition in Russian); Social Studies (one women's lib course); Spanish (8 semester courses); and Study Skills ("Power Reading").

- **Muchos foreign languages!** With four years of French, Spanish, and Russian available, not to mention additional literature and composition courses, three years of German, and one year each of Polish and Latin, this program deserves your attention if you are seriously interested in languages.

- **No diploma option**—instead, you apply courses towards a diploma from your school or state.

- **No honors courses** available.

- **No dual-credit courses** available. However, many of their university courses can be taken for "Advanced Standing," meaning for *deferred* college credit. Once you're in college, the deferred credits are credited to you. With deferred credit, you may or may not get high-school credit for these courses, depending on your school and state.

- **Science courses are not lab courses,** unless you count the packet of bean seeds included with General Biology I. There are no Chemistry or Physics high-school courses, but university survey (*not* lab) courses are available in these area.

- **A large Resource Directory** included in the catalog gives individual phone numbers, and in some cases, fax numbers and email addresses, for individual instructors by course, as well as full contact information for the 72 local Extension offices where you can take proctored exams, one for each Wisconsin county.

- **Most exams must be proctored.** A proctor can be any school official (grade school, high school, counselor, etc.), a college testing center, or a certified public librarian. In remote locations, pastors or military chaplains are allowed.

- **Take up to one year** to finish your course. You can apply for a three-month extension, for a $25 fee. The fee for a second three-month extension is $50. Extensions are with the approval of the relevant academic department.

- **Lessons are graded by instructors;** these are not just computerized multiple-choice courses. They supply the envelopes for mailing them in. You must put each assignment in a separate envelope, and you need written permission to submit more than four assignments per week per course. They ask you to allow two weeks for an assignment to be graded and returned.

- **Some instructors,** but not all, **accept email lesson submissions.** Lessons can be submitted by fax for any course upon payment of an additional $20 fax fee.

- **No "used textbook" option.** However, textbooks and materials are purchased separately, so if you already own the textbook, you don't have to buy it again.
- **Increasingly friendly** to homeschooled students, but not yet up to the level of friendliness of, say, Indiana University. One good sign: they are beginning to advertise in homeschool publications.
- **Web courses** are only currently available at the college level, for business and nursing. There are no plans for high-school online courses at this time.

If you're interested in science, math, or engineering as a future career, this is not the program for you. It's just too lightweight in the math and science departments. Try the high-school programs from University of Nebraska-Lincoln or Texas Tech instead. But if you're interested in the fine arts and languages, or in the "Advanced Standing" option in which you take some of the many fine university courses also offered by UWEX in the very same catalog (I especially recommend their college courses in creative and freelance writing), then give UWEX a look. *Mary Pride*

CHAPTER 41

High School with a Difference

In this chapter you'll find three totally unique high-school curricula, plus audio and video courses that can be a curriculum in themselves.
I included audio and video curriculum in this chapter, because most people still aren't used to thinking of tackling high-school subjects in this fashion. Too, the particular product lines we reviewed often include instruction that differs markedly from the traditional classroom lecture format.

Now, an interesting point: It so happens that the three "high-school programs with a difference" you'll find reviewed below were all written by Christians for Christians. These are serious attempts to develop a distinctive education *not* based on the public-school model.

In each case, the print curricula in this chapter were written by just a few people and published by small businesses, usually owned by one family.

Does that make them better or worse than the curriculum from textbook publishers or state universities? Well, it makes them

- More personal
- More consistent
- More fun (my personal opinion!)

Committee-written materials tend to be either uniformly bland or uneven in tone. This won't be a problem here! And I can tell you that any of these programs far exceeds the amount of content you can expect from a traditional high school, in the areas they cover.

So do you want to go the road less traveled by? It's up to you!

NEW!
KONOS History of the World
Grades 9–12. Each volume, $150 (includes student book, teacher book, maps, and time line). Shipping extra.
KONOS, Inc., PO Box 250, Anna, TX 75409. (972) 924-2712. Fax: (972) 924-2733. Email: konos@konos.com. Web: www.konos.com.

High School With a Twist

They're here—the first two volumes of the long-awaited KONOS high-school program!

KONOS History of the World Year I: The Ancient World starts with the civilizations of the Fertile Crescent and ends with the founding of Rome. Along the way your high schooler will perform work equal to a year's credit in English (composition and literature), world history (including Bible history) and geography, and art (history and studio). For a complete curriculum, you will need to provide separate math and science courses.

What you get: a 400+ page *consumable* Student Book, with all assignments plus space for keeping track of hours, and a Teacher's Guide with discussion/essay questions and tests. The Student Book is broken into lessons, each with Bible verses to study, 153 characters and a time line,

Timeline Figures

four large maps to study, vocabulary words to write on 3x5 cards, resource list, a list of related KONOS units, many activities with detailed directions, and questions to evaluate your progress (e.g., "Have you compared the technology available to the people in Sumeria to that of today?").

Activities have a Christian worldview and are typical KONOS. You make things, draw things, research things, act things out, and even do a little cut-and-paste. To find out the difference between ancient and modern farming methods, for instance, you take a sharp stick and try to break up the ground enough to plant. Then you make a simple plow by attaching a rope to your stick which one person pulls while another guides the stick. In another typical activity, you make a fabric painting of the Royal Standard of Ur, using Batik dye and wax. (A picture of the Royal Standard is provided in the book.)

Unlike many other history-based programs, the KONOS Student Book includes a wealth of background information about each historical topic studied. This is not a book that just assigns you X pages to read from someone else's book! The background information is clear, understandable, and clearly written by someone who cares that students walk away from this course understanding and remembering what they have studied. To this end, students are also encouraged to use various learning strategies— such as flashcards, sorting historical information into baskets, and playing memory games—to increase retention.

The English activities are designed to cover different types of writing skills, from note-taking to persuasive essays. These are not Mickey Mouse assignments: KONOS co-author Jessica Hulcy takes the "150 hours per credit, and that does *not* include time spent reading" requirement seriously.

Overall, the Student Book is easy to use. Text is large, there's lots of white space in the margins, information is provided in charts and lists when possible, there are a fair number of illustrations, and handy check boxes are provided so you can record when each activity is completed.

The Teacher's Guide includes learning objectives in each subject studied (English, history, and art, as well as general learning skills), lists of supplies required for each week's work, and answers to the questions and exercises in the Student Book. The answers are often quite extensive, explaining the reasons why a particular answer is right. Evaluation questions are also included, to help students "dig into" the subjects studied, and to help the parent assess student progress. KONOS suggests several ways the questions can be used, from weekly written essays, to oral exams, to complete essay exams.

While KONOS does recommend two supplementary textbooks (the ubiquitous *Streams of Civilization* and *Picturesque Tales of Progress*), most research is intended to be done in the library.

History of the World Year II covers Rome, the early church, the Byzantine and Holy Roman empires, Charlemagne, the Moslems and Vikings, China, and the Middle Ages. Like the first volume, each week's lessons cover the subjects of history, English, Bible, geography, and art. Like Year One, it comes with a large Student Text (over 500 pages), a 100-page Teacher Guide, 150 timeline characters with a timeline to mount them on, and several large maps, all included in the basic price. Like Year One, it provides a full year's credit in world history/geography, English, and art. More than that, this volume also includes a beginning Latin course, with 36 lessons, that should count as a semester's credit.

Year II is loaded with classic literature and plays related to the time period studied, such as Shakespeare's *Julius Caesar,* Augustine's *City of God, Quo Vadis, Beowulf,* Dante's *Inferno, Canterbury Tales,* the Magna Carta, *The Black Arrow,* and much more. You'll also find an introduction designed to train your student in study skills and learning methods. Your student will not only learn how to approach new and difficult material, but also how to retain it and actually enjoy the process!

Year II is much more challenging than Year I. Consider the first year as your way to woo your student from the relative ease of elementary unit studies to the stricter study requirements needed for a college preparatory high-school course.

KONOS History of the World Year III, covering the Reformation, Renaissance, and the rest of European history, is currently under development.

The KONOS high-school curriculum has also been used by some students to obtain *college* credits in history. For more information about this option, contact the KONOS office.

If you want your high schooler to learn to learn on his own, and you prefer for him to enjoy doing it, I would take a good hard look at this curriculum. *Mary Pride*

TRISMS Volume II: Creation of the World Through the Middle Ages was originally designed for one full year of high-school education, but most families use it for two years, as it takes that long to do justice to this wealth of material.

This Christian program switches the emphasis from social studies to humanities. Civilizations that were surveyed briefly in Volume 1 are now studied in depth, with assignments growing out of interaction with source documents and the art, architecture, science, music, and literature of each civilization. Eastern and Western civilizations are covered in a logical sequence. Language arts now becomes studies in composition and literature.

NEW!
TRISMS Volume II & III
Grades 9–12. Creation Through the Middle Ages, $125. Rise of Nations (due Fall 2000), $75. Student Pack, $30. Timeline book, $10. Questionnaire answer keys, $35. Add 10% shipping.
TRISMS, 1203 S. Delaware Pl., Tulsa, OK 74104. (918) 585-2778. Email: linda@trisms. Web: www.trisms.com.

All the literature, which consists of excerpts from dozens of ancient writings, is provided within the curriculum volume itself, except for common classics such as the *Iliad* and *Odyssey,* Bible selections, and other reading material easily available through bookstores and libraries.

The reference material and background readings are a different story. These are *not* provided, although you do get a week-by-week list of suggested readings; so expect to spend a lot of time in the bookstore and library or ordering through book catalogers.

The heart of this volume is the 34 lesson plans, each in a week-at-a-glance format. Each week includes columns for art, music, architecture, science, civilizations, literature, and vocabulary. At the bottom of each two-page spread are found a list of resource books for that week, a list of historical events, geographical areas of interest, and a comparison question, e.g., "Compare Queen Hatshepsut's obelisk with that of men pharaohs." Each year of TRISMS takes 38 weeks in all, including the 34 weeks of lessons and four weeks for the quarterly test and projects.

Be aware that you don't get as much background information in the TRISMS text itself as you find in KONOS History of the World or Worldviews of the Western World. You also won't find any illustrations. The outside reading selections are essential for fleshing out the civilizations studied.

This volume also includes time tables listing the civilizations and time periods studied in chronological order, a student/teacher orientation to the program, a 25-page annotated Reading and Resource List divided into what's needed for each lesson, science assignments, literature assignments, the 34 literature selections I already mentioned, and a section with definitions of literary terms used in the assignments.

Students write mini-reports on 3x5 note cards for every biography and work of historical fiction they read. Students also fill out questionnaire forms to answer questions about the people studied: Who? Motivation? Changes they caused? Consequences of the changes? Dates? New vocabulary? Students also complete an extensive Civilization Questionnaire for each civilization studied. The questionnaires, worksheets, maps, quizzes, and tests are all packaged separately in the Student Master Pack included with this volume.

Civilizations studied include Sumeria, Indus Valley (ancient India), Egypt, Phoenicia, Minoa (Crete), ancient China, Babylon, Hittites, Aryan India, Mycenea, Olmec, Nubia, Old Testament Israel, Greece, Assyria, Etruscans, neo-Babylonian (Chaldean), China (more dynasties), the Maya, Persia, Athens and Sparta, Alexander the Great and Macedonia, Mauryan Empire of India, the Roman Republic, the Roman Empire, Germanic tribes (if you can call *those* civilized!), the Celts, the early Christians, the Byzantine Empire, the early Middle Ages and Vikings, Islam, the

"Romanesque" or Dark Ages, the High Middle Ages, the Mongol Empire, and Japan. If this sounds like a *lot* more than *you* remember ever studying in school, you're right! What a terrific, thorough background your student will have after studying all of this!

Although you are allowed to photocopy the forms in the Student Master Pack for subsequent students, it's so much more convenient—and more impressive as far as recordkeeping goes—to get an extra Student Master Pack for each additional student. Considering that each student will likely be using this course for two years, it's not that much extra per year to have neat, easy-to-grade records.

Oh joy, questionnaire answer keys *are* available for this volume! I would strongly advise you to purchase these answer keys, which are sold separately. Answer keys to the quizzes and tests are provided in your basic Volume 2 purchase price.

After three years' experience with Volume 2, the consensus is that it does provide a good foundation for future college studies. Using it as a two-year course brings the price per year down to just a little over $50, with everything included. Plus, the entire curriculum is resalable after use!

TRISMS volume III, The Rise of Nations, is due out in Fall 2000. It will continue your history and associated theme studies into the modern age. *Mary Pride*

Dr. Francis Schaeffer was many things in his lifetime: Reformed Presbyterian pastor, missionary to Europe, writer, thinker, speaker, and theologian, to name just a few. He is best known today for his work in defining and defending the Christian worldview, and showing why the popular non-Christian worldviews of our day are self-contradictory and unlivable.

Building on Dr. Schaeffer's work, and incorporating many of his books and videos, David Quine's **World Views of the Western World** is an ambitious attempt to create a three-year high-school curriculum designed to build Christian kids into worldview champs.

Currently only the first and second years are available. The "syllabus" (actually, a huge 630-page oversized lay-flat workbook/textbook) forms the heart of the course. This is supplemented with books, videos, audiocassettes, and Cornerstone Curriculum Project's own *Adventures in Art* and *Classical Composers & the Christian Worldview* curricula.

The books for **Year 1** include a mixture of classics (*Iliad, Odyssey,* Plato's *Republic,* and the *Aeneid*), works by Dr. and Mrs. Schaeffer and their co-workers (*Affliction, The Gift of Music, How Should We Then Live?, The God Who Is There, Escape from Reason, He Is There and He Is Not Silent*), and apologetics and worldview (Augustine's *City of God* and Sire's *The Universe Next Door*). This same mix continues in future years, as we shall see. Francis Schaeffer's classic *How Should We Then Live?* video series is employed throughout all three years, along with a video from course author David Quine in Year 1 and John Whitehead's *The Second American Revolution* video in Year 3. The "dramatized audio cassettes," referred to cryptically as D.A.C. in the syllabus, are mostly from the following Knowledge Products series:The Giants of Philosophy (four tapes from this series are used in the first year), Great Economic Thinkers, and The United States Constitution (these series will be used in Years 2 and 3). See reviews of these series elsewhere in this volume.

NEW!
World Views of the Western World

Grades 9–12. Year 1 Syllabus, $125. Resources for Year I: Adventures in Art I/II/III, $180; optional portfolio, $30. Building a Biblical World View Video, $15. Classical Composers, (call for price). Virgil's Aeneid, $8. Augustine's City of God, $9. Homer's Iliad and Odyssey, $8 each. Plato's Republic, $9. Sire's The Universe Next Door, $13. Edith Schaeffer's book Affliction, $12. Quine's Let Us Highly Resolve, $10. Dr. Francis Schaeffer: Trilogy, $25; Genesis in Space and Time, $12; Job audiocassette, $18. Dramatized audiocassettes about Aristotle, Plato, Augustine, Aquinas, and Socrates, $15 each. Total Year 1 Package, $600. Total Year 2 package, $576. Year 3, TBA. Add 5% shipping.
Cornerstone Curriculum Project, 2006 Flat Creek Pl., Richardson, TX 75080. (972) 235-5149. Fax: (972) 235-0236. E-mail: dquine@Cornerstone Curriculum.com. Web: www. CornerstoneCurriculum.com.

Years 2 and 3 will weigh in at 5½ Carnegie Units each, meaning you will only need to add a couple of math courses and a science course to meet state graduation requirements. If you are college-bound, I suggest you make it a lab science and add a foreign or classical language, typing, and driver's ed.

The Year 1 package price of $600 is more than homeschool parents have been used to spending for K–8 curriculum, but well within bounds for a year of high school. Don't forget that, since most of the resources are books, videos, and cassettes that can be used again and again, you won't need to buy them for a second or third student. This brings the price per child down considerably, if you use the course for several children in a family.

The course would be very easy to use with groups. This would have the advantage of lowering the price per student, since all can listen to cassettes and watch videos together, as well as making it possible to discuss the thought questions as a group. Each student will still need his own syllabus.

Year 1 is designed to cover the following topics: composition, ancient literature, philosophy/theology, music history and appreciation, art history and appreciation, western civilization, humanities, and world history. An outline of how you may assign credit for these topics shows the entire year being worth four Carnegie Units—the equivalent of four year-long courses. Years 2 and 3 continue to cover all these topics. They finish up the literature sequence with medieval and modern literature respectively, and fill in requirements for American government and American history. Politics, economics, and science history will also be covered in these years.

In **Year 2**, you will be studying the Renaissance, the Reformation, the revolutionary age (1700s through the early 1900s, with a little stop-off at *Animal Farm*), and the rise of modern science. **Year 3** continues into and through the 20th century with the age of non-reason (when the philosophers gave up on the notion of absolute truth), the age of fragmentation (when artist and musicians started tearing art and tone apart), the new theology (with its abandonment of biblical truth), the age of personal peace and affluence (where we're at right now), and final choices (where do we go from here?). At this point, you should be well prepared for any philosophical or theological question college professors or fellow students can throw at you.

The course is well-organized in an unusual way. First, you have a week-by-week schedule, with assignments separated into "Biblical World View" and "Greco-Roman World View" sections. This makes sense, because the bulk of the syllabus is made up of 295 page of Biblical World View pages and 260 pages of Greco-Roman World View. Each week's assignment tells you which pages of each section to do, plus which books to read, videos to watch, and cassettes to listen to.

An introduction, itself written in the style of the weekly pages, explains how the course works and walks you through an initial assignment. You discover that your notes and course work is to be written directly in the syllabus. Specific reading/writing/watching/drawing/etc. assignments are given in the margins of the pages. Space is provided in the body of the page for taking notes during each reading/watching/listening session. Major headings for your notes are provided. Following each such session, you are supposed to write out complete answers to each question. This may involve sketching the image in Nebuchadnezzar's dream, or copying a diagram from one of Francis Schaeffer's books. You are also supposed to be creating a "My Book of the Ages" timeline on continuous computer paper.

A teacher's manual for this course, showing a completed timeline and suggested answers to the discussion questions and assignments, is sorely needed. Most parents don't have the background in philosophy, history, and theology to be confident about whether the student's answers are dead-on right or wildly off the mark. Even questions about facts take a lot of time to look up in the appropriate book. If parents and students are learning together, which is often the case, the parents need to be able to check their own work—and don't forget, at this age the students might dispute the parent's answers! If no impartial judge of your answers is available, this can be a problem. If the student is learning on his own, a quick way to check on his progress is even more essential.

This is very much a course for abstract thinkers. The vast majority of your time is spent with words and ideas, and a good vocabulary and quick understanding are essential. Most of the books and thinkers you will be studying are normally found in college-level courses. This should not pose a problem for most teens who have been homeschooled for a long time, but you'll find it quite a switch if you've been doing unit studies up to now! On the other hand, future lawyers, future college professors, and future pastors should love it. *Mary Pride*

Audio Courses for High School & Beyond

Here is a tremendous resource for high school and college at home. Each two-tape **Knowledge Products** set comes in a handy small binder, often with a short introduction to the subject material on the jacket, and includes between 2½ to 3 hours of listening. You can purchase an entire series at once, or do it the easy way, one set per month billed to your credit card. This amount of listening is easy to get through as you drive around in the car—which is the way Bill does it.

- Narrated in authoritative style by Charlton Heston, this 13-part **Giants of Philosophy** series discusses works of philosophy and the men behind them. Written by a professor of philosophy, the narrations include a biography of each philosopher which places his work in its historical context, followed by a good chunk of his major work(s), with commentary and explanations. It's all done very objectively, presenting each philosopher's main points, how he contrasts with other philosophers, and how much of a difference his philosophy made, but no comment on whether the philosophy was right or wrong. This objective approach makes the series usable by just about anyone. Philosophers covered range from Plato (c. 430–350 B.C., Greece) to Jean-Paul Sartre (1905–1980, France). A very enjoyable and informative series.

- Narrated by Craig Deitschmann, this 12-part **Giants of Political Thought** series discusses works of political literature and their respective authors, with each writer's voice dramatized to match his region or nationality. You get a biography of each political writer, along with a brief history of his period, plus extensive readings from his major works, and explanations of what the writers were trying to say. Unbiased presentation makes it usable by just about anyone. The series includes every book you'd expect to find in a classical-education course on the subject (which nowadays means a handful of 19th-century thinkers are included as well). Extremely well done; recommended.

- Narrated by Louis Rukeyser (of Wall Street Week fame), the 13-part **Great Economic Thinkers** series discusses works of economic literature and the development of economic thought, with a balanced overview of liberal, conservative, and libertarian economics. From Karl Marx to Lord Keynes to the Austrian and Monetarist schools, it's all here.

- The 15-part **Science and Discovery** series, narrated by former NBC-TV News journalist Edwin Newman, starts with *Science in Antiquity* and takes you right up through chaos theory.

- Narrated by Ben Kingsley, the 13-part **Religion, Scriptures and Spirituality** series discusses the origin and practice of the world's major religions, including the varieties of Christianity, classical religions, native religions, and even skepticism.

- Narrated by Harry Reasoner, Peter Hackes, and Richard C. Hottelet, the 20-part **World's Political Hot Spots** series discusses the world regions which historically have been politically unstable—which turns out to be just about everywhere except Canada and the USA. Packed with history and geography!

NEW!
Knowledge Products audio-cassette series

High school–adult. Science and Discovery series, $224 plus shipping. Giants of Philosophy and Religion, Scriptures & Spirituality, Great Economic Thinkers: each complete series, $194 postpaid. Giants of Political Thought, $179 postpaid. World's Political Hot Spots series, $299 postpaid. Individual two-tape sets, $17.95 plus $3 shipping. *Knowledge Products, 722 Rundle Ave., Suite A-13, Nashville, TN 37210. (800) 876-4332 or (615) 742-3852. Fax: (615) 742-3270. Email: crom@edge.ercnet.com. Web: www.cassettes.com.*

Other series are available as well. You'll find their reviews in Volume 3.
Bill and Mary Pride

Video Courses for High School & Beyond

Additional Video Courses Reviewed in Volume 3

- Bob Jones University Press *Manners at Work* video course
- Chalk Dust Math Videos
- Don Aslett's *Is there Life After Housework* video
- Firebaugh's Algebra on Videotape
- Homespun Tapes music training courses
- How Great Thou Art courses
- Lightbearers Christian Worldview Curriculum
- Piano for Quitters
- Saxon's Algebra on Videotape
- School of Tomorrow Science Courses
- Standard Deviants (detailed reviews of individual video series)
- Summit Ministries Understanding the Times Curriculum
- Superstar Teachers (many subjects)
- Sybervision Language Courses
- Video Tutor Math courses

The last two years of high school are amazingly like the first two years of college. True or false?

True *and* false. Socially, high school isn't all that much like college. But academically, many of the same courses are studied. The difference is that college courses cover more material in less time and in a much more opaque way.

While it is generally understood that American high schoolers need all the help they can get, colleges still seem to feel that the best way to impress students with their teaching authority is to make the teaching hard to understand. To that end, college texts utilize harder vocabulary, more complex sentence structure, and less helpful explanations than high-school texts. College professors also carry on the good work of confusing students by a variety of means: incoherent lectures, reading lectures straight out of the book, or assigning their teaching chores to "teaching assistants." Many of these overworked grad students do not speak English with exceptional clarity and have no noticeable teaching ability.

Take (1) a huge number of confused college students who (2) desperately need to do well in their courses and (3) are willing to pay for help, and what do you get? In this case, the **Standard Deviants Video Series**. ("Standard Deviant" in this context is a word play referring both to how your grades will improve—i.e., *deviate* from the *standard*—and to the fun-loving rule-breaking folks today's college students fondly imagine themselves to be.) Designed to make tough college subjects easy to understand, the 60 videos in this series mix solid instruction with offbeat humor in a mostly successful attempt to make the facts and concepts you need to remember memorable.

Employing the something-new-to-see-every-10-seconds style of MTV, this series doesn't just *present* information: it socks you in the eye with it! Off-the-wall comedy skits illustrate (and sometimes parody) course concepts. Serious content is often delivered in a droll way, via a lineup of dozens of characters that range from Captain Helium (a flying superhero) to a male and female janitor with attitudes. Cartoon bits that remind you of Monty Python mingle with snatches obviously inspired by Saturday Night Live.

The faces you'll see are young. Most people involved in this company are recent college graduates. Genuine college professors are paid to edit the videos for accuracy, but the videos themselves are designed by the young, for the young.

So, these tapes are fun to watch and hold your attention. What about their content? Amazingly, they are all well-organized and quite complete in what they cover. This means some subjects require two, or even three, tapes of two hours or more duration. This also means that savvy kids and teachers are discovering you can use these tapes for more than just review. Some profs are even showing these videos in class!

As of this writing, academic titles available in the the Standard Deviants series are:

- *Accounting 1 & 2*
- *Algebra 1 & 2*
- *American Government 1 & 2*
- *Astronomy 1 & 2*
- *Basic Math*
- *Biology 1 & 2*
- *Business Law*
- *Calculus 1 & 2*
- *Chemistry 1, 2, & 3*
- *Differential Equations*
- *English Composition*
- *English Grammar 1 & 2*
- *English Punctuation 1 & 2*
- *Finance 1, 2, & 3*
- *French 1 & 2*
- *Geology 1 & 2*
- *Geometry 1 & 2*
- *Internet Basics*
- *Italian: Nouns, Verbs, & Adjectives*
- *Italian: The Basics*
- *Learning HTML*
- *Macroeconomics*
- *Marketing*
- *Microeconomics*
- *Nutrition*
- *Organic Chemistry 1, 2, & 3*
- *Physics 1 & 2*
- *Pre-Algebra 1 & 2*
- *Pre-Calculus 1 & 2*
- *Psychology*
- *Public Speaking*
- *SAT Math*
- *SAT Verbal*
- *Shakespeare: Origins, Othello, and Titus*
- *Sociology 1 & 2*
- *Spanish 1 & 2*
- *Spanish: Intermediate Grammar*
- *Spanish: Intermediate Verbs*
- *Statistics 1, 2, & 3*
- *Trigonometry 1 & 2*
- *World Geography: Northern and Southern Hemispheres*
- *Auto Care, Car Buying*
- *Creating Web Pages*
- *Interviewing*
- *Personal Finance*
- *Public Speaking*
- *Quick & Easy Cooking*
- *Resumés and Cover Letters*
- *Taxes*

Workbooks to accompany the videos are currently available for Accounting, Algebra, Basic Math, Chemistry, Finance, Geology, Psychology, and Spanish. These are really course books in themselves, explaining the material covered in each course. Time codes and video notes sections cross-reference the videos. Practice exams and quizzes double-check what's been learned. Fun activities and simple one-person games (we're talking crossword puzzles and the like) add yet more reinforcement. There's some humor, but it's mostly of the "funny names in the word problems" sort. Chatty educational content outweighs humor in the workbooks about 20 to 1.

If you feel the need to take Psychology, I particularly recommend that workbook. It outlines the major non-Christian schools of thought with less words and more objectivity than any other text I've seen.

If you want to get a real jump on your college education . . . if you need help in college . . . or if you'd like to review what you learned in high school and maybe add something to it, this series is just great. *Mary Pride*

Important note: the high school subjects have recently been edited to make them suitable for all audiences. The first editions of these tapes, which were originally designed with secular college students in mind, did include quite a few mildly naughty bits. The new "Edited For All Audiences" versions of high school titles, which will now replace the old versions, should be just fine. If you're buying from a retailer, or directly from Cerebellum, be sure to ask for the Edited For All Audiences version. These can be identified by the yellow video shell. Just turn the tape over and check the bottom.

Now available: DVD courses, "combo" sets of videos (e.g., Part 1 and 2 of Algebra 1), at a discount off individual tape prices; combo sets of DVDs. All courses will eventually be available in both video and DVD.

NEW!
SuperStar Teachers Audio and Video Courses

High school and college. Most courses priced between $99.95 and $199.95. Some titles go on sale from time to time at up to half off. Shipping extra.
The Teaching Company, 7405 Alban Station Court, Suite A107, Springfield, VA 22150. (800) 832-2412. Fax: (703) 912-7756. Email: custserv@teachco.com. Web: www.teachco.com.

Teaching Company founder Tom Rollins had a vision: to capture the best university professors in America on video, thus making their courses available to adults who wanted to refresh their memory of college courses or pick up knowledge they had missed on the way by. Thus the first **SuperStars Teachers** video and audio courses, now numbering over 80 at the college level.

Then Mr. Rollins had another idea: find the best high-school teachers in America, and make

their courses available, too! The call went out, and hundreds of video samples came back. From those, he and his staff chose what they considered the most memorable and educationally superior. They then contacted the winning teachers, and arranged to create full video courses in the following subjects:

- Algebra 1
- Algebra 2
- American History
- Basic Math
- Chemistry
- Geometry
- World History

Each course comes in a convenient video binder, with a guidebook outlining the lectures—very handy for adding your own personal notes. These are not "review" or "refresher" courses, *a la* Cerebellum's Standard Deviants courses reviewed above, but courses designed to teach you the subject from scratch.

Don't expect MTV-like hijinks, or even any visual content more exciting than a blackboard and occasional computer graphic. In the History courses, teacher Lin Thompson impersonates various historical characters in period costume. In the science and math courses, you just get excellent classroom teaching.

For detailed reviews of individual courses, see Volume 3. *Mary Pride*

CHAPTER 42

Online Academies for Homeschoolers

Over the years since 1897, when Calvert School signed up its first homeschool student, hundreds of thousands of families have taken part in distance education. As with the Calvert curriculum, for the past hundred years the vast majority of distance education has centered around correspondence courses. This type of arrangement combines the flexibility and environment of home study with the opportunity to interact with and have work assessed by someone other than the parent.

The popular explosion of the Internet in the last three years has led to the growth of a new flavor of distance education. Dozens of Internet-based classes and online academies have been formed. Through email, newsgroups, Web-based bulletin boards, and real-time video and audio, these offer students around the world the opportunity to interact with teachers and other homeschooled students in a group setting.

Where We Are in 2000

For the last five years, my family has personally experienced the ups and downs of all kinds of online courses. From serving as guinea pigs for the "beta test" of Scholars Online Academy, to listening to *loud* RealAudio lectures delivered live via modem by Fritz Hinrichs of Escondido Tutorial Service, to their experiences with A.P. courses from Pennsylvania Homeschoolers, our kids have taken a total of several dozen online courses. Meanwhile, for *Practical Homeschooling* and its cousin, the now-defunct *Homeschool PC* magazine, our editorial staff reviewed a half-dozen additional online academies.

What you see in this chapter therefore pretty much represents *all* the online academies of note currently popular with homeschoolers. This is just the beginning of what I fully expect to be a tidal wave of online instruction— possibly requiring an entire book of its own in the *next* edition!

How to Choose and Use an Online Course
by Mrs. Wendy Pierce

The most critical requirement necessary for successful online education is gaining an understanding of what to expect from the potential online program and what the program will require of both student and parent. Factors we at the Institute for Study of the Liberal Arts and Sciences (ISLAS) have found key when considering an online program are the following:

Parental Involvement

The more actively parents are involved with their children's online learning experience, the more success they will experience. ISLAS recommends parental involvement at the following levels:

Junior High Student (ages 10–12)

Starting out, the parent may need to sit with the student during class to help him adapt to scrolling text on the computer screen. In the beginning, the parent may also need to periodically type for the student if typing skills have not been minimally developed. If necessary, the student will need help in navigating between different applications like web browser and conferencing software. Organization of electronic email (email) is an absolute necessity and easily accessing all applications from the desktop is extremely helpful.

Early High School Age (Freshman and Sophomore)

If the student has already participated in a junior high class, parental involvement needed at the high school level in regard to technology is less than at the junior high level; however, because of the increased number of classes and academic levels, the need for organization increases when compared with the junior high student. Early high school students needs help organizing email, scheduling offline learning time, meeting homework deadlines, and wisely scheduling extra curricular activities. Parent review of class logs helps monitor class participation and validates understanding of material while also providing material for dinner table discussions of the student's course work. Students should email teachers on their own if questions surface about their studies. Parents should communicate with the teacher at least once a month even if it's just to let the teacher know everything is going well.

Late High School Age (Junior and Senior)

By this level of online learning the student should need very little organizational help. Interaction between the student and parent should be centered around actual academic studies. Dinner table discussions, along with reading class logs, should continue to be a means by which parents can assess the student's work and provide material for parent/student discussion. Students should be scheduling the completion of assignments and communicating with teachers to clarify understanding of presented material. Parents should oversee the organizational process, be available for questions, and proctor tests; however, completing studies in a timely manner should be the student's responsibility. Parent communication with the teacher should continue, at a minimum, once a month.

Student Assessment

Answering the following questions prior to enrollment in an online program will help you determine the type of program which will be best suited for your child as well as help determine the number of classes in which he should enroll.

What prior academic preparation is necessary for successful participation in the program? Does your child want to be home schooled? Is he academically motivated? Does he like computers?

Learning the Ropes—Attend a Student Orientation Course

All ISLAS students attend an orientation course where they learn how to use the applications necessary for class participation. Orientation classes are generally one hour per evening for 7–10 days, hence minimizing the anxiety that sometimes accompanies learning a new skill.

Most ISLAS families are surprised to learn that computer illiteracy is the most easily overcome problem in achieving success with the online learning medium. Students don't need the latest, fastest and most up-to-date computer, (though there are reasonable minimum requirements); furthermore, it's not necessary to pay for expensive computer training classes to participate in an online class. Yes, some training must occur focusing on basic computer skills (email, conferencing software, audio files, and web browser), but 6–10 hours of orientation training is enough to teach the student the basic computing skills and instill user confidence. Technology is a school bus to the classroom; once the initial novelty wears off, technology fades to the background, calling little attention to itself. Learning the skills needed to participate in an online class are few and simple.

Attend a Parent Orientation Course

A parent orientation class should include alumni of the program in which you have enrolled. In this class, parents obtain practical advice concerning offline study time, organization of email, and additional information concerning safe use of the internet. Experienced parents share methods of study that don't work or which were frustrating to their student; hence helping "newbies" to avoid the same mistakes. On the other hand, parents learn of hints and ideas that will enhance learning and which are key in making online learning a success; hence being spared the reinvention of the wheel. ISLAS has found this open forum where parent "oldies" and "newbies" can share ideas to be as important an element in preparation as is the student orientation course.

Enroll in a Summer Course

There is nothing like jumping in and trying it! Participation in a summer class prior to the fall term will more than adequately prepare students for the world of online learning in the fall.

The Nuts and Bolts—Organization of Email

Choose an email program that has an easy filing system. ISLAS recommends Eudora. Each class should have a separate folder which contains sub-folders in the following areas: assignments to do, assignments completed, tests to take, tests completed, quizzes to take, quizzes completed, answered questions, and misc.

Email should be retrieved from the outbox and filed in the correct class folder. In an electronic medium email can get lost so filing completed correspondence is absolutely necessary to prevent the student from having to redo assignments.

Have email attachments and class logs placed directly on the computer desktop so students merely click the appropriate folder to retrieve documents.

Organization of the Browser

Bookmark (Netscape) or add to the Favorites Folder (Internet Explore) all class web sites and conference center web site locations. Our students file them in a folder named ISLAS.

Plan Parent Computer Time

As a parent, learn how to find the class web sites and how to email your student's teacher. Plan 15 minutes a day to review student email and parent email. The student should have a separate email account from the parent allowing him to be responsible for his own email; however, until the student is proficient in managing email the parent should receive a courtesy copy of all correspondence. ISLAS provides two email accounts upon registration for this purpose and has found that students are quite capable of email management once taught the necessary organizational skills.

Offline Study Time

Success in online learning can only be achieved when adequate offline preparation has occurred. The following section provides methods that ISLAS students have found to be of help when organizing offline study time.

1. After the online class session, obtain the next assignment. Write it down or print it out and file it in a three-ring notebook for that particular class.
2. The day after a class meeting, assess the assignment portioning it into manageable blocks of time each day of the school week. Some families use a daily checklist for this and others note the assignment on a calendar. Print out the class log or gather notes and enter them into the class notebook. We have found that writing down class notes into a notebook helps cement concepts more concretely than just reading them from the computer screen.
3. Administer weekly quizzes prior to the class meeting.
4. Whether initiated by the older student or by the parent, implement checkpoint Friday to be certain the work for the week has been completed—check that notes are entered in the class notebook, quizzes taken and paired with the results, reading assignments completed, out-basket filed, and email organized.

Sample of Student Organization for a Student Taking Latin II, World History, Theology, English Literature, Geometry, and Writing Program with Scholars' Online Academy (ISLAS)

Monday
Class Meetings: Latin II
History: Finish up reading assignment, submit quiz and make sure History assignment for Tuesday is complete
Geometry: Offline, do daily assignment
English: Finish up reading assignment, submit quiz and make sure English assignment for Tuesday is complete
Theology: Continue with reading and writing summaries
Writing Program: Do prewriting portion of assignment

Tuesday
Class Meetings: English and World History
Latin II: Check assignment for the week, enter log notes in notebook, translate 4 sentences and complete $\frac{1}{10}$ of the worksheets due in two weeks, spend 10 minutes memorizing forms.
Geometry: Offline, do the daily assignment
Theology: Make sure assignment for Wednesday is complete.
Writing Program: Begin writing outline and thesis statement

Wednesday
Class Meetings: Theology
History: Plan assignment for the week, enter log notes in notebook
English: Plan assignment for the week, enter log notes in notebook
Latin II: Translate 4 sentences and complete $\frac{1}{10}$ of the worksheets due in two weeks, spend 10 minutes memorizing forms, submit quiz
Geometry: Offline, do daily assignment
Writing Program: Finish outline, begin essay

Thursday
Class Meetings: Latin II
History: Begin new assignment
English: Begin new assignment
Theology: Plan assignment for the week, enter log notes in notebook
Geometry: Offline, do daily assignment
Writing Program: Finish outline, begin essay

Friday
Latin II: Enter notes in notebook, translate 4 sentences and complete $\frac{1}{10}$ of the worksheets due in two weeks, spend 10 minutes memorizing forms
History: Continue assignment
English: Continue assignment
Theology: Continue assignment
Geometry: Offline, do daily assignment
Writing Program: Finish essay and submit it

To check before the weekend
Check to make sure notes have been entered in notebook, necessary quizzes completed, writing program work submitted, assignments progressing as they should. Latin II workbook pages and geometry assignments should be mailed to the respective teachers via regular post. TAKE A BREAK!

Randy and Wendy Pierce homeschool their five children, three of whom are of online age, and are Administrative Assistants to the online schools Regina Coeli Academy and Scholars' Online Academy. For more information on these academies, see the Scholars' Online Academy review in this chapter, or visit www.islas.org.

Switched-On Schoolhouse sign-on screen

If you're familiar with the popular Alpha Omega line of worktext curriculum, you've probably noticed that the worst part of using it is the endless grading—and averaging—of grades. Or, I should say, that *was* the worst part, if you're ready to switch to the new computerized version. Called *Switched-On Schoolhouse*, it includes a host of neat features—and some extra material—not found (or possible!) in the worktext curriculum. And an online academy using this CD-ROM curriculum—**Alpha Omega Online Academy**—is now available.

Just like Alpha Omega's worktext curriculum, each grade of *Switched-On Schoolhouse* consists of five subjects: Bible, Language Arts, Math, Science, and Social Studies. Currently grades 3–12 are available with more grades in development.

Each subject of each grade requires a separate installation, though once you have installed the first grade, the installations from then on are almost instantaneous. Each installation requires that you type in the serial number provided with the program. (Don't lose it!)

Switched-On Schoolhouse has two sets of menus: one set for the teacher, the other for the students. In the teacher mode menus, the teacher can enter new students, review or edit student grades, enable or disable lessons, and set overall program options. In student mode, the students study their lessons, do practice exercises, and take tests.

The program starts in student mode. The entry screen shows a list of up to five students. When you first install the program, this list is blank. The teacher has to add the students using teacher mode.

Switched-On Schoolhouse provides security for teacher mode. When you enter teacher mode the first time, you can define a password. If you ever forget the password later, you can bypass security and erase the password with a simple key sequence. You then enter teacher mode and enter another password. The manual notes that any student who knows the key sequence can do this too, but the teacher will soon discover their handiwork!

Once into teacher mode, you click "Add a Student" and enter the student's name. You can then choose what subjects the student will be taking from the list of available options. In order for a subject to appear on the available list, you need to install it first. If you want to disable certain subtopics of any subject, you can go into the grading screen and click "disable" for that lesson. This screen is also used later to report grades or enter grades for student projects.

You can also reach the options menu from teacher mode. On this menu you can specify what percent grade corresponds to what letter grade; whether to display the percent grade, the letter grade, or both in the student menus; whether to use focused learning or not; the percent penalty for spelling errors; how much weight each portion of a subject contributes to the final grade; and what word processor you will use and the 3-character DOS extension to use for its files.

Switched-On Schoolhouse uses a method called "focused learning." While a student is studying a lesson and doing the exercises, he may get one of the answers wrong. If he does, then at the end of the lesson, the program will send him back to the portion of the lesson with the question he missed. He then can review the lesson and try the question again. If he gets it right, the program will note the fact and he will never see that les-

NEW!
Alpha Omega Online Academy

Grades 5–11. Individual subjects, $61.95. Whole grade, $259.95. Shipping extra. Bridgestone Online Academy program: placement/registration fee, $100/child; tuition, $750/child/grade 3–6. $875/child/grade 7–12. $50 tuition decrease for each additional student. Requires Pentium 133, Windows 95 or 98 (not NT), 16 MB RAM, and 4x CD-ROM drive. *Alpha Omega Publications, 300 N. McKemy, Chandler, AZ 85226. (800) 622-3070. Fax: (480) 785-8034. Web: www.home-schooling.com.*

Two other online academies are licensed to use the Switched-On Schoolhouse software:

- **Summit Christian Academy**
  DFW Corporate Park, 2100 North Hwy 360, Suite 503, Grand Prairie, TX 75050. Orders: (800) 362-9180. Inquiries: (972) 602-8050. Fax: (972) 602-8243. Web: www.scahomeschool.com.

  This academy also offers traditional curriculum programs, using mostly A Beka, Alpha Omega, and Bob Jones University Press materials. Diagnostic testing, and national standardized testing using the Iowa Test of Basic Skills, are also available separately.

- **Sycamore Tree**
  2179 Meyer Place, Costa Mesa, CA 92627. Orders: (800) 779-6750. Inquiries: (949) 650-4466. Fax: (800) 779-6750. Email: sycamoretree@compuserve.com. Web: www.sycamoretree.com.

  Sycamore Tree also has an extremely flexible full-service traditional correspondence program, which you can mix and match with online courses. See their writeup in the Very Different Curriculum chapter.

Switched-On Schoolhouse assignment screen

Switched-On Schoolhouse Bible lesson screen

Switched-On Schoolhouse history lesson screen

son again unless he chooses to review it. If the student finds that one question is totally impossible, he can skip that question by holding down shift and clicking on the question. He will of course get a zero for that question. If you opt to turn off focused learning, the program proceeds through the lesson in order with no review whether or not you get an answer wrong.

When a student starts *Switched-On Schoolhouse* and reaches the screen with the list of student names, he clicks on his name to bring up his assignment screen. He will see an icon for each of the subjects he is currently taking. These do not all have to be in the same grade. For example, the student could be taking grade 9 science at the same time as grade 7 language arts.

The student selects a subject by clicking on its icon. *Switched-On Schoolhouse* remembers where you left off the last time you were doing that subject and starts you there.

A lesson consists of teaching material—either a QuickTime movie, an audio recording, or an illustrated text lesson. You proceed to the next screen either by clicking the next button in the left margin of the screen, which soon becomes tedious, or, as I discovered by making use of the detailed help menus, by pressing F2—much easier.

After the program presents a section of a lesson, it asks review questions about it. The questions can be fill-ins, multiple choice, matching, true/false, or even a crossword puzzle using the lesson's vocabulary words. This is all "open book." Students can scan back through the lesson material to find the correct answers. The program gives a student one shot to get the answer right and if he misses, the program displays the "wrong answer" screen and at the same time tells him verbally he got a wrong answer. It then proceeds to the next question.

If the teacher has focused learning turned on, then at the end of the lesson, the program will return the student to the first wrong answer and give him another opportunity to answer correctly. Once he has answered everything correctly, the program congratulates him and then asks if he would like to go right on to the quiz that follows, warning that he will not be allowed to stop halfway. If he says OK, then on he goes to the quiz. Quizzes and tests are all "closed book."

Once the student has passed the quiz, *Switched-On Schoolhouse* will either assign a project or go on to a new section of the course. For example, the assignment sequence for 8th grade Science goes like this: Science 801:

> 1. Science Today
>   Science 801 A (project)
>   Quiz 1
> 2. Today's Scientist
>   Quiz 2
> 3. Science and Technology
>   Science 801 B (project)
>   Quiz 3
> 4. Conflicts with Society
>   Quiz 4
>   Test

Projects include assignments such as: "Write a short well-organized essay describing Gregor Mendel, his discoveries, and the impact of those discoveries." The teacher has to read and grade projects, and enter the grades into the grades screen under teacher mode in order for project grades to be factored into a student's final grade.

The course material for *Switched-On Schoolhouse* is the same kind of solid material contained in Alpha Omega's LIFEPACs. I asked if the material was taken out of the LIFEPACs and was told some is, but much of the instruction in *Switched-On Schoolhouse* is unique to it.

Nothing in *Switched-On Schoolhouse* should offend any Bible-believing Christian. The Science is taught from creationist, young-earth presuppositions. The Bible courses are based on the foundation of an inerrant, God-inspired Bible. Government is taught from a strict constructionist point of view.

The lessons are well written and lavishly illustrated. You would miss a lot if you didn't do these lessons in color! The video clips are high quality and interesting to watch. In wordy subjects—e.g., social studies or language arts—the exercises vary in type enough to keep a student on his toes, and the questions are challenging and well enough chosen to make sure he had to read the lesson in order to answer them.

For those who believe math proficiency comes by practice, this is just the thing. The exercises in grade 9 math seemed to go on endlessly, but I was in a hurry. The problems vary and become progressively more complicated as each lesson progresses and as each new subtopic adds a new kind of problem to the mix. Because it's computerized, it practically eliminates the parent's need to grade, and automatically provides just the reviews that students need.

Switched-On Schoolhouse presents its lessons simply and straightforwardly. It actually makes very little use of the flashier abilities of the computer except to run QuickTime movies, animate small graphics, and show you everything in full color. I'm not sure this is all bad. This program might not appeal to students who like to meander through a computer program, seeing the sights and clicking on every graphic. But for those who like a traditional approach to presenting coursework and who want an assist in keeping track of what Junior is doing in his schoolwork, these programs—and their associated online academies—are ideal. *Bill Pride*

Apex Learning originally began as a way for schools to offer Advanced Placement courses that they didn't have the resources to offer themselves. The brainchild of Paul Allen, co-founder of Microsoft, Apex currently offers 10 AP courses, all of which meet The College Board's recommendations for Advanced Placement course content, with more slated to come out in 2001.

Apex courses feature online tutorials, reading materials, writing assignments, and interaction with fellow students and the instructor. All this is done "asynchronously," meaning classwork can be done at your convenience, rather than having to sign on at specific times to attend a "live" class. However, you do have to start on one of five particular dates, since course work must be completed by the time the AP exams are offered in May.

Courses offered in Fall 200:

- AP U.S. Government & Politics (1-semester course)
- AP Microeconomics (1-semester course)
- AP Macroeconomics (1-semester course)
- AP Statistics (2-semester course)
- AP Calculus AB (2-semester course)
- AP U.S. History (2-semester course)
- AP English Language (2-semester course)
- AP English Literature (2-semester course)
- AP Chemistry (2-semester course)
- AP Physics B (2-semester course)

If you enroll in the online academy, the software will upload your assignments and quiz results to the academy staff. Their tutors will then interact with you, grading written assignments and commenting on them and offering help as needed. The academy will also compile a transcript documenting your work, which may be helpful later on.

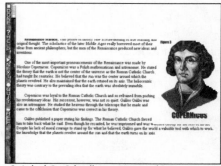
Switched-On Schoolhouse History of Science screen

NEW!
Apex Learning Advanced Placement Courses
Grades 10–12. $395/semester course; $375/course if family signs up for 4 or more at one time. *Apex Learning, 110 110th Ave NE, Suite 210, Bellevue, WA 98004. (800) 453-1454. Fax: (425) 468-6501. Email: inquiries@apexlearning.com. Web: www.apexlearning.com.*

Minimum System Requirements for Apex

PC: Pentium 90/16 MB RAM, Windows 95. **Mac:** Power PC 601, 32 MB RAM, System 8.1, 32MB RAM. **Both Mac and PC:** 20MB available hard disk space, 28.8 modem, ,sound card, speakers or headphones, CD-ROM drive, printer, access to fax machine, MS Internet Explorer 4.01/AOL 4.0/Netscape Navigator 4.08, JavaScript and Cookies enabled, Acrobat Reader 4.0, RealPlayer 7, Flash Player 4.0, monitor with support for 800 x 600 pixel resolution and support for thousands of colors (16-bit color), Internet email account.

Recommended System Requirements

PC: Pentium II 233/64 MB RAM, 56.6 modem. **Mac:** PowerPC 604/^$ MB RAM, System 8.6. **Both Mac and PC:** MS Internet Explorer 5.0/AOL 5.0, JavaScript and Cookies enabled. Other specs same as minimum recommendations.

AP Exam Review

Each spring, Apex also offers AP Exam Review to students who have taken their AP courses elsewhere. The Apex Exam Review system allows full access to their multimedia tutorials, plus a diagnostic test that creates a custom study plan for each student, complete with syllabus. In addition, students will practice with sample exam questions, and participate in online study groups. Technical requirements are the same as for regular Apex courses.

Courses offered in Spring 2001:

- AP U.S. Government & Politics
- AP Microeconomics
- AP Macroeconomics

Scuttlebutt says that the following courses *may* be added by Fall 2001: Biology, Physics C, Calculus BC, and European History. All are two-semester courses.

Fall 2000		**Spring 2001**	
Start (Monday)	End (Friday)	Start (Monday)	End (Friday)
Aug 21	Jan 5	Jan 8	May 18
Aug 28	Jan 12	Jan 15	May 25
Sept 5	Jan 19	Jan 22	June 1
Sept 11	Jan 26	Jan 29	June 8
Sept 18	Feb 2	Feb 5	June 15

Exam Dates

AP Courses	AP Exam Date
Calculus AB	May 10 (a.m.)
Chemistry	May 14 (p.m.)
English Literature	May 7 (a.m.)
English Language	May 10 (a.m.)
Microeconomics	May 17 (a.m.)
Macroeconomics	Mary 17 (p.m.)
Physics B	May 16 (p.m.)
Statistics	May 17 (p.m.)
U.S. Govt & Politics	May 15 (p.m.)
U.S. History	May 11 (a.m.)

As you can see, the only scheduling conflict is between Statistics and Microeconomics. You can take any number of the other offered AP courses without experiencing an exam schedule conflict. Be aware your local school is under no legal obligation to allow you to sign up for the exam, and exams can *only* be signed up for through local schools. Thus, you would be wise to get it in writing from your local school that they will allow you to sign up for the exam *before* signing up for any AP course.

Also note, that although most courses end *after* the exam date, Apex is well aware of this, and will work with you to ensure that all course content necessary for the exam is completed by the exam date. In real life, most AP high-school classes never finish the book, anyway!

The student has to take a pre-test (provided at no charge by Apex) before signing up for either Physics or Calculus. You grade the test yourself at home, and provide Apex with the score. They then, with your help, determine if your student is ready to take the course.

The Statistics and Calculus courses require use of a graphing calculator. Apex recommends the TI-83 model. If you want the Physics course to be a lab course, you'll also need to purchase Schaum's *Outline of College Physics*, available at bookstores or through Apex, and do the labs, which in turn will require purchasing the lab equipment from one of the sources listed in Volume 3 of *The Big Book*.

Apex student enrollment was a little over 500 in 1999; they are expecting between two and four thousand enrollments in 2000. Towards this end, Apex recently inked a deal with Michigan Virtual University to offer AP courses to public and private schools in Michigan.

Apex estimates your student will need 10–12 hours per week per AP course, about half of which will be spent online. Some of the rest may involve sitting in front of a computer, working with the course CD-ROM provided by Apex (for some courses only). The online teacher grades your student's work, which is submitted via email, and recommends the final course grade. Parents can request that regular status reports be emailed to them, so you can be sure your student is keeping up with the work.

The advantages of completing an AP course are many, provided you do well on the exam:

- Most colleges grant college credit for AP exams with scores of 3 or above (5 is the maximum possible score).
- All colleges are impressed with students who have done well on one or more AP courses.
- If you have a child who is "too young" for college, AP courses can fill up a year or two while enabling your child to earn college credit at home.

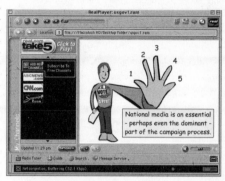

Sample Apex tutorial screen

Apex courses cost about twice as much as the AP courses from Pennsylvania Homeschoolers, which I know from experience do an excellent job of preparing students for the AP exams. However, Apex currently offers some courses PA Homeschoolers do not, and some PA Homeschoolers teachers can be quite picky about who they allow to take their course. While my 14-year-old daughter Sarah was allowed to sign up for U.S. History through PA Homeschoolers, the English Language and Composition teacher refused to accept her solely on the basis of her age. Apex has no age requirement; they don't even ask for your child's birthdate, just for the year he will graduate high school. Apex also is not likely to run out of teachers, no matter how many students want to enroll. Beyond that, all I can say is that I have signed up two of my own children for two Apex courses apiece in 2000, as well as for two courses from PA Homeschoolers. *Mary Pride*

What organization has been offering quality education for half a century without embracing educational pop psychology, and now is making its unique educational style available online?

The answer: **Clonlara School**. A long-time favorite of homeschoolers, with a complete "correspondence" program, Clonlara now also offers online education via their Compuhigh Academy.

Established in 1994, and presently enrolling some 275 full- and part-time students, Clonlara Compuhigh is actually the world's oldest online high school.

That's good to know, but you want to find out what makes Compuhigh special. The best way to see how Clonlara differs from other online academies such as Willoway, Scholar's Online Academy, Potter's School, or Escondido Tutorial Service, is to ask and answer some questions. So let's start!

Clonlara tries not to cater to any specific belief. The school mostly avoids debatable topics in science or history altogether. For example, geology as a hard science need not concern itself with *why* rock layers are in any specific order, just how to discern the layers. Biology need not concern itself with *why* the body is structured the way it is, just how the body is structured. And history need not concern itself with what we *speculate* happened, just what events we have proof of and *know* happened. Even so, some of their courses do present some evolutionary "old-earth" beliefs, but mildly enough so that a reasoning child can skip over them.

NEW!
Clonlara School Compuhigh
1289 Jewett St., Ann Arbor, MI 48104.
(734) 769-4511. Fax: (734) 769-9629.
Email: clonlara@delphi.com.
Web: www.clonlara.org

What courses does Clonlara offer?

Compuhigh has courses on Algebra 1, Algebra 2, American Government, Biology, Computer Networking, Earth Science, English as a Second Language, Geometry, Native American Literature, World Geography, and American History. These together will give you enough credits for a year of school; you have math, science, writing, history, and geography. The school is accredited, meaning that if you complete one of their 22-credit plans, not only does it count as a valid school year, but also the results are accepted by most colleges, public schools, and the United States military.

How much does it cost?

Clonlara has family enrollment rates. For a family with one student to enroll, the price is $550. Two or three students, $575. Four or more students, $600. High-school juniors enrolling for the first time in Clonlara, $650. High school seniors enrolling for the first time, $1100. Please note that this does not include textbooks, postage, or telephone costs for sending material to Clonlara, SAT test costs, graduation fee ($50 per student), or the costs of the individual courses ($50 each). It's a tad expensive, but still attainable and very useful if you can afford it.

NEW!
Eagle Christian High School
Grades 9–12. Registration costs vary by date you sign up: see article for details. Tuition: $175 per semester class or $750 per semester for a full courseload (6 classes). 5% tuition discount for accounts paid in full by the first day of classes. Payment plan available. Multiple child discounts available. Books, software, and materials not included in tuition price. *Eagle Christian School, a ministry of Valley Christian School, 2526 Sunset Lane, Missoula, MT 59804. (888) 324-5348. Fax: (406) 549-5047. Email: principal@eaglechristian.org. Web: www.eaglechristian.org.*

Compuhigh allows you to sign up any time in the school year; you will not be held back or pushed along by the other students.

Compuhigh also leaves the actual methods and structure of education largely up to the parents. There are a number of options. You could learn from formal textbooks if you wanted to, you could perform extensive Web or other research on whatever topic they're working on, or you could suggest most any other method which seems feasible.

Naturally, there are some constraints to this method. For math, they use formal textbooks universally. For their popular English Writing course, much of the instruction comes from their teachers on the bulletin boards, via email, and in live chats.

Furthermore, this philosophy simply will not work for a lazy, indecisive, or disorganized student. The student and parent must define their own learning style, choose their own books, and stick with it! Therefore, unless you are already fairly disciplined, this course may not be for you.

The general course outlines, lessons, assignments, projects, or anything else of that nature is posted on your course's Web page

You have some say in how you'll communicate. You could work largely by email or talk to the teachers regularly via chat. You could post back and forth on the message board. Again, this is what makes Clonlara unique; there is no one way which they use for everybody. It depends on what you plan on doing within CompuHigh.

To view the Web pages, any browser and modem speed will do (though faster is better and you'll need Netscape 2 or up to see the animated GIFs). To deal with the bulletin boards, however, I would recommend you have at least a 14.4 modem; like any well-used bulletin boards, they have miles of posts and it can take a long time to load. To use their chat, you need a Java-capable Web browser and a fairly good computer. Web chat reloads every two seconds and when you have a lot of messages to look through and a Web page to generate every two seconds, it can get bogged down and have errors. I would personally recommend Clonlara look into getting Internet Relay Chat server software.

Clonlara Compuhigh is well-staffed and the lessons are well-planned. You do need marginally good computer power and marginally good modem speed to use it, but due to its nature, you can use it with any system that has Java-capable Web browsers: Mac, PC, possibly Web TV, maybe even Amiga.

If you already are well-disciplined, organized, can make yourself do your work without being told to, can afford the price, and are looking for an online academy with no particular religious point of view, Compuhigh is an excellent way to handle a course—or a year—of homeschool. *Joseph Pride*

Eagle Christian High School does not have regular "meetings," like a number of other online academies, but rather offers its courses on the Web through correspondence. You visit the Web page for the class you're taking. There you read the assignments for the week and download audio and video clips for the lessons. You then do the required reading as specified in the assignments, write up the required exercises, and email the completed work to your teacher.

None of the books or software required for the courses come free with them, though most of the required software is available free from its author. Some of the software necessary to run the courses may not be available for the Mac; in this case they recommend you obtain a PC emulator, such as *PC Access* or *RealPC*.

Each course comes with a complete list of books. You can buy them from Eagle Christian High School or most bookstores. Also, most courses require you have a CD-ROM encyclopedia handy.

One unique item in Eagle Christian High School's curriculum is its eighth grade math book. While it's not printed in color or in very high resolution, it still has enough visuals to teach math effectively. You probably have never seen a textbook which combines Christianity, math history, and math so seamlessly.

Eagle plans to produce a CD-ROM to accompany this math course in the future. They plan to include video clips of the teacher explaining each math lesson and demonstrating how to do the problems, color illustrations, and so on. CDs are under development for other classes as well. Likely the CD-ROMs will be only compatible with Windows. Sorry, Mac users!

When a student is admitted, a parent manual is sent. This manual includes a checklist to make sure all requirements have been met before the first day of classes. This includes information to help you make sure your computer system and Eagle Christian High's computer system are compatible. You and your student will be asked to send e-mail messages, include attachments, scan and send documents, etc. The Eagle staff will do the same on their end to make sure that the student can read messages from the school and that the school can read theirs.

Eagle Christian High School 2000–2001 School Calendar

Fall Semester:

Classes begin	Sept. 5, 2000	(Wednesday)
Thanksgiving Break	Nov. 23–24, 2000	(Friday–Sunday)
Finals Week	Jan. 3–7, 2000	(Monday–Friday)

Spring Semester:

Classes begin	Jan. 18, 2001	(Monday)
President's Day	February 19, 2001	
Easter Break	April 13–16	(Thursday–Monday)
Finals Week	May 21–25	(Monday–Friday)

Summer Semester

Classes Begin	June 5, 2000	(Monday)
Progress Report	July 5, 2000	(Wednesday)
Last Day of Classes	July 28, 2000	(Friday)

Eagle Christian High School gives official grades, by a standard grading scale. If you so request, Eagle Christian High School will send out your high school transcript to the university or high school of your choice. The first three transcripts are free, and additional transcripts cost $3 each.

Eagle Christian High School most definitely does not like cheating of any kind, and your test proctor may not be a member of your family, but rather should be an "official" such as a pastor, librarian, or the like.

Each course lasts two semesters. You may sign a full-time student up for $750 per semester, for which you get six classes. Alternatively, you could sign up for individual classes at $150 each. If you sign up by June 1, there is no registration fee. If you sign up by July 1, the registration fee is $50. If you sign up by August 1, the registration fee is $100. You may still sign up after August if space is available, but you'll have to pay an additional $100. If you pay in advance, you get a discount of 5 percent. Otherwise, you must pay 40 percent by September, 30 percent more by October, and the last 30 percent by November.

Students starting classes during Spring semester or Summer Semester will be required to pay a nonrefundable $25 registration fee to accompany the application. The deadline for applying for admission for Spring Semester 2001 is December 15, 2000. The deadline for Summer Session 2001 is May 3, 2001.

At the moment, Eagle Christian High School offers the following courses:

Bible

- Life of Christ—The Beginning Years of Ministry—Grade 7
- Life of Christ—The Final Two Years of Ministry—Grade 8
- Old Testament Survey—Grade 9
- New Testament Survey—Grade 10
- Life in Christ—Grade 11
- Evidences—Grade 12

Business Skills

- Keyboarding—Grade 9
- Accounting—Grade 10
- Beginning Web Design
- Advanced Web Design

English

- English 7—Grade 7
- English 8—Grade 8
- Communications—Grade 9
- American Literature—Grade 10
- British Literature—Grade 11
- Great Books—Grade 12
- Writing for Publication
- AP English Composition

Fine Arts

- Introduction to Art—Grade 9
- Music Appreciation—Grade 10
- Grade 11 courses are still under development
- Music Theory—Grade 12

Foreign Language

- German 1—Grade 9
- German 2—Grade 10
- Spanish 1—Grade 9
- Spanish 2—Grade 10

Physical Education

- Junior High Physical Education—Grade 7–8
- Health and Physical Education—Grade 9–10

History

- The 20th Century: 1900–1950—Grade 7
- The 20th Century: 1950–2000—Grade 8
- World Studies—Grade 10
- U.S. History—Grade 11
- Government and Economics—Grade 12

Math

- Arithmetic 7—Grade 7
- Pre-Algebra—Grade 8
- Algebra 1—Grade 9
- Geometry—Grade 10
- Algebra 2—Grade 11
- Advanced Math—Grade 12
- Consumer Math—Grade 12

Science

- Life Science—Grade 7
- Physical Science—Grade 8
- Biology—Grade 9
- Environmental Science—Grade 10
- Chemistry—Grade 11
- Physics—Grade 12
- Anatomy and Physiology

Minimum System Requirements for Eagle Christian High School

Pentium133, 4x CD-ROM, 33.6 modem. Windows 3.1 or higher; browser such as Internet Explorer or Netscape.

Recommended System Requirements

Pentium 200 or higher, a 8x or higher CD-ROM, and a 33.6 or higher modem. Windows 95 is recommended, and Internet Explorer 4.0 or higher is also recommended. A scanner and the ability to fax is recommended and is required for some classes. Black and white scanners are fine for all classes except Art classes, which require the use of a color scanner.

NEW!
Escondido Tutorial Service
Grades 6-12. Each semester course, $105.
2634 Bernardo Avenue, Escondido, CA 92029. (619) 746-0980. Email: gbt@gbt.org. Web: www.gbt.org.

Fritz Hinrichs as he appears on realtime video from his monitor-top video camera

If you sign up additional children at the same time, you can save 25 percent off the course price for the second child, 40 percent off the price for the third, and 50 percent off the price for the fourth and any beyond that.

Eagle Christian High School operates on a two-semester schedule, plus one summer session. The fall semester begins the first week of September and ends in early January. The spring semester begins mid-January and ends in late May. The summer session begins in early June and continues until the end of July. If you intend to sign up for both semesters of any course, starting right in the middle of December, you're out of luck. Also, this means the schedule is much more difficult to adapt to your own life or your normal learning speed; the entire class has to go by the same schedule.

Eagle Christian High School is probably the closest you can come to a private high school while still performing the schoolwork in your own home. The structure is already supplied, the teachers evaluate every student regularly, and you have an official high school transcript and record, including Grade Point Average, which may both be difficult to manage in a non-traditional education like many homeschools. This venue of study is recommended for those who love having everything structured, planned, and professional, and not for those who like some latitude in schedule and method. The books are well-chosen, the courses are carefully planned, and the whole thing will look excellent on a college application. I imagine other high schools and colleges will be offering their courses online before long; this is a great way to get an official school record while still operating out of your own home. *Joseph Pride*

Escondido Tutorial Service

If you want to attend the cutting edge in Internet classrooms, **Escondido Tutorial Service** will take you there. What started as a simple text-based tutorial service has grown into a full-fledged conferencing system for interactive education.

Fritz Hinrichs is the man behind it all. He is a graduate of St. John's College in Annapolis, Maryland, and has also studied at Westminster Seminary. Effecting a merger of his scholastic backgrounds, Fritz adds a dose of classical theology and Christian thought to the "classical education" approach that St. John's is known for.

While in seminary, Fritz Hinrichs initially planned on becoming a philosophy professor. But he saw that most of the conventional college teaching situations were very unstimulating—consisting of lecturing, extensive publishing, and little interaction with students. In his opinion, colleges were taking a cookie-cutter approach to training their students; they were educational "factories" where mass production rather than individual crafts-

manship was the norm. (Perhaps as an extension of this interest in "individual craftsmanship," Fritz also works as a cabinet maker. When not running tutorials, he uses his summers to build furniture, including Jack Bean and early-American reproductions.)

Nate and Rachel Ahern

Fritz became convicted about the poor quality of high-school education, realizing that by the time most students get to college, it's really too late to set them on a path of real intellectual life. After determining that there was a need to start teaching important materials to students when they are younger, Fritz began meeting lots of homeschoolers. According to Mr. Hinrichs, "I basically said, 'These kids are mature, they're ready to learn, and these are the types of kids who are ready to engage in mature discussion of good literature.'" He started volunteering, working with local students and putting on classes on math and Shakespeare as needed. He also taught part-time at a local Christian school.

After working with the local students for a year, Fritz decided to start the Great Books Tutorial, operating it out of his home. Now he could offer homeschoolers a solid education in classic literature, in a small-class environment conducive to discussion.

Thanks to Internet technology, the walls of his classroom environment now extend to include students all over the United States. There are now

Members of the geometry tutorial (clockwise from top): Fritz Hinrichs, Eric Youngdale, Becky Erickson, Jacob Smith, Josh Stacey, David Wojnicki, David Newheiser.

over 50 students participating in one or more of Escondido Tutorial Service's classes.

The heart of Escondido Tutorial Service is the Great Books Tutorial. Designed as a six-year program, the Great Books Tutorial is a comprehensive study of the writings and ideas which have shaped our culture and history.

Instead of artificially parsing the humanities into separate distinct subjects, a classical education looks at the great works of history and brings together the ideas that influenced our history, government, philosophy, theology, and literature.

Ideally, a student would begin the GBT at age 12, so they can complete the full tutorial by the time they complete high school. "But that's pretty challenging," says Fritz. "It takes a really good student." To accommodate individual needs, students have started the tutorial as late as the age of 16.

We interviewed a number of Fritz Hinrichs' students, and will be including their comments throughout the rest of this article.

The great books curriculum spans a variety of authors, languages, and centuries. Starting with Homer's *Iliad* and *Odyssey*, the reading list for the tutorial continues with works such as Aristotle's *Poetics*, Plato's *Republic*, Virgil's *Aeneid*, Augustine's *Confessions*, Dante's *Divine Comedy*, Shakespeare's *Hamlet* and *Macbeth*, Descartes' *Discourse on Method*, Hume's *Treatise on Human Nature*, Smith's *Wealth of Nations*, Nietzsche's *Beyond Good and Evil*, and Tocqueville's *Democracy in America*. Students who complete the tutorial will have been exposed to the great pivotal works of Western thought.

Nate Ahern, age 15, says:

"Geometry is taught using an approach very different from what is common in modern schools. Using Euclid's *Elements* as a text, we see how each proposition is constructed from nothing—how it is proved. In this way, geometry facts such as the famous Pythagorean Theorem are not taken for granted, but understood. Each week we are assigned several propositions to complete as homework, and we must articulate the reasons for each step of the proposition. When class time arrives, a die is rolled to randomly choose students to prove each proposition for the class. This procedure can be quite intimidating, but it usually ensures that every student is prepared with his or her homework before class."

Rachel Ahern, age 16, says:

"In addition to the Great Books Tutorial, I am taking a course from Mr. Hinrichs on Euclid's *Elements*. Aristotle discusses the necessity of a 'first principle,' or foundational assertion, behind everything. Such a principle is demonstrated by the 'elements,' the basic proofs governing all geometry. By going through the geometric proofs one by one, seeing how each builds upon the things previously proven, I can understand the reason behind all the rules we must simply assume in a modern geometry course.

"As with all ETS courses, reading Euclid enables me to go back to the original source material of an academic field instead of simply reading about it from a textbook. I have enjoyed and learned much from the Great Books approach to education afforded by ETS."

David Newheiser, age 15, says:

"One area of schooling which is often overlooked in our day is the reading of the classics. Some say that because we live in a modern age, the classics are irrelevant. But the classics are especially relevant in our day; only by learning from the past can we be prepared the future.

"The reason the reading of the classics is overlooked is obvious; very few have the knowledge required to understand, much less teach, the classics. Fritz Hinrichs not only has a knowledge of literature in general, but also a passion for the classics which he imparts to his students. I have had the privilege of taking several classes from Mr. Hinrichs including the Great Books Tutorial.

"Mr. Hinrichs knows the classics backward and forward, but he also serves to make the books interesting. Because he uses the Socratic method, the class is not a lecture, but interactive instead. He questions us on key sections of the text, leading to lively debate among students while Mr. Hinrichs gently guides the course of debate. He challenges us to think independently and figure out the answers.

"It is not always easy to read classics. But the GBT class does alleviate some of the strain. In each class we read over the crucial parts of the text. As we go along, Mr. Hinrichs asks us to explain the passage. If we cannot, he explains it to us. This serves to help us better understand the text.

"Another big part of the class is writing. This is the part on which we are evaluated. After we finish reading each book, we are usually asked to write a paper on that particular work. I'm not talking about a typical book report here; but a deep, in-depth paper. The style of paper we write often differs depending on the type of book we are studying, but we are definitely encouraged to examine the text in-depth. It proves whether or not we actually know the text.

"After we turn in our papers, Mr. Hinrichs proceeds to tear apart the grammar, writing, and content. I have to say that, even though getting my

The number of classes offered through ETS is growing, and includes:

- Biblical Courtship/Christian Home
- Classic Christian Literature
- C.S. Lewis
- Essay Writing
- Geography
- Geology
- Geometry Tutorial
- Great Books Tutorial
- Global Science
- God's Law and Civil Government
- Greek Tutorials (Koine and Classical)
- History of Christianity
- The History Forum
- Latin Tutorial
- Logic Tutorial
- New Testament Survey
- Rhetoric Tutorial
- Saxon Tutorials (Algebra 1/2, Algebra 1, Algebra 2, Advanced Math, and Physics)
- Shakespeare Tutorial

All courses involve a combination of readings outside class, various writing assignments, and group discussion during the two-hour class sessions each week.

Each course runs during the traditional school year.

Interested parents and students need to bear in mind that Escondido Tutorial Service is just that—a tutorial service, and not a school. Consequently, ETS does not offer grades at the conclusion of each course. Fritz describes himself as "talking curriculum," and he best describes his program this way: "For the homeschoolers who have their own independent study program or their own service that they're going through to keep their records, I am just coming in and giving the teaching." For some courses, he does offer an evaluation at the end of the semester. But that is more his way of keeping in touch with the parents than something that you could take to a school as a record of the student's performance.

After experiencing the chat sessions on America Online and realizing, "Hey, this would be a great way of getting people together," Fritz Hinrichs first took his Great Books Tutorial online in the fall of 1994, running class sessions on America Online. When AOL became too expensive, it migrated over to the Town Hall forum on Compuserve. But when Compuserve also became too expensive, Fritz took ETS off and got a real Internet account. That's when things really took off.

He began using Internet Relay Chat (IRC), a text-based interface similar to the chat features of AOL and Compuserve. There were about eight students at that time, and they used IRC the whole school year. Then, in the summer of 1996 Fritz discovered RealAudio and began moving the tutorials over to that format. As he describes it, "With this one-way audio, I started doing broadcasting. It was like having a radio station, though nobody could talk back to you." That's when Fritz decided he needed additional telephone lines. With six phone lines, students could respond via audio by calling in.

Though students could now participate in a live audio tutorial, Fritz conceded that this arrangement was somewhat unsatisfactory "because they'd have to initiate the call. And because RealAudio had about a 10-second delay, I would say something and about 10 seconds later they would start to respond over the telephone. That was a hindrance."

The next development came with CU-SeeMe. With CU-SeeMe came two-way audio, text chat, and whiteboarding capabilities. This was the answer to the audio delay problem. As an example, Fritz described his Great Books 2 class. "There are four students that have two-way audio, and we just have a normal conversation—it's like a conference call. It's really delightful. I got so frustrated with the typing that it's a really wonderful thing now to have these kids talking and articulating themselves, and really interacting in a very human way."

Fritz Hinrichs' office and classroom has the appearance of a mini radio station. He has two computers, one to handle the RealAudio broadcasting, the other to handle the CU-SeeMe audio. To the left of his desk is a mixing board which takes in the various audio inputs and combines them for broadcast back out over the RealAudio and CU-SeeMe. There are five microphones—two on the speakerphones, one condenser mike that sits on the table to pick up the live students' voices, another voice mike, and an announcer's mike for Mr. Hinrichs.

For the geometry tutorial, there are eight local students and five online students. With audio coming from the speakerphones, the live students, and the CU-SeeMe, plus the text input from the students without two-way audio, it really is a collaborative situation between the local and the online students.

The other benefit of CU-SeeMe is its whiteboarding capability. Fritz can display a picture, and then add notes by "drawing" on the picture. Essentially, it is a digital chalkboard. Fritz can paste a geometric diagram on the whiteboard, and then ask students to mark the congruent angles. Or, he can paste up a map of Greece and mark the various military campaigns.

But the CU-SeeMe audio isn't ideal for all situations. Fritz says that he'll use CU-SeeMe when he ask a student a question in class at random. But he adds, "If I'm going to have one student read a part of the text or demonstrate something, I'll have them call in. When you're using CU, there's about a three-second delay between the time your comment is done and you hear the other person responding. But when you're on the phone, you can just go back and forth."

Not all of his students have the computer capability to use CU-SeeMe, however, so he still keeps the text chat and RealAudio broadcasting going. The RealAudio is used by Mac people so they can receive one-way audio, while the IBM folks can get the two-way through CU-SeeMe. But for people on Macs, the software has not been developed for them to do the two-way audio successfully, even though CU-SeeMe has promised a Mac version. So there are still students who need to type back and forth.

Fritz concedes that this is a problem. "The people who are just typing their responses get blown away because a conversation moves so much faster than they can move their fingers." By not adopting a standard system, more students have been able to participate in the tutorials. Nevertheless, working with diverse systems has its problems. Taking a bold step toward system compatibility, the decision was made that anybody who is a new student with ETS will have to have a Pentium Windows 95 machine. "After a year with trying to do cross-platform teaching and dealing with the instabilities," Fritz said, "I have resigned myself to the fact that I will not be able to handle the technical aspects of getting all the different platforms to work together."

But Fritz is excited about the change. Everyone having the same platform offers the added benefit of being able to transfer files back and forth without conversion problems, whether it be students turning in assignments or Fritz distributing class notes.

first paper back covered with red marks wasn't a pleasant experience, it definitely taught me to write better. While my writing is still not as good as some, it is definitely better than when I began the Great Books Tutorial.

"I am beginning to discover that life is enigmatic. That is, the answers are not always clear-cut. By taking the GBT I have learned to think, to debate, to write, and to read difficult books. As I see the rest of my generation search in futility for answers, I count myself fortunate to have been taught to think and reason."

Maggie Porter, age 12, says:
"I've been a student at Escondido Tutorial Services for two years now. The textbooks we are using for the Logic course are *Introductory Logic* and *Intermediate Logic*. I have found most of the assignments in Logic class to be fun. I've learned to identify fallacies and listen for validity in people's arguments. Most of the time we have three exercises to do for homework. During class, we are asked to do individual problems from that week's homework, then we cover the next week's lesson and Mr. Hinrichs gives us a few examples and explains new concepts.

"One of the most interesting and challenging assignments we had in Logic this year was to debate a topic. I had to argue that Odysseus would be a better hero than Achilles for athletic youths to admire at the local gym. I had never done a debate before and I was very nervous, but somehow I made it through; and in the end it was fun."

Since the original review of ETS was published, Escondido Tutorial Service has become a truly virtual classroom, supporting two-way audio and video of professor and student, at least for those with fast modems, As Fritz says about the video, it's just "a little window with my face in it," which redraws every half minute or so, meaning you catch the prof in a variety of odd facial expressions.

Fritz adds, "Until the video becomes high-resolution, there's not much teaching benefit to it. It's basically, 'Oh neat, look at the teacher's face.' I could never do anything like have a video of my chalkboard, write on it, and have students be able to look at it. That won't be feasible until you have a much-higher-resolution video signal, which will take a lot more bandwidth. I don't see that happening very soon. But to have them see my face and hear the audio at the same time is actually something that is fairly near in the future."

Instead of focusing on the video, Fritz Hinrichs sees the digital whiteboard as the real future and development of online schooling. The video will simply be there to let you see people's faces. ("What would be really valuable is the capability to see all the students' faces in order to see who's paying attention," Fritz says. Spoken like a teacher!) But being able to do multi-point video—e.g. having 15 faces on the screen at once, with each one transmitting video—that will take a lot of bandwidth.

Escondido Tutorial Service has grown to the point that Fritz cannot take many more live students himself. Additional teachers have been added: even Mike Farris, founder of HSLDA, taught a course in person once! (That course is still available, minus the personal interaction with Mr. Farris.)

As the next big step, Fritz sees ETS as basically becoming an Internet broadcasting network rather than just a provider of individual live classes. He can save the class content and, using the RealAudio like a radio station, broadcast it so that people can freely visit the ETS web page and listen to the classes. People who are interested in the courses, can basically audit the courses for free. He hopes to be able to finance the service by offering advertising on his web site.

Fritz Hinrichs is excited about his ideas for the future, and the prospect for making the class content widely available. "Working with RealAudio in this way," he says, "I can basically take thousands of students, and have a much wider impact on Christian education beyond just the students I can teach one-on-one."

This tutor of the Great Books has a vision for teaching. Guided by that vision, Escondido Tutorial Service is well on its way to having a world-wide impact, offering a quality, classical, Christian education from a simple office in Escondido, California. *Christopher Thorne*

NEW!
Laurel Springs School

Grades 5–12. About $2,500 per year (one 10-month period). Enrollment fee, covers entire family for one year, is based on highest grade: preschool, $125; 1–8, $275; 9–12, $315. Transcript fee, $25; Curriculum fee, $85/course, covers basic materials and books; Tuition: Two courses, $850; three courses, $1,150; four courses, $1,450; five courses, $1,750; six courses, $2,050. Families can elect to pay the fees in 10 monthly installments.

Southern California may be the home of Hollywood and Disneyland, but it is also home to one of the country's most innovative independent study programs, **Laurel Springs School**.

From its home in the city of Ojai, Laurel Springs is working with nearly 2,000 students to provide them with customized curricula and flexible learning programs. Laurel Springs first offered an online learning program in 1994, and it has grown in size and recognition since then. There are now approximately 1000 students taking part in online classes, and the school has received significant media attention, including a feature story on the *Today Show.*

Laurel Springs began their independent study program back in 1991, under the leadership of Marilyn Mosley, the school's director. The goal is to provide families with an educational program which gives them maximum flexibility to pursue their own interests, and offers many different learning options.

Laurel Springs School, PO Box 1440, Ojai, CA 93024-1440. (800) 377-5890. (805) 646-2473. Fax: (805) 646-0186. Email: info@laurelsprings.com. Web: www.laurelsprings.com.

> "Everyone has their own style of learning, and Laurel Springs is fit to your individual needs as a student."
> —*Alissa Ivanovich*

The Online Learning Program continues that tradition. In addition to families having the freedom to set their own school schedules, students also gain experience with the latest computer technology. Through Internet research and email correspondence, students put their reading and writing skills to the test, and broaden their education beyond the textbook.

> *"Our mission is to create innovative educational programs that elicit young people's innate love of learning, and pride in their own achievements and abilities. We believe children benefit most from an educational process which respects an individual approach to learning. Our purpose is to spark each child's natural curiosity, and to direct their enthusiasm for learning in ways that will help them mature and engage meaningfully in the world around them."*

Laurel Springs director Marilyn Mosley

What is a typical online class like? Each week, students receive their class assignments via email. Then, students visit specific web sites to fulfill class assignments, or to do self-directed research. At the end of each week, the students email their assignments back to their teacher for comment and review.

"We try to combine different kinds of assignments, each of which require different skill levels," says Marilyn Mosley. "Usually in an online course the students are looking at web sites, reading the material and assessing the information, and answering a number of questions that involve critical thinking. Then they're normally asked to do one essay."

According to Marilyn, the high-school online program is modeled after colleges in that they emphasize essay-writing. Any time a student sends in a paper, he will receive an in-depth response from the teacher. Though some teachers offer final exams, many times they opt for research papers. The big difference is that Laurel Springs students are never forced to take a timed test, or to compete for grades with other children.

Jill Watkins conversing with a student

"I like Laurel Spring school very much because I can work at my own pace every week. Also, I think the curriculum is written very well and the assignments are easy to understand."
—*Paul Christal*

Students Eva Beck, age 14 & Katie Rosinsky, age 10

An online class is like email with an IQ!
—*Alissa Ivanovich*

The students really seem to enjoy this new learning method. Kai, a Laurel Springs student who lives in Japan, says, "Using the Internet makes it possible to get a wide variety of information—much more than I had access to before. My early years of homeschooling were hard because we live in the country in Japan and there is no English library nearby. We had to order books ahead of time and use the encyclopedia, but something was always missing." Kerrick Hodge says, "I come across more information in one day's research on the Internet than I could glean in a month from some 40-year-old textbook."

The teachers obviously play a vital role in the Online Learning Program. All of the 60 teachers who are part of Laurel Springs are trained to do the online program. Marilyn emphasized that they are very conscientious about assigning a teacher to each student for every class they take. That teacher is responsible for staying in touch with that child, sending them email, and working with them on their coursework.

Vicky recently moved to the United States from Australia. One of the first things she noticed was how quickly she heard back from her teachers. "I always hear back within a couple of days of sending in my assignment," she says.

Combining Internet resources and software, students receive true multimedia instruction. Of course, students are welcome to supplement their courses with field trips or experiments. For example, science instructors will work with students to construct appropriate lab exercises.

When asked about the issue of creation vs. evolution, and its place in their science curriculum, Marilyn said that they don't want anyone to do work that they don't believe in or that they are unhappy about. "If a family comes to us and their perspective on origins is creation, we have a couple of teachers who know this information, and they will use their own textbooks, such as ones from Bob Jones or A Beka. Although it is not in our normal curriculum, we will create a program to make sure they can work in that fashion."

Laurel Springs offers a full selection of online high-school courses for its students:

- Computer Science (Introduction to the Internet)
- English (Reading Literature, World Literature, American Literature, and English Literature, Creative Writing, and honors and non-honors English Fundamentals)
- Math (Algebra 1, Algebra 2, Trigonometry, Geometry, and Calculus)
- Social Studies (Cultural Geography, World History, American History, and Government and Economics)
- Science (Biology, Physics, Chemistry, honors and non-honors Earth Science, Oceanography, General Science, and Health)
- Foreign Language (Spanish and French)
- Fine Arts (Art History)

The school, which considers "life and learning to be one and the same," will also work with students to provide elective credit for other educational experiences. Physical Education credit can be given for aerobics, baseball, martial arts, and even surfing. Fine Arts credit can be given for art, dance, acting, instrumental or vocal music, and fashion design. Students can also receive credit for travel, gardening, mentoring, an apprenticeship, or workstudy.

Laurel Springs is an official, fully licensed California private school. In every course, and at every grade level, each child's performance is graded. These academic records are maintained in the administrative office, and the teachers update these records every semester. This allows your child to graduate with a complete transcript, and makes transferring to another private or public school simple.

Graduation requires completion of 225 units of credit. Each year-long class earns the student 10 units of credit. A year consists of 36 weeks of work, with a minimum of 4 hours of study per week in each major subject.

Every graduating teenager will receive an academic diploma for their school work. It is valid towards any college or university they choose to attend after graduation. And if you want to make the trip to Ojai, California, they provide a formal graduation ceremony at the end of each school year.

Though Laurel Springs has a traditional school year for those families that want to follow it, they operate year-round. Many of their students do coursework during the summer, or just take one class for the summer. When asked about their school schedule, Marilyn said, "From my experience of having directed independent study for 25 years, some families need to have the feeling that they can stop for the summer because the parents get so burned out. So we wanted to make sure the parents had the permission to do that. But we also wanted to make sure that if a child was really motivated and they want to work during the summer that they have the freedom to do that as well. So we stay open year-round."

Laurel Springs is always looking for innovative ways to make their courses more exciting, and listening to what parents want. For example, they created a project-based curriculum for children in grades K–8 that's much more hands-on, combining art and good literature and history.

The high-school hands-on program was added because if students—especially young boys —have been in a regular public high school and they're unhappy, by the time they're 16 they are so burned out on school that to bring them to Laurel Springs and still hand them a textbook won't work; they can't make that transition. Marilyn tells us, "I think that burnout is a result of the public school problem. So we're creating more project-based curriculum for those children who need it. I'm really happy that we can do this for students."

That's not all that is in the works. An honors program has been started, and Laurel Springs is also working towards becoming licensed by the authors of *Discover Your Child's Learning Style* as one of the first schools to implement their Learning Styles Model. (See chapter 11 for details.)

As an added bonus to students and their parents, Laurel Springs also has a college counselor on staff. She reviews every child's records and will work individually with each family to make sure that they're ready for the college of their choice. It can be difficult to keep up with the changing laws and college-admission criteria, but Laurel Springs wants to be prepared and support its families with their college plans.

With a focus on pursuing an "active style of learning," Laurel Springs is helping students—from California and beyond—take full advantage of the educational resources available from around the world. All from your home computer. *Christopher Thorne*

Howard and Susan Richman, periodic contributors to *Practical Homeschooling*, are also the directors of **Pennsylvania Homeschoolers**— one of the first homeschool state groups to actively move to the Internet. Through their work with academic competitions and college-preparatory exams, the Richmans have paved the way for helping homeschoolers move to the next level of educational success.

The Richmans and their colleagues have done a lot of work in bringing AP exams (national advanced placement exams administered by the College Board) to the attention of homeschoolers. Through Advanced Placement, students can receive college credit in a variety of subject areas, if the college of their choice so chooses, by earning a passing score on the corresponding exam. (Just about every college does grant AP credit.)

> "Instead of regurgitating information from a book and lectures to please the egomaniacal whims of some uninterested, uninteresting teacher, I am actually researching and applying all of the required information for my classes."
> —*Kerrick Hodge*

*Ramaa Mosley,
graduate of Laurel Springs & Bennington College*

NEW!
Pennsylvania Homeschoolers Online AP Courses

Grades 9–12. Course fees, from $225 to $400 each online AP course.

Course materials (books, videos, etc.) extra.

Pennsylvania Homeschoolers, R. D. 2, Box 117, Kitanning, PA 16201. Phone/fax: (412) 783-6512. Email: richmans@pahomeschoolers.com. Web: www.pahomeschoolers.com.

Main menu shows courses available, how they work

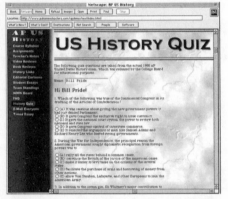

The very cool U.S. history demo site includes this self-checking quiz

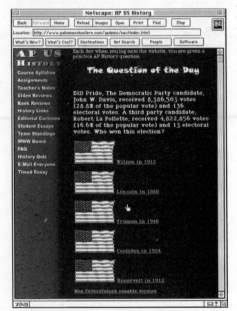

Students get points for completed work and extra research. Student points count towards their team's total. Competition is fierce!

To help homeschoolers prepare for and pass the AP exams, Susan and Howard Richman have organized a number of online courses, taught by a variety of teachers and tailored to the subject matter of the AP exams.

Considering the present cost of higher education, the registration fee for an AP exam (about $70) is minimal compared to the price of college tuition for just one course (the average is around $1,500). By successfully taking several AP exams, your student could eliminate the equivalent of one semester of college—or more! Also, the first two years of college traditionally focus on liberal arts requirements in the humanities and social sciences; and "liberal arts" is increasingly taking on a politically-correct flavor—something to which we might want to minimize our children's exposure. And of course there's cost. Who wouldn't want the chance to save thousands of dollars on college tuition by getting college credit out of the way while still in high school?

To get a better idea of what the Advanced Placement program is all about, Susan Richman suggests you spend some time at the College Board web site (*www.collegeboard.com*) looking over the background information for each exam.

So what can you expect from a Pennsylvania Homeschoolers online course? Each course has different computer requirements (some will tax your modem more than others), but all courses require basic email capability. Some courses, such as AP US History, have a full multimedia web site devoted to the course on which students can view course information, take interactive quizzes, post messages to other students, and more. To see a "demo" version of the AP US History web site, take a look at *www.pahomeschoolers.com/apdemo*.

The courses currently being offered for the 2000–2001 school year are:

- AP Art History
- AP English Language & Composition (2 sections)
- AP English Literature & Composition
- AP French Language & Composition
- AP Macro Economics
- AP Music Theory
- AP Psychology
- AP U.S. History
- AP U.S. Government and Politics

Each course starts in September and runs for the traditional school year.

Before you consider signing up for an AP-level course, you should make sure you have a solid background in the material being studied. Take the time to look at the College Board descriptions of the exams and prepare yourself for the courses. One of my kids missed taking AP English because he didn't send the email form in on time, so don't wait until the last minute to sign up your student. Be sure you contact the course instructor a few months prior to the start of the course to check on space and availability.

Once you have registered for the course, you can expect to spend a lot of time. For some courses, spending two hours a day for reading and writing assignments is not unusual. Depending on the course, you will receive course assignments via email or read them on the web. You can also send comments to other students in the class by email, or you can post questions and comments on the class web site.

Even if you are not presently interested in having your children actively prepare for the AP exams, take a look at what Pennsylvania Homeschoolers is doing with the World Wide Web. Their U.S. History course design is a model for what I'd like to see other people doing with their courses. Quizzes, reading assignments, and comments from other students and the teachers are all available right on the web. This is the future of high-school and college homeschooling. And you heard about it here first! *Mary Pride*

Lessons from Outer Space

HomeSAT

Grades K5–12. Complete HomeSAT startup kit, $279.90. HomeSAT services, $39.95 a month for 10 months/year. Registration fees: $10/course, K5–grade 8; $40/course, grades 9–12. *HomeSAT, 800-739-8199. Fax: (888-525-8398. Email: hsatinfo@bju.edu. Web: www.homesat.com.*

All around this big round hunk of dirt and water we refer to as "earth," Christian home educators are using signals beamed from space to teach their children.

Are the transmissions coming from aliens? No, these homeschoolers are using **HomeSAT** courses, broadcast by satellite from Bob Jones University, to teach their children.

Why would homeschoolers want to use a literal "satellite" program?

Here are some answers:

- Many homeschool parents either do not have the time or do not have the confidence to properly teach the more difficult courses like chemistry, foreign languages, or advanced math.

- Many missionaries and home educators in remote lands cannot receive steady mail service and do not have quality schools near them.

- Many people in the military have children, but have to move all the time, cannot settle their children in any school for long, and do not have the time left over to teach more difficult school subjects.

In all these cases, these families need steady help, anywhere in the world, any time of the year, to give their children a quality education.

For many, the BJUP satellite courses are invaluable.

What does HomeSAT offer over its three channels of education and entertainment?

- Preschool, elementary, and high school courses especially for homeschoolers

- Christian living seminars and other family-oriented programming

- College courses, Bible courses, and 24-hour Christian music

When you sign up for a course, HomeSAT not only provides lessons for the students, but also instructions for the parents, with activities, assignments, and everything you need to teach your children, *except* the actual textbooks, science lab supplies, and whatnot. Those you'll still

HomeSat

need to purchase from Bob Jones University Press.

For the elementary courses, offered via HomeSAT's BJ Help Network, the teachers try to spice it up with puppets, little video clips for examples of various topics, experiments, and more.

The "BJ LINC" high school courses don't have quite as much of this. They have the lesson material and some visuals. Also, the high school courses don't seem to move quite as fast. These are classes offered to high schools all around the United States, by which the whole class can actually interact with the teacher. Very beneficial for the high schools, but not so beneficial for homeschoolers who

don't have the LINC keypads and communicators. Home educators must still sit through tests given via the keypads and ten or twenty minutes per class of the teacher speaking to various high school students.

As I know from experience, having used their chemistry and French courses, the classes take 45 minutes a day and could probably be compressed into 15 minutes if they were offered without BJ LINC. Perhaps in the future Bob Jones University could persuade its tutors to stay 15 minutes longer in order to perform a shorter version of the same class for homeschoolers. I know I would appreciate it!

HomeSAT used to only be available for several hours a day. Recently they have increased to 24-hour, 7-day service, and upgraded their signal to digital, allowing a clearer picture.

The complete starter kit includes the dish, antenna, cables, and receiver. To keep the service going you pay a monthly fee. While you can *watch* the classes for free, and even tape them for further viewings and restudy, don't forget that you need to pay the course registration fee to get the syllabus, assignments, grading info, and to allow your child to receive an official certificate of course completion.

All in all, this service, despite its minor drawbacks and the fact that it may be too expensive for some homeschoolers, is excellent for the homeschool mom who is unable to give the amount of time or expertise necessary to teach some classes. I would also highly recommend it to homeschoolers in "the middle of nowhere" or homeschoolers who are forced to move all the time. Just be sure that the child you intend to use it has a large enough attention span to sit through a 45-minute class. *Joseph Pride*

NEW!
The Potter's School

Grades 9–12. Each course $200–$300 tuition. Materials extra.
(360) 697-5819 Email: information@ pottersschool.com. Web: The Potter's School, www.pottersschool.com; The Potter's School Cooperative, www.pottersschool.com/cooperative; MrsG's Math Tutorials, www.pottersschool.com/mrsgsmath.

Mrs. Kerri Dennis, Parent, says:

"My husband and I have been so very impressed with Janna Gilbert, as a teacher of math (geometry in our case), as a guide to the technical world of online schooling, and for her excellent advice on the order and type of mathematics courses our children should pursue. The CU-SeeMe format seems to be ideally suited to online math instruction."

Jordan Mantha, Student, says:

"In the past two years I have taken Algebra II and Geometry online with Mrs. Janna Gilbert of Mrs. G's Math Tutorials. My online math classes have not only been a technological treat, but have also prepared me for my college-level math courses."

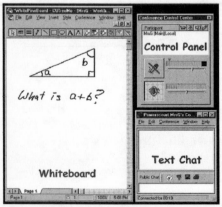

Whiteboard software allows the teacher to come up with freehand drawings and text

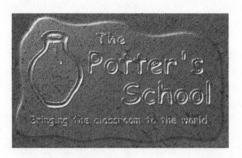

Online classes are often structured to foster cooperation, like students working with each other on collaborative essays or other projects. The Potter's School has extended that spirit of cooperation to its own design. Instead of one institution providing instruction in many subjects, The Potter's School brings together a number of teachers—a cooperative—who each independently teach their respective subjects. This buffet-style approach may in fact be the way that online instruction is headed.

What started with a limited but innovative number of course offerings in mathematics has grown into **The Potter's School Cooperative**, a full high-school level home education service specializing in the use of Internet videoconferencing to support distance learning. Its founders, Jeff and Janna Gilbert, are "seasoned veterans" in the world of online instruction—they have performed consulting for schools and corporations, and conducted numerous online education seminars and workshops.

The Potter's School is best known for their popular online math courses, Mrs. G's Math Tutorials, featuring direct instruction with live audio, an integrated whiteboard, and video. Now, in an effort to improve the quality and variety of online courses available to homeschoolers, The Potter's School has begun to assist other teachers in bringing classes to the Internet via videoconferencing. Together they have formed The Potter's School Cooperative, a growing group of independent online instructors.

Each instructor pledges to provide personalized instruction to the student, to honor the parent as the principal of the homeschool, and to be responsive to the needs of the customer—that is, the family. In addition to their academic credentials, the instructors have a wealth of teaching and homeschooling experience. The Cooperative's charter also includes a non-denominational statement of faith which declares commitment to the Christian Bible as "the perfect standard for faith and moral conduct and as the foundation for all instruction."

Cooperative instructors are truly independent, constrained only by their own voluntary pledge to support homeschooling ideals and standards of customer service. So teachers in the Cooperative are free to make the most of their courses.

All courses offered by The Potter's School Cooperative employ Internet videoconferencing for direct instruction. In addition to audio, visual aids—such as an integrated whiteboard, video for demonstrations, and web-based interactive slide shows—are employed extensively. Some courses also include collaborative projects, allowing students in geographically separated areas to work together.

Avoiding the temptation to pigeonhole students into a particular educational philosophy (such as "classical education"), The Potter's School prefers to let each homeschooling family choose the courses which best suit their needs. With this in mind, they will only sponsor a class if it meets their quality standards and if it does not compete with other existing high quality online courses. This is an innovative step—they will not provide courses simply for the purpose of rounding out their own curriculum. If another organization offers a high-quality online course that would suit the needs of students, why duplicate the effort?

Though it started in fall 1998 with a broad secondary core curriculum, The Potter's School Cooperative ultimately intends to feature a complete junior and senior high program. Toward that end they are continually interviewing additional instructors and planning new courses.

> **Minimum System Requirements for Potter's School**
>
> At least a Pentium 100 running Windows 95 with 24 MB RAM, a 28.8 kbps modem, and a sound card. To enhance your experience, they also suggest you also consider a drawing pad or even a camera (each costs approximately $100). All courses require White Pine's CU-SeeMe software. Unfortunately, CU-SeeMe for the Macintosh does not currently support a whiteboard, so students must have a PC to participate in their tutorials.

Potter's School Classes for 2000–2001

- **Christian Education:** Bible Survey, Understanding the Times.
- **English:** Grammar Review and Compositional Writing, American Literature (with a strong writing component), A Journey Through Narnia (junior high literature and writing), Writer's Workshop
- **Fantasy Literature** (2nd Semester)
- **Journalism**
- **Math:** Pre-Algebra; Algebra; Geometry; Advanced Algebra; Functions, Statistics, and Trigonometry
- **Science:** Biology, Chemistry, Logo to Legos
- **Science Fiction** (1st Semester)
- **Shakespeare**
- **Social Studies:** American History, World History, World Geography, Church History
- **Foreign Language:** German, Spanish, Latin 2

Scholar's Online Academy (SOLA) is sponsored by the non-profit Institute for Study of the Liberal Arts and Sciences (ISLAS), as is their sister Catholic online academy, Regina Coeli. SOLA has been offering quality online instruction since 1995, when my two oldest sons, Theodore (Ted) and Joseph (Joe), each took a slate of six courses apiece from SOLA. They and two other students participated as "beta testers" for the academy that year.

In its second full year of instruction, SOLA added 50 students to their college preparatory program. Currently, the level of participation has grown to approximately 100 students in their programs, which continue to emphasize a rigorous classical education that challenges the mind and nourishes the spirit.

These are genuine college-level courses, but with far more teacher input than a typical college course, making them suitable for serious high-school students. It has been tough, however, for many incoming students to adjust to the rigorous academic program. So in order to prepare students ages 10–13 for the college preparatory classes of SOLA, the staff formed the Agnus Dei Junior High in 1997–98, offering seven classes in literature, math, Latin, philosophy, and history.

All courses are taught from a classical Christian perspective. This means that you study works which traditionally have been considered the heart and soul of a college education, rather than today's trendy "politically correct" writings. This is especially evident in SOLA's Philosophy sequence. After the first year in which students are made familiar with philosophical terminology, logic, issues, and some major philosophers, two more courses are offered (Philosophy II & III), which delve deeper into metaphysical principles and philosophical ideas while still being grounded by and compared to fundamental truth.

SOLA emphasizes the classical liberal arts as goods within themselves rather than as mere utilitarian means to the end of "better jobs." And SOLA's course listing (given in the sidebar) is exactly what the doctor or-

NEW!
Scholar's Online Academy

Tuition: Most college preparatory courses, $300; Courses that meet twice a week, $350; Junior High courses, $250 per student. Summer course, $150. Registration fee: 3–5 classes, $100/student; 1–2 classes, $80/student. $350/class that meets for 90 minutes once or twice per week. $400/120-minute, twice-weekly class. $500/AP class, except AP Latin. Summer course, $30. Orientation class, $35.

ISLAS, 3 Nellis Terrace, Bedford, MA 01731. (520) 751-1942. Fax: (520) 751-2580. Email: admin@islas.org. Web: www.islas.org.

Assignments, course schedules, and other important information is in a password-protected area available to students only

2000–2001 ISLAS Academic Course Offerings

Scholars' Online Academy Courses
- **Science:** Natural Science, Biology, Chemistry, Physics, Astronomy
- **Languages:** Greek I–II, Greek III–IV, Latin AP, Introduction to Mediaeval Latin
- **Literature:** World Literature, Western Literature to Dante, English Literature, American Literature, AP English
- **History:** World History I, World History II
- **Writing Program:** Grammar I, Grammar II, Dialectic Course, Rhetoric Course

Regina Coeli Academy Courses
Regina Coeli Academy (RCA) is SOLA's sister school for Catholics
Algebra I, Geometry, Advanced Algebra, American History, American Government, History of the Catholic Church, Philosophy I, Latin I, Latin II, Latin III, Theology I–IV, Confirmation Class

dered for anyone whose student has been following the "classical education" method up to the high school level.

What's it like to actually *take* one of these courses? Here's our impression from our family's early experiences.

SOLA courses have books to read and assignments to complete just like regular courses. SOLA provided the 800 numbers so we could order the books from the publishers. In our case, it took a few weeks before all the books arrived, even though we paid for express shipping. Happily, you can now order all SOLA texts through their "St. John's Bookshoppe," accessible online through SOLA's main web address.

Meanwhile, we were getting to know the teachers. They introduced themselves through email, and also via a "Welcome to SOLA!" online chat before the semester started. The course syllabi and assignments also were sent to us by email.

Once the semester began, courses followed a more-or-less regular schedule. Chats for a given class would be scheduled for a particular day and time. The chats themselves consisted of teacher and students using the on-line medium to discuss readings and assignments, ask questions, and also enjoy fellowship together.

In fact, the degree of "togetherness" surprised many participants. As a matter of fact, an effort had to be made to cut down the online jokes and hi-jinks so classes could run more smoothly!

For our free-spirited sons, who were used to arranging schoolwork and studies around their hobbies, instead of the other way around, the SOLA schedule meant making some adjustments. Both quickly got in the habit of showing up for chats on time. Getting assignments in on time took a bit longer, with Ted (who is a year and a half older) finding it easier to get in the groove than Joseph, who was just the age for ninth grade. When they put in the effort, though, both boys found they could do the work, and even found it enjoyable.

Online homework does take longer, in some cases. For math class, at first the students were typing in the answers and sending them via email. As the algebra work became more difficult, this became unwieldy, so the instructor is considering moving towards having the students grade their own work and send in only the problems they got wrong. For most other courses, just sending the assignment answers is sufficient. However, this usually is a two-step process, with the student first writing down the answers, then transcribing them to the computer. English essays take no extra time, of course, since most students write them on the computer.

On the other hand, email interaction with the professor is more reliable than waiting around during a college professor's few visiting hours. And class discussions tend to be much more lively, especially Latin class, which can get downright hilarious. Linda Robinson, or "Magistra Robinson," as she likes to call herself online, gives the students a Latin sentence to translate, and counts down online: "Five-four-three-two-one-SPLAT!" As soon as she types "SPLAT!" everyone races to type in his or her translation. These range from correct to highly amusing, but nobody hangs back from "splatting" the best they can. Together the class figures out any dubious words or cases, until finally the right answer shines forth in all its grammatical glory.

Other classes, such as Biology, are considerably drier, but still fraught with interest as students and professor discuss not only answers to problems, but the implications of what they are learning.

New for interested parents: ISLAS is offering a tuition-free class in scholastic philosophy for parents only; tax-deductible donations will be accepted but are not required. It's a great way for you to test the waters of online learning for your family.

If the best indicator of success is the end product produced, then Scholar's Online is well on its way to a successful future. Last year, their three graduating seniors were all accepted to colleges of their choice with substantial academic scholarships. They are Rachel Ahern, attending Harvard; Ian Boudreau, attending Franciscan University; and Micah Valine, attending Canisius College. This is a very real testimony of the level of academic achievement fostered through SOLA's tutorials.

Here's something to watch for: SOLA also has plans to offer direct college credit as well as AP credit for students taking their upper-level courses. To that end, they are presently negotiating with one established accredited distance learning institution and with a new liberal arts college being established in New England.

ISLAS currently provides a safe chat environment for homeschooled students, including those not enrolled in their program. You will need standard IRC chat software. Email them for directions and channel signon information.

All SOLA students are registered and use a password to access the private area of SOLA's server, where class assignments and other course information is stored.

To expand the opportunity for more students to take advantage of online learning, a scholarship fund has been established.

Two of my three older children have taken SOLA's college-prep Latin courses, and my two "middler" students took their junior-high Latin. I still plan to learn Latin myself . . . someday . . . but in the meantime, SOLA has done the job for us. *Mary Pride*

Willoway's Main Page

Even the best online academies I've researched have done relatively little to tap the power of the Internet. The **Willoway CyberSchool** is different in many ways. For one thing, it offers the junior-high years. Most other online academies concentrate on the high-school years only. Willoway also offers a fully accredited high-school program.

For another thing, Willoway pushes the limits of what can be done educationally with the World Wide Web. Its emphasis: "producing technically literate students able to contribute in an ever-increasingly digital world." Its methodology: "We help the child develop the ability to recognize problems, take charge of their learning, and to take an active role in the responsibility of their education. Teachers act as guides in the teaching-learning process."

This is not just hot air. There's an awful lot of researching and hands-on Web work built into the Willoway curriculum, as you'll see.

Students at Willoway learn four different ways; through online collaborative projects, interactive online tutorials, conferencing, and the

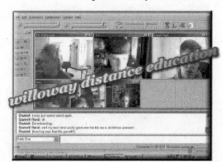

Willoway CyberSchool
Grades 7–12. Grades 7 & 8: Tuition, $2,250/year; $1,125/semester; monthly payment option: $125 due upon enrollment, $225/month September through June. Grades 9–12: $2,400/year; $1,200/semester; or $125 on enrollment and $240/month. Tuition is prorated if you enroll after September. 10% discount for second child. Software and books extra.
Willoway CyberSchool, 267 Mountain Top Rd., Reinholds, PA 17569.
Phone/fax: 610-678-0214.
Email: jbhale@ptd.net.
Web: www.willoway.com.

Main Student Entry to Assignment Arena and Student Center

Willotropolis Learning Community

Role Playing Robert E. Lee

daily assignment sheets. Examples of all four are provided on the web site. Be sure to explore the web site to see the virtual world Willoway students have created!

If your child isn't already Internet-savvy, Willoway will work to make him or her a World Wide Web whiz! Your child will learn how to use email, FTP (file transfer protocol), chat skills, video conferencing, 3D graphic design, animation, realaudio publishing, and all skills related to Web design. In addition, students learn how to use software packages relevant to different curriculum areas. These packages are not included in your child's curriculum price.

All this emphasis on technological savvy is intentional. Unlike other online academies, which basically substitute online technology for a traditional classroom environment (e.g., a RealAudio lecture instead of an in-person lecture, online chat instead of in-class discussion, online syllabi instead of classroom handouts), Willoway considers learning as much as possible about computers and the online world to be a major part of their curriculum. Willoway kids don't just get their assignments online: they create projects, individually and in teams, that are posted on Willoway's web site. The curriculum doesn't just include a few extra web links to explore for fun; much of the curriculum *is* following up web links and accessing the text, graphics, videos, and such stored at reliable sites about the subject currently being studied. Instead of writing pen-and-pencil reports, students create web pages, complete with graphics, detailing what they learned.

Willoway's learning methodology is based on the theory of constructivist learning. Under this theory, students "construct" meaning—figuring out how the world works—by creating their own "microworlds" which mirror or explain aspects of the real world. Thus Willoway students create 3D virtual worlds where they show what they have learned, all within Willoway's 3D learning world called Willotropolis. They role play historical characters, put on plays for other Willoway students, and create interactive games . . . all at a distance. Willoway encourages students to form their own questions and issues, to go about answering and analyzing them, to take responsibility for their own learning, and to become problem solvers and, perhaps more important, problem finders, led by their own ideas and informed by the ideas of others. Willoway students are taught to think for themselves and to create on a daily basis. This is the basis for the Willoway Method.

These students ask for, if not demand, the freedom to play with ideas, explore issues, and encounter new information. The way a teacher frames an assignment usually determines the degree to which students may be autonomous and display initiative. For example, students in a 9th grade Willoway English class read *Journey to the Center of the Earth* by Jules Verne. The novel was integrated with a Willoway science unit on volcanoes. After discussing the text in online literature study groups, students went on to incorporate fact with fiction by creating their own virtual volcano world.

Journey to the Center of the Earth play

The play must go on . . .

. . . and on. Each frame has dialog & directions.

Characters from the novel then came alive inside Willoway's 3D learning community called Willotropolis. Students wrote a play where the main characters took other Willoway students on an interactive journey to the center of the earth. Each character had a chance to "speak" and explain the setting and context of the volcano game. Students then acted as tour guides and partnered with other Willoway students to take them deep inside the volcano. Various earth science facts were embedded into the 3D game exemplifying student knowledge.

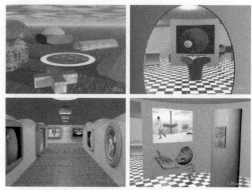

Inside of a student-created depiction of a Mars colony. Students used Bryce 3D to create room backgrounds.

Another good example where the constructivist learning model has been applied at Willoway was during the Mars2030 project. Students created their own online 3D virtual Mars world. They integrated science knowledge learned about Mars, and then created their own version of what it might be like to live in a Mars colony. They programmed a 3D world as well as learned how to use *Bryce 3D* to make room backgrounds. They wrote journal entries "looking" out their Mars colony portals and shared what they "saw."

This means Willoway students spend a lot of time online: an average of 40 minutes a day online in their virtual classroom, two to three hours online researching the current class topic, and about thirty minutes online talking with their peers. This averages out to about 4½ hours a day online, which as I know from my own experience is no problem at all for kids who love using the computer.

Willoway uses a variety of conferencing software packages. The main conferencing applications used are CU-SeeMe, The Palace, and ICQ. Willoway also has developed an interactive "whiteboard" workspace where students work on collaborative projects and complete daily assignments. This whiteboard learning community allows users to interact with documents via an onscreen area on which teachers and students may write or draw, just like you can on a regular chalkboard.

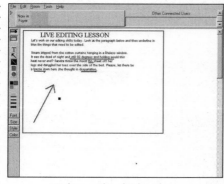

Working on the whiteboard area

Although Willoway focuses on Internet technologies and collaborative projects at a distance, they also recognize the importance of outside learning activities and parental involvement. How do they work these two ideas into the program? Community service requirements and parent volunteers. Many Willoway parents like to maintain direct input into their child's educational program. After all, that is the main reason most people homeschool. Parents help to design individual elective courses and volunteer to organize local outings and field trips with other Willoway students. One student was interested in learning about the effects of local runoff into a stream by his home. His parents helped him to organize the learning activity and guided the student during this elective study.

Parents also help to organize social gatherings and field trips. Recently parents and students traveled to the end-of-the-year

Gathering water for stream study

Analyzing data for stream study

Willoway students having fun at the Hershey Park Picnic

school picnic in Hershey, PA, where students spent a fun afternoon riding roller coasters and seeing the physics behind it after completing an end-of-the-year unit on roller coasters.

Willoway has no special religious emphasis. Although a number of the web sites children visit include evolutionary content, Willoway itself steers clear of taking a position on this subject. I get the impression that the school's founder, Janet Hale, is very willing to accommodate parental convictions and will work with you if you find any activity objectionable.

The students apparently love Willoway, according to the testimonials they have posted on Willoway's site. They love their teacher, their classmates, and the new computer skills they are learning. They love being encouraged to ask, "Why?" and learning how to find the data to answer their own questions. Often these students' career goals either include going directly into a computer-related job upon graduation from Willoway or starting their own business.

BOTTOM LINE: If your child is in the right age range, has to be dragged away from the computer, and doesn't enjoy school (if he's enrolled in school) or doesn't terribly enjoy the traditional methods you have been using so far to homeschool her (if she's homeschooled), and if you can afford the tuition, Willoway might be just what you are looking for! *Mary Pride*

EXTRA INFO

Appendixes

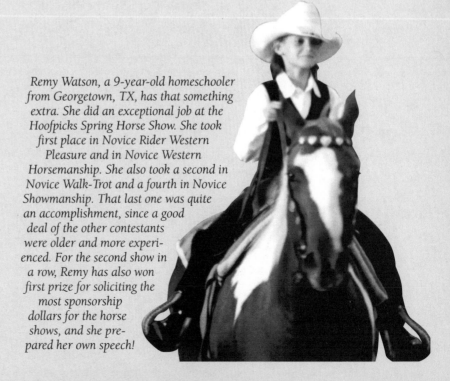

Remy Watson, a 9-year-old homeschooler from Georgetown, TX, has that something extra. She did an exceptional job at the Hoofpicks Spring Horse Show. She took first place in Novice Rider Western Pleasure and in Novice Western Horsemanship. She also took a second in Novice Walk-Trot and a fourth in Novice Showmanship. That last one was quite an accomplishment, since a good deal of the other contestants were older and more experienced. For the second show in a row, Remy has also won first prize for soliciting the most sponsorship dollars for the horse shows, and she prepared her own speech!

What the Research Says About Homeschooling

Do you need hard facts to convince others—or even yourself—that homeschooling works? Are you simply curious about homeschool family income, spending, and test scores?

Then you've come to the right place.

The following 10 pages illustrates the state of homeschooling as of 1997—the most recent year for which I could get permission to reprint an in-depth report.

You can purchase a more recent report, *Homeschooling on the Threshold*, reviewed in the sidebar, if you need an inexpensive handout or simply crave the latest data. But the information in this appendix can help you right now.

Aside from the growing numbers of children involved (now 1.7 million up from 1.23 million), the rest of the data in this appendix has not changed much in the past three years. If anything, it has been more fully corroborated by additional studies. Go ahead, read . . . and be impressed!

We would like to thank Dr. Brian Ray of the National Home Education Research Institute, the foremost home education researcher in the world, and the Home School Legal Defense Association, for graciously granting us permission to reprint the following pages from their booklet, "Home Education Across the United States."

Dr. Brian Ray also has published about 30 research reports, a video, and audio tapes. He publishes a newsletter *The Home School Researcher* which collects and comments on research having to do with homeschoolers. It costs $25/year for 4 issues. For information contact: National Home Education Research Institute, 925 Cottage Street, NE, Salem, OR 97301. (503) 364-1490. Fax: (503) 364-2827. Web: www.nheri.org.

ABOUT THE RESEARCHER

Dr. Brian D. Ray

DR. BRIAN D. RAY is president of the National Home Education Research Institute. He holds a Ph.D. in science education from Oregon State University. NHERI conducts basic, data-gathering research; serves as a clearinghouse of information for researchers, home educators, attorneys, legislators, policy makers, and the public at-large; and provides speaker services on various topics. NHERI also publishes research reports and the unique, academic, refereed journal *Home School Researcher*.

Strengths of Their Own—Home Schoolers Across America: Academic Achievement, Family Characteristics, and Longitudinal Traits is available from NHERI for $19.95, plus $2 shipping.

National Home Education Research Institute

P.O. Box 13939, Salem, Oregon 97309

(503) 364-1490 ∾ http://www.nheri.org

Home School Legal Defense Association

17333 Pickwick Drive, Purcellville, Virginia 20132

(540) 338-5600 ∾ http://www.hslda.org

HOME SCHOOLING is a flourishing phenomenon within the United States. In the early 1980s, the general public had never heard of home schooling, but today, almost everyone has.

Still, society at large knows little about home schoolers: their backgrounds, their activities, or their achievements. *Strengths of Their Own: Home Schoolers Across America*, a recent study conducted by Dr. Brian Ray, president of the National Home Education Research Institute (NHERI), provides some answers.

Dr. Ray collected data on 5,402 home school students from 1,657 families for the 1994–95 and 1995–96 academic years. Nearly 6,000 surveys were sent to home school families using a variety of sources and methods. Some were mailed directly to families (both those randomly selected from numerous mailing lists as well as longitudinal participants from Ray's similar study in 1990). Others were blindly forwarded to families through the leadership of independent home school support groups and networks operating in every

How Many Home Schoolers Are There?

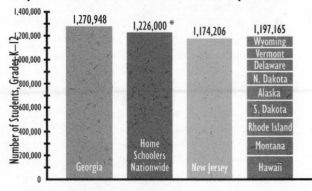

Figure 1.0 – Home School Students Nationwide Compared to Selected State Public School Populations

Footnote: *This study calculated that there were 1.23 million home school students in the U.S. during the fall of 1996. The estimated margin of error for this calculation is ±10%, yielding a range of 1,103,000 to 1,348,000. This is similar to the total public school enrollment of Georgia or New Jersey (ranked 9th and 10th largest respectively among state public school populations nationwide).

Public school state enrollment figures are for 1994 and the most recent available, based on a table from the U.S. Department of Education, Office of Educational Research & Improvement, National Center for Education Statistics (1996, November). *Digest of Education Statistics (1996)*. Washington, DC: U.S. Department of Education.

How Do Home School Students Score?

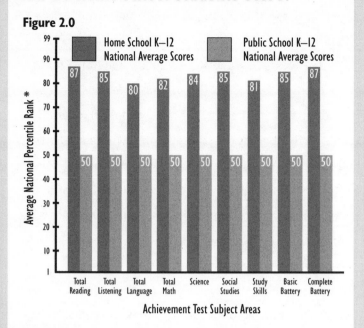

Figure 2.0

Legend: Home School K–12 National Average Scores / Public School K–12 National Average Scores

Y-axis: Average National Percentile Rank *

Achievement Test Subject Area	Home School	Public School
Total Reading	87	50
Total Listening	85	50
Total Language	80	50
Total Math	82	50
Science	84	50
Social Studies	85	50
Study Skills	81	50
Basic Battery	85	50
Complete Battery	87	50

X-axis: Achievement Test Subject Areas

Footnote: Data collected for standardized academic achievement tests for the 1994–95 academic year.

*For more detail about the non-equal-interval nature of a simple percentile scale which has distortion especially near the ends of the scale, see the complete study by Brian D. Ray, *Strengths of Their Own—Home Schoolers Across America: Academic Achievement, Family Characteristics, and Longitudinal Traits*, 1997, Salem, OR: National Home Education Research Institute.

state. Unquestionably, this research represents the largest and most comprehensive study on home schooling ever undertaken (see *Ray*, 1997).

In a collaborative effort to provide solid answers to common questions about home schooling, HSLDA and Dr. Ray have highlighted some of the key findings of this study. Where available, comparable public school student data were also obtained. This publication, *Home Education Across The United States,* is the result.

Just how prevalent is home education today? The data indicate there are approximately 1.23 million American children being taught at home. This finding (which has an estimated margin of error of ±10%) exceeds the total public school enrollment for the state of New Jersey, which has the 10th largest student population in the nation. Put another way, there are more home school students nationwide than there are public

school students in Wyoming, Vermont, Delaware, North Dakota, Alaska, South Dakota, Rhode Island, Montana, and Hawaii—*combined*. In fact, America's home schoolers collectively outnumber the individual statewide public school enrollments in each of 41 states (Figure 1.0).

Why are so many parents choosing to home school? Because it works. This study shows that home educated students excel on nationally-normed standardized achievement exams. On average, home schoolers outperform their public school peers by 30 to 37 percentile points across all subjects (Figure 2.0).

In fact, home schoolers' test scores sometimes increase in relation to the number of years a student has been taught at home. The data for eighth grade home schoolers suggest that those who have completed two or more years at home score substantially *higher* that those who just completed one year of instruction (Figure 3.0). This suggests that students who move

How Do Long-Term Home Schoolers Compare to Those Who Switch to Home Education Midstream?

Figure 3.0 – Achievement for Eighth Grade Home Schoolers Segmented by Years Taught at Home

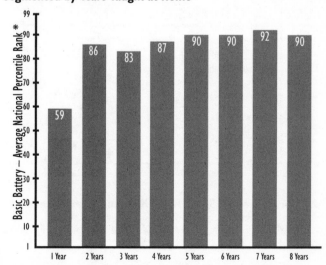

Y-axis: Basic Battery – Average National Percentile Rank *

Years Taught at Home	Score
1 Year	59
2 Years	86
3 Years	83
4 Years	87
5 Years	90
6 Years	90
7 Years	92
8 Years	90

Footnote: *See *Ray* (1997) for more detail about the non-equal-interval nature of a simple percentile scale which has distortion especially near the ends of the scale.

Is Teacher Certification Necessary for High Achievement?

Figure 4.0

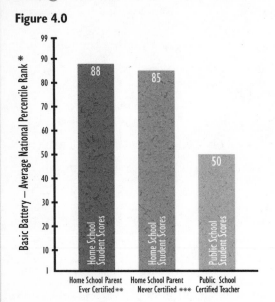

Footnote: *See *Ray* (1997) for more detail about the non-equal-interval nature of a simple percentile scale which has distortion especially near the ends of the scale.
**Either parent ever certified.
***Neither parent ever certified.
Home school data are for grades K–12.

from an institutional school to home school may experience a brief transition period. Students home schooled from early grades tend to score higher in subsequent years in some subject areas (see *Ray*, 1997).

Critics often claim that only parents with teaching credentials can effectively home school. The data from this study suggest otherwise. Home school students' test scores segmented by whether their parents have ever held a teaching certificate reveal a differential of only three percentile points—the 88th percentile versus the 85th percentile (Figure 4.0).

Furthermore, a parent's education background has no substantive effect on their children's home school academic performance, according to this study. Home educated students' test scores remain between the 80th and 90th percentiles, whether their mothers have a college degree or

Does Parent Education Level Predict Student Achievement?

For Home Schoolers: NO!

Figure 5.1 – Home School Achievement – Basic Battery Test

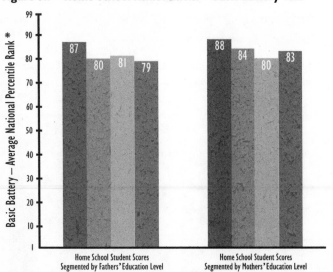

For Public Schoolers: YES!

Figure 5.2 – Public School Achievement – Writing Test**

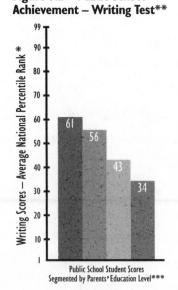

Figure 5.3 – Public School Achievement – Math Test**

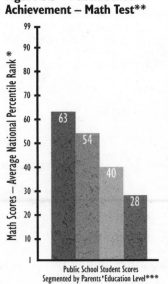

Key for Figures 5.1–5.3: Parents' Highest Education Level Attained

Graduated College | Some Education after High School | Graduated High School | Less than High School Education

Footnote: *See *Ray* (1997) for more detail about the non-equal-interval nature of a simple percentile scale which has distortion especially near the ends of the scale.
**Basic battery achievement test scores not available for public school students.
***Public school data are for eighth grade writing scores and 13-year-old's math scores based on tables from the U.S. Department of Education, Office of Educational Research &

Improvement, National Center for Education Statistics (1996, November). *National Assessment of Educational Progress (NAEP) trends in academic progress* [trends report and appendices]. Washington, DC: U.S. Department of Education.
Home school data are for grades K–12.

did not complete high school (Figure 5.1).

For public school students, however, a parent's education level *does* affect their children's performance (Figures 5.2 & 5.3). In eighth grade math, public school students whose parents are college graduates score at the 63rd percentile, whereas students whose parents have less than a high school diploma score at the 28th percentile. Remarkably, students taught at home by mothers who never finished high school score a full 55 percentile points higher than public school students from families of comparable educational backgrounds.

Does race make a difference in academic performance? Math and reading scores for minority home schoolers show no significant difference when compared to whites. In reading, both white and minority home schoolers score at the 87th percentile. Only five points separate them in math—the 82nd percentile versus the 77th percentile (Figures 6.1 & 6.2).

A similar comparison for public school students, however, demonstrates a substantial disparity. White public school eighth grade students score at the 57th percentile in reading and at the 58th percentile in math nationally.[1] Black public school eighth grade students score at the 28th percentile in reading and the 24th percentile in math in the same national sample. Hispanic students score at the 28th percentile in reading and at the 29th percentile in math nationally. However, national figures are not available which allow proportional weighting of various minority groups to match the same proportions as are found among home schooling racial minority groups.

Scores are available from the Virginia Department of

[1] Footnote: Public school achievement data are for eighth grade based on tables from the U.S. Department of Education, Office of Educational Research & Improvement, National Center for Education Statistics (1996, November). *National Assessment of Educational Progress (NAEP) trends in academic progress* [trends report and appendices]. Washington, DC: U.S. Department of Education.

How Do Minorities Fare in Home Education?

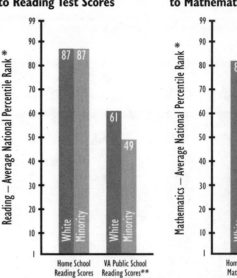

Figure 6.1 – Race Relationship to Reading Test Scores

Figure 6.2 – Race Relationship to Mathematics Test Scores

Footnote: *See *Ray* (1997) for more detail about the non-equal-interval nature of a simple percentile scale which has distortion especially near the ends of the scale.

**Public school achievement data are based on eighth grade scores from Table 4 of *The Virginia Assessment Program: Results for the 1995–1996 School Year* (1996, July). Richmond, VA: Virginia Department of Education.

The Virginia minority scores were weighted according to the proportions of minorities in this study of home schoolers to arrive at the numbers in this figure. The minority groups were American Indian/Alaskan Native, Asian/Pacific Islander, black, and Hispanic. Of home school minority students tested in this study, about 63% were black or Hispanic.

Public school achievement data are similar for the U.S. in general but the same detail of data was not available for all public schools. See U.S. Department of Education, Office of Educational Research & Improvement, National Center for Education Statistics (1996, November). *National Assessment of Educational Progress (NAEP) trends in academic progress* [trends report and appendices]. Washington, DC: U.S. Department of Education.

Home school data are for grades K–12.

What About the Gender Gap in Academics?

Figure 7.0

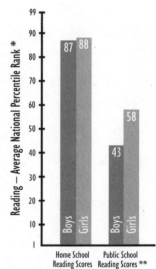

Footnote: *See *Ray* (1997) for more detail about the non-equal-interval nature of a simple percentile scale which has distortion especially near the ends of the scale.

**Public school achievement data are for eighth grade based on tables from the U.S. Department of Education, Office of Educational Research & Improvement, National Center for Education Statistics (1996, November). *National Assessment of Educational Progress (NAEP) trends in academic progress* [trends report and appendices]. Washington, DC: U.S. Department of Education.

Home school data are for grades K–12.

Is Family Income a Predictor of Academic Achievement for Home Schoolers?

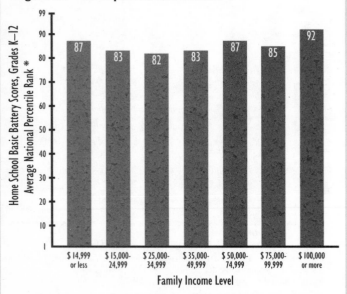

Figure 8.0 – No Impact on Achievement

Footnote: *See *Ray* (1997) for more detail about the non-equal-interval nature of a simple percentile scale which has distortion especially near the ends of the scale.

centile versus the 87th percentile). Public school student performance in math follows a similar pattern, but public school boys' reading scores are markedly behind girls', the 43rd percentile versus the 58th percentile—a 15 point difference (Figure 7.0).

Segmenting student test scores by family income shows that socioeconomic status is not a determinant of academic performance for home schoolers (Figure 8.0). Regardless of family income bracket, home school students score between the 82nd and 92nd percentiles.

According to some researchers and officials, family income does have a significant impact on public school students' test scores. Concerned about a recent study of student achievement in the Denver public schools, a school board member wrote, "The conclusion is clear.

Public Education which allow the scores to be weighted in a manner which matches the proportions exactly in the same ratio as are found in the home schooling sample. When the scores are weighted in this fashion, Virginia white eighth grade students score at the 61st percentile in reading while the weighted minorities score at the 49th percentile. In math the same scores show whites at the 60th percentile and minorities at the 50th percentile.

Home schoolers have been able to substantially eliminate the disparity between white and minority scores even when the samples are adjusted to reflect the exact same proportion of American Indians, Asians, blacks, and Hispanics.

When segmented by gender, test scores for home schoolers reveal that boys are slightly better in math (the 84th percentile versus the 79th percentile), and girls are somewhat better in reading (the 88th per-

Does Spending Correlate with Achievement?

Figure 9.0

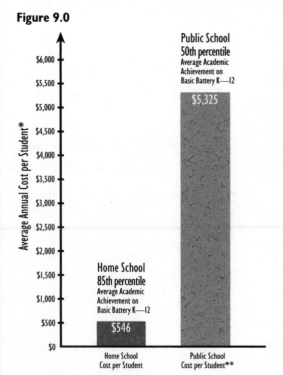

Footnote: *All cost-per-student amounts in this figure exclude capital costs.
**United States Department of Education, National Center for Education Statistics (1996). *Statistics in brief, June 1996; Revenues and expenditures for public elementary and secondary education: School year 1993–1994. [From: Common core of data: National public education financial survey.]* Washington, DC: U.S. Department of Education.

Is Government Regulation Necessary for High Achievement?

Key for Figures 10.1 & 10.2

Low Regulation
No state requirement for parents to initiate any contact with the state.

Moderate Regulation
State requires parents to send notification, test scores, and/or professional evaluation of student progress.

High Regulation
State requires parents to send notification or achievement test scores and/or professional evaluation, plus other requirements (e.g. curriculum approval by the state, teacher qualifications of parents, or home visits by state officials).

Figure 10.1 – State Regulation: No Impact on Home School Achievement

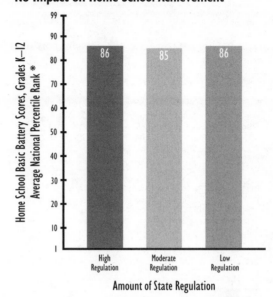

*Footnote: *See Ray (1997) for more detail about the non-equal-interval nature of a simple percentile scale which has distortion especially near the ends of the scale.*

Figure 10.2 – Breakdown of States by Regulatory Policy

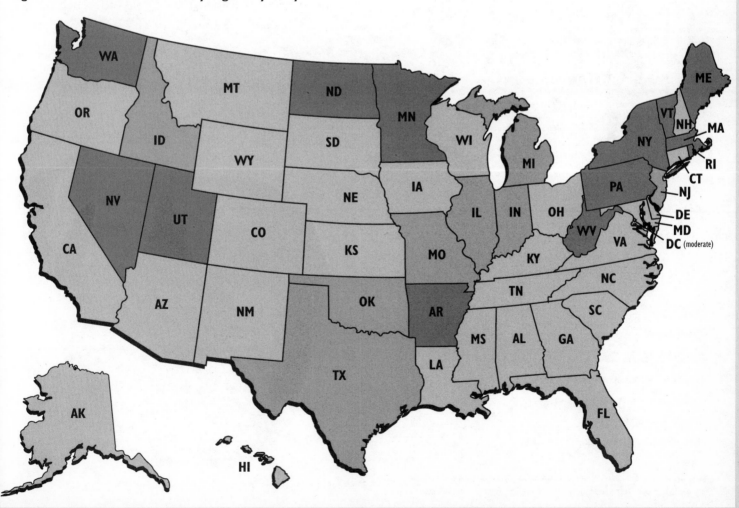

Family income and class are stronger indicators of educational success than race."[2]

A cost-benefit analysis reveals that an average of $546 spent per home school student per year yields an average 85th percentile ranking on test scores. Compare this to the average annual expenditure of $5,325 per public school student to achieve only an average 50th percentile ranking. These figures do not include capital expenditures, like buildings and land, etc. (Figure 9.0).

The degree of governmental regulation from state to state has no significant effect on the academic performance of home schoolers. Whether a state imposes a high degree of regulation (i.e., notification, standardized testing, professional evaluations, curriculum approval, teacher qualifications, home visits, etc.) or no regulation, home school student test score averages are identical—the 86th percentile for both segments (Figure 10.1). Legitimate questions may be asked concerning the purpose of such regulations since there is no apparent effect on student learning.

Standardized tests for home schoolers are administered in various ways. Little difference was found in scores among students tested by a parent, a private school teacher, a public school teacher, or

[2] Footnote: *Denver Business Journal*, February 21, 1997, p. 40A. See also, Coleman, James S., Thomas Hoffer, & Sally Kilgore, (1982) *High school achievement: Public, Catholic, and private schools compared*, New York, NY: Basic Books, and Snow, Catherine E., Wendy S. Barnes, Jean Chandler, Irene F. Goodman, & Lowry Hemphill, (1991) *Unfulfilled expectations: Home and school influences on literacy*, Cambridge, MA: Harvard University Press.

Do Test Scores Vary by Who Administered the Test?

Figure 11.0

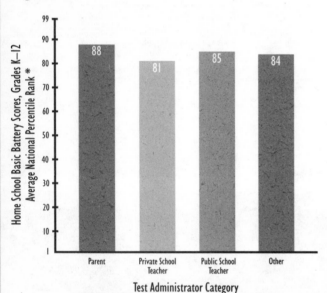

Y-axis: Home School Basic Battery Scores, Grades K–12 Average National Percentile Rank *

Bars:
- Parent: 88
- Private School Teacher: 81
- Public School Teacher: 85
- Other: 84

X-axis: Test Administrator Category

Footnote: *See *Ray* (1997) for more detail about the non-equal-interval nature of a simple percentile scale which has distortion especially near the ends of the scale.

What Kind of Curriculum Do Home Schoolers Use?

Table 1.0

Type of Curriculum	Usage*
Parent Designed (major components are hand picked)	71.1%
Complete Curriculum Package	23.8%
Satellite School (as source)	3.0%
Home School Program from Local Private School	0.7%
Other	6.5%

Footnote: *Some parents marked more than one category, so total exceeds 100%.

How Many Times Do Home Schoolers Visit the Library Per Month?

Figure 12.0

- 6 + Visits: 9%
- 3–5 Visits: 38%
- 1–2 Visits: 53%

Footnote: Data are for K–12 home school students.

Are Computers a Part of Home Schools?

Figure 13.0

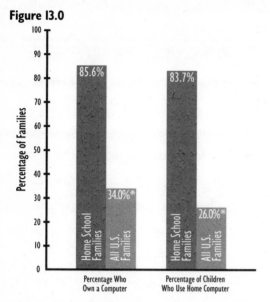

Footnote: *Data for all U.S. families based on table from United States Department of Education, National Center for Education Statistics. (1996). *Digest of education statistics 1996, Table 417: Access to and use of home computers, by selected characteristics of students and other users: October 1993.* Washington, DC: U.S. Department of Education.

What About Socialization?

Figure 14.0 – Home Schoolers' Activities & Community Involvement

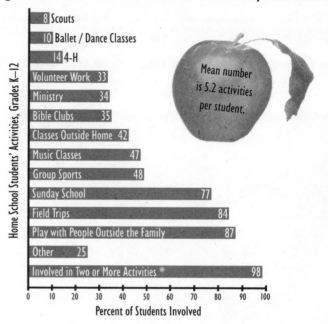

Footnote: *Participation in two or more of the 12 activities does not include "other activities." See Table 8 of *Ray* (1997).

How Many Hours Per Day Are Spent Watching Television & Video Tapes?

Figure 15.0

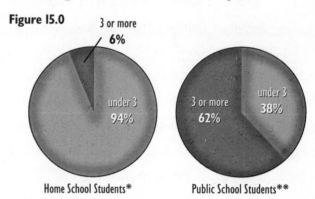

Footnote: *Data reported for K–12 home school students' weekday viewing.
**Data reported for 13-year-olds are fairly representative of 9-, 13-, and 17-year-olds, based on tables from the U.S. Department of Education, Office of Educational Research & Improvement, National Center for Education Statistics (1996, November). *National Assessment of Educational Progress (NAEP) trends in academic progress* [trends report and appendices]. Washington, DC: U.S. Department of Education.

some other test administrator. And again, the average scores range between the 80th and 90th percentiles (Figure 11.0).

What kind of curriculum do home schoolers use? The vast majority of home school parents (71.1%) hand-pick their instructional materials, custom designing the curriculum to presumably suit the needs of their children, their family's lifestyle, and applicable government regulations. Nearly 24% use a complete curriculum package purchased from one of numerous providers. Other options include enrollment in private satellite schools or special programs operated by the local private school. The data also revealed that some parents employ more than one approach to assembling their children's curriculum (Table 1.0).

This study found that home schoolers (53%) visit a library at least once or twice each month (Figure 12.0). Nearly half (47%) reported that they go even more often. As a group, home schooled students frequent the library an average of 3.8 times

each month (see *Ray*, 1997).

Apparently quick to employ the cutting-edge technology of personal computers, 85.6% of home school families reported owning a computer and 83.7% say their children use it in their education. Compared to

Ages of Home School Students in Study

Figure 16.0

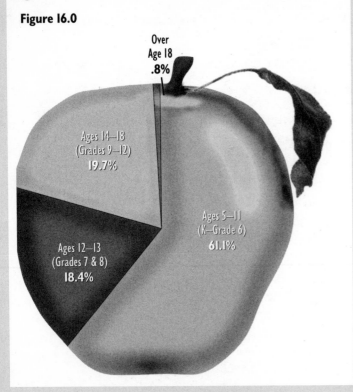

Over Age 18 .8%

Ages 14–18 (Grades 9–12) 19.7%

Ages 12–13 (Grades 7 & 8) 18.4%

Ages 5–11 (K–Grade 6) 61.1%

public school children (Figure 15.0).

Of the 5,402 children included in this study, all grades (K–12) are substantively represented. The majority of the sample (61.1%) is comprised of grades K–6, probably because the movement is relatively young and has grown so rapidly (Figure 16.0).

According to the data, home school parents are employed in a full range of typical occupations. Most notable, however, is the finding that 87.7% of mothers and 0.5% of fathers have elected to stay home full-time to teach and raise their children (Table 2.0).

How enthusiastic are home school parents about their success? The vast majority (89%) intend to continue teaching their children at home all the way through high school (Figure 17.0).

On average, home school graduates had 6.9 years

the national norms for all U.S. families (34% and 26%, respectively), home school families are setting a trend for equipping their children with resources for the 21st century (Figure 13.0).

Home schoolers are often asked, "What about socialization?" The data on home school students' activities and community involvement reveal that, on average, these children are engaged in 5.2 activities outside the home, with 98% involved in two or more. Activities ranging from scouts, dance class, and 4-H to sports, field trips, and volunteer work demonstrate that home schoolers interact with people of all ages, from all sorts of backgrounds, and in all types of social settings (Figure 14.0).

This study also measured the time home schoolers spent watching television and video tapes each weekday. These data were compared to those for public school students. Simply put, home school children spend substantially less time watching TV than do

What Are the Occupations of Home School Parents?

Table 2.0

Occupation	Father	Mother
Farmer, Farm Manager	3.4 %	0.2 %
Homemaker, Home Education	0.5 %	87.7 %
Laborer	2.4 %	0.1 %
Manager	8.9 %	0.3 %
Military	4.3 %	0.1 %
Office Worker	1.1 %	0.8 %
Operator of Machines	3.7 %	0.1 %
Small Business Owner	10.7 %	2.1 %
Professional 1 (Accountant, RN, Engineer, etc.)	17.3 %	4.8 %
Professional 2 (Doctor, Professor, Lawyer, etc.)	16.9 %	1.1 %
Protective Service	1.7 %	0.0 %
Sales	4.3 %	0.1 %
School Teacher	2.2 %	0.9 %
Service Worker	1.0 %	0.4 %
Technical	8.1 %	0.1 %
Tradesperson	6.9 %	0.3 %
Other	6.5 %	0.9 %

How Long Are They Going to Home School?

Figure 17.0 – Parents' Intent to Continue Home Education

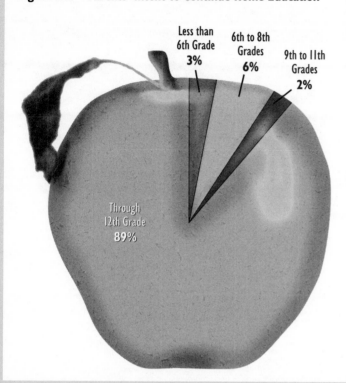

Less than 6th Grade **3%**

6th to 8th Grades **6%**

9th to 11th Grades **2%**

Through 12th Grade **89%**

How Many Years Were Home School Graduates Taught at Home?

Figure 18.0

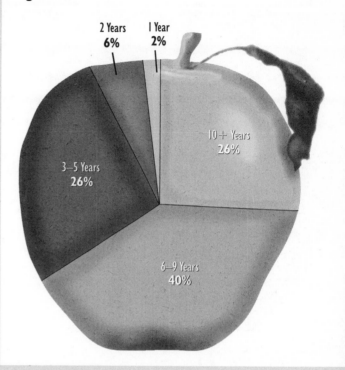

2 Years **6%**

1 Year **2%**

10 + Years **26%**

3–5 Years **26%**

6–9 Years **40%**

of home education (see *Ray*, 1997). The data reveal that 92% of graduates were taught at home for three or more years (Figure 18.0).

Once they graduate from high school, home schoolers closely parallel their public school counterparts, whether they pursue more formal education or enter the job market (Figure 19.0).

This study demonstrates that home schooling works. It suggests that direct parental involvement and hard work are the keys to educational success. Regardless of race, gender, socioeconomic status, parent education level, teacher certification, or the degree of government regulation, the academic achievement scores of home educated students significantly exceed those of public school students. Home school students are fully engaged in society and experience a wide range of opportunities outside the home. They are smart users of both technology and their time. And

What Happens After Graduation?

Figure 19.0

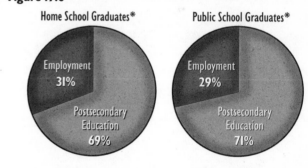

Home School Graduates*

Employment **31%**

Postsecondary Education **69%**

Public School Graduates*

Employment **29%**

Postsecondary Education **71%**

Footnote: *Percentages do not include military, unemployed, missions, ministry, volunteer work, etc., since these categories were not available for both groups.

Public school graduate data based on table from National Educational Longitudinal Survey (NELS) *1988–1994 Descriptive Summary Report*. Washington, DC: U.S. Department of Education.

graduates are equipped to pursue their aspirations— work or college. Contrary to the often speculative opinions of critics, the facts from this study demonstrate success.

Homeschool Groups by State, Province, & Country

This list includes *state* groups; *city* groups for large cities; and *large* independent groups (covering a region of a state). We couldn't include local support groups because, 1) there are too many of them, and 2) they change much too frequently. Finding and keeping up with this data is difficult, so we apologize if we left your large state, city, or regional group out. Visit the "Groups" area of www.home-school.com and fill out the online form to have your group added to our next listing and our web site.

For the most recent listing of groups, and a listing of events by state and date, visit **www.home-school.com and click on "Groups" and "Events"**

United States: States & Territories

Alabama

Alabama Home Educators Network
3015 Thurman Road
Huntsville, AL 35802
Phone: (256) 534-6401
Email: KaeKaeB@aol.com
Web: members.aol.com/kaekaeb/ahen.html
Motto: Many Voices, One Mission . . . Educating Our Children. Alabama Home Educators Network offers information to new homeschoolers and veterans alike, via an email list or/and information packet.

Christian Educators At Home of Anniston (CHEAHA)
2044 Alexandria-Jacksonville Highway
Jacksonville, AL 36265
Phone: (205) 848-9944
Email: Lisa@bama.starhosting.com
Web: www.teachus.com/cheaha/
Convention: Yearly

Christian Home Education Fellowship of Alabama (CHEF-AL)
3325 Crestwood Dr.
Semmes, AL 36575
Phone: (334) 645-5003
Fax: (334) 645-9243
Email: hls@prodigy.net
Web: www.alhome.com
Member Families: 15,000
Convention: Yearly
Month(s): May
Attendance: 2,200

getAHEAD
P.O. Box 1012
Foley, AL 36536
Phone: (334) 989-7007
Email: getahead@gulftel.com
getAhead is a publication dedicated to helping Alabamians find the assistance they seek, and to improve the future of homeschooling.

Alaska

Alaska Homeschool Association
P.O. Box 874075
Wasilla, AK 99687
Phone: (907) 373-7404

Alaska Private and Home Educators Association (APHEA)
P.O. Box 141764
Anchorage, AK 99514
Phone: (907) 566-3450
Fax: (907) 373-5779
Email: mvandiest@matnet.com
Web: www.aphea.org
Convention: Yearly

Arizona

Arizona Families for Home Education (AFHE)
P.O. Box 2035
Chandler, AZ 85244-2035
Phone: (480) 503-2400
Email: afhe@primenet.com
Web: www.afhe.org
Member Families: 5,000
Graduate recognition night, leadership seminar.
Convention: Yearly
Month(s): July
Attendance: 3,000

Havasu Christian Home Educators
3920 Flying Cloud Dr.
Lake Havasu City, AZ 86406
Phone: (520) 855-5802
Monthly meetings.
Convention: Yearly

Arkansas

Arkansas Family Council
414 S. Pulaski, Suite 2
Little Rock, AR 72201
Phone: (501) 375-7000
Convention: Yearly

ome Educators of Arkansas
O. Box 192455
ittle Rock, AK 72219
hone: (501) 847-4942
ax: (501) 821-4379
mail: heareport@juno.com
Veb: www.geocities.com/heartland/
arden/4555/hear.html

California

California Homeschool Network (CHN)
P.O. Box 55465
Hayward, CA 94545
Phone: (800) 327-5339
Email: Mail@cahomeschoolnet.org
Web: www.cahomeschoolnet.org
Member Families: 750
Quarterly Seminars: Homeschooling Your Family

Christian Home Educators Association of California (CHEA-CA)
P.O. Box 2009
Norwalk, CA 90651-2009
Phone: (800) 564-CHEA
Fax: (562) 864-3747
Email: cheaofca@aol.com
Web: www.cheaofca.org
Member Families: 5,000
CHEA also hosts a yearly Bay Area conference with attendance of 2,000, and leadership conferences.
Convention: Yearly
Month(s): July
Attendance: 6,000

Homeschool Association of California (HSC)
P.O. Box 2442
Atascadero, CA 93423
Phone: (888) HSC-4440
Web: www.hsc.org
"See our web site for a thorough discussion of the legalities of homeschooling in CA, excerpts from the educational code books, and links to the state dept. of education web sites. HSC is a sponsor of the annual California Home Education conferences."
Convention: Yearly

The Link
587 North Ventura Park Rd.
Suite F-911
Newbury Park, CA 91320
Phone: (805) 492-1373
Email: hompaper@gte.net
Web: www.conejovalley.com/thelink/
Convention: Yearly

Sacramento Council of Parent Educators (SCOPE)
P.O. Box 163178
Sacramento, CA 95816
Phone: (916) 646-0401
Fax: (916) 646-0401
Email: macknbecky@juno.com
Convention: Yearly
Attendance: 750

Colorado

Christian Home Educators of Colorado (CHEC)
3739 E. 4th Ave.
Denver, CO 80206
Phone: (303) 388-1888
Email: office@chec.org
Web: www.chec.org
Convention: Yearly

Colorado Home Educators Book Fair
7072 Singing Springs Lane
Evergreen, CO 80439
Phone: (303) 670-0673
Fax: (303) 674-3431
Email: monte@magmachem.com
Web: www.hearth-n-home.com
Convention: Yearly
Attendance: 1500

Northern Colorado Home School Association
12150 Rist Canyon Rd.
Bellvue, CO 80512
Phone: (970) 493-2243

Rocky Mountain Education Connection (RMEC)
20774 E. Buchanan Drive
Aurora, CO 80011-5401
Phone: (303) 341-2242
Email: connect@pcisys.net
Web: www.pcisys.net/~dstanley/
A complete copy of Colorado's Home School Statute can be found on RMEC's home page.
Convention: Yearly

Connecticut

Connecticut Home Educators Association (CHEA)
P.O. Box 611
Ivoryton, CT 06442
Phone: (203) 781-8569
Email: Aronhome@worldnet.att.net
Web: www.connix.com/~dschroth/chea/
Member Families: 400
23 support groups located in all geographic regions of the state.
Convention: Every other year
Month(s): May

The Education Association of Christian Homeschoolers (TEACH)
4 Grieb Court
Wallingford, CT 06492
Phone: (860) 231-2930, (800) 205-7844
Fax: (860) 677-4677
Email: 103161.415@compuserve.com
Web: www.teachct.org
Convention: Yearly

Delaware

Delaware Home Education Association
500 N Dual Highway, PMB 415
Seaford, MD 19973
Phone: (302) 337-0990
Email: jcpoeii@juno.com

Tri-State Homeschool Network
P.O. Box 7193
Newark, DE 19714-7193
Phone: (302) 322-2018
Email: brew@dpnet.net
Serves New Castle County, DE, Cecil County, MD, Southeastern PA, and the Pennsville, NJ area.

Florida

Allendale Academy
7208 Amhurst Way
Clearwater, FL 33764
Phone: (727) 531-2481
Fax: (727) 531-6491
Email: adacademy@aol.com
Web: www.allendaleacademy.com
Member Families: 217
Allendale Academy is a private school acting as a homeschool umbrella in the state of Florida and in other states across the country.

Christian Home Educators of Florida (CHEF)
6280 - 150th Avenue North
Clearwater, FL 33760
Phone: (727) 539-1881
Fax: (727) 539-1678
Email: CHEFFCCPSA@aol.com
Web: www.FLHomeschooling.com
Member Families: 79
CHEF offers statewide newspaper, academic and sports competitions at state level, annual homeschool convention.
Convention: Yearly

Circle Christian School
4644 Adanson St
Orlando, FL 32804
Phone: (407) 740-8877
Fax: (407) 740-8580
Email: circle@ao.net
Convention: Yearly
Attendance: 1,300

El Shaddai Ministries of Florida, Inc.
1151 Emma Lane
Leesburg, FL 34748
Email: ForHIM3@aol.com
Homeschool Mom's Retreat.
Convention: Yearly

Faith Christian Academy
2940 Winter Lake Road
Lakeland, FL 33803
Phone: (941) 668-8084
Member Families: 500
Faith Christian Academy is a private, accredited umbrella school for homeschoolers. They offer sports teams, yearbook, school pictures, math classes, choir, traditional cap and gown graduation for seniors, record keeping, support, and lots more.

Florida at Home
4644 Adanson
Orlando, FL 32804
Phone: (407) 740-8877
Email: circle@ao.net
Convention: Yearly

Florida Coalition of Christian Private Schools Association, Inc. (FCCPSA)
6280 - 150th Avenue North
Clearwater, FL 33760
Phone: (727) 539-1881
Fax: (727) 539-1678
Email: CHEFFCCPSA@aol.com
Web: www.FLHomeschooling.com
"40 member schools and growing. We are here to support and assist those who wish to form private schools for home education, as well as support and assist existing private schools. We offer a legal department, accreditation, a resource manual, and administrator leadership conferences."
Convention: Twice a year

Florida Parent-Educators Association (FPEA)
P.O. Box 50685
Jacksonville Beach, FL 32240-0685
Phone: (877) 275-3732
Fax: (904) 241-5538
Email: office@fpea.com
Web: www.fpea.com
Member Families: 6,000
FPEA publishes the bi-monthly newsletter *The Almanac*. They also publish *The Guide to Home Schooling in Florida*, given free upon request.
Convention: Yearly
Attendance: 6,000

Home Education Resources and Information
711 N St. Johns Bluff Rd.
Jacksonville, FL 32225
Phone: (904) 565-9121
Email: herijax@juno.com

Tallahassee Homeschool Group
Rt. 5, Box 42
Havana, FL 32333
Phone: (904) 877-8304
Related newsletter *The Teachable Moment*.

West Florida Home Education Support League
P.O. Box 11720
Pensacola, FL 32524
Phone: (850) 995-9444
Web: www.wfhesl.org
Convention: Yearly
Attendance: 1,200

Georgia

Catholic Home Educators of Georgia
74 Williamson St.
Jefferson, GA 30549
Phone: (7060 367-2437
Email: kadonald@juno.com
Convention: Yearly
Attendance: 900

Georgia Home Education Association
245 Buckeye Lane
Fayettville, GA 30214
Phone: (770) 461-3657
Fax: (770) 461-9053
Email: ghea@mindspring.com
Web: www.ghea.org
Convention: Yearly
Attendance: 2,000

Harvest Home Educators
P.O. Box 1756
Buford, GA 30516
Phone: (770) 271-2360
Fax: (770) 271-2967
Email: harvesthomeeducators@juno.com
Convention: Yearly
Attendance: 3,000

Hawaii

Christian Homeschoolers of Hawaii
91-824 Oama Street
Ewa Beach, HI 96706
Phone: (808) 689-6398
Fax: (808) 689-0878
Email: oamastpro@aol.com
Member Families: 400
User book fair, Moms' Lunch.
Convention: Yearly
Month(s): March
Attendance: 500

Idaho

Christian Homeschoolers of Idaho State
7722 Wayside Dr.
Boise, ID 83704
Phone: (208) 322-4270
Email: info@chois.org

Home Educators of Idaho
3618 Pine Hill Drive
Coeur d'Alene, ID 83814
Phone: (208) 667-2778

Illinois

Association of Peoria Area Christian Home Educators (APACHE)
P.O. Box 5203
Peoria, IL 61601-5203
Phone: (309) 589-1307
Email: PeoHmEdu@aol.com
Convention: Yearly
Attendance: 1,800

Illinois Christian Home Educators
P.O. Box 775
Harvard, IL 60033
Phone: (815) 943-7882
Convention: Yearly
Attendance: 2,000

The Illinois Beacon
c/o Iowa-Illinois Christian Home Educators Association
P.O. Box 246
Aledo, IL 61231
Phone: (309) 582-3121
Email: iailchea@mcol.net
State homeschool newsletter published monthly by Iowa-Illinois Christian Home Educators Association. Monthly calendar of events, legislative, and support group news, recipes, prayer requests, articles, more.

Indiana

Indiana Association of Home Educators (IAHE)
8106 Madison Avenue
Indianapolis, IN 46227
Phone: (317) 859-1202
Fax: (317) 859-1204
Email: iahe@inhomeeducators.org
Web: www.inhomeeducators.org
Mothers' Retreat, Legislative Day, Support Group Leadership Seminar.The IAHE maintains a mail list of 8,000 families and provides support for 250 support groups.
Convention: Yearly
Month(s): June
Attendance: 6,000

Iowa

Network of Iowa Christian Home Educators (NICHE)
P.O. Box 158
Dexter, IA 50070
Phone: (515) 830-1614, (800) 732-0438
Email: niche@netins.net
Web: www.the-niche.org
Member Families: 900
Monthly newsletter.
Convention: Yearly

Kansas

Christian Home Educators Confederation of Kansas (CHECK)
P.O. Box 3968
Wichita, KS 67201
Phone: (316) 945-0810
Email: info@kansashomeschool.org
Web: www.kansashomeschool.org
Publish the excellent newsletter *C.H.E.C.K. News*. Dozens of support groups
Convention: Yearly

Johnson County Parent Educators
P.O. Box 14391
Lenexa, KS 66285
Phone: (913) 791-8089
Email: AprilMiller@juno.com or jcpe@unicom.com
Conference: Yearly
Attendance: 1,700

Kentucky

Christian Home Educators of Kentucky (CHEK)
691 Howardstown Road
Hodgensville, KY 42748
Phone: (270) 358-9270
Fax: (270) 358-9270
Email: chek@kvnet.org
Web: www.chek.org
Member Families: 800
State graduation, leadership symposiums. Directors speak about Kentucky home education for support groups, churches, etc.
Convention: Yearly
Month(s): July
Attendance: 1,600

Kentuciana Homeschooling
Louisville, KY
Email: cdaffy@cybergal.com
Web: start.at/ourhome
This site lists the local area support groups, field trips and activities, co-op school info, classes, things to do, swap 'n shop, etc.

Louisiana

Christian Home Educators Fellowship of Louisiana
P.O. Box 74292
Baton Rouge, LA 70874-4292
Phone: (888) 876-2433, (504) 775-9709
Convention: Yearly

White Dove Fellowship Home School Co-op
3600 Manhattan Blvd.
Harvey, LA 70058
Phone: (504) 362-0798
Email: sonex@bellsouth.net, timcausey@juno.com
Quarterly meetings during the school year, formal End of School Year banquet, and monthly newsletter. Also trips, events, and various classes.

Maine

Home Education and Family Services
51 West Gray Rd.
Gray, ME 04039
Phone: (207) 657-2800
Fax: (207) 657-2404
Email: royala@mindspring.com
Web: www.homeeducator.com
Convention: Twice a year
Month(s): July and August
Attendance: 900

Homeschoolers of Maine (HOME)
337 Hatchet Mountain Road
Hope, ME 04847
Phone: (207) 763-4251
Fax: (207) 763-4352
Email: home@homeschool-maine.org, homeschl@midcoast.com
Web: www.homeschool-maine.org
Member Families: 600
Convention: Yearly
Month(s): April/May
Attendance: 800

Maine Catholic Home Education Network
210 Beech Ridge Road
Scarborough, ME 04074-9151
Phone: (207) 839-6351
Web: members.aol.com/moosenews

Maryland

Christian Home Educators Network, Inc. (CHEN)
P.O. Box 2010
Ellicott City, MD 21043
Phone: (301) 474-9055
Email: chenmaster@chenmd.org
Web: www.chenmd.org
Member Families: 1,000
Convention: Yearly

Maryland Association of Christian Home Educators
P.O. Box 247
Point of Rocks, MD 21777
Phone: (301) 607-4284
Convention: Yearly

Massachusetts

Massachusetts Homeschool Organization of Parent Educators (MassHOPE)
5 Atwood Road
Cherry Valley, MA 01611-3332
Phone: (978) 544-7948, (508) 755-4467
Email: info@masshope.org, CalvinL158@alo.com
Web: www.masshope.org
"We do not have membership, but do have approximately 3,500 families in our database."
Convention: Yearly
Month(s): April
Attendance: 2,500

South Shore Homeschoolers
87 Snell Avenue
Brockton, MA 02402
Phone: (508) 588-1529

Michigan

Christian Home Educators of Michigan
Southfield, MI
Email: garykath@flash.net
Convention: Yearly
Attendance: 800

Homeschool Support Network of Michigan
P.O. Box 2457
Riverview, MI 48192
Phone: (734) 284-1249
Email: HSNMom@aol.com
Web: www.outrig.com/hsn/
Convention: Yearly
Month(s): January

Information Network for Christian Homes (INCH)
4934 Cannonsburg Road
Belmont, MI 49306
Phone: (616) 874-5656
Convention: Yearly
Attendance: 3,500

Traverse City Bulldogs
P.O. Box 5931
Traverse City, MI 49696
Email: croz@gtii.com
Boys and girls basketball program for homeschool children. Usually about 15–20 games per season, including state championship tournament.

Minnesota

Home-Based Educator's Accrediting Association (HBEAA)
P.O. Box 32122
Fridley, MN 55432
Phone: (612) 223-0333

Minnesota Association of Christian Home Educators (MACHE)
P.O. Box 32308
Fridley, MN 55432-0308
Phone: (612) 717-9070
Email: mache@isd.net
Web: www.mache.org
Member Families: 2,000
Graduation, high school dinner/cruise, SG
Leader conference. Publish *The Paper
MACHE,* a 16–20 page, bi-monthly
newsletter.
Convention: Yearly
Month(s): April
Attendance: 4,000

Minnesota Homeschoolers Alliance (MHA)
P.O. Box 23072
Richfield, MN 55423
Phone: (612) 288-9662
MHA is a volunteer organization that covers the state of MN. MHA offers a quarterly
newsletter and homeschooling handbook,
and also hosts regional events for fun and
information to homeschooling families.

Mississippi

Mississippi Home Educators Association (MHEA)
P.O. Box 945
Brookhaven, MS 39602
Phone: (601) 833-9110
Fax: (601) 833-9110
Email: mhea@juno.com
Web: www.mhea.org
Non-membership organization.
Convention: Yearly
Month(s): May

Missouri

Christian Home Educators Fellowship (CHEF)
1344 N. Bend Road
Union, MO 63084
Phone: (314) 521-8487
Convention: Yearly
Attendance: 2,000

Families for Home Education (FHE)
6209 NW Tower Drive
Platte Woods, MO 64151
Phone: (417) 782-8833
Email: fhe@microlink.net
Web: www.microlink.net/fhe/index.htm
Member Families: 4,600
Rally Day, workshops, speaking engagements.
Convention: Yearly
Month(s): June
Attendance: 2,000

Missouri Association of Teaching Christian Homes (MATCH)
2203 Rhonda Dr.
West Plains, MO 65775-1615
Phone: (417) 255-2824
Email: match@match-inc.org
Web: www.match-inc.org
Convention: Yearly
Attendance: 500

Montana

Montana Coalition of Home Educators (MCHE)
P.O. Box 43
Gallatin Gateway, MT 59730
Phone: (406) 587-6163
Email: white@gomontana.com
Web: www.mtche.com
Member Families: 1,200
Convention: Every other year
Month(s): May
Attendance: 750

The Grapevine, Montana Homeschool News
P.O. Box 3228
Missoula, MT 59806
Phone: (406) 542-8721
Published monthly during the school
year—September through May.
Subscriptions are $20 per year.

Nebraska

Nebraska Christian Home Educators Association
P.O. Box 57041
Lincoln, NE 68505-7041
Phone: (402) 423-4297
Convention: Yearly
Attendance: 1,200

Nevada

Home Education and Righteous Training
Box 42264
Las Vegas, NV 89116
Phone: (702) 391-7219

New Hampshire

Christian Home Educators of New Hampshire
P.O. Box 961
Manchester, NH 03105
Phone: (603) 569-2343
parison@chenh.mv.com
Convention: Yearly

New Hampshire Home Schooling Coalition
P.O. Box 2224
Concord, NH 03301
Phone: (603) 539-7233
Email: nhhc@dimentech.com
Web: www.nhhomeschooling.org
Convention: Yearly

New Jersey

Education Network of Christian Home Schoolers
P.O. Box 308
Atlantic Highlands, NJ 07716
Phone: (732) 291-7800
ENOCHNJ@aol.com
Convention: Yearly

Unschoolers Network
2 Smith Street
Farmingdale, NJ 07727
Phone: (732) 938-2473
Web: www.geocities.com/Athens/8259/
Convention: Yearly

New Mexico

Christian Association of Parent Educators - New Mexico (CAPE-NM)
P.O. Box 25046
Alburquerque, NM 87125
Phone: (505) 898-8548
Fax: (505) 294-7582
Email: cape-nm@juno.com
Web: www.cape-nm.org
Member Families: 600
Convention: Yearly
Month(s): April
Attendance: 1,200

New Mexico Family Educators (NMFE)
P.O. Box 92276
Alburquerque, NM 87199-2276
Phone: (505) 275-7053
Newsletter called *The Connection* published
ten times per year.

New York

Long Island Family Teachers United in Prayer (LIFT UP)
753 Greenlawn Ave.
Islip Terrace, NY 11752-1701
Phone: (516) 277-6646
Newsletter, parent meetings

Long Islanders Growing at Home Together (LIGHT)
186 East Avenue
Freeport, NY 11520
Phone: (516) 868-5766
Email: Devww2@aol.com
A non-profit organization that welcomes members of all denominations. The purpose of LIGHT is to offer information, organize activities for member children and their families, hold meetings that support members in their home education choice and help members introduce themselves to one another.

New York State Loving Education at Home (LEAH-NYS)
Box 438
Fayetteville, NY 13066
Phone: (716) 346-0939
Email: info@leah.org
Web: www.leah.org
Member Families: 2,700
Convention: Yearly

NY State Home Education News
P.O. Box 59
E. Chatham, NY 12060
Phone: (518) 392-6900

North Carolina

Heritage Education, Inc.
227 Clement Rd
Brevard, NC 28712
Phone: (828) 885-2311
Fax: (828) 885-2311 (call first)
Email: blamm@sitcom.net
Conference: Annual
Attendance: 750

North Carolinians for Home Education (NCHE)
419 North Boylan Avenue
Raleigh, NC 27603-1211
Phone: (919) 834-6243
Fax: (919) 834-6241
Email: nche@mindspring.com
Web: www.nche.com
Member Families: 5,000
Convention: Yearly
Month(s): May
Attendance: 6,100

North Dakota

North Dakota Home School Association
P.O. Box 7400
Bismarck, ND 58507-7400
Phone: (701) 223-4080
Email: gailb@wdata.com,
ndhsa@wdata.com
Convention: Yearly
Month(s): March
Attendance: 800

Ohio

Christian Home Educators of Ohio (CHEO)
430 N Court St.
Circleville, OH 43113
Phone: (740) 474-3177
Fax: (740) 474-3652
Email: cheohome@bright.net
Web: www.cheohome.org
Convention: Yearly
Attendance: 4,000

Christian Parents' Educational Fellowship
310 Blue Bonnet Drive
Findlay, OH 45840
Phone: (419) 422-9371
Fax: (419) 425-5209
Email: rwiseman@bright.net
Web: www.bright.net/~rwiseman/
Convention: Yearly
Attendance: 600

Ohio Home Educators Network
P.O. Box 23054
Chagrin Falls, OH 44023-0054
Fax: ohiohen@aol.com
Web: www.speedynet.net/~haas/ohen/

Oklahoma

Christian Home Educators Fellowship of Oklahoma
P.O. Box 471363
Tulsa, OK 74147-1363
Phone: (918) 583-7323
Email: chefofok@aol.com
Convention: Yearly

Home Educator's Resource Organization of Oklahoma (HERO-OK)
302 N. Coolidge
Enid, OK 73703-3819
Phone: (580) 438-2253
Email: mjmiller@pldi.net
Web: oklahomahomeschooling.org/
Fall conference, quarterly newsletter, annual directory, *Oklahoma Homeschooling Handbook*, open email list for OK residents.
Convention: Yearly

Oklahoma Central Home Educators' Consociation (OCHEC)
P.O. Box 270601
Oklahoma City, OK 73137
Phone: (405) 521-8439
Web: www.telepath.com/ochec/
Support groups, Legislative Watchdog Committee, bi-monthly newsletter, record-keeping, home school center, Capitol Day, conference, and book fair.
Convention: Yearly

Oklahoma Home Educators' Network (OHEN)
P.O. Box 1420
Blanchard, OK 73010
Phone: (405) 980-3863
Email: OKHEdNet@aol.com
"The purpose of the OHE network is to distribute factual information. Our primary focus is legislative affairs, though we also seek to provide other resources and useful information regarding homeschooling in Oklahoma."

Oregon

Lane Inter-Christian Guild of Home Teachers (LIGHT)
P.O. Box 70498 9111
811 Trivoli Street
Eugene, OR 97401
Phone: (541) 782-2466
Email: light@efn.org
Convention: Yearly

Oregon Christian Home Education Association Network (OCEAN)
17985 Falls City Rd.
Dallas, OR 97338
Phone: (503) 288-1285
Email: oceanet@oceanetwork.org
Web: www.oceanetwork.org
Convention: Yearly

Oregon Home Education Network (OHEN)
4470 SW Hall Blvd., #286
Beaverton, OR 97005
Phone: (503) 321-5166
Email: ohen@teleport.com
Web: www.teleport.com/~ohen/

Pennsylvania

Christian Homeschool Association of Pennsylvania (CHAP)
P.O. Box 115
Mount Joy, PA 17552
Phone: (717) 661-2428
Email: CHAPKimH@aol.com
Convention: Yearly

Pennsylvania Homeschoolers
RD 2 Box 117
Kittanning, PA 16201-9311
Phone: (724) 783-6512
Email: richmans@pahomeschoolers.com
Web: www.pahomeschoolers.com
Publish a quarterly newsletter called
Pennsylvania Homeschoolers. Sponsor
Homeschool Excellence Day at the capitol.
Pennsylvania Homeschoolers Accrediting
Agency is one of three groups that can issue
PA state-approved high school diplomas.
Annual PHAA High School at Home
Conference. Run many AP level Internet
courses. Over 100 affiliated support groups.

Puerto Rico

**Christian Home Educators
Association of Puerto Rico**
Luchetti 7 Ramon Fdz.
Manati, PR 00674
Phone: (787) 854-0167
Email: aarmaiz@hotmail.com

Rhode Island

**Rhode Island Guild of Home
Teachers (RIGHT)**
P.O. Box 11
Hope, RI 02831
Phone: (401) 821-7700
Convention: Yearly

South Carolina

**South Carolina Home Educators
Association (SCHEA)**
P.O. Box 3231
Columbia, SC 29230-3231
Phone: (803) 754-6425
Email: SCHEA1@aol.com
Convention: Yearly

South Dakota

**South Dakota Christian Home
Educators**
P.O. Box 9571
Rapid City, SD 57709-9571
Phone: (605) 341-3257
Convention: Yearly
Attendance: 450

**South Dakota Home School
Association**
P.O. Box 882
Sioux Falls, SD 57101-0882
Voicemail: (605) 338-4959
Convention: Yearly
Attendance: 500

Tennessee

**Chattanooga Southeast Tennessee
Home Educators**
7420 Short Tail Springs Rd.
Harrison, TN 37341
Phone: (423) 266-4663
Fax: (423) 344-4753
Email: carola@voy.net
Convention: Yearly
Attendance: 1,000

**Mid-East Tennessee Home
Education Association**
425 County Rd. 783
Etowah, TN 37331
Phone: (423) 263-3308
Fax: (423) 263-7026
Email: mideastthea@juno.com

**Middle Tennessee Home Education
Association**
P.O. Box 1382
Franklin, TN 37065
Phone: (615) 794-3259
Publish newsletter, *Jonathon's Arrow*
Convention: Yearly
Attendance: 2,000

**Tennessee Home Education
Association**
3677 Richbriar Court
Nashville, TN 37211
Phone: (615) 834-3529
Convention: Yearly

**West Tennessee Home Education
Association**
P.O. Box 10013
Jackson, TN 38308-9936
Phone: (901) 664-9936
Email: nod-llmoments@juno.com

Texas

**Christian Home Education
Association of Central Texas**
P.O. Box 141998
Austin, TX 78714-1998
Phone: (512) 450-0070
Email: cheacentx@juno.com
Convention: Yearly
Attendance: 1,200

**Family Educators Alliance of
South Texas (FEAST)**
4719 Blanco Road
San Antonio, TX 78212
Phone: 210-216-7068

Hearth and Home Ministries
P.O. Box 835105
Richardson, TX 75083
Phone: 972-231-6841 or 972-272-6965)
Fax: 972-231-6841
Email: info@homeschoolbookfair.org
Web: www.homeschoolbookfair.org
Convention: yearly
Attendance: 6,000

**North Texas Home Educators
Network (NTHEN)**
P.O. Box 830207
Richardson, TX 75083
Phone: (214) 804-8516
Email: info@nthen.org
Web: www.nthen.org
Convention: Yearly
Month(s): August

SE Texas Homeschool Association
4950 FM 1960 W Suite 297
Houston, TX 77069
Phone: (281) 370-8787
Fax: (281) 655-0963
Email: sethsa@sethsa.org
Web: www.sethsa.org
Convention: Yearly
Attendance: 4,000

**Texas Home School Coalition
(THSC)**
P.O. Box 6982
Lubbock, TX 79493
Phone: (806) 797-4927
Email: staff@thsc.org
Web: www.thsc.org
Convention: Yearly

Utah

**Utah Christian Home School
Association**
P.O. Box 3942
Salt Lake City, UT 84110-3942
Phone: (801) 296-7198
Email: utch@utch.org
Web: www.utch.org

Vermont

**Christian Home Educators of
Vermont**
7 Green Rd.
Wilmington, VT 05363
Phone: (802) 464-0746

Virginia

**Home Educators Association of
Virginia (HEAV)**
1900 Byrd Ave., Suite 201
Richmond, VA 23230
Phone: (804) 288-1608
Fax: (804) 288-6962
Email: HEAV33@aol.com
Web: www.heav.org
Member Families: 1,400
Convention: Yearly
Month(s): June
Attendance: 5,000

Washington

Washington Association of Teaching Christian Homes (WATCH)
554 Pletke Rd.
Tieton, WA 98947
Phone: (509) 678-5440
Email: Rlisk@aol.com
Convention: Yearly

Washington Homeschool Association (WHO)
6632 S 191st Place, Suite E-100
Kent, WA 98032-2117
Phone: (425) 251-0439
Fax: (425) 251-6984
Email: whooffice@juno.com
Web: www.washhomeschool.org
Convention: Yearly
Attendance: 3,300

West Virginia

Christian Home Educators of West Virginia
P.O. Box 8770
S. Charleston, WV 25303-0770
Phone: (304) 776-4664
Email: chewvadm@aol.com
Convention: Yearly

Wisconsin

Wisconsin Christian Home Educators Association (WCHEA)
2307 Carmel Avenue
Racine, WI 53405
Phone: (414) 637-5127
Fax: (414) 638-8127
Email: jang@execpc.com
Web: www.execpc.com/~jang/
Member Families: 780
Convention: Twice a year
Month(s): Sept/May
Attendance: 1,500

Wyoming

Homeschoolers of Wyoming
P.O. Box 3151
Jackson, WY 83001
Phone: (307) 733-2834
Email: mungermtrr@compuserve.com
Convention: Yearly

Overseas/Abroad

Christian Home Educators on Foreign Soil
HHC 160th
SIG BDE Box 948
APO 09164
Phone: 11-497-217-3912

Canada

Alberta

Wisdom Home Schooling
Box 78
Derwent, Alberta T0B 1C0
Phone: (780) 741-2113
Fax: (780) 741-2204
Email: wisdomhs@telusplanet.net
Web: www.telusplanet.net/public/wisdomhs

Home School Legal Defense Association of Canada
#203-1601 Dunmore Rd SE
Medicine Hat, Alberta T1A 1Z8
Phone: (403) 528-2704

Alberta Home Education Association
Box 40
Bluesky, Alberta T0H 0J0
Phone: (403) 236-1176
Web: www.abhome-ed.org

British Columbia

Chea (Canadian Home Educators Association of British Columbia)
Colleen Erzinger, President
c/o #8-4800 Island Hwy N
Nanaimo, British Columbia V9T 1W6
Phone/Fax: (250) 493-0338

Victoria Home Learning Network
#106-290 Regina Ave
Victoria, British columbia V8Z 6S6
Phone: 383-7618

Newfoundland

Peter & Pamela Hynes
52 Cottinwood Cres
St. John's, Newfoundland A1H 1A1
Phone: (709) 747-2041

Manitoba

Manitoba Association of Christian Home Schoolers (MACHS)
Interlake Region
Box 1006
Arborg, Manitoba R0C 0A0
Phone: (204) 376-523
Email: ghuebner@ecn.mb.ca

South Central Region
Box 499, RR #1, Grp 45
Winkler, Manitoba R6W 4A1
Phone: (204) 32-8686

New Brunswick

Bluenose Natural Home School
P.O. Box 243
Newcastle, New Brunswick E1B 3M3

Home Educators of New Brunswick
c/o Barbara Brewster
9 Garrison Drive
Renforth, New Brunswick E2H 2V1
Phone: (506) 847-4663
Email: 104302.1060@compuserve.com

Nova Scotia

Nova Scotia Home Educators Association
RR #1
Rose Bay, Nova Scotia B0J 2X0
Phone: (902) 766-4355
Contact: Marion Homer

Ontario

Catholic Home Schoolers Association
c/o Miriam Doylend
Box 24145, 300 Eagelson Rd.
Kanata, Ontario K2M 2C3

Homeschoolers of Colour Connection
2850 Lakeshore Blvd W #80068
Etobicoke, Ontario M8V 4A1
Email: Cher@sympatico.ca
Web: www3.sympatico.ca/cher

Ontario Christian Home Educators Connection
Box 2
Iona Station, Ontario N0L 1P0
Phone: (519) 764-2841

Toronto Christian Homeschool Association
1403-2550 Kingston Rd.
Scarborough, Ontario M1M 1L7
Web: www.netcom.ca/~vcolling/torch.html

Ontario Christian Home Educators Connection (OCHEC)
c/o Jake & Heather Zwart
RR #1
Millgrove, Ontario L0R 1V0
Phone: (905) 689-7762
Fax: (905) 689-9620
Email: secretary#ochec.org
Web: www.ochec.org

Quebec

Association of Christian Home Educators of Quebec (ACHEQ)
12 Reaume
N.D. Ile Perrot, Quebec J7V 7X4
Phone: (514) 425-1135
Web: achequ-acefq@uni-signal.ca

Saskatchewan

Saskatchewan Home Based Educators
207 Adolph Way
Saskatoon, Saskatchewan S7N 3K2
Phone: (306) 249-2636

Christian Home Educators of Saskatoon and Surrounding (CHESS)
c/o Menno & Karen Wedel
1801 Grosvenor Ave
Saskatoon, Saskatchewan S7H 2T5
Phone: (306) 373-6194

MYRRH Newsletter
#197-919C Albert St
Regina, Saskatchewan S4R 2P6

Foreign Countries

Australia

Christian Academy of Life Ltd.
P.O. Box 300
Laidley, Queensland 4341
Phone: 07-5465-1076
Email: HomeSchoolingLife@uq.net.au

Families Honoring Christ
Box 310
Mount Waverly, Victoria 3149
Phone: 03-9544-8792

Homeschoolers Australia
P.O. Box 346
Seven Hills, New South Wales 2147
Phone: 02 629 3727
Fax: 02 629 3278
Application for dispensation through the State Education Dept required.

England/United Kingdom

Education Otherwise
P.O. Box 7420
London N9 9SG UK
Web: www.education-otherwise.org

Home Education Advisory Service
P.O. Box 98
Welwyn Garden City, Herts. AL8 6AN
Email: 100752.1061@compuserve.com
Web: ourworld.compuserve.com/home-pages/home_ed_advisory_srv

Home Service
48 Heaton Moor Road
Heaton Moor, Stockport SK4 4NX
Phone: 161-432-3782

Learning In a Family Environment
PSC 37 Box 1215
APO AE 09459
Phone: 01638-533516

Germany

HEART for Germany (Home Educators are Real Teachers)
ICOAC4, Messtetten Unit 30405
APO AE 09131
Phone: 7579-921873
Email: wagnerwn@swol.de

Japan

Kanto Plain Home Schoolers
PSC 473 Box 184
FPO AP 96349-5555
Email: msbunny@surf-line.or.jp

Korea

Yet to be named... Cornerstone?
P.O. Box 24
Sachon City, Kyungnam Province
660-360, Republic of Korea
Phone: 82-591-758-5201
Contact: Jan

Mexico/Central America

El Hogar Educador
APDO 17
Arteaga Coahuila 25350
Phone: 018-483-0377
Email: vnm@characterlink.net

New Zealand

Christian Home Schoolers of New Zealand
4 Tawa Street
Palmerston North 5301
Phone: 06-357-4399
Email: keystone.teach@xtra.co.nz

Learning as Families
35A Primrose Street
Hamilton
Phone: 07 847-8248
Email: salpow@ihug.co.nz

Homeschool Laws by State

This section should quell the fears of relatives and friends!

As you can clearly see, homeschooling is legal everywhere in the U.S., including its territories. The laws regarding homeschooling do vary quite a bit from state to state, though.

The listing below is a snapshot summary of the laws at one point in time—June 19, 2000. State laws change, so for the most recent listing for your state, visit *www.hslda.org/central/states/*.

The information below does not constitutes the giving of legal advice. It is for your benefit in getting a broad picture of the laws nationwide, and as a starting point for your own study of the actual laws.

Also please note that while some states *require* a notice of intent to homeschool, others only *allow* for it. Where the chart says you "may" file a notice of intent to homeschool, generally state homeschooling groups advise against this. Contact your local state group for detailed information on how to comply with the homeschool law in your state.

State or Territory	Compulsory School Age	Legal Options to Home School	Attendance Required	Subjects Required	Teacher Credentials	Notice Required	Recordkeeping Required	Testing Required
Alabama	Between the ages of 7 and 16	Establish and/or enroll in a church school	None specified (175 days required for the public schools)	None	None	File a notice of enrollment and attendance with the local superintendent on a provided form (not required annually)	Maintain a daily attendance register	None
		Use a private tutor	140 days per year, 3 hours per day between the hours of 8am and 4pm	Reading, spelling, writing, arithmetic, English, geography, history of the United States, science, health, physical education, and Alabama history	Teacher certification	File a statement showing children to be instructed, the subjects taught and the period of instruction with the local superintendent	Maintain a register of the child's work	None
Alaska	Between 7 and 16	Establish and operate a home school	None	None	None	None	None	None
		Use a private tutor	180 days per year	Comparable to those offered in the public schools	Teacher certification	None	None	None
		Enroll in a state department of education approved full-time correspondence program	180 days per year	Comparable to those offered in the public schools	None	None	None	None
		Request school board approval to provide an equal alternate educational experience	180 days per year	Comparable to those offered in the public schools	None	None	None	None

State or Territory	Compulsory School Age	Legal Options to Home School	Attendance Required	Subjects Required	Teacher Credentials	Notice Required	Recordkeeping Required	Testing Required
Alaska (cont.)		Qualify as a religious or other private school	180 days per year	None, but standardized testing must cover English grammar, reading, spelling, and math	None	File a Private School Enrollment Reporting Form with the local superintendent by the first day of public school; also file a Private and Denominational Schools Enrollment Report and a School Calendar with the state department of education by October 15 each year	Maintain monthly attendance records; also maintain records on immunization, courses, standardized testing, academic achievement, and physical exams	Administer a standardized test in grades 4, 6, and 8
American Samoa	Between 6 and 18 years of age inclusive, or from grade one through grade twelve	Request department of education authorization to operate a private school	Same as the public schools	A curriculum that is approved as being in the interest of good citizenship by the director of education	Teacher certification	A de facto part of the authorization process	Maintain permanent report cards; submit monthly enrollment reports and an annual report to the department of education	None
Arizona	Between 6 and 16; by noting so in affidavit (see Notice Required), instruction in a home school setting may be delayed until 8 years of age	Establish and operate a home school	None	Reading, grammar, math, social studies and science	None	File an affidavit of intent with the local superintendent within 30 days of the start (even if instruction will be delayed until age 8) or end of home schooling	None	None
Arkansas	5 through 17 on or before September 15 of that year; a child under age 6 on September 15 may be waived from kindergarten with submission of a state-provided form	Establish and operate a home school	None	None	None	File written notice of intent with the local superintendent by August 15 (for those starting in fall semester), December 15 (for those starting in spring semester), or 14 days prior to withdrawing child mid-semester from public school; re-file annually thereafter at beginning of school year	None	Participate in same state-mandated norm-referenced tests given to public school students (in grades 5, 7, and 10); no cost to parent unless alternate testing procedures are approved
California	Between the ages of 6 by December 2 and under 18 years of age	Qualify as a private school	None	Same as the public schools and in the English language	Must be capable of teaching	File an annual affidavit with the local superintendent between October 1 and 15	Maintain an attendance register	None
		Use a private tutor	175 days per year, 3 hours per day	Same as the public schools and in the English language	Teacher certification	None	None	None
		Enroll in an independent study program through the public school	As prescribed by the program	As prescribed by the program	None	A de facto part of the enrollment process	As prescribed by the program	As prescribed by the program
		Enroll in a private school satellite program, taking independent study	As prescribed by the program	As prescribed by the program	Must be capable of teaching	None	As prescribed by the program	As prescribed by the program
Colorado	7 and under the age of 16. Also appl[ies] to a six-year-old child who has been enrolled in a public school in the first [or higher] grade, unless the parent or legal guardian chooses to withdraw such child.	Establish and operate a home school	172 days per year, averaging four hours per day	Constitution of the United States, reading, writing, speaking, math, history, civics, literature, and science	None	File notice of intent with the local superintendent 14 days prior to start of home school and annually thereafter	Maintain attendance records, test and evaluation results, and immunization records	Administer a standardized test for grades 3, 5, 7, 9, and 11 or have the child evaluated by a qualified person selected by parent
		Enroll in a private school that allows home instruction	None	As prescribed by the program	None	None	None	None
		Use a private tutor	None	Constitution of the United States, reading, writing, speaking, math, history, civics, literature, and science	Teacher certification	None	None	None
Connecticut	Five years of age and over and under sixteen years of age; five- or six-year-olds can opt out when the parent goes to the school district and signs an option form	Establish and operate a home school	Generally, 180 days per year	Reading, writing, spelling, English, grammar, geography, arithmetic, United States history, and citizenship, including a study of the town, state and federal governments	None	None, but parents may voluntarily comply with State Dept. of Education guidelines by filing a Notice of Intent form with the local superintendent within 10 days of the start of home school	The guidelines require that parents maintain a portfolio indicating that instruction in the required courses has been given	None

State or Territory	Compulsory School Age	Legal Options to Home School	Attendance Required	Subjects Required	Teacher Credentials	Notice Required	Recordkeeping Required	Testing Required
Delaware	Between 5 years of age and 16 years of age; can delay start (if in best interests of the child) with school authorization	Establish and operate a home school providing regular and thorough instruction to the satisfaction of the local superintendent and the state board of education	180 days per year	Same as the public schools	None	Report enrollment, student ages, and attendance to Department of Education on or before July 31 each year; also submit annual statement of enrollment as of last school day in September in form prescribed by Department of Education	None	Administer a written examination as prescribed during the approval process
		Establish and/or enroll in a home school association or organization	180 days per year	Same as the public schools	None	Association or organization must register with the Department of Education; report enrollment, student ages, and attendance to Department of Education on or before July 31 each year; also submit annual statement of enrollment as of last school day in September in form prescribed by Department of Education	None	None
District of Columbia	Age of 5 years by December 31 of current school year until minor reaches the age of 18	Provide private instruction not affiliated with an educational institution	During the period that the public schools are in session	None	None	None, unless the child is being removed from the public school	None	None
Florida	Attained the age of 6 years by February 1, but have not attained the age of 16 years	Establish and operate a home school	None specified (180 days required for the public schools)	None	None	File notice of intent with the local superintendent within 30 days of establishment for home school (not required annually)	Maintain a portfolio of records and materials (log of texts and sample work sheets)	Annually, either: 1) administer any standardized test or a state student assessment test; must be given by a certified teacher, 2) have child evaluated by a certified teacher, or 3) be evaluated by a licensed psychologist, or 4) have child evaluated by another valid tool that is mutually agreed upon
		Qualify and operate as part of a private school corporation (a legally incorporated group of home school families)	None specified (180 days required for the public schools)	None	None	None	None	None
Georgia	Between 7th and 16th birthdays; Before 7th birthday if a child has attended public school for more than 20 days	Establish and conduct a home study program	180 days per year, 4 hours per day	Reading, language arts, math, social studies, and science	High school diploma or GED for a teaching parent; baccalaureate degree for any private tutor used	File a declaration of intent with the local superintendent within 30 days of commencing the home study program and by September 1 annually thereafter	Maintain attendance records and submit monthly to the superintendent; write and retain an annual progress report	Administer and retain the results of a standardized test every 3 years beginning at the end of the 3rd grade
Guam	Between the ages of 5 and 16 years	Private instruction by a private tutor or other person	170 days per year	Same as the public schools and in the English language	None	None	None	None
Hawaii	Have arrived at the age of at least 6 years and not at the age of 18 years by January 1	Establish and operate a home school	None	Curriculum must be structured and based on educational objectives as well as the needs of the child, be cumulative and sequential, provide a range of up-to-date knowledge and needed skills, and take into account the interests, needs, and abilities of the child	None	File a notice of intent with the principal of the public school the child would otherwise be required to attend before starting to home school (not required annually); notify this same principal within 5 days after ending home school	Maintain a record of the planned curriculum	Administer standardized achievement test of parent's choice in grades 3, 6, 8, and 10; Submit annual report of child's progress to local principal comprised of either: 1) standardized test results, or 2) written evaluation by certified teacher, or 3) written evaluation by parent
		Enroll in a superintendent-approved appropriate alternative educational program	As prescribed during the approval process (about 3 hrs per day)	As prescribed during the approval process	Baccalaureate degree	None	None	Participate in statewide testing program at the public schools

State or Territory	Compulsory School Age	Legal Options to Home School	Attendance Required	Subjects Required	Teacher Credentials	Notice Required	Recordkeeping Required	Testing Required
Idaho	Attained the age of 7 years, but not the age of 16 years	Provide an alternate educational experience for the child that is otherwise comparably instructed	Same as the public schools	Same as the public schools	None	None	None	None
Illinois	Between the ages of 7 and 16 years	Operate a home school as a private school	Generally, 176 days per year, but not mandated for private or home schools	Language arts, biological and physical science, math, social sciences, fine arts, health and physical development, honesty, justice, kindness, and moral courage	None	None	None	None
Indiana	Earlier of the date the child officially enrolls in a school or reaches the age of 7 until his 18th birthday	Operate a home school as a private school	Same as the public schools; Generally, 180 days per year	None	None	None, unless specifically requested by the state superintendent of education	Maintain attendance records	None
Iowa	Age 6 by September 15 until age 16	Establish and operate a home school	148 days per year (37 days each quarter)	None	None	Complete an annual Competent Private Instruction Report Form; file 2 copies with the local school district by 1st day of school or within 14 days of withdrawal from school	None	Complete by May 1 and submit to the local school district by June 30: 1) test results from an acceptably administered standardized test, or 2) a portfolio for review
		Establish and operate a home school that is supervised by a licensed teacher	Same as above	None	None for teaching parent; license for the supervising teacher	Same as above	None	None; however, must meet with supervising teacher twice per quarter (one may be conducted by telephone)
		Use a private tutor	Same as above	None	Teaching license	Same as above	None	None
Kansas	Reached the age of 7 and under the age of 18 years	Operate a home school as a non-accredited private school	Substantially equivalent to public school: 186 days per year or 1116 hrs per year; 1086 hrs for 12th grade	None	Must be a competent teacher (however, local school board has no authority to define or evaluate competence of private school teachers)	Register name and address of school with the state board of education (not subject to approval)	None	None
		Operate a home school as a satellite of an accredited private school	As prescribed by the supervising private school	As prescribed by the supervising private school		None	As prescribed by the supervising private school	As prescribed by the supervising private school
		Qualify for a state board of education approved religious exemption in the high school grades	As prescribed during the approval process	As prescribed during the approval process	As prescribed during the approval process	A de facto part of the approval process	As prescribed during the approval process	As prescribed during the approval process
Kentucky	Has reached the 6th birthday and has not passed the 16th birthday	Qualify a home school as a private school	185 days per year, or the equivalent of 175 six-hour days	Reading, writing, spelling, grammar, history, mathematics, and civics	None	Notify the local board of education of those students in attendance within two weeks of start of school year	Maintain an attendance register and scholarship reports	None
Louisiana	From the child's 7th birthday until his 17th birthday	Establish and operate a home school as approved by the board of education	180 days per year	At least equal to the quality of that in the public schools including the Declaration of Independence and the Federalist Papers	None	File an application and a copy of the child's birth certificate, with board of education, within 15 days after start of home school and annually thereafter	Whatever form(s) of documentation is(are) planned to satisfy the testing requirement	Submit with renewal application documents showing satisfactory evidence that the program is at least equal to that offered by the public schools
		Operate a home school as a private school	180 days per year	Same as above	None	Submit notification to the state department of education within the first 30 days of the school year	None	None
Maine	7 years of age or older and under 17 years	Establish and operate a home school as approved by the local school board and the commissioner of the state department of education	175 days per year	English, language arts, math, science, social studies, physical and health education, library skills, fine arts, Maine studies (in one grade between grade 6 and 12), and computer proficiency (in one grade between grade 7 and 12)	None	Complete a state-provided Application for Equivalent Instruction Through Home Instruction form; submit a copy to both the local school board and the commissioner of the state department of education 60 days prior to start of home school	None	Annually, either: 1) administer a standardized test, or 2) take a local test, or 3) have child's progress reviewed by a certified teacher, a superintendent-selected local advisory board, or a home school support group that includes a certified teacher
		Operate a home school as a non-approved private school that teaches at least 2 unrelated students	175 days per year	None	None	None	None	None

State or Territory	Compulsory School Age	Legal Options to Home School	Attendance Required	Subjects Required	Teacher Credentials	Notice Required	Recordkeeping Required	Testing Required
Maryland	5 years old or older and under 16 with one-year exemption available for 5 year-olds	Establish and operate a qualified home school	Must be of sufficient duration to implement the instructional program	Must provide regular, thorough instruction in the same subjects as the public schools including English, math, science, social studies, art, music, health, and physical education	None	File a notice of intent with the state department of education at least 15 days before the start of home school	Maintain a portfolio of relevant materials, reviewable by the local superintendent up to 3 times per year	None
		Provide supervised home instruction through a church school or a state-approved correspondence course	As prescribed by the supervising program	As prescribed by the supervising program	None	File a notice of intent with the state department of education at least 15 days before the start of home school	As prescribed by the supervising program	As prescribed by the supervising program
Massachusetts	6 to 16 years of age	Establish and operate a home school as approved in advance by the local school committee or superintendent	None specified, though 900 hours at elementary level and 990 hours at secondary level are expected	Reading, writing, English language and grammar, geography, arithmetic, drawing, music, history, and constitution of United States, duties of citizenship, health (including CPR), physical education, and good behavior	None	A de facto part of the approval process	None	Annually, either: 1) administer a standardized test; must be administered by a neutral party, or 2) submit progress reports to the school district
Michigan	Age of 6 to the child's 16th birthday	Establish and operate a home education program	None	Reading, spelling, mathematics, science, history, civics, literature, writing, and English grammar	None	None	None	None
		Operate a home school as a non-public school	None	Must be comparable to those taught in the public schools	Teacher certification (unless claiming a religious exemption)	Submit, to the local superintendent, at start of each school year a statement of enrollment	Maintain records of enrollment, courses of study, and qualifications of teachers (must be submitted to the Department of Education upon request)	None
Minnesota	Between 7 and 16 years of age	Establish and operate a qualified home school	None	Reading, writing, literature, fine arts, math, science, history, geography, government, health, and physical education	None	File with the local superintendent by October 1 of each school year the name, age, and address of each child taught	If teaching parent is not at least a college graduate, submit a quarterly report to the local superintendent showing the achievement of each child in the required subjects	Administer an annual standardized test as agreed to by the local superintendent
Mississippi	Age of 6 on or before September 1 and has not attained the age of 17 on or before September 1	Establish and operate a home school	Whatever number of days that each [home] school shall require for promotion from grade to grade	None	None	File a certificate of enrollment by September 15 of each school year to the district's attendance officer	None	None
Missouri	Between the ages of 7 and 16 years	Establish and operate a home school	1,000 hours per year; at least 600 hours in the five required subjects; 400 of these 600 hrs must occur at the regular home school location	Reading, math, social studies, language arts, and science	None	None required; parents may provide a notice of intent within 30 days of establishment and on September 1 each year thereafter	Maintain records of subjects taught, activities engaged in, samples of the child's academic work and evaluations or a credible equivalent	None
Montana	7 years of age or older prior to the first day of school and the later of the following dates: the child's 16th birthday; the day of completion of the work of the 8th grade	Establish and operate a home school	180 days per year, 4 hours per day for grades 1–3 and 6 hours per day for grades 4–12	Same basic instructional program as the public schools	None	File annual notice of intent with the county superintendent	Maintain attendance and immunization records; must be available for inspection by local superintendent upon request	None
Nebraska	Not less than 7 nor more than 16 years of age	Establish and operate a home school as a private school	1,032 hours per year for elementary grades, 1,080 hours per year for high school grades	Language arts, math, science, social studies, and health	None, unless the teacher is employed by the family	File an annual notice of intent with the state commissioner of education by August 1 (or 30 days prior to the start of home school)	None	None

State or Territory	Compulsory School Age	Legal Options to Home School	Attendance Required	Subjects Required	Teacher Credentials	Notice Required	Recordkeeping Required	Testing Required
Nevada	Between the ages of 7 and 17 years	Establish and operate a home school	180 days per year; 240 minutes per day for grades 1 and 2; 300 minutes per day for grades 3–6; 330 minutes per day for grades 7–12	Parents must provide the local school board with satisfactory written evidence that the child is receiving at home . . equivalent instruction of the kind and amount approved by the state board of education, including U.S. and Nevada constitutions	Either: 1) possess a teaching certificate for grade level taught, or 2) consult with a licensed teacher or 3-year home school veteran, or 3) use an approved correspondence course, or 4) obtain a waiver; Options #1, #2, & #3 are waived after 1st year	File, with the local school board, annual satisfactory written evidence that the child is receiving at home...equivalent instruction of the kind and amount approved by the state board of education	None	None
New Hampshire	At least 6 years of age [on September 30] and under 16 years of age	Establish and operate a home school	None	Science, mathematics, language, government, history, health, reading, writing, spelling, U.S. and New Hampshire constitutional history, and art and music appreciation	None	Within 30 days of withdrawing from public school or moving into the school district, file a notice of intent with a private school principal, the state commissioner of education, or the local superintendent	Maintain a portfolio of records and materials including a log of reading materials used, samples of writings, worksheets, workbooks or creative materials used or developed by the child	By July 1, file either: 1) results from a standardized test, or 2) results from a state student assessment test used by the local school district, or 3) a written evaluation by a certified teacher, or 4) results of another measure agreeable to the local school board
New Jersey	Between the ages of six and 16 years	Establish and operate a home school	None specified (180 days required for the public schools)	U.S. and New Jersey history, citizenship, civics, geography, sexual assault prevention*, health*, safety, and physical education *may opt out	None	None	None	None
New Mexico	At least five years of age prior to 12:01am on September 1 of the school year to the age of majority unless the person has graduated from high school; children under eight can be excused	Establish and operate a home school	Same as public schools	Reading, language arts, mathematics, social studies, and science	High school diploma or equivalent	File notice of intent with the school district superintendent within 30 days of establishing the home school and by April 1 of each subsequent year	Maintain attendance and immunization records	In grades 4, 6, & 8 either: 1) take the district-administered state achievement test, or 2) participate in the Bob Jones University Press Testing Service (must notify the school board of intent by January 15)
New York	A minor who becomes six years of age on or before the first of December in any school year until the last day of session in the school year in which the minor becomes sixteen years of age or completes high school	Establish and operate a home school	Substantial equivalent of 180 days per year; 900 hours per year for grades 1–6; 990 hours per year for grades 7–12	Grades K–12: patriotism and citizenship, substance abuse, traffic safety, fire safety; Grades 1–6: arithmetic, reading, spelling, writing, English, geography, U.S. history, science, health, music, visual arts, and physical education; Grades 7–8: English, history and geography, science, mathematics, physical education, health, art, music, practical arts, and library skills; At least once in grades 1–8: U.S. and New York history and constitutions; Grades 9–12: English, social studies—including American history, participation in government, and economics, math, science, art or music, health, physical education, and electives	Competent	File annual notice of intent with the local superintendent by July 1 or within 14 days if starting home schooling mid-year; complete and submit an Individualized Home Instruction Plan (form provided by district)	Maintain attendance records (must make available for inspection upon request of the local superintendent); file, with the local superintendent, quarterly reports listing hours completed, material covered, and a grade or evaluation in each subject	File, with the local superintendent, an annual assessment by June 30; must be from a standardized test every other year in grades 4–8, and every year in grades 9–12; other years can be satisfied by either another standardized test or a written narrative evaluation prepared by a certified teacher, a home instruction peer review panel, or other person chosen by the parent with the consent of the superintendent
North Carolina	Between the ages of seven and 16 years	Establish and operate a home school	At least nine calendar months per year, excluding reasonable holidays and vacations	None, but annual standardized tests must cover English grammar, reading, spelling, and mathematics	High school diploma or GED	File notice of intent with the state division of non-public education upon starting home school	Maintain attendance and immunization records and results of standardized tests	Administer an annual standardized test measuring achievement in English grammar, reading, spelling, and mathematics, the results of which must be available for inspection

State or Territory	Compulsory School Age	Legal Options to Home School	Attendance Required	Subjects Required	Teacher Credentials	Notice Required	Recordkeeping Required	Testing Required
North Dakota	Any educable child of an age of seven years to sixteen years	Establish and operate a home school	175 days per year, four hours per day	Elementary: spelling, reading, writing, arithmetic, language, English grammar, geography, U.S. history, civil government, nature, elements of agriculture, physiology and hygiene, effects of alcohol, prevention of contagious diseases, U.S. Constitution; High School level: English, math, science, social studies, health and physical education, music, combination of business, economics, foreign language, industrial arts, or vocational education	Possess either: 1) a teaching certificate, or 2) a baccalaureate degree, 3) a high school diploma or GED and be monitored by a certified teacher during first two years or until child completes 3rd grade, whichever is later; monitoring must continue thereafter if child scores below the 50th percentile on required standardized achievement test, or 4) proof of meeting or exceeding the cut-off score of the national teacher exam	File annual notice of intent with the local superintendent 14 days prior to the start of the home school or within 14 days of establishing residency inside the district For Autistic Children: In addition to above, file a copy of the child's diagnosis from a licensed psychologist along with an individualized education program developed and followed by the child's school district and parent or by a team selected and compensated by the parent.	Maintain an annual record of courses and each child's academic progress assessments, including standardized achievement test results For Autistic Children: Also file with the local superintendent progress reports from an individualized education program team selected by the parent on or before November 1, February 1, and May 1 of each school year	Take a standardized achievement test in grades 3, 4, 6, 8 and 11; must be administered by a certified teacher; results must be provided to the local superintendent; a composite score below the 30th percentile requires a professional assessment for learning problems and submission of a plan of remediation to the local superintendent
		Operate a home school as a county- and state-approved private school	Same as the public schools	Same as above	Teacher certification	A de facto part of the approval process	None	None
Northern Mariana Islands	Between the ages of six and sixteen	Seek approval to operate a home school	180 days per year with at least 300 minutes of secular instruction daily	Same as the public schools	None	Submit a waiver application to the commissioner at least 60 days prior to start of school year	Submit to the commissioner monthly, quarterly, and annual reports on program progress	None
		Seek approval to operate a home school as an chartered non-public school	Same as above	As prescribed by the board in issuing a charter	None	Submit to the board of education an application for a charter	As prescribed by the board in issuing a charter	None
Ohio	Between six and eighteen years of age	Establish and operate a home school	900 hours per year	Language arts, geography, U.S. and Ohio history, government, math, health, physical education, fine arts, first aid and science	High school diploma, GED, test scores showing high school equivalence, or work under a person with a baccalaureate degree until child's test scores show proficiency or parent earns diploma or GED	Submit an annual notice of intent to the local superintendent	None	Submit with renewal notification either: 1) standardized test scores, or 2) a written narrative showing satisfactory academic progress, or 3) an approved alternative assessment
Oklahoma	Over age of five (5) years and under the age of eighteen (18) years	Establish and operate a home school as an other means of education expressed in the state constitution	None	Reading, writing, math, science, citizenship, U.S. constitution, health, safety, physical education, conservation	None	None	None	None
Oregon	Between the ages of 7 and 18 years who have not completed the twelfth grade	Establish and operate a home school	None	None	None	Notify education service district in writing when child starts being taught at home; when moving, notify new district in same manner	None	Participate in an approved comprehensive test in grades 3, 5, 8, and 10 administered by a qualified neutral person; if child was withdrawn from public school, the first test must be administered at least 18 months after child was withdrawn; children with disabilities are to be evaluated as per their individualized education plan

State or Territory	Compulsory School Age	Legal Options to Home School	Attendance Required	Subjects Required	Teacher Credentials	Notice Required	Recordkeeping Required	Testing Required
Pennsylvania	From time the child enters school, which shall not be later than the age of eight (8) years, until the age of seventeen (17) years	Establish and operate a home education program	180 days per year or 900 hours at the elementary level or 990 hours at the secondary level	Elementary level: English spelling, reading, writing, arithmetic, U.S. and Pennsylvania history, civics, health and physiology, physical education, music, art, geography, science, safety and fire prevention Secondary level: English language, literature, speech and composition, science, geography, civics, world, U.S., and Pennsylvania history, algebra and geometry, art, music, physical education, health, safety, and fire prevention	High school diploma or equivalent	File a notarized affidavit with the local superintendent prior to start of home school and annually by August 1st thereafter	Maintain a portfolio of materials used, work done, standardized test results in grades 3, 5, and 8, and a written evaluation completed by June 30 of each year	Administer standardized tests in grades 3, 5, and 8; submit results as part of portfolio
		Establish and/or operate a home school as an extension or satellite of a private school	Same as above		None	School principal must file a notarized affidavit with the department of education	None	None
		Use a private tutor who: 1) is teaching one or more children who are members of a single family, 2) provides the majority of instruction, and 3) is receiving a fee or other consideration for the instruction	Same as above		Teacher certification	File copy of certification and criminal history record with the local superintendent	None	None
Puerto Rico	Between six and eighteen years of age	Establish and operate a home school as a non-governmental school	Same as the public schools	Same as the public schools	None	None	None	None
Rhode Island	Completed six (6) years of life on or before December 31 of any school year and not completed sixteen (16) years of life	Establish and operate a home school as approved by the local school board	Substantially equal to that of the public schools	Reading, writing, geography, arithmetic, U.S. and Rhode Island history, principles of American government, English, health and physical education; U.S. and R.I. constitution in high school	None	A de facto part of the approval process	Maintain an attendance register	As prescribed during the approval process; may require report cards
South Carolina	5 years of age before September 1st until 17th birthday or graduation from high school; 5-year-olds may be excused from kindergarten with submission of written notice to the school district	Establish and operate a home school as approved by the local school board	180 days per year, 4 hours per day	Reading, writing, math, science, and social studies; also composition and literature in grades 7–12	High school diploma or GED or a baccalaureate degree	None	Maintain evidence of regular instruction including a record of subjects taught, activities in which the student and parent engage, a portfolio of the child's work, and a record of academic evaluations, with a semiannual progress report	Participate in the annual statewide testing program and the Basic Skills Assessment Program
		Establish and operate a home school under the membership auspices of the South Carolina Association of Independent Home Schools (SCAIHS)	180 days per year	Reading, writing, math, science, and social studies; also composition and literature in grades 7–12	High school diploma or GED	None	None	None
		Establish and operate a home school under the membership auspices of an association for home schools with no fewer than fifty members	180 days per year	Reading, writing, math, science, and social studies; also composition and literature in grades 7–12	High school diploma or GED	None	Maintain evidence of regular instruction including a record of subjects taught, activities in which the student and parent engage, and a portfolio of the child's work, with a semiannual progress report	None
South Dakota	Six years old by the first day of September and who has not exceeded the age of sixteen years; children under age 7 can be excused	Establish and operate a home school	Similar to that of the public schools; generally 175 days per year	Language arts and math	None	Submit a notarized application to the local superintendent using the standard form provided by state department of education	None	Administer a standardized test to children in the same grade levels tested under the state testing program (grades 4, 8, and 11)

State or Territory	Compulsory School Age	Legal Options to Home School	Attendance Required	Subjects Required	Teacher Credentials	Notice Required	Recordkeeping Required	Testing Required
Tennessee	Between the ages of six (6) and seventeen (17) years, both inclusive; also applicable to children under age 6 who have enrolled in any public, private, or parochial school for more than six weeks; a parent of a six-year-old may make application for a one-semester or one-year deferral with the principal of the public school in which the child would be required to attend	Establish and operate a home school	180 days per year, 4 hours per day	For grades K–8: None For grades 9–12: English, mathematics, science, social studies, and wellness; also must take college preparation subjects according to declared path—foreign language and fine arts for University path; focus area for Tech path	For grades K–8: High school diploma or GED For grades 9–12: College degree (or an exemption granted by the commissioner of education)	Submit a notice of intent to the local superintendent by August 1 of each school year	Maintain attendance records; must be kept available for inspection and submitted to the local superintendent at the end of the school year	Administer a standardized test in grades 5, 7, and 9; must be given by commissioner of education, his designee, or a professional testing service approved by the local school district
		Establish and operate a home school in association with a church-related school	As prescribed by the church-related school	As prescribed by the church-related school	For grades K–8: None For grades 9–12: High school diploma or GED	For grades K–8: None For grades 9–12: Register with the local school district each year	None	Administer the same annual standardized achievement test or Sanders Model assessment used by the local school district for grades 9–12
		Operate as a satellite campus of a church-related school	As prescribed by the church-related school	As prescribed by the church-related school	None	None	None	As prescribed by the church-related school
		Operate as a satellite campus of a non-recognized religious school, based upon an assertion that the church-related school option unconstitutionally excludes certain religions	As prescribed by the religious school	As prescribed by the religious school	None	None	None	As prescribed by the religious school
Texas	As much as 6 years of age, or who is less than 7 years of age and has previously been enrolled in 1st grade, and who has not completed the academic year in which his 17th birthday occurred	Establish and operate a home school as a private school	None	Reading, spelling, grammar, math, good citizenship	None	None	None	None
Utah	Between six and 18 years of age	Establish and operate a home school as approved by the local school board	Same as the public schools	Language arts, math, science, social studies, arts, health, computer literacy, and vocational education	None specified; however, the local school board can consider the basic educative ability of the teacher	A de facto part of the approval process	None	None
		Establish a group of home school families as a regular private school	None	None	None	None	None	None
Vermont	Between the ages of seven and sixteen years	Establish and operate a home school	175 days per year	Reading, writing, math, citizenship, history, U.S. and Vermont government, physical education, health, English, science, and fine arts	None	File a written notice of enrollment with the commissioner of education any time after March 1 for the subsequent year	None	Submit an annual assessment from: 1) a certified (or approved Vermont independent school) teacher, or 2) a report from a commercial curriculum publisher together with a portfolio, or 3) results of an acceptably administered standardized test
Virgin Islands	Beginning of the school year nearest [child's] 5th birthday until the expiration of the school year nearest [child's] 16th birthday, except those who graduate from high school earlier	Seek commissioner of education approval to establish and operate a home school	As prescribed during the approval process	As prescribed during the approval process	As prescribed during the approval process	A de facto part of the approval process	As prescribed during the approval process	As prescribed during the approval process
		Apply for accreditation to operate a home school as a private school	As prescribed during the accreditation process	As prescribed during the accreditation process	As prescribed during the accreditation process	A de facto part of the accreditation process	As prescribed during the accreditation process	As prescribed during the accreditation process

State or Territory	Compulsory School Age	Legal Options to Home School	Attendance Required	Subjects Required	Teacher Credentials	Notice Required	Recordkeeping Required	Testing Required
Virginia	Has reached the 5th birthday on or before September 30, and has not passed the 18th birthday; 5 year-olds can be excused	Establish and operate a home school	Same as the public schools; generally 180 days per year	If operating under teacher qualification #4, math and language arts; for all others, none	Either: 1) possess a baccalaureate degree, or 2) be a certified teacher, or 3) use an approved correspondence course, or 4) submit evidence parent can teach and use curriculum that includes state objectives for language arts and math	File an annual notice of intent with local superintendent by August 15; if starting mid-year, file notice as soon as practicable	None	Administer a standardized test or have child otherwise evaluated every year (for those six years or older on September 30 of the school year); submit results to local superintendent by August 1
		Operate a home school under the religious exemption statute	None	None	None	File a notice of intent with the local superintendent (optional)	None	None
		Use a private tutor	None	None	Teacher certification	Same as above	None	None
Washington	Eight years of age and under eighteen years of age	Establish and operate a home school	Equivalent to: 2,700 total hours in grades 1–3; 2,970 total hours in grades 4–6; 1,980 total hours in grades 7–8; 4,320 total hours in grades 9–12	Occupational education, science, math, language, social studies, history, health, reading, writing, spelling, music and art appreciation, U.S. and Washington constitutions	Either: 1) be supervised by a certified teacher, or 2) have 45 college quarter credit hours or completed a course in home education, or 3) be deemed qualified by the local superintendent	File an annual notice of intent with the local (or applicable nonresident) superintendent by September 15 or within two weeks of the start of any public school quarter	Maintain standardized test scores, academic progress assessments, and immunization records	Annually, administer and retain a state approved standardized test by a qualified person or have the child evaluated by a certified teacher currently working in the field of education
		Operate under extension program of an approved private school designed for parents to teach their children at home	180 days per year or same as above	Same as above	Must be under the supervision of a certified teacher employed by the approved private school	None	None	Progress must be evaluated by a certified teacher employed by the approved private school
West Virginia	Compulsory school attendance shall begin with the school year in which the 6th birthday is reached prior to the 1st day of September of such year or upon enrolling in a publicly supported kindergarten program and continue to the 16th birthday	Seek local school board approval to operate a home school	Same as the public schools; generally 180 days per year	English, grammar, reading, social studies, and math	Be deemed qualified to teach by the local superintendent and school board	A de facto part of the approval process	As prescribed during the approval process	As prescribed during the approval process
		Establish and operate a home school	None	English, grammar, reading, social studies, and math	High school diploma and formal education at least four years higher than the most academically advanced child to be taught (waived for 2000-2001 academic year)	File a notice of intent with the local superintendent two weeks prior to starting to home school	None	Annually, either: 1) administer an acceptable standardized test, or 2) be evaluated by a certified teacher, or 3) assess progress by another agreeable means
Wisconsin	Between the ages of 6 [by September 1] and 18 years	Establish and operate a home-based educational program	Must provide at least 875 hours of instruction each year	Must provide a sequentially progressive curriculum of fundamental instruction in reading, language arts, math, social studies, science, and health; such curriculum need not conflict with the program's religious doctrines	None	File a statement of enrollment with the state department of education by October 15 each year	None	None
Wyoming	Whose 7th birthday falls before September 15 of any year and who has not yet attained his 16th birthday or completed the 10th grade	Establish and operate a home school	175 days per year	A basic academic educational program that provides a sequentially progressive curriculum of fundamental instruction in reading, writing, math, civics, history, literature, and science	None	Annually submit to the local school board a curriculum showing that a basic academic educational program is being provided	None	None

Contests

Art Contests

American Morgan Horse Art Contest

All ages. $5 fee per piece.
AMHA, Box 960, 3 Bostwick Road, Shelburne, VT 05482. (802) 985-4944. Web: www.morganhorse.com/gen_art. html.

Deadline: Oct 1. Mediums: Pencil, pen, ink, pastels, oils, acrylics, water colors, sculpture, carving, embroidery. Judged on breed promotion, creativity, artistic quality, and overall appearance.

Dick Blick Linoleum Block Print Contest

Grades 4–12 (three divisions by grades).
Dick Blick, Box 1267, Galesburg IL 61402. Web: www.dickblick.com.

Annual contest for kids, focusing on linoleum block printing (no wood cuts, or styrofoam or other types of prints accepted), a technology that is easy enough for the homeschool. Prizes include art supplies. Deadline: April 28, 2000.

NewsCurrents Editorial Cartoon Contest

Grades 1-12.
Knowledge Unlimited, Inc., P.O. Box 52, Madison, WI 53701-2303. (800) 356-2303. Web: www.thekustore.com.

Create original editorial cartoons on any current events topic.

Practical Homeschooling Art & Photo Contests

Envelope Gallery contest open to all homeschool students. Photo contest open to all members of homeschooling families. Must be subscriber to enter. No fees.
Home Life, Inc., PO Box 1190, Fenton, MO 63026. Entries must be submitted via mail.

Envelope Gallery Draw, color, or paint a picture on an envelope and send it in. You may get your envelope published in *Practical Homeschooling*.

Annual Photo Contest Send in your best family photo. Honorable mentions get published inside the magazine. Winners get published on

Most of the contest listings in this appendix originally were compiled by Laurie Bluedorn of Trivium Pursuit and were taken in part from "Trivium Pursuit's List of National Contests Open to Homeschoolers." *Big Book of Home* Learning readers can obtain the entire Trivium Pursuit list free by writing: Trivium Pursuit, 139 Colorado Street, Suite 168, Muscatine, IA 52761. Phone: (309) 537-3641. Email: trivium@muscanet.com. Web: www.muscanet.com/~trivium.

The other main contributors to our contest listings are Susan and Howard Richman, founders of Pennsylvania Homeschoolers. Over the years, their children have won more contests than any other children I know, and their state newsletter always is packed with announcements of other winning Pennsylvania homeschoolers. Remaining listings were compiled by Mary Pride.

Sarah Pride researched and updated all listings as of January 2000, making this list more up-to-date than that available in the current crop of "Contests" books. All contests listed welcome homeschoolers.

the cover and receive a $100 gift certificate from the Home Life catalog.

Tandy Leather Art Competition
Grade 12.
Tandy Leather, PO Box 791, Ft. Worth, TX 76101. (888) 890-1611 8:00AM–7:00PM M–F or 8:00AM–5:00PM on Saturday. Fax: (817) 551-9601.

Create an artwork from leather, take a photo, and enter it. The scholarship program is designed to promote the use of leather as an art material and to advance the craft of leather art. The competition is open to any public, private, or homeschooled high school senior who plans to attend a college or university. Scholarships are awarded for first place ($2,000), second place ($1,500), third place ($1,000) and fourth place ($500). Scholarship winners may choose their own course of study.

Students entering the Tandy Leather Art Scholarship Competition are required to complete a "work of art" made of at least 50 percent leather. Entries are judged on originality, workmanship, and the contents of a written summary. Judging is done by a panel of leathercraft professionals and art educators.

Tandy Leather Company offers a free, 25-minute instructional videotape about leather art to support groups. The video, entitled *Leather Sculpture, Wet Forming Leather and Mask Making*, shows helpful tips and techniques, plus gives students ideas and suggestions for creating their own leather art.

Essay & Fiction Contests

Ayn Rand Essay Contest
Grades 9–12. No fee.
Ayn Rand Essay Contest, Box 6004, Inglewood, CA 90312. Web: www.ayn-rand.org/contests.

Essay contests with a libertarian twist. Deadline: April 15, 2000. Essays written on certain Ayn Rand books. 9–10 and 11–12 have separate book topics. Prizes up to $1,000 for 9–10; up to $10,000 for 11–12.

Center for the American Founding
Center for the American Founding, 1401 Chain Bridge Rd., Suite 100, McLean, VA 22101. (703) 556-6595. Email: info@founding.org. Web: www.founding.org/tour/html/compass.html.

This essay competition focuses on the question "How the founding of America has changed the world," and homeschoolers have been specifically invited to take part. Judges will look at originality of thought and quality of execution. Essays must be one-page, single-spaced, typed. State and national winners. Prizes include a scholarship to *Close Up Washington*, a one-week tour of Washington DC, plus cash awards and publication.

Concord Review
Grades 9–12.
The Concord Review, PO Box 661, Concord, MA 01742. (800) 331-5007. Web: www.tcr.org.

Not exactly a competition in the usual sense, the *Concord Review* is a scholarly journal that publishes high-school students' history research essays. Excellent guidelines on their website, including a full range of past-published essays. Looking for in-depth papers on any aspect of world or US history, in the 4000-6000 word range. Homeschoolers welcome.

DuPont Challenge Science Essay Awards Program
Grades 7–12.
DuPont Challenge, General Learning Communications, 900 Skokie Blvd, #200, Northbrook, IL 60062-4028. (847) 205-3000. Web: www.glcomm.com/dupont.

Open-ended, 700–1000 word science essay competition in two divisions (junior and senior high). Student can choose topic of current interest. Poster available giving details, along with last year's winning essays to give students a feel for the quality being sought. Deadline for submission: January 28.

Eldred World War II Essay Contest
Grades 9–12. No fee.
Eldred WWII Museum, Box 273, Eldred, PA 16731. (814) 225-2220. Web: www.eldredwwiimuseum.org.

Sponsored by the small but wonderful *Eldred World War II Museum* in north central PA. This is only the second year for this contest, and I heard about it when Rachel Bell, a homeschooler from Pennsylvania, was named 2nd-place winner in the 1999 competition. This year the contest is expanded and open to students in many more states, and it will really be a wonderful spur to in-depth learning about WWII. This year's question: How did the United States' economic and industrial system contribute to the allied victory in World War II? Excellent guidelines on website. Many substantial cash awards—$25,000 in total prize money, including up to 30 honorable mentions of $250 each. Deadline March 15.

Letters About Literature 2000
Grades 4–7 (level I). Grades 8–12 (level II).
LAL 2000 - Level I(or II), King's College, c/o The Graduate Reading Program, 133 N. River St., Wilkes-Barre, PA 18711. (203) 705-3500. Web: www.weeklyreader.com/features/readct3.html.

Annual competition sponsored by Weekly Reader and The Center for the Book in the Library of Congress. Students are asked to write a letter to the author of a book that has had a great impact on them, sharing how the book affected them. They are not looking for the typical book report (the directions point out that the author already knows the plot of the book!)—students are instead urged to reflect on what impact the book made on their lives, how it made them act differently, see issues in a new light, etc. Kids in the Richman's writing club (they've often used this as their monthly assignment) have won honorable mentions many times in this competition, and their daughter Molly was once a national finalist for her letter to

Anne Frank. Cash awards, certificates. Mid-December deadline. Weekly Reader also sponsors several other writing contests in poetry, fiction, and personal essays—check out their website regularly to see what's coming up.

Mothers Against Drunk Driving Essay Contest

Grades 4–12.
Mothers Against Drunk Driving. (800) GET-MADD. Web: www.madd.org/under21.

Annual essay contest. Students write a brief 250-word essay related to the theme for the year—currently it's "Strong Enough to Say No." Great info on website, with winning entries from previous year.

National History Day

Grades 6–12. Entry fee.
University of MD, 0119 Cecil Hall, College Park, MD 20742. (301) 314-9739. Email: hstryday@aol.com. Web: www.nationalhistoryday.org.

This annual competition for junior high and senior high students has both project, presentation, and essay categories. Students first compete at regional, then state and national competitions. Many homeschoolers have qualified for state level competitions, and at least one homeschooler has been a national winner. Each year a broad theme is chosen. For 2000 it's Turning Points in History, which students can examine through any era in history, local to worldwide. Use of primary documents is a must. Exemplary guidelines and handbook are available right on-line, helping you to design a whole curriculum with History Day at the core. Scholarship awards.

National Peace Essay Contest

Grades 9–12.
National Peace Essay Contest, 1200 17th St. NW, Suite 200, Washington, DC 20036-3011. Web: www.usip.org/ed/Programs/NPEC/npec.html.

This is a serious foreign policy essay contest, sponsored by the US Institute for Peace. Excellent and rigorous guidelines on website, including sample winning essays from previous

years. Jesse Richman won second and third place in PA state competition when he was in high school at home, and his homeschool friend Brandon Geist won first place from PA, earning a trip to Washington, DC for a special weeklong program on foreign policy. College scholarship awards for all state and national winners.

Optimists International Essay Contest

All high school students 19 & under. *(800) 678-8389 x 224. Web: www.optimist.org/prog-essay.html.*

A civics essay competition, with students responding in year 2000 to the topic "Where would I be without freedom" in a 400–500-word essay. Students enter at local club level (contacts listed on website), then on to district level, and winners earn an all-expenses-paid weeklong trip to Valley Forge Freedoms Foundation 4-day workshop. Deadline for club level is end of February, districts mid-April.

Practical Homeschooling Story Contest

Ages: 10 and under and 11 and up. Must be subscriber to enter. No fees. *Home Life, Inc., PO Box 1190, Fenton, MO 63026. (636) 343-7750. Fax: (636) 343-7203. Email: orders@home-school.com. Web: www.home-school.com.*

Practical Homeschooling magazine gives you a story starter and you write the ending. Winners receive some desirable educational toy or book.

Scholastic Writing Awards

Grades 7–12. $5 per submission. *Scholastic Books, 555 Broadway, New York, NY 10012. (212) 343-6493. Web: www.scholastic.com/artandwriting/*

This very prestigious annual competition, sponsored by *Scholastic Books*, encourages a wide range of writing; there are categories for personal essays, short stories, plays, poetry, journalistic writing, even science fiction. Some special options for high school seniors who may submit a full portfolio of writing. Excellent guidelines. Cash awards. Due date: mid January.

Sons of the American Revolution Essay Contest

Grades 11–12.
Chairman, NSSAR Knight Essay Contest, 1000 S. 4th St., Louisville, KY 40203. Email: K2000essay@aol.com. Web: www.sar.org/youth/knightrl.htm.

Now called the *Knight Essay Contest*, this annual competition asks students to examine any aspect of the Revolutionary War, the Declaration of Independence, or the US Constitution, in a 500- to 750-word essay. Many states have local competitions, leading to state and national competition—large submissions are also welcomed. Cash awards and publication.

USA Weekend Student Fiction Contest

Grades 9–12.
USA WEEKEND Student Fiction Contest, PO Box 4252, Blair, NE 68009-4252. Web: www.usaweekend.com/classroom

Sponsored by *USA Weekend*, the insert that goes in many Sunday newspapers across the country, students are asked to write an original short story of no more than 1500 words, that takes place at least partially in summer in the 1990's. A homeschooler from Pennsylvania, Dillon Wright-Fitzgerald, was one of the 5 national finalists in this competition last year, earning a gift certificate, and publication on the *USA Weekend* website, plus a great full-page newspaper article in her hometown paper. The guidelines on their website are quite helpful, including many intriguing ways to use a newspaper to help you gain ideas for stories. Homeschoolers are specifically welcomed. Mid-February deadline.

Young Naturalist Awards 2000

Grades 7–12. $3 entry fee.
Young Naturalist Award, c/o Alliance for Young Artists & Writers, Inc., 555 Broadway, 4th Floor, New York, NY 10012-3999. (212) 343-5582. Web: www.amnh.org/youngnaturalistawards.

Sponsored by the American Museum of Natural History in NYC, this annual competition encourages wide ranging science research and thinking. Students write essays related to the selected theme for the year. For 2000, projects could involve looking back 100 years to see what we knew in a science area now compared to then, and what we might know in another 100 years. Or students could write about a possible science museum exhibit they'd like to see, or about a science exploration. Sample winning student essays are on their website. Scholarship awards at each grade level. Deadline: January 3.

Computer Science Contests

Computer Learning Foundation
Grades 1–12.
Computer Learning Foundation, 1066 W. Evelyn Ave., Sunnyvale, CA 94086. (408) 720-8898. Web: www.computerlearning.org.

Numerous computer-related contests, for example, the Our Town website competition where you build a site for your town. Two iBooks for grand prizes and ten software prizes. Deadline April 1.

Lycos CyberSurfari
All ages.
Web: www.cybersurfari.org

This contest used to be a once-a-year, two-day fest of caffeine and battling bandwidth, where you raced to find all the clues you could in over 100 Web sites. Now Cybersurfari, in addition to three contests guaranteed to raise your blood caffeine content to unhealthy levels, has events all year! In the CyberSurfari Virtual Classroom, You can now find all sorts of "practice clues," and links to neat and educational sites. Even if you don't have a T1 in your basement, you can win prizes in CyberSurfari.

Divisions of Play: Individual Child, Individual Adult, Family Team, Elementary School Team, Middle School Team, High School Team, and Teachers-only team

USA Computing Olympiad
Grades 9–12.
Web: usaco.uwp.edu

Computer programming competition for high-school students. Each year four students are chosen to represent the USA in international competition in programming using the C++ language. Two homeschoolers were among the 16 who made it to the finals and training camp in 1996. Many ongoing "challenges" throughout the year in addition to the big final competition in the early spring. Students compete as individuals.

Math Contests for Individuals

American Statistical Association's Poster or Project Competitions
www.amstat.org/education/poster1.html

How about a competition where you develop an original statistics project? Try the website for full details, registration info, sample winning posters, and much more. Also, if you live in Pennsylvania, check out the special web page for the PA Statistics Poster Competition at renoir.vill.edu/~short/posters/ . . . you'll get to see lots of fun samples of winning posters from recent years (even some really cute ones by kindergartners!), helping you get your ideas together for your own project. You'll realize here that doing work with math does indeed involve the real world. No fee to enter.

Casio Online Classroom
education.casio.com/contests.htm

This is a really neat contest with six divisions for elementary through high school levels. And guess what the prize is—a super Casio calculator . . . each week! Kids email in answers to fascinating problems developed by various university math departments, and a random drawing from all correct entries chooses the winner. All students with correct answers are listed right on the website each week. Fun to see that kids from all over the world take part in this contest. A great perk: they have archives of back problems, giving you lots of practice and fun challenges.

The Mandelbrot Competition
www.mandelbrot.org

Started by several friends who'd all enjoyed various math competitions while growing up, this is both an individual and team competition, with three or four rounds of problems. Costs are very reasonable: $40 to $50 a year per team of four students (and more students can take part as individuals). There are two high-school-level divisions, plus a middle-school competition, and there are both individual and team components. Billed as "the competition that teaches as much as it tests'"—and I can see it does just that. No calculators.

The Math Forum Problem of the Week
forum.swarthmore.edu

This site has been going for about five years, and includes weekly math challenges for all level. What's unique here? Students are expected to write out full solutions to problems, describing their solution strategy and thinking process. Recognition for correct solutions, and special notice for outstanding written explanations. The Math Forum also takes suggestions for original math problems to use on the site, and welcomes new people (even students!) to serve as mentors and readers of student solutions. There's also a full archive of past problems, along with many other resources for both students and teachers. Many students from all around the world take part. For all levels, elementary on up—and it's free!

Quarter Mile International Math Tournament
Barnum Software, 3450 Lakeshore Avenue, Suite 200, Oakland, CA 94610-2343. (800) 553-9155. Outside USA: (510) 465-5070. Fax: (800) 553-9156. Email: quartermil@aol.com. Web: www.TheQuarterMile.com.

Grades 1–12 and adult categories. Small entrance fee buys you special "tournament" version of Quarter Mile software. The software drills you in math skills related to your grade category and saves your best "races." You mail in the disk by the tournament deadline and get back a certificate and a listing showing how everyone (including you) did in your grade level. Homeschooler Sarah Pride was the Grand Champion for two years running, and a number of other homeschooled children have placed first in their grade-level categories. Next tournament in the spring, 2000.

SA Math Talent Search

www.nsa.gov/programs/mepp (then go to link for USAMTS).

Tired of multiple-choice exams or speed tests? Want to take your time to really think and ponder and develop your mathematical ideas carefully? Then the USAMTS may be for you. This unique program was started by a professor at Rose Hulman Institute of Technology, based on the math competitions he'd remembered from his younger days in Hungary where speed was not the main goal, but rather well-reasoned and thoughtful work. This is an individual distance competition, where students have 4 weeks to solve a very challenging set of five math problems, developing full written solutions, proofs, or explanations, not just an answer. You are even allowed to research any topics to gain more background and information—just you can't discuss the problems with other people. Top students receive special recognition for each of the four sets of problems, and many prizes are awarded at the end of the year (my son Jacob received a set of great math books one year). This program is free to students, and problems and full info are now up on the Internet. Although there is not a team or social aspect to this competition, all the students keep in touch through a newsletter. Excellent student solutions are published to help others see ways to develop their proofs. The emphasis is on encouraging students to only compete against themselves, learning to set high goals, work hard at very difficult tasks, and learn to achieve a higher level of competence than at the start of the program. Taking part and doing very well is another route to being

chosen for the AIME mentioned above.

Solve-It

www.udel.edu/educ/solveit

Want to try a summer distance math contest with a big emphasis on fun and parent involvement? Try Solve-It, sponsored by the University of Delaware, for a great program for 4th- to 8th-graders. Cost is $50 per student, and you can choose between two difficulty levels (you get to choose whichever would better match your child's current abilities—grade level is not crucial here). You'll receive problem sets in the mail, along with follow-up mailings and solutions, and prizes and awards for completing the program. Involves students writing out full solutions and telling how they went about working on the problem, rather than just giving the correct answer.

USA Math Talent Search

High-school level (or younger if *very* good in math).
COMAP Inc., Suite 210, 57 Bedford ST, Lexington, MA 02173. Web: www.comap.com/highschool/contests.

Year-long free correspondence math competition. Advanced problem-solving, four sets of five problems each. Students must not only discover the correct answer but must also write out a succinct and elegant proof of how they worked out the solution. Excellent program, very encouraging to all students who take part. Prizes of math books to all students who reach certain levels of achievement over the whole year program.

Science and Engineering Contests

Duracell/ NSTA Scholarship Competition

Grades 6–12.
Duracell, 1840 Wilson Blvd, Arlington, VA 22201. (888) 255-4242.

Create and build a working device powered by batteries.

Intel Science Talent Search

Grade 12.
Science Service, 1719 N Street, NW, Washington DC 20036. Email: sciedu@sciserv.org. Web: www.intel.com/education/sts. Entry forms are available on the Science Service web site at www.sciserv.org.

Formerly Westinghouse Science Talent Search, one of the most prestigious science awards for high school seniors, involving presentation of a major research project in any of the sciences (life sciences, behavioral and social sciences, engineering, math and physical sciences, etc.) done under supervision of a scientist (not necessarily a teacher).

In 1999 a homeschooler won the competition! Intel awards $1.2 million in prizes: $1,000 to each of the 300 semi-finalists and $1,000 per semi-finalist to their schools. The 40 finalists receive awards ranging from a $5,000 scholarship to a $100,000 4-year scholarship. Deadline for entries is early in December.

The information packet includes the rules (of which there are many), the guidelines for what the judges would like to see, and the process for entering the competition (quite convoluted and involving several officials outside your family). This science competition is probably the most difficult a high-school student can enter.

Invent America!

Grades K–8.
Invent America!, 1505 Powhatan Street, Alexandria, VA 22314. (703) 684-1836. Web: www.inventamerica.org.

Student invention contest. Schools & home schools may submit one invention per grade. One $1,000, one $500, one $250 and two $100 bonds are awarded at each grade. Deadline: June 15.

Junior Engineering Technical Society

Grades 9–12.
Junior Engineering Technical Society 1420 King Street, Suite 405, Alexandria, VA 22314. (703) 548-5387. Web: www.engineeringnet.org/jets/ welcome.htm.

Engineering examination and other engineering competitions.

National Science Teachers Association
Grades 3–12.
NASA/Space Science Student Involvement Program, 1840 Wilson Boulevard, Arlington, VA 22201. (703) 243-7100. Web: www.nsta.org/programs/ssip.htm.

Five different space science contests. Win trips to NASA centers, internships with NASA scientists, Space Camp scholarships, medals, ribbons, certificates, and recognition. Deadline January 10.

Science Service
Grades 9–12.
Science Service 1719 N Street, NW, Washington, DC 20036. (202) 785-2255. Web: www. sciserv.org.

International Science & Engineering Fairs. Grade 12: report of an independent research project.

The Thomas Edison/Max McGraw Scholarship Program
Grades 9–12.
National Science Education Leadership Association, PO Box 5556, Arlington VA 22205.

Student compile a proposal for a project idea which deals with a practical application in the fields of science and/or engineering. Deadline mid December. They are looking to find students who best exemplify the creative genius of Thomas Edison (homeschoolers' favorite homeschooler!).

National Academic Contests

Medusa Mythology Exam
Students of Latin and Greek in grades 9–12. Fees: $2/student plus a $15 school fee.
Medusa Mythology Exam, 6416 Park Hall Drive W, Laurel, MD 20707. (800) 896-4671. Fax: (202) 663-8007 att: M. Webb. Web: medusaexam.cjb.org.

Too old for the National Mythology Exam (see its listing in this category)? Try this one! Top achievers win certificates and medals and can apply for

several cash prizes. Registration thru March 1 for year 2000 exam, given April 3–7. Registration packets can be downloaded from the web.

National French Contest
Grades 1–12. Small fee for each child entered.
American Association of Teachers of French, Box 32030, Sarasota, FL 34239. Web: aatf.utsa.edu.

There are exams (listening, oral, and reading) at all levels, for beginners to very advanced, with good outlines showing exactly what is expected at each stage. Regional and national recognition. Submission deadlines: Grades 1–6—March 2–12; Grades 7–12—March 2–20. Must order tests at some point before then.

National German Examination
Grades 9–12, at least 16 years old. $4 per student.
American Association of Teachers of German, 112 Haddontowne Court No. 104, Cherry Hill, NJ 08034. (609) 795-5553. www.aatg.org/testing.htm.

Year 2000 is its 29th year. Test is administered from early December to late January. Over 25,000 participants in 1999. Winners must be in 90th or higher percentile and may not be German. Prize is a month-long trip to Germany. Various cash, book, t-shirt, and other prizes.

National Greek Examination
All grades. $3 per student.
American Classical League/National Junior Classical League, Department of Classical Studies, 2160 Angell Hall, 435 South State Street, University of Michigan, Ann Arbor, MI 48109. (313) 647-2330.

Classical Greek exam. Year 2000 is its 20th year. One $1,000 scholarship is available for the high-scoring senior.

National Latin Examination
All grades. $3 per student.
American Classical League/National Junior Classical League, Box 95, Mount Vernon, VA 22121. (800) 459-9847. Web: www.vromo.org/~nle.

Written Latin exam. Signup deadline mid-January. The exam is given the second week in March. Twenty $1,000 scholarships are awarded for seniors who earn gold medals in Latin III or higher exams. Others get gold or silver medals and/or certificates. Exams are offered for four levels,:Introductory, Level II, Level III, and Level IV (AP Latin).

National Mythology Exam
Grades 3–9. Modest fee per student.
The American Classical League, Miami University, Oxford, OH 45056-1694. (513) 529-7741.

Mythology exam. The exam focuses mostly on Greek myths (using the wonderfully illustrated D'Aulaires books of Greek Myths for most of the required readings), with additional sets of questions for grades 6 to 9 on specific chapters of the Iliad, Odyssey, Aeneid, and a selection of African myths and American Indian myths. This group also sponsors the National Latin Exam. Can be done individually at home or (more fun!) as a home-school group (how about having everyone come dressed up as a favorite character from a myth?).

National Social Studies Olympiad
Grades 2–12. $10 each student for homeschools.
NSS, Box 2196, St. James, NY 11780. (631) 584-2016. Web: members.xoom.com/Quartararo.

Social studies contests. Signup deadline February 10, 2000.

Other Individual Contests

The American Legion Oratorical Contest
Grades 9–12.
The American Legion, Box 1055, Indianapolis, IN 46206. (317) 630-1249. Web: www.legion.org/orarules .htm.

National oratorical contest. Local contests sometime between Jan. 1 and Mar. 12. Orations must be about the U.S. Constitution.

Discover Card Tribute Award Program

Grade 11.

American Association of School Administrators, PO Box 9338, Arlington VA 22219. (703) 875-0708. Web: www.aasa.org/discover.

A scholarship award program, based on special talents, leadership, obstacles overcome, unique endeavors, and community service. State and national level scholarship awards. Deadline for applications: mid January.

International Children's Art Exhibition

Grades K–9. No fee.

ICAE, Pentel of America, Ltd., 2805 Columbia St., Torrance, CA 90509. (800) 421-1419.

Original 2D artwork, any theme.

International Jugglers Association

All ages. Fee to attend the convention, no additional fee for competing.

International Jugglers Association, Inc., PO Box 218, Montague, MA 01351. (413) 367-2401. Fax: (413) 367-0259. Email: secretary@juggle. org. Web: www.juggle.org.

Hosts a regular "Juggling Festival," with many competitive events like combat juggling, joggling, 3-Ball Simon Says, and more, plus world-renowned competitions for overall performance. Small prizes, but lots of fun. Meet the older Pride kids there!

International Whistlers Convention

All ages. No fee.

International Whistlers Convention, Box 758, Louisburg , NC 27549. (919) 496-4771.

Whistling contests at convention. 2000 convention in Louisburg, NC, from April 13-16.

National Chess Competitions

All grades.

United States Chess Federation, 3054 NYS Route 9W, New Windsor, NY 12553. (914) 562-8350. Web: www.uschess.org.

Rise through well-defined ranks of chess mastery by competing in local, state, national and international competitions.

National Horticultural Contests

Ages 22 and below.

National Junior Horticultural Association, 1424 North Eighth Street, Durant, OK 74701.

Numerous contests.

National Model Rocketry Contest

All grades.

National Association of Rocketry, Box 177, Altoona, WI 54720. (800) 262-4872. Web: www.nar.org.

Model rocketry contests. Must join NAR to compete. Signup is generally in July or August.

Team Competitions

In this context, "team" may mean either that you compete as a team, or that you must assemble a group to hold your own first-rung local competition, from which winners will be chosen to compete at higher levels.

American Express Geography Competition

Grades 6–12.

P.O. Box 672227, Marietta GA 30067-9077.

Original research paper related to one of three broad themes. This can be done as an individual or as a cooperative team effort. Free program, with big prize money awards. The Richmans' son Jesse was a National Finalist two different years—so they know about homeschoolers!

American Mathematics Competitions

Grades 7–12. Registration fee $30 (going up in 2000).

University of Nebraska-Lincoln, Box 880658, Lincoln, Nebraska 68588. (800) 527-3690. Web: www.unl.edu/amc.

Homeschool groups are welcome to register for these challenging annual multiple-choice test competitions. Junior high and senior levels, state and national recognition.

American Statistical Association Competition

Grades K–12. No fee.

American Statistical Association, 1429 Duke St., Alexandria VA 22314-3403 (703) 684-1221 x165. Web: www.amstat.org/education/poster1.html.

Create an original statistical research project or poster. The project must involve at least two students. Deadline April 15.

Global Challenge Exam Competition

Grades 7–12. Fee in $50 range, for up to 100 students.

Global Challenge, P.O. Box 9700, Coral Springs, FL 33075.

An annual multiple-choice exam competition on current events and geography, with local and national awards at each grade level. Based on facts, not political bias.

MathCounts Math Competition

Grades 7 and 8. About $30 per team.

MathCounts Foundation, 1420 King Street, Alexandria, VA 22314-2794. (703) 684-2828. Web: mathcounts.org.

Junior high level math competition, involving full-year coaching program plus regional, state and national competitions. A team is four students chosen from your school or homeschool group. Great coaching materials available. Mathcounts is also sponsoring an ongoing project of encouraging students (both junior high and Mathcounts alumni) to send in original math word problems for possible inclusion in future books of sample problems for their excellent coaching program. Registration date differs by state. The program starts at the beginning of the school year.

Mathematical Olympiads for Elementary & Middle Schools

Grades 4–6 and 7–8. Registration fee: Grades 4–6: $60 for up to 35 students. Grades 7–8, $75.

Math Olympiads, 2154 Bellmore Avenue, Bellmore, NY 11710-5645. (516) 781-2400. Web: www.moems.org.

A broadening year-long program introducing kids to non-routine problems that really make kids think. Homeschoolers very welcome. Contest begins at the beginning of each school year. Grades 7-8 division is new in 2000.

Modern Woodmen of America Contests

Grades 5–8.
Modern Woodmen of America, 1701 First Avenue, Rock Island, IL 61204. (309) 786-6481. Web: www. modern-woodmen.org/cepf.htm.

Civic oration contest and essay contest. Must have at least 12 students from homeschool group to enter. More than 90,000 participants each year. Can win $500 to $1,000 savings bonds.

National Geographic Society Geography Bee

Grades 4–8. Fee: about $20/school.
National Geographic Society, 1145 17th ST NW, Washington DC 20036-4688. (202) 828-6659. Web: www.nationalgeographic.com.

Follow links to get to the Geo Bee—sample questions for kids online!

An oral bee that tests a wide range of geography and current events knowledge—way beyond dreary states and capitals. Cost: about $20 per "school"—and for homeschoolers this means a *minimum* of *six* students from grades four through eight taking part together at your local bee. Local winner takes written test to see about qualifying for one of the 100 spots at the state level bee. State winner advances to nationals, and homeschoolers have made it to these levels. Homeschooler David Biehl won the Bee in 1999! The 10 top finalists get $500 apiece, and the tothree divide $50,000 in scholarship money. Registration deadline for your home-school group is usually mid-October.

National History Day Competition

Grades 6–12. Fees at each level.
University of MD, 0119 Cecil Hall, College Park, MD 20742.

(301) 314-9739. Email: hstryday@aol.com. Web: www.nationalhistoryday.org.

History project competition. Student research projects, papers, or performances related to a yearly broad history theme (students are very free to pick whatever specific topic they want, as long as they can show how it relates to the broad theme). Students are encouraged to use primary resource materials wherever possible. Excellent student guide book available. Regional competition that advances to state and national levels. Starts at the beginning of each school year. Can be done as team project. Fees vary with region.

National Reading Incentive Program

Grades K–6. No fee.
National Reading Incentive Program, (800) 4-BOOK-IT. PO Box 2999, Wichita, KS 67201. Web: www.bookitprogram.com.

An easy-to-organize group activity. Each family sets individual goals for reading each month, and kids win coupons for free pizzas. If everyone in your group meets their goals, you can have a group pizza party at the end of the year. Great geography and reading resource booklet. Mid-June registration date each year.

Odyssey of the Mind

Grades K–12. $135 signup for entire homeschool group.
Odyssey of the Mind, c/o Creative Competitions, 1325 Rt. 130 S., Suite F, Gloucester City, NJ 08030. (856) 456-7776. Web: www.odysseyofthemind.com.

Problem-solving contests. Seven members per team. Solve five problems in the time before the contest and present the results at the contest.

Robotix 2000 Classroom Competition

Grades 4–8.
Learning Curve International, 314 West Superior Street, Chicago, IL 60016. (800) 704-8694 ext. 1. Fax: (312) 470-9400. Web: www.learningcurve.com.

Build the best mobile space exploration robot using Robotix parts and a single Robotix controller. The purpose of this robot is to clear an area of "volcanic rock debris" and deposit it in a designated canister. The robot that clears the most debris in the least time wins.

Robots are built by "clubs" of more than one student, and as large as 35 students. This can include brothers and sisters in the age group, neighbors' kids, or support-group members. All entrants have to be legal U.S. residents, and not associated with Learning Curve, the judging committee, or the Astronauts Memorial Foundation.

Scripps Howard National Spelling Bee

Grades 1–8.
Scripps Howard National Spelling Bee, Box 371541, Pittsburg, PA 15251. (800) 672-9673. Web: www.spellingbee.com.

Have a local spelling bee, then send your top three kids to regionals sponsored by large city newspapers, and maybe make it to the state or national level. Contact your local homeschool group in July or August to set up your bee. Homeschooler Rebecca Sealfon won the Bee in 1998; homeschoolers swept all three top places in 2000! First prize is $10,000 plus a cornucopia of smaller prizes.

ThinkQuest

Ages 12–19. No fee.
Advanced Network and Services, 200 Business Park Drive, Suite 307, Armonk, NY 10504. (914) 765-1100. Web: www.thinkquest.org.

Website-building contest with a team of 2–3 people. Start working on your project anytime and finish by August 15, 2000. Finalists in 2000 go to Cairo Egypt. One to three finalists and their coach in each of five categories will receive cash awards/scholarships from $5,000–$25,000. Application deadline is May 1.

Selling to Homeschoolers

Over the years, I have been approached by many companies who want to start selling to homeschoolers. Sometimes these are huge multi-billion-dollar companies; much more frequently, they are small family businesses.

Having spent literally hundreds of hours on the phone trying to help these people, I have a pretty good idea of the kinds of questions you must have—and that you should be asking—if you have a product you would like to get into the homeschool market.

First, let me ask you some questions.

- **Why do homeschoolers need your product?** Homeschoolers need phonics programs, because every child has to learn to read. Similarly, homeschoolers need academic curriculum in all subject areas. Homeschoolers are always looking for ways to make learning academics more fun, thus creating a market for educational games and software. And skills not taught in school—such as the medicinal use of herbs or how to clean a house—often fit right in to what homeschoolers may consider the "necessities."

- **What makes your product unique and superior?** Yes, every homeschool family needs a phonics program, as I mentioned above. But there already are dozens of excellent phonics programs. Before you spend any time producing and marketing yet another such program, it needs to have features markedly different from the others that make it superior in some way. The same applies to any homeschool product. The most common mistake that producers of "kitchen-table" products make is to not be familiar with the *existing* competition. A look at the relevant chapters in the relevant volumes of *The Big Book of Home Learning* should help you quickly determine just how widespread and successful your competition is.

- **Do you have glowing testimonials from people who aren't your friends or relatives, and who had to pay for your product?** Such testimonials are even more valuable if those writing them already had experience with competing products. But if your only testimonials come from your sister and your best friend, don't let these well-meaning people lead you into what could be a huge waste of money, dreams, time, and energy.

Let's say you've sailed by these questions. Your product is either superior to existing products in its category or creates a brand-new category of its own. And you have wads of testimonials from folks who have tried it and love it.

Now, I'm going to try to help you make the right financial moves.

The Price is Right!

Don't underprice. The temptation is to sell your product for just a tad more than it costs you, so as not to be considered greedy. You think this will make everyone love you, and help you sell lots of product. In reality, it is the royal road to bankruptcy and heartache.

Anyone can sell bunches of a quality product they practically give away. What they *can't* do is:

- **Wholesale it.** Wholesalers expect from 40 to 70 percent off the retail cost, depending on the quantity sold to them and the type of wholesaler.
- **Advertise it.** Advertising isn't free, and no matter how clever you are with press releases and review samples, any such mention will appear in one, and *only* one, magazine, radio show, or TV show. It's true that "it pays to advertise," and *more* true that "it pays to constantly advertise." Marketing experts have said that it takes, on the average, 14 exposures to a product before a consumer will buy it. One lone press release can't do the entire job.
- **Pay for more batches of your product.** If you make just a tad on the first batch of your product, and sell every bit of that batch (none are damaged, lost, or returned), you then have the price you paid for your first batch plus just a tad more. Now, you will have to purchase a second batch, and you only have enough money for just that, considering that you undoubtedly had phone bills, office supply bills, postage expenses, and the like. Many well-meaning people have gone around and around on this treadmill for years before figuring out that every speck of profit just got sunk into overhead and paying for more product, with nothing left over for them. Don't be dazzled by what you think are large sales. It doesn't matter if you take in $100,000 a year; the question is, how much of that do you get to *keep*?
- **Continue developing more products.** If you are the product creator, you aren't making any money for the time you spend developing additional products until those products come to market and pay back your initial investment in them. If you are collaborating with others, they need to eat, too.

This is why you shouldn't flinch when I tell you that the rule of thumb is to charge 7 to 10 times as much for your product as it costs you for the raw materials—the printing, binding, boxing, and whatnot. By now I hope you can see that the majority of the final retail price goes to the costs of doing business, with hopefully a reasonable, although not excessive, amount left over payable to you for the value of your ideas and labor.

If you can't sell your product at that price, you have an alternative: **find a way to make your product costs less expensive**. When your print runs get to 1,000 or more, switch from photocopying to printing to save big money. In fact, you might pay less for a larger print run than a smaller photocopied run. Get multiple bids on your printing. Ask others with similarly packaged, noncompetitive products, who does their binding, printing, tape duplicating, and boxing. Use less expensive packaging. If you're selling mail-order, you don't need four-color boxes and custom binders. Homeschoolers are capable of buying our own binders, and you'll save a bundle by shipping flat three-hole-punched and shrink-wrapped pages rather than heavy, bulky binders, which may get crushed in shipping.

If you have samples of your final product, you might be able to get wholesalers and catalogers to **share the cost of your next printing** by offering juicy pre-pub discounts on that printing. A typical deal might be 70 percent off on pre-pub orders of 50 or more. Since the normal cataloger's discount is 50 percent of retail cost, and assuming you are following the rule of thumb and your actual cost is 10 to 13 percent of retail cost, it might be possible to sell enough heavily-discounted pre-pub orders to cover the entire cost of the printing, leaving you with a stock of product that effectively cost you nothing, which you can advertise directly to consumers through homeschool magazines and card decks, the Web, and so forth, as outlined below.

Ways to Market Your Product to Homeschoolers

The first step you should take if you are serious about marketing to homeschoolers is to obtain a copy of the latest edition of the *Authentic Jane Williams Guide to the Homeschool Market*. At the time I'm writing this, in September 2000, the 1999 edition is still the most current. See the review on the next page for more details.

Now, here's what you need to know to get started:

Reviews. While a good review alone will not lead to marketing success, it can open a lot of doors and build credibility for your product. Here are some basic guidelines for sending review samples:

- **Carefully select who you want to review it.** Natural sources for reviews are homeschool magazines, *The Big Book of Home Learning*, and Cathy Duffy's *Christian Home Educators' Curriculum Manuals*. All are listed in the *Authentic Jane Williams Guide*, along with lesser-known reviewers. If you want to go farther, perhaps trying to get reviewed in state newsletters, your best bet is to send a letter with an SASE, offering to send a review sample if they send back the letter promising to run a review.
- **Always send the complete product**, not a "demo" version. Reviewers need to see the whole thing.
- **If you have an extensive series** (of books, for example), you might want to check with the individual reviewer or organization as to whether they need the entire series or just a few representative samples.
- **Do not try to be clever** by attaching stickers all over your product saying, "Review Sample Only! Not for Resale!" This merely prevents the reviewer from photographing your product and comes across as cheesy and amateurish. Trust me: no homeschool reviewer rushes out to street corners to make millions by hawking review samples.
- **Dittos for sending review samples with invoices** announcing that the full amount is due if product is not returned in 30 days or 60 days. My unfailing policy is to stuff such "samples" directly back in the box and return them to the person who sent them. In the case of a magazine, such as *Practical Homeschooling*, we send samples to dozens of review-

---

Print and Save!

Generally, the cost of printing a book is lower than the cost of photocopying it when you get 500 to 1,000 or more copies printed at a time. And, now, if you are able to provide electronic files, some companies can print your book in runs of 500 or 1,000 for less than ever before. One such company is **Delta Direct Access**, 27460 Avenue Scott, Valencia, CA 91355, (661) 294-2200, fax (661) 294-2208, Web: www.ddaptis.com.

ers, and couldn't get them back to the sender in the time period even if we wanted to. But most importantly, the point of reviewing is to *review*, which means having kids try out the workbooks, playing the CDs, watching the videos, and in general marring the perfect pristine product. The reviewer or reviewing organization is investing considerable time and effort in giving your product free publicity through their magazine, book, or radio show, and it is not good manners or good business to suggest that they should pay you for the privilege.

Testimonials. These are a fabulous marketing tool that too few companies use. Ideally, every print ad should include a testimony or two, and your web site should have scads of them. Keep in mind that homeschoolers especially like to hear what fellow homeschoolers think about a product. Endorsements from schoolteachers or school-oriented publications or organizations carry less weight. Homeschoolers consider some organizations the "bad guys"; endorsements from them might actually hurt your product.

Homeschool conventions should be considered first and foremost a market testing device rather than a market, when it comes to new products, in my opinion. Sales at homeschool conventions have taken a nose dive in the last few years, due in my opinion to the wide availability of

NEW!
The Authentic Jane Williams Guide to the Homeschool Market, 1999 edition

Adults. $150 plus $15 shipping.
Home Life, Inc., PO Box 1190, Fenton, MO 63026.
Orders: (800) 346-6322. Inquiries: (636) 343-7750.
Web: www.home-school.com.

If you're thinking of marketing to homeschoolers, you must buy this book. Even if you're only in the "I-have-a-great-idea" stage, **The Authentic Jane Williams Guide to the Homeschool Market** can save you thousands of dollars and hundreds of hours.

What is this most excellent book? It's 456 oversized, spiral-bound pages, divided into three sections.

The first section, the "grey" pages, is 50 pages of savvy, up-to-date marketing advice. Is exhibiting at curriculum fairs and conferences worth it, and exactly what does it involve? Would you be better off with card deck or magazine advertising? How should you package your product to appeal and not offend? These, and many more questions you may not even have thought of, are dealt with.

The second section, the "white" pages, is the heart of the book. These are over 450 detailed alphabetical listings. 165 catalogs. 125 conferences and workshops. 85 stores. 195 newsletters and magazines. 160 reviewers and resource columns. Speakers. Consultants. Card decks. Direct mail lists. Each listing includes full contact information (address/phone/fax/email/web site) and detailed information relevant to the type of listing. For example, homeschool group listings have 1999 projected attendance at their conference, attendance at each conference from 1994–1998, the number of 1999 on-site exhibits, the 1998 conference location, the 1999 exhibit dates, the conference title, who is stuffed the bags handed out to attendee, what type of a homeschool group it is (e.g., "inclusive" or "Christian"), the year it was established, and the percent of members who are homeschoolers. In addition, each listing comes with a series of one- or two-letter codes, which let you know what marketing opportunities are available through that group. *A is advertising opportunities, bc is book club, cf is conference/curriculum fair*, etc.

This would all be impressive, but hard to sort out, if it were not for the book's third section: the "pink" pages. These are the "specialty indexes": lists, in order, of the listings that fall in a certain category. Want to see conferences listed in order of the greatest to the least attendance? Then flip to that specialty index. It lists the conferences and the page numbers on which each can be found. Want conferences by date? By state? Want mailing lists? Speakers? Stores? Card decks? Catalogs? Wholesale distributors? In all, you'll find 29 specialty indexes, covering every imaginable marketing need.

Updated every year or two by one of the most professional and meticulous people I know, *The Authentic Jane Williams Guide to the Homeschool Market* is just plain invaluable. I used to spend hours on the phone every week explaining to would-be marketers how to get started in the homeschool market. Now I just tell them to buy this book. Very highly recommended. *Mary Pride*

products via catalogs and the Internet. However, a homeschool convention is still a great place to interview people as to what they think about your packaging, your content, your price, the way your product is positioned, and the like. If you have a new, hot product you may at least cover your exhibiting costs while getting an emotional boost and some useful marketing advice.

Homeschool magazines are a tried and true way to establish a product's name and credibility. The key is to match the ad size to your product's net profit and its market universe. This means an expensive product that everyone needs gets a full page, while an inexpensive product that relatively few people see the need for gets a tiny ad. However, even an inexpensive magazine ad can lead customers to a much more detailed sales message on your web site.

Since its inception, *Practical Homeschooling* has always bent over backwards to help the new homeschool advertiser. If you're looking for a homeschool magazine in which your only cost is the actual ad, regardless of how much design and copywriting help we provide, you need to contact us.

Homeschool card decks are an inexpensive way to reach large numbers of homeschoolers at once through direct mail. Each advertiser has his own card or cards, which are all packed together in a clear wrapper and mailed directly to the deck publisher's list of homeschool families. Just as with magazines, many card decks are listed in the *Authentic Jane Williams Guide,* including the deck published by *Practical Homeschooling* magazine. Again, we offer the same free design and copywriting help in our card deck that we do in our magazine.

Homeschool catalogs are a way for you to wholesale to homeschoolers. I've listed my favorites in Chapter 7. Many more are listed in the *Authentic Jane Williams Guide,* where they are also indexed by size of print run. This is another group to which you should consider sending review samples. Be aware that many catalogs rely on homeschoolers already knowing about your product, so you will need to keep advertising on your own even if you go the wholesale-to-catalogs route.

Teacher stores are a relatively untapped market for homeschool products. More and more are beginning to add "homeschool corners." To sell directly to these people, your best bet is to join the National School Supply and Equipment Association (*www.nssea.org*). They sponsor several yearly selling shows where you can exhibit your products and sell directly to store and chain buyers. NSSEA also rents its mailing list, so you can mail your own direct offers, and publishes a journal for its members, *Tidings,* that you can advertise in.

Online selling is becoming an essential part of the homeschool marketing mix. At present, the homeschool companies I talk to who have good web sites get from 10 to 40 percent of their sales through those sites. Those companies whose sales are slacking are generally those that do not offer online shopping, indicating to me at least that a certain percentage of people now insist on buying through the Web.

To get into online marketing, you need to:

- **Sign up with a domain hosting service.** My son Ted the webmaster recommends Value-Web (*www.valueweb.net*), as they do not charge for letting you list them as your service, enabling you to register your domain name and save it for yourself while not having to immediately start paying for hosting a site you don't have up yet.
- **While you're on Value-Web,** type the domain name you'd prefer into their search engine, in order to see if it's already

To request a free media kit with information about advertising in *Practical Homeschooling* magazine, call 636-343-6786 or fax 636-225-0743. Be sure to include your name, company name, address, phone number, fax number, and the name of the product you hope to advertise.

A recent issue of the Practical Homeschooling Power Pack card deck

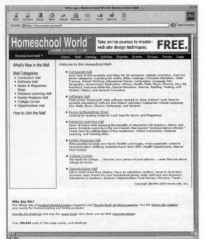

Our Homeschool Mall area is divided into "halls"

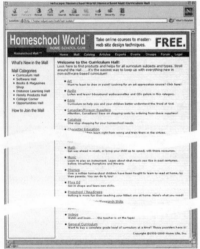

Here we are in the Curriculum Hall

Now we're in the Phonics Category of the Curriculum Hall. Each link is placed in the appropriate category, to make it easy for homeschoolers to locate the products they need. Click on a link and it takes you to that company's site.

taken. If it hasn't been taken yet, you can sign up right then to obtain rights to it for two years for $70. If you have a trademarked company name or product name, that should be your first choice. Sometimes if you can't get the dot-com name (e.g., *thenameyouwant.com*) you can get the dot-net name (e.g., *thenameyouwant.net*).

Ted says books on how to learn HTML are not terribly useful. What you need is a HTML 3.0 reference guide. That should be enough to help you translate your print brochure or catalog to the web. If you still can't figure it out, Ted recommends you purchase the *Dreamweaver* web design program.

Setting up online shopping is a different story; for that you might need professional help. For PC owners, there are some programs out there that claim to help you do this. Often they are tied into a particular hosting service, who demands a cut of your sales, so you'll want to carefully check out your commitment to the service before getting into this.

Your site is only as useful as the amount of visitors it attracts. I already mentioned that your can build traffic by including your web site address in your advertising. You should also register your site with the major search engines, and purchase or exchange links with sites that have a large amount of the kind of traffic you want.

Since we're talking about marketing to homeschoolers, you might wish to **purchase an inexpensive link** from the "Homeschool Mall" area of our "Homeschool World" web site (*www.home-school.com*). Ours is the most-visited homeschool web site in the world, with over 350,000 visitors a year, 1.7 million pages served per year, and 5 million hits per year at the time of writing. Our traffic has risen constantly since we opened the site five years ago, and it continues to grow. A link from our site is the quickest and simplest way to direct this traffic towards your site.

Opportunity Still Knocks!

There is still room for more great new homeschool products. Part of the proof is *The Big Book of Home Learning* itself. As each edition was finished, I thought, "What more can people possibly come up with?" Then the time rolled around to do the next edition, and once again we were reviewing hundreds of brand-new clever and useful products.

Read and re-read this appendix. Think through the questions and study the suggested resources. Who knows . . . the next time we revise this book, one of the products may be yours!

Meet the Reviewers

Anne Brodbeck is a graduate from the University of South Alabama with a BS in Secondary Education. She is the mother of five homeschooled children, ages 5, 11, 21, 23, and 26 (the oldest three have graduated and moved out). Anne has homeschooled for 16 years.

Barbara Buchanan is a college-educated full-time mom, who has been homeschooling for 15 years. Barbara has four boys, from toddler to teen, an 8-year-old girl, and one on the way. She has homeschooled all her children since birth.

Irene Buntyn has been homeschooling her three children for five years. She has an associate's degree in Sign Language interpreting and speaks Spanish fluently. She served as a sign language interpreter for eight years in her local church and began Bible studies for the deaf. Irene is currently working towards her bachelor's in Christian Education degree through Oral Robert's University.

Charles & Betty Burger are homeschool parents from the Berkshire Hills of rural western Massachusetts. Betty now writes for *Homeschooling Today*, and Charles is a technical analyst for Gilder Publishing. The Burgers have homeschooled their eight children for 12 years.

Marcella Burns and her husband Richard have homeschooled since 1983. Her oldest daughter, Carol, 28 this October, graduated from Baptist Bible College in Pennsylvania with a Missions degree. Her daughter Kathleen is at Central Michigan University, pursuing a performance major in violin. The seven children still at home range in age from 4 to 16.

 Terri Cannon is a pastor's wife and the mother of six homeschooled children. She's been homeschooling for 11 years and has published a homeschooling record-keeping system for about 8 years. She has worked with computers for 17 years, taught in a Christian school, and edited curriculum for Accelerated Christian Education.

 Tammy Cardwell, a mother of two and a homeschooler since '91, is the author of *Front Porch History*, published by Greenleaf Press. She spent a year on her Journalism major in college, then left to get married.

 **Toni Clark** is a homeschool mom of two girls, ages 3 and 10. She has homeschooled her older daughter since age 5 and intends to keep homeschooling through high school. Toni has a Bachelor of Science in finance, has worked as a financial analyst, and has volunteered with special education children and vacation Bible school classes.

MacBeth Derham has conducted field programs in science for a consortium of school districts. She and husband Don homeschool their four children just outside New York City. MacBeth's children are ages 10, 8, 6, and 4, and have been homeschooled from birth. MacBeth is an active member of her local support group, and has helped out in various ways, including organizing and leading field trips.

Sherry Early is a graduate from the University of Texas with a Masters in Library Science. She and her husband, Tim, an engineer at NASA, have been homeschooling their seven children for ten years. Sherry is one of the directors for her local homeschool co-op.

Christine Field is the author of *A Field Guide to Homeschooling*. Christine was formerly an HSLDA referral attorney. She has now written five books, the most recent being *Life Skills for Kids*. Christine has four kids, age 10, 9, 6, and 3, and has homeschooled them from the start.

Michelle Fitzgerald is a mother of two, ages 16 and 12. Michele has homeschooled for 12 years. She has a master's in business and founded, organized, and runs her local homeschool support group.

 **Sharon Fooshe** attended Tennessee State University. She is active in her church, teaches a youth group, and also travels all over the US with her three homeschooled children and her husband on his monthly business trips. Sharon has homeschooled for three years. She's an active member of her local support group.

Kathy Goebel has been married for 25 years. Kathy homeschooled her kids, Katrina (now 21) and Peter (19), until both graduated, making Kathy a veteran homeschooler of 11 years. She's helped with a local support group in various ways, and served as a Secretary on the North Carolinians for Home Education Board for three years.

 **Kristin Hernberg**, her husband Michael, and her four teens live in upstate New York. Although each one of Kristin's kids has attended school outside the home for a short time, Kristin has homeschooled since 1986. Kristin has also helped lead a homeschool support group, and taught children from the slow to the gifted.

 Fritz Hinrichs, a graduate of St. John's College in Annapolis, MD, and Westminster Seminary, is the founder of Escondido Tutorial Service, a prominent homeschool online academy.

Tammy Kihlstadius is one of the original founders of the Home Computer Market, which sells and critically reviews all kinds of educational software. She is the mother of seven totally homeschooled children.

Brad Kovach is a graduate of Indiana State University and a former copy editor for *Practical Homeschooling* and *Homeschool PC*. He has since been a news editor and photographer for the Topics Newspapers in Indianapolis, Indiana.

Rebecca Livermore has been homeschooling her children, ages 11 and 12, for 9 years, and is primarily a unit study person. Rebecca is also a freelance writer. She has frequently contributed to *Discipleship Journal*, *New Attitude*, *Homeschooling Today*, and a number of other publications, including of course the book you're holding. The Livermores just came back from a trip to North India; they're currently teaching a photography/journalism course in their local support group.

Cindy Marsch has four children, ages 11, 9, 7, and 2, who she homeschools. She has college and graduate school training in advanced writing and literature. Cindy serves as an instructor on AOL's Online Campus, teaching several writing courses. She offers writing tutorials and evaluations through her website, *www.writingassessment.com*.

Cindy & Barney Madsen met at BYU in an English class. Barney is a practicing attorney and Cindy is the editor of the homeschooling periodical, *The LEARN Newsletter*. Together they've been homeschooling their four children for five years.

Renee Mathis's educational background includes majors in home economics, journalism, and child development. A homeschooler for 13 years, she is currently active in leading the West Houston Home Educators support group with her husband Steve, teaching logic classes to homeschoolers, teaching their five children, and doing curriculum consulting.

Teresa May Married to a retired military man, Teresa has two teenage boys—David, age 18 and Joshua, age 16. She is now going into her eleventh year of homeschooling.

Barbara Meade homeschools her six children, who range from mid-high-school to early elementary age. She has been homeschooling for 12 years. Barbara started and was active in several homeschool support groups in Colorado.

Lisa Mitchell has been married twenty years, is the mother of two teenagers, and was an employee in the public school system five years before deciding to homeschool. Her children, now 21 and 19, have graduated homeschool and gone on to college.

John Nixdorf has a Bachelor of Fine Arts degree with a minor in Art Education. He and his wife homeschool four children, with one more having graduated and joined the Air Force. The Nixdorfs have homeschooled for 15 years. John is an elder at his church, an active member of his homeschool support group, and spent the last year and a half starting a homeschool-friendly scout troop.

Kim O'Hara has homeschooled her three kids, ages 9, 13, and 18, for seven years. She studied Analytic Geometry and Calculus in high school and Advanced Calculus at the University of Chicago. For two years, she managed a homeschool bookstore in her home, which gave her many additional opportunities to compare resources, and is frequently called on for advice.

Marla Perry lives with her husband and two teen boys in northern California. She says homeschooling for the past nine years has been the best education; her history degree trails in second place.

Barbara Petronelli is now in her sixteenth year of homeschooling. She has six sons and daughters and has tested many methods and curricula on them over the years. Barbara had a high-school education and studied music in her freshman year at college, then went on to full-time homemaking. Barbara is currently attending Penn State University. She is an avid fiddle player, and plays and teaches Celtic music in northeastern Ohio.

Rebecca Prewett, a pastor's daughter, resides in Nipomo, California, where she homeschools her six children, from toddler to teen. Rebecca's oldest child is 15, and has been homeschooled since birth. She served for some years as a sysop on the old Practical Homeschooling forum on America Online.

Bill Pride has been a homeschool dad for 21 years. He earned his B.S. in Mathematics from M.I.T. and his M.A. in Missions and M.Div. from Covenant Theological Seminary. If there's anything scientific or mathematical Bill doesn't know, Mary has never discovered it.

Mary Pride is the mother of nine totally homeschooled children, ages 7 to 21, the publisher of *Practical Homeschooling* magazine, and the author of seven other books, not counting editions of the *Big Book of Home Learning*. Mary holds the BS in Electrical Engineering and a M.Eng. in Computer Systems Engineering from Rensselaer Polytechnic Institute, and has worked with every kind of computer systems from the days of punched cards to the present.

Joseph Pride, a National Merit Semi-Finalist (it's too early to know if he'll be a Finalist), has been a homeschooled student since he was born 19 years ago, and has seen it all, from workbook work to many kinds of online academies. He has helped out in the family business, Home Life, Inc., since he was 5, doing everything from triple-folding piles of paper to editing *Practical Homeschooling* magazine and working for years on the book you're holding. Joe hopes to head off to college in less than a year.

Sarah Pride, another National Merit Semi-Finalist and international math champion, has been homeschooled all 17 years of her life, and has seen just as many flavors of homeschool as Joseph has. Sarah has also helped out in the family business, doing any job that needs to be done, from janitor duty to making a thousand or so telephone calls in order to fact-check this book. She intends to graduate homeschool high school this year.

Ted Pride has been homeschooled for all his life and considers himself a graduate. Ted still lives at home due to health problems. You can see Ted's area of expertise on our website, *www.home-school.com*. Ted runs his own web design business, Websitters, at *www.websitters.com*.

Gail Rivera is a homeschool mom of 13 years with five children. She helps out at her homeschool co-op and teaches a class a week.

Teresa Schultz-Jones attended Marymount College and Boston University where she earned a BS in Math and Computer Science, and went on to earn her Masters in Computer Science. She has lived in Belgium and France before for about 5 years. Today her and her husband Gerry homeschool two of their three children in Medway, Massachusetts.

Tony Silva has worked for years in the music industry. He was one of the few and proud homeschoolers who made the GENIE homeschool message boards so lively.

Lynn Smith is a homeschool mom of two, ages 17 and 12, and has reviewed educational products for *Practical Homeschooling* for about half a decade. Lynn has homeschooled for 11 years, and was one of the leaders of her local support group for four years.

Christopher Thorne served for two years as editor of *Practical Homeschooling*. Holding a bachelor's degree in physics, a minor's in astronomy, and earning a master's in computer science, he currently works for Boeing, which proves it *does* take a rocket scientist to edit our magazine!

MaryAnn Turner is a homeschool support-group leader, and a past *Practical Homeschooling* columnist. She has seven children and another on the way, and has homeschooled for 15 years.

Michelle Van Loon, homeschooling mother of three, is a writer of plays and short stories for children, a voracious reader, and a researcher with academic strengths in history and literature. "Educating my children has taught me how to educate myself as well." Michelle is the author of *From Heart to Page: Journaling Through the Year for Young Writers*, written up in *Big Book* Volume 2.

Katherine von Duyke is the mother of eleven children, and has homeschooled for fourteen years. Kathy has written numerous articles in *Practical Homeschooling*, and is the former publisher of the *KONOS Helps* newsletter. She is also the author of the *Home Education Copybook* and the *Month-By-Month Spelling Guide*, both reviewed in the *Big Book* series.

Allison Waibel and her high school sweetheart **Steve** have been married for 19 years. They have three children and have enjoyed homeschooling for the last 7 years. Steve owned his own construction business for most of his adult life, but after discovering the wonders of computers and online services he closed his business and went to work for America Online. He is also back in school working towards a Computer Science degree.

Anne Wegener and her husband Tim are in their eleventh year of homeschooling their seven children. Anne has a B.S. in chemistry from Indiana University. She leads her homeschool support group. Anne lives on a farm in the rolling hills of southern Indiana.

Melissa Worcester and her husband David live in Galway, New York where they homeschooled their son for four years.

FIND IT FAST

Index

Speaking of fast . . . Homeschooler Stephen
Dickerson (9) of New Woodstock, New York,
collected three medals in his first season of
running in 5 km and 8 km road races. He
placed first in his age group in the "Human
Race," held in Syracuse, New York, and
placed second in his age group in two other
regional races, the DeRuyter Tromp Town
Run and the Madison Hall run.
He shows remarkable speed and endurance
for his age, regularly besting many adults
(including his out-of-breath father!).

Find It Fast

Index

Yes, I want to keep up with the latest in homeschooling!
Sign me up for:

☐ Three years of Practical Homeschooling, $45
☐ Two years of Practical Homeschooling, $35
☐ One year of Practical Homeschooling, $19.95
☐ Trial subscription (3 issues), $10
Foreign and Canadian subscribers, add $10 per year.
MO residents, add 5.975% tax. Please pay in U.S. funds.

Name _____

Address _____

City, State, Zip _____

Country _____

Phone (in case we need to check on your order): _____

I'm paying by ☐ check made out to Home Life, Inc. ☐ credit card (MC, Visa, AmX, Disc)

Card #:_____ Exp: _____ / _____

Signature: _____

Return with payment to Home Life, PO Box 1190, Fenton MO 63026

Or call **1-800-346-6322** for fastest service

New!

from Mary Pride!

Alpha Omega Publications

300 North McKemy Avenue

Chandler, AZ 85226-2618
